Praise for Torah as a Guide to Enlightenment

"In my book *Times for Redemption* I point out how important it is for us to prepare the vessels to hold the spiritual energy needed for redemption. *Torah as a Guide to Enlightenment* is an inspired offering to help us prepare our vessels."

—Rabbi Matityahu Glazerson, author *of Letters of Fire, Above the Zodiac, From Hinduism Back to Judaism,* and *Times for Redemption*

"Rebbe Gabriel Cousens's deep and profound book is reopening a door to Judaism and Torah that has been closed in my heart for a long time. Through *Torah as a Guide to Enlightenment* I can now begin to understand the spiritual teachings of the Torah, how inspiring and beneficial they are for me as well as for the many Jewish members within our Sufi spiritual community. I appreciate the rebirth into the Jewish tradition within my heart and experience."

—Jason D. Groode, senior director of Sufis Hawaii

"*Torah as a Guide to Enlightenment* is a fascinating gateway into some of the most profound mysteries of creation. Rabbi Gabriel Cousens, MD, attempts to unlock the gate to give us a taste of some of the sparks of the inner Torah through modern science and Kabbalah. Thirty years ago I saw a similar work on Bereisheet called *Beginning and Upheaval* written by Rabbi Meir Leibush Malbim and translated by physicist Dr. Zvi Faier, a close disciple of Rabbi Dr. Chiam Zimmerman, one of the great rabbis of the last generation. After seeing that work I am not at all surprised by what Rabbi Cousens is doing here. This book should be used as an eye and mind opener and we should all value what King David asked: Open my eyes so I can see the wonders of your Torah. For us there is no greater wonder than to see the integration of wisdom and Torah rolled into one."

—Rabbi Moshe Schatz, author of *Maayan Moshe, Tikun Lail Shavoout of the Rabbi Shalom Sharabi, Keter Malchut on Seferot H aʾomer,* and *Sparks of the Hidden Light*

Other Books by Rabbi Gabriel Cousens, MD

Tachyon Energy (co-authored with David Wagner)
Conscious Eating
Depression-Free for Life
Rainbow Green Live-Food Cuisine
Spiritual Nutrition
There Is a Cure for Diabetes
Creating Peace by Being Peace

Torah
as a Guide
to Enlightenment

Rabbi Gabriel Cousens, MD

FOREWORD AND HASKAMAH BY RABBI GERSHON WINKLER

North Atlantic Books
Berkeley, California

Published by
North Atlantic Books
P.O. Box 12327
Berkeley, California 94712

Cover design © Ayelet Maida, A/M Studios
Book design by Susan Quasha

Printed in the United States of America

"The Tabernacle and Enclosure" illustration on page 292 by Jared Krikorian

Torah as a Guide to Enlightenment is sponsored by the Society for the Study of Native Arts and Sciences, a nonprofit educational corporation whose goals are to develop an educational and cross-cultural perspective linking various scientific, social, and artistic fields; to nurture a holistic view of arts, sciences, humanities, and healing; and to publish and distribute literature on the relationship of mind, body, and nature.

North Atlantic Books' publications are available through most bookstores. For further information, visit our website at www.northatlanticbooks.com or call 800-733-3000.

Library of Congress Cataloging-in-Publication Data
Cousens, Gabriel, 1943–
 Torah as a guide to enlightenment / Gabriel Cousens ; foreword and haskamah by Gershon Winkler.
    p. cm.
 Includes bibliographical references.
 Summary: "Focusing on a deep metaphysical interpretation of the Torah, Torah as a Guide to Enlightenment presents, for the first time, the original intention of the Jewish tradition: an explicit guide to liberation from the mystical Jewish enlightenment point of view"—Provided by publisher.
 ISBN 978-1-58394-249-9
 1. Bible. O.T. Pentateuch—Commentaries. 2. Mysticism—Judaism. 3. Spiritual life—Judaism. 4. Self-actualization (Psychology)—Religious aspects—Judaism. I. Title.
 BS1225.53.C68 2011
 222'.107—dc23
                            2011018454

1 2 3 4 5 6 7 8 9 SHERIDAN 16 15 14 13 12 11

Dedication

To Hashem, the source of divine inspiration (Ruach HaKadesh)
for the emanation and birth of this book
and for sustaining us on all levels.

This book is dedicated to Abraham Avinu,
the grandfather founder of this great Torah lineage of deveikut/chey'rut
and a personal inspiration to me.
It is dedicated as well to all the bold awake sages, prophets, and rabbis
eternally alive in deveikut/chey'rut,
who have sustained the Torah light of enlightenment
throughout the history of this great and ancient lineage.

Acknowledgments

At the top of my acknowledgment list is my Rav Gershon Winkler. In 1983, after my forty-day fast, I received a *chasmal* (gentle divine voice) to deepen into my Levitical Jewish tribal roots. I talked to about five different rabbis requesting help in translating my inner experiences into Torah language. At that time no one understood what I was sharing, but Rav Winkler, who admitted he also did not understand, agreed to help me bridge and edit my direct knowing *(chokhmah)* into language helpful to Am Yisrael. He has served as my key Jewish reference source and my personal teacher on Jewish perspectives since 1983. All this time he has shared many aspects of mystical and shamanic Judaism and kabbalah that are not particularly available today. His formative ultra-Haredi rabbinical background, along with his present earth-based shamanic lifestyle, has been perfect in our many years of discussion and reflection on my mystical enlightenment Torah teachings and insights. In this context it was natural that he became my personal Rav as well as my Hebrew consultant and translator of ancient texts. He has been a footnote source for areas we deemed important to document for the *haskamah* of *Torah as a Guide to Enlightenment.* His inspired Foreword and haskamah have captured the spiritual magic of this Ruach HaKodesh-inspired creative process. His in-depth, comprehensive, wise, and scholarly review of my text and the Hebrew have added an important dimension to this work. I am grateful, appreciative, and thankful for his extraordinary feedback on my teachings.

I also want to acknowledge Yehoshua Sedam for his understanding and being able to work with great enthusiasm with the depth of the teachings, which translated into helping with the transcriptions and rough copyediting of many of these parashahs. I acknowledge him for working with the organization of the Hebrew fonts for print, as well as for working so well with Emily Boyd, my book production manager at North Atlantic Books. Yehoshua saved me an enormous amount of computer time in preparing this book for print, for which I am very grateful. I also want to acknowledge Michael Bedar for his transcriptions of some of the earlier parashahs.

My gratitude goes to Emily Boyd, who has been the production manager for almost all of my books through the years. She has been a delight and a joy, as always, to work with. My gratitude also goes to Winn Kalmon, a patient copyeditor and an astute reader of this text, offering valuable outsider perspective. And last, but not least, my wonderful spouse, Shanti Golds Cousens, who patiently supported me in the writing of this book, and who was always eager to hear me present these parashahs on each Shabbat before sharing them publically. Her feedback has been lovingly invaluable. I also want to appreciate the loving interest of my students both in the U.S. and Israel, who have shown so much appreciation for the value of these Torah teachings in the spiritual evolution of their lives.

Contents

Foreword

Torah scrolls abound. They are confined to arks, beautifully adorned closets that grace synagogues and temples around the world. They live far beyond the words they contain, and far beyond the walls that contain them. Their words fly out constantly in endless streams of sacred symbols, each encrypted with fathomless mystery wisdom, dormant with seeds of ever-flowering lessons waiting to be brought to fruition on the lips of those who chant them, read them, study them, teach them.

The words of the Torah are black fire inscribed upon white fire, burning fiercely, yet lovingly, into the hearts of those who truly know how to listen to the crackling sounds of their message in cadence with the call of their own souls.

But alas! In our era of political correctness, the flames of both have been dampened by attempts to dilute both the soul of Torah and the soul of her adherents. The noise of the world around us has by now become amplified by decibels that are deafening to the soul, severing her from the infinite horizons of possibility she had come to know at her very genesis in the bosom of the One Who Spoke and the World Came into Being. Inhibited by the constraints of the confining webs woven around her by the Dark Side, the soul now finds herself languishing in a subtle form of slavery, yearning for the Liberation and Connectedness she once knew with her Creator.

Torah seeks to free her. And she seeks the light of Torah. After all, in Aramaic, we always referred to Torah as *O'rai'ta* (אורייתא), which means "illumination." The word Torah (תורה) itself, while it translates literally as "guide," is at the same time also rooted in the word for "light"—*o'rah* (אורה), or better yet, "enlightenment."

The two walk often together, the Torah and the Soul, albeit separated by chasms ranging from language barriers to dangerous misconceptions planted by the forces that seek to control our deepest sense of Self by slowly and subtly dissolving our connection with the Divine Mystery. Each seeks the other like lovesick romantics, each almost touching the other, but not quite, their attempts at connecting thwarted again and again by the interruptive forces of doubt and skepticism. For the voice of Torah remains a delicate whisper against the resonating roar of Bible critics and other sowers of disbelief and uncertainty. Even many so-called rabbis downplay her credibility and uniqueness from pulpits hewn of cardboard and plastic, and thus many are misled and further driven from their soul's deepest longing of Liberation and Connection—chey'rut and deveikut (חירות and דביקות, respectively).

But then along comes a warrior brimming with the brazen, audacious qualities of the likes so rarely found amid the rabbis of today, a man deeply immersed not only in the word but more so in the spirit that conceived the word. Casting aside all inhibitions around political correctness and all restraints of ego and id, he dares to compose a treatise of the Torah that raises the decibels of her voice so that all souls, regardless of their external identities, can hear her message and experience her magic.

A master of medicine, a healer of souls, an awakener of hearts, Rabbi Gabriel Cousens, MD, has freed up Torah to free up souls, flinging wide open her rusty gates to enable her wisdom to gush forth unabatedly and in fullness of intent and application. This work, this book, these messages that emanate from every segment of the five books of the Faithful Shepherd (Moses) are here brought to life and to light, carried on the wings of loving words from a loving heart. They flow from a teacher whose life aim is to liberate souls from their confinement in the realm of illusion, the *alma d'shikra* (עלמא דשקרא), and gently guide them through the wisdom of Torah, Talmud, Midrash, and Kabbalah out into the *alma d'kushta* (עלמא דקושטא), the realm of truth.

This book is a great deal more than another commentary on the Torah. Gabriel challenges each of us individually to dare move beyond the illusory patterns we carry, to cleanse the lens of our perspectives and soar on the wings of our souls to heights we might never have thought possible. He skillfully weaves the wisdom of the sages through the ages into a cohesive and fruitful brew of lessons that speak directly to the deepest depths of our spirits. In the tradition of the holy sages of centuries past, Gabriel endeavors to address us at our very core, challenging us to reach out toward the already-outstretched arm of God that waits so very patiently for our grasp. At every junction of the

Torah, he pleads with us that we take the leap of faith, like a flying trapeze, and release our grip on what we know, or think we know, so that we might free our palms to receive what we truly need to know. His mantra throughout this important work is Liberation of Soul and Connectedness with God, and that this is the foundational intent and message of the Torah. But it is not just a repetitive theme of Gabriel the man; it is indeed the central objective of the Torah as it has been taught and understood for thousands of years, albeit forgotten over time, especially in our own time. Gabriel has restored this theme, and clarified it in the context of the Torah writ, demonstrating through the narratives of the Torah and the exhaustive commentaries on the Torah through the ages that Liberation of Soul and Connectedness with God is indeed the aim of this sacred body of divinely inspired wisdom. "None can truly claim to be liberated," the ancient rabbis taught, "other than those who immerse themselves in the study of Torah" (Midrash Bamidbar Rabbah 10:8). For the Torah inspires wholeness and restores the soul (Psalms 19:8). "Her ways are ways of pleasantness, and all of her paths are paths of peace. She is the Tree of Life for all who take hold of her" (Proverbs 3:17–18).

This book, then, promises to make Torah relevant to our lives, to help us apply the ancient writ to our timeless Now, so that we might gradually shift from *mo'cheen de'kat'nut* (מוחין דקטנות), ever-limiting consciousness, to *mo'cheen de'gad'lut* (מוחין דגדלות), ever-expanding consciousness.

So may it be.

RABBI GERSHON WINKLER
9th Day of Second Adar, 5771

הסקמה לספר הזאת

מאב הרב גרשון וינקלר

בס"ד מעיד אני עלי את השמים ואת הארץ שקראתי ויגעתי בספר היקר ולא מצאתי בה שום מאומה או שמץ רק מרגליות טובות מלא חכמה הזה

ותבונה ומוסר השכל לפתוח לבינו לאבינו שבשמים ולהגדיל תורה ויאדיר. והמחבר הרב גבריאל קוסינז באר היטיב תורת משה רבינו והסביר לנו כל פרשה ופרשה של התורה הקדושה דרך מפרשי התורה ועל ידי התלמוד והמדרש והקבלה בין בפשט בין ברמז בין בדרוש בין בסוד. וגם זכה הרב גבריאל בחידושי תורה שבאו עליו משפע רב והביא לנו מתנה גדולה בכתיבתו הספר הזאת לזכות את דורינו בדביקות וחירות ולראות בטוב ה' בארץ החיים. ולכן שמחתי בקול רגלי מבשר משמוע שלום מבשר טוב בהוצאת לאור העולם ספר היקר הזה, והנני נותן בו הסקמתי ואני מקוה שילמדו כולם בספר הזה בלב למען ה' ולמען תורתו, ועל ידי זה יושפע עלינו שפע רב מכל העולמות. נכון

כן יהי רצון, נאום אני הקטן הרב גרשון בן הרב מנשה צבי שליט"א ואסתר רבקה – זכרונה לברכה – ממשפחת וינקלר.

יום תשע לירח אדר שני, שנת תשע"א

With Heaven's Support, I hereby call as my witnesses the heavens
and the earth that I have read and explored this precious book
and have found neither flaw nor wrongfulness, only precious
jewels filled with wisdom and understanding and sensible intro-
spective lessons intended to open up our hearts to Our Father
Who is in the Heavens, and to spread and glorify the Torah. And
the author, Rabbi Gabriel Cousens, has clarified well the Torah
of Moses our Teacher and explained for us each and every portion of the Holy Torah through the path of the commentators
of the Torah and through the Talmud, Midrash, and Kabbalah,
on the literal plane, the cryptic plane, the explorative plane, and
the mystery plane. And Rabbi Gabriel has also brought forth
fresh insights into Torah understanding with which he has been
inspired from the realms of higher inspiration, and has brought
to us a great gift in his having written this book to merit our
generation with connectedness to God (deveikut) and liberation
(chey'rut), and to enable us to "perceive the goodness of God in
the land of the living" (Psalms 27:13). And therefore do I rejoice
in "the sound of feet running about with the declaration of news
of peace and news of goodness" (Isaiah 52:7 and Nahum 2:1)
through the emergence into the light of the world of this precious book. And I hereby grant my approval of this book and
it is my hope that everyone will study this book for the sake of
Hashem and for the sake of the Torah. And by so doing, may we
draw great inspiration from the realm of inspiration in all of the
universes. So may be the higher will, says I, the small one, Rabbi
Gershon son of Rabbi Menashe Tzvi (may he live a long whole-
some life) and Esther Rivka (may her memory be for a blessing),
of the family Winkler. 9th Day of the Moon of Second Adar, in
the year 5771.

Introduction

לשם ייחוד קודשא בריך ושכינתיה על ידי ההו

בדחילו ורחימו לייחד שם י–ה בו–ה ביחודא שלים

l'shem yee'chud kud'sha b'reech'hu u'sh'cheentey ahl y'dey ha'hu,
beed'chee'lu ur'chee'mu, l'ya'chey'd shem yah b'vah b'yee'chudah
sh'leem

"For the sake of the unification of the Sacred Wellspring and the
shekhinah through this, in awe and in love, to unify Yah in Vah
[God transcendent in God immanent] in complete unification."

THIS classical kabbalistic declaration of intent speaks to the deeper inner sod
(סוד) essence of the Torah, from which the outer essence of the Torah emerges
as love. When Hillel the Elder was asked to synopsize the entire Torah in
a single phrase, he responded: "What is disconcerting to you, do not do it
unto your neighbor.... The rest is commentary" (Talmud Bav'li, Shabbat 31a).
With all due respect to Rabbi Hillel the Elder, and even to myself, as I bring
this relatively new level of interpretation, the Torah remains a deep mystery
beyond the ability of the human mind and psyche to fully comprehend. This
is particularly true of the complexity and depth of Bereisheet, which, for example, took me more than a year of focused study to even begin to penetrate.
For that reason, I write this book in complete awe of the messages and gifts of
the Torah to our world.

The inner essence of Torah is about the merging of the heavens and the earth
within us. On the sephirotic tree, it is the unification of malchut (מלכות) with
tiferet (תפארת); the unification of Elohim and YHWH; the unification of the
sephirotic partzufim (faces of God) of nukba/nok (נוקבא—sacred daughter),
with zeir anpin (זעיר אנפין—sacred son). *Torah as a Guide to Enlightenment*
is about opening our eyes to this greater truth that deveikut (God-merging)/

chey'rut (enlightenment) is the ultimate inner purpose of Torah. As David wrote: "Open thou my eyes, that I may behold wondrous things out of thy Tora" (Tehillim 119:18). In this way, we become the expression of the living God as the unification of the Holy One. It is then that we become the living image of the Divine as expressed as love in our daily life.

> Thus is the Torah the bond between God and the Human. And this is clearly known, how the Torah is the central conduit between God and the human, and therefore the Torah is referred to as "Covenant" throughout the Scriptures, for the Covenant is the relationship between God and the Human, and the Torah, she is the essence of that relationship.
>
> (sixteenth-century Rabbi Yehudah Loew of Prague [MaHaRaL] in *Gevurot Hashem*, Chap. 47, folio 192)

In 1983, during a deep meditation, a voice from the realm of silence (hashmal) resounded with these very words: "You must go back to your roots and help your people."

This book is a result of the divine will reflecting this Torah offering. *Torah as a Guide to Enlightenment* is an interpretation of the Torah from a mystical *deveikut/chey'rut* (divine union/liberation) perspective. Correspondingly, each *parashah* (segment of the Torah) is a lesson on the path of enlightenment. It is a flow of knowledge that goes beyond a rationalist (*pashtan*) viewpoint and into the deeper realms of the soul. It is a visionary sharing modeled after the initial teaching to Avraham of *"lekh lekha"* ("go to the Self"), as the deep essence of the Great Torah Way. Students of the Great Way, at some point (if they want to experience a deep revelation of Hashem), will naturally find themselves going beyond their intellectual understanding (*binah*) to directly experience the knowledge of the living Torah internally (*chokhmah*) with love and awe of the One. At the deepest level, they must ultimately merge and disappear into the Infinite One (*Ayn Sof*) and disappear into the *ayin* as the heart of the Ayn Sof. This book is written to follow that inner-directed mystic, or enlightenment model, which is based on my direct experience and evolution over the last sixty years. It explicitly goes beyond, while simultaneously incorporating, the traditional, academic, scholarly, left-brain *p'shat* approach, as well as the *remez*, *drash*, and metaphysical *sod* understanding of the Zohar.

To create this text, intense Torah study and a variety of the teachings from the great Torah sages were incorporated on the mental and spiritual planes. I studied each parashah many times, contemplated it, meditated on it, became inspired through the *Ruach HaKodesh* (רוח הקודש), and then wrote. Although some aspects of all four levels of Torah interpretation—*p'shat* (literal), *remez* (symbolic), *drash* (interpretive), and *sod* (metaphysical and spiritual)—are covered to make certain points, this book is written primarily at the spiritual enlightenment levels of sod, focusing on deveikut (God-merging) and chey'rut (enlightenment). It emanates from love and awe of God. It emanates from the desire for divine merging with God in the context of Torah (*t'shukat deveikut*—תשוקת דביקות). It emanates from the urge induced by the divine kiss (*neshikat elohut*—נשיקה אלהת). The integration of all these levels of interpretation and intention are important for this work to be what it is intended to be *a guide to enlightenment*.

Torah as a Guide to Enlightenment deliberately avoids traditional, rationalist, academic, outwardly directed analysis, except when absolutely needed to support a point. Instead, the book comes from an internally directed, insight-driven, ongoing mystical experience. I remember, more than ten years ago, being in the book-laden office of a world famous kabbalist and asking the simple question that takes one beyond intellectual philosophy: "Do you meditate?" He answered with some remorse, "No." In this book we go beyond kabbalah as an intellectual, metaphysical philosophy to the deepest level of awareness the Torah gives us.

> In the eyes of God, personal insight is more precious than divine revelation. For if you depend exclusively upon the scriptures and the teachings of religions and of the masters but have no personal insights of your own, it is all worthless.
>
> (second-century Rabbi Akiva
> in *Midrash O'ti'ot D'Rebbe Akiva, O't Bet*)

Perhaps this path is a powerful method for all to perceive the deeper meanings of the Torah Way. Through this interpretation, we will come to understand that we possess a 4,000-year-old lineage path of enlightenment, at the very least, equal to all other liberation paths in both Eastern and Western cultures. Yet we need to keep in mind that we cannot technique our way to God. The final shattering of the glass ceiling of the mind is an act of grace. In this process, we go beyond understanding the "Torah as Law," and the idea of the "people of the Law," to the "people of the light of God," as in the "people of enlightenment." As it says in Shemot (Exodus) 19:6, "You will be a kingdom of priests and a holy nation to Me." This is both a collective and a personal statement about the Torah's role as a guide to creating the conditions for personal and collective enlightenment. This collective focus, as a nation of enlightened priests, is a unique emphasis of the Torah. Through this understanding, we can go beyond the limited perspective of the Torah as Law and the idea of the people of the Law. Torah as Law is an important foundation for the ultimate gift of the Torah and the purpose of life, which is deveikut/chey'rut.

Torah is a feminine word related to *mo'reh*, which means "guide." It is also related to the words *ho'rah* and *o'rah*—"parent" and "illumination," respectively. These direct Hebrew interpretations of the word accurately reflect this book's title and intent. They suggest that the Torah is a loving parent and a guide to the illumination of enlightenment. The concept of Torah as Law not only keeps us in our comfort zone. The Law is extremely important and foundational to the Great Torah Way, but the deepest truth of the Torah cannot be limited to the Law. I avoid, as much as possible, any concept that puts God in a box or creates the delusion that we can technique our way to God. The name of God is beyond any one word such as "Law" or "Love." The Ayn Sof is beyond any limitations.

The whole written Torah is actually one unbroken living name of Hashem, forever making a new enlightenment statement in each generation (Zohar, Vol. 3, folio 35b). The Great Way of the Torah is beyond any technique. It is about living according to the Torah in a way that takes us *beyond* concepts and the mind. It is the original calling of Avraham to walk into the Self (Bereisheet 12:1 and 22:2). It is the original directive of Moshe to walk up the mountain into the unknown (Shemot 19:3 and 24:12). It encourages us not to stay at the base of the mountain in our spiritual comfort zone worshipping the Golden Calf. The Golden Calf shifts us away from the profound revolutionary Torah teachings of a nondual, nonmaterial, yet personal, God, beyond the limitations of Elohim. Elohim is the God of nature. It is an aspect of the infinite face of God known as *YHWH* (ה-ו-ה-י). YHWH is reflected in Elohim, but is prior to and transcendent of the existence of Elohim. The creation of the Golden Calf came out of the consciousness of the *ey'rev rav* (ערב רב) (Tikunei Zohar 42a), which were the multitudes of non-Hebrews who joined Am Yisrael (the collective nation of Israel) in their liberation from Egypt (Shemot 12:38). These did not, however, have that direct divine connection, nor were they open to the nondual unknown. The image of the Golden Calf gave people the false security of thinking they were seeing the face of God. This, of course, completely undermined the deeper message of the name of God as *Grace*, which takes us to enlightenment by disappearing into the face-lessness of YHWH. This is the deepest purpose of life.

This is not an attack on the idea of the Law, because the *mitzvot* are fundamental to the Great Way of the Torah. I am pointing out that we need to transcend the influence of the ey'rev rav, who want people to stop at the comfort zone of the Golden Calf rather than transcend into the ultimate Truth. Moshe Rabbeynu's message to Pharaoh and Am Yisrael is that there is a God named YHWH, who is above the divine face of Elohim. YHWH is both personal and more powerful than Elohim. Our destiny ultimately is to disappear into YHWH, as Moshe disappeared into the cloud going up the mountain (Shemot 20:18). It is no accident that the Hebrew name Elohim (אלהים) has the same numerical value (81) as the Hebrew word for nature, which is *HaTeva* (הטבע). Enlightenment necessarily takes us beyond the confines of nature.

Today, many of our youth are no longer willing to live in the egocentrically and ethnocentrically safe, illusionary, secure knowledge of having a visible God in a box to relate to. This box includes a full cultural overlay, in which liberating ceremonies and prayers have degenerated into meaningless, but culturally familiar, powerless rituals. This point was made in our modern times, as early as the eighteenth century, by Rabbi Yisrael Ba'al Shem Tov, who refused to enter certain synagogues because they were cluttered with broken, un-ascended prayers, like birds with broken wings, hopping about on the floors. It is incumbent on us to bring a new authenticity and inner power to the Great Torah Way that allows our prayers to fly to the heavens. People know there is "something more," and they are leaving our tradition because it has become dominated by the ey'rev rav energy that seeks to put God in a box. This is happening in many organized religions around the world. Indeed, the reader of this book will find that there is something more to Torah than the Law. It is the noncausal, incredible, delectable, ecstatic, erotic, satiating, love-filled, compassionate, contented, and peaceful experience of YHWH within our very own being.

The Law, stiff with formality, is a cry for creativity, a call for the nobility concealed in the form of the commandments. It is not designed to be a yoke, a curb, or a straitjacket for human action. Above all, the Torah asks for love. All observance is training in the art of love. To forget that love is the purpose of all the mitzvot is to vitiate their meaning. It is a distortion to say that Judaism consists exclusively of performing ritual or moral deeds, while forgetting that the goal of their performance is in transforming the soul. The Torah consists of five books. The Code of Law (*Shulchan Aruch*) consists of only four books. Where is the missing part of the law? Answered Rabbi Israel of Rizhin (nineteenth century): "The missing part is the person. Without the living participation of the person the law is incomplete" (Rabbi Abraham Joshua Heschel in *God in Search of Man*, pp. 307, 310, 311). When we put God in a box with fixed meanings and an exclusive authoritarian *p'shat* interpretation, we have moved from the Tree of Life (*Etz Chaim*—עץ חיים) to the Tree of Knowledge of Good and Evil (*Etz HaDa'at*—עץ הדעת).

The egocentric, combative, and disruptive energy of the ey'rev rav then manifests in a variety of divisions, disrupting the unity of Am Yisrael. It also creates conflict among the various religious communities themselves. In the time of the Golden Calf and today, the outer ey'rev rav could have no effect if there were not an inner ey'rev rav resonating in each person. As in those ancient times, the true Levites must stand up to the ey'rev rav. In this context, the work of the ey'rev rav, then and now, is to disconnect Am Yisrael from YHWH and the Great Torah Way, as a powerful path to deveikut/chey'rut (divine union/liberation). In this way the ey'rev rav are continuing to share and multiply their mental slavery among us. Although we may think that the ey'rev rav influence was something that only existed in the time of Moshe, be aware that it is actively with us today as well. According to the Zohar, ey'rev rav souls have incarnated into Am Yisrael and have worked their way into leadership roles in both secular and religious communities (Zohar, Vol. 1, folio 25a).

As then, so now. The story of the Golden Calf is a revelation about today. Unfortunately, the ey'rev rav are as powerful a minority now as they were then, and they have driven thousands away from our tradition in pursuit of YHWH through other paths. This book is an open door for these sincere spiritual seekers to return to the deeper enlightenment level of their roots. This level of Torah interpretation is offered as an inspiration to help us transcend the ey'rev rav tendencies within ourselves and in our communities. It is offered to help us return to the revelatory awareness of Mount Sinai (*Har Sinay*—הר סיני), as our deeper truth. As a guide, the Torah outlines, and is, the process by which the Divine guides all of creation toward enlightenment. This creates a pathway for us to return to the Divine. We have a model for this journey based on our people's ancient account of creation: Bereisheet (Genesis).

In the process of Torah interpretation, there is no need for a binding opinion in matters that do not involve *halakhah* (הלכה), or principles of faith. Halakhah interpretations, on the other hand, demand clear action and decisive positions, applicable for specific situations in specific moments. Yet, even then, opposing opinion, although vetoed by a majority, were respected and recorded as precedence for related or future situations (Babylonian Talmud, Edi'ot 1:5 and Tosef'ta Edi'ot 1:2). When the schools of Hillel and Shamai were arguing over various halakhic interpretations some 2,100 years ago, a heavenly voice proclaimed "Both are the words of the living God" (Talmud Bavli, Eruvin 13b). Non-halakhic questions, on the other hand (like what is the age of the universe), are always open to any opinions found in a recognized Torah source. In non-halakhic questions there is no need for a final verdict or a majority consensus. There is only a need for sincere discussion for the "sake of the heavens." It is in this context that this book gives an in-depth discussion of the Great Torah Way from the deveikut/chey'rut (enlightenment) perspective.

The teachings offered in this book are drawn from repeated readings of the Torah, the Zohar, a variety of kabbalistic literature and teachings, midrashic teachings, and study of the ancient and modern sages and scholars including Rabbi Shlomo ben Isaac (Rashi), Rabbi Moshe ibn Maimon (Rambam), Rabbi Moshe ben Nachmon (Ramban), Rabbi Isaac Luria (the Ari'zal), Rabbi

Chayim Vital, Rabbi Moshe Haim Luzzato (the Ramhal), and some of my favorite enlightened tzaddiks Rabbi Israel Ba'al Shem Tov, Rebbe Elimelech, Rebbe Zusha, the Rebbe of Kotzk, and Rabbi Nachman of Breslov. Current Torah teachers whom I have been strongly inspired by include Rav Gershon Winkler, Rav Ariel Bar Tzadok, Rav Avraham Yitzchak Kook, and Rabbi Shlomo Carlebach (whom I served as personal physician for a number of years). Others who have also inspired me in the writing of this book include Rabbi David Aaron, Rabbi Binney Freedman, and Rabbi Zvi Leshem. The *Me'am Lo'ez*, written by Rabbi Ya'akov Culi in the fifteenth century, is a twenty-one-volume midrashic commentary that was a profound inspiration for me, as has been and is the ancient mystical Sefer Yetzirah.

The Torah is a divinely inspired communication that came through Moshe Rabbeinu (משה רבינו), "Moses, our teacher." It has provided us with a guide for how to live as full, enlightened human beings in harmony with the living planet. We do this so that we may evolve (*mitaken*—מתקן) and wake up to the truth of who we are. This becomes the living purpose of life, to live in deveikut/chey'rut (enlightenment). The deepest way to understand the Torah is to be lived by it. In that process we connect, at the soul level, to its source. It is my prayer that those who read this book become inspired to live by the Torah on this level. The book is written in a mystical style for this purpose.

There are four levels of Torah interpretation. These help us to understand that we are multidimensional beings living simultaneously on all these levels. The first is p'shat, a literal, physical, and scientific level of interpretation. Remez is an intellectual metaphorical interpretation. Drash is the heart and allegorical level; it includes morals, emotions, the Midrash, and subjective teachings. The sod interpretation is a deeper metaphysical-psychospiritual perspective of how to walk as a full human being on the earth. Sod is derived from kabbalah and the Talmud. At a deeper level, the book's primary focus, sod is about deveikut/chey'rut (divine union/enlightenment), the ultimate purpose of life. The sod interpretation gives us a full multidimensional understanding with an emphasis and perspective that is often missing even in popular kabbalistic teaching.

The Great Way of the Torah is a paradoxical path to full enlightenment. This is metaphorically explained in the talmudic PaRDeS story. (PaRDeS is an acronym composed of the four levels of scripture interpretation: p'shat, remez, drash, and sod = PaRDeS.) The story reveals the kabbalistic path of the ascent of the second-century master, Rabbi Akiva, who journeys into the world of the Ayn Sof (the nothing) and returns completely whole and integrated. The story compares him with three other rabbis. Rabbi Ben Azzai gazed at the Divine Presence (experienced the nothing) and died. Rabbi Shimon ben Zoma experienced the Divine Presence and went mad. Elisha ben Avuya (*Acher*, "the other one") became mired in nondual perception and lost his faith. Rabbi Akiva, however, entered into the world of both the *b'limah* (the nothing) and *mah* (the something) as a fully integrated, enlightened person (Talmud Bavli, Chagigah 14b). His walk is a model of the Great Torah Way. Before they entered this mystical journey, Akiva's message to his colleagues was "When you arrive at the pure marble stones, do not proclaim 'Water! Water!'" The deeper meaning is that the stones represent the different planes of awareness. Therefore, if we label them with a particular definition in the moment (such as seeing them akin to water), we create separation consciousness. Separation consciousness in turn inhibits the truth inherent in enlightened consciousness, which is a fully integrated walk not confined to any one particular definition. Only through enlightened consciousness can we become the liberated light illuminating the walk between the b'limah and the mah.

These rabbis were some of the greatest of their generation and are mentioned frequently throughout the Talmud. Each experienced a different fate according to his level of spiritual development. In this context the teaching of PaRDeS is archetypical regarding the Torah as a guide to enlightenment. Shimon ben Azzai, who was said to have experienced the great nothing, studied the Torah so intensely day and night that he never married or raised children. His sole focus was on the holiness of the Torah. His piousness was renowned and he was the ultimate *Hasid*. He was considered a *parush* (פרוש), one who is completely separated from the physical pleasures of the world. As a result he became very ethereal and ungrounded. Paradoxically, his piousness and separation from earthly pleasures were the cause of his death. When he experienced the merging with the One, he felt the heavenly intoxication and simply decided to leave the earth for heaven. Through this we learn that if we are not properly grounded, we are more likely to leave before our time and not fulfill our mission on the earth.

This communal mission of Am Yisrael is the spiritual rectification of the earth plane, contaminated by the dark side brought in by the actions of Adam and Cha'vah (Eve). By being channels of the *shefa* (שפה, the *Or Yashar* [אור ישר]—heavenly, downward flowing spiritual energy), we bring this healing energy to earth for *tikkun ha'olam* (תיקון העולם)—repairing the world. In other words, to create a tikkun for the blemish of humanity that occurred at Eden, we must become liberated. It is the battle to rectify our fallen collective soul. At that time, the satanic forces outside of us moved inside of us, and became the *yetzer hara* (יצר הרע), the impulse toward no-good. Through our earthly grounding we can overcome the temptation to remain in the intoxication of the heavens, so that we may complete our work on the earth plane, even while basking in divine union and enlightenment.

Shimon ben Zoma is the next great teacher for us in the story of PaRDeS. Ben Zoma was considered a mighty man. He was well grounded and committed to his earthly mission. He exemplified strict spiritual discipline and was a master of all his desires. He had learning, strength, and wealth. He had but one weakness: he was not in complete piousness and spiritual clarity. He was also not satisfied with his portion and was trying to force union with the One. Because of this weakness, when he entered the endless light of Hashem, it was more than his mind could handle, and he went psychotic (*nit'rafah da'ato* [נטרפה דעתו]—his mind was torn). Ben Azzai was too separated, and Ben Zoma was too mingled. To enter PaRDeS, one needs the devotion, spiritual capacity, and piety of Ben Azzai, combined with the wisdom and discipline of Ben Zoma. These rabbis show us that although they were elevated spiritual beings, they had egocentric goals and intentions. Goals and intentions build ego and limit our capacity for enlightenment, making the final pathway dangerous and difficult to wake to. The safest approach is to both desire the Divine intensely while living on all levels and ways to enlightenment. We must completely surrender to the will of God for us, and allow the *shekhinah* to guide us without having any intention but the desire for God. This was the failure and disaster of all three.

Elisha ben Avuya (Acher) was the third. Having the combined qualities of the first two, he was considered one of the great sages of that time. He was able to experience the great merging (*Yihud Elyon*—ייחוד עליון) of the supernal union. But his mistake, which led to his spiritual downfall, was that he separated Yihud Elyon (*atzilut*) from *Yihud HaTahton* (יהוד התחתון), the union with the earth plane of *malchut*. He thought that the Torah and its mitzvot were only for those who have not experienced Yihud Elyon. In the consciousness of the world of atzilut, there is only the One; there is nothing other than God, and all is nullified before the God of the Ayn Sof. In his perception, therefore, there was no need or place for Torah and mitzvot. He continued to cling to Yihud Elyon, and therefore felt he no longer had to live in the earth plane by the Great Torah Way, including the Torah teachings and the mitzvot. He knew that all was God as he perceived the Now, but he did not know how to integrate the worlds. As a result, he "cut the young saplings," which is the unbroken union between the "sod/atzilut of Yihud Elyon" and "p'shat/assiyah of Yihud HaTahton." Somehow he thought that one who perceives the One cannot perceive the "other." He did not understand that we are multidimensional beings, and, in the enlightened awareness of the One, we must learn how to live simultaneously in all dimensions.

This is the enlightened walk between the b'limah and the mah. The two are both one. The light and power of sod (atzilut) tends to make the light of p'shat (assiyah) seem dark. The best way to live in the world of assiyah is to see it as the illuminated illusion of the dancing shekhinah. This is why, even after enlightenment, respect for halakhah and Torah study are foundational. Without sod and p'shat united, we do not have a channel through which to bring the light of the *mashiach*. The light of the mashiach is the higher light of sod, which must come into the world of p'shat to rectify it. Without the direct connection to p'shat, sod cannot bring the light of the mashiach. In this context Elisha ben Avuya became an apostate and was directly blocking the purpose of Am Yisrael, the will of God, and of the awareness of enlightenment. For this it is said that not only did he lose his place on earth, but also in the heavens; in the end, his disciple Rabbi Meir turned him around and he died in purity (Midrash Kohelet Zuta 7:7).

It is unfortunate that Elisha ben Avuya did not heed the warning of Rav Akiva: "When you come to the place of pure marble stone, do not say, 'Water! Water!' For it is said, 'He that works deceit shall not dwell within my house'" (Tehillim [Psalms] 101:7). The two marble stones represent the two (יי) *yuds*

of the world of atzilut and of malchut. They are the two yuds joined by the
(ו) *vav* of (א) *aleph*. Elisha ben Avuya did not understand that in the world
of atzilut there is purity both above and below, and the stones (as the two
worlds) are a continuum. The white stone also represents mayim de'kurin
(מיים דכורין), the masculine waters (the *Or Yashar* or the descending light),
and mayim nukvin (מים נוקבין), the feminine waters (the *Or Hozer* or the
ascending light, activated by our prayers). When the Or Hozer ascends into
the heavens, she activates the downward flow of mayim de'kurin. They both
flow through the *kavim* (קוים—channels) of *tiferet*. There is no separation as
these two worlds offer a continuum in the singularity of the Etz Chaim consciousness of the world of atzilut. In this context, "Do not say, 'Water! Water!'"
would mean "Do not think that there are two types of water and thereby create a separation, activating disunity and destroying the channels between the
worlds." The world of atzilut and assiyah are one. It says in Yesha'yahu 44:6,
"I am the first, and I am the last." There is only separation in the world of assiyah, which is the world of spiritual impurity. In the world of atzilut, there is
no impurity, and they are united by the pure firmament of tiferet.

In this enlightened context, we can identify three general, interrelated
ways of relating to God. The first level is a literal mapping of the way to enlightenment, which is outlined by the mitzvot and halakha of the Torah. The
second is the sweetness (*hamtaka*—המתקה) of the love of divine communion,
which requires separation in order to happen. Paradoxically, separation is
the driving force toward complete merging. At the level of enlightenment, it
continually renews the intense love, longing, and Eros of Hashem. These two
levels are absolutely essential, and not linear in relationship. The third level
is total dissolution into the Divine (*achdut*—אחדות). This is complete deveikut. Moshe tells us in Devarim (Deuteronomy) 4:4, "Only you, the ones who
remained attached to God your Lord, are all alive today." This holds, except,
in the case of deveikut, there is no "you" left with which to cling—there is
only God.

Moshe, walking up the mountain into the unknown, is a model and an
example of deveikut. Perhaps his state of being "half angel/half human" and
radiating so much light that he had to wear a veil explains this level of merging and emerging. His activation of the seventy elders by serving as a cosmic

conductor of God's grace (BeMidbar [Numbers] 11:16–17), and his activation of Yehoshua by touch (BeMidbar 27:22–23) are also part of the path of Torah enlightenment process. This activation is known as *s'micha m'shefa* (משפע סמיכה). Today it is known more commonly as *Hanihah* (הנחה). It is the descent of grace that activates the permanent unfolding of the Ruach HaKodesh/ shekhinah energy that transforms Etz Chaim within us into *Etz Ayin*. This energy of s'micha m'shefa, with the use of the *Tetragrammaton* (יהוה) mantra, or *hagiyah* (הגיה), to activate the consciousness of God and to focus the mind, was the ancient prophetic way of the Great Way of the Torah lineage. This Tetragrammaton *hagiyah* (יהוה הגיה) was, and still is, also a way to draw grace and to prepare to receive the transmission of the grace in the prophetic lineage, as evidenced by Samuel, who activated both King Saul and King David with s'micha m'shefa (First Shemu'el [Samuel] 10:1 and 16:13). Grace can also be received directly from Hashem, as with Avraham, Moshe, and Ezekiel. In these examples, as with s'micha m'shefa, there are often rumblings and thunder, lightning, and darkness, as well as spontaneous movements and shakings. Before the merging there can also be either a black void or a blinding white light. It is associated with a state of existence, where all that is left is a subtle sense of "I am" before this "I am" disappears into the nothing (ayin—אין).

In the physical reality of this world, our bodies can sustain this dissolution for about seventy-two hours, before the body begins to physically dissolve. In my personal experience, many times, when fasting for three days without food or water, I have had a complete dissolution of form for extended periods. It is not a death like the subtle body walking down a tunnel of light, in which there still remains a subtle body having left the physical form. It is a complete disappearance of all form and I Am-ness. In approximately this state, but with a subtle "I am" perspective still present, I have also painlessly gone through two hernia operations and dental surgery without anesthetic, because there was no body to feel. There was truly a complete disappearance of all form. I first discovered this seventy-two-hour dissolution cycle on a forty-day water fast. The last three days of my fast were essentially spent without moving in unbroken deep meditation. I went spontaneously beyond the mind and I Am-ness into complete deveikut/dissolution. Near seventy-two hours (when calculated later), as my body began to dissolve, and my soul cord began to disintegrate, a spark of

"I am" consciousness returned so that I could hear the *hashmal* (חשמל) saying, "It is not time to merge finally in Me, but you must go back and share my teachings with the people of your roots." This is the source energy behind this book. The noncausal ecstasy, love, peace, oneness, contentment, and compassion were seductively overwhelming during my lengthy fasting rite, but God spoke again promising that I could come back to this direct communion/dissolution whenever I chose, within seventy-two hours of fasting and meditation.

A key element in this process, beginning in 1975, is that there has been no intention. Intention was the trap of the three rabbis who failed in PaRDeS. They intended and wanted something. This resulted in being egotistically motivated, rather than being driven or drawn along in a surrendered way to the shekhinah. She, as the expression of God, and she alone, can take us safely into the One, as achdut, and lead us safely out again. Not even the greatest, with Rav Akiva as their guide, could protect themselves on their quest. To be fully alive in enlightenment is to be lived without quest, driven and drawn by the shekhinah. It is simply enough to do one's best to keep up with what she is asking. To enter and leave PaRDeS safely and whole, one cannot desire anything but the One to come in its own time, while letting ourselves be lived by love, by chey'rut, and by mitzvot and halakhah. There are many dead bodies on the path to enlightenment. The Torah is a guide for us, so that we do not have to be one of them.

> Divine Urge
> The seed of Truth,
> Eternally planted
> Within the body-mind-I am complex,
> Is awakened by your touch.
> This seed of cosmic fire
> Ignites the Eternal Divine Urge
> Into a roaring flame.
> This one is like a bull in heat,
> Seeking to mate with the One,
> Crashing through
> The illusion of all barriers
> Beyond imaginary physical and mental limitation,

Charging into the endless bliss of meditation,
Whose experiences deprogram
The mind and body from the illusion of the world,
A form of Divine behavior modification,
Slamming this one into the emptiness of Divine Stillness.
A wild love-crazed moth,
Irresistibly pulled toward the Divine fire.
All this one has to do is show up
And be willing to die.
A flame of the Divine Love,
The I-ness is burnt to a crisp,
And Yah's breath blows away the ashes.
Empty and full
As I am That.
Complete Peace.
The urge completes its mission.
Nothing is left.
Nowhere to stand.
No one standing.
Nothing to Do, Be, or Become,
Free to move in any direction,
As this one becomes
The wild Divine Dance of Yah.

(Poem by Rabbi Gabriel Cousens, MD)

Previous to this experience of total merging for seventy-two hours, and even before the time of the acknowledgment of my permanent stabilization in deveikut/chey'rut by my two enlightened spiritual teachers, I had begun to dwell for hours in this disappeared state of complete deveikut/chey'rut, but it was not permanently internalized in enlightenment. Rather, these were enlightenment experiences on the way to stabilizing in deveikut/chey'rut. The paradox of permanent enlightenment is that it happened in a flash after many years of intense focus on and merging into the Divine. One can only stay in full dissolution for a limited time; the rest of the time one resides in the

TORAH AS A GUIDE TO ENLIGHTENMENT

play of the world, in the subtle dualistic divine communion of the noncausal subtle ecstasy of love (ahava—אהבה), peace (shalom—שלום), contentment (shalvah—שלוה), sweetness (hamtaka—המתקה), oneness (achad—אחד), and compassion (rachamin—רחמים), as the natural human enlightened state. When we live and walk around in enlightenment, there is a delightful sense of separation, which actually activates the divine awe, love, and erotic experiencing of the noncausal delight of the Divine in all things. This is the permanent internal awareness associated with a stabilized enlightenment compared with an enlightened moment or an enlightened thought. It is living in the world in bitul ha'yesh (emptiness), yet in the fullness of the individualized expression of God's will as keter.

One of my enlightened teachers taught me, after acknowledging my permanent stabilization, "We cannot have a permanent merging until after leaving the body." This is an important message. Even in the depth of those three days, the "I am" was subtly alternating between emerging and dissolving; it was neither one nor the other. My teacher also instructed me to always honor the mitzvot and the halakhah throughout my life as part of the mission to bring light to the world. In this way I would not create a break between the worlds (don't say "water, water"). It took about eight years to fully integrate this message into a mature enlightened walk between the b'limah and the mah. The temptation of the nondual world of atzilut is strong, but the noncausal love, peace, bliss, contentment, oneness, and compassion remain fully active while walking in the physical body and assiyah, world of the mah. Full liberation takes time to mature. Part of the maturation process is to move beyond identifying enlightenment as simply being in the nondual state of atzilut. This maturity is the ability to walk the path between the b'limah and the mah on the physical plane as our natural way of being; simultaneously knowing that even "enlightenment" is just a concept and that one just is.

A second part of this maturation is the experience of the unbroken, endless, divine emptiness within, and yet reflected in the Will of God (keter—כתר) as our unique expression in the world. We become naturally, actively, and consciously aware, expressing as a unique flame of the universal fire of God. This happens spontaneously and naturally when one is completely surrendered to the shekhinah. It is then that we walk the full Torah path of chey'rut enlightenment, including the external Torah way, the Torah way as erotic communion with the Divine, and the temporarily complete deveikut. The divine erotic dance between the b'limah and the mah, in this larger context, is a Torah model of mature enlightenment. It is an inspirational and spiritually sophisticated model (at least) equal to any other enlightenment model in the world. In this awareness, one begins to think of himself or herself in the third person, as others in my rabbinical lineage have done (such as the Rav Premislaner and Rav Zusha). In this book, the understanding of this natural tendency is transmitted by the linguistic description of the inner experience of achdut, as inspired and expressed by Rav Abraham Yitzhak Kook. Rav Kook explains that "I" is the "I am the Lord your God" of the Ten Commandments (Shemot [Exodus] 20:2). He says it is one's essential "I." Using the first person in this way works for the author and is far more comfortable and familiar for the reader, though speaking in third person is closer to the truth.

This first-person, achdut (union) experience is not new in our Jewish tradition, but it is also not as commonly shared as mystical communion, Torah study, and the practice of mitzvot. However, mystics did share and have these experiences, as noted in Eliot Wolfson's book *Spiritual Ascent in 16th Century Mysticism*, as well as the Torah's account of Moshe's ayin, God-merged experiences on Mount Sinai. The Torah scholar's resistance to the achdut experience is the idea of complete annihilation. As pointed out before, annihilation of form for more than three days does not happen without permanently leaving the body. What actually happens is that the *identification* with the ego is dissolved. (We still retain the ego in the sense of a personality and physical form, which we must take care of and nourish.) Even the relationship with the witness disappears. In fact, all relationships and duality disappear. The experience of all separation disappears, and one walks in the world from the perspective of the b'limah playing in the world of mah. It is a perspective in which nothing is happening and everything has already happened. One is free to move in any direction as the intended will of God (*ratzon Hashem*—השם רצון) plays out through our personalized expression of the divine will. We are able to move in any direction to fulfill the will of Hashem as it moves through us in individual expression.

The Torah teachings, alluding to both individual enlightenment and the collective enlightenment of Am Yisrael, are found in more than a few places, additional to the PaRDeS teaching. For example, in Yirmeyahu (Jeremiah) 31:30–33:

> Behold, days are coming, says the Lord, when I will make a new covenant with the house of Yisra'el, and with the house of Yehuda: not according to the covenant that I made with their fathers in the day that I took them by the hand to bring them out of the land of Mizrayim; which covenant of mine they broke, although I was their master, says the Lord; but this shall be the covenant that I will make with the house of Yisra'el after those days, says the Lord; I will put my Torah in their inward parts, and write it in their hearts; and I will be their God, and they shall be my people, and they shall teach no more every man his neighbor, and every man his brother, saying, "Know the Lord"; for they shall all know me, from the least of them to the greatest of them, says the Lord; for I will forgive their iniquity, and I will remember their sin no more.

Yesha'yahu (Isaiah) 11:9–10 says:

> They shall not hurt nor destroy in all my holy mountain: for the earth shall be full of the knowledge of the Lord, as the waters cover the sea. And in that day it shall be, that the root of Yishay, that stands for a banner of the peoples, to it shall the nations seek: and his resting place shall be glorious.

Daniyyel (Daniel) 12:1–4 says:

> And at that time shall Mikha'el stand up, the great chief angel, who stands for the children of thy people: and there shall be a time of trouble, such as never was since there was a nation till that same time: and at that time thy people shall be delivered, every one who shall be found written in the book. And many of those who sleep in the dust of the earth shall awake, some to everlasting life, and some to shame and everlasting contempt.

And they who are wise shall shine like the brightness of the firmament; and they who turn many to righteousness like the stars
forever and ever. But thou, O Daniyyel, shut up the words, and
seal the book, until the time of the end: many shall run to and
fro, and knowledge shall be increased.

The Torah, our prophets reminded us, is about deveikut/chey'rut (divine
union/enlightenment), which is the ultimate religion for all humanity. The
Torah is about our total lifestyle, which acts as a precondition for drawing grace. Grace leads us into deveikut (God-merging)/chey'rut (enlightenment). Chey'rut consciousness takes us prior to duality. It takes us prior
to time, space, and matter, and this is how the Torah begins. The first two
words of Bereisheet are Bereisheet bara, meaning "the something emerged
from the nothing." The twelfth-century Rabbi Moshe Ibn Maimon (chief
physician to the sultan of Egypt) pointed out that the Torah explains an
order of the unfolding of universal consciousness that has a divine direction. All creation has as this guided direction the ultimate enlightenment
of all beings. On the literal plane, the Torah gives levels of the blueprint of
creation. We see the spiritual blueprint of creation as the creation of the true
heavens, and a physical blueprint of creation as the creation of the earth.
From this perspective the Torah provides an outline of the evolution of consciousness we are able to understand in the world of duality. Before Bereisheet there is nothing we can comprehend because it is beyond the mind
as prior to time, space, and being. It is the awareness of enlightenment as
suggested in the Sefer Yetzirah.

The role of the Torah as a guide to enlightenment is also reflected in the
blue and white colors of the Star of David on the flag of modern Israel. The
upward facing triangle represents the Or Hozer (ascending energies) rising
to the heavens. It represents mayim nukvin (מים נוקבין), the feminine waters rising to meet the descending triangle of *zeir anpin* (זעיר אנפין) and the
descending masculine waters of or yashar (אור ישר), also known as the descending blessings and energies of mayim de'kurin (מיים דכורין). As these
heavenly and earthly energies merge into one, they emanate a singularity of
oneness. Their singularity depicts the simultaneous, synchronous deveikut/

chey'rut of enlightenment. This is reflected in the liberated one's earthly walk of enlightenment between the descending triangle of b'limah (nothing) and the ascending triangle of mah (something). In the center of this walk, between the b'limah and the mah, is the nothing of the *bitul hayesh* (ביטול היש), symbolic of the complete cosmic emptiness. The blue and white colors represent the colors of the supercausal plane of the sephirotic energy of *chokhmah* (חכמה), the consciousness of enlightenment as the direct apperceptive knowledge of YHWH. It is no accident that at the deepest understanding, the Israeli flag represents God-merged enlightenment. The spiritually hungry intuitively know that this is our birthright, but do not realize that this flag is an emanation and reflection of the Great Torah Way of enlightenment.

The Torah gifts us with a radical understanding of life. It teaches us that all human beings, regardless of class, are created in the image of God (Bereisheet 1:27 and 9:6). The word image is not about anything on the physical plane. It refers to divine consciousness at the level of the soul, in the world of the pure mind (*beriah*—בריאה) through the sephirah of *binah* (בינה). It includes a synthesis of both the inner and outer female and male, reflecting the full image of God, a "he-Adam" and a "she-Adam." It is written: "On the day that God created man, He made him in the likeness of God. He created them male and female. He blessed them and named them Man [Adam] on the day that they were created" (Bereisheet [Genesis] 5:1–2). Both he-Adam and she-Adam reside in every human being, as do the dimensions of chokhmah (the direct knowing, beyond the mind, as our ultimate potential) and keter (divine will). This image of God is the reflection or shadow of God consciousness in all humans of the Adamic race.

The Torah takes us beyond the shadow of the divine consciousness and into direct God knowledge in deveikut/chey'rut prior to Bereisheet. It reveals the purpose of relative consciousness on the earth plane and our journey into absolute consciousness in the upper heavens of our inner selves. It is an awesome transmission that gives earthlings the opportunity to evolve their own consciousness. It therefore had to wait twenty-six generations before being transmitted to us (Midrash Bereisheet Rabbah 1:4), for some degree of maturity was required to even begin to comprehend the Torah's awesome scope and depth.

It is, of course, difficult to describe "prior to existence" from a subjective experiential understanding, or any other type of understanding. But the phrase "Bereisheet bara" describes it succinctly: Prior to consciousness and existence in the *aleph* (א), one may experience the complete dissolution of the I Am-ness into the nothing or the ayin (אין). Many repeated experiences of this in the past thirty years include the primordial death (*his'tal'kut*) of the I Am-ness into the ayin. It was difficult to find previous literary validation of these rare experiential insights, but in the Zohar, in an eloquent statement it exists: "beginning of all beginnings, *Atika Kadisha* [עתיקא קדישא—Ancient Holy One], highest of all mysteries, beginning of all beginnings and of no beginnings, who is not known: and what is in His mind cannot be made known for there is no connection to *chokhmah* and not to our mortal minds ... and thus is Atika Kadisha, called ayin, for nothing hinges there" (Zohar, Vol. 3, folio 288b).

It is my experience from the repeated mystical death experiences (*his'tal'kut*) that ayin is the heart of the nothing, which then becomes the something. Out of the ayin emerges the Ayn Sof (אין סוף). At the ayin, there is no I Am-ness standing and nowhere to stand. Ayn Sof is beyond the mind, time, and space. It is both paradoxically prior to existence and unending existence. It is the unknowable perfection as the realm of the silence. Ayn Sof is the *All*. It is an infinitely expanding, undifferentiated unity. From this complete absence of ayin, prior to existence, Ayn Sof rises from the heart of ayin, then as the hidden All. Out of the All of the Ayn Sof comes what Schneur Zalmen calls the "primal affirmation," as the *Or Ayn Sof* (אור אין סוף), the light of the infinite. The "no-experience" of Ayn Sof is the essence of perfection and there is no spiritual evolution to it. Being prior to the mind is prior to the nondual reality that we know in the mind. The core of the Ayn Sof (*Hamiddat Ha Ayin*) is the source from which the nothing becomes the something in the dialectical process prior to, and including, the mind. Somewhere in this process the I Am-ness emerges in the play of the dual and the nondual. Though we are typically at a loss for description of this complete obliteration, and little personal description of it is found in the mystic literature, a Sufi prophet named Muhyiddin ibn'Arabi, in his book *Fusus al-Hikam*, written in 1165, succinctly spoke of his experience of complete dissolution of form and existence. It is rarefied, but it is significant for the purposes of sharing this teaching to validate this experience shared among the few.

Maimonides explained that the process of creation has an order. My sharing here is also an attempt to explain the unexplainable order from the ayin, the "heart of the nothing," to the "something." Shemot 33:20 says "And he said, Thou canst not see my face; for no man shall see me, and live." This awareness is a continual mystical death in the play of the world. In other words, as the sixteenth-century kabbalistic master, Rabbi Yeshayahu ben Avraham (the Sh'LaH), in *Toldot Adam Bayt Dovid*, said, there are levels within deveikut; as one dances through these post-enlightenment states, one may be "taken" (le'kee'chah—לקיחה), as were Hanokh (Enoch) and Eliyahu (Elijah). There are thousands of phases even beyond this. The life force touches eternity always and is illuminated from light to light. (Olam Haba overlays Olam ha'Zeh.) Beyond this ascended state is his'tal'kut (disappearance—הסתלקות). One may enter into this disappearance without death by ascending up to the Above, with body and soul intact, for all is. The way that Rabbi Yeshayahu ben Avraham talked about the experience of mystical death implies that he knew about it from an experiential point of view as well as theoretical.

In the beginning we have the "prior to the unending light" as the Ayn Sof, the "No-End." The Ayn Sof exists prior to time and space and light (i.e., subatomic particles), and before the pure existence of the Divine beyond our comprehension. It is in this "prior-to-consciousness" arena from which relative consciousness unfolds, and where relative truth permeates creation. In this spiritual evolutionary unfolding, God is a verb, rather than in the Absolute, where God is an unchanging noun.

Although having a nondual understanding does not make one enlightened, nor does it mean that one already *is* enlightened, it is nonetheless a sign of enlightenment, or, at least, often a sign of enlightened thinking, and a theme running through the Torah. The Torah teaching is even deeper than nondual awareness, because inherent in the nondual concept is the *existence* of the dual. The Torah's opening statement "Bereisheet bara" (בראשית ברא), which implies that *something* emerged from *nothing*, is a statement that the ultimate truth of God and deveikut/chey'rut is prior to existence and prior to the mind.

In my own ongoing awareness, the I Am-ness or the Self, which is the subtle "I am" identity, actually disappears, as does the illusion of light and dark, and time and space. When I first began to go spontaneously into these "prior-to-nothing" states people thought I had died, as all breathing appeared to have stopped. It is from this non-awareness prior to the mind that I began to understand the opening line of the Torah, "Bereisheet bara." Before the creation, there was the nothing from which the something emerged. The nothing is prior to the mind, time, space, and I Am-ness. In the morning *Shacharit* prayer, we recite "You were the same before the world was created; you have been the same since the creation of the world." This is a clear enlightenment teaching. The nondual awareness is expressed in a variety of ways but a simple way is *Ayn Zulato* (אין זולתו), or "there is nothing other than [God]." In the ancient mystical writ known as Sefer Yetzirah, God is beyond time, space, and being (I Am-ness). In this context, God is not a verb, but is rather unchanging existence and complete and absolute oneness without other. The period between Rosh Hashanah (the dualistic idea of God as both king and judge) and Yom Kippur (day of nondual at-onement) teaches us this through the purification and awakening processes of the ten *sephirot* during those ten days, and is yet another reflection of this oneness teachings of the Torah. Another term for this concept, voiced by the prophet Moshe is *Ayn od milvado* (מלבדו אין עוד)—"There is none else beside him [God]" (Devarim 4:35). *Ayn* (אין) is rooted in, and is spelled the same as, the word ayin (אין), which translates as nothing. We can therefore just as easily read it as "There is no other nothing but God"—God, in other words, is the sole nothing. All else is something, created from the absolute nothing. Both terms represent a sense of an unbroken wholeness through which one may experience the world. In the enlightened state, this awareness is almost constantly present.

Since it was first taught to us by Moshe, some 3,300 years ago, every observant Jew has recited the declaration known as *sh'ma* at least twice a day, morning and night, if not three times, as commonly done in our modern times. It is the first prayer we learn as a child and the last prayer we are instructed to say before we die: *"Sh'ma Yisra'el Adonai Eloheinu Adonai Echad"* (אלהינו יה אחד שמע ישראל יה)—"Listen, Israel, God is our Lord, God is One" (Devarim 6:4). Understood from the nondual perspective, the sh'ma reminds us to always experience the singleness of God in the plurality of creation. On the other hand, from a "prior-to-the-mind" awareness, understanding the sh'ma, as it is more popularly understood, is a reminder that "there is only one God." This creates significant duality and limitation, because it creates boundaries around God, and a definition. From our deeper sh'ma awareness, however (which was also the theme of my bar-mitzvah), we are naturally led to constantly experience the glory of God in all things. And therefore we recite *"Baruch shem k'vod malchuto l'olam va'ed"* (ברוך שם כבטד מלכותו לעולם ועד), following our proclamation of the sh'ma—"Blessed is the name, the glory of whose reign is forever and ever." This is similar to yet another such awareness expressed in the mantra *"shiviti Hashem l'neg'dee ta'mid"* (שויתי יה לנגדי תמיד)—"I have set the Lord always before me" (Tehillim 16:8). In this context, the Shiviti affirmation can be interpreted not only as a spiritual practice, but also as an ongoing awareness in which we naturally experience the luminosity of Hashem, radiating out of all creation, all the time. We see this further articulated in the phrase *"m'lo kol ha'aretz kvodo"* (מלא כל הארץ כבודו)—"The whole world is filled with [God's] glory" (BeMidbar 14:21; Tehillim 72:19; Yesha'yahu 6:3).

These are the seminal chey'rut-enlightenment teachings of the Torah that are repeated again in the Prophets, the Psalms, and the Zohar. Mal'akhi 3:6 says "For I am the Lord, I do not change," and Yesha'yahu 45:5 again teaches "I am the Lord, and there is none else." In the Zohar, it says *"leht atar panui mineha"* (לית אתר פנוי מניה)—"There is no place devoid of [God]" (Tikkunei Zohar, folio 122b). All of these are the essential teaching of the Torah's non-dual teachings of Ayn Zulato.

The second part of the teaching around enlightenment is alluded to in the account of the PaRDeS (פרדס), the shamanic journey involving four rabbis, led by Rabbi Akiva in the second century, as described earlier in this introduction. The lesson there is that a fuller enlightenment requires the constant paradoxical holding of the walk between the b'limah and the mah. Although there are other dual levels of interpretation of the Torah, which may represent the majority perspective, it is significant that these chey'rut teachings are also found in the works of major mystics such as Moses Cordovero in *Pardes Rimonim* ("The Orchard of Pomegrantes") and by mystics like the Ba'al Shem Tov: "Nothing exists in this world except the absolute Unity which is God"

(Va'EthChanan 13, translated by Aryeh Kaplan, *The Light Beyond,* p. 37). The Ba'al Shem taught that one should be in a constant state of the *yechudim* (unifications), which involves experiencing and liberating the God light in all things. The Tanya, the founding teaching text of Chabad Hasidim authored by the eighteenth-century Rabbi Schneur Zalman of Liadi, is another powerful focus on the nondual understanding of the Torah.

The teaching of Ayn Zulato helps us understand that all comes from God, including evil, or the yetzer hara, the evil impulse. In this context, by the illusory mechanism of "free will" and our exposure to the yetzer hara, we are given the opportunity to evolve spiritually by overcoming the seduction of the dark side and choosing the good. We are presented with both the challenge and the potential penalty, which is to lose our *nefesh* (נפש—life force) to the *Sit'ra Ach'ra* (סטרא אחרא—forces of darkness). Generally speaking, with the exceptions of Hanokh, Noah, Malki-zedek, Avraham, Yitzhak, Ya'akov, Yosef, and Moshe, who were the *tzaddikim* of their times, humanity, and Am Yisrael, as a whole, has not done too well in resisting the Sit'ra Ach'ra. One of the metaphysical reasons the Torah was given was to show us how to protect ourselves from the Sit'ra Ach'ra and as an antidote to prevent or repair the loss of nefesh to the Sit'ra Ach'ra.

In this metaphysical context, sinning and *tum'ah* (impurity) are acting in ways that lose nefesh. Building nefesh happens through living the mitzvot and the teachings of Torah. The forty-day purification from the month of Elul through Yom Kippur was, and is, an effort to build the nefesh by atoning for our missing the mark. The Temple sacrifices on that day, culminating in transferring the lost nefesh of Am Yisrael to the goat, and then sending the goat to *Azazel,* is about "giving the devil his due." This was also a Torah mechanism to put a cap on how much of the nefesh the Sit'ra Ach'ra could take. In general, the Temple sacrifices replaced the lost nefesh, which resulted from our dark-side activities by replacing what was lost with the life force/nefesh of the animal. The fall of the first Temple and the eventual Diaspora, in both 586 BC and in 69 AD, abolished this mechanism and allowed for the unprecedented thievery of nefesh by the Sit'ra Ach'ra, as there was no longer a cap on it. At a certain subtle level, the attempts to delegitimize Israel, and anti-Semitism in general throughout the ages, as well as now, can be understood to be driven by the powerful efforts of the Sit'ra Ach'ra to prevent limitation on the amount of nefesh it is allowed to steal. That only works, however, if Am Yisrael continues to act in ways that lose nefesh. If people were to return to the Great Torah Way, the luminosity and intensity of the nefesh would be so strong that the Sit'ra Ach'ra would not be able to steal it or even *approach* the people of the light. The nefesh of Am Yisrael would be so bright as to illuminate the entire world.

Regarding the various interpretations of the Torah, we can view p'shat as what is literally written. Remez is a hint pointing to possibilities beyond the literal. As Maimonides pointed out, we can look at this process as order, and in this order, the heavens came first and spirit preceded matter. According to drash, spirituality took precedence over earthly pursuits, and this is how we are directed to live our lives. We are to dedicate our lives to spiritual development, not to gathering material things. The heavens on the drash level are primary, and earthly activities are secondary, although they are here to help us to learn our spiritual lessons. We are on the earth plane to evolve spiritually through lessons available to us solely here and now.

Physics tells us that there is a great singularity to the universe, although it is difficult for us to see this unity in the relative world of separation. This singularity precludes a coherent conscious society, which will emerge and predominate during the messianic times. The Torah is a guide for how to awaken to this truth. The Torah shows us the progression of order as a spiral evolution of consciousness, instead of viewing it as linear history. Bereisheet explains a process about the order and timing of creation. Prior to time space, and energy we have existence. Existence is prior to the creation of the heavens and the earth. This gives a clue to the next phase of evolution. After creation, we see a consistent pattern of Hashem intervening throughout history to guide evolution.

Each parashah in the five books of the Torah, then, is a multilayered teaching in the Way of the Torah as a guide to enlightenment. I have for many years been lecturing on the parashahs as lessons in enlightenment. It has been joyous to see many who have felt disenfranchised from their roots by the ey'rev rav, within themselves and externally, happily waking up to their tradition as a profound enlightenment path. May all who read this book be blessed to realize the Great Enlightenment Way of the Torah.

Rabbi Gabriel Cousens, MD

The
Book
of
Bereisheet

Bereisheet

Bereisheet (Genesis) 1:1 is the key to understanding the Torah as a guide to enlightenment. Bereisheet 1:2–6 is also called m'aseh Bereisheet (בראשית מעשה), the work of creation. However complicated it is, I shall attempt to address it from a variety of angles that will give us some understanding among its many subtleties. Regarding the p'shat (literal) level of understanding Bereisheet, Maimonides wrote in his Guide for the Perplexed, "Study astronomy and physics if you desire to comprehend the relation between the world and God's management of it." This interesting concept leaves us with much to understand, and it gives us a clue.

Taking Maimonides's suggestion, we begin by asking the question, How do we reconcile the scientific estimate of the age of the universe (fifteen billion years according to physicists—the earth herself being more than 4.5 billion years old, according to archeologists and paleontologists), with the Torah's creation date occurring merely 5,771 years ago? This question must be addressed before we can look at the spiritual significance of Day One. Our sages taught that a theology devoid of knowledge of the physical universe is a contradiction of terms. We will now attempt to resolve that contradiction from a larger perspective. Before we do that, we have to understand that we are really talking about two distinct levels of creation: (1) the first fifteen billion years, and (2) the creation story of Adam that took place 5,771 years ago. Somewhere we must resolve this discussion before going deeper into these two different creation stories.

There is a midrashic teaching that whenever a Torah passage begins with the phrase Ve'eleh (ואלה—"and these"), it is a continuation of a preceding section. When it begins with Eleh (אלה—"these"), it represents a break from the preceding section. Bereisheet 2:4 begins with Eleh (אלה). This is a hint that this account is not to be associated with the previous section having to do with tohu and bohu (primeval chaos and emptiness) that constituted the dynamics of creation ex-nihilo.

An understanding of the distinction between Einstein's specific theory of relativity and his general theory of relativity will help us to begin making sense of this. Prior to Einstein's theories, proposed in 1905 and 1916, time was always regarded as an absolute concept regardless of who measured it or where they were measuring it. This has changed in both space and time to a new understanding. Of course, unbeknownst to most, the theory of relativity was already discussed in the Judaic tradition by such mystics as the sixteenth-century Rabbi Yehudah Loew of Prague (in *Sefer Gevurot Hashem, Hakdamah Sh'neeya*, folios 15 and 16; see also Chaps. 36, 68, and 70). The aspect of relativity related to *time dilation* is the key to understanding the discussion of time between the pre-Adamic era (six days of creation) and the post-Adamic time. Although this makes the discussion more complicated, it is essential for a deeper understanding. The six-day cycle suggests that although the creator could have done this in an instant, for reasons beyond our understanding, a gradual unfolding was chosen. The Talmud teaches us that it was to demonstrate the preciousness of our universe: "With ten utterances did God create the world. But could God not have created the world with a single utterance? Rather, it is to teach you how precious is our earth, and how great the reward for those who cherish her and how great the consequences for those who abuse her" (Mishnah, Avot 5:1).

By understanding the rules of physics in their current manifestation, we can see that there was a need for a gradual development beginning with the Big Bang and progressing all the way to the development of humanity. We must also appreciate that the physical earth and its inhabitants are not necessarily direct products of the Big Bang. In the beginning the earth was void, and then it was formed—*tohu va' bohu* (תהו ובהו). From a modern perspective, we see that particle physicists now refer to tohu and bohu as the basic building blocks of matter. The force of the Big Bang compressed tohu and bohu into hydrogen and helium. These were the only elements formed at that time. The alchemy of the cosmos converted hydrogen and helium into the rest of the elements. Over time stars were born and died.

As pointed out by the ancient rabbis, God created and destroyed many worlds in the process of establishing life on earth (Midrash Bereisheet Rabbah 3:7). This, of course, agrees with the science of modern physics. It was not until Adam appeared that the present functioning time era began. At that point, time as we now know it began. Prior to this, it was God's time. God had not manifested on earth in relationship to Adam. Earth did not exist for Day One and Day Two in Bereisheet. Bereisheet (Genesis) 1:1 says, "In the beginning God created the heaven and the earth," but Bereisheet 1:2 says, "the earth was without form and empty"—so obviously it did not yet exist. This is a statement about primordial material being created. It then goes on to say that out of this primordial substance the earth was created. When we are speaking of the earth, we are referring to time and space prior to creation. Time, space, and I Am-ness did not exist before the Big Bang. This then gives us insight into several levels of the creation.

First, there was the nothing, prior to creation out of which the Big Bang occurred. Next, the heavens unfolded and the earth was created. "Earth" in this context, could also be interpreted as our particular universe. In the divine intervention, in the first second of creation, there was a *Ruach Elohim*. The wind of God, called the Ruach Elohim (רוח אלהים), gave birth to a perpetual expansion of the universe. As it expanded, multiple universes were formed, patterned after the Tree of Life. This is the mystical tree of the ten energies of nothingness condensed into four evolutionary realms: primal thought (*atzilut*—אצילות), conceptualization (*beriah*—בריאה), shaping (*yetzirah*—יצירה), and manifestation (*assiyah*—עשׁיה). This pattern can be seen from the macrocosmic to the microcosmic subatomic levels of the multiple universes.

When the expanding universe creation interfaced with our empty universe of potential (which was tohu and bohu—empty and void), the energy, based on the pattern of *Etz Chaim* (Tree of Life—עץ חיים), was injected into this universe of emptiness. The pattern of the Torah as Etz Chaim, forming the subtle organizing fields for this universe, began to manifest and consolidate into form. This explanation corresponds with the primordial creation story of the formation of the universe as recounted in the Zohar. There, we are told that prior to creating this universe Hashem looked into the Torah as he manifested this expanding universe as a Torah/Etz Chaim pattern. This primordial, etheric pattern filled our empty universe. This pattern then manifested physically (Zohar, Vol. 1, folio 134a). Consequently, the physical and energetic local universe became a manifestation of the Torah. In this way, Hashem, the

Torah, the creation of his universe, and Adamic humanity, as the image of God, became, and remain, one (Zohar, Vol. 3, folio 73a). This is the deep meaning of the *shema* (שמע), the traditional Hebrew declaration of the one-ness of God, transmitted from Moshe some 3,300 years ago (in Devarim 6:4).

Interestingly enough, the name *Elohim* (אלהים), the name of God as *natural law*, shares the same numerical value, or gematria (גמטריא), as the Hebrew word for Nature herself (*HaTeva*—הטבע). In this way we can begin to understand that the Torah is beyond a particular religion. Rather, on one level, the Torah is as the natural and unfolding law of this universe. Thus, by understanding the Torah in this way, we are able to align with the natural laws of the universe, which include the Ten Speakings (commonly mistranslated as the Ten Commandments), and all the 613 *mitzvot*, or sacred instructions. By aligning with the Torah we are able to fulfill the meaning of *halakhah* (הלכה), which is commonly translated as Jewish law, but actually implies *the divine and natural way to walk as a full human being on the planet*. Unfortunately, since the time of Adam and Eve (Cha'avah), since they ate of *Etz HaDa'at* (הדעת עץ—the Tree of Knowledge) instead of *Etz Chaim* (עץ חיים—the Tree of Life), and since the time of Kayin, who saw himself as separate from Hashem (השם), preferring technology/science over the Divine, we have slowly, repeatedly, and progressively lost our natural, psychic, and spiritual harmony with the Torah as a guideline to live as full and awake human beings on the planet. In order to rectify this, Hashem has made a variety of *tikkunot* (תיקונות—divine interventions or corrections) to help humans. One of the most well known was the interdimensional communication of the Torah at Mount Sinai as a way to help *Am Yisrael* (עם ישראל—the spiritual nation represented by the collective Jewish people, as it says in Yeshiyahu 43:21 [Isaiah], "this nation that I formed, in order to relate my glory"), and all of humanity, reconnect to the divine walk and way of God.

When we understand the opening words of the Torah, they give us a clue to life's ultimate purpose, which is to know God. To know God is to go back before creation, prior to time, space, and I Am-ness. The first chapter and verse tells us to go prior to the mind to a place that none can know on the level of the mind. It is only after the creation occurred that the mind (*binah*, or understanding) began to exist. Prior to understanding is the mystery of the unknown prior to time and space. This is the awareness of *deveikut/chey'rut* (דביקות/חירות—enlightenment). For six days God made the heavens and the earth. What exactly did God make this *from*? God made it from the primordial soup created by the initial Big Bang.

In discussing time, we must remember that there was no earth in the beginning of the universe, so there was no ability to blend time frames. Cosmic time had no relationship to earth time, because the earth did not exist yet. According to the law of relativity (an inherent trait of the universe), it is impossible at the time of creation for a common frame of reference to exist between the creator and each part of the mix of the universe. According to Einstein's law of relativity, local time varies among different parts of the universe. There are differences in gravitational forces and movement of stars and galaxies. The passage of time is a local observation. It varies from place to place. As we look at all the stars, we must understand that these are billions upon billions of cosmic clocks that all started at the moment of the Big Bang. The unfolding of the Big Bang makes it clear that we are but fragments of previously created and exploded stars. In other words, we human beings are made of stardust.

How do we chart time prior to Adam? We are forced to choose a reference point, and we choose the time frame of the creator rather than earth time. In this frame of reference, we view the whole universe as a single entity, until the great relative shift occurs, initiating us into local earth time. Our physical world comes from stardust (Zohar, Vol. 1, folio 231a). This is the ground of our being. Bereisheet 1:30 says that all creatures were given a soul. This is *nefesh*, and it is the lowest of soul levels in kabbalistic teachings. It has been discovered that humanity has lived on this planet for at least one million years. However, in the creation of the Adamic race, Adam was given something more than human creatures previously possessed. In Bereisheet 2:7, Adam was given the living breath of God. At this instant, the creator and the created became one. God's breath became the breath of Adam. At this point we transition into earth time. Since the time of Adam, no one can disagree about the unfolding of this local time.

These six days are not referring to twenty-four-hour cycles. These are epoch times. The reference for these six days was the time frame for the total universe. Only now, the modern physicists can give us another insight, through string theory. Whatever intelligence transmitted the Torah to Moshe was actually giving us the physics of the creation of the universe. It has taken us nearly 5,700 years to decipher this advanced spiritual physics statement. Even the subtlety of the words is a clue. It was not a "rest" on the Shabbat, but, rather, *repose*—to encompass, or set, the universe after the first six days. As this concept relates to Shabbat, in Shemot (Exodus) 20:11, Zekharya (Zachariah) 5:11, and Shemu'el (Samuel) 21:10, the same word for resting (הנחה—*ha'nachah*) is used.

In discussing the six days, Nehunia ben haKana, to whom is attributed authorship of *The Bahir*, points out that in *The Bahir*, page 30, section 82, Bereisheet does not say "in six days" but rather "six days." This understanding gives us a useful perspective in discussing the meaning of the six days beyond a literal, fundamentalist interpretation. In this context, each day of the six days is attributed a certain power. The power of each of these six days is related to the sephirotic energies from *tiferet* through *yesod* (six of the ten sephirotic energies). As I will explain later, from the perspective of Maimonides, these six days of power describe a cosmic and subtle spiritual order of unfolding. Time, in this context, is a relative function that comes out of order.

Maimonides also made reference to this. The first Shabbat was a resetting, in which, afterwards, the laws of time and space would then function in a "normal" (earthly) way. Two sets of time are spoken of here. According to the logic of pre-advanced physics, the first six days were pre-logical. The first Shabbat marks the start of Adamic time. The relativity of time, Einstein's law of relativity, the Doppler effect, and other perceptions have now created validity for the meaning of the six days on a quantum physics level of understanding. They can provide us with an encompassing understanding of the unfolding prior to Adamic time without contradiction.

I am not proposing a Darwinian theory, as the overall research does not support Darwinism in any scientific way. There is no dynamic evidence in the fossil record, or in the variety of life around us, that proves one species changes into another, or that complex life forms arise from simpler ones. This theory not only has not been proven, but it is most likely false according to some of the leaders of the scientific community concerned with this question.

In 1980 an important conference on macroevolution was held, which shared a complete reevaluation of origins. The world-famous paleontologist at the American Museum of Natural History, Dr. Niles Eldridge, unequivocally declared, "The pattern we were told to find for the last 120 years doesn't exist." We have been looking for Darwin's pattern of evolution, and it cannot be found. There is now overwhelming evidence from both statistical and paleontological perspectives that life could not have been started by a series of random chemical reactions. Though it is theoretically possible, top physicists and mathematicians estimate that there is not enough time in the fifteen billion years of the multi-universe's existence, or the age of the earth, for random chemical reactions to get life going. We may thus reasonably conclude that a divine force has metaphysically directed the evolution of life. By letting go of Darwinism, we can begin to consider a directed evolution in the creation of the life of the universe and specifically life on earth.

Many clues appear to allow for this understanding. Rabbi and physician Moshe ben Nachman (Nachmanides, or "the Ramban") taught in the introduction of his commentary on Bereisheet that all that was transmitted to Moshe was written into the Torah directly or implicated, including the numerical values of the letters. I will consider some of these while talking about Bereisheet. Everything in the Torah is a hint or clue. Everything is a teaching, including the very *shapes* of the letters. Shir Hashirim (Song of Songs) 1:4 says "The king has brought me into his chambers." The Torah is the chamber the Divine brings us into giving us understanding of God's way in the universe.

When discussing the age of the universe, it is fascinating to understand that more than 800 years ago, Rabbi Isaac of Acco, both a student and colleague of the Ramban, developed an understanding and interpretation from the *Sefer ha'Tenunah*, computing the age of the universe at fifteen billion years (in his work *Shoshan Yesod Olam*). It is significant that this calculation did not originate with modern-day astrophysicists, but from a thirteenth-century rabbinic scholar. Jewish mystics have known it for some 800 years!

Any opinion found in a recognized Torah source is considered acceptable, when we are discussing non-halakhah concepts (such as the age of the universe). Sa'adiah Gaon, the greatest Torah scholar of the tenth century, taught that life on other worlds was consistent with Torah teachings. It is an accepted Torah teaching that extraterrestrial life exists.

An understanding of pre-Adamic times is not necessarily specific to the context of the Big Bang. In the Big Bang worlds were created and destroyed, and we are the stardust emerging from this. However, I am also talking about sabbatical cycles. From this we get an idea of the age of the universe. One of the key texts is the Sefer ha'Tenunah, a kabbalistic work attributed to the first-century *tanna* rabbi Nehuna ben ha-Kanah. It discusses the Hebrew letters and their shapes, and is a frequently cited opinion in halakhic literature. This book specifically discusses the sabbatical cycles. It states that the world will exist for 6,000 years, and for the seventh thousand-year period, it will be destroyed. Each sabbatical cycle is 7,000 years. It is prophesied that we are going through seven sabbatical cycles, which means that we may propose the existence of a world cycle to be 49,000 years (close to two times 26,000). This does not seem too far away from the Mayan and general astrological calculations in which there is an intersection of the plane of the Milky Way with the zodiacal plane in alignment with the galactic center every 26,000 years. This understanding, however, was not shared by the sixteenth-century rabbis Moses Cordova (the RaMaK) and Isaac Luria. They did not agree with this concept in general. However, there are enough kabbalists that follow this 49,000-year theory to establish it as a valid perspective.

According to the Sefer ha'Tenunah, there were other civilizations before the Adamic race was created; these were the worlds of previous sabbatical cycles. While we do not know which sabbatical we are in, we certainly have some clues. In Bereisheet 1:5 we read "It was evening and it was morning, one day." This implies that there was time before the Adamic cycle. This reinforces the distinction between the Big Bang and the Adamic cycle. The Talmud also supports the theory of sabbatical cycle. According to the Talmud and some of the midrashim, there were actually 974 generations before the time of Adam (Talmud, Shabbat 88b and Zevachim 116a). Tehillim (Psalms) 105:8 says "He has remembered his covenant forever, the word which he commanded to a thousand generations." This suggests that the Torah was destined to be given after a thousand generations. Since Moshe was twenty-six generations *after* Adam, it stands to reason that there were 974 generations *before* Adam. These were the previous civilizations manifested and were destroyed (Midrash Bereisheet Rabbah 3:7). The early *rishonim* (ראשונים—early rabbinic authorities) such as Bihya Recanati, Ziyyoni, and the *Sefer Hinnukh*, along with the commentaries of Ramban, also suggest pre-Adamic cycles.

This is relevant because these pre-Adamic time cycles account for the dinosaurs, Neanderthals, mastodons, and the unearthed fossil records without creating a contradiction with the Adamic cycle. These ancient, extinct species and other paleontological findings were part of these pre-Adamic cycles. Rabbi Isaac of Acco did a particular mathematics of the cycles. In his rare work, *Ozar ha'Hayyim*, he wrote that because these cycles existed before Adam, they must be measured in divine years. He understood this eight hundred years ago. According to the midrashic sources, a divine day is 1,000 earth years. A divine year is 365,250 earth years. If we do the math, this makes the world 42,000 years old when Adam was created (which is the theory of the six cycles). If we multiply this by 365,250, we get 15,340,500,000 years, which matches the calculations of astrophysicists.

There is no conflict in what we mean by the six days and the six cycles. Toho va bohu (chaos and void) was happening fifteen billion years ago. Bereisheet 1:1–2:3 is the first account of creation. Bereisheet 2:4–2:23 is the second account of creation. Bereisheet 1:27 says: "God [thus] created man with His image. In the image of God, He created him, male and female He created them." This suggests that Adam and Cha'vah (Eve) were created simultaneously. The second version says that Cha'vah was created from Adam's rib. Perhaps the Torah is speaking of two different things here. Perhaps this is thought and manifestation. Man and woman were created simultaneously in thought (maybe as Adam and Lilith) on the astral plane. Man and woman may have been created separately, as Adam and Cha'vah, on the physical plane.

When was the world created? Which month in the Hebraic lunar calendar system does its creation correspond with? Was it made in the moon of autumnal *Tishrei* or vernal *Nissan*? That is the question posed in the Talmud. Rabbi Yehoshua held that the world was created in the month Nissan, and Rabbi Eliezer was of the opinion that it occurred in Tishrei (Talmud, Rosh Hashanah 10b–11a). Actually, both are correct, based on our understanding of these two different planes—thought and manifestation. In the month of Tishrei, the world was created on the binah level in thought. In Nissan, it was created in deed in *malchut*.

The Big Bang is where the spiritual infrastructure of the universe was created prior to the existence of time and space. In enlightenment, we naturally go *prior* to time and space. To return to this state is the ultimate purpose of life. It is wonderful that this is shared in the very first chapter and verse of Bereisheet. As the universe unfolds, 5,771 years ago we had the creation of Adam. The breath of God was introduced here, and man was able to communicate with the Divine. This was the next evolutionary step in the development of humanity.

There is no conflict whatsoever between the Torah and sophisticated modern astrophysics. Science has finally caught up with the teachings of the Torah. The minute we begin to talk about the seven sabbatical cycles of 7,000 years each, we need to look at the question of reincarnation and the Jewish faith in resurrection. As we look at this further we get a different perspective on the issue. The oral teachings, aligned with both resurrection and reincarnation, are basically identical. At the end of each cycle, the world and human beings go to a higher order of perfection. At the end of the seven cycles, all the holy sparks of humanity become perfected and return to the One. All beings become illuminated in the permanent state of deveikut/chey'rut (God-merging/enlightenment). The historical spiral purpose of creation is that all beings return to the One in perfect enlightenment. Each lifetime and each cycle is a preparation for the following cycle. When we understand this, it gives meaning, purpose, and direction to life. This is why the Torah is a handbook for deveikut/chey'rut.

It is said in the teachings, "Blessed be he who set the lights in the sky" (Talmud, Sanhedrin 42a). The Torah is seen as a light in the sky illuminating the earth. It is the subtle organizing energy field for the earth and this local universe. On the fourth day, two lights were fashioned. The greater light, ruling the day, is the Torah. The lesser light, ruling the night, is man's intellect. Man's intellect rules the world and leads us into the danger of rationalism, where we become disconnected from the heart and morality. As we witness these cycles of destruction and renewal, we can better understand the teachings coming through Yesha'yahu (Isaiah) 65:17, "For behold I create new heavens and a new earth." He is referring to the cycles in progression. This may seem to contradict the statement that the world stands forever, but it does not. The world does stand forever, but there are different cycles in the world.

In the first parashah of the Torah, all knowledge is contained as concentrated understanding. It is the superconcentrated mass before the Big Bang. We can view the heavens as an element. The word *shamayin* (שמים—heavens) is a combination of the words for fire (אש—*esh*) and water (מים—*mayim*). The Elohim took fire and water and mixed them. The shamayin was a vapor, not the atmosphere. The firmament (*raki'a*—רקיע) was the atmosphere made for breathing. The Torah is specific. Elohim said let there be an expanse of raki'a, but they did not give a similar command for the heavens.

Another question arises with the first chapter of Bereisheet. Why are the four elements (fire, air, water, and earth) not explicitly mentioned? In the second verse, the earth was empty and desolate. It would be unnecessary to say, "before the creation of the world, not even the *light* of the world existed." This suggests we are talking about two different levels of creation. The Torah may have been referring to the lifeless earth in one of its seventh thousand-year cycles of desolation. This becomes clearer when we see the spirit of God hovering over the waters in Bereisheet 1:2. The eleventh-century commentator Rabbi Shlomo Yizchaki (Rashi) pointed out that this refers to the glory throne of God. The Torah strongly suggests that this present world is not in its first cycle. The elements were created in earlier cycles and did not need to be mentioned.

What was happening before "the beginning"? According to the Torah tradition this is unknowable and beyond the realm of mortal questioning (Talmud, Chagigah 11b). The Hebrew letter (ב—*bet*) begins the first chapter. The letter opens only in a *forward* direction. It is closed on three sides—it can only go forward. Because it is bound in this way, all that is given for us to use is what comes after creation. We can access nothing before creation. Scientists can get to minus 1/43rd of a second, but they cannot go further back into the Big Bang unfolding. This is pretty far back, however, 10 to the minus 43rd power of seconds is ten million, million, million, million, million, million, millionths of a second. At this point the universe is as big as a speck of dust and is now expanding outward. The temperature of this speck of dust was 10 to the 32nd power degrees Kelvin, or 100 million, million, million, million, million degrees Kelvin. There is no measurement older or hotter than these numbers. A physics term referring to beyond these is *singularity*.

These are our limitations as we attempt to approach prior to the Big Bang—the understanding prior to creation cannot be reached by the mind. The level of binah, the pure mind (בלי—b'lee) cannot be transcended mentally. Prior to the beginning there was no time or space or mass. Prior to the beginning there was only the energy of the Divine. This is a message. When we look at beriah, we realize that to return to God is to go beyond the beginning. It is to go into the nothing from whence all came. It is the place all humanity will go when we go through all seven cycles of creation and destruction. It is the place of chey'rut and ultimate truth. It is our source. It is in the very first letter of the very first word of the Torah. This is the purpose of the Torah. It is a guidebook and a pathway to going prior to creation into the mystery of deveikut/chey'rut.

After creation began, initially there was no order; only chaos. From the physics perspective of tohu va bohu, there was a high incidence of random high-energy collisions that prevented any organization in the particles present. Without order there was no information (light) to be conveyed. The brilliant thirteenth-century "physicist" Rabbi Nachmanides quoted a commentary supporting this position written six hundred years before him. Prior to the existence of the universe, time did not exist. He gathered this wording from Bereisheet 1:5, "It was evening and it was morning, one day." If it had said "the first day," it would have implied a continuum of time. Instead the implication is "no time" prior to Day One. Maimonides and Nachmanides shared similar opinions that prior to the creation of the universe neither time nor space existed.

The creation of the universe brought forth time and space. Time allows for the flow of the universe. Space allows for the expansion of the universe. The creation of the primordial substance brought forth the existence of time and space. In the classical theory of Arizal (sixteenth-century Rabbi Yitzchak Luria), creation happened when God contracted space into a point from which the universe could expand. In this expansion are the ten aspects of the Divine as the ten sephirotic energies. These are hinted at when we have ten repetitions of the phrase "and God said."

The ten sephirot (ספירות) contract to the four dimensions of height, width, depth, and time. The physicists now propose string theory with its ten dimensions that contract into four. Of course, we are simply describing the Tree of Life. The middle six dimensions of the Tree of Life are called zeir anpin collectively (זעיר אנפין), and we are ultimately left with the remaining four—*keter* (כתר), *chokhmah* (חכמה), *binah* (בינה), and *malchut* (מלכות). The coherence between modern astrophysicists and the Torah is fascinating. Nachmanides, in his commentary on Bereisheet, was able to speak about an expanding universe (essentially, the Big Bang theory) in a very similar way. We have no idea where Nachmanides received this information, aside from his own contemplation. Without a scientific background it was amazing that he was able to outline it in a powerful way.

According to the Torah, the heavens and the earth were created from nothing. This is an accurate statement based upon the consciousness of chey'rut. The Hebrew word *bara* (ברא) means "the creation of something from nothing" (*Pirush HaRamban ahi HaTorah*, Bereisheet 1:11). It was a major revelation for me to understand that the opening words of the Torah—the very seed energy of the Torah—are a statement of deveikut/chey'rut as the founding teaching and the essence of the Torah. Nachmanides wrote that this was incomprehensible unless one had received the "hidden wisdom," known as *chokhmah nishtarah* (חכמה נסתרה). This is accessible in modern times through quieting the mind and receiving this divine gift in meditation. Nachmanides recognized that a descent of grace is required for this reception, and this can only happen through a righteous way of life as a precondition. It is a mystical intuition that from *nothing* comes *something*. It is only described one time in the Torah as the second word of the first sentence. It says "Bereisheet bara" (בראשית ברא). This is the profound opening of the Torah.

The best the astrophysicists can do is to *describe* a condition, in which all matter is compressed into a space of zero size and infinite density, as a theoretical concept. This is similar to the biblical concept that the universe started as a tiny, but finite speck of space the size of a grain. Both theorize that matter was present in miniscule amounts as compared to energy. This is profoundly different from the Greek cosmology, which states that matter is the basis of the universe and is therefore eternal. When we understand this, we know that our walk upon the earth is a walk between the *b'limah* (בלי מה—nothing) and the *mah* (מה—something). Our job is to integrate the nothing and the something. The b'limah is the absolute reality. The mah is the relative reality. This mystical walk is the spiritual art of our lives and our evolution. Its synergy is connected in the unfolding of enlightenment. In the consciousness of chey'rut we hold these simultaneously by abiding in the nothing, while walking in the dualistic relative world of the something.

One wonders, in awe, how these rabbis had this understanding of an expanding universe. Most likely, they got their information in the conventional spiritual and intuitive way. The Torah and the astrophysicists agree that there was a Big Bang, and that the expansion of the universe is not self-limited. They agree that the universe continues and that there is not a state of expansion and contraction. It says in Tehillim (Psalms) 148:4–6: "Praise him, heavens of heavens, and you waters that are above the heavens. Let them praise the name of the Lord: for he gave command, and they were created. And he established them for ever and ever: he has made a decree which shall not pass." We can be assured that the process will continue. The heavens, in essence, are eternal.

How did this expansion occur? It is interesting that both modern physics and the Torah understood that we are dealing with black-hole physics, and that there had to be an intervention to reverse the contraction, which occurred at the very beginning. Physicists explain this intervention by proposing an "inflationary energy." This was, in other words, an expansive energy, or pulse, that occurred 10 to minus 35 seconds after the beginning of the universe. At this time, the universe itself had a diameter of 10 to minus 24 centimeters—pretty small. The term "wind of God" is used only once in Bereisheet to describe this cosmic influx of expansive energy. Bereisheet 1:2 says "with darkness on the face of the depths [black hole], but God's spirit [God's wind] moved on the water's surface." In the beginning was a black hole, and there was an intervention by "God's wind," which began the reversal of the contraction and initiated the expansion of the black hole. Since then we have an eternal uninterrupted expansion of our universe. The astrophysicists, as explained before, have also projected a one-time event called an "inflationary epic," in which this expansive energy occurred. The wind of God is called the Ruach Elohim (רוח אלהים). What is the significance of this wind of God? This event clearly points out that we do not live in a random universe. As we examine the evidence, Big Bang evolution in general, and human evolution in specific, have all been intervened upon by the Divine throughout history, for the purpose of expanding consciousness.

Fossils occurred 3.5 billion years ago. This is not possible by random selection. Harold Morowitz, a physicist at Yale, published a book in 1968 called *Energy Flow in Biology*, which made the very clear point in presenting his mathematical model refuting the Darwinian theory of evolution. Based on his calculations, optimistically rapid rates of reactions for mere formation of bacteria would take longer than the fifteen-billion-year age of the universe. When we consider that sedimentary rocks formed 3.8 billion years ago, we cannot help but theorize periodic divine intervention from the very beginning of the Big Bang.

The Torah and modern astrophysics have proven the Big Bang; they have also proven that the universe is divinely organized. Instead of entropy (increasing chaos), we have enthalpy (increasing order). This is not possible in a random universe. Enthalpy is a sign of divine intervention. This is hard to understand but the evidence is present.

Bereisheet 1:31 says, "God saw all that he had made, and behold, it was very good." What is being said here is that there is a divine purpose for life. We exist to participate in this purpose in a way that brings all humanity into God-merging. The Torah makes this subtly clear through the descriptions of all the divine interventions that there is a divinely directed cosmic and human evolution. We are given the *illusion* of free will on the plane of malchut so we can choose to consciously or unconsciously cooperate with these purposeful series of divine interventions. Some of these nodal interventions include: (1) the Ruach Elohim that reversed us from contracting into a black hole; (2) the formation of the Adamic race; (3) the great flood; (4) the defeat of Pharaoh with the ten plagues and the freeing of the Jews; (5) the events of *Har Sinay* (הר סיני); and (6) the receiving of the Torah as a gift from God. The list is longer, but this makes the point. As conscious participants we can choose to be a joyous holy part of evolution, or be dragged along by the tide in a half-drowned, uncomfortable manner.

As a joyous holy participant (living in the Way of Torah in which knowing and experiencing Hashem is overwhelmingly joyous), we can continue to align with the enlightenment process as the core of our being by letting it bring us to deveikut/chey'rut, which is the purpose of all life. In this context, faith is not a belief system. It is putting God at the center of our life's context. It is knowing that there is only God and returning to God. It is a knowing that this is the purpose of creation. An atheistic, secular understanding of life makes everything appear random, meaningless, and dull. This mindset makes it easy to be seduced by money, power, and sex. We need not be mired in the material world. We need not be part of the idol worship of money, power, politics, slavery, and sex. God continually intervenes throughout history to prevent this from happening, if only we are open to these interventions.

As the expansion of the universe continued, temperatures began to fall, and as this began to happen, light separated from matter and emerged from the darkness of the universe. Bereisheet 1:2–4 says: "The earth was without form and empty, with darkness on the face of the depths, but God's spirit [God's wind] moved on the water's surface. God said, 'There shall be light,' and light came into existence. God saw that the light was good, and God divided between the light and the darkness." From a physics perspective, prior to cooling down to 3,000 degrees Kelvin, the mix of photons and free electrons (or light and matter) was at the level of chaos. The light, in a sense, was trapped in the electrons. As it cooled the electrons were able to bind and slow down into their atomic orbits, while the photons were separated and released as light.

There was a continuum here. The light in Bereisheet 1:3 existed prior to the separation of the light from the darkness in Bereisheet 1:4. It was the light held in the electrons above 3,000 degrees Kelvin. The light held in the electrons, or the *black fire* (חשך—*hoshek*), was invisible. Physicists call these gamma rays, and they are invisible to the eye. After these rays, the light became visible. The metaphor of hoshek used in Bereisheet could also be known as "the void." In meditation we are able to enter the void. It is a visceral experience of total darkness, in which we disappear into this darkness and void. The black fire is a deeper energy of consciousness than the light. The deeper energy of the darkness *creates* the light. We often view darkness as "evil," but this is not the case. The creative energy is in the darkness. After Bereisheet 1:4, the Torah moves to the human perspective, perceiving light and darkness (as the absence of light).

Nachmanides pointed out that the darkness, in verse 2, is the creative substance of the universe, from which the next level of universe expansion emerges. "I form light and create darkness." This black fire is an energy that emits no light. As light is released from matter, we see this matter as consisting of seventy-five percent hydrogen and twenty-five percent helium. It was therefore able to coalesce, creating galaxies and stars. After this time, the heavy elements needed to produce all life began to form from the permutation of hydrogen and helium. In this unfolding process came cycles of creation and destruction of whole galaxies as all the elements were created. In this context, on the physical plane, we are stardust.

The next step in the Torah/astrophysics creation chronology is the creation of our local universe, in which the sun and the moon appear on the fourth day. In Torah and physics reality, the earth, as we know it, did not exist in the first three days. When earth is mentioned prior to this, it is a reference solely to the creation of primeval matter, from which God conjures the unfolding of corporeal existence. Yesha'yahu 48:13 says, "My hand also has laid the foundation of the earth, and my right hand has spanned the heavens." In Bereisheet 1:1, the Big Bang happened. Shemot 20:11 says "It was during the six weekdays that God made the heaven, the earth, the sea, and all that is in them."

The process of creation happened in epochs with increasing organization of chaos into order. This is emphasized when it says there was evening and morning six times. Evening is *erev* (ערב) and is translated as chaos. Day, as *boker* (בקר), literally means "discernment," as in "order." There were six epochs (days) that we went through in the evolutionary process to prepare us for the creation of humanity. All was created in the beginning, but it has taken us fifteen billion *human* years to get to where we are now—and the process continues... Again, the nature of the universe expanding is entropic (increasing chaos), but in our small section of the universe enthalpy (increasing order) is happening. This has something to do with nuclear, magnetic, and electromagnetic forces, but it is most easily understood from the point of view of divine intervention. Bereisheet 1:31 says "and behold, it was very good." Onkelos, a great Torah sage who lived around 200 AD, interpreted the words "and it was good" as "and it was unified order," which is a profound understanding for 1,800 years ago, as well as today. This is an accurate and essential point. This unified order is awesome in its divine process.

Somewhere in this orderly process the special conditions of the earth took place for the creation of human life here. There was not only human life, but also variations of life. On the third day plant life appears. This is interesting because it happens before the sun and moon appear. Prior to this, water appears as the substance that fills the seas. There was light at this time, but it was a translucent light that infused the atmosphere. Nachmanides stated that the firmament formed on the second day, which intercepted the light that existed from Day One. The atmosphere was able to hold this light.

Biologically speaking, plants create oxygen, which allows all other life to exist on the earth. Oxygen became available about two billion years ago from plant photosynthesis. Photosynthesis also allowed carbon materials to exist, which provided food. So we see that the Torah gives an accurate sequence of appearances. By the Torah account, animal life appeared in the water on Day Five and on the land on Day Six. It is an amazing biologically accurate and mystical unfolding.

Finally, the pre-Adamic human era began at least 3.2 million years ago. For the creation of human DNA, some people suggest extraterrestrial sources of life as already discussed as a valid Torah teaching. Sir Francis Crick, who with his Nobel Prize-winning co-researcher Dr. James D. Watson, were able to decode the structure of DNA, have also offered this as a possibility for the introduction of human DNA. The creation of the Adamic race began approximately 5,771 years ago. The Neanderthals existed at least 100,000 years ago, and their brain size was up to one hundred cubic centimeters larger than today's human.

There is a difference between pre-Adamic humans and Adamic humans, unrelated to brain size but rather to mental capacity and consciousness. We see consistent examples of divine intervention occurring again at the time of Adam. We are all stardust from the Big Bang, but on Day Six the Divine chose to make the Adamic race in God's image: "God created mankind in his image." In Bereisheet 2:7 man became a living nefesh (נפש—animal soul), but in Bereisheet 2:19 God breathed the *neshama* (נשמה) into the humanoid and it became the Adamic race. At that point, Adamic human time began. This is the story of the Adamic race.

What is this image of God? It appears that Cro Magnon man and Neanderthal man were similar to our current race. Image refers to something deeper.

The root of the Hebrew word for image (צלם—*tzelem*) is *tzel* (צל), meaning "shadow." This likeness is not physical. Rather, it implies that humanity became the shadow of the influence of the Divine through our actions and our lives. This is the clearest way of understanding the concept of "likeness." The spirit that was breathed within us allows us to be this shadow (image) of the Divine.

In summation, we can say that in the beginning the universe was concentrated into a *super-space* that was primarily energetic and fractionally material. At some point in space and time, the Big Bang began by divine intervention over a black hole by the Ruach Elohim, creating an ever-expanding universe by reversing the contraction into a black hole. The universe began to cool, separating photons from elections. Light was separated from mass. From the energy of the darkness the light emerged. The Torah and astrophysics show us that even the darkness was made of energy. This was the hoshek, or "black fire," spoken of in the kabbalah. Etymologically, the Hebrew word for darkness, hoshek, implies a withholding, a holding back, a contraction, of light. In other words, darkness is basically withheld, or dimmed, light: "Even the darkness is not dark for thee, but the night shines like the day: the darkness and the light are both alike to thee" (Tehillim 139:12).

The Second Law of Thermodynamics suggests that expansion of the universe should create chaos, but in certain parts of the multiple universes' chaos, there is instead increasing order … by divine intervention. We are constantly moving locally from erev to boker—from night into day, from chaos into divinely organized order. Darwinism cannot account for this ordering process, or for life on earth. There is not enough time for this. The only accounting for this rapid ordering is divine intervention for the creation of life on earth and the creation of the human race. Further evidence for this is that the special conditions existent on earth, for the creation of life, could not have happened randomly. As we are learning from global warming, life on earth exists in a narrow margin, and the elements that support life on earth are rare. These are divinely organized conditions for us.

When God said, "it was very good" in Bereisheet 1:31, it is a reference to the divine energy in all creation. Onkelos said, "it was unified order." This goodness is the *shekhinah* (שכינה) in all of creation. When we wake up we begin to see this dance and this goodness. According to kabbalah, life is joy and creation in the scintillating play of consciousness as God's illuminated illusion. And, yes, the deep Zohar teaching is Ayn Zulato—there is only God as the non-dual singularity.

This creates the mindset that helps us celebrate the Divine in our everyday lives. We can see this process, without too much imagination, by simply looking at the opening of Bereisheet, which reveals these deep spiritual teachings. This is the root meaning of the Torah as "showing the way" to deveikut/chey'rut as the ultimate purpose of life. Although the Torah is the Law, on one level, it is also the hidden design of creation, and on the highest spiritual level, it is a guidebook to enlightenment. We are the people of God reverberating in the image of God; we are not limited to the narrow concept of the "people of the Law."

The Torah teachings understood, at their highest octave, as a guide to enlightenment help to establish us as a people of God. As a guidebook, Torah is the template of how the Divine guides all creation, thus forging a pathway for us to return to God. The seven sabbatical cycles add the concepts of reincarnation and resurrection. Understanding these two teachings will help us to live in an increasingly perfected earth consciousness as well as an increasingly perfected soul consciousness over lifetimes. We now have a model in Bereisheet as a description of the unfolding order of creation and the enlightenment path. Beyond physics, this is a description of the path of deveikut/chey'rut and clarifies the purpose of life—to return to, and merge with, God.

Having addressed the p'shat (literal) understanding of the Bereisheet account of creation, we will now move into deeper layers of Torah interpretation. In review, there are four levels on which to interpret the Torah. The first is *p'shat* (פשט), a literal, physical, and scientific level of interpretation. The second is *remez* (רמז), an intellectual, metaphorical interpretation. The third is *drash* (דרש), a heart level interpretation. Drash includes morals, emotions, the midrash, and subjective teachings. The fourth is *sod* (סוד), a deeper, metaphysical, psychospiritual perspective derived from kabbalah and the Talmud. The sod interpretation gives a multidimensional understanding.

One's personality and degree of spiritual evolution often contribute to the level of Torah interpretation that he or she can comfortably understand. Some may only understand the Torah literally. Some see it metaphorically or morally. Some see it on the spiritual level. Others feel that all four levels must be considered for a full understanding. The Torah taken literally shows the blueprint of creation. The Torah's spiritual blueprint shows the creation of the true heavens. The Torah's physical blueprint shows the creation of the earth. This perspective provides an outline of the evolution of consciousness, and allows us understanding of the world of duality. The levels of interpretation, however, must be consistent one with another. I am attempting to present an integration of these four avenues of interpretation. Such an alignment will provide us with a more complete, holistic teaching. Because people understand the Torah according to their level of consciousness, it is not beneficial to debate right and wrong. We are multidimensional beings, and we are only able to understand Torah according to our fluidity.

The Torah, based upon the intricacy of details given in Bereisheet 1:1–2, is a radical understanding of the unfolding and ultimate meaning of life. It teaches that all humanity, regardless of class, is created in God's image (Midrash Tana D'Bei Eliyahu Rabbah 10:1). As implied before, this image is divine consciousness in the mind in the world of beriah (the pure mind) and the sephirah of binah. This holographic soul image resides in every human being, as do the dimensions of chokhmah and keter, which emanate direct knowledge beyond the mind, as our ultimate potential.

Throughout this play of consciousness, it helps to keep in mind that this is a paradox. As we look at the ayin/Ayn Sof (סוף אין—the nothing) unfolding, we understand that there is no humanity or world, and that there is only God. But from a dualistic perspective, as we see in Bereisheet, we know that this divinely illuminated illusion is necessary for the evolution of consciousness. We live in the paradox between the b'limah and the mah. In this context, my interpretations of the Torah teachings are most productively seen as intuitive understandings in alignment with the basic teachings of the Torah and our sages.

The Torah is holy poetry in motion. It is alive and speaks freshly in every generation. It allows us to live fresh and poetic truth as this one name of God speaks to us. Paradoxically, although the Torah is the cornerstone of the Jewish religion, the word *religion* does not appear in the text of the Torah. Torah is about deveikut/chey'rut, which is the ultimate "religion" for humanity. Torah teaches us to create a lifestyle of *kedusha* (קדושה—holiness) and *midot* (character) as common preconditions for grace, leading us into deveikut/chey'rut or enlightenment.

This enlightenment takes us prior to duality. It takes us prior to time, space, and matter. One aspect of enlightenment is the realization of God as the great nothing prior to the Big Bang, out of which all creation emerged. "Bereisheet bara" means "the something emerging from the nothing." Rabbi and physician Moses Maimonides pointed out that the Torah creates a teaching of a divine order of evolutionary unfolding as "universal consciousness having a divine direction" (Midrash Bamid'bar Rabbah 10:8; Zohar, Vol. 3, folio 7a). The goal of creation is ultimate liberation for all beings and their merging back into Hashem. Before Bereisheet there is nothing we can intellectually comprehend, because it is beyond the mind as prior to time, space, and being. God is beyond our intellectual comprehension in binah, but the essence of the Divine can be aperceived in chokhmah.

The Torah takes us beyond the shadow of the divine consciousness and into direct God knowledge in deveikut, prior to Bereisheet. It is an awesome transmission of consciousness that gives earthlings the opportunity to evolve their consciousness. It had to have been given after one thousand generations, to the twenty-sixth generation after Adam, for some maturity was required to even begin to comprehend the Torah's awesome scope and depth. This maturity was not present in the previous 974 pre-Adamic generations. Physics confirms that there is a great singularity to the universe, although it is difficult for us to see this unity in the relative world. This singularity will soon emerge as a coherent, conscious society during the messianic times. The Torah is a guide for how to awaken to this truth. The Torah shows us the progressive spiral order as an evolution of consciousness instead of viewing it as linear history.

Here we are talking about the divine power unfolding. The Lurianic teachings give us some insight into this unfolding order here. We begin with ayin (אין), the complete nothing prior to time, space, mass, and being. There is a movement from the ayin prior to the Ayn Sof (אין סוף), which is the first endless emerging from the nothingness containing everything and its opposite in total unity. From the Ayn Sof unfolds tohu and bohu (תהו ובהו). From these two qualities, which begin with the Ayn Sof withdrawing space and creating a vacuum, a *tzim tzum* (צם צום), or spark of light, emerges from the divine concealment. From this contraction and expansion, a void (*tehiru*—טהרו) comes out from the Ayn Sof with a residue (*reshimu*—רשימו) of divine light. This Or Ayn Sof (אור אין סוף) emanates into this primordial void in a line of energy called *kav* (קו).

From this comes the primordial pattern (the primordial man, known in kabbalah as *Adam Kadmon*—אדם קדמון). From Adam Kadmon's eyes, nose, mouth, and ears flashes this light as the twenty-two letters. From these letters are formed *kelim* (כלים—vessels) containing further light. These vessels create a world of points. These points become the ten sephirotic energies. They are the circles of nothing, but we attach meaning to them. They are oneness in that they are circles and they are also the ten spheres of the Tree of Life: At the top of this pattern is keter (כתר)—the divine will. It is the highest level of consciousness in which we are merged in enlightenment with our individual expression of the divine will. In it, we are not a void, but a being (individual personality) that is truly an expression of the divine will as it plays through us.

From keter comes chokhmah, the direct knowing. It is the direct apperception of the truth. From chokhmah comes binah (בינה) as direct understanding. The direct apperception becomes the pure intellectual understanding from which all creation comes. Next is *chesed* (חסד), loving-kindness. *Gevurah* (גבורה) follows. (Gevurah is sometimes called *deen* [דין]—justice.) Gevurah is about boundaries and discrimination. *Tiferet* (תפארת—beauty) is next. *Netzach* (נצח) is the power of the prophets—the ability to persevere on the spiritual path, to recover from failures and continue on the spiritual path. *Hod* (הוד) is the power of divine splendor, awe, and appreciation. From netzach and hod comes *yesod* (יסוד), the energy of the *tzaddik*, the one who walks in balance, like the ancestor Yosef. Hod is represented by Aharon (Aaron), and netzach is represented by Moshe (Moses). Chesed is represented by Avraham (Abraham), and tiferet is represented by Ya'akov (Jacob). Gevurah is represented by Yitzhak (Isaac), and Yosef (Joseph), the *tzadok,* represents yesod by showing great sexual restraint (Bereisheet 39:8). He overcame sexual temptation so that he could evolve spiritually. This is a great challenge on the spiritual path. We then move to malchut (מלכות), the sphere of the moon. This is the shekhinah energy and the energy of David. It is the feminine receptive principle.

These ten sephirotic energies make up the *Odeot Yesod* (אותיות יסוד), the twenty-two letters from which all creation comes. These letters emanate into five worlds: Adam Kadmon, Atzilut, Beriah, Yetzirah, and Assiyah. Adam Kadmon is linked with keter, yet is prior to keter, as the four worlds come out of Adam Kadmon. Atzilut (אצילות) is the direct knowing connected with chokhmah. It is the male principle. Beriah (בריאה) is the pure mind, connected with binah. It is the female principle. Yetzirah (יצירה) is the astral plane, containing the sephirot of chesed, tiferet, gevurah, netzach, hod, and yesod. Assiyah (עשיה) is malchut, the physical plane. This flow reflects the divine order unfolding out of "Bereisheet bara."

An imbalance in these energies, and the vessels, created a shattering, classically known as the "breaking of the vessels"—*shevirat ha'key'lim* (הכלים שבירת). Metaphorically speaking, for a person to evolve spiritually, he or she must live in a way that strengthens the vessels. This means following the 613 mitzvot—248 positive commandments and 365 negative commandments. Fulfilled perfunctorily they work against us. Performed with a sense of awe, opening oneself up to what each one does, opens a channel for the Divine to bring the *Or Yashar* (אור ישר) down into our lives to complete the cycle created when the *Or Hozer* (אור חוזר) ascends upward. If these are not performed this way, it is a desecration. To do these for the sake of doing them creates a negative spiritual result. The breaking of the vessels is a critical metaphor for living a life in which we repair our vessels and our inner Tree of Life. Balancing these ten sephirotic energies in our lives will allow us to transcend them, and go prior even to keter.

When the vessels ruptured, the energy between chokhmah (male) and binah (female) were fractured. The pieces fell to the earth as sparks (ניצוצים— *nee'tzo'tzim*) trapped in husks (קליפות—*k'lipot*). The sum of the husks is the *Sit'ra Ach'ra* (סטרא אחרא—the realm of darkness). We must be aware that in Judaism everything is an aspect of the Divine. Evil and good are not separate from the Divine. In this context, the forces of darkness are here to provide tests for the elevation of the light. Sit'ra Ach'ra has great relevance on the spiritual path. It need not overwhelm us. God usually gives us only what we can handle.

The lights emanating from the head of Adam Kadmon are the seventy-two mystical names of God. These help us rebuild the broken vessels. They help us to understand the five faces of the Divine (פרצופים—*partzufim*). These are metaphorical personalities. *Arich Anpin* (אריך אנפן) is the "Ancient One" in keter, otherwise known as *Atik Yomen* (עתיק יומין). Above this is the great grandmother, "Grace"—*Ey'ma Ila'ah* (אימא עלאה). *Abba* (אבא) is chokhmah, the father. *Ima* (אמא) is binah, the mother. *Zeir anpin* (זעיר אנפין), the son, or astral plane, includes the six middle sephirotic energies. *Nukvah* (נוקבא) is malchut. The path between nukvah and zeir anpin is the pathway of enlightenment, in which male and female energies become one again, and Abba and Ima again face each other in erotic divine unity. The point here is that we cannot mitzvot our way to God. We should still perform the mitzvot because they connect our hearts to God; however, it is grace that leads us beyond time and space. We cannot merely sit and wait for grace. The mitzvot comprise a way of being that prepares us to go to a higher level of awakening, so that grace can lead us beyond.

The nineteenth-century mystic Rabbi Mordechai of Izbica, in my interpretation, suggested that *yosef* (intense practice) leads us into *yehuda* (the flow of the Divine). Here one operates at a higher octave of relationship with God. It is exceedingly rare to just jump to the consciousness of yehuda; almost always we work our way up to this consciousness through the focused Torah kedusha way of Yosef. This is all part of the unfolding of divine order. This process in the Lurianic matrix is *tikkun ha olam* (תיקון העולום). This is accomplished by raising the sparks of consciousness that came from the broken vessels. We are repairing these vessels by our actions in the world, and by our lifestyles. Ultimately tikkun ha olam represents the return to the beginning in which the Ayn Sof (which is always already unified) becomes *apparently* unified. This is a sophisticated path, in which one is forced to live with this paradox. It is said that the kabbalah is not a path to paradise, but a path to paradox. The ability to hold the b'limah and the mah in a paradoxical synergy is the mystery our existence as multidimensional beings and transcending this in the oneness.

These categories of *partzufim* (faces of God) represent the divine unfolding, evolution of, and purpose of life. This description is a hint at the complexity of the divine unfolding as the evolution of consciousness that is hinted at in Bereisheet. We see from the *Rashei Tevot*, the power to create or destroy the universe comes from these twenty-two letters. We are literally given this power of creation. Moshe demonstrated this power when he killed the Egyptian using the sacred letters (Midrash Tanchuma, Sh'mo't, Chap. 10). We are also told that he divided the Sea of Reeds (*Yam Suf*) through specific permutations of the letters encoded in the divine names (Midrash Pesik'ta D'Rav Kahana 19:6).

As we go farther, we come to extremely profound spiritual insights and another way to understand. Heaven is not the sky, but is a different dimension. Heaven starts at the astral plane and expands into the more subtle planes of the pure mind in the world of beriah as well. Ultimately, prior to creation of even the heavens we had the first harmonics beginning as what is now called the physics of the string theory, which is analogous to the first speaking of the "word." There was a "speaking" that set the harmonic energies of the strings into motion and those strings vibrated into the next levels of creation. This creation moved from the ultimate image of God as "prior-to-consciousness" (God's true nature beyond comprehension) into the world of duality. In this "physics account" God *spoke* the universe into being. As the tenth-century BCE Hebrew chieftain King David put it: "For he spoke, and it was; he commanded, and it stood fast" (Tehillim 33:9). The divine word activated the subatomic particles moving into matter.

"The heavens" represents another etheric dimension, while the earth represents the physical plane. The earth of Bereisheet 1:1 is not the literal planet Earth, but rather the time, space, and matter of this universe. This is why the Torah starts with bet (ב) and not aleph (א). Bet connotes duality. Bet opens to the left. It is the house of creation. The other letters emerge from it. It has above and below aspects. It has visible and invisible dimensions. We cannot call heaven "prior-to-creation." Both emerged, but heaven emerged first (Midrash B'reishit Rabbah 1:15). Bet teaches "as above, so below, linked by spirit." The vertical line represents humanity holding the multidimensional consciousness connecting the physical and spiritual planes. Here we have Elohim (אלהים—a numerical value of 86) as natural law and YHWH (יהוה—a numerical value of 26) as two different aspects of creation. The primordial expression of the divine will takes us to the concept of singularity. We move beyond that oneness now from Or Ayn Sof (אור איי סוף—pure light of God in the darkness) to the center of the infinite in the One (though at this point, there is only a potential).

The primordial light is not light as we experience it. This is not particles and waves (*agulim* [עגולים]—spheres), but this original light is the life force of the universe. It is the nefesh (נפש)—the *prana*, the *chi*, and the true energetic substance of the universe from whence all else is energized. It is the prime currency of the universe. Neither gold nor silver is the real currency. It is this life force that entities are in competition for. When we understand this point, it gives an interesting perspective on our global drama. (We will discuss this later in the book.) In the evolution, this nefesh begins to congeal into matter. This energy and matter separate and from it comes light. This begins with faster-than-light particles called tachyons. This is concealed light beyond time and space. This is the heavens and the astral plane. Different entities, such as angels, live on this plane. This is the aleph (א) level of the invisible universe from which the strings create the visible universe of duality.

As stated before, bet (ב) also implies a prior aleph (א). These two dimensions may be consciously linked through the mind in meditation. In this process we may discover that we exist in both the heavens and the earth as multidimensional beings. This is why we say humans are a merging of heaven and earth (Midrash B'reishit Rabbah 8:11 and 12:8).

As we understand the creation of Adam we realize that humanity descended from the astral plane existence. The he-Adam and she-Adam were attempting to bring elevated consciousness to earth. They became entangled in the physical plane and their ability to come and go between the worlds was lost. The Adamic race became stuck in the physical, mortal body. Immortality will occur again when we return to this light body as our primary body. It is when we become the pure nefesh of creation again.

This helps us move in a way that makes sense of the wild, disorderly, and chaotic process of tohu (תהו). Tohu is the primordial chaos, but it is also the seeds of creation. It is the undifferentiated forms from which all matter comes. We call this *yeshmʾayin* (ישׁאמין). From tohu comes bohu (בהו). Bohu is the vacuum, the empty primordial form from which all creation comes. Here emerge all the basic elements. Tohu and bohu are *pre-dimensional*. From the darkness comes the concealed energy, or fire. Then we have the earth, water, and air. These primordial elements become active between these two planes of the heavens and the earth. To clarify again, the heavens are not *above* us. The heavens are, rather, a parallel dimension. Aleph represents the invisible. From the level prior to creation aleph brings nefesh (life force). It is pre-light. When God says, "let there be light," this is the creation of the nefesh. In the second *pasuk* (פסוק), or passage, of Bereisheet, we have the emergence of nefesh, the primordial life force that emanates from the first letter of the Hebrew aleph-bet, the א (aleph). Aleph represents the invisible. It is pre-light. When the Torah says the righteous will live forever (in Tehillim 92:13 and Mishle 10:30), it means they will live in the heavens as eternal light bodies.

As said before, when we move into Day Two, we arrive at the creation of the first set of angels. Those created on this day are the intermediaries from which all creation comes. They are the Elohim. This is based upon the deep rabbinical teachings. These angels are the "creator gods" or Elohim. They are higher self-souls or *maggidim* (מגידים). In the oral teachings it is said that these souls existed to create the astral plane and earth. These are the pre-heaven angels from which all creation came. They are the light of *Yah's* garment. The realms of beriah, yetzirah, and assiyah come from these pre-heaven souls/angels. These are the ones that said "Let us make man in our image"— the shadow of the Divine. They are what is referred to as the "power of God." They are the expression of the pure nefesh, which the dark forces are always trying to steal. The heavens, in this case, are created from the light of Hashem; it is the pre-light light that exists at the beginning of Bereisheet. Though they are the beginning of time and space, they are also prior to time and space. They are the life-force energy underlying all creation. God saw that this primordial light was good.

In the overview of this way of seeing creation, the creation process begins in the non-activity of the darkness and moves into the activity of creation. The Elohim are not God, but are rather primordial forms of the *expression* of Yah. Therefore God is concealed in nature, but nature is not God. Believing nature to be God leads us into the dangers of pantheism and nature worship. Pan-entheism, by contrast, is seeing the dance of God in all things. Judaism is primarily a panentheistic religion. Day One is the first level of creation. In Day

Two the pre-heavenly angelic Elohim were created, and the separation of the waters into the waters below and above occurred (separation of heaven and earth dimensions), called *raki'a*. The higher waters were the astral plane, from which the earth comes. The ten levels of angels, as outlined by Maimonides (Mishnah Torah, Hilchot Yesodei HaTorah 2:7), live here. Above these are the archangels, the *neshemot*, literally "the breaths," as in the primal thought or breath, so to speak, of God, what the ancient Sefer Yetzirah calls *Ru'ach Elohim Chayyim* (רוח אלהים חיים), "breath of living God" (Chap. 1, Mishnah 1). Rakia in this context is the intermediary between the earth plane and the heavenly plane. It could be considered outerspace between the dimensions (sky or *shamayin*). These waters allow us to move from the b'limah (nothing) to the mah (something).

Proverbs 16:8 gives us a way to merge with God by keeping God's name before us always. When we focus on this, the rest of the mitzvot naturally occur. We keep the name of God before us so that the name of God reverberates within us endlessly. "I have set the Lord always before me," wrote King David some 3,000 years ago. When we do this we become the mitzvot. Our frequency becomes that of the light of the heavens. As we ascend into the planes of yetzirah (astral), beriah (mind), atzilut (direct apperception), we can even enter into prior-to-consciousness.

The Way of the Torah is not a philosophy; it is a lifestyle designed to transform us into the frequency of the name of God in every moment. The Torah Way in this process also helps to reestablish us back into holy time, which is an astrological framework time.

Twelve refers to the physical plane: the twelve tribes, twelve constellations, and, in essence, the boundaries of time and space emerging (including the stars, sun, moon, and planets). It refers to the emergence of astrological divine time, which helps us tune into the Divine through the movements of the heavenly bodies. In our tradition, the moon, sun and stars, as well as the earth, are considered components of a living self-reflective consciousness (Maimonides in Mishnah Torah, Hilchot Yesodei HaTorah 3:9). The introduction of the Gregorian time system eventually cut people off from this more organic reckoning of the time of the universe and from living in harmony with that aspect of God's reflection inherent within it. The Gregorian time of a 28-day moon,

24-hour day, and 60-minute hour is "machine" or "matrix" time. Living in this "machine time" may be superior for living in the post-Industrial Revolution as a human economic unit in the social machine, but it separates us from God and the holy cosmic time frame of the Divine. God's time is superior for our spiritual wealth and health. Vessels again become one, and we again consciously know oneness with the Divine. This is the ultimate purpose of life and the purpose of the great guidance of the Torah.

Another way of understanding the message of Bereisheet is to see it through the progression of the days of the week and the interface of the energies of the sephirot as *levels of consciousness*. Parashah Bereisheet is one of the more complicated (and possibly the deepest) parashah in the Torah. Bereisheet is, in essence, the power of the seed of human consciousness and of all creation that unfolds from it. It holds within it the spiritual evolution of all humanity. From the point of deveikut it describes the evolution of consciousness and the meaning of enlightenment. As pointed out before, the ultimate seed starts with the words Bereisheet bara describing the something emerging from the nothing. The nothing is the steady state of deveikut/chey'rut.

On Day One we are primarily in *hitpashtut*, the simplicity of the awareness of "no-boundary" consciousness. This is associated with *olam ha-ba* (עולם הבא) the "world to come." This is the direct knowing of the Divine in the sephirotic realm of chokhmah. On Day One we are in non-dual oneness, or *omek* (עומק)—unfathomable depth consciousness. Day One is the essential oneness, and represents in this sense the merging back into the One. Therefore it is called "Day One," rather than "the first day," because "the first" suggests there is more than one, but the word "One," as in "Day One," implies wholeness and uniqueness.

On the second day, the sephirotic attribute of gevurah emerged, which created separation and consequently duality—and the unity of Day One is disrupted. On Day One was wholeness as simple nondual unity unconscious of itself. Metaphorically, the message is that hell was created on Day Two (Talmud, Tosefta Berachot 5:36). Hell-consciousness is associated with the problems we find in disunity and disharmony among people living in the separation consciousness. This was the beginning of *alma d'peruda* (עלמא דפרודא), the world of duality, and *alma d'shikra* (עלמא דשקרא), the world of illusion. Day Two was when this became activated. The work on Day One, which is Sunday, is the ability to unify the parts of the whole so they can work together as a synergy. The second day of creation, which correlates to Monday, is a fragmented day. The sages advise us to avoid beginning anything new on that day. The second day correlates to the negative pole of the Tree of Life column—"to receive for self, alone"—and correlates to the sephirotic realm of gevurah. In Day Two, the level of understanding is gevurah consciousness, which means seeing the world primarily through the lens of duality.

On the third day, the central column of Etz Chaim was created. It corresponds to our ability to resist the desires of the ego and to choose a life that is aligned with the truth of our soul. This brings us into *binah shebalev* (בינה שבלב), the understanding of the heart. It is a combination of binah and tiferet consciousnesses. It flows from the right column of the sephirotic tree, which corresponds to the force of sharing, and from the left column, which corresponds to ego—both then blending within the central column, which corresponds to the illusion of free will at a lower level, and the path of liberation at the highest level. The third day, which is Tuesday, gives us the strength to balance and shift the energy from ego, or left column, to the right side, which is "receiving in order to share." Our ability in the central column, to overcome the tendency of the "evil urge" or selfish behavior, creates a healthy and spiritual life.

The fourth day, or Wednesday, is the seed energy of jealousy, or ego energy out of balance. Many kabbalists associate this with the root of evil; it is deeper hell energy. The fourth day was when the moon and the sun (at first equal in size) were in conflict because the moon was not satisfied with sharing her position with the sun. The moon wanted to be more important than the sun. Of course, the moon was "rewarded" with becoming always "lesser than." We can use the fourth day to immunize ourselves to jealousy and envy. The fourth day is also not a good day to begin anything new because the deepest level of evil began on the fourth day. The sephirotic qualities of netzach (the power of perseverance and spiritual victory) and *hod* (experiencing the glory of Hashem in all things) help us to rise above and defeat the dark tendencies of Day Four.

The fifth day, according to the Zohar, connects us to the deep light of the Torah. The Torah consciousness on this day is *shimusha* (שימושא). This means becoming the living expression of the Torah, or serving the Torah in an unlimited way, as one's soul expression. It is different from *limudah*, which is learning Torah in a bound, scholarly way. This day connects us to the tzaddik—the enlightened persona—within and without. It is a celebration of the divine teacher. It is yesod consciousness on the sephirotic tree. The word *yesod* means "foundation."

On the sixth day, which is the level of malchut, humanity was created, and the illusionary idea of free will was more fully established in alma d'shikra (world of illusion). As that whole picture goes further, we get a better insight into this because it says in Bereisheet 1:27, "So God created Mankind in his own image, in the image of God he created him; male and female he created them." He did not create them separately but together, in the image of God. This is a very interesting statement because it says, in a sense, that an individual person who sees himself separate from God does not reflect divine energies. However, an individual who sees himself in unity with at least one "other" *does* reflect the image of God. And what is that image? It is love, as the merging of male and female reflects it. This is the mystery that comes together on the sixth day—the creation of the human Adamic soul in the image of the spirit of God, as the image of God. We will return to Day Six, but first a few words on the resetting energy of Shabbat.

Day Seven, which is Shabbat, in essence, completed the cycle. Although it is called "the day of rest," it really means we have a rest from the world of duality; it is a resetting. If our consciousness is ready, it takes us to the realm beyond time, space, and being. It takes us back to the fundamental unity that is outside the world of duality and illusion. Rather than having the illusion of a "day of rest," Shabbat is when we work spiritually the hardest to let go of our egocentric qualities. On Shabbat we are more powerfully linked to the sephirotic realm of keter, which is the purest expression of the divine will. At this level we become the cosmic expression of *bitul hayesh* (ביטול היש) or emptiness. It is through this emptiness that the Divine most lucidly expresses. On a subtle plane we have the potential to become an individual expression of the Divine as we become the face of God. However, our creative ego can easily become confused and mistake the void for the Divine. It takes years of subtle spiritual maturity in bitul hayesh for this level of expression to be cultivated.

Shabbat is the experiential remembrance of moving from prior-to-existence to creation. This is movement from the aleph energy of liberated consciousness to the creation energy of Bereisheet. Shabbat reminds us of the continual and direct intervening of God in the creation process. Shabbat at a deeper level is the commemoration and celebration of the continual presence and intervention of Hashem in our everyday lives. Day Seven, which is Shabbat, in essence, completed the cycle.

On Day Six we are introduced to the Garden of Eden, which was considered at least a mystical location for the emergence of Adam and Cha'vah (Eve). In the Garden of Eden we had two parallel universes: The Tree of Life (Etz Chaim), or the nondual universe of oneness, unity, love and inner pleasures of the Divine, and, by contrast, the Tree of Knowledge (Etz Ha Da'at) of Good and Evil. When we are feeling unity in the ultimate truth, our connection to the Tree of Life is strengthened. When we are feeling doubt, selfishness, and separation, these actions of themselves weaken our connection to the Tree of Life and deepen our enmeshment with the Tree of Knowledge of Good and Evil.

In the kabbalistic understanding, the phrase "Adam and Cha'vah" is a metaphor for the unified soul that existed before our immediate universe came into being. This "larger," more cosmic soul is called Adam Kadmon (קדמון אדם), and includes all the souls of humanity. Adam and Cha'vah are collectively referred to as "the vessel," and that is what has to be strengthened. Eventually, the vessel shattered, and Adam and Cha'vah became countless sparks of souls who descended into the physical world and took on physical bodies. Before the shattering of the vessel and the Adamic fall in Gan Eden, a group of very pure souls collectively known as Metatron separated from the Adam soul before it was destined to fall. This Metatron soul group is part of the messianic soul energy, which will intervene to uplift humanity.

We, who are the vessel of God, were created by God to receive and become the noncausal love, joy, peace, bliss, compassion, oneness, and contentment that Adam inherited as the natural emotions and inner experience from the divine force. Adam received the DNA of being God-like; but he needed, at another level of evolution, to become the co-creator of his own light. We are responsible for creating heaven on earth, and thus become as gods. At the time Adam ate of the apple, he didn't have the ability to make free-will choices, so this so-called "sin" was on an evolutionary level part of his spiritual development. And so, at this bifurcation point, the Torah interpretation suggests that this was not necessarily an act of ego, nor a "missing of the mark."

The duality of Etz Ha Da'at was given to us as our path of evolution to help us learn the way of overcoming duality, when we were given the illusionary gift of free will. We have since become accountable for the amount of light that we generate in our lives. Part of our work is to activate the inner Torah, so that we can become a generator of light to all the nations. At a deeper level, Adam's fall to earth was not a punishment, because his "failure" created the preconditions for the world of duality, which allows us to work in profound ways to overcome our selfish impulses and to evolve into a higher perfection in the world. If divine consciousness was just handed to us, we would really not be able to grasp the meaning of its value and truth, nor could we appreciate the Tree of Life and light that is in our inheritance. There would be no process of spiritual evolution available.

Inner knowledge and character development (midot) is one of the most important components on the spiritual path. Overcoming duality in the midst of the world is a way to tap into the spiritual light and build the midot. It is taught that the Torah scroll shines as brightly as a galaxy of stars, and our job is to activate and switch on the Torah as a power generator of the divine presence. The ten generations from Adam to Noah represent the ten sephirotic energies that allow the light of the creator to flow through all ten dimensions. We enter this world with great appreciation for the mysteries and for the seed of consciousness that is planted in all of us as the eternal void, as the nothingness to which we all ultimately return. It is through the awareness of non-duality beyond light and darkness that we wake up to our complete oneness. At first it is known temporarily as an experience of oneness and may evolve into a steady awareness beyond time, space, and being. At this point it is called deveikut/chey'rut, full God merging in its steady manifestation. May we all be blessed with this awareness.

Bereisheet 2:1 says, "Heaven and earth, and all their components, were [thus] completed." In Bereisheet chapter 2, we move into the issues of Adam and Cha'vah in Gan Eden and get another understanding of Gan Eden. In Bereisheet 2:8, "God planted a garden in Eden to the east." This implies that there was a smaller garden within the larger Eden. This Eden with its four rivers was approximately 10,000 square miles and included India, Egypt, and the Middle East. In the oral tradition (such as that of Yonatan Ben Uzziel, who created the first translation of the Torah two thousand years ago) there is an important teaching that Gan Eden was not on the surface of the planet. This particular tradition, as revealed to the second-century Rabbi Shimon bar Yochai by his spirit teacher, the prophet Eliyahu, reports that there are seven worlds underneath the surface of the earth, and that Gan Eden was located on the sixth level down. The names of the seven levels, from the deepest to the surface, are: (1) *Eretz* (a completely dark world with no radiance, to where it is said Adam was exiled); (2) *Adamah* (a place where the original Gan Eden is said to be; it is also taught that this Gan Eden is directly under Hebron); (3) *Arka*; (4) *Gey'*; (5) *Neshee'ya* (area where the "grays inhabit"); (6) *Tziah*; and (7) *Tevel* (Hash'matat Ha'Zohar, Vol. 1, folio 253b–254a). These names represent the seven hollow spheres, each with a "sky" approximately 100 miles high and a land base of 100 miles. This implies that there are many civilizations living with us simultaneously on the planet and within the planet.

In the Adamah level there are giants who are said to be the offspring of Adam's mating with the female *shey'dim* during his 130 years in exile. Shey'dim are demonic ancestor creatures that eat, mate, and are mortal. In Adamah there is no joy. It is also said in the oral tradition that they were made by the Divine at twilight on the sixth day (Midrash Tanchuma, Bereisheet, No. 17). This is where Kayin (Cain) and Hevel (Abel) were born. Shet (Seth) was also born here and then, with the birth of Shet, Adam and Cha'vah moved to Tevel (the earth's surface). It is also taught in the oral tradition that in the underworlds there exist nonhuman races such as centaurs and other pre-Adamic entities. Because of their slightly different genetics, if they rise to the earth's surface they cannot contain the light and are thus prone to evil behavior. Some of these entities that inherit the genetic predisposition for evil include the fallen angels, who also dwell below the surface and who are explicitly antagonistic to the success of the God-created human experiment on the surface of the planet.

At some point, the oral tradition tells us, Kayin was taken to the realm of Arka, where there was light, and he sired what may be the entire population of Arka. It is taught that there are no holy seven grains or seven fruits in Arka, and that there are fifteen-feet-tall giants as well as three-feet-high "hobbits" in the world of Arka. Perhaps this is the basis for J.R.R. Tolkien's "Middle Earth" and the Lilliputians of *Gulliver's Travels*.

The next layer up is called Gey' (also known as *Gey' Hinum,* or hell). It is considered a place of spiritual fire and is inhabited by Korach, who was swallowed by the earth in the time of Moshe. The next level up is Neshee'yah, which has a cooler climate. It is inhabited by people who are masters of witch-craft and technology and where those from Gey' may migrate. From here, there are tunnels up to Tevel. Neshee'yah is where the various levels of "grays" exist. They may be tall or short and have no noses, gray skin, and large black eyes. Some feel the "grays" may be some form of shey'dim. Some feel these people are the source for some of the UFOs, and that they often enter Tevel through underwater passages as well.

Worlds underneath the earth's surface are not solely an ancient Hebraic concept. A number of aboriginal cultures share such teachings in common, namely, that their ancestors came from under the earth. Native Americans such as the Hopi, Cherokee, and the Lakota, the New Zealand Maori, as well as different South American tribes, teach about this emergence of their tribes from underneath the earth. They also teach that there are tunnels leading to these lower levels. The doorways to these tunnels are situated in the Hopi lands, in the Lakota Black Hills, on Mount Shasta, and all over the world. In the Hebrew tradition, the gates to these tunnels are located at the Cave of Machpelah in Hebron. This is the cave where many believe Adam and Cha'vah are buried, along with the earliest ancestors of Am Yisrael including Avraham and Sarah, Yitzhak and Rivkah, Ya'akov and Le'a.

A traditional shamanic teaching for all indigenous groups is that the vital importance for the survival of a tribal culture spiritually is to have energetic and physical control of the burial sites of the ancestors. This may give some insight in to the Hopi/Navaho (Denai) struggle over the land containing their burial sites as well as control in the Black Hills for the Lakota. It certainly gives some insight into the deeper issues around who controls Hebron and spiritual importance for Am Yisrael.

I have chosen to allude to these ancient esoteric teachings to make a few important practical points in understanding spiritual life historically and in the present on the surface of the earth (Tevel). These seven layers still hold these different civilizations, which are still actively involved with our race. The Adamic race was not the first on this planet, and there is a need for us to walk more humbly on the surface of the planet, and to respect and be wary of these other civilizations that were here before us and which may interact with us in unfavorable ways.

In levels four through six dwell *nephilim* and other malevolent forces that activate and support the dark forces, which operate on the surface of the planet. Based on oral teachings, it is my understanding that there are two major themes being played out. One is the technology-versus-God conflict highlighted in the argument between the first two human brothers Kayin and Hevel and repeated before the flood and at the Tower of Babel. Sadly, this conflict remains present even today in the religion of scientific secularism with its misuse of technology, such as genetically engineered foods and nuclear energy, and with its agenda of dominating the world, of separation from God, and vying to be more powerful than God.

The second, which is connected to the first, is the destruction of life on the planet to harvest nefesh, or life force, and the attempted elimination of the Jews, the *B'nei Yisra'el*, and their brothers, the righteous gentiles, or *B'nei Noach*, who are steadfastly maintaining the channels for bringing the light of God onto the planet. An example of this struggle was and is the activities of the Thule Society, a documented black-occult group said to have made contact with these underworld forces. The Thule Society, backed by world financiers from both the US and Europe, is believed to have brought Hitler to power. It is well documented that Hitler and his inner circle were masters of the black-occult and used these forces in their efforts to dominate the world.

The Jews specifically, plus millions of others, were part of the human/blood sacrifice that was part of this power effort to dominate the planet. Without an understanding of this current 6,000-year struggle, which is active today, we do not have the full perspective to understand, cope with, alleviate, and spiritually respond appropriately to the present world situation. In our Torah/ kabbalah teachings, the best and simplest way to make oneself immune to the black-occult forces is to be *shomer mitzvot* and to constantly repeat the Tetra-grammaton (יהוה), which is the "name of grace" that protects and draws grace in all four worlds. The B'nei Noach at least must do the Sheva mitzvot, seven Noahide Teachings, and repeat the name of God as well. All of us need to be living by VayYiKra (Leviticus) 18:19—"You must love your neighbor as [you love] yourself"—and performing all actions with a heart-centered energy of love. These actions, as a way of life, build the vessel of light that can more actively draw the divine energy. This can, in turn, dispel the darkness. In essence, it means to return to the natural way that God has guided us to live on the planet, as open-hearted, God-awe inspired beings of love.

Bereisheet 1:26–28 says:

> God said, "Let us make man in our image and likeness. Let him dominate the fish of the sea, the birds of the sky, the livestock animals, and all the earth—and every land animal that walks the earth." God [thus] created man with His image. In the image of God, He created him, male and female He created them. God blessed them. God said to them, "Be fertile and become many. Fill the land and conquer it. Dominate the fish of the sea, the birds of the sky, and every beast that walks the land."

There are a few significant things to note here. First, God is speaking in the plural. It says "Let us [Elohim] make …" and "our image and likeness." It is likely that this is referring to the pre-angelic souls who were a template for all the souls of humanity, which was mentioned earlier in Bereisheet. In this subtlety, the Elohim, as the emanations of the Divine, are saying that "our soul prototypes are going to be the basis for all humanity." Those soul prototypes will, in the process of working out their own spiritual evolution, have the opportunity to exercise their dominion. However, dominion is not the right to pollute, destroy, or desecrate God's planet. Dominion is the power to affect creation in a stewardship of responsibility that uplifts all of creation.

Next, it says in the singular "God created man with His image." Here the frequency of the Divine is a "prior-to-creation" frequency as the spirit of

God in all people. The individual Elohim souls emerged from the primordial energy of creation on Day Two. From this, the different soul groups evolved, including the frequency of the Divine that is in all people. These are two distinct blessings. This seeming redundancy expresses that the universal spark of God, as well as the individual soul (neshama) as part of that divine spark, has the right and ability to subdue and have dominion over the planet. This is not the right to destroy the ecology, but to work in harmony *with* the ecology, in order to have a hand in shaping the divine process: "to work it [Eden] and watch it" (Bereisheet 2:15). Correctly understood, this often-misquoted passage is not about the right to exploit, but implies a spiritual test to see if we can mimic Hashem in a mini-trial of benign dominion for the benefit of all.

Immediately after the creation of man and woman, the Torah talks about food, and so once humans are created, Bereisheet addresses how to feed them. Bereisheet 1:29: "God said, 'Behold, I have given you every seedbearing plant on the face of the earth, and every tree that has seedbearing fruit. It shall be to you for food.'" Bereisheet 1:30–31 adds an additional piece of often-overlooked message: "[God said,] 'For every beast of the field, every bird of the sky, and everything that walks the land, that has in it a living soul, all plant vegetation shall be food.' It remained that way. God saw all that he had made, and behold, it was very good. It was evening and it was morning, the sixth day." This is the dietary blueprint for humanity. God does not make mistakes. That blueprint is a live-food, plant-source-only diet, not only for humanity, but also for all the animals. Why was such a blueprint given for the spiritual evolution of the planet? There are a variety of reasons.

First, to avoid eating animals is to avoid creating cruelty, misery, and pain in the animal world. Today we see gross, unconscious mass cruelty to animals, especially in the case of factory farming, where the animals are treated as soulless machines that are no more than economic units to be exploited. This is a clear desecration of the divine plan. Dominion does not mean desecration of any life for the sake of financial gain. Today approximately thirty billion animals are killed each year to feed the carnivorous appetites of humanity. Additionally, forty-five million fish are killed each day, depleting natural habitats and creating ecological imbalances. We are responsible for our actions.

In doing this, we are downgrading our opportunities to spiritually evolve by creating so much death and destruction. Can we expect to achieve, on a mass level, the evolution of consciousness and deveikut/chey'rut that is our birthright when we are consuming the life force of sentient animals and generating so much pain and suffering?

Second, God's dietary plan preserves our personal health. Statistically speaking, the countries with the highest animal flesh consumption have the highest amount of chronic disease. Diabetes is two to four times higher in meat eaters. Cancer is two to four times higher in meat eaters (including meat, fish, and chicken), which includes three to four times higher breast and prostate cancer. Leukemia and lymphomas are three times higher, and lung cancer is two times higher in dairy drinkers. Vegetarians under the age of sixty-five are forty-five percent less likely to suffer a heart attack than meat eaters. Because of the acidity and high phosphorous associated with flesh consumption, osteoporosis is four times higher in meat eaters. The list goes on, but the point is very clear: high intake of animal flesh is directly proportional to chronic disease in its consumers.

Bereisheet 1:29 presents an organic, plant-source-only diet, which creates minimal disease. The use of pesticides and herbicides was an alien concept in Torah times, but the pesticide concentration today is approximately fifteen times higher in flesh foods than in vegetables. Breast milk from a woman who is on a plant-source-only diet has only one percent the toxins of the breast milk of a flesh-food-eating woman. The Torah as a model of natural, harmonious living certainly implies that we should eat organic. The current science shows that many pesticides and herbicides are either carcinogens, metabolically poisonous, and/or neurotoxins. One research study released by the Environmental Defense Counsel showed that the average newborn umbilical cord blood in the U.S. contains approximately 200 toxins (180 carcinogens, 217 neurotoxins).

These were not problems at the time of Adam and Cha'vah, and we do not need to have these problems today. The so-called green revolution has not proven to be superior to organic food production and GMO produce either equals or has up to ten percent less yield than organic foods per acre. GMO foods also contaminate, on a mass scale, organic and commercial produce, and are being shown to cause a series of health problems in living organisms. The Torah also teaches that we have a spiritual obligation to take care of our health. The great rabbi/physician Moses Maimonides taught, "Since maintaining a healthy and sound body is among the ways of G-d, for one cannot understand or have knowledge of the Creator if one is ill; therefore one must avoid that which harms the body and accustom oneself to that which is helpful and helps the body become stronger" (Mishnah Torah, Hilchot Deʾot 3:2).

Third, the vegetarianism of Bereisheet 1:29 protects and preserves human life. Currently, 40–60 million people starve to death each year. An estimated 29,500 to 42,000 children starve to death each day according to the UN. The primary reason for this is that a meat-centered diet results in a hoarding of resources. A flesh-centered diet takes 22–29 times more petrol to produce a pound of meat as opposed to a pound of wheat. The grain it takes to feed 100 cows can feed 2,000 people. Today people are choosing to feed that grain to cattle instead of to starving children. It is estimated that if meat eaters would cut down just 10 percent of their meat consumption, there would be enough food to feed all humanity. If everyone were to eat plant-source-only, there would be enough food to feed the planet seven times over. A flesh-centered diet is indeed a hoarding of resources. Animal agriculture uses 50–75 percent of the planet's potable water. It pollutes the air we breathe. When we pollute the air and water and feed cattle instead of starving people because we are motivated for capital gain, we demonstrate our disregard for life.

Fourth, the plant-source-only diet outlined in Bereisheet 1:29 protects the ecology. A flesh-centered diet pollutes water and air. It is also the main cause of global warming and/or weather instability. Dr. David Hanson of NASA, head of the global warming project, has stated that animal agriculture is the major cause of this phenomenon, not carbon dioxide. Cattle methane contributes at least 37 percent of the global warming gases. Methane is between 25 and 100 times more warming than carbon dioxide. Nitrous oxide, from the billion pounds of manure produced each year in the US alone, contributes 300 times more to global warming than carbon dioxide. It takes 9–13 years to get methane out of the atmosphere and over 100 years to get CO_2 out of the atmosphere, so the global weather instability from the methane and NO_2 would dissipate in a short time if the world went to plant-source-only cuisine.

Animal agriculture also contributes to acid rain, which is responsible for degradation of the coral reefs. Switching to a plant-source-only diet greatly aids in stopping the ecological destruction and creating a renewal of the earth.

Finally, the plant-source-only diet leads to peace. When people are fed and healthy and the environment is not being destroyed, it is far more likely that peace will prevail, because people will not be fighting over resources. This is *sh'leimut,* or total and complete peace. These five mitzvot are the result of the prescription God gave humanity in Bereisheet 1:29. We were given a preventive, healthy diet for maintaining a healthful, natural life for our planet and ourselves. However, in Bereisheet 9:3 flesh-food was ultimately allowed as a dispensational ordinance. Rav Avraham Yitzhak Kook, the first chief rabbi of Israel, describes Bereisheet 9:3 as a compromise, because people were not ready to adhere to a plant-based diet. This compromise was allowed with the theoretical idea that the people would eventually move toward a plant-source-only diet. The Torah often compassionately meets people where they are in order to move them toward the ideal. Bereisheet 9:3 meets people where they are and leads them to the ideal of Bereisheet 1:29.

Another example of this consenting principle is that the Israelite soldiers were not allowed to rape enemy women during war. If a soldier saw a woman he was inclined toward, he had to take her home, shave her head, dress her in plain clothing (to enable her to grieve); then, if, after a month, he still desired her, he had to marry her and accord to her all the responsibilities of a husband to his wife (Devarim 21:10–13). This process was designed to curb lust. The process palliated the urges, so that the behaviors were more reasonable and consistent with spiritual life. The meat allowance was for the same purpose.

A final piece of all this is that, based upon my direct observations of thousands of people, when people transition from a flesh diet to a plant-source-only diet, their spiritual energies, aptitudes, and desires improve. They become more interested in spirituality. This is also coupled with learning to eat less. There were great sages who ate a little meat, but ate very little food in general. They ate very minimal amounts of meat for ritual and ceremonial purposes. This includes ceremony where we release those devolved souls who incarnated into animals, in which a bite of the flesh is taken to release the trapped soul along with the appropriate prayer. According to kabbalistic tradition this is only to be done by Torah scholars or kabbalists, and is only to be done with authentic kosher food (not with animals who are either factory farmed or not slaughtered according to halakhah). Such conditions are very difficult to obtain these days. Along with this we have the mitzvot of releasing souls trapped in the plant kingdom through a vegetarian diet, although this sort of devolvement is less common in the plant kingdom than in the animal kingdom.

The other implied teaching of reincarnation regarding flesh eating is that in looking at prophecies in the Hebrew scriptural Book of Yesha'yahu (Isaiah) about the coming of the messiah, there is a subtle suggestion that the world will return to a Bereisheet 1:29 diet as part of the shift of energy that will draw the messiah. The more we eat this way, the more we create the preconditions for the messianic energy to manifest. It is no accident that Hashem gave us the dietary cuisine of Bereisheet 1:29 as our highest Torah ideal, and Bereisheet 9:3 as nothing more than a compromise pointing us in the direction of the Torah ideal.

Bereisheet 2:9–15 says:

> God made grow out of the ground every tree that is pleasant to look at and good to eat, [including] the Tree of Life in the middle of the garden, and the Tree of Knowledge of Good and Evil. A river flowed out of Eden to water the garden. From there it divided and became four major rivers. The name of the first is Pishon. It surrounds the entire land of Havilah where gold is found. The gold of that land is [especially] good. Also found there are pearls and precious stones. The name of the second river is Gihon. It surrounds the land of Cush. The name of the third river is the Tigris which flows to the east of Assyria. The fourth river is the Euphrates. God took the man and placed him in the Garden of Eden to work it and watch it.

Then Bereisheet 2:16–17 says: "God gave the man a commandment saying, 'You may definitely eat from every tree of the garden. But from the Tree of Knowledge of Good and Evil, do not eat, for on the day you eat from it, you will definitely die.'" Here the plot has been established for what will happen to humanity.

Adam was alone and God created a mate for him—Cha'vah. She was the bone of his bone, flesh of his flesh. In a clue to the larger setting, Bereisheet 2:21 says:

> God then made the man fall in to a deep state of unconscious-ness, and he slept. He took one of his ribs and closed the flesh in its place. God built the rib that he took from the man into a woman, and He brought her to the man. The man said, "Now this is bone from my bones and flesh from my flesh. She shall be called Woman [*ishah*] because she was taken from man [*ish*]."

The statement "this is bone from my bones and flesh from my flesh" refers to a kabbalistic teaching that Adam appeared first in the world of yetzirah (astral plane) and the first woman on the astral plane was Lilith, not Cha'vah. Lilith was simultaneously created with Adam, and rebelled against Adam and began to work with the dark side, the fallen angels and demons, becoming the consort of the angel Sama'el (Satan). Thus Cha'vah, who represents the more mature and maternal woman, was actually a creation that came out of man. She was a much more aligned frequency with the man so that they became more unified.

Commenting on the Torah's account of Cha'vah's interaction with the serpent, Yonatan ben Uzziel recounts a tradition that Cha'vah mated with the serpent, and that Kayin (Cain) was an offspring of that union. (The implication of the word "mating" is probably not a literal sexual intercourse; most likely it is a heavy psychic contamination that primarily affected Kayin and, to a significantly lesser extent, his brother, Hevel.) This is why, at the birth of Kayin, Cha'vah says "I have gained a man," as if she had perhaps antici-pated something other than a human baby. Hevel (Abel), on the other hand, came from her union with Adam. The serpent was probably a reptilian being associated with warlock, wizard, and/or the energy of the nephilim (fallen angels who tried to disrupt God's plan of the evolution of the Adamic race). The rebellion of the fallen angels is still happening. Unfortunately, their fallen angel genetics cannot hold the energy of the light, causing them to incline toward alignment with the dark side, or Sit'ra Acha'ra. The genetics of Kayin's offspring, who were half human and half nephilim, also could not hold the energy. They too moved to the dark side along with their father.

After 130 years, Adam and Cha'vah conceived Shet (Seth). Shet brought forth Enosh, who lived 815 years. Seven generations from Adam, Hanokh (Enoch) was born to Yered. Hanokh was the first enlightened being on the planet. Hanokh lived 65 years before having sons and daughters. Bereisheet 5:24 says, "Enoch walked with God, and he was no more, because God had taken him." According to the Mishnah he was taken up alive. He received a month to a year of training, where he was given visions of the cosmic and planetary plan and was imparted with astrophysical knowledge of the angelic realms and patterns (Tosefot L'Zohar, Vol. 2, folios 277a–b). He then returned to earth to teach and was taken up alive at the age of 365, where he became the head of the archangels as part of the Metatron soul energy, which sits at the right hand of God and endeavors to lead humanity back to God. Metatron also battles against Sama'el (Satan) and the fallen angels.

Hanokh could have (and may have) studied with Adam, because their life spans overlapped. As the angel Zagzakel, Metatron was Moshe's angelic teacher, so in this way Hanokh was also Moshe's teacher. It is said that Hanokh's soul is the guardian angel of the messiah, and so Metatron's soul is the soul of the soul of the messiah. Hanokh also created through his life the Aliyah of Ascension. At least ten people in this tradition have ascended alive to be with the Divine as B'nei Aliyah—"children of the Ascension." It is taught in the Mishnah that the soul energy of Metatron will incarnate on earth as the messiah. The essence of Hanokh's soul did not fall at the time of Adam, but is part of the Metatron soul energy that incarnates as the high priest or spiritual leader of each generation.

In the tenth generation from Adam came Noah. At the age of 500, Noah begat Shem, Ham, and Yefet (Japheth). God saw the wickedness of humanity in this time period, which included cannibalism, cruelty, sexual perversion, genetic manipulation and engineering, exploitation and slavery, marriage of humans to animals, and generally an unimaginable desecration of creation. God realized that the reset button needed to be pushed, and brought forth a flood to erase the genetics of the fallen angels from the planet. Creation on the earth almost had to start over with a new genetic upgrade. Noah represented this genetic change. He was born without webbed feet and hands contrary to previous generations, and he was born circumcised. He represented a great change away from reptilian genetics.

Many people have lived separate from the technology of destruction throughout history. These separate ones were called *Ushenim,* or Essenes. They were able to step out and join the natural path bonded to the earth, in contrast to Kayin and Nimrod who were actively evil and hedonistic. There were people throughout the ages who stood up against the power of the fallen angels and their servants on the surface of the earth. Some of these fallen angels merged into different levels of the underworlds to escape the flood. They have not left the planet and have been assigned a certain domain under the earth. They are currently activating the energies of great darkness upon the planet.

It is predicted that these forces of darkness will rise again and try to disrupt the balance. The oral kabbalistic tradition predicts that an apocalyptic intervention will be made by the messiah, who will be accompanied by a force of higher angels. These *seraphim* will appear as flaming serpents. They will, in a single day, destroy the forces of darkness upon the planet as implied in Zekharya (Zechariah) 14:9–10: "And the Lord shall be king over all the earth: on that day the Lord shall be one, and his name One." The table has been set and the play of light and darkness continues. The darkness, paradoxically, is ultimately a gift from the Divine to help us evolve spiritually if we so choose. It is our greatest challenge, and our greatest source of ennoblement. For deep within the darkness lies the ember of divine light, waiting for us to fan it into full force by our actions and our choices.

Amen

Noah

This is a very interesting parashah. It is somewhat painful because it so closely reflects our society today. It also holds some messages about the process of enlightenment. One of the most important teachings in this parashah is that we are definitely influenced by those around us. Nachmanides pointed out that violent energy was so strong in the days of Noah that "all flesh had perverted its way on the earth" and had become violent (Bereisheet 6:12). The egocentric culture of death and separation from God literally affected all flesh on the planet. In the Midrash, it is said that even sheep and cattle turned carnivorous, and all the birds turned predatory. It was this level of violence that brought the flood. The "corruption of the way," in the form of genetic engineering, all levels of sexual perversion and bestiality, and marriages between humans and animals, was secondary to the extreme violence practiced at that time. Noah, in this context, was considered "a tzaddik in his time" because he was able to stand firm and remain righteous amid such collective negativity.

Amazingly, only a thousand years after this cycle of Bereisheet began, God decided to undo creation. Why? On almost every level, people were guided by the original misunderstanding they inherited from the Tree of Knowledge of Good and Evil: receiving for self, alone, rather than receiving in order to share. Additionally, there were the negative effects of the genetic field created by the fallen angels and their offspring, the nephilim. Consequently, great imbalances resulted across the planet. Perhaps the most negative forces were the so-called fallen angels, who thought they knew better than God. As pointed out earlier, they mated with the daughters of man and created offspring that were half human and half angel in their genetics. This was a delicate and dangerous blend that activated and amplified evil tendencies among them. Appealing to our primitive minds, these extraterrestrials came to the planet to undermine God's plan, as implied in many sources going back to Talmudic times.

The Zohar teaches that a group of 200 fallen angels led by Aza and Azael became the source of this negativity. However, Noah's connection to the light was so strong that no evil person or group could move him from his righteous center. All of this negativity contributed to the separation that began with Kayin (Cain). Kayin emphasized man-made technologies and introduced the concept of cities (culture of death), which separated people from the Divine and from the culture of life and liberation of the Great Torah Way. This is the essential difference between Kayin's "way of man" and Hevel's (Abel's) "way of God"—living in harmony on earth. A focus on the physical world and technology separates humanity from the light of God as it shines solely through the light of the Self. Ego builds through a sense of separation consciousness and desires for money, power, and material gain. In Noah's time this orientation began to dominate over social harmony and focus on the Divine as central to the meaning of life. This split continued to widen in the antediluvian times until chaos reigned, led by the nephilim.

Along with this separation of heaven and earth came the breakdown of intimacy and trust between people. In other words, this generation of Noah created a breakdown in intimacy processes. Intimacy is necessary for divine merging and for deepening our experience of oneness with the Divine. In this way, intimacy helps to heal the separation between heaven and the earth. Unfortunately, this degradation of intimacy is occurring today, and we as a people would do well to learn from our history. Today there is incredible violence, genocide, idolatry, sexual perversion, rape, theft, murder, slavery, disruption of the ecology, and active efforts by the few to control the minds of the many. The spiritual warning here is that as in the days before the flood, so will it be in the days before the coming of the messiah.

In the antediluvian times, they laughed at Noah as he built an ark the length of three football fields. They laughed at him because they believed they had the technology to control the weather and all of nature. They believed that through their science they had become more powerful than God. Does this sound familiar? Today we are going a step further. Codex, which operates under the United Nations World Health Organization, is trying to outlaw organic foods. How far from the way of God we have wandered.

Some people adopt the view that Noah stood out because everyone else around him was mediocre, but that is irrelevant. Noah held to the "way of God," as guided by the Way of the Torah, regardless of the *status quo*. A major challenge for us on the spiritual path is that we see so many people doing actively unholy things and pressuring us to do the same. Worse than this, they become upset if we do not follow their co-dependent and unconscious ways.

Interestingly, the word *noach* (נח) means "comfortable"! The man whose name meant "comfortable" chose an uncomfortable path. The uncomfortable path is *almost a precondition* for enlightenment, because the ego wants to keep us in our comfort zones, so that we do not desire liberation. This is the way the ego structure works—it helps us to fall asleep in the comfort zone of social applause, power, and the short-term results of greed. Walking the spiritual path is a journey into the unknown. It is not about comfort. We see this exemplified by the ancestor Ya'akov (Jacob), who said to the pharaoh, "The days of my life have been few and hard" (Bereisheet 47:9). As King Solomon wrote, everything has its time, and it truly was not time for *Ya'akov Avinu* (Ya'akov our father) to be comfortable. He gained his comfort in the last few years of his life. On the spiritual path, even after one reaches the level of self-liberation, there is still a tendency for delusion and desire for the "comfort zone." We must always walk on the razor's edge and remain attentive to this temptation at any spiritual stage.

The covenant that Noah made with God following the Great Flood was very important. Humanity had become seduced by egocentric needs. There was a great variety of sexual sin. Genetic engineering was violating life's sacred DNA code. There was mating between species. In a sense, there was a disregard for life's basic plan. They had moved away from an organic way, and it is said that the nephilim, in their crossbreeding, had created human cannibals. New archeological research suggests that antediluvian cannibalism and pre-Adamic cannibalism was common. The genetic breeding of the nephilim with the human population contributed to great darkness. Noah's covenant was intended to reconnect us with the light of binah, so that this light would dissolve (or at least balance) the negative forces of his time.

Another disconcerting parallel between these antediluvian times and our current times is that water was used to cleanse the people of their imbalances. Water, in fact, cleansed the planet of people. Today we see water, and every aspect of our environment, fighting back—with tornados, hurricanes, strains of antibiotic-resistant bacteria, viruses, and fetid lagoons poisoned by

animal agriculture and other toxic wastes. These are undermining the quality of our drinking water, air, and soil, and, ultimately, our immune systems.
As we traverse the six-thousandth year, we are bottoming out. The question
remains: Will we create a spiritual ark that will bring light and transform the
consciousness of the living planet, or are we going to go the way of antediluvian times?

From a kabbalistic perspective, the story of Noah and the ark is a metaphorical message. Noah is a metaphor of the upper-world dimension known
as yesod, the ninth sephirah, through which all the energy moves into the
last one, malchut, the receptivity of the earth's physical plane. The ark represents malchut. Obviously, the "wicked" men are the people who are committed to receive for self, alone. This is the flourishing of the ego over anything
else. When Noah (who represents the heavens or higher sephirotic energies)
enters the ark, it represents the merging of the heavens and earth. Traditionally, this is the way imbalances are repaired. Merging the heavens and earth
creates tikkun. Just as Noah enters the ark, we can create a conduit that allows
heavenly light to come onto the planet and transform consciousness. This is
our spiritual challenge.

Reading between the lines reveals a message about the relationship of humans to animals, our interconnectedness with them, and the holiness of that
relationship. It is said in the Midrash that Noah and his sons and daughters
spent almost their whole time caring for the animals in the ark's living zoo
(Midrash Tanchuma, Noach, Chap. 14). There were many animals—not just
two of each, as the song goes. The birds were in pairs of sevens, as were the kosher animals. Noah's dedication to the animals' wellbeing is deeply significant.

Avraham once asked Malki-zedek (Shem, the son of Noah), "Through
what merit did you survive the Great Flood in that ark?"

He replied, "Through the deed of charity that we performed in the ark."

Said Avraham, "What? Charity? Were there beggars in the ark? Wasn't it
just your family and the animals?"

Said Malki-zedek, "True, but we were busy night and day tending to the
welfare of all those many birds, animals, and wildlife. We never even got to
sleep. Rather, day and night we fed them and tended to their very different
and unique needs" (Midrash Tehilim 37:1).

Today, we do not consider the fact that for every two billion fast-food hamburgers eaten, one thousand species become extinct! When a species becomes extinct, there is a subtle shift in the natural balance and holiness of our world pattern, because that living creature's created light is now gone. Because Noah and his family were feeding everyone in every moment, their hearts were continually open. It rained only forty days, but they served the animals intensely day and night for ten months before the ordeal in the ark was completed.

Another way of understanding the ark's code is as a symbol of the covenant with Hashem. This covenant creates a safe space for humanity during times of severe judgment. Some kabbalists feel that the ark of our times is the holy book of the Zohar, containing the mystical teachings of the second-century school of Rabbi Shim'on bar Yochai. Today's catastrophe is not a forty-day torrent of rain, but rather a gradual eroding of our ecology, slowly making our earth uninhabitable. Global warming or weather instability, all the pollution of our rivers and groundwater, destruction of our land, and the general pollution of the whole atmosphere are all part of this creeping destruction. It is no longer subtle because so many see it happening.

Oral tradition also suggests a shift in the water's nature. In antediluvian times, in the time of Gan Eden (גַן עֵדֶן), water had the ability to create physical, emotional, mental, and spiritual purification. All the water was naturally healing (Midrash Vayikra Rabbah 34:15 and Otzar HaMidrashim, Ma'asiyo't, Keta 42). The flood created a shift in the water's molecular and spiritual structure. Water, the cosmic ocean, lost much of its healing power, though water is still the lifeblood of the planet. The molecular weight of water is 18. Eighteen is also the numerical value for the Hebrew word *chaim* (חיים), meaning "life."

After the ark launched, all the humans and nephilim were destroyed except for those nephilim who escaped into the tunnels beneath the earth. Some Torah scholars believe that these are still generating negative forces from the inner earth realms. Og, one of the largest of the nephilim (Devarim 3:11), survived the flood by hiding along the outside of the ark (Talmud Bavli, Zevachim 113b). A thousand years later, Moshe killed him in battle (BeMidbar 21:35). He attached himself to the ark when Noah went to retrieve some grape leaves he had gathered earlier from Gan Eden. Og sneaked in during Noah's absence. This is the way the darkness works; it sneaks in during a moment of distraction. The Midrash tells us that Noah had compassion on Og, drilled a hole in the side of the ark, and fed the giant as the flood raged (Midrash Pirkei D'Rebbe Eliezer, Chap. 33).

When the rains finally ceased, Noah opened a window. Metaphorically, he opened the window of his soul to the heavens, and sent out a raven to see if the waters had subsided. The raven represents anger in the world and is a biblical metaphor for the *contrary* (Talmud Bavli, Gitin 54a). Sending out the raven is also a symbol of our effort to eliminate anger from the world. Noah and his family wished to emerge from the ark, a symbol of the womb opening to the new world into which humanity was to be reborn. It was too soon to eliminate even spiritual anger, and so the raven returned after a brief flight. Then Noah sent out a dove to explore the situation, and she too returned, unable to find a dry perch. After waiting another seven days, he sent the dove out again, but this time she returned with the proverbial olive branch of peace in her beak. This was a sign of hope for the world. Noah waited another seven days and sent the dove out once more. This time, she did not return, and he knew for certain that the flood had sufficiently subsided and dry land was to be found.

Upon his safe return to land and leaving the ark, Noah offered sacrifices to complete the energetic cycle. The covenant of the rainbow was made with God, and God promised never again to eliminate the creatures of the earth by heavenly floodwaters. The covenant was established not only with humanity, but also equally among all the animals and other life on the planet. The raindrops reflect light into a prism at forty-two degrees. This is the power of the *Ana BeKoach* (אנא בכח) forty-two-letter name of God that becomes a rainbow. The bow is arched upward, reflecting the importance of humanity living in a way that creates holiness of the Or Hozer (אור חוזר). The Or Hozer is the upward flowing of light to the Divine, keeping the merging of heaven and earth in a perpetual cycle.

God gave humans dominion over all the earth and its life. This included the right to alter the ecology, but not the right to exploit the ecology. As it says in the mystical book of the Bahir, "The hand of God is in the earth as a hand is in a glove." The forces of nature provide a classroom for us to commune with and learn from God. Nature is not a pawnshop to sell trash for egocentric, greedy purposes.

God gave the blessing for all the souls of all the animals and of the humans to be fruitful and multiply. We were also given permission to eat flesh in Bereisheet 9:3. It is unclear why this permission was given. Perhaps people were not ready for the vegan ideal. The Torah gave them an approach to guide them toward that ideal (Talmud Bavli, Kidushin 21b). With permission to eat flesh, the average life span of humans dropped from 300–900 years to an average of 120 years (Bereisheet 6:3). Beginning with Noah (the first human born circumcised without webbed feet and hands, according to Midrash Tanchuma, Noach, Chap. 5), these times reflected major genetic changes. The Great Flood also resulted in a climate change, and perhaps also an atmospheric change. All of these things, including flesh consumption, contributed to the reduced life span in humans.

Our work is to return to pre-fall, Gan Eden consciousness. There we were living in immortal light bodies. Our work is to make our physical bodies conductors of our internal, immortal light bodies, so that we may again move between the heavens and the earth.

The rainbow code activated the seven lower sephirotic dimensions and upgraded their transformative expression in the world. Considering this, not all people were ready to activate their light bodies and to live by the higher energies of the original non-flesh Bereisheet 1:29 diet. (This does not exclude the kabbalistic rites of eating flesh to release the souls of humans who have regressed back into animals from bad actions in their previous lives.) Having moved from a period of intense murder and cannibalism, perhaps it was enough that they would not kill and eat each other. As God told Noah, it is forbidden to spill the blood of man by man, man by animal, or our own blood through suicide (Bereisheet 9:5). Perhaps the blood lust of cannibalism was redirected here, by allowing consumption of livestock, fowl, and fish. In later rabbinal teachings, such as taught by the Rambam (Maimonides), eating meat was tolerated because the collective Am Yisrael was not yet spiritually ready to return to the Bereisheet 1:29 herb, grass, vegetable, fruit, nut, and seed cuisine. It is interesting to note, however, that today, outside of India, Israel has the largest number of vegetarians per population.

According to oral tradition, after the flood, Noah created a vineyard from a grapevine he had secured from Gan Eden and became drunk on these grapes.

The vineyard is a metaphor for higher spiritual dimensions, and the resulting intoxication was thus, at some level, a divine intoxication. Like Adam, Noah could not handle these higher energies. He could not handle the energy of the grape juice as a conduit or a transmitter. Instead, it opened up a focal point of negativity, because he had not purged all his subtle egocentric desires, although he "walked with God and was whole."

According to the Talmud, when Noah's younger son Ham found him naked and drunk in his tent, he raped him according to one sage and castrated him according to another (Talmud Bavli, Sanhedrin 70a). Others posit that it was Ham's son Kena'an (Canaan) who abused Noah while he lay drunk, and that Ham discovered what happened and laughed (Midrash Pirkei D'Rebbe Eliezer, Chap. 23). This is a metaphor for how we have been seduced and raped by our own egos, which channel these negative forces. We face these stories as part of our purification as we journey toward the higher realms. We cannot reach the higher realms until most, if not *all*, of our egocentric tendencies are dissolved. Sometimes, if we are not prepared to dissolve them, these tendencies come back to bite us. This is why the Torah is a manual for enlightenment. As we live the mitzvot, we naturally quiet the mind so we can go to the higher realms. Noah curses Kena'an, the son of Ham, and his descendants, to be slaves to Noah's other sons, Shem and Yefet (Bereisheet 9:25), who took action and covered their father's nakedness (Bereisheet 9:23). Accordingly, the children of Yefet merged with and "lived in the tents of Shem" (Bereisheet 9:27). This is symbolic of the reality of Arabs and Jews living together successfully.

It is important to note that Noah did not curse *all* the sons of Ham to be slaves, a false justification used by Bible-toting pioneers to justify black slavery. Only Kena'an was so cursed. The other sons of Ham were Kush (Ethiopia), Mizrayim (Egypt), and Put (allied with Egypt and Ethiopia and in that region). (These later became allies of Israel [Nahum 3:9–10].)

From Kush came Nimrod, the first one-world dictator. He possessed the ability to captivate the minds of men, and ruled by force. Until Nimrod there had been no wars or rulers. Nimrod ruled over what later became known as Babylon, and was the leader and bringer of radical atheism. Openly rebellious against God, he refused to follow God's agenda to populate the world. Instead he built the Tower of Babel as part of his rebellion against God's forces. Nimrod and the Tower of Babel represent the full separation between man and God.

Bereisheet 11:2 says, "When [the people] migrated from the east, they found a valley in the land of Shinar, and they settled there." Moving away from the East represents moving away from God and the natural world. The Tower of Babel was not just a gigantic ego trip. These people had access to antediluvian knowledge and technologies (including nuclear technology). They believed that the power that brought the flood came not from God, but from a certain group of corporeal-bodied "fallen angels" (or extraterrestrials), and they discovered their home planet. They made plans to attack them in revenge for creating the preconditions for the flood. It says in Bereisheet 11:6, "Now nothing they plan to do will be unattainable for them!" This is the power of the dark side, when unified. In return, the "watcher angels" (as identified in Daniel 4:14) acted first to confound their minds by creating mental confusion and chaos. These are the same watcher angels who created mental illness in the mind of Kayin and later in the mind of Nevukhadnezar.

Nimrod's life did not get easier with the arrival of Avram (later Avraham/Abraham), who at the age of twenty-four made a fool of Nimrod by challenging his claim to be a god. Avram survived being thrown into the same furnace where they fashioned the bricks for the Tower of Babel (Midrash Tana D'Bei Eliyahu Zuta 25:3). Several generations later, Avram's grandson, Esau, killed Nimrod (Midrash Pirkei D'Rebbe Eliezer, Chap. 24). The Jewish history of fighting the one-world Babylonian government, and awakening the general population to the Divine, goes back to the time of Nimrod. There is a prophecy that Nimrod will be reborn as the anti-messiah, *Armulis*.

We understand the power of unity even for the sons and daughters of darkness. The construction of the Tower of Babel happened because all the people had one common language, and the forces of the light could not overcome the power of their unity. They were too strong. Unified darkness will always defeat the side of good if there is *dis*unity among the good. The only way to defeat unified ego, or evil, is through unity on the side of good with the addition of divine intervention.

The task of light workers in the world today is to unify the good. People must realize that the forces of darkness are much more organized than the forces of light. We create a tremendous field of unity for the forces of light as we link with one another in meditation and use the power of the light. When God took away the unified language, which was Hebrew, disunity happened, and the forces of darkness were scattered all over the planet.

There were ten generations from Adam to Noah, representing a cycle of ten sephirotic energies. From Noah to Avraham, there were also ten generations. It is no accident that from Noah we trace the lineage that leads us to the creation of Avraham, and ultimately the initiation of Avraham by Malki-zedek. This work with Avraham, which is where this parashah ends, shows another opportunity for the seed of the Torah Way to be replanted, for the blossoming of full Tree-of-Life consciousness, enlightenment, and deveikut on the planet. The central message here is that the seed unfolding from Noah to Avraham is a significant part of our spiritual evolution. It implies that, certainly, in time, our world will transform into a world of deveikut. Blessings to all who follow this Torah Way of unfolding—this path of enlightenment—given to the people who study Torah, kabbalah, and Zohar. Such people will live in the consciousness of the full fruition of the seed that was planted at the time of Hanokh, preserved by Noah, and then planted and activated again in the time of Avraham.

Amen

Lekh Lekha

PARASHAH Lekh Lekha is the foundation statement of Judaism as a full enlightenment path. It is our introduction to Avraham as seed of the Jewish people. Often, in a play or a movie, its essence is apparent in the opening lines. Similarly, the message that Avraham received from El Shaddai (אל שדי), "lekh lekha" (לך לך), contains the Jewish Way essence and the mystery of enlightenment for all the great liberation traditions.

The phrase "lekh lekha" means "go to your self"—but what does that mean? Avraham is told in a Ruach HaKodesh experience, "Leave your country, leave your birthplace, and leave your father's home." These are the elements for the normal ego structure that make up our illusory sense of self. Nation, birthplace, and family are the materials that we build our ego identity upon, and it is from these that we establish our illusory sense of self. They create the illusion of personal security, citizenship, property rights, and inheritance. God was not only commanding a geographical move. El Shaddai, the great nurturer and protector, had much more in mind.

It is the ultimate purpose of life to know the divine presence; to know the Self, which is rooted in the Self of God. This Ruach HaKodesh experience, a heavenly s'micha m'shefa, was the neshikat elohut (נשיקת אלהות), divine kiss, activating the t'shukat deveikut (תשוקת דביחות), the urge for divine merging. The Self includes the soul essence and the spark of God in all people and in all things. It is prior to consciousness.

Lekh lekha means traveling to a new land, the deveikut consciousness of Israel. It means, at another level, to create a new and more conscious identity, independent of nationality, land (our personal dirt and dysfunctional egocentric thought forms), and family (relationship patterns). "Israel," or the "promised land," is a code word for a higher level of spiritual existence. Kena'an (כנען), the "promised land," on the physical plane, is called Ha'aretz Asher Ar'eka (הארץ אשר אראך)—"the land where I [God] will reveal myself to you." This is both a metaphor and a physical reality. It is the living field of the land of heightened spiritual energy and inspiration for *at least* the Jewish people.

This may also be a clue as to why so many people have been fighting over this high-spiritual-energy holy land for millennia. The paradox is that no one who has conquered the land has been able to remain there, because they are not able to handle the energy of the land. In the twelfth century, when Saladin drove out the Crusaders, he was asked how long he would occupy the land. His answer: "We will stay here as long as we maintain our holiness. If our people cannot maintain a holy way, we will be forced to leave." Saladin reflected a profound and prophetic understanding of the land. He realized that occupancy of that land was determined by collective ability to relinquish worldly self-definitions, and devotion to God was life's central context.

In this evolutionary process, as with Avraham, we become more and more the individualized expression of the Divine on this physical plane. One level of Avraham's new identity was its foundation on his service and love for God, as he walked before God in his wholeness and became a blessing to the world. Ultimately, as Avraham spiritually grew with each of his ten trials, he became fully identified as a spark of God, as "I am"—the total, whole, and complete liberated person, living in steady deveikut, whether awake or asleep, whether in *hitbonenut* (concentration) or *hitbodedut* (meditation).

Avraham was not a pushover, according to the oral tradition's stories of how he began his teachings: One day his father Terah, who was a builder and seller of idols, left him in charge of the shop. A man came to buy an idol, and Avram asked him his age. He answered, "sixty." Avram said, "That's interesting. Woe to the man who is sixty years old and worships an idol that is only a day old." Demonstrating the stupidity of idol worship was not the best way to sell idols.

There is a classic story of a woman who brought a flour offering for the idols in Terah's shop. Left in charge of the shop again, young Avram took a hammer and smashed to smithereens all the idols in the shop except the largest one. He then placed the hammer in the hand of the remaining idol. When his father came back, he was very upset. "You destroyed the idols!" he yelled at his son.

Avram replied, "What are you talking about? It was amazing! A woman brought some flour as an offering, and when I placed it before the idols as an offering, the idols began to fight among each other. The largest idol then took the hammer and smashed the others."

His father became very angry. "Why are you lying? You think these idols have the ability to think and move?"

And Avram laughed and said to his father, "Listen to what you are saying."

Avraham not only confronted his father. The king of Avraham's native empire was none other than Nimrod. According to the sages, he was a powerful being, who had a vision of God and rebelled against it. Nimrod was also notorious as a hunter of human souls. He was a powerful occult figure, who knowledgably and consciously attempted to control the minds of the people. He represented the first attempt at a one-world dictatorship, and it is predicted by the kabbalistic sages of old that he will one day incarnate as the "anti-Christ" to attempt it again.

Although not yet enlightened, Avraham, as a highly evolved being, undermined the power of Nimrod to control the masses by encouraging them to question. Avraham was a threat to their system because he taught people to go beyond the bio-computer, body-mind complex, to access the Divine. Conscious people are a natural threat to all dominator political systems. Avraham was not only promoting the main purpose of life as deveikut, but human emancipation, which, in most cases, is preconditional to waking the masses. Avraham taught about the Divine from his own direct inner experiences and used his understanding to guide people toward their *own* direct experience. Letting go of idolatry was part of getting free and part of the Avrahamic tradition of independent thought and discovery.

Eventually, the oral tradition tells us, Avraham was summoned to the court of Nimrod, who set about challenging the now-seventy-five-year-old rebel: "Do you not know that I rule the world, and that the sun, moon, and stars all respond to my beck and call? And yet you dare to cross me and challenge my faith!"

Avraham replied: "Nature has decreed the sun to rise in the east and set in the west. If you can decree that tomorrow it will rise in the west and set in the east, then indeed I can declare you the Lord of the World. And in addition, if you are really the ruler of all things, you must know what is in everyone's thoughts, so tell me what I am thinking."

Avraham had boldly and daringly called Nimrod's bluff, and Nimrod's response was one of violent arrogance. He sentenced Avraham to death by fire. It is said in the Mishnah that the kiln they had made was so hot that when they threw Avraham into it, the soldiers standing nearby spontaneously burst into flames as well. However, Avraham remained unscathed. The entire population of Ur Kasdim witnessed this miracle, and Avraham immediately became famous and attracted many followers. Nevertheless, he left Ur Kasdim, went to Charan, and began publically sharing the singularity and power of God wherever he went. Later in our lineage, Moshe, at the direction of the Divine, and in the liberation energy of the Avrahamic tradition, created the biggest political liberation action in the history of the world with the exodus of the Hebrews from Egypt.

On the outer plane, Avraham's path might appear to us as a lonely journey, but deep inside of us the flame of Hashem waits for each us to choose to illuminate our personal path beyond the illusion of normalcy into the metaphorical arms of Hashem. In that light, it is anything but lonely. It is the ultimate inner fulfillment beyond any attraction for power, money, or pleasure on the outer plane. Avraham was asked to give up the safety and illusion of idolatry and to walk, like Moshe, up the mountain into the unknown. Every path of liberation requires walking into the unknown—letting it all go, knowing we cannot lose what we never really had, and realizing that we cannot attain what we already are. The walk was easier because Avraham was strongly inspired and driven by t'shukat deveikut and the love of God.

A profound and mystical teaching that arises from this great tradition is *ma'aseh avot siman labanim* (מעשה אבות סימן לבנים), "the deeds or actions of the ancestors serve as signs or guides for the behavior of their descendants, as well as what they might be challenged with" (Midrash Tanchuma, Lech Lecha, Chap. 9). Avraham's actions, character, and personality became a model of liberation for us through the Jewish Way. In this context, Avraham may be the most influential person to ever have lived. From his seed have grown three great traditions: Judaism (the trunk), and Christianity and Islam (the branches).

Avraham also, like most liberated people, was an iconoclast, a rebel, and even a guerilla warrior, who with only 318 warriors defeated four mighty kings to free his nephew Lot and hundreds of other captives. He functioned on every level as a whole and complete person. Avraham did not hoard his awareness. Instead he became a blessing for the nations by sharing his deep teachings with them.

On an egocentric level, one could say that Avraham overcame his desire for "self alone," which was the primary cause of the original fall of Adam and Cha'vah. Some of the Midrash even teaches that Adam and Cha'vah reincarnated as Avraham and Sarah to correct their initial fall (Midrash Kohelet Rabbah 3:15). Avraham chose to go against his desire to receive for "self alone," and moved instead to the higher level of understanding. This higher understanding is to "receive in order to share." He moved fearlessly through the identification with the ego to break free of his self-interest and the illusory comfort zone of temporary ego appeasement. He let go of old ways of thinking and negative behavior patterns to connect with the light. He liberated his soul from the prison and the bonds of his physical body. This is the story of a great being and his path of deveikut/chey'rut.

Yah tells him, "I will bless those who bless you, and he who curses you, I will curse. All the families of the earth will be blessed through you" (Bereisheet 12:3). As pointed out earlier, Avraham was told to "walk before God and be whole." In that "walking before," he became a blessing to all of creation. This was his very function. It is said that Avraham and his blessings influenced both the heavens and the earth. Initially, it was "the Lord YHWH of the heavens" who took him out of his father's house, but later, Avraham refers to God as "possessor of heaven and earth" (Bereisheet 14:22).

How did that change happen? When God first communicated with Avraham, his limited perception was that it was the ancient monotheistic God of the heavens. The understanding of a personal God, who could intervene on the earth, was not recognized or understood. But as Avraham began his mission and his consciousness evolved, he recognized and taught the existence of God's active presence on the earth. The paradigm shifted through the actions and faith of Avraham, so much so that Malki-zedek—who is described as the "Priest of the God of the Above"—initiated Avraham with the consciousness of Yah, as the God of the heavens *and* the earth, of both Above *and* Below (Bereisheet 14:18–19).

Avraham's new vision reunited the heavens and the earth. He helped to heal the rift between the heavens and the earth that started with Kayin, as a reflection of the negative consciousness of the fallen angels. He presented a worldview that, although it had been taught earlier by Shem and Eber, was new to most of the population. He fused the spiritual with the physical, and in this process attracted large numbers of people away from idol worship and inspired them to make the Divine the center of their lives. In that way, Avraham taught that God ruled over the heavens and the earth, merging the physical, mundane life with the spiritual in every moment. In this way he also established a core understanding of the Great Torah Way.

Our everyday life is a path to holiness. It is a journey in which the awareness of God is not a distant concept hidden away out of reach in the heavens, but is actively revealed in our mundane life and in nature. As Moshe would later phrase it:

> "It is not in heaven, so [that you should] say, 'Who shall go up to heaven and bring it to us so that we can hear it and keep it?' It is not over the sea so [that you should] say, 'Who will cross the sea and get it for us, so that we will be able to hear it and keep it?' It is something that is very close to you. It is in your mouth and in your heart, so that you can keep it."
>
> (Devarim 30:12–14)

It is a fundamental Jewish teaching, that each of us has the potential, through our day-to-day choices and actions, to unite the holy and the mundane and to unite the heavens and the earth. If we live our lives awakened with divine consciousness, we free and unify the holy sparks of the divine light that are trapped in the klippot (קליפות), the husks of darkness. It is no wonder that the word for "evil" in Hebrew, ra (רע), when reversed, spells ar (ער), Hebrew for "awake."

In living wakefully, Avraham earned two beautiful mitzvot according to the Talmud: one is the *techelet* (תכלת) and the other is the *tefilin* (תפילין). The techelet are the blue fringes we affix to four-cornered garments, or to the ritual shawl as *tzitzit* (ציצית); the blue color represents the heavens of higher consciousness. The leather straps of the tefilin (which we wrap around our arm and head in prayer) allow us to fuse the spiritual aspect with our physical body. If we did not have the tefilin, we could not fuse the physical to the spiritual. In order to fulfill the divine will, we must bind our head (our upper consciousness) with our arms and hands (our lower bodily action consciousness), thus joining the heavens with the earth.

Avraham exemplified this merging, and therefore was rewarded both the techelet and the tefilin (Talmud Bavli, Sotah 17a). Avraham's fusing of the holy and the mundane was one of the great gifts to us. He created the foundation of the essence of the Jewish way of life. This is the discovery of the dance of Eros in the world, and living that dance. Added to this is the commitment to share that way of life throughout the world in ways so that people can incorporate it into their lives. It is a very, very powerful message that Avraham gave us.

Soon after Avraham arrived in the Holy Land they were stricken with a famine. Deep inside he knew the land of Kena'an was indeed the inheritance of the Eternal, but he most likely was wondering, "Why have you sent me to the Holy Land only to experience a famine?"

Nevertheless, he went "down" into *Mizrayim* (מצרים—Egypt). Mizrayim represented another test for him, namely, going into the darkness of the ego. There, he had to deal with his fear for his life, and he asked Sarah to say she was his sister. Truly, they were soulmates. She was the shekhinah, and so in a way she was his sister. Actually, literally, physically, and genetically, she was his half-sister because they shared the same father but had different mothers. Because of her unusual beauty Pharaoh abducted her, as Avraham had feared would happen, and tried to sleep with her and marry her. All kinds of problems arose. The Midrash says that Pharaoh and his household were stricken with boils (Midrash Tanchuma, Lech Lecha, Chap. 8). This is a precursor to the ten plagues that helped to free his descendants from Egypt (Midrash Pirkei D'Rebbe Eliezer, Chap. 26). Eventually, Pharaoh figured out that being with Sarah was the cause of the plagues, and he gave Avraham and Sarah gifts, asking them to leave. Pharaoh could not handle this powerful, spiritual, shamanic energy. In this process, Avraham and Sarah defeated the negative temptations of Mizrayim (the ego), whereas Adam and Eve could not. They rose to the occasion, created a tikkun for Adam and Eve, and left.

Avraham and Sarah returned to Kena'an to live happily ever after ... until another famine struck the land. This time they traveled to the territory of King Avimelekh, who was also attracted to Sarah, and the same scenario began again. Avimelekh took Sarah to his bed and attempted intimacy with her. God intervened once again and rendered him impotent. The wombs of the women in his household became sealed up; they became stuck in childbirth. Avimelekh, however, had a better understanding. He *honored* Avraham and asked him to live among his people. Good things happened.

Part of this message about conquering negativity is that Avraham played out the future. He had a vision in which his people were taken into Egypt and made slaves. But just like Avraham would return with the gold and money, overcoming the dark side, ultimately so would the people. The plagues that occurred to Pharaoh were a warning of the plagues that would later fall upon the Egyptians, when Moshe took the people out again exposing them to the prospect of mass liberation for all of Am Yisrael. This was not only Avraham's liberation. It was the forthcoming liberation of all the people.

In the course of descending into and returning from Mizrayim, something happened to Avraham's nephew Lot. This is an instructive point. When they went down to Mizrayim, Lot was connected with them; it was "Avraham, Sarah, and Lot, and all of their possessions." However, when they came back, it was "Sarah, their property, and Lot." It is said in that time that Lot walked opposite to Avraham. In other words, Lot was unable to rise above the egocentric lifestyle of the Egyptians. He was seduced by the dark side. This, in turn, influenced Lot's shepherds, who fought with Avraham's shepherds over wells and land use.

Lot had been changed. He had been captured by the ways of negativity. Avraham knew this and realized that Lot was unable to live with them at their elevated level. In essence, Avraham asked him to leave and go his own way. Though Avraham was the total expression of chesed (חסד—loving kindness), he could not undermine his spiritual evolution for the sake of the kindness and love of chesed.

Lot could no longer live in the tent of Avraham. Yet, still cloaked in the attribute of chesed, Avraham introduced this separation with dignity and respect for the other, offering Lot ample choices rather than simply driving him away:

Abram said to Lot, "Let's not have friction between me and you, and between my herdsmen and yours. After all, we're brothers. All the land is before you. Why not separate from me? If you [go to] the left, I will go to the right; if to the right, I will take the left."

(Bereisheet 13:8–9)

Avraham's action gives us a deeper understanding of what we sometimes have to do on the spiritual path. Some people simply are not ready to be in that light. Either the spiritual energy forces them out, or they cannot comprehend it yet. They have to be asked to leave, lest their presence impedes, or outright dims, our own light. Even so, we must do what is necessary, with respect and gentleness, as modeled by Avraham.

The principle of ma'aseh avot siman labanim ("What happens to the patriarchs is both a sign, and even prophecy, of what will happen to their descendants") is incredibly awesome, mystical, and profound. It applies to almost every event of Avraham's life, as noted below in nearly two dozen specific instances.

- He awoke via the Ruach HaKodesh and a heavenly initiation s'micha m'shefa; received the neshikat elokut (divine kiss); and became highly motivated by t'shukat deveikut (desire for union with the Divine).
- He began living in the way of the mitzvot and a completely moral life. (This dedication to morality separates Judaism from the pagan belief in the survival of the fittest, which Hitler, as a pagan, taught.) The way of the mitzvot creates an upward flowing energy of divine flux, or shefa (the Or Hozer), which brings a downward shefa (the Or Yashar), further increasing the light and directing one's spiritual evolution toward the Self (lekh lekha). This is the path of deveikut and ultimately toward a permanent state of deveikut, the quality of enlightenment that exists prior to consciousness, played out in the world as the endless walk between the b'limah and the

mah, which is both the divine walk between, and the synergy of, the nothing and the something. At the highest stage it is a permanent experience of the Divine in the merging of the heavens and the earth. Avraham became, thereby, a permanent master of and dweller of the realm of *yechudim*, the divine forces of unification. Creating and fostering the yechudim is a powerful Torah Way of life, emphasized by the Arizal and the Ba'al Shem Tov, two liberated masters of later centuries.

- He also started the way of hit'bonenut (התבוננות—mindful concentration or contemplation) and hit'bodedut (התבודדות—solitary meditation) as evidenced by his initial experiences of the Ruach HaKodesh following his circumcision when he sat meditating under the ancient oaks in the fields of Mamre (Bereisheet 18:1). This practice is repeated by his son Yitzhak, who we find meditating in the fields prior to the arrival of his bride-to-be, Rivkah (Rebecca) (Bereisheet 24:63). These practices continued for thousands of years, as we find them being observed by the Arizal (sixteenth-century Rabbi Yitzhak Luria), who meditated for seven years on Elephantine Isle in the Nile before coming to Safed; by the Ba'al Shem Tov, who taught in the eighteenth century that meditation was seven times as important as Torah study (*Tza'vot Ha'Besht*), and who spent many years in the mountains in complete solitude; and also by the Ba'al Shem Tov's great-grandson Rabbi Nachman, who emphasized the practice of hitbodedut.

- When Avraham came to Kena'an, Hashem said to him, "I will give this land to your offspring" (Bereisheet 12:7). We, the Jewish people, keep coming back to this holy land (as did Avraham and Sarah), as our spiritual DNA is programmed to the land. In fact, some 2,700 years ago, when the Assyrian warlord Sancherib invaded the northern tribes of Israel and replaced them with peoples from other lands, the newcomers kept getting attacked by lions. They saw this plague as something spiritually related and realized soon enough that the land did not connect with them: "We do not know the rule of the god of this land." As a result, they were assigned Jewish teachers to familiarize them with the ways of Judaism in order to align their DNA, so to speak, with that of the land, and they were never again plagued by such attacks (Second Kings 17:24–28). Accordingly, they became known as *gey'rey araot* (גירי אריות—"converts by lions") (Talmud Yerushalmi, Kidushin 42a). This is, of course, a shamanic understanding that many of the aboriginal peoples, Native Americans, and, most important, the Arab world understands: the very fruit, vegetable, grain, and tree seeds of the land contain the historical consciousness and evolution of our people on the land. Our power as Am Yisrael (עם ישראל) is connected to the land of Israel. Thus its potency is determined by how we relate to her, in particular to Jerusalem, the Temple Mount, and the ancestral burial sites; the most important of which is, of course, the Cave of Machpelah in Hebron, the burial place of Adam and Cha'vah, Avraham and Sarah, Yitzhak and Rivkah, and Ya'akov and Le'a. This fundamental understanding may provide us with some insight into the territorial struggles that continue in these areas, just as it gives insight into the Hopi and Navaho struggles around *their* land and burial sites.

- Avraham was told by God that all the families of the earth shall be blessed on his account (Bereisheet 12:3). The trunk of Judaism and the branches that later emerged from it, as Christianity and Islam, are recipients of this blessing. There are approximately two billion followers of Christianity in the world today and about one billion followers of Islam. This is two-thirds of the earth's population, with most of the world having been exposed to the Hebrew scriptural accounts known as the Torah.

- Avraham led his life with the unbroken consciousness that moved him daily to question, "What light can I reveal today?"

This way of life was seen in the great master the Ba'al Shem Tov and other Hasidic masters.

- Avraham was spiritually and politically forced to leave Ur of the Chaldees, where the people could not receive his teachings and even harassed him, and where he had been arrested by Nimrod and thrown into a burning furnace. When he left Ur, however, the people he encountered along the way began to listen to him, and his fame had already spread far and wide by the time he reached the Land of Canaan. He had become the original *ivri* (עברי—boundary crosser), crossing not only geographical boundaries but, most important, spiritual boundaries that took him and his students beyond the spiritual limitations and traps of idolatry. This has been true also with many teachers in our tradition such as the R. Ba'al Shem Tov, R. Nachman of Breslov, and R. Moshe Chaim Luzzato.

- Hashem told Avraham that the Divine will bless those who bless him and curse those who curse him (Bereisheet 12:3). Throughout history this has been the case. The Avrahamic role is to "walk before me and be whole" (Bereisheet 17:1). The "walking before God" means that all of our actions are to be a blessing to the world. To be a blessing to the world is to be a conduit for bringing the awareness of God into the world; that is the ultimate and only blessing. It is the deepest gift of Am Yisrael to the world.

- It is taught that Avraham went to Shekhem to prophetically pray, in advance, for Ya'akov and his sons, and for Ya'akov's daughter Dinah, who would later be abducted by the prince of Shekhem (Rashi on Bereisheet 12:6). Then he moved on and pitched his tent between Beth El and Ai, as this was the place that Yehoshua would capture first, centuries later, after crossing the Jordan (Ramban ahl HaTorah, B'reisheet 12:6).

- Hashem appeared to Avraham at the Oaks of Moreh, to reassure him again that the land, which Noah had originally apportioned to his son Shem (Malki-zedek), and which had been later conquered by Kena'an, would eventually be returned to Avraham's descendants since they are of the seed of Shem (Rashi on Bereisheet 12:6). In response to this promise of restoration, Avraham built an altar to Hashem and publicly worshipped God there. He was also near Mount Gerizim and Mount Ebal where the Israelites would gather in Moshe's time before crossing the Yarden into the land of Kena'an. He also visited the Oaks of Mamre in Hebron to prophetically establish the pattern for the importance of Hebron. Hebron later became the burial ground for our ancestors in the Cave of Machpelah, which Avraham must have known was also a gateway into the inner earth and to Gan Eden. Avraham, we see, was literally walking prophetically in front of his children.

- The Midrash teaches that God only appeared to Avraham via the Ruach HaKodesh, or in dreams at night, and not in *mar'eh* or *machzeh*, which are different terms for levels of higher prophetic vision. Nonetheless, from the beginning of his teachings to the end of his life, including the 600 chapters he wrote in the mystical Sefer Yetzirah about the problems and evils of idolatry, he taught the eternal truth of the one God and stood firmly against idolatry, not only as a primitive distraction, but also as a mental trap that keeps people from becoming enlightened.

- When he returned safely from Egypt with much wealth, Avraham separated from his nephew Lot, who had become seduced by the egocentric ways of Egyptian culture. According to some of the sages, by not trusting Hashem, Avraham had put Sarah at risk with the pharaoh when they descended into Egypt during the famine. Also, in going to Egypt altogether, he missed the mark, because if he had stayed in Kena'an, he would have been rescued from death by his faith in Hashem. The most important lesson from this is that we are influenced by the company we keep. At this point Avraham was willing to touch, but not blend with, Lot. This was again repeated with Ya'akov and 'Esav when Ya'akov chose not to associate with 'Esav (Bereisheet 35:12–17) except at the time of Yitzhak's death (Bereisheet 35:29). The importance of separating oneself from negative forces is a major teaching on the path of liberation, and the reason it has been important for those following the great Torah Way to maintain our holy ways by keeping ourselves somewhat separate from the secular world, and instead, like Avraham with Lot, to touch, but not blend with, this world. This is also illustrated later in the story of Lot's rescue by Avraham, and in the story of Sodom and Gomorrah, where he both defended and had compassion for their existence and their level of awareness along the spiritual path. Part of his profound chesed awareness was exemplified in his practice of leaving the flaps of his tent open to all four directions, as an invitation and welcoming gesture to everyone, as both a friend to the world and as a way to share his liberation teachings universally. In the next generation his experience with Avimelekh, the Philistine king, is repeated with Yitzhak, although to a lesser extent (Bereisheet 26:6–10).

- In their interactions with the local leadership, Avraham and Sarah introduced a new model for male-female relationships that was, and remains, the most advanced in the Middle East. In the Midrash it is said that Avraham brought the teachings to the men, and Sarah brought them to the women (Midrash Bereisheet Rabbah 84:4). For women at this time to be in this leadership role was a breakthrough in male-female relationship dynamics.

As the history unfolded, Avraham gathered 318 of his servants and defeated the armies of four kings, who attacked five neighboring kingdoms and took Lot and many others captive (Bereisheet 14:14). How did such a small group of people defeat four kingdoms? The key here is found in the number 318, which is the numerical value of the Hebrew word for speech, or communication—*siach* (שׂיח). Avraham knew the power of speech. Siach also refers to the speech of the angels, which is the power of mind over matter.

Along the way Avraham, like everybody who initiates positive spiritual change, continually faced difficulties. He was thrown in the oven by Nimrod, he faced the Egyptian pharaoh, the Philistine king Avimelekh, and the four kings. Avraham was spiritually rewarded in many ways for his trials and tribulations. When he defeated the four kings, he was offered by the king of Sodom all the spoils of his success. He declined these spoils, saying: "I will not take anything that is yours! You should not be able to say, 'It was I who made Abram rich'" (Bereisheet 14:21–24). In other words, Avraham said that no human being should take credit for the success and prosperity that he knows has come directly from God. In the process of Avraham's victories, Malki-zedek, the king of Shalem, came to him, acknowledging Avraham and passing on to him the lineage from Adam, Hanokh, Noah, and now Shem (son of Noah, also known as Malki-zedek). Malki-zedek had been sharing the teachings of the lineage of the God of heaven and earth all this time, although silently, in the city of *Yerushalayim*. He passed the lineage on with blessings to Avraham.

Avraham also tithed to Malki-zedek. The secret of the tithing is that we live in a physical world where the negative forces of the Satan are allowed nourishment, and that nourishment comes from the energy of our ego. Thus, if we feel our financial sustenance is coming from anything other than God, we are tainted by the presence of the Satan. By tithing a portion of our money, we sever the connection with the Satan. The first ten percent is to disconnect our livelihood from the influence of the Satan, and so the ten percent is not just charity, but is also protection from the Satan. It is taught that when we give more than ten percent, that is an act of true charity as long as it is given with no expectation of return. If it is given as a business deal, in which one expects a return, then not only does one not get any benefit, but it also may result in a negative outcome because the principle of *tzedeka* (charity— צדקה) is violated.

- After defeating the four kings, Avraham had a daytime vision in which Hashem promised to be his shield (*ma'gen avraham* [מגן אברהם]—the shield of Avraham) against any revenge from the four kings, and that his reward for walking with God would be great (Bereisheet 15:1). On one level it was a promise of physical protection, but on a deeper level it represented what naturally comes from the liberation awareness that Avraham was deepening in his life.

The shield of Avraham eventually became known as the Star of David, an explicit symbol of enlightenment. The merging of the upward-rising and downward-flowing triangles in this symbol represents the merging of the heavens and the earth, which is, and was, a key part of the enlightenment teachings of Avraham and this lineage. The merging of the two triangles also represents the merging of *dekura v'nukva* (דכורא ונוקבא—the sacred female and sacred male into one), which is also symbolic of liberation.

In the center of the overlapping merged triangles is the emptiness and zone of nullification, the *bitul hayesh* (ביטול היש), which is the permanent inner experience and awareness of deveikut/chey'rut (divine union/liberation). The merging of the triangles also represents the sacred and liberated walk of the enlightened one, of the walk between b'limah and the mah. It is not an accident that the Star of David, a symbol of enlightenment, is the center of the Israeli flag.

The flag is made in blue, which represents the heavens and is also in the color of the supercausal body, which is the highest, most conscious subtle body. The supercausal body may be seen and experienced in meditation as the blue light of consciousness. In other words, the flag of Israel is a complete symbol of enlightenment, whether people choose to be conscious of this, and whether they choose to live up to the meaning of the flag is another question. The Torah narrative recounts God as saying or thinking that clearly Avraham's commitment to enlightenment and the fulfillment of his spiritual mission included his commitment to instruct his children, as well as to continue the work of creating an enlightenment lineage (Bereisheet 18:19).

- Soon thereafter, Avraham was promised a successor child and told that his children would be greater in number than the stars in the heavens (Bereisheet 15:5). He was also told that he would be given all the land he saw in any direction, including all the boundaries of the land of Kena'an (Bereisheet 15:18–21). At this stage, just as his offspring would need in the future, he needed some assurance. But there is no assurance for the righteous as much as they may want it. As part of this assurance, and an important teaching in the Jewish tradition, God alters the astrological predeterminations dictating that neither he and nor Sarah would bear children. The grace of YHWH intervenes and alters both their childbearing destinies by changing the energies of their names from Avram and Sarai to Avraham and Sarah. The stars have it that Avram and Sarai will not bear children, but the names Avraham and Sarah through grace will (Midrash Kohelet Rabbah 5:4). This, the Midrash posits (Midrash Tanchuma, Shof'tim, Chap. 11), is implied when the Torah tells us that God "took [Abram] outside and said, 'Look at the sky and count the stars, if you be able to number them. That is how [numerous] your descendants will be'" (Bereisheet 15:5). They would have a son, and he would be a carrier of the Avrahamic tradition. Hashem also made a covenant with him that he would inherit the land under all circumstances. One way to interpret this is that no matter what, the land is guaranteed, but those who sinned still have to do *teshuva* (תשובה) before they can return to the land in peace. Teshuvah means changing one's ways that are taking us away from God and thus returning to the way of God and God.

- God instructed Avraham to perform a shamanic ritual involving a bullock, a ram, a goat, a sparrow, and a dove, which was a whole offering, a sin offering, and a peace offering, which were repeated in the desert following the exodus from Egypt, and during the First and Second temples. Alas, a vulture came down to eat the offering, which is symbolic of how alien nations would try to interrupt the sacrificial rites. But, like Avraham, Am Yisrael will shoo them away (Bereisheet 15:9–11). Every nation that is accustomed to pass judgment on Am Yisrael will suffer the consequences if they exceed their mission. Those who have already paid the consequences include Egypt, Assyria, Babylon, Persia, Greece, Rome, and Germany.

- The final step Avraham was told before he had a child through Sarah was that he must circumcise himself. A lot of people do not understand this. At its very basic level, it is a covenant with God, a permanent blood bonding and a statement that God made the earth not in perfection, but to be perfected by man, including our own bodies. It is taught in the kabbalah that the phallus corresponds to the spiritual world of yesod. Yesod is the energy channel through which all positive spiritual energy flows from the upper sephirotic energies into malchut, into the physical world. The teaching is that the negative forces hover around the realm of yesod to capture the positive light that flows through it down to the immanent realm of malchut. Ritual circumcision removes these negative forces from the baby, and in a sense helps heal the whole world and so it is a powerful covenant. With this new flow of energy through Avraham (now that he had been circumcised),

Sarah made it possible for them to have a child, and there was no negativity in the creation of that child.

We now see the whole cycle. Avraham became the first enlightened person in the Jewish tradition (with Hanokh being the first in the broader universal lineage, as it goes back to Adam). The energy was purified through him with the circumcision so that it would continue to flow through the creation of his son Yitzhak. Avraham's covenantal ceremony of circumcision, which has continued in our tradition to this day, indirectly resulted in a divine statement that Am Yisrael would have possession of the land forever (Bereisheet 17:4–10). The circumcision ceremony was a living covenant with Hashem and, again, was specifically intended to create a purified transfer of energy from yesod (the heavens) into the earth plane of malchut.

Present medical research suggests that circumcision has some medical benefits. It holds perhaps as much as 2–5 percent better preventable health effect and significantly lessens the transmission of AIDS and STDs. But this is not really a holy justification for circumcision. It should be done for its shamanic tribal covenant value. Today some are concerned about its theorized traumatic effect on the infant, physically and mentally. In my own medical research on the question of theoretical trauma of circumcision, only one out of forty male adults had any negative affect, on any level, and this one result was nullified in thirty seconds of infrared light treatment. It appears that for the first eight days of a child's life, the tissue is such that no physical scarring occurs.

- Avraham greeted the three angels with love and amazing hospitality, and valued hospitality above even revelatory experiences (Bereisheet 18:1–3). This later emerged as the teaching of the second-century Rabbi Akiva that the summation of the entire Torah is the injunction in VayYiKra 19:18: "You must love your neighbor as [you love] your [higher] Self" (Midrash Sif'ra, Kedoshim 4:12).

- Frustrated over her inability to bear a child, Sarah, while still Sarai, bid her Egyptian handmaiden, Hagar, to mate with then Avram, so that she might bear a child through her (Bereisheet 16:1–2). When Hagar became pregnant, she was told by an angel that her soon-to-be-born son, Yishma'el, would father many nations and would be a "rebel." He would afflict the seed of Avraham and Sarah with all kinds of problems: "His hand will be against everyone, and everyone's hand will be against him. Still, he will dwell undisturbed near all his brothers" (Bereisheet 16:12). The prediction in the Torah is that Yishma'el's hand will be against every man, and he will be victorious at first over the nations, and then all the nations will be against him, and he will be defeated. This, of course, has been historically played out and is being played out again in our times. But in the end, the exiled Hagar returned and remarried Avraham after changing her name and energy to Keturah (Bereisheet 25:1), and Yitzhak joins with Yishma'el in peace to bury their father Avraham (Bereisheet 25:9). The potential for peace between Arab and Jew can be great once the right to exist is acknowledged.
- Avraham was the carrier of the lineage of deveikut/chey'rut, from the mystery school of Shem and Eber, but he was still missing one thing: God had promised him children who would be like the stars of the heavens. This is very interesting, since Avraham was a skilled astrologer, and he knew in his astrological readings that he was not destined to have children. But being the first Jew, he prayed for grace, and his astrology was transcended. God told Avraham to forget his astrological concerns and rise above the planetary influences! The Zohar says directly: "Do not look to the wisdom of the stars, for that is not the way to know my name. Rather, seek out the secret of my name. [When you accept the power of grace by the power of YHWH which transcends Elohim or the laws of nature and the stars,] then 'you shall father a son'" (Zohar, Vol. 1, folio 90b and Vol. 3, folio 148a).

This is a most important clue as to whether Avraham knew the Tetragrammaton. Because of the miracles in his life (such as surviving the fires of Nimrod, the birth of Yitzhak, and the defeat of the four kings with 318 men), it is highly suggestive that he knew of the energy of God as grace, encrypted in the divine name YHWH. Avraham then knew the potential of the name of YHWH as the promise of the name, but not the public manifestation of the name. However, his awareness of the name, as the promise and as grace, foretells the actualization of it, because the name YHWH was later given to Moshe (Shemot 6:3). Although he did not fully ask for the name as Moshe did, Avraham certainly must have experienced the seed awareness of it and thus knew it on some level: ma'aseh avot siman labanim.

So, indeed, after circumcision and changing their names, Avraham and Sarah gave birth to Yitzhak. In order to activate the consciousness that rises above the stars, we must activate the understanding that we are one with God. We are deveikut, and we must emulate the heroic way of life that Avraham lived. In the transformation, which overcame the effects of the stars, they changed their names from Avram to Avraham and from Sarai to Sarah. This was, in effect, changing their spiritual genetic code. Part of the blessing of their son Yitzhak may be in the name shift that occurred for Avraham at the age of 99. God said: "No longer shall you be called Abram. Your name shall become Abraham, for I have set you up as the father of a horde of nations" (Bereisheet 17:5). The new name has two parts: *ham* from the word *ha'mon* (המון), meaning "many," and *Av* (אב), meaning "father." *Avraham* is translated now as "father of many nations." It is interesting to note that the numerical value of Avraham's new name is 248, the same as the number of positive mitzvot listed in the Torah.

I have great admiration for Avraham and what he still brings to the world. I feel particularly blessed and connected to Avraham because I had several visionary visitations by Avraham. The first occurred once during Rosh Ha-shanah as I sat in total silence in 2003. The energy of Avraham flowed into me and inspired me to share the truth of the One of the heavens and earth, of the One who is the spark of the creation in all and the truth of enlightenment for all peoples. A second daylight vision occurred during my aliyah ceremony in 2007, while I sat, without food and water, for seventy-two hours in a cave-cliff setting near Arad, deep in the Judean Desert. Avraham appeared for a minute in silence, just long enough to identify himself and to nonverbally communicate his essence into me.

May we all be blessed that we share the deep meaning of enlightenment and love of Avraham with all of creation.

Amen

VayYera

PARASHAH VayYera truly conveys to us the depth of the greatness of Avraham, and provides many lessons for our spiritual path of deveikut. The very first lesson is the account of Avraham sitting in the doorway of his tent on the third day following his circumcision. As he sat and healed, he was immersed in a direct revelation of the Divine. It is quite radical that Avraham, at the age of ninety-nine, chose to circumcise himself and all his men, including boys aged eight days and older. The blood of circumcision stamps us with our covenant to God throughout at least our physical existence. The seed of Avraham had, through the shamanic ceremony of circumcision, received a special level of connection, at a deep soul level. It is through circumcision that we change our natural, physical, and astral form in the realm of yetzirah. Spiritually, this means overcoming lower sexual desires and committing our sexual energies for merging with the Divine. It is like a farmer who tills the land, plants the wheat, harvests it, and turns it into bread, thus arguably creating a higher perfection of nature. So removing the foreskin is not a subtraction, but a completion, in line with the will of the Divine. It elevates the connection between soul and body.

Tyranus Rufus (the second-century Roman governor of Judea) asked Rabbi Akiva, "Which is more pleasant? The works of humans or the works of God?"

Rabbi Akiva replied, "The works of humans."

Tyranus Rufus was shocked. "What?" he exclaimed, "you, a man of God, proclaim the works of humans more pleasant than the works of God?!"

Rabbi Akiva said, "Kindly bring me a bushel of wheat and a slice of cake." They brought him these. Said Akiva, "Tell me, then, which is more pleasant? The raw wheat stalk, or the cake?" Akiva then asked for a bale of flax to be brought, along with a garment made of flax. These he then held out and asked, "You tell me, now, which is more pleasant, the bale of raw flax, or the garment?"

Said Tyranus Rufus, "I was expecting you to say that the works of God are more pleasing, and then I was going to challenge you on your ritual of circumcision; how can you alter what God has created? After all, if God desired for you to be circumcised, would God not have created you so?"

Said Akiva, "I knew you were intending to ask that, and thus I replied as I did. For according to your argument, we ought not to cut the umbilical cord since if God wanted us to walk about without the umbilical cord and placenta attached, God would have created us so. Rather, the ritual instructions of our people are intended to connect us to the divine through our co-participation in creation, as King David taught (Tehillim [Psalms] 18:31), 'All of the instructions of God are intended to connect us'" (Midrash Tanchuma, Taz'ria, Chap. 7).

There is a midrashic story that gives us a deeper insight into the story of Avraham's circumcision (Midrash Tanchuma, Va'yera, Chap. 3, and Bereisheet Rabbah 42:8). It is said that Avraham had three friends, Aner, Eshkol, and Mamre. When Yah told Avraham to circumcise himself, he went to ask their advice. This is interesting in itself because Avraham always unquestioningly did whatever Yah asked. Why did he ask for their advice?

Aner said to him, "Do you really want to cripple yourself? What if the relatives of the kings that you killed come to kill you? You would be unable to flee them or any other of your enemies!"

Avraham took note of his counsel and then went to Eshkol, who said, "You are already 100 years old, and if you circumcise yourself you will lose a lot of blood, and you may even die from it."

Avraham thought that this, too, was something to consider. Then he went to Mamre, who said, "You came to ask for my advice in this manner? God saved you from the fiery furnace in Ur Kasdim and performed many miracles for you and delivered you from the might of the four kings; without His strength and power they would have killed you and your tiny army. He saved your whole body numerous times and you come to me to inquire about one part of your body? Of course you should be circumcised if that is what God has asked."

It is said that YHWH (יהוה) said to Mamre, "Because you counseled Avraham to circumcise himself, I will speak to him in your territory." Therefore, this parashah opens with "God appeared to [Abraham] in the plains of Mamre" (Bereisheet 18:1).

Why was Avraham concerned about this *mitzvah* (good deed)? Avraham understood that his task was not only to serve God, but also to publicize his teachings as widely as possible, and to spread the word of this new wisdom tradition of liberation. At that time, people were listening to him because many were uncomfortable burning their children in the fire and performing other similar rituals mandated by the authorities in that age of idolatry. They were seeking something more compassionate and more personal. When Avraham shared with them the word of YHWH, it was very powerful and uplifting for them. He was teaching faith in the living One, God, merging the heavens and the earth.

However, with this latest divine instruction regarding the ritual of circumcision, Avraham had the same concern that Paul had had when James and Jesus were both completely in favor of circumcision. He feared that he would possibly lose the support of the people he was attempting to convert. That is perhaps why Avraham felt the need to seek counsel from his friends. He felt he was a messenger of Yah, not only for his own tribe, but also for the whole of humanity. He saw that he had a universal responsibility to teach morality, spirituality, holiness, and ethics to all people. And he was not sure whether the rite of circumcision would jeopardize his success.

On the other hand, the message Mamre gave Avraham was that one of the most powerful aspects of his nature and his new way of life involved more than abolishing cruel rituals. Rather, it involved Avraham's willingness to dedicate his life as a living example of the expression of God's will in the world. People felt Avraham's conviction tangibly and witnessed his true belief in the life that he had chosen for himself. The power of the certainty of a spiritual teacher is a strong inspiration to the students. The personal act of his circumcision was further proof of Avraham's total allegiance to God's will.

Having survived circumcision, let us look at the next layer of the parashah, and the importance of welcoming guests. Hospitality is a great heart-opening mitzvah and helps us to serve the Divine in all beings. Avraham sat at the door of his tent, symbolic of being conscious of that moment's flux of the Ruach HaKodesh opening into the heavens. He was basking in the heavenly direct-knowingness of chokhmah awareness of God. It is the heat of the day, which symbolizes the heat of chesed and the grace of chokhmah. This quality of light heals and regenerates the righteous, but at the same time, the light burns those on the dark side. This is often why, when people go to a spiritual place where there is a lot of light, it is uplifting for some people. It is also why some people have very difficult reactions and actually must leave because it is too hot or bright for them.

Avraham sat there on the third day of his circumcision in the pain and the heat, and yet he was in the bliss of communion with God. He sat in the doorway of his tent communing with God. He was ready to serve any travelers on the road because he refused to let the heat and the pain disrupt his mitzvah of hospitality. When the three men appeared, he rose to greet them, even though he was in the midst of a direct revelation from God. What a powerful message!

Kabbalah teaches that inviting guests into your home is greater than receiving the very face of the shekhinah! If Avraham had said instead, "Hey guys, I'm deep in meditation right now, please don't bother me," it would have been an entirely different message. It would have shown us, in essence, that his attachment to the supernal God-experience was actually a form of selfish desire. It would have been the pursuit of spiritual riches over material riches, motivated by his egocentric selfish desires. The manner in which he responded is a beautiful testimony to him and a great teaching. This is the difference between a God-experience tainted by selfishness, and therefore one that dulls our awareness of the Divine and dims the God light within us, and a God-experience that brings us into God awareness and refines our character, or midot (מדות).

The first two lines of this parashah offer us a tremendous amount of insight. The welcoming of guests with love represents a higher level of consciousness than even welcoming the shekhinah energy. It is hard to say exactly how Avraham knew this, except to presume that he knew it from his own inner wisdom. The eighteenth-century mystic, Rebbe Zusha, a deveikut/chey'rut rabbi in my personal rabbinical lineage, explained that Avraham had activated all 248 parts of his body and all 365 ligaments with the intention that they should always fulfill the desire of the creator. He had fortified himself with the intention, or kavanah (כונה), that his body should never do anything against God's desire.

His visitors represented three angels: Mikha'el, who came to bless Sarah that she be with child; Rafael, who came to heal Avraham from his circumcision; and Gabriel, who came to fulfill God's decision to destroy Sodom and Gomorrah. There is more code going on here; these three angels also represented the sephirot of chesed, gevurah, and tiferet, or the heavenly realms, which had been opened up to Avraham through the circumcision rite. These would continue to be expressed through Yitzhak (Isaac) and Ya'akov (Jacob).

After inviting the three strangers to his home, Avraham washed their feet. The Zohar teaches us that water corresponds to the purifying light of the creator (Zohar, Vol. 3, folio 246b), and feet correspond to the sephirah of malchut, which is the material plain of existence. The act of washing their feet tells us about the power of Avraham's light to purify and heal the world (Zohar, Vol. 1, folio 102b). This is a power we all have, and connects us to the whole idea of *mikveh,* the specially constructed ritual pool our people use for cleansing the entire body and soul of impurities.

While Avraham offered food to his guests, no message was yet communicated; the highest service is service for the sake of service alone, without any agendas. So, while Avraham welcomed his guests with "Let some water be brought, and wash your feet. Rest under the tree," not a single word had been exchanged. They were still in this whole interaction at another level of communication. He invited them to sit under a tree, and according to the Zohar, this tree had unique properties (Zohar, Vol. 1, folio 102b). The tree accepted those with a high level of spiritual awareness, or completeness. Avraham was actually testing them. Whoever was impure could not sit under the tree without first being purified by water. The tree was unique in that it would stretch out its branches and offer cool shade and protection for anyone who was at a high level of spiritual completeness. With negative people, the tree would shrink, offering them little shelter from the sun. This is the way it works when most people enter a spiritual setting. If they are at the right vibration, they are engulfed in love; if they are not, it is a very difficult place for them to be. That does not mean that such people should leave a spiritual place, but they should attempt, as their negativities arise, to use their situation to further purify themselves and cleanse their minds so that no material or external situation will control their emotions.

Idolatry is not about worshipping statues, but rather allowing oneself to be controlled by any external situation, or by emotions such as anger or sadness. It is allowing oneself to be possessed by a symbol as one's source of energy or source of wellbeing. Therefore, such things as worshipping wealth, power, and lust as central to one's life, are all forms of idolatry. In idolatry, we sever our connection to the divine presence within us—that source of noncausal joy, peace, love, compassion, oneness, and contentment. This is a key message about enlightenment: "Do not believe that anything outside of you is your source." For this reason idolatry is antithetical to the Torah Way of enlightenment and to liberation in general. The tree of Avraham actually acted as the Tree of Life rather than the Tree of Knowledge (of Good and Evil). The Tree of Life has flawless reality: noncausal bliss, love, contentment, compassion, oneness, peace, infinite wisdom, and immortality beyond time, space, and being. The Tree of Knowledge is *matrix* time, space, being, death and chaos. Avraham would purify people so they could move into Tree of Life reality, and dissolve darkness and death from their midst.

As we have seen from all these teachings, everything in Avraham's life was about awakening. After he fed his guests, they revealed the purpose of their visit. The angel Mikha'el informed him that Sarah, now age ninety (well past menopause), would have a son. This is an unimaginable situation, and the angel Mikha'el, who corresponds with the sephirah of chesed, brought this merciful message, and blessed Avraham and Sarah so they could bring forth a child within a year. Sarah overheard this discussion from her tent and laughed at the idea. Her laughter may have been triggered by a little doubt, but it was also a prophecy, because her son would be given the name Yitzhak, which means "he will laugh." The verse "Sarah laughed within herself" pertains to her son. In that moment, when she laughed, the spiritual seed of Yitzhak was implanted in her womb. At another level of interpretation, the laughter refers to the bliss, peace, love, and *simcha* (spiritual joy—שמחה) that we will experience in the messianic age (Tehillim [Psalms] 126:2).

There is yet another metaphorical interpretation of Sarah's laughter. In Bereisheet 18:14, the term "appointed time" (referring to Yitzhak's birth) is also a clue that in the time to come, the dead will be resurrected, and we will return in the same bodies and enjoy laughter and rejoicing. The messianic time is the time of immortality, of noncausal love, joy, laughter, peace, compassion, oneness, and contentment (Midrash Tehilim 98:1). In fact, the name "Sarah," as with many of the names and words in the Torah, is encrypted with a code. It is symbolic of the state of humanity after it has become spiritually, emotionally, mentally, and physically whole. While the body is still alive in this world, it lacks completion. But if one has lived a life of rightness and walks a path of truth, and dies in that state of being, then one leaves this world completed, and is called "Sarah" (Zohar, Vol. 1, folio 115a).

After fulfilling their mission at Avraham's tent, two of the angels (Mikha'el and Gabriel) left for their next assignment: the destruction of Sodom and Gomorrah. (Rafael was not needed there, since the mission involved warning and destruction.) When Avraham learned of God's plan to obliterate these two cities, he tried to plead their case, but their darkness was too overwhelming. He asked, "How can I accept a world where the righteous (and maybe the innocent) die along with the wicked? If there were fifty righteous people, would God destroy them along with the guilty? What about forty-five? Forty? Thirty-five?" However, he could not find even ten righteous men, and Avraham relinquished his advocacy.

Avraham returned to meditate and pray in the fields of Mamre, content that he had made some difference. The deeper teaching here is that it is not who we are, but whether we can make a difference. Avraham's compassion and sense of oneness was different from Noah's, who did not plead for the people. He is similar to Moshe, who advocated for the people. Avraham understood that regardless of how dark and mean-spirited people may be, each individual still possesses a spark of the Divine. He was pleading on behalf of the most negative people for God's tolerance, because they too have a divine spark within them. However, everything in Sodom and Gomorrah was upside down: People who gave food to beggars, who did good deeds, who took care of strangers and brought them into their homes, were sentenced to death. Sexual perversion and oppression of the poor were common practice. Sodom and Gomorrah also represent our dark side, and not merely external cities, though these cities did exist.

Avraham had gone as far as he could in his argument with God, but to no avail, and the next day, when the destruction was looming, he was at peace meditating in the fields of Mamre. From there, he sent a (supposedly psychic) message to his nephew Lot in Sodom, telling him that these angels were on their way. Lot prepared to receive the angels, who later saved his life. The angels told Lot to urge his family to escape. Lot hesitated, but the angels seized him, his two daughters, and his wife and said, "Here, [we're] helping you out … let's leave!" They literally had to pull him out of the city. Why was that? It was because his ego was still attracted to the "dark side" of his life, and he needed the help of the Divine to break his ties with Sodom. Many of us need divine assistance in severing ourselves from places within us where the dark forces thrive. The angels also instructed Lot and his family, "Don't look back." This is a powerful metaphor. Lot's wife could not help herself. She looked back and was turned into a pillar of salt.

What is looking back about? Why is this such a serious message? We have to let go of past stories that continue defining us today. People often stay in their past stories their whole lives and keep playing them out as dysfunctional, repeating patterns. Clinging to our past desires and patterns that keep regressing us into trouble (drugs and sugar addictions, sexual excesses, overeating, bad memories, and so on) keeps us from the joy of waking up to the Divine. Holding onto materialistic lifestyles (which are not evolutionarily functional) when, in fact, life is about spirit, keeps us from breaking free beyond the matrix of our lives and beyond our own Sodoms and Gomorrahs.

"Don't look back" is a warning to the ego addict. All of us must incessantly stand up to those temptations because even a little sip of the ego-addicted way of life brings us back into that way of life. As the Essene Teacher of Righteousness said so beautifully, "Dost thou forsake the eternal for that which dieth in an hour?" "That which dieth in an hour" is connected to looking back. The *eternal* is living in the presence of God in our life. This does not mean that we should refrain from grieving or forget the lessons of the past. Rather, we need to be aware of how easily we can sever our connection with the Divine if we let our dysfunctional and egocentric patterns dominate our lives. It is possible to get so caught in our past stories that they control our lives. At that point they become forms of idol worship.

Lot and his daughters were initially resistant to the angels' instruction to flee into the mountains, but, out of fear, they went there anyway and settled in a cave. Lot's fear in the mountains was the fear of recognizing and admitting his negative traits. His daughters feared that the rest of the world had been destroyed, leaving no survivors except them and their father. Feeling responsible for the continuation of humanity, they decided they had no choice but to mate with Lot. They made him drunk and, on two successive nights, had sexual intercourse with him and became pregnant. The eldest daughter had a boy she named Moab, who would later father the Moabite nation. Her sister had a boy she named Ben-Ami, who would later father the Amonite nation.

The Talmud reveals that the child born to the older daughter was the seed of King David, and also the messiah through Ruth, who was a direct descendant of Moab (Talmud Bav'li, Nazir 23b–24a; Ho'rayot 10b–11a). That is a really interesting phenomenon, because from this most low situation, from incest, comes the messiah. How does that happen? The messiah, as an individual, is destined to generate the greatest possible spiritual light in the world! In kabbalistic understanding, the greatest light comes from the people who have had the most transition in their lives (Zohar, Vol. 3, folio 47b). Therefore, it makes sense that the messiah must emerge from the lowest realm. Most everyone this rabbi knows certainly has not been born pure, or is living a perfect, sinless life.

What is the message? Instead of getting tangled in guilt or useless shame for our actions by looking back (which takes us away from the light), we should be inspired to do teshuvah (תשובה), turning back to our divine center in order to reshape our souls toward becoming a great light.

The metaphor of the potter comes from the Zohar, which tells us that the world and a human soul are a slab of clay spinning on a potter's wheel. As long as the wheel is turning, we are able to remodel the shape of the clay to any form. We are the potter, and our nefesh (נפש—body), our *ruach* (רוח—heart/emotions), and our neshama (נשמה—unique soul spark) are the clay. As long as we keep turning and churning through our life cycles with the intent of improving our openness to the Divine, we can transform ourselves into a beautiful expression of divine creation. Sometimes we can accomplish this in a single lifetime, sometimes across many lifetimes. There is nothing competitive about it, and there is no expiration date. In this way we become co-creators of the light in our lives. This is a powerful message, and an inspiration for anyone who opens to the spiritual path. The motto of tiferet (תפארת) is, yes, we can transform this pot, as the pot and the potters, enlightening the clay of our lower soul manifestations. We even see also how the low energetic origin of the messianic energy can nonetheless slip under the radar of the dark side in its manifestation process.

Before Sarah gave birth, they traveled to the city of Gerar, in the land of the Philistines, in the Negev (now Israel) west of Be'ersheva and east of what is now Gaza. To protect him from being killed by those who would covet his wife's beauty, Avraham told everyone that Sarah was his sister. "Sister" is a code word for divine presence, or shekhinah (Zohar, Vol. 3, folios 77b–78a). Gerar is another code word for negativity and darkness.

Meandering about in the darkness seems to be a part of development for the people of light, as part of their evolutionary process, in order to rise above it. Adam and Cha'vah were not able to transcend, but Avraham and Sarah, as incarnations of Adam and Cha'vah, were, because they were so deeply connected to the Divine and receiving in order to share. So often in our lives we get trapped in negative situations; it is then that we need that divine connection to transcend and evolve from those very situations.

The chieftain of Gerar, Avimelekh, took Sarah. He found her exceedingly attractive and intended to add her to his harem. Sarah, remember, personifies the energy of spiritual completeness, so it did not take Avimelekh long to realize that something was unbalanced when he attempted intimacy with her. The wombs of his wife and all the women in his royal family were suddenly blocked and they could not conceive children. Unlike the pharaoh of Egypt, however, Avimelekh was aware that something was off. He had a vision that Avraham was a great shaman and a great prophet, and that he would do well to honor him and return Sarah to him. Avimelekh gave Avraham gold, cattle, silver, and, unlike the pharaoh, who asked the couple to leave Egypt as soon as possible, he offered them housing in his region. He realized that they would bring abundance to the place. They did this via the wellsprings of Be'ersheva. Later, they made the first peace treaty over a well. Peace is possible when there is a sense of honoring each other's right to exist, and to exist in a way that works for everyone. This is the secret to establishing peace. Their interaction is a model for a quality of peace that comes when we consciously choose to face the darkness.

The last part of this parashah involves the birth of Yitzhak and the *akeidah* (עקידה—the binding and offering of Yitzhak). The name Yitzhak means "laughter" and is a metaphor for immortality, and for the immortal human being who lives beyond time, space, and being. "He will destroy death for ever; and the Lord God will wipe away tears from off all faces" (Yesha'yahu [Isaiah] 25:8). The one who knows that there is no death for the Self knows immortality. Through meditation (hitbodedut—התבודדות) and faith (*emuna*—אמונה), we can awaken to this immortality consciousness, and thus know our own immortality.

One of the mysteries of this story is the role of Hagar and Yishma'el (Ishmael). They are used as a metaphor for the dark side. Their banishment is a metaphor for the expulsion of our selfish desires from our innermost being, and even this act of sending them away is hard for Avraham. However, Sarah, because of her prophetical knowledge, understood the importance of this. She also understood that Yitzhak and Yishma'el represented two poles: Yishma'el the pole of chesed, and Yitzhak the pole of gevurah. They had to be separated for the energy to flow and create tiferet, which comes later in the form of Ya'akov, and brings great light to the planet. It is said that when Hagar and Yishma'el were sent out into the wilderness, Yishma'el was between thirteen and seventeen years old. He was not a little baby as many infer from the typical biblical tales.

Distraught, Hagar was visited by an angel in Be'ersheva, where there were wells. The angel said, "Your son will be the father of a great nation." The angel also said, "His hand will be against all nations; he will be a rebel." After Sarah died, it is said in the Midrash that Avraham remarried Hagar, because she had transformed herself into a higher frequency. She had become Keturah (Midrash Bereisheet Rabbah 61:4). When Avraham died, Yishma'el and Yitzhak were peaceful with each other at his funeral. A healing took place at that time. This healing needs to take place again on the physical plane between the Arabs and Jews.

The Zohar points out that Yishma'el was not named in the story following the birth of Yitzhak, as long as the two lived in the house of Avraham and Sarah (Zohar, Vol. 1, folio 118b). What does this mean? The light of our soul cannot exist in the presence of our ego, and the ego must be separated in order for our higher soul forces to shine through and guide our lives. It does not mean that we must destroy the ego altogether, but rather that we must separate from identifying with the ego. Once this happens, we can then work with it to enhance our evolution. On another level, just like any battery, the positive and negative poles need to be separated from each other in order to avoid a short circuit.

The last teaching in this parashah involves Avraham's tenth trial by God: the near-sacrifice of Yitzhak, known as the akeidah, or "the binding." This was the call by God to sacrifice the very child whom Avraham was promised would father the whole Jewish lineage. This is why the Torah Way is not about paradise, but paradox. It is through the path of paradox that our spiritual awareness grows.

The akeidah is a very difficult story. Avraham rose early in the morning, and he and Yitzhak traveled for three days. This provided enough time to fully contemplate the situation and cool down from any "heat of the moment" zeal. He took Yitzhak up the mountain, built an altar, and bound him to it. Yitzhak was not a little two-year-old as is popularly presumed. Yitzhak was thirty-seven years old! (Sarah was ninety when he was born, and 127 when the akeidah took place.) At thirty-seven, Yitzhak could easily have said *no* to his 137-year-old father, but instead, he chose to co-participate as part of his own spiritual development.

Avraham raised his arm with a knife to sacrifice Yitzhak, but at the last moment an angel appeared and said, "You don't really have to do that." God created a ram caught in the bushes, and they sacrificed the ram instead and made the first *shofar* from the ram's horns. Some of the more secular Jewish sources have called this child abuse, as unbelievable as it seems, but that is, in a sense, child's play next to the significance of this. What needed to happen spiritually for their mutual enlightenment development was a switching of the polarities. Avraham represented almost fixed chesed, and Yitzhak represented almost fixed gevurah. Neither could become complete, accessing every part of their higher soul function, until they blended their polarities.

A liberated person is free to move in any direction to serve the Divine. Yitzhak desired to tie up his ego on the altar and completely sacrifice it. This was an act of compassion and pure chesed, because it was his choice to do what his father had asked of him. Avraham, who was all about chesed and sharing, was forced to take on the quality of gevurah, and access that part of his essential self. At that moment, when he was about to sacrifice Yitzhak, Avraham accessed gevurah and became complete. At that moment, when the knife was raised, Yitzhak accessed chesed and became complete. Yitzhak surrendered himself to the Divine and opened his heart fully to the whole situation, and Avraham completed himself by donning the cloak of gevurah. And thus, for both Avraham and Yitzhak, tiferet was created—the perfect balance, the perfect wholeness, called "spiritual wholeness," which is a characteristic of enlightenment.

On a psychospiritual level, the Zohar explains that Avraham represents the energy of mercy, and Yitzhak represents judgment and boundaries. The paradoxical great Torah Way is always about the need to sweeten and temper judgment with mercy, and vice versa. The tying up of Yitzhak represents sacrificing the ego, or the yetzer hara (יצר הרע). As left-column energy, the dark side of Yitzhak represents our reactive, self-centered desire to receive in our physical body. Avraham corresponds to the right column, sharing, soul, and excess pleasure. The final success in this tenth trial is for Avraham to restrict his selfish, reactive desires, and to release the power of his soul. The ram represents those soul traits of selfishness. In that moment, the wholeness comes because we have bound our ego, and we have eliminated the yetzer hara. It is through the power of meditation every day that we offer ourselves in constant yechudim (יחודים), burning up the yetzer hara of our powerful egos. Both Avraham and Yitzhak then returned to the mundane world as whole, enlightened (deveikut/chey'rut) human beings.

When Avraham returned, he settled in Be'ersheva. There he discovered that Sarah had died. The Midrash suggests that she could not handle the news of her son's near-sacrifice and preferred to leave her body (Midrash Tanchuma, Va'yera, Chap. 23).

The end of the parashah talks about the birth of Rebecca (Rivkah), Yitzhak's future wife, who represents the rebirth of the shekhinah to take the place of Sarah. The shekhinah is always there, and somehow, some way, if we do not choose to help, someone else will.

This parashah speaks to the whole process of spiritual enlightenment in a most profound and awesome way. It speaks to the heroic deveikut/chey'rut journey of Avraham and his ten trials, and the spiritual completeness, which includes, but is different from, temporary spiritual bliss and joy (simcha), spiritual trance-state experiences, getting high, and even love of Eros. The message is that a fully liberated or deveikut/chey'rut person is a complete person, one who understands and acts on that sense of connection with all of creation. It is being a *mensch*. Being a mensch, however, does not make one enlightened; rather, being enlightened includes being a mensch. May we all know the enlightened greatness of Avraham and Sarah in our own lives.

Amen

Chayay Sarah

THIS is a particularly interesting and subtle parashah. It begins: "And Sarah was a hundred and twenty-seven years old: these were the years of Sarah's life. Sarah died in Kiryat Arba, also known as Hebron.... Abraham came to eulogize Sarah and to weep for her" (Bereisheet 23:1–2). There are different ways to interpret this. It is a little strange, for it says, "And Sarah was a hundred and twenty-seven years old: these were the years of Sarah's life." But when we interpret it from the point of enlightenment, it makes sense. The point is that the days of Sarah's life equal the days she actually lived. In other words, it is saying Sarah was in the divine presence all the days of her life. She knew the secret of being present. Some people would say that when she was 100 she was as virtuous as a girl of twenty, and at twenty as innocent as a child of seven (Midrash Bereisheet Rabbah 58:1). This is a result of her being present through every phase of her life. It has to do with intention, or kavanah. It is the intention to be in the presence of the Divine in every moment that brings joy on the spiritual path. This is of one of the most important teachings of the Ba'al Shem Tov: to be intently focused on the presence of the Divine in every moment, and always being in the process of turning the mundane world into a holy world and thus bringing spirit into the mundane. This is what we call yechudim (יחודים), or unifications.

What this parashah is saying about the life of Sarah is that we are always to have the kavanot (intentions) to be in the presence of the Divine in all ways, as exemplified by Sarah. This is a very central message for us. The Midrash suggests that she was the reincarnation of Cha'vah (חוה), or that she was able to repair what Cha'vah had broken. The kabbalah also suggests a future incarnation of her as Esther (Midrash Bereisheet Rabbah 58:3, and Sh'lah, Sefer Bereisheet, Chayyay Sarah, Torah Ohr, Chap. 3).

In this parashah another subtle teaching emerges from the oral tradition: Avraham wept only a little bit at the time of Sarah's passing, which is unusual because they had been together for more than fifty years. They were soulmates and prophets who shared the great mission of being the seed of Am Yisrael. It is also said that Yitzhak did not attend her funeral. The explanation given is that he was too busy studying the Torah. There is something of a mystery to this. The understanding is that Yitzhak and Avraham, having both become enlightened, understood and experienced that Sarah's presence was still with them. In the awareness of deveikut/chey'rut they knew the deeper truth, that she was not the body, but instead the eternal soul and the light of the shekhinah energy. However, the oral tradition also says that the light in Sarah's tent went out when she left the earth plane (Midrash Bereisheet Rabbah 60:16). So there was a loss of light at this point, and that is really why Avraham wept. Avraham was focusing on the light and spirit of Sarah with the understanding that whatever God does is for the best. Yitzhak was studying the Torah because it helps reveal the light of the Divine, which would recreate the light that was no longer being revealed with Sarah's body gone. This is a different way of looking at the world. From the point of view of chey'rut, how do you grieve the eternal light that is never gone? There is nothing to grieve because nothing has been lost.

From another perspective, in the next chapter, Bereisheet 24:1, Avraham was more than 137 years in age, and Hashem had blessed Avraham with everything. As an enlightened being, he had everything. Later in the Torah's unfolding of the story of Ya'akov, Ya'akov expresses this chey'rut awareness when he tells 'Esav, "I have everything" in response to 'Esav telling him "I have a lot" (Bereisheet 33:9–10). This happened right after Avraham became liberated from the akeidah revelation. At that time, as discussed earlier, Yitzhak too became liberated, and had been given everything on the spiritual and physical plane. All of this suggests that the full self-realization that Avraham had experienced so empowered him that he was able to be much more at peace, as was his son Yitzhak, at the death of the physical body called Sarah. It gives an enlightened perspective on how to see and live naturally in the bigger picture versus getting caught in the little picture. It lets us know that in the deveikut/chey'rut perspective of the world, we move from reactive to proactive. Here we can celebrate the mystery of the Divine in our lives as it unfolds, without being deluded by how it appears on the physical plane.

The account of Sarah's death also brings us to yet another level of understanding when we ask the question, "Why did she die?" Some sages posit that when Sarah was told of the binding of Yitzhak, Avraham's readiness to sacrifice him, and how his knife came within millimeters of her son's throat, the shock of it all drove her soul out of her body and she died (Midrash Pirkei D'Rebbe Eliezer, Chap. 31). This is a message about a projected, unawake human awareness. If this can happen to Sarah, meaning that the pain was so great for someone of such great stature, considered "untainted" at the age of 127, it can happen to anyone. This unawake interpretation gives the impression that even if Sarah was enlightened, she could not handle the situation. It tells us that a person can be damaged by unbearable suffering. It tells us that while suffering is okay, sometimes it becomes unbearable, and then you may have to leave. It also implies that God can "mistakenly" give us too much suffering.

The enlightened message is that God gives us what we can handle, and that perhaps Sarah died for the protection of the Jewish people in the future. One teaching on suffering is that it helps purify a person as part of the awakening process. Another interpretation, from an enlightened perspective, is that Sarah's mission in life had been completed now that her two men, Avraham and Yitzhak, had become enlightened. It is taught in the esoteric aspects of our tradition that soulmates come together to help each other become enlightened. Often it is the woman who incarnates to help her mate wake up. Perhaps Sarah's earthly job was done. As the ancient rabbis declared: "Everything is from the woman" (Midrash Bereisheet Rabbah 17:7).

Avraham is said to have buried Sarah "in dirt," but this is a reference to a special cave. He specifically chose a cave that was situated in Kiryat Arba where Sarah died. Today, as in biblical times, this locale is known as Hebron (Bereisheet 23:2 and 19). This particular cave, known as *Machpelah* (מכפלה), or Cave of the Pairs, is believed to be the burial site of Adam and Cha'vah, and, according to some kabbalists, is perhaps even the passageway to the underworlds and into Gan Eden. At the very least, it is important that they were both buried and living in areas of positive energy. Every indigenous population knows the importance of being in charge of the burial sites of their ancestors. In a not-so-subtle way those who control the gravesites of the ancestors can affect the energies of their progeny lineage.

The parashah moves on to the importance of reactivating the light of the feminine in the lives of Avraham and Yitzhak. Yitzhak was thirty-seven years old at this point, and had "always rejoiced in the light of his mother's tent." Avraham instructed his chief servant, Eliezer, to return to Avraham's homeland and relatives and find a wife for Yitzhak. This was an interesting spiritual challenge for Eliezer, who was a great power of service. He indeed did the right thing by requesting of God that he find a woman whose ethics and kindness were unusual. Eliezer had some doubts about being able to do this, but Avraham, with the certainty of an enlightened being, says to him, in Bereisheet 24:7: "God, the Lord of heaven, took me away from my father's house and the land of my birth. He spoke to me and made an oath, 'To your offspring I will give this land.' He will send His angel before you, and you will indeed find a wife there for my son."

In surrendering to God's will, Eliezer made what seems to be an outrageous prayer when he reached Haran and stood by the well. He negotiated with God:

> "O God, Lord of my master Avraham: Be with me today, and
> grant a favor to my master Avraham. I am standing here by the
> well, and the daughters of the townsmen are coming out to draw
> water. If I say to a girl, 'Tip over your jug and let me have a drink,'
> and she replies, 'Drink, and I will also water your camels,' she will
> be the one whom You have designated for Your servant Isaac. [If
> there is such a girl,] I will know that You have granted a favor for
> my master."
>
> (Bereisheet 24:12–14)

Not only was this woman, who was to be Yitzhak's wife, going to give him water to drink by pouring it down his throat, but she was to volunteer to water all his camels, if she were to past the test. (If it were only ten camels, this would entail hauling close to fifty gallons of water.) This woman would have to be in deep service. Eliezer was firmly fixed on finding someone who was the female energetic equivalent of Yitzhak. Such a person had to be living completely in the consciousness of receiving, not only for self, but equally for others as well, in order to share. A woman with this quality would certainly possess the spiritual energy necessary to propagate Am Yisrael.

His prayer was so much to ask that the only course of action for such an evolved being was to surrender to God. When Rivkah came to the well, she spontaneously offered to do exactly what he had prayed for. As she approached the well, the water rose to greet her, an event that Eliezar had only seen happen with Avraham. In an overwhelmed state, without checking her background any further, he symbolically gave her a gold nose ring and two bracelets and asked to be taken to her home. He was further amazed when he found out that Rivkah was the daughter of Betu'el, who was the son of Avraham's older brother Nahor. Rivkah was also the daughter of Milcah, who was the daughter of Avraham's brother Haran. It was family on both sides.

Although they wanted Eliezar to stay ten months or longer, Eliezar only wanted to stay for ten days, symbolic of sharing the Tree of Life (Etz Chaim) with them. Eliezar gave Rivkah a choice, and she naturally chose to leave as soon as possible. When Rivkah left, her family understood something very profound about her, and in Bereisheet 24:60 they said: "Our sister, grow into thousands of myriads. May your descendants inherit the gate of their foes." Rivkah could do what the rest of her family could not do because she was at such a high spiritual level.

Kabbalistically, the world of assiyah (malchut) is in single digits. The realm of yetzirah has to do with 10s, which includes chesed, gevurah, tiferet, netzach, hod, and yesod. Hundreds represents the world of beriah, and 1000s represent the world of chokhmah, or the yod ($\textrm{'}$) of YHWH (יהוה). And 10s of 1000s, which are known as "myriads," correspond to the world of keter, the highest of the sephirot. The symbolism of all this suggests that Rivkah was living as the embodiment of the divine will (keter). She brought much to the relationship as this enlightenment lineage unfolds.

On the return journey Rivkah saw Yitzhak in the field without knowing who he was, and she was so struck by him that she almost fell off her camel. "Who is that man?" she asked. When Eliezar informed her that he was Yitzhak, she put her veil on. There was instant soulmate recognition. This, however, was a different kind of marriage than Avraham's and Sarah's or Ya'akov's and Rahel's, as yet to come. Rivkah was agreeing to marry someone she did not know, but energetically she knew the truth. In the play between free will and destiny she naturally aligned with the unfolding of the divine will. Yitzhak went to greet Rivkah and brought her into his mother's tent. The moment Rivkah entered the tent it became filled with light once again (Midrash

Bereisheet Rabbah 60:16). This was significant because, as it was pointed out, the light of the shekhinah consciousness in Sarah's tent had gone out. But as Rivkah joined with Yitzhak, the male-female was joined in the alchemical union of the One as Ayn Zulato (אין זולתו—there is nothing other than God). A powerful light was created that exceeded either of them. It symbolizes that Yitzhak's union with Rivkah would channel the light for the whole world. This has some very interesting implications for the meaning of a spiritual relationship and the power of an enlightened sacred relationship.

In this tradition there are several different models of sacred relationship. Yitzhak and Rivkah did not even meet until they were married. How is this the basis for a relationship? On a deeper level, however, as soulmates connect, they characteristically often come from long distances, and may be of different ages. They have often done a significant amount of spiritual work, and they know where they stand in all aspects of their life, including spiritually. They also bring a spiritual track record to the union. Soulmates are aligned in purpose, aligned in the meaning of what life is about. They are not motivated simply by chemistry, but by the higher spiritual life mission. Of course, in any relationship, soulmate or not, you have to make an effort to make it work, and this is implied in the passage: "And Yitzhak brought her into his mother Sarah's tent, and took Rivkah, and she became his wife [*ishah*—אשה—also the word for "sacred fire"]; and he loved her: and Yitzhak was comforted after his mother's death" (Bereisheet 24:67).

Love followed; it did not precede. It was fanned ablaze from a spark of realized truth. When you bring light into a relationship, it opens up the ability to bring light into yourself and transform yourself. The word for love in Hebrew is *ahava* (אהבה), and it is related to the word *hav* (הב), which means "to give." So how do people who do not really know each other make an agreement that they should get married? By intuitive trust in one another, and trust that God has brought them together so they might give, nurture, and elevate one another. Ultimately it is not really different from a spiritual marriage today, which is also based on faith in the alignment with the Divine and divine love.

I am not advising people to just run out and get married. Soulmates are highly evolved people, who have a deep understanding of their own lives and their own purpose. They have earned each other through their spiritual efforts.

The important point is that it is more powerful to focus primarily on one's personal spiritual development, plus effort and not solely prayer, in drawing one's soulmate. Rivkah and Yitzhak understood instantly and intuitively that they were soulmates, but still they had to have a certain trust that this was the case. They needed a certain willingness to develop the relationship into love, to fan the spark into flame. Rivkah realized the greatness of her destiny with Yitzhak, and perhaps from the moment she saw Eliezar, she intuitively knew that she needed to leave Haran and her family to materialize this destiny.

Yitzhak was different from Avraham, and he needed a different type of soulmate. Avraham was the power of chesed, the giving of energy. He took a very active role in the world; he was the father of many nations. Yitzhak was able to highlight the teaching of *avodah* (עבודה), divine service, which required the inner strength of gevurah. Unlike his father, who dug wells, fought wars, defeated kings, traveled with God, and was even willing to sacrifice his son, Yitzhak never left Israel, and never dug more than one new well (the other wells he dug had already been dug by his father and had been sealed by the Philistines). Yitzhak accepted and integrated all that he was given. Avraham, on the other hand, needed a mate who would not "accept all that was given," but who would join him in the struggle to transform the world. And so, in Rivkah, a different partner was given. She was aligned with the God relationship, as filtered through the inner world of gevurah that Yitzhak represented.

Avraham was, by this time, "old and full of years" (Bereisheet 25:8). He had lived an amazing life of service. Not only did he have Yitzhak as a successor to carry on the mission with Rivkah, but he also had the gratification of having fulfilled his divine mission with his beloved Sarah. Most important, he had *become* the ultimate purpose of life, having merged with God in full deveikut/chey'rut awareness. He lived in noncausal contentment, noncausal love, noncausal peace, noncausal oneness, noncausal compassion, and noncausal spiritual joy. There is no greater wealth than this. The sages say that "full of years" includes a vision of the reward that God gives the righteous before they die (Midrash Bereisheet Rabbah 62:2).

As the seed of Am Yisrael, Avraham may be considered the greatest model of deveikut/chey'rut in the history of Am Yisrael. Although not gifted with the power of prophecy, as was Moshe, he represented the power of living in the present, being open to Hashem in every moment. His spiritual strength allowed him to let go of his comfort zone of pure chesed and move into gevurah. In this he demonstrated the characteristic quality of an enlightened being—the freedom to move in any direction beyond thought form and belief limitations. This was also a powerful sign of his chey'rut state. His complete surrender to God at the akeidah, in which the lifting of the knife and willingness to sacrifice Yitzhak (who represented his future in time and space) also symbolized his death to any aspects of ego that he may have invested in Yitzhak. This took him beyond the duality of I Am-ness of separation from God and into complete deveikut as God's will. This was the most powerful statement of his awakening to deveikut/chey'rut awareness as the ultimate purpose of the Torah. His historical role was almost beyond comprehension and established him as one of the most influential people in the history of spiritual evolution of the planet as well as perhaps the greatest in the history of Am Yisrael:

- He was a God-merged person and the seed energy of Am Yisrael and its ultimate purpose.
- He was revolutionary and evolutionary, standing up against the most powerful force of his day, Nimrod, the first one-world dictator and future Armulis (anti-Christ).
- He defeated the four kings with only 318 warriors.
- His tent was open to the world in all four directions, as a symbol of universal compassion.
- He was the living seed of three great religions.
- He was the bringer of a new evolutionary level of male-female relationships, and the model of sacred relationships.
- He personified the revelation of a loving personal relationship with both a transcendent and immanent God intervening in our lives for the purpose of enhancing our personal spiritual evolution and that of humanity (tikkun ha'nefesh and tikkun ha'olam).
- His spiritual greatness to walk before God and be whole, as a blessing to the world, as the expression of God (the "walking before"), could also be understood as the conduit of God's

energy and the presence of the shekhinah entering into the physical world.

- He became the carrier and transmitter of the Malki-zedek lineage.
- Avraham and Sarah's work went beyond tribal consciousness to uplifting the universal consciousness of the planet.
- He activated the idea of living a moral life connected with the heart of all people, dedicated to the service of all people and the seed understanding of loving your neighbor as yourself.
- He created the ending of idolatry.
- He brought the teaching of celebrating holiness in all life, merging continually with the heavens and the earth.

After the death of Sarah, the Torah tells us, Avraham married Keturah, who was actually Hagar (Midrash Bereisheet Rabbah 61:4). Hagar had, by this point, risen to a higher level of evolution, at which she was able to resonate with Avraham. They had many children, whom they sent to the East to spread the teachings of Avraham. They were a reflection of Avraham's intention to share the light with all nations of the world, and to be a father of many nations.

How Avraham and Sarah lived is a great example for humanity. They always asked themselves the question, "What light can we reveal today?" They never retired. They were always looking for more opportunities to share the deeper truths. Even the events around Avraham's physical death remain important teachings. Avraham left his physical body at the age of 175.

It is very significant for the current relationship between the Muslim world and the Jewish world to pay attention to these final teachings that emerge from the Torah's account of Avraham's passing. The first is that both Yishma'el and Yitzhak came together in peace to bury Avraham. Second, Avraham reunited with Hagar, known also as Keturah, showing that, at the end of the story, the sons and daughters of Avraham and the people of Hagar will be at peace with one another. That is a powerful prophecy and legacy.

We see, as we talk about Avraham and his role, that in a sense, all humanity belonged to Avraham. He truly was the father of many nations that will ultimately be at peace. While Avraham and Sarah were concerned with the existence of the nation they were creating, they also understood, from the larger perspective, that spiritually evolved people need not be limited to their own particular tribe, but be one with all humanity. Avraham's deep teaching of deveikut/chey'rut was not only universal, but also particular to the individual chey'rut expression of each person. It acknowledged the importance of recognizing the spark of God in each person. From that it evolved into seeing the light of God in all the nations.

May we be blessed with both the particular and the universal in our lives, and the deveikut/chey'rut energies and intense way of life of these two sacred people. May we be blessed with the chesed quality of life of Sarah and Avraham; and the power, trust, and inner strength of Yitzhak and Rivkah, in all that we do.

Amen

Toledot

Parashah Toledot is very interesting. The first line starts: "These are the chronicles of Isaac son of Avraham: Avraham was Isaac's father. When Isaac was 40 years old, he married Rebecca…." (Bereisheet 25:19). Then: "His wife was sterile, and Isaac pleaded with God for her sake. God granted his plea, and Rebecca became pregnant." So we have, again, the continuation of the spiritual energies, and there are great parallels between Avraham and Yitzhak (Isaac). First, they each had two sons, and the younger carried the spiritual energy over the elder. With Avraham there was Yishma'el, and later came Yitzhak. Second, as we read in this parashah, 'Esav (Esau), the elder by a fraction, is eclipsed by Ya'akov (Jacob), the younger, who receives the lineage transmission. Although he was the elder of the twins, 'Esav was not able to hold the energy of the lineage (Bereisheet 25:32–34). Thus, it was Ya'akov who received the birthright and the blessing. (The power of the shekhinah always kept events on track, as Sarah and Rivkah actively directed the inheritance of the tradition to its highest octave.)

Another parallel between Avraham and Yitzhak is that famines spread through the land during their lifetimes. Avraham was forced to go down to Egypt during his first famine, and to Gerar during his second famine. In the time of Yitzhak, a third famine struck the land. However, during Yitzhak's famine God told him not to leave the land (Bereisheet 26:2). This was because Yitzhak possessed the quality of gevurah as judgment. If that judgment had been unleashed upon the world, which may have happened if he left Eretz Yisrael, the world might not have survived. Yitzhak's judgment was withheld to protect the world from unrestrained strength and intensity. This was also why, in the previous parashah, Avraham emphasized repeatedly to his servant Eliezer that Yitzhak must not leave the land—"Do not bring my son back there!" (Bereisheet 24:5–6).

Another parallel involves Avimelekh, king of the Pelishtim (Philistines), and his chief of staff, Pikhol, who drew up a pact with Yitzhak, just as they had done earlier with his father. Avimelekh's chief of staff had said to Avraham:

"God is with you in all that you do. Now swear to me here by God that you will not deal falsely with me, with my children, or with my grandchildren. Show to me and the land where you were an immigrant the same kindness that I have shown to you" (Bereisheet 21:22–23). Avimelekh and Pikhol understood the power of blessing. When they later disputed with Yitzhak over well rights, they visited him near Be'ersheva and repeated the wording of the pact they had made with Avraham:

> "We have indeed seen that God is with you. We propose that there now be a dread oath between you and us. Let us make a treaty with you, that just as we did not touch you, you will do no harm to us. We did only good to you and let you leave in peace. Now you are the one who is blessed by God." [Isaac] prepared a feast for them, and they ate and drank. They got up early in the morning, and made a mutual oath. Isaac then bid them farewell, and they left in peace.
>
> (Bereisheet 26:28–31)

Avraham and Yitzhak named the place where they made the pact Be'ersheva, literally "the well of the oath" (Bereisheet 21:31 and 26:33).

The deeper point among these accounts is that God gave Avraham and his descendants the power to bless others. As it is written in the Torah, "All the families on earth will be blessed through you and your descendants" (Bereisheet 12:3 and 28:14). The teaching is that until the time of Avraham, God was blessing the world, but now "you" are responsible for the blessings: "Whomever you see fit, you may bless." This power was passed on to Yitzhak (Bereisheet 21:12). This is the core of this parashah. God also said, "All the nations on earth shall be blessed through your descendants" (Bereisheet 22:18 and 26:4).

It is also noted that Yitzhak and Avraham were identical in appearance. When Avimelekh took Sarah, there was a question of who made her pregnant. When they saw how closely Yitzhak resembled Avraham, it was obvious that Avraham was indeed his father. The Torah makes this point by opening this parashah with "Avraham begat Yitzhak" to imply that nobody questions this (Midrash Tanchuma, Toledot, Chap. 1).

Another important message that the couples, Avraham and Sarah, and Yitzhak and Rivkah, communicated through their lives, was their introduction of a whole new level of male-female relationship dynamics. Avraham and Yitzhak are described as being married to the shekhinah through their relationships with their wives. In Avraham's case, Sarah was his half sister as well. More important, they demonstrated in their relationships that the role of women was not only about procreation, merely carrying the seed like an animal. Rather, for the first time in history, women and men were seen as partners for bringing the message of the Divine to the world.

People slowly began to comprehend this. When Avraham and Sarah went down to Egypt, and the pharaoh took Sarah to sleep with her, things started happening to the pharaoh and his household that helped him to realize that God was intervening. He grew afraid of them and the power of their relationship, when he saw that this was not just another woman; this was Sarah, the wife of Avraham, and they were one. So he gave them riches and said "Please leave." The situation was slightly different in Avimelekh's case. Avimelekh was able to contain his awe of them and honor them by inviting them to settle in the land of the Pelishtim around Gerar and Be'ersheva. Avimelekh, too, had tried to take Sarah for his wife, but realized the power and sanctity of her relationship with Avraham. Later, when Yitzhak and Rivkah came to Avimelekh (or his son as the successor), Yitzhak offered the same story that she was his sister. However, this time Avimelekh had already perceived that they were in a divine partnership.

In kabbalistic terms, this partnership is called *achoti kalla* (אחותי כלה), meaning "my sister bride" (Shir Hashirim [Song of Songs] 4:9). This is based on the Song of Songs, which refers to the connection between God and the Jewish people in terms of husband and bride. The image *achoti kalla* implies the deep mystical link between man and woman as partners in bringing forth the message of God. And you can see the nations starting to get this symbolically as you read through these stories. Beginning with the pharaoh, who did not understand it, but felt its power, and moving to Avimelekh, who comprehended it to a certain extent with Avraham and Sarah, and finally with Yitzhak, the Pelishtim king fully understood. So when Yitzhak came to Avimelekh, they did not need divine intervention, because Avimelekh recognized the spiritual intimacy between Yitzhak and Rivkah. This was symbolic of the nations understanding and accepting relationship between men and women as spiritual partners and the power it generates. It was the beginning of a global cultural shift denouncing the objectification of women for pleasure and procreation alone. Women were to be seen as equal partners in the great plan to serve the creator through an elevated, sacred relationship.

Like Sarah, Rivkah was a powerful woman, and one wonders why both of these giants were unable to conceive for a long time. The Midrash tells us it was to foster their endearment to their husbands in order to firmly solidify the relationship with their partner before introducing the responsibility of raising children. In this way, it was more likely that raising children would become a source of further bonding rather than a distraction (Midrash Shir HaShirim Rabbah 2:41). In Rivkah's case, it was the prayer of Yitzhak that finally opened her womb. The additional message here is that there is more power in praying for another. We should, of course, pray for our own needs, but we must remember to also include in our prayers the needs of others. Even though Rivkah was born without a uterus, the prayer was so powerful that a miracle occurred, and she was able to conceive (Midrash Bereisheet Rabbah 63:5).

During her pregnancy, Rivkah became puzzled by the sensations of extreme turbulence that she experienced inside her womb, and sought an explanation from God. God informed her that two future nations were struggling within her (Bereisheet 25:22–23). The Midrash teaches us that every time Rivkah would pass the entrance to a place of learning, a great commotion erupted inside her womb as her son Ya'akov would push and shove his way past his twin 'Esav in order to listen to the teachings. On the other hand, when she would pass a place of idolatry, her son 'Esav would push and shove, trying to make his way toward the site of the idol (Midrash Bereisheet Rabbah 63:6).

Rivkah began to wonder whether a baby was unable to tell the difference between good and evil, but then she got the message from God that she had two very different nations in her womb. This is the first blatant introduction to the intimate play, connection, and struggle between the forces of good and evil. From Avraham we learn the power of mercy, and how to make people feel welcome and safe, and what it meant by surrender to God. From Yitzhak we learn the power of gevurah, or discernment and judgment, as a tool for revealing the light. From Ya'akov we learn the power of the truth, as it is written, "Thou wilt show truth to Ya'akov, loyal love to Avraham" (Mikha 7:20). But as we go farther into the story, we begin to wonder, "What is this 'show truth to Ya'akov'?"

When Ya'akov and 'Esav were born, Ya'akov emerged from the womb holding onto the heel of 'Esav, and 'Esav was completely red, as red as clay. Although they were twins, they were very different from one another. Ya'akov was born into spirituality and the mystical Torah; he basically sat in the tent of his mother, or the divine shekhinah. 'Esav, on the other hand, was drawn by his desires; he knew how to hunt and was a man of the field (Bereisheet 25:27). The beauty is that we have both Ya'akov and 'Esav within us, just as Rivkah did, and our spiritual task is to integrate these energies. There is perhaps a neverending battle between these two energies, the impulsive yetzer hara ('Esav) and the spiritually awake *yetzer tov* (Ya'akov). The more we live the mystical Way of the Torah, the easier it becomes to rest in yetzer tov consciousness.

The battle never ends. This is one of the great Torah teachings. Even when a person is totally liberated, and this battle may appear to be primarily done, one should remain always at the razor's edge (Talmud Bav'li, Sukah 52a). Those who reach high levels of awareness and forget this principle often create great difficulty for themselves and others. We need to understand that Ya'akov and 'Esav represent the powers of the positive and negative together, and each serves the divine purpose in a unique way. The message is that we can serve through both desires, for the flesh and for the spirit. A person may have an unbalanced ego, but if you put that ego in the right direction, toward "the achievement of God" (although that is the wrong understanding), ultimately, by the time you arrive there, the ego no longer dominates, and you may come to understand the fuller picture (Talmud Bav'li, Pesachim 50b). The spiritual path, and chey'rut itself, is not a goal; it is our birthright (to know God). It is already encrypted within us (Devarim [Deuteronomy] 30:14). In this context there is nothing to strive for other than the ability to awaken to the experiential awareness of truth.

The power of blessing that came from Yitzhak is the power of the blessing of the righteous. In our prayers for the Shabbat, we say, "By the mouths of the upright you shall be exalted, and by the lips of the righteous you shall be blessed, and by the tongues of the pious you shall be sanctified, and among the holy ones you shall be lauded." Here is an important thing to keep in mind about blessings: through our own holiness we empower our blessings.

'Esav and Ya'akov lived out the basic patterns of their lives. Ya'akov studied in the tent, and 'Esav wreaked havoc in the world. One day, 'Esav came upon Nimrod, and the two big egos collided. It is significant that 'Esav, who was still under the influence of our tradition as the grandson of Avraham, defeated and killed Nimrod, the first one-world dictator. By the principle of *ma'aseh avot siman labanim* (מעשה אבות סימן לבנים) it is a powerful message for the future. It ultimately means that Am Yisrael will defeat Armulis (the anti-Christ who will become the leader of the "one-world order," which is trying to dominate the world today). 'Esav then donned Nimrod's clothing—the same clothing that Adam had worn in Gan Eden. He hurried back home, exhausted from his day of plunder and death, to find Ya'akov brewing a red lentil soup. Famished, he asked Ya'akov for some soup. Now, 'Esav was Ya'akov's brother, so Ya'akov should have just given him the soup. What was the big deal? But Ya'akov was very clever, and said, "Yes, you can have the soup, but in return, I want your birthright as a firstborn."

'Esav said, "Behold, I am at the point of death, and what profit shall this birthright do to me." At this point he represents those who do not honor their lineage and birthright.

His younger twin responds: "'Make an oath to me right now,' said Jacob. He made the oath, and sold his birthright to Jacob" (Bereisheet 25:32–34).

In essence, 'Esav said: "Why do I need the firstborn responsibilities? I'm hungry!" He gave up his birthright, he got the soup, and he poured it down his throat. This is very interesting, because most people, through the way we eat, give up our birthright as spiritual beings.

We eat unconsciously, and, in a way, this blocks our consciousness and the flow of spiritual energy. We block this flow by the quality and quantity of foods we eat. This is, thus, a very prophetic statement. How often do we give up our birthright for a bowl of soup, or for a Hostess Twinkie, or for a steak? Later, before Yitzhak offered to bless 'Esav, there was an illusionary split happening between Rivkah as the shekhinah energy and Yitzhak. Yitzhak gave the illusionary appearance of favoring 'Esav more, whereas Rivkah tended to favor Ya'akov (Bereisheet 25:28).

As the story unfolds, there was another famine in the land, but Yitzhak was told by God that he could not leave the land like his father did:

> God appeared to Isaac and said, "Do not go down to Egypt. Remain undisturbed in the land that I shall designate to you. Remain an immigrant in this land. I will be with you and bless you, since it will be to you and your offspring that I will give all these lands. I will thus keep the oath that I made to your father Abraham. I will make your descendants as numerous as the stars of the sky, and grant them all these lands. All the nations on earth shall be blessed through your descendants. All this is because Abraham obeyed my voice, and kept my charge, my commandments, my decrees, and my laws."
>
> (Bereisheet 26:2–5)

Historically, it is important to note that these statements were made close to 3,900 years before the present Middle East conflicts about this very land, and written down about 3,400 years ago. Contrary to uneducated, nonhistorical, but popular, political beliefs, these claims to the land of Israel obviously did not start in 1948.

Another level of concern was that Yitzhak had grown so holy that Hashem did not want him being contaminated by the energies of the nations outside the boundary of the promised land. Yitzhak then took his family to the village of Gerar, whose Philistine chieftain was, again, Avimelekh. Because of his past experience with Avraham, Avimelekh understood quickly that Rivkah was Yitzhak's wife. He invited Yitzhak to stay there, and Yitzhak became very bountiful: "Isaac farmed in the area. That year, he reaped a hundred times [as much as he sowed], for God had blessed him" (Bereisheet 26:12).

The Philistines became jealous of Yitzhak's success, and when he realized this, he knew that he needed to move on. As he traveled back toward Be'ersheva he began to re-dig and uncover the wells that his father Avraham had dug. These had been sabotaged by the Philistines and sealed following Avraham's death (Bereisheet 26:18). Part of Yitzhak's role was to maintain the power of the Avrahamic teachings as living waters. The well of living water is also a metaphor for the great Temple. The first well was called *Esek* (עסק—contention), the second well *Sitnah* (שטנה—enmity), and the third well *Rechovoth* (רחובות—spacious). This well at Be'ersheva represents the third Temple, which will be built quickly and without quarrel or difficulty. Every time Yitzhak would dig up one of Avraham's ten wells, the shepherds of Avimelekh would dispute it. In this way he slowly kept moving toward Be'ersheva rather than engaging in conflict with Avimelekh's shepherds, until he finally found the tenth well that Avraham had dug, which they did not dispute. This is very interesting because he chose to act humbly and patiently, and give up a little bit, in return for finding his base. This could be a model for negotiations in the Middle East as well in our own times. He said, "For now the Lord has made room for us, and we shall be fruitful in the land." He went up from there to Be'ersheva, and YHWH appeared to him the same night, and said: "I am God of your father Abraham. Do not be afraid, for I am with you. I will bless you and grant you very many descendants because of my servant Abraham" (Bereisheet 26:24). Yitzhak built an altar there, as was the custom of the early Hebrews following a vision. Soon thereafter, Avimelekh arrived along with his captain, Pikhol, and his friend, Ahuzzat. Yitzhak said to them, "Why are you coming to me? You chased me away." They replied, "No, no, we see that you are a holy person, and we want your blessings." It was on that day that Yitzhak's servants had informed him concerning the well they had dug: "They said, 'we have found water.' And they called the well *Sheva*." Therefore the name of the city is *Be'ersheva*. In that process, he began to bless the water and raise it to its highest frequency again, as it was before the fall of Adam.

The narrative now unfolds with 'Esav, who was forty years old and trying to emulate his father, at least externally. He married two women. The first wife was Yehudit, the daughter of Berid the Hittite, and the second was Basamat, the daughter of Elan the Hittite. Unfortunately these two wives became a major source of harassment for Yitzhak and Rivkah. 'Esav's Hittite wives did not understand who Yitzhak and Rivkah were and the nature of their lineage, so they became a bane on their lives.

Yitzhak felt he was near death, and he had lost his physical vision, perhaps connected with the severity of gevurah. Or perhaps because, as the Midrash tells us, the tears of the angels in the heavens had fallen into his eyes as he lay upon the altar on Mount Moriah (Midrash Bereisheet Rabbah 65:10). Yitzhak called upon 'Esav, his eldest son, and said: "Now take your equipment, your dangler and bow, and go out in the field to trap me some game. Make it into a tasty dish, the way I like it, and bring it to me to eat. My soul will then bless you before I die" (Bereisheet 27:3–4). Rivkah overheard this, and she said to Ya'akov: "This is the time to get the blessing. It is your responsibility to continue the lineage at its highest octave. This is the time when truth must win out over the darkness." Ya'akov replied, "Well, I don't know; I may get cursed if Father realizes that I'm not really 'Esav." Rivkah said "I will take it upon me." That was the mother's love in Rivkah and also the power of the shekhinah, whose role is to stand up and preserve the lineage and the higher truth. So she took the clothing from Gan Eden that 'Esav had taken from Nimrod when he had killed him. She put it on Ya'akov, and wrapped Ya'akov in goat's skin, so that he would appear very hairy.

This cosmic scenario continued as Ya'akov went to his father, and his father said, "Who are you?" Now, this "Who are you?" was a very profound question! His father tuned into Ya'akov's spiritual evolutionary confusion and asked the key question that the spiritual teacher (tzaddik) asks of students to help wake them up. In the literal, yet metaphorical sense, he said: "Who are you? Are you 'Esav or are you Ya'akov?"

Ya'akov was in the midst of personifying two identities. He was wearing his brother's clothes and his energy, and he had the aroma of Gan Eden. He felt a need to ask, and to be asked, who he was, and he was stricken with confusion because he was being forced now to go beyond just hanging out and meditating in the tent of his mother. He was being challenged to evolve toward a more mature spiritual integration. He was forced to integrate becoming a wild man of the field *and* a guardian of truth, simultaneously.

So when Ya'akov came to Yitzhak and said, "My father, *hineini*, here I am," Yitzhak said "Who are you, my son?" Yitzhak knew that something was "off," or, rather, "on."

"What are you doing?" he asked. "What are you up to?" What Yitzhak was really wanting of Ya'akov was for his son to look deep inside himself.

Ya'akov did just that, and said: "I am … 'Esav, your firstborn. I have done what you asked of me."

Ya'akov, supposedly a paragon of truth, appeared now to be lying! Or was he? When he said *Anochi* (אנכי—"I am"), perhaps he was referring to the "I am" of the Divine Self. The spiritual evolutionary issue was that Ya'akov was struggling with his own identity, and what his identity must become. Yitzhak still did not quite trust him, possibly because Ya'akov was not yet integrated within himself.

So he said: "Let me touch you, my son. Are you really Esau or not? The voice is Jacob's voice, but the hands are the hands of Esau. But are you really my son Esau?" (Bereisheet 27:21–24).

Ya'akov said *Ani* (אני—"yes, it is I"). Yitzhak then sniffed him, and he smelled the energy of Gan Eden on the clothes, and he gave him the blessing. The blessing, of course, is very profound. Yitzhak said:

> "See, my son's fragrance is like the perfume of a field blessed by God. May God grant you the dew of heaven and the fat of the earth, much grain and wine. Nations will serve you; governments will bow down to you. You shall be like a lord over your brother; your mother's children will prostrate themselves to you. Those who curse you are cursed, and those who bless you are blessed."
>
> (Bereisheet 27:27–29)

The Zohar tells us that the blessing that Ya'akov received from his father helped him to overcome the angel Samael ('Esav's angel) when Ya'akov wrestled with him years later (Zohar, Vol. 1, folios 144b and 170a). It empowered Ya'akov to make peace with this angel and therefore also with 'Esav. As the Zohar points out, there can be no peace for oneself until one is at peace with one's enemy. Importantly, the other blessings that Ya'akov received, he reserved for the future:

> "The rest of the blessings I shall reserve for the time when my children will need them to fight the kings and rulers in the world who will rise against them.... When that time arrives, all the blessings will be aroused on all sides toward Israel, and the world will be properly established from that day on.... The supernal Kingdom will then arise."
>
> (Bereisheet 27:27–29)

On an internal level, "the kings and rulers of the world" represent our inner negativities that we need to overcome through the power of love, prayer, grace, and self-work, as well as work aimed at improving the state of affairs of the governments and ruling societies of the world. This opens us up to both peace with ourselves and, ultimately, the experience of world peace. Perhaps, according to the principle of ma'aseh avot siman labanin, it is in our own times that these ancient blessings are meant to be activated. We have to assume that Yitzhak knew exactly what he was doing in his choice to pass the lineage on to Ya'akov. In retrospect, it was a historical moment with too much significance to think Yitzhak was simply a blind man being fooled.

As physician for the great Rabbi Shlomo Carlebach for many years, I was always greatly moved by his tremendous compassion and his ability to understand the "other side" of a discussion or human interaction. I admired his capacity to always choose to interpret a situation at its highest octave. His ability to give another the benefit of the doubt was a great peace teaching and an antidote to the plague of sin'at chinam (שנאת חנם—random animosity). The persistant plague of sin'at chinam is a core aspect of our inability to activate the blessing from Yitzhak to Ya'akov.

As it says in Devarim (Deuteronomy)16:20, "Pursue perfect honesty, so that you will live and occupy the land that God your Lord is giving you." Also written there is the importance of judges not taking bribes and, on the same level as bribes, having any agendas about the person being judged (verse 19). The teaching is that if there were any agendas or bribes involved, the judge is to remove himself from the case. In order to activate the blessing, we need to go beyond the egocentric practices and the comfort zone of judgment of those not living the same way as we. We are encouraged, instead, to see the inherent holiness in *all* of Am Yisrael. This is the key to activating the blessing from Yitzhak to Ya'akov.

There are those of us who study Torah, but do not practice the mitzvot, and there are those of us who practice the mitzvot, but do not study the Torah. There are those who neither study the Torah nor practice the mitzvot, but perform deeds of loving kindness, and there are those who study the Torah and practice the mitzvot, but do not perform deeds of loving kindness. Let them all bind together as one community and each will compensate for what the other lacks (Midrash Vayikra Rabbah 30:13). This Midrash teaching needs to be put into active practice in Am Yisrael today.

The practice of name-calling among some of us, whether we call someone a "Jewish anti-Semite" or a "self-hating Jew" for holding compassion for the Palestinians, or "impure" for not yet fully living according to the Torah teachings is a form of intellectual violence. This kind of intellectual violence is in direct contradiction to the very clear teaching of VayYiKra 19:16–17 and the lesson that sin'at chinam was the cause of the fall of the second Temple (Talmud Bav'li, Yoma 9b). A general definition of sin'at chinam is hating someone simply because their opinion or spiritual practice is different from your own. Of course, we can and often must agree to disagree. But ethics demands that while disagreeing with someone, we also respect the perspective from which their life choices and opinion arise, as long as it is for the sake of heaven. To disagree does not mean we stop respecting someone and/or stop seeing the spark of the Divine in a person. Each individual has a unique spiritual journey, a unique way of walking this life path.

While our ancestors trekked through the desert following their exodus from Egypt, they made forty-two stops, and they made each stop "to make known the loving kindness of God." It was to bring chesed into the experience. It was in appreciation of the unique gift of their own journey and the journeys of others. When we do this, we stand again at the foot of Mount Sinai in the radiance of divine communion. See how great is peace. For it is written, "And they journeyed and they settled, and they journeyed and they settled" (BeMidbar 33:6 and onward). This implies that they argued with one another throughout these journeys. However, when they arrived at Mount Sinai, it is not written "And the children of Israel settled there," but rather "Israel camped opposite the mountain" in the singular (Shemot 19:2). This is to teach us that in that moment they became as one and were in harmony with one another. At that point, God said, "Now is the proper time to give them the Torah, seeing that they are united as one and there is peace between them" (Midrash Vayikra Rabbah 9:9).

We left the narrows of Mizrayim to live in the expansiveness of Israel. As it says in Tehillim (Psalms) 118:5: *"Min ha'meitzar karati' yah. Anani bamerchav yah"*—"From the narrow confines I call out to God, and he answers me from the wide open spaces" (from the space of the liberated heart). So activating the blessing is an invitation to us to see all of this from beyond the limitations of our own "narrows," or personal points of view, and to create the space. We are invited to create peace as God created in Bereisheet. We are invited to create for the world, and for the "other" to exist. This is the invocation of chesed into the world. Can we appreciate others' journey as different from our own, and respect where they are coming from? Can we respect where their lifestyle choices have led them, even if into great difficulties for themselves? This is the secret of the healing of Am Yisrael and activating the blessing that will help to save Am Yisrael.

Please note that I am not writing this as a rationale for not living the path of mitzvot, because actually I *am* living the path of mitzvot, as I have chosen to live a Torah-observant life. On the other hand, instead of denigrating and dishonoring those who do not live this way, I see my role as Shlomo Carlebach did; that is, to help reconnect Am Yisrael to its core spiritual essence one step at a time and adhering by the Torah teaching of moving toward the Torah ideal. Not everyone is ready, or has the full capacity, to absorb the full light and spiritual energy of the sod level of the Torah at one time.

This is always the question for healing: Are we able to connect at the level that Shlomo did by his outstanding example of this quality of awareness that he modeled with consistency and conviction? Are we able to leave the narrows of our own particular viewpoint and speak instead from the open spaces? Are we able to connect to each other from the open spaces of our hearts for this higher purpose? Are we able to respect, though not necessarily agree, with everyone else's journey?

Another aspect of these teachings is that when Moshe chose to send a thousand warriors from each tribe, including the Levites, to fight the Midianites, each tribe traveled in a specific formation connoting their different roles. In other words, Moshe recognized the different meaning and contribution of each tribe to the overall completeness of Am Yisrael. The teaching here was not about creating a *hitnak'dut* (התנכדות), an oppositional force, but of creating unity in diversity.

There are two words in ancient Hebrew for "tribe." Both words imply a scepter or staff of some sort. One is *ma'teh* (מטה), the kind of staff or stick we might use to support our walking, and the other is *shey'veht* (שבט), more like a club we might use to beat something or someone. In the Torah account of Moshe's rallying the people to war against the Midianites, he addresses each tribe not as shey'veht, but as ma'teh. One would have thought it would be the other way around in a time of war. But Moshe was a staunch teacher whose main goal was the unification of the masses into a single nation, yet, at the same time, respecting the individual components of each tribe comprising that nation.

More than anything else, he desired to preserve the value and majesty of Am Yisrael's oneness, while simultaneously seeing the value and beauty of each individual. They were to be tribes not by clubbing one another with the splintering quality of shey'veht, but in supporting one another with the unifying quality of ma'teh. If we are to activate the power of the blessing by Yitzhak of Ya'akov, which are based on Am Yisrael respecting and loving each other's unique soul spark, then we need to do just that, rather than trying to kill someone's soul spark for the sake of the self-righteousness (sinat chinam). By respecting each of our very unique soul sparks, we manifest more and more of the messianic hope of forgiveness and understanding, which is the prophetic and divine direction of our times.

Throughout the Torah, there is a teaching of the different roles of the tribes. The Levites were charged with holding the spiritual energy, as the other tribes had different roles in what we now call the "secular" world. Politics, economics, farming, and so on were all imbued with kedusha (קדושה—sanctity) regarding their role in creating the collective holiness of Am Yisrael, as well as the collective action of war (if necessary) to fulfill their divine mission. The teachings of Rav Avraham Yitzhak Kook, a vegetarian and the first Chief Rabbi of Israel in modern times, made this rather clear. The split of Israel today into "secular" and "religious" is a direct antithesis to these ideals and goes directly against the overall Torah mission as Rav Kook has interpreted it. This split does not allow the blessing of Yitzhak to Ya'akov to be activated and, on the contrary, becomes a serious threat to Am Yisrael and to its divine mission as a light to the world. When the blessing given by Yitzhak to Ya'akov is activated, the Torah's purpose for Israel to be a positive light to all the nations will be activated. Then Israel will become an undefeatable beacon of *shalem* (שלם—completeness) and *shalom* (שלום—peace).

Having thoroughly explored the profound implications of the blessing of Yitzhak to Ya'akov for our current world situation, let us return to where we left off in the story. Yitzhak was about to offer the blessing he had intended for 'Esav, who was in the field hunting game for his father's dinner. Ya'akov knelt before his old, blind father, who was not sure of the identity of the man kneeling before him. And he was not quite sure the blessing he had intended for 'Esav ought to now go to another—to his brother Ya'akov, who had disguised himself as 'Esav. Was it really possible, though, that Yitzhak did not recognize Ya'akov's vibration? Did he really not know that Ya'akov was the intended carrier of the lineage? Even his father Avraham had known this long before Ya'akov was conceived (Zohar, Vol. 1, folio 120a). Had not Yitzhak and Rivkah, as most parents do, talked about these things beforehand? I question whether Yitzhak was actually deceived.

When 'Esav returned from the hunt and brought his father his (second) dinner, he invited his father to eat "so that your soul will bless me." Yitzhak was puzzled and asked him, "Who are *you*?"

'Esav was shocked: "I am your son, your firstborn, 'Esav!" Simultaneously, the two realize that Ya'akov had received the blessing intended for 'Esav.

Yitzhak then communicated both his confusion and his firm intention of nevertheless making the blessing stick: "Isaac was seized with a violent fit of trembling. 'Who … where … is the one who trapped game and just served it to me? I ate it all before you came and I blessed him. The blessing will remain his" (Bereisheet 27:33).

At this point, 'Esav was really upset. He bitterly cried out "Bless me too, Father!"

Yitzhak said, "Your brother came with deceit, and he already took your blessing."

'Esav lamented: "Isn't he truly named Jacob (Ya'akov)! He went behind my back [*akav*] twice. First he took my birthright, and now he took my blessing!"

This is a very important scenario; the truth finally came out about what had been going on all along. "First he took my birthright," 'Esav cried, "and now he took my blessing!" 'Esav had missed the point: If you give up your birthright, you give up your right to the blessing due the firstborn. Yitzhak, however, understood this; he said, "Actually, Ya'akov *has* those blessings, he *has* the birthright."

Some of our sages have taught that Yitzhak knew, by the Ruach HaKodesh, that it was Ya'akov whom he had blessed, and was using his innocence to let the shekhinah do the work. He was therefore not about to reverse the blessing in any way. The blessing was also a statement that in the end, Ya'akov would prevail over 'Esav. But the teaching, by implication, is that we must be the true Ya'akov/Israel to merit this manifestation. If Yitzhak knew all along that the mysterious stranger was Ya'akov, then why did he tremble? Why was he filled with dread when he and 'Esav made their "discovery"? What frightened Yitzhak about Ya'akov? Or was it about Ya'akov?

Perhaps what made him tremble at the realization moment was that all this time 'Esav had been wearing the same clothes of Gan Eden that Ya'akov had just worn, but now the clothes wreaked of the smell of the power of hell. Yitzhak felt the power of hell in 'Esav, and yet he decided to give him a blessing anyway, but only as a servant. It is very interesting that even though Yitzhak admitted he had been "fooled" by Ya'akov, his reaction was a realization of something he had already known, that Ya'akov indeed had been the firstborn. He discovered by 'Esav's own admission that he had forfeited his own birthright for a bowl of lentil soup. So Yitzhak basically told 'Esav: "I did indeed bless the firstborn as promised … or the one who held the birthright of the first born. And so will he remain blessed."

The blessing incident was also a momentous occasion of transformation for Ya'akov, because he now was indeed the firstborn and the legitimate lineage carrier. He had to stand up and realize that there was a contrast between 'Esav, living for the pleasure of the moment, and Ya'akov, living in the ways of Yah and contemplating his purpose in the universe. The birthright, which Ya'akov accepted to grow into in his life, is the birthright of us all. The birthright of being a whole, complete, liberated human being is a big yoke for all of us to accept upon ourselves. It is what the ancient sages referred to as *o'l malchut shamayin* (עול מלכות שמין), the "yoke of the kingdom of heaven."

Ya'akov's life represents all the responsibility and hard work that it takes to be that person and to carry that yoke. It was not a light thing to be blessed with so huge a responsibility. Making the world a more ethical, moral, and spiritual place is a lot of work. The blessing represents the beginning of that work. 'Esav wanted the reward, but he was ill prepared to invest the effort. He was too busy seeking the fulfillment of his desires. These are choices we all eventually make when presented with the Torah Way of deveikut/chey'rut. Yitzhak intuitively knew this, but when he really understood what 'Esav was about, he realized that 'Esav was the son who would sell his birthright for a pot of soup, who would trade in this awesome and holy responsibility for the momentary and temporal pleasure of lunch. He would sell the dream of Avraham and all the long, hard efforts of a lifetime for a pot of soup. Yitzhak understood truly that Ya'akov was willing to carry out the divine mission, or he would never have sought out the birthright with all of its weighty and challenging demands.

"Your voice is the voice of Ya'akov," Yitzhak had proclaimed as he probed earlier to validate Ya'akov's identity. "Your hands are the hands of 'Esav." What prophetic words were these? His mother had instructed him to dress up as 'Esav. And as he stood before his father in the garb of 'Esav, hearing Yitzhak ask him who he was, he must have wondered about this himself: Indeed, who am I? What underlies this question that my father is asking me? On a deeper level, then, it is a story about the struggle between Ya'akov and *Ya'akov*, not Ya'akov and *'Esav*. Ya'akov was asking the *berur* (בירור) question, the *clarification* question: "Who am I?" Am I ... Ya'akov, who sits in the tent of my mother and of the masters? Or am I 'Esav, who is willing to fight for what the truth is? Am I the voice, or am I the hands? This is the choice that he has to make before responding to Yitzhak's question, and he has to say "yes" to both, because he must inherit 'Esav's hands of action in order to bring forth to the world the spiritual treasures of Ya'akov's voice.

If you don't know who you are, how can you hope to become the essence, and give the world your gift? To do so, you must be willing to give of yourself from the place of apperceiving the ultimate truth of who you are, beyond even the hands of 'Esav or voice of Ya'akov. The qualities of either are but functions of the personality, not the ultimate truth of your essential self. It was not enough for Ya'akov to *possess* the blessings; he still had to earn and activate them! He had to make that internal shift within himself that would integrate, in every action and word, his role as inheritor of the Divine. In that process, he had to learn to bring holiness into the world, to bring the truth into the world. This is true for all who choose the great way of deveikut/chey'rut. This was the struggle of Ya'akov, represented by the word anochi, when he responded to his father's question with "I am." Anochi has to do with that relationship with God that is deveikut. The "I am" consciousness is anochi, which goes back to the very first word uttered by the Divine when we received the Ten Speakings (or Ten Commandments): *Anochi Hashem*—"I am YHWH, your God." The "I am" is YHWH, your God. Until we change that relationship with the God within us, until we make that choice that Ya'akov made, to stand up for and become the embodiment of Ultimate Truth, our relationship with the Divine cannot fully develop. When we can be lived by Shabbat, when we can be lived by the Great Torah Way of deveikut/chey'rut, when we tap into that yetzer tov within us, and we feel the spark of God within us begin to fan into a flame, it is then that we begin to recognize who we really are. From that comes our heightened ability to fulfill our worldly and divine purpose in life. That is the choice that Ya'akov activated in order to be open to receive the blessing. That is also the challenge that Ya'akov had to rise to—that we all have to rise to. The question, again, is Who am I on *every* level? Not only the personality level. Am I Ya'akov or am I 'Esav? Am I open to becoming the ultimate purpose of life and merge in full deveikut/chey'rut? This is the spiritual question that everyone entering the path of enlightenment needs to ask of themselves.

On a personal level, before Ya'akov could receive the blessing, he had to make the internal decision to be the *full* Ya'akov that he was meant to be and to realize that God exists in the hands of 'Esav, as well as in the tent of Ya'akov. In the Great Torah Way of deveikut/chey'rut we must bring the tent of the shekhinah out into the field of the world. Ya'akov had in that moment opened the door to becoming truly and fully Ya'akov. And so, in that very moment, the blessing truly belonged to him.

It is significant that God does not enter into the story at all. Ya'akov alone must make the choice, without divine guidance or help, to become a vehicle for the creation of a great nation, built on the foundations of Avraham and Yitzhak. Ya'akov alone must choose to manifest the fine and fragile balance of gevurah and chesed, and to be the mediating force between the field (actions of the hands) and the tent of the shekhinah (meditating on the shekhinah). This is the challenge we all have as spiritual students: How do we build the world in partnership with God?

It was only when Ya'akov came into his own, and 'Esav was seen for what he really was, that Yitzhak realized how dangerously close the world came to the hell that he was smelling. Thus "Yitzhak trembled a great tremble." May we all be blessed that in each moment of each day, we continue to hear the inner voice, calling us to discover who we really are, calling us to walk the way of deveikut/chey'rut and to be the dancing, ecstatic, wild expression of the Divine. May we realize our personal essence and ability to give and share that essence with the world. May we always sit in the tent of the shekhinah, the tent of Ya'akov, but may we always be filled with the sweet smells of the Gan Eden fields of 'Esav's clothing. And when we walk in that field, may we bring holiness to every moment of our existence in that field.

Amen

VayYetze

⏤⟶

THE word vayyetze (ויצא) means "And he went out." This parashah is about Ya'akov going out of his mother's tent into the world. This was the second step in his spiritual development. It is a step many of us have to take. How do we move from our egocentric comfort zones to the next step in our spiritual evolution? Even though Ya'akov was meditating in the tent of his mother, which was a special blessing, he had yet to develop the "hands" of 'Esav. For his spiritual evolution it was necessary for him to integrate all aspects of his life. On the Torah Way to deveikut/chey'rut, it is not enough to meditate in a cave. More is asked of us.

Ya'akov was approximately seventy-seven years old and was now beginning the second part of his journey with a foundation of years of meditating in his mother's tent and in the tent of the mystery masters, Shem (Malki-zedek) and Eber (Midrash Bereisheet Rabbah 63:10). Earlier, we discussed the principle of ma'aseh avot siman labanim, meaning that the actions of the ancestors are symbolic of what will occur for the descendants. This means that the actions of the ancestors are not only "assigned" to the descendants, but are also prophetic, in that they provide us with important information regarding what their children will probably face. As such, it is for our own good, for we are able to then read back into the accounts of the ancestors for clues as to what we will face, or what we are already faced with, and how we are to deal with it. Thus, as the ancestors are able to master these trials and temptations in their own lives, we, the children, are better able to survive and continue to evolve spiritually.

Like Avraham, Ya'akov too brought the light of the Divine outside the borders of Yisra'el. Rivkah sent him out because 'Esav was so angry with himself for having given away his firstborn rights and the accompanying blessing that he wanted revenge on Ya'akov. He not only wanted the rights and blessings back; he also wanted to kill Ya'akov for what happened. Yitzhak's intention in sending Ya'akov out was his marriage from his own tribe. Yitzhak was a prophet and understood that there was a greater mission involved here; he also needed to spare Ya'akov from the dark intentions of his brother. In our own lives we are guided in certain directions, and we trust that whatever God does is for the best (Talmud Bav'li, Berachot 60b). Likewise, these family dramas combined to gently push Ya'akov out, to move him toward the next level of his own spiritual path for his own spiritual evolution. This was part of his training to become the father of Am Yisrael. This was an important example of how to turn the difficulty and opposition in our lives into our spiritual advantage and evolution.

Ya'akov first traveled to Be'ersheva, as Avraham did before him. There is a teaching that the shekhinah went with him (Midrash Tanchuma, Bamidbar, Chap. 19), so he had a little help, just as Avraham did in his journeys. Several of the Midrashic traditions teach that before Ya'akov went to Haran, he spent fourteen years training in the mystery schools of Shem and Eber (Midrash Bereisheet Rabbah 63:10). He had gone from his mother's tent and had been additionally trained, as was Avraham, by Shem and Eber. Like Ya'akov, everyone on the spiritual path needs a spiritual teacher or teachers to support them on their way to deveikut/chey'rut. Additionally, he was now more prepared to deal with the black magician Lavan.

Bereisheet 28:10–16 reveals a prophecy to Ya'akov:

Jacob left Be'ersheva and headed toward Charan. He came to a familiar place and spent the night there because the sun had already set. Taking some stones, he placed them at his head and lay down to sleep there. He had a vision in a dream. A ladder was standing on the ground, and its top reached up toward heaven. God's angels were going up and down on it. Suddenly he saw God standing over him. [God] said, "I am God, Lord of Avraham your father, and Lord of Isaac. I will give to you and your descendants the land upon which you are lying. Your descendants will be like the dust of the earth. You shall spread out to the west, to the east, to the north, and to the south. All the families on earth will be blessed through you and your descendants. I am with you. I will protect you wherever you go and bring you back to this soil. I will not turn aside from you until I have fully kept this promise to you."

Ya'akov, like his son Yosef, was a dream-master, and this is partly how they survived in the very difficult and darkly occult world of their times. What was being shown to him in this prophetic dream was that whatever happens on earth happens also in heaven through the angels as conduits of divine energy. God's angels walk on the earth carrying out their mission and are direct expressions of the divine will. God showed Ya'akov that God stands above the ladder and promised him that he would not be under the power of the angels, but that he would be under divine direction without any intermediaries. The presence of God would always be with him.

Another way of interpreting the vision of Ya'akov's ladder is that it was a prophecy for the Am Yisrael that in the end they would ascend and stay there, but before that, they would be dominated by the four kingdoms (Babylon, Persia, Greece, and Rome). Second, the grace given to the Jewish people is that they operate directly under the guidance and protection of God, rather than under angelic protection. Third, the walk of all liberated people is between the b'limah and the mah—between the top of the ladder and the bottom of the ladder. This walk begins prior to enlightenment and continues afterward. The ladder represents the merging of the heavens and the earth. This mystical walk is something that people begin to develop in their lives as they grow spiritually. As it is taken further, we move into the nondual awareness that we are simultaneously the nothing and the something. In an enlightened state we walk as Ya'akov's ladder—where the heavens and the earth kiss, where the b'limah and mah merge into a divine synergy.

This is a different definition of enlightenment than is emphasized in the East, where the emphasis is primarily on the b'limah (the nothing). The emphasis in the Great Torah Way of deveikut/chey'rut is an ability to become Ya'akov's ladder. It is the ability to walk simultaneously with one's head (consciousness) in heaven and one's feet on earth. It is also taught that when Am Yisrael is acting unconsciously there is a separation between heavens and earth and the ladder is withdrawn from the earth. In this, the powers of darkness on the earth prevail. When Am Yisrael walks in full consciousness, as a model of

Ya'akov and as his children, then the ladder touches heaven and earth. In this, the light prevails. This is a profound teaching of the deeper spiritual mystery behind Ya'akov's dream. When we understand the principle of ma'aseh avot siman labanim, we understand that these are prophecies made for *all* of Am Yisrael in every era, not just for Ya'akov in his. The divine communication in Ya'akov's vision clearly informed him that the land belonged to him and his descendants, and that God would be with him and his descendants always.

How can we say that during the Inquisition years and the Holocaust, for example, that God was with Am Yisrael? God being with us does not mean that we can do whatever we please. We cannot act as negatively as possible, and not follow the Torah Way, while expecting that everything will be fine. Rather, God will be with us, and we will survive the results of our actions. But we will also have Inquisitions and, as Moshe foretold, other great tragedies if we do not follow God's way. We will be kicked out of the land and will only be able to return once we have been purified. That is hard medicine to swallow, but if we look at the Holocaust, we can see that we did survive, and we have flourished since. The Holocaust was so horrifying that the world had to give the land of Yisra'el back to Am Yisrael. When we say "Remember the Holocaust," we might want to remember that perhaps something more than our suffering at the hands of the occultist Nazis played out. It also helps to consider that anti-Semitism might be the result of not following the Torah Way, which Moshe warned us not to forsake. This in turn might have created the conditions for the dark energies of an Inquisition and Holocaust to be activated. We should also remember Moshe's prophecy, that if we do not live in the land of God, as it is laid out in the Torah, we might again be kicked out of the land as happened to the people before us (VayYiKra 18:28). This must be remembered in modern Israel as part of our survival and evolutionary understanding.

In Bereisheet 28:16–18, Ya'akov woke up from the dream about the angel-occupied ladder and God's promise, and said: "God is truly in this place.... It must be God's temple. It is the gate to heaven!" This shows us one of the meanings of Jacob's ladder: It was a portal to the heavens. In Bereisheet 28:18–22, the story continues:

Jacob got up early in the morning and took the stone that he had placed under his head. He stood it up as a pillar and poured oil on top of it. He named the place ... God's Temple [Beth El]. The town's original name, however, had been Luz. Jacob made a vow. "If God will be with me," he said, "if He will protect me on the journey that I am taking, if He gives me bread to eat and clothing to wear and if I return in peace to my father's house, then I will dedicate myself totally to God. Let this stone that I have set up as a pillar become a temple to God. Of all that You give me, I will set aside a tenth to You."

This was the beginning of the practice of the tithe. The first ten percent goes to neutralize the dark side. Above this amount is considered charity if it is not given as a "business deal," in which we expect something back in return. The interpretation of this passage gives us much to understand and much more to study. Another metaphor teaching in this parashah is the inversion of the heavens (astral plane) and the earth plane. On the earth plane the forces of darkness are more powerful, until there is divine intervention. When Ya'akov finally reached his destination, the home of his conniving uncle, Lavan, he was taken advantage of in a variety of ways. In the end, divine intervention completely defeated Lavan. Ya'akov was then able to cleverly leave Lavan, calculating a seven-day headstart for travel.

The forces of darkness work on both the higher and lower planes. For example, on the lower planes, although Ya'akov was the second child to emerge from Rivkah's womb, on the higher planes, he had been conceived first (Midrash Bereisheet Rabbah 63:8). One oral tradition suggests that the dark angels had switched the order of the twins' emergence from the womb so that 'Esav was born first. On the higher planes, the truth of Ya'akov's spiritual greatness overwhelmed the energies of 'Esav on every level, including his angel, as we will see in the story of Ya'akov wrestling with the angel of 'Esav. This principle of spiritual inversion, as exemplified in this story, teaches that Ya'akov was forced from the very beginning of his conception to learn how to deal with the Sit'ra Ach'ra (סיטרא אחרא—the dark side, or literally, "the other side"). This is not an incidental message on the spiritual path, as the dark side is always there as a force of judgment and tends to get more severe as we ascend spiritually. We need to learn how to deal with the dark side, including the most basic approach: living with as much holiness as possible in our everyday lives. Ya'akov's subsequent training in dealing with Lavan is something that all those on the spiritual path should pay attention to. Unfortunately, this emphasis on dealing with the dark occult has been lost in the current ways of Am Yisrael. This explains why so many failed to see what was happening as the Nazis' dark occult power began to build. The Am Yisrael were no longer holding the teachings of Ya'akov and learning from him how to defeat and/or avoid these dark forces. The defeat of Lavan and later of Balaam, in Moshe's time, is a clear message—ma'aseh avot siman labanim.

Except for a few well-trained kabbalists today, the knowledge of how to deal with the dark side on the occult level has been lost. However, the righteous and those who live in the ways of the Torah are naturally protected from the energetics of the dark side through their kedusha (holiness). The dark side cannot penetrate the energetic field created by those living in the light of the Great Torah Way. The basic way of occult protection is simple: *Lead a righteous life*. This approach automatically provides protection, and it applies to all people who are living in that way. This is why this passage is a prophecy. Mark Twain pointed out that this ancient, tiny group (the Jews) survived the Egyptians, Romans, Greeks, Persians, and Babylonians (and in our time, the Nazis). How did this happen? How did Am Yisrael survive constant and consistent genocidal attacks on its existence? How is it that each nation that has attempted to destroy Am Yisrael has been annihilated? Mark Twain did not know why this was the case, but he noted that it was so, and he was intrigued by it. Twain felt by historical observation that the Jewish nation was immortal.

Some sages in the Torah tradition feel that Ya'akov's ladder is also akin to Avraham's vision, when he made his covenant between the parts (of the animals). Ya'akov was seeing the four kingdoms, their dominion, and their ascent and descent upon the ladder, as was also described by Daniyyel concerning Babylonia, Persia, Greece, and Rome. Their angels would ascend and descend. Ultimately, after Rome, the angel of Edom would descend, and the angel of Ya'akov would permanently ascend. This is the prophecy of this dream.

We are living this prophecy today. The sages understood that this ladder was a gateway to the heavens. It was grounded in Be'ersheva, where he was sleeping. It is said that a well traveled before him from Be'ersheva to Mount Moriah (Midrash Pirkei D'Rebbe Eliezer, Chap. 35). According to the Midrash, he arrived at the site at noon and God spoke to him and told him to stop and set up camp. Ya'akov was confused. After all, the sun had not yet set. God then caused the sun to set prematurely, and he went to sleep (Midrash Bereisheet Rabbah 68:10).

There is some confusion about how fast Ya'akov traveled between locations. This is the first teaching of the "springing of the earth," or what we call the "folding of the road" (Talmud Bav'li, Sanhedrin 95b). This is akin to the Ba'al Shem Tov, who traveled in his wagon through time and space. It appears this phenomenon was happening to Ya'akov as he moved from Be'ersheva to Moriah to Haran in a very short time.

According to the Zohar, when he was on Mount Moriah, he gathered twelve stones, representing the twelve tribes that were to come from him, and placed three in each of the four directions. He then went to sleep in this circle of stones and had his vision of the ladder (Zohar, Vol. 1, folio 147b). When he woke, the twelve stones had become one stone (Bereisheet 28:18), just as the twelve tribes were to become one nation. This finalized itself at Har Sinay, in the giving of the Torah, when the Jewish nation became one soul. Although this vision occurred at Moriah, the Midrash implies that Luz, Beth El, Moriah, and Jerusalem were all the same place (Midrash Bereisheet Rabbah 69:7), and therefore constitute a gate to heaven.

What happened to this stone? It is said that oil flowed down from the heavens and initiated the stone, which, by an act of God, entered the earth and became what is now known as *Even HaShetiyah* (אבן השתיה—the Foundation Stone). Today this stone is housed in the Dome of the Rock on the Temple Mount in Jerusalem. It is a powerful stone replete with the energetics of God's house. The Even HaShetiyah generates massive energy. The power of Jerusalem is greatly amplified by this stone and may be the cause of what we call "Jerusalem madness." This could be one of the things that people are unconsciously fighting over. No nation has been able to sustain being in that energy, except for Am Yisrael, who has had an unbroken presence there over thousands of years except for the two hundred and ten years they were slaves in Egypt. Am Yisrael otherwise lived there for some four thousand years since the time of Avraham, although obviously not being in political control for this full time. This energy also caused the diaspora of Am Yisrael for not following the Torah, after the fall of the first and second Temples. Today, Am Yisrael has a third chance to establish and live in harmony with the higher frequencies of God as amplified by the Even HaShetiyah.

As already pointed out, Ya'akov was trained in the power of the positive occult energies. Most of the Midrashim acknowledge the "springing of the earth" as having occurred for Ya'akov, allowing him to travel great distances in a brief time. His next stop was Haran. At Haran Ya'akov came to a well in a field and saw three flocks of sheep. The symbolism of the three flocks of sheep is interpreted in a variety of ways. They represent the three levels of Am Yisrael: *Kohan'im, Levi'im*, and *Yisra'elim*. It also relates to the three festivals during which the nation was reenergized at the sanctuary: *Sukkot, Pesach*, and *Shavuot*. The well that is said to have traveled with Ya'akov is symbolic of the Temple, which originally had been a portable sanctuary. The flocks of sheep may be symbolic of the pilgrims who would ascend to the sanctuary. The well at which he arrived in Haran may represent the teachings of the Torah as flowing out from the wellspring of divine wisdom and reaching the whole world. It was here that he met Rahel (Rachel). Ya'akov was attracted on many levels to Rahel, who showed up at the well as the only female shepherd, which in itself was unusual. She was exceptionally powerful, as was her father. No one dared to mess with Lavan's daughter.

The shepherds gathered at the well were waiting for enough strong people to show up so they could move the huge boulder sitting atop the well. Ya'akov was so touched by the sight of Rahel that he singlehandedly moved the stone. He then ran over to Rahel, kissed her, wept, and told her his story. Having developed his skills of prophecy, he wept because he saw the difficult life they would lead, and that she would die in childbirth outside the borders of the land promised to their children.

Ya'akov then asked to meet her parents, and she introduced him to Lavan (Laban), who was the brother of Ya'akov's mother, and grandson to Nahor, the older brother of Avraham. Lavan was not an ordinary person. He was a black occult magician, perhaps the black occult master of the Middle East. Although Ya'akov was strong spiritually, he met his match on "the other side" in the occult power of Lavan. It would be twenty to twenty-two years before he developed enough strength to defeat Lavan. Some sages have suggested that Lavan and Balaam were the same person (Midrash Tanchuma, Va'yetze, Chap. 13). As Balaam, then, he was one of three advisors consulted by the pharaoh in Moshe's time regarding whether to release the Hebrews from slavery. The other two were Iyyov (Job) and Yitro (Jethro). Iyyov kept silent and suffered because of it. Yitro abandoned the court of the pharaoh and was blessed for not participating. But Balaam advised the pharaoh not to release Am Yisrael (Midrash Sh'mo't Rabbah 1:9). Later, Balaam was hired by the Moabites to curse the Israelites as they camped out in the desert of Sinai. He was eventually killed by Am Yisrael, for his relentless attempts at bringing their downfall (BeMidbar 31:8).

Ya'akov was blessed in this struggle with Lavan because he was well trained in the mysteries of the heavens and empowered by his personal experience of knowing God directly. He became a dream-master and had the ability to transcend into the heavens as we see with the ladder dream-vision. Ya'akov's dreams were constantly flowing and teaching him as a primary connection with the Divine. The teachings were that even when he was asleep, the light was consistently a part of his consciousness. In a sense, he was *awake* while sleeping. This quality of Ya'akov the dreamer is the case with all liberated beings. And now, because of his interaction with Lavan, he had the opportunity to learn about the forces of darkness, and how to be strengthened as part of his continued training and spiritual evolution. If we have the right understanding, all that comes to us in our life is for our spiritual empowerment.

A principle that Ya'akov faced throughout his life was *midah k'neged midah*, which translates as "measure for measure." As Ya'akov appeared to "deceive" his father, Yitzhak, to attain his blessing, he too was deceived—by Lavan and his daughters Rahel and Le'a (Leah). Later, he was deceived and tricked by Lavan in the counting of sheep owed to him, and when Lavan changed his wages ten times. His own sons, who told him that Yosef had been killed by a wild animal, also deceived him with a fabrication that sent him into mourning for twenty-two years. Ya'akov's paradoxical character as a deceiver serves as a subtle example for us on how to live a righteous Torah life with powerful baseline protection against the dark side, while at the same time holding the earthly wisdom of how to survive and succeed in a dark field. In this context, Lavan actually became a great teacher for Ya'akov.

The struggle of spiritual powers against the dark occult powers played out in the story of Ya'akov and Lavan, as the power of God was able to overcome all the tricks that the black magician Lavan used against Ya'akov. This happened both immediately and later in the desert during the exodus when he, as possibly Balaam, was defeated by Am Yisrael. In this struggle between good and evil (both of which originate from God in the Torah tradition [Yesha'yahu 45:7], lest we conceive evil as coming from a separate source, and thus enter into idol worship), Ya'akov's two wives aided him. They had grown up in Lavan's family and were thus experts in the occult. They were also prophets in their own right (Midrash Bereisheet Rabbah 72:6). They understood deception as evidenced by their initial deception of Ya'akov and later with Lavan. Rahel, the younger, did not wish to undermine her elder sister Le'a. According to Lavan's custom, Le'a had to be married first, being the eldest. Rahel also had concern about Lavan's powers, which could have jeopardized all their lives if his plan to deceive Ya'akov by having him marry Le'a first had been thwarted.

Later, Lavan as Balaam would stand clearly against the house of Ya'akov. Lavan did everything he could to prevent Rahel from being married, because she would bring Yosef and Binyamin (Benjamin) to the twelve tribes. Why was this a problem for him? The lineage of Yosef would eventually defeat Lavan (as Balaam) 240 years later. Lavan foresaw this, and his attempt to block the marriage of Rahel was part of his effort to block the emergence of Am Yisrael and its existence as a nation. Ya'akov's wives trained him in occult ways so that he could overcome the dark side. This also highlights the teaching that the combined power of the male and female energies is far more powerful than when they are separate. In this case it was the power of God working through Rahel, Le'a, and Ya'akov that defeated Lavan. This struggle was necessary because God does not do everything for us. What growth is there in that?

The forces of darkness try to siphon off energy from the forces of light. Lavan was an energetic parasite, living off the energetic life force (nefesh) of Ya'akov. Ya'akov's spiritual connection allowed him to bring down *shefa* (heavenly spiritual energy) into the physical plane. Lavan was siphoning off the blessings from Ya'akov, and thus Lavan became rich while Ya'akov remained poor until he figured out what to do. At the same time, however, Ya'akov was aware that he was a vessel for the divine blessing. Lavan, too, must have known this, which would explain why he spent so much energy trying to keep Ya'akov trapped there, all the time draining his nefesh and preventing him from manifesting Am Yisrael. In this twenty-two-year struggle, Ya'akov's dreams guided him, as did divine intervention in other ways.

After Rahel gave birth to Yosef, Ya'akov consulted with his wives and asked them if they were ready to leave. They agreed and the family finally left. Taking with them the flocks owed to Ya'akov, they snuck out during the night. As they made their escape, the prophet Rahel stole the source of her father's occult powers, the idols, also known as *terafim* (תרפים). She placed an energy field around them so that Lavan would not sense they were gone. They were therefore able to escape from and defeat Lavan, as well as retrieve the blessings that Ya'akov had brought down, which Lavan had taken from him.

Later, Yosef, Rahel's son, mastered the power of dreams, and was trained in the power of the occult, becoming the greatest occultist in Egypt. This is the principle, again, of ma'aseh avot siman labanim. He became second to Pharaoh, based upon the power of the Divine focused through his own occult power and knowledge. This occult knowledge was also a part of the training of the ancient rabbis of the Great Sanhedrin. Though it may seem like a wild idea today, it was, at that time, a standard part of their training (Talmud Bav'li, Sahnedrin 17a). This was the way of Ya'akov and his children, though we have lost much of this over the millennia in the course of our lengthy, scattered exile. There is evidence that this occult power was used to defeat the Germans, and other adversaries of Yisra'el in the Middle East, during World War Two and shortly thereafter. Kabbalists used this power to draw a line of blood that Rommel's tanks in the desert could not pass. Rommel came near the line, but never passed it. The ways of the fathers are indeed a message and a prophecy for the children.

Ya'akov became the main target for Lavan, but the righteous Torah Way of living is a source of real power, which brought grace to Ya'akov. In our lives, we must give no opening for the dark side to slip in. We must live as close as possible to a 100-percent righteous life, so that we are not susceptible to dark forces. If we maintain a high level of physical health, as well as emotional, intellectual, and spiritual health, the dark side cannot easily violate us, and our divine energy cannot be stolen and used against humanity. Although this is not necessarily a message some want to hear, nevertheless leading a righteous Torah Way and understanding the Torah principle of ma'aseh avot siman labanim is an intuitive opening for understanding what is happening in the world today as a replay of these ancient struggles of light and dark, when we discuss the one-world government. This is important because, unfortunately, as many understand, the world today is subject to a general black occult effort at complete domination.

One of the major strategies of the dark side is based on the principle that a stronger mind can dominate a weaker mind. In our times, our health has been compromised by our subjection to a variety of toxic forces, such as vaccines, chem-trails, and GMO foods. These weaken the immune system and cause the brain to swell for up to two years. Chemical trails, which are toxic materials sprayed from jets, fall on many regions of the world. The excessive prescription of psychotropic drugs, in spite of the mounting published research declaring them to be ineffective, at best, and dangerous, at worst, may permanently damage the brains of those subjected to their effects. Junk foods, genetically engineered foods, and fluoride and lithium in our water supply further weaken the minds (and willpower) of the masses. These influences disable us from transcending our five-sense bio-computer minds and make us subservient to stronger minds and intentions. Thankfully, the general public is slowly catching on, and this is one reason, for example, why people do not trust the media and are using the internet instead. The mainstream media have perpetually spread confusion, misinformation, and disinformation that weaken and confuse the public. It is not a coincidence that a high percentage of medical doctors and educators speaking out against the potential dangers of vaccination are Jewish. These men and women, as part of Am Yisrael, are consciously or unconsciously battling the forces of darkness. Only when we become conscious of all this, are we able to protect ourselves. Because of these dynamics, it is important to maintain good physical health and avoid the drug and alcohol use that is rampant today. Drugs and alcohol, by weakening the mind, make everyone more vulnerable to the mind-domination efforts of the negative forces of the Sit'ra Ach'ra.

The oral tradition tells us that the first Jewish Holocaust occurred 3,400 years ago in Egypt during the ten plagues that befell the pharaoh and his people. During the ninth plague of darkness, eighty percent of Am Yisrael died (Midrash Sh'mo't Rabbah 14:3), because they could not let go of, or break out of, the black magic forces of the Egyptians. The more recent Holocaust is considered by some to also be a result of black magic forces, employed by the Nazis, and based on the black occult teachings of the Thule Society, a Bavarian black occult group that is well documented to have brought Hitler to power. It is no accident that the Nazis were the first to put fluoride in the water to weaken the spiritual will of the people, to decrease the power of their minds, and to make the women sterile. Unfortunately, these are historical and scientific facts that more than a few are aware of. The Sit'ra Ach'ra took the lives of 6 million Jews, and 54 million deaths altogether, during World War II alone. It is important not to become paranoid, but rather to care for our body, mind, and spirit, and live a Torah Way lifestyle so that we will become less susceptible to these forces. (This strongly suggests that we unplug our televisions, and do not do drugs or alcohol except for ceremonial wine.) I also suggest reading this version of the ninety-first Psalm, as translated by Rabbi Gershon Winkler, one of the most powerful protection prayers.

> You who now desire to sit in the mystery realms of the
> Beyond; to enter the Sleep of the Shadow of Shaddai;
> Say unto the Infinite One, "You are my shield and my power;
> My God, in whom I trust.
> For you rescue me from the embers of possible harm,
> And from the rumblings of disconcertment;
> You pass over me, sheltering me always;
> And under your wings am I shielded.
> Your truth and your presence are my strength;
> And I shall therefore not fear the terror of night,
> Or of the arrows that fly by day;
> Or of the challenges that approach me in the darkness,

Or of the sudden assaults that confront me at mid-day.
No. For a thousand shall fall at my side;
Tens of thousands at my right side;
Toward me they shall not approach,
Appearing only as illusion, a mere sight to behold.
And I shall witness the downfall of evil.
Because you, O Infinite One, are my shelter;
The wellspring of your essence you set firmly in the Beyond;
Therefore, no evil can touch me; nor approach my tent."
For God instructs the angels to watch over you in all your
Ways; upon their palms shall they carry you lest you stumble
With your feet upon a rock. You shall be empowered to
Overcome your obstacles; Lions and serpents will not
Overwhelm you. For God says to you,
deep within your soul,
"Because you have directed your passions toward me,
I will make myself felt by you, known by you,
For you have acknowledged my essence.
Therefore, when you call me, I will answer;
I am with you in times of trouble;
I will lift you up and I will bring you honor.
I promise you long life, and I will show you my support;
I promise you long life, and I will show you my support."

The power of blessing is great. It is so great, this parashah teaches us, that even an unconscious blessing has potency. We see this in the story of Yitzhak blessing Ya'akov, thinking he was blessing 'Esav, and subsequently passing on the lineage to its true heir. Still, it is likely that Yitzhak was at least partially aware of what was happening at the time. We see this dynamic repeat itself again with Le'a and Rahel, when Lavan switched brides on Ya'akov during the wedding ceremony, and his intended bride, Rahel, was switched for Le'a. Here again, Lavan used his occult powers to block Ya'akov's perception that Le'a was not Rahel. An unconscious blessing may have even more power, actually, because a conscious blessing is only as strong as its intent. An unconscious blessing can be more powerful because the person is merely a conduit for the will of Hashem, and the ego is not necessarily in the way interfering with the blessing. Ya'akov became then an unconscious conduit for blessing Le'a. Through Le'a and her lady-in-waiting, Zilpah, two-thirds of Am Yisrael was manifested, and through Le'a the power of the inner world becomes available to Yisra'el.

It is taught in mystical traditions that a picture can access the subconscious mind best. The subconscious gives us a closer experience of our soul. Subconscious blessings come from a soul level. One cannot help raise the question of why even a small part of the creation of Am Yisrael is associated with what appears to be trickery, as evidenced by Le'a getting the energy for a child that was meant for Rahel, and by Ya'akov receiving a blessing meant for 'Esav. Le'a's first child, Reuven, did not receive the holiness of the firstborn as a result of this deception. His energy was scattered and he was unable to function as the eldest brother. Levi, Le'a's third child, became the high priest, and Yehuda, Le'a's fourth, became the king. Rahel's firstborn, Yosef, eventually took on the role of the eldest brother. Many of Reuven's descendants lost their firstborn status and were among the 250 of Am Yisrael's firstborn who were burnt up in the story of Korach (BeMidbar 16:1 and 35). It is taught in the Midrash that a drop of semen used to fertilize the egg of Reuven was saved later to conceive Yosef (Zohar, Vol. 1, folio 155). This is also related to the power of the subconscious blessing. Although there is a superficial suggestion that some of the energy of Ya'akov involved the energy of trickery, we understand, on a deeper level, that when the mind and ego disengage, as happened with this "deception," then the powerful blessings from the deeper subconscious source of the divine presence are able to come through more clearly. It all remains a mystery best interpreted by "whatever God does is for the best." The creation and power of Am Yisrael comes from the source of blessing at the neshama level of soul.

Today I teach meditation that involves visualizing the letters of the Tetragrammaton, and in that process we are able to bypass the conscious mind and access the subconscious and unconscious mind, because a picture is worth a thousand words. The picture is resonating with an aspect of subconsciousness. Ya'akov created, through his life's actions and choices, a tremendous vehicle for the closest possible contact with the Divine through his neshama level of soul. Ya'akov and his unconscious behavior naturally became the divine balance of tiferet, in that his father Yitzhak represented gevurah, and Avraham represented chesed. It was a natural balance that manifests as truth, beauty, and completeness. Ultimately, it was deeply and unconsciously connected to the divine will at the level of keter.

There is an important symbolic role difference between Rahel and Le'a. Rahel represents *alma d'itgalia* (עלמא דאתגליא), which is the revealed world of malchut in the physical plane and of the outer world. She was part of the legacy of Avraham and Yitzhak in bringing the teachings to the whole world. In this context, Rahel was not buried with Ya'akov. Le'a, on the other hand, represents *alma d'itkasia* (עלמא דאתכסיא), the *inner* teachings of Ya'akov. Her inner teachings are the secrets of the Torah, also known as kabbalah. Rahel brought the teachings to the nations. Le'a held the teachings, and remained at home symbolically, guarding the teachings of the people. As Rahel is described as being beautiful and well endowed (the outer existence and attractiveness in the world), Le'a was of weak vision and not particularly attractive. Le'a was the energy of binah, the energy of the heavens. They both played important roles in the divine mission of Am Yisrael.

Each was uniquely suited to her task. Le'a and Zilpah created eight of the twelve sons of Ya'akov and his only daughter, Dinah. Rahel's nature was to express the outward energy of Avraham, Yitzhak, and Ya'akov, to spread the Torah teachings to the world and to fulfill that universal responsibility. Rahel was also a fighter. Before leaving her father, she disempowered him by stealing his idols. She was not merely trying to disempower him, however, but was trying to wake him up and empower him spiritually, *freeing* him from idol worship. Unfortunately, today these inner and outer roles are seen as polar rather than complementary toward creating a total functional expression of Am Yisrael. I look forward to a time when the sons of Rahel and the sons of Le'a will understand that there is only one Am Yisrael, and they each had their particular roles.

Rahel died in childbirth with the emergence of Binyamin, and was buried outside of Bethlehem, as a message and protector of her people. This is a beautiful teaching of the importance of God's plan and of acknowledging the legitimacy of healthy differences. The symbolic teaching and way of life of the archtypes of Yosef (Rahel) and Yehuda (Le'a) are not ultimately contrary, but expressing different ways and levels in which enlightenment occurs along a continuum.

The Divine was playing very deeply in all this. The subconscious blessing of Yitzhak to Ya'akov, and Ya'akov to Le'a, was God acting fully. The defeat of La-van came from the drawing down of Ya'akov's blessings. (Proverbs) 29:25 says, "He who puts his trust in the Lord shall be protected." When we are living a holy life, we are protected against the forces of darkness. While we are not bulletproof, we are nevertheless preserved. Ma'aseh avot siman labanim is the principle at work throughout this parashah. May we be blessed to understand the deeper aspects of Ya'akov's life. May we be able to take these aspects to the highest potential within ourselves and be a light unto the nations.

Amen

VayYishlah

THIS complex and amazing parashah really lays down the whole foundation of the nation of Am Yisrael. Directly translated, vayyishlah means "And he sent." What exactly did Ya'akov send? He sent scouts ahead of him as he made his journey back home after decades with Lavan. Some of the sages believe that these scouts were not human, but actually angels (Midrash Bereisheet Rabbah 75:4). Ya'akov was hoping that it would be safe by now to finally return home even though he had just crossed over the River Yabok in order to pass through the Lands of Sey'ir, the place where 'Esav had settled. Still fearing that his brother wanted revenge for what happened twenty-two years earlier, Ya'akov sent scouts to make sure the road ahead was safe for his now multiplied family and all his flocks. If the scouts were to meet up with 'Esav, they were to try and appease him ahead of time before Ya'akov and his clan arrived.

> He instructed them to deliver the following message: "To my lord
> Esau. Your humble servant Jacob says: I have been staying with
> Laban, and have delayed my return until now. I have acquired
> cattle, donkeys, sheep, slaves and slave-girls, and am now sending
> word to tell my lord, to gain favor in your eyes."
>
> (Bereisheet 32:5–6)

The scouts returned with frightening news: "We came to your brother Esau, and he is also heading toward you. He has 400 men with him." Ya'akov was terrified. He looked around and realized he had no army, no weapons, and was responsible for the welfare of a large number of women and children. He felt extremely vulnerable. Quickly he devised a plan and divided up the family into several hiding places, hoping that at least some of them would survive the possible onslaught. That night, with everyone tucked away safe and sound in a hiding place, Ya'akov hurried back across the River Yabok to retrieve the rest of his belongings, when he was suddenly attacked by someone. He struggled with this stranger, mustering all of his strength to deal with this sudden un-expected challenge.

According to some traditions, the "stranger" was none other than the angel of 'Esav (Midrash Bereisheet Rabbah 77:3), named Sama'el. He is also known as the Satan (Midrash Tanchuma, Vayish'lach, Chap. 8). Although angels are considered to be noncorporeal by many sages, this angel was clearly capa-ble of manifesting in the corporeal, as did the angels who visited Avraham. Ya'akov's whole struggle is symbolic of the spiritual struggle that every person ultimately goes through. Ya'akov was not struggling simply with something outside himself, but with the forces of evil within (yetzer hara) that were ac-tivated by the world outside of himself. In essence, this was the struggle of the power of light (yetzer tov—יצר טוב) versus the power of darkness (yetzer hara—יצר הרע).

VayYishlah points out something very important on the spiritual path: Good and evil are not separate, and the power of the Satan, as gevurah, is important for us to use for inspiring tikkun. When we overcome the satanic, demonic forces of temptation, accusation, and prosecution, we raise ourselves spiritually. This battle between Ya'akov and 'Esav's angel went on overnight, until dawn. For most everyone it is indeed a lifetime battle. In the kabbalistic teachings, during the period from midnight to the rising of the morning star (known as A'lot Ha'shakhar—עלות השחר), the energy is very strong, and this is the best time to meditate, because it connects us to zeir anpin (זעיר אנפין), or the central column. Zeir anpin is the sacred sun who, when fully awake, merges with malchut, the sacred female, making full enlightenment. It is also the energy of tiferet, which is beauty and full compassion. So after midnight toward sunrise, Ya'akov was being energized. In addition to the cycle of the day, he was also being energized by the power of light generated by the 248 positive mitzvot and the 365 negative mitzvot. When we follow these, we plug into the positive energetic grid of Yah. That is what gave Ya'akov the power to defeat the angel. There is a strong metaphysical-kabbalistic message here because the mitzvot, and our direct connection to the Divine, are truly our protection against the dark occult forces that are just as active today as in previous times. For people who are aware of these active dark forces in our personal life and on the planet, we derive the most potent protection from devotion to the Divine, generating light and love in all actions, and living by the mitzvot.

On another level, Ya'akov was wrestling with his own inner dark force along with the external dark forces represented by the angel, and he was winning as the dawn approached. In losing the battle, the angel touched him on the left sciatica. This is the place where negativities are stored and the place where the dark side can make deeper contact. In essence, not only was Ya'akov touched and tainted, but so were all his progeny. All of us have to accept this taint, but also know that we have the ability and power to overcome this taint. Having overcome the seat of evil, he did not destroy it. Rather, he sent it away. He released it. That is a significant statement because, at the same time, the angel *too* was transformed and was now ready, for the first time, to sing the praises of God (Midrash Bereisheet Rabbah 78:1).

This transformation of the darkness through our own internal transformation was part of what the struggle was about. When we look upon it as the darkness outside of ourselves, we understand that Ya'akov was willing to wrestle with the forces of evil because it was his divine mission to amplify his love for God and model for us the liberated awareness of God's oneness prior to duality. In this struggle, he had to overcome the duality within himself, rolling around in the dust of the earth. Ya'akov, as Yisra'el, had mastered Ya'akov's ladder because he was able to merge the heavens and the earth by living as the dance between the b'limah (the nothing) and the mah (the something).

There is another subtle piece to this story. Even though Ya'akov defeated the forces of evil, he was not unharmed. His left hip was dislocated, and this was the price he had to pay for victory. We have to understand that in dealing with the world of evil, often we do get "slimed." However, the result is complete victory in the form of unity consciousness as part of the path of deveikut/chey'rut (divine union/liberation).

The Torah repeatedly has our patriarchs and matriarchs going into the dark side (symbolized by Egypt) as a test to see if they are able to overcome it. Ya'akov's struggle was then an essential part of the spiritual path blazed by those who came before him. In this context we understand, as the kabbalah teaches us, that evil exists to elevate our consciousness by trying to defeat us and seduce us.

Interestingly enough, the angel in the end said, "Let me leave; dawn is breaking." Why did he say that? It is a very profound teaching about power and the dark side. He said, "I am an angel, and from the day I was created, my time to see the face of God did not arise until this moment" (Talmud Bav'li, Chulin 91b). In other words, Ya'akov's struggle within himself activated the holographic pattern of God's love within the angel. Now, the angel Sama'el was transformed into a different consciousness, so that he too could also sing God's praises. The subtle teaching here is that our work includes elevating the dark side, demons and all, back to God. This is not recommended work for just anyone, as it requires someone who is well trained, Torah observant, and a righteous hero of God. These prerequisites are vital before even thinking about entering into hand-to-hand combat with the physicalization of the dark side as Ya'akov did.

When we take this a little further, we discover in the ancient kabbalah that in the future, the name of the satanic angel will be changed from Sama'el (סמאל) to El (אל), which is a sacred divine name. The part of his name that is *sahm* (סמ) is his death-causing name, as *sahm* means poison. Yesha'yahu 25:8 says, "He will destroy death forever." It does not say "the angel of death," but only death itself; death shall be swallowed up, and there shall remain a holy angel. In other words, Sama'el, the angel of death, will remain and he will be called El, for he will transform into a holy angel, the quality of sahm removed from him (sixteenth-century Rabbi Yeshayahu ben Avraham in *Sh'lah, Toldot Adam, Bet Dovid*, No. 5).

Another tradition has it that his name will change from Sama'el to Sa'el (סאל). The numerical value, or gematria, for Sa'el is 91, which is the sum of the letters composing יהוה (Tetragrammaton, 26) and אדני (Adonai, 65). In this process, the angel becomes holy and takes its place among the other holy angels. This is the result of us holding the place of peace with the dark side, so that we can eventually transform the dark side into the light. It is part of the true struggle of what is happening today on the planetary level. It is important that Sa'el became holy after the struggle and wanted to act for the good of Yisra'el.

Before Ya'akov released the angel, he asked for a blessing. The angel then asked Ya'akov, "What's your name?"

Ya'akov answered, "Ya'akov."

There is limitation to this name, because it means "grasping at the heel of," which was the state in which he was born. But the struggle has been completed. In liberation there is no striving or "grasping." We just *are*. He was free of the heels that had been treading on him, because the energies of the angel of 'Esav had been corrected, and the angel now desired good for the people. And so he gave him the name Yisra'el, which means "who struggles with God." He said to Ya'akov, "You struggled with angels and mortals, and you won." The Hebrew word for struggle is *sar* (שׂר), which means "warrior."

The name of this parashah, VayYishlah, as noted, has to do with sending away, and on one level, it is relating to the awareness of the energy needed to let go of and "send away" the dark side within us. This includes negative people and situations with which we have surrounded ourselves, and which, in a certain way, reflect our inner darkness. It is primarily through the power of prayer that Ya'akov/Yisra'el was able to do this.

As part of the amelioration of the negative state of 'Esav, Ya'akov also offered a sacrifice to 'Esav. This is an important kabbalistic teaching, because we always must give something to the dark side, as we are honoring it. We give it its due, so that we will be left alone, distracting it so that we can be in control of the rest of our own energy. In this context, when Ya'akov defeated 'Esav's angel, and the angel said, "I want to go," Ya'akov persisted: "Wait, wait, it can't be as simple as that. Is it just that I defeat you, and, after suffering in pain and damage, all I get is my survival? That's not a great deal." So, he asked for a blessing. The blessing, in a sense, was not only that he and his ancestors would survive their enemies, but that there would be God's grace intervening in their lives. This is a very profound blessing that has sustained Am Yisrael throughout the generations. It goes beyond even being left alone by the dark side. The blessing that Ya'akov received is, of course, his name, but there was another part to that. He was asking that 'Esav's angel let go of his claim to the blessing that Yitzhak gave to Ya'akov. Through this defeat of the angel, and with the angel letting go of that desire for the blessing, 'Esav too was able to let go of the desire for the blessing, and that source of hate disappeared as 'Esav's angel gave up the subtle claim to the blessing.

This is a rather profound teaching. We see in this how the incredible hatred that 'Esav harbored toward Ya'akov underwent drastic change because his *angel's* spiritual essence had been transformed. And so, as we see later in the story, 'Esav was able to feel great mercy in his heart toward his brother and even kissed him when they met. This *is* a way that hatred becomes transformed. When we are in a state of love, our feeling-based prayer is one of love and peace, and we thereby activate the holographic pattern of love, peace, and compassion that extends from us. This is why it takes us beyond the focus on 'Esav's hatred, and brings us to mercy. The reverse of that principle demonstrates that when we bring judgment on others, it comes right back to us.

After he defeated the angel, Ya'akov called the place Peni'el (פניאל): "I have seen the Divine face to face, and my soul has withstood it" (Bereisheet 32:31). Sending away can also connote letting go or separating out. It is very interesting, when we understand this on a national level. Creating Am Yisrael requires separating from the world, just as Ya'akov/Yisra'el separated from his brother 'Esav after their friendly reunion. This meant separating from the whole world that 'Esav represented. In a sense, this parashah gives us the strength to be able to do just that. It is essential on the path of liberation that we do not hang around with and blend with the forces of the dark side, even if our egos are attracted to them. It is okay to touch, but not to blend. In the end we are all one, but we are not *at* the end yet, and one's spiritual development usually requires some protected germination time.

Another very important message in the awareness of liberation is the teaching of Bereisheet 2:18: "It is not good for man to be alone"—*lo tov he'yot ha'adam le'vado* (לא טוב היות האדם לבדו). This is important because even to *think* that you are alone is not a good thing. The Torah mentions that Ya'akov was alone when the angel jumped him. Bereisheet 32:25 says "And Ya'akov was left alone: and there wrestled a man with him until the breaking of the day" (*va'yivater Ya'akov levado va'ye'avek ish imo ad a'lot ha'shachar*—השחר ויבתר יעקב לבדו ויעבך איש עמו עד עלות). What made Ya'akov so vulnerable in that moment to the attack of the angel was that he experienced himself as alone. Even the consciousness of isolation means that one does not perceive the oneness of all we are. Ya'akov had to struggle with that separation consciousness, as dark side thinking. He had to struggle in that time with himself, trying to be someone he was not. In fact, he was *born* that way, holding the heel of his brother. But, in essence, that was not who he was. That birth of the twins shows the mingling of the good and the evil, as well as the existence of the dark side within oneself.

Ya'akov, in that time, as he struggled with the angel, was also struggling with his role in life. This was a continuation of the same struggle he had had when he received the blessing from Yitzhak. Was he Ya'akov, dwelling in the shekhinah tent of his mother, or had he become 'Esav, the wild man of the field? He started dreaming of angels and ladders and God, and he was on his way to higher understanding. And now, some twenty-two years later, after living in the house of Lavan, he had devolved into dreaming of sheep. He had to struggle again in his spiritual path with his own essence: Was that what life is about? Materialism? How many sheep did he have? Or was it about being one with God? How much was he in touch with his purpose when he left Lavan? That was a deeper part of the struggle here.

Ya'akov's sense of aloneness had to do with his lack of consciousness and remaining sense of separation. When he was given a new name, proving he was able to rise to the higher consciousness through the struggle with the darkness, he realized who he was meant to be, as Yisra'el, the people of Yisra'el, the oneness of Yisra'el, and the one soul of all the people. In the end, Ya'akov becomes Yisra'el, not 'Esav. He remained true to the spiritual light he was meant to be. Ya'akov's struggle is an essential struggle for most people today on the spiritual path. Are we able to stay true to who we are meant to be? That is what the struggle was and still is. On a national level, it represents a misunderstanding on the part of Am Yisrael, because Am Yisrael thinks it stands alone. When we think we are alone, we are Ya'akov, alone in the night, struggling in the consciousness of separation. When we realize we are one with *all* peoples, we become Am Yisrael, the people of Yisra'el. Hashem's promise to Ya'akov, "I will be with you," is always true. We are never alone because the spark of God is within all of us. It is that loyalty to the spark of God guiding us that allows us to become our sacred design, and not the design of Lavan or 'Esav. When we become the truth of who we are meant to be, as one with God and as our specific expression of God's will on this planet, we encourage all peoples to reach their full potential!

Going back to the historical beginning of this parashah (Bereisheet 32:4–6):

> Jacob sent messengers ahead of him to his brother Esau, to
> Edom's Field in the Seir area. He instructed them to deliver the
> following message: "To my lord Esau. Your humble servant Ja-
> cob says: I have been staying with Laban, and have delayed my
> return until now. I have acquired cattle, donkeys, sheep, slaves
> and slave-girls, and am now sending word to tell my lord, to gain
> favor in your eyes."

As mentioned earlier, these messengers were perhaps angels of light. When
Ya'akov reported to 'Esav that he had been staying with Lavan and had delayed
his return until now, he was saying that he had struggled with the dark side and
had defeated the dark side, and had become very powerful and wealthy as a result. He was not just saying "I'm coming on hands and knees to you." His meta-
communication was "Hey, I defeated Lavan, the heaviest black-art occultist in, at
least, the Middle East, and now I am ready to really deal with you." But he made
his message very gentle and humble: "I have acquired cattle, donkeys, sheep,
slaves and slave-girls, and am now sending word to tell my lord, to gain favor
in your eyes." In other words, he wanted harmony between him and his brother.

"The messengers returned to Jacob with the report: 'We came to your
brother Esau, and he is also heading toward you. He has 400 men with him.'"
There is a kabbalistic tradition that they were actually 400 evil angels. Ya'akov
was, of course, concerned when he heard this: "He divided the people accompanying him into two camps, along with the sheep, cattle and camels"
(Bereisheet 32:8–9). Later, it says, "I crossed the Jordan [ירדן] with [only] my
staff, and now I have enough for two camps" (Bereisheet 32:11). This tells us
of the complexity of what is going on. Contrary to the belief in many systems,
a central teaching on Ya'akov and 'Esav is that they were twins, born from the
same womb in the same hour. As is clearly stated in Yesha'yahu (45:7), "I form
the light, and create darkness; I make peace, and create evil; I, the Lord do all
these things." In other words, in the Torah tradition, good and evil both come
from the Divine. Both come from the same source—God.

Adding further complexity is the Torah teaching "As above, so below." The
Zohar points out that at the level of the heavens, the good is energized from

above by Metatron (מטטרון), and the evil is energized by Sama'el. This obviously implies a mysterious connection between these two angelic forces.
Evil energies are ultimately meant to elevate the people of light. They act as a
stimulus to elevate the righteous.

The only major physical difference between Ya'akov and 'Esav was that
Ya'akov had smooth and hairless skin, and 'Esav had hairy skin. The hair of
'Esav was a sign of extreme severity, of gevurah being out of balance. The
other difference was their voices. Yitzhak, the father of Ya'akov and 'Esav, was
therefore able to discern the hands of 'Esav and the voice of Ya'akov. On a metaphorical level, the hands of 'Esav represent the logical aspect of the intellect,
which sees the world as black and white in the context of Torah only as "law,"
and the voice of Ya'akov represents the intuitive, compassionate aspect of seeing life through the consciousness of zeir anpin or tiferet. Both are needed to
help us distinguish between good and evil.

The Torah guides us to choose good over evil, although God, manifesting
as life in the world, presents us with complex choices in which good and evil,
symbolized by the face of Ya'akov and the face of 'Esav, are hard to distinguish.
Unfortunately, we often choose the appearance of Ya'akov, when underneath
it is the face of 'Esav. This is why the Midrash related the mythos of 'Esav to
the pig more than any other animal (Midrash Vayik'ra Rabbah 13:5). The pig
appears kosher on the outside, having split hooves, but is not kosher on the
inside, lacking two stomachs. A key question in life is, "How do we distinguish which is which?"

This is made even more complicated, because the voice of 'Esav and the
hands of 'Esav can perform what look like good actions and speak what sound
like the right words. Often, the only way we can distinguish the difference is
our intuitive ability to tune into the kavanah, the intent, of a person. Another
clue is to be able to sense when a person is coming from an intellect detached
from the intuitive heart, symbolized as the voice of Ya'akov, the expression of
spiritual depth and deveikut (bonding with God). At another level of metaphor, when one has not first eaten at the Etz Chaim, then one cannot spiritually integrate the experience of the world of duality and the confusion that
comes from living in that world, for then one walks this world with only the
perspective of the detached intellect.

It is this disconnected intellect that causes so much confusion and lack of discrimination between good and evil in the world today. If we are not conscious as multidimensional beings, walking between the b'limah and the mah, Ya'akov's ladder never lands, and we fall off during our climb. When we are integrated, however, Ya'akov's ladder is where heaven and earth kiss. When Ya'akov's ladder touches both heaven and earth, we enter into a nondual state in which heart and mind become one. It is then that we are best able to make those necessary distinctions.

It is important to note that Ya'akov's response to 'Esav's approach, by dividing his camp, was not just a military strategy, but it helps us get in touch with the complexity of who Am Yisrael is. Before he was attacked by the angel, he was still called Ya'akov, and at this point he was (already) saying "I have become two camps," meaning "there are two of me." The name Ya'akov represents the physical nature, Elohim, and the name Yisra'el is about spirituality, miracles, and grace. As we see throughout the Torah, he alternated between the names. First there was a collective Etz Chaim-conscious aspect of Am Yisrael that really encompasses the physical and the emotional, the light and the dark, and the balance represented by what we call tiferet, or beauty. Tiferet also represents *emet* (אמת—truth).

What is this truth? It is the truth of God. It is being aligned with the expression of the will of God, being aligned with the absolute truth, the Ayn Sof (סוף אין). Ya'akov had four wives, but his chief wives, Rahel and Le'a, represent two key aspects: Le'a represents alma d'itkasia, the hidden transcendental world of binah, while Rahel represents alma d'itgalia, the revealed world of malchut, and sharing the teaching of the Torah with the entire world in the tradition of Avraham. Le'a represents the Yisra'el part, and Rahel represents the Ya'akov part. However, this dichotomy is not exactly a polarity. They go hand in hand—the spirit and body, the soul and body are all connected.

There are five levels of soul: (1) nefesh (נפש), the physical life force energy and body; (2) ruach (רוח), the emotional-heart life force (these two are considered the lower levels of the soul); (3) neshama (נשמה), the individual soul; (4) *chaya* (חיה), the oversoul; and (5) *yechida* (יחידה), the level of the soul that is hardwired to the realm of Ayn Sof (these last three are considered the higher levels of the soul). In all, they represent complex and corresponding aspects of Ya'akov and Yisra'el, of Am Yisrael, and of all humans.

Ya'akov divided his family into two camps to survive a possible negative outcome from his encounter with 'Esav, and yet, at the same time, he was also ready to claim his leadership and begin the nation of Am Yisrael, as was his destiny. On a prophetic level, the act of dividing his family into two camps was quite significant, because it was the story of Am Yisrael, and what Am Yisrael had to ultimately do in order to survive: play two roles. The first was the role of Avraham, seconded by Yitzhak, which was generally to take the name of God to all the peoples, but they never founded a nation. That was not their explicit role. Their work was to take the name of God to the world. Ya'akov's work was to create a nation, a distinct entity that would embody the name of God. That is why vayyishlah, "to send away," is the key word here. The two camps represent these two major functions. What is interesting is that Avram had his name changed one time to Avraham, and that was final. However, Ya'akov/Yisra'el was always going back and forth; sometimes he was called Yisra'el, and sometimes he was called Ya'akov. What does that mean? It means that *both* aspects had to keep expressing themselves in different ways. He had to be the father of the Jewish nation, and he also had to be spreading the light of God to all the nations. And so, to be the father of the Jewish nation, his name was Yisra'el, and for this he had to have the higher wisdom. But for the universal responsibility, the name remained Ya'akov. That is what makes Ya'akov so complex, whereas Avraham, one of the greatest, if not *the* greatest, person in our history, had a single purpose, so he did not have that complexity of merging the polarities. All of this is encrypted in Ya'akov's declaration of the two camps: the camp of Le'a, alma d'itkasia, which was to provide and create the nation of Yisra'el, and that of Rahel, alma d'itgalia, which was to go into the world.

Feeling vulnerable at the news of his brother's approach, Ya'akov called out to God (as if God needed reminding), "Rescue me from 'Esav." This may appear as a subtle contradiction, but it was also part of the consciousness, because he alternated his consciousness and awareness. He feared 'Esav, feared that he and all of his wives and children might be attacked. He said, "And you did say that 'I will surely do you good, and make your seed like the sand of the sea that cannot be numbered from the multitude.'" Basically he was say-ing: "God, I thought I'd remind you that you said everything was going to be okay." At this level of the teachings, we are reminded of the prophecy in Yermeyahu 31:11, that Ya'akov, and therefore Am Yisrael, would be delivered from a physical force stronger than they, and that they only needed to have faith. There is a teaching in Ya'akov's actions that we as a people will be de-livered by three things: (1) prayer and faith in Hashem; (2) giving an offering to the dark side to appease the negative energies; and (3) by warfare, as a last result. Some of the sages even criticize Ya'akov for sending messengers to alert 'Esav of his presence as he passed through the land of Edom to reach Yitzhak. The best move would have been to trust in God and in his sovereignty *under* God, and simply pass through Edom without fanfare.

His approach turned out okay in the end because he defeated 'Esav's angel, and touched his brother, but did not blend with his energy. As "the deeds of the ancestors influence those of the descendants," it certainly did not turn out well for the latter-day Hasmonean kings who entered into a covenant—thus touching *and* blending—with the Romans (descendants of 'Esav), which resulted in their inviting the Romans into Yisra'el for protection. Inviting the Romans resulted in the fall of the second Temple, the destruction of the Second Jewish Commonwealth, and the slaughter of an estimated one mil-lion Jews, thousands of whom were crucified for dissension. "There was not enough space for all the crosses," reported the first-century historian Jose-phus, "and not enough crosses for all the victims" (Josephus's *War of the Jews*, Book 5, Chap. 11, end of para. 11).

Part of Ya'akov's strategy with his brother was to give an offering to his brother, which was very shamanistic in the sense that we always give an of-fering to the dark side, so that it can be controlled. The Jewish people did this ritually in ancient times on Yom Kippur, when they offered a goat to Azaz'el (VayYiKra 16:8–11), which represents the other side (Zohar, Vol. 2, folio 184b). The dark side can be controlled. Its forces always require an of-fering; when we give a small piece, like we do with the *challah* for Shabbat, they are satisfied. You actually find this in other traditions as well—the point being that there are classic ways of handling the dark side in many ancient traditions.

When Ya'akov and 'Esav finally met face to face the day after the struggle with the angel, they embraced and kissed. And Ya'akov said to 'Esav, "After all, seeing your face is like seeing the face of the Divine, you have received me so favorably" (Bereisheet 33:10). This takes us into another understanding of this story: When we shift our consciousness, we shift how we see the world and how the world sees *us*. The world is as you see it; the world is as you believe it to be. This was also about ameliorating hatred, as both brothers shifted their perspectives of one another and came to see the light of God in each other.

There is a teaching from the second-century Rabbi Abba that although 'Esav hated his brother, he was overcome with mercy in that instant, and he truly greeted him with all his heart (Zohar, Vol. 1, folio 172a). This was because Ya'akov, in mastering the angel, had come to peace with his brother and could now love him with all his heart. Ya'akov was no longer judging his brother, and it created a space for his brother to let go of *his* judgment of him. The shift that took place is an important spiritual lesson.

This struggle has other dimensions to it. Prior to the encounter with 'Esav, Ya'akov, as we mentioned earlier, had been in the house of Lavan for twenty-two years and had begun to dream of sheep instead of a ladder ascending to God. He had been seriously distracted because of his wealth and his worries in relationship to Lavan and 'Esav. Before wrestling with the angel he was therefore not in balance, nor truly at the highest level of a vibrant soul. Ya'akov was struggling then with yetzer tov and yetzer hara. His core questions at the time were, "Who am I?" "What am I doing?" This is what most people struggle with. They have so much noise and distraction and soul pain in their life that they cannot experience the exquisite beauty of the inner experience of peace.

The common tendency is that if you have a little bit of pain in your soul, turn the music louder, eat more food, take some drugs and alcohol … so you can go numb. Painlessness or numbness is not happiness, because painlessness and numbness do not provide us with meaning. We have a deep longing within us for connection with God known as the t'shukat deveikut (דביקות תשוקת), the divine desire for the Divine. This was what was burning within Ya'akov, and what saved him as he struggled with himself as yetzer tov versus yetzer hara.

The more we live the mitzvot of the Torah Way, the more we live in alignment with love and the divine will, the more the t'shukat deveikut is activated and the more the divine alchemical process of spiritual transformation takes place so that we can be in full surrender to the Divine and awaken to deveikut/chey'rut. That is what gives us meaning, spiritual inspiration, and happiness in our lives. It is the great love, t'shukat deveikut, that Ya'akov had for God that empowered him to continue the struggle and not go numb. As the Talmud says, they made such a commotion that the dust ascended to the throne of glory itself (Talmud Bav'li, Chulin 91a). Ya'akov knew, through divine inspiration, that this struggle was required of him. He had to be willing to wrestle with the forces of evil in the outer world, but also within himself, as part of his personal struggle to wake up and know the One. He had to overcome the illusion of duality characteristic of alma d'peruda (עלמא דפרודא), the path we all have to walk. He was struggling for the sake of Am Yisrael and for the sake of God. We do have the option to stay in our comfort zones and dream about sheep, like Ya'akov. We have the option not to take any challenges into our lives and just stay comfortable and take care of our physical needs, but there is no spiritual evolution in that. There is no life in that. There is no deep inner peace, love, contentment, joy, and meaning in that. Whenever we are talking about evolution, divine evolution, we are driven by love, t'shukat deveikut, to face the challenges. It is love, the divine urge, that gives us the strength to face the challenges of our lives. This is the potential gift of the dark side: Like 'Esav, it inspires us into the light. That is an important message about the spiritual path. And the beauty of it all lies in Ya'akov's willingness to face the challenge of the struggle with evil and to become profoundly elevated by it.

Wrestling with his brother, Ya'akov had to think like a warrior, but he was not yet fully a warrior. His full identity was the complexity of Am Yisrael, the complexity of operating on all levels. His full identity, as a multidimensional being, was given to him in the vision of the ladder, where there are so many rungs in the ladder that his head was in the heavens and his feet were on the ground. When he woke up, he was awakened to his inner truth and greatness, and it was then that his profound identity became clear to him. Because of this, he understood that he needed to separate from his brother, who represents the energy of the dark side, but also has the face of God in him.

This encounter inspired Ya'akov to a higher experience of Hashem than ever before! In this process, Ya'akov realized that God was always with him, inside and outside, as an integral weave of which each person is a strand. He rediscovered his dream, he rediscovered his purpose, he rediscovered his divine mission, which was to create Am Yisrael and know deveikut/chey'rut. This is a great and powerful insight that he received through his struggle with his brother.

After he had struggled with the angel of his brother, he offered 'Esav gifts, which is part of how you placate the dark side. Esav said, "I have a lot" (*rov*—רוב).

Ya'akov replied, "I have *everything*" (*kol*—כל).

Ya'akov insisted 'Esav receive his gifts. What was really going on in this interchange was that 'Esav did not feel full. He may have had a lot, but he could always take more. That is the condition of people in the world today in the world of materialism, whereas Ya'akov was saying that he was no longer dreaming about sheep and possessions but felt content within himself. His response highlights the later teachings of Ben Zoma (second century), that a wealthy person is one who is completely happy with what he or she has (Mishnah, Avot 4:1), whereas 'Esav highlights the teaching of Solomon: "He who loves silver [material possessions] shall not be satisfied with silver" (Kohelet [Ecclesiastes] 5:9).

In the language of enlightenment, we are filled with the noncausal love, peace, bliss, oneness, compassion and contentment, and that inner contentment is part of what it means to be a liberated being. You are then so filled with the light of the Divine, so filled with these beautiful natural emotions, that you do not need anything. Ya'akov was speaking from this place, that he really did not need anything, as compared to someone who had a lot, but … well, would not mind having more.

VayYishlah is usually read during the month of Kislev, which is when Chanukah is. 'Esav's materialism represents the Jewish people who were attracted to the materialism of the Greeks in those days, versus the Jewish people who were inspired by the Hasmonean high priests to focus on God. The light of Chanukah is a symbol of the inner light, the light we experience when we realize that we *are* everything, and that we are complete within ourselves. This is the secret of those who choose to be in love with God and who are truly following the Great Torah Way of deveikut/chey'rut. In this awareness we understand that we have received everything in every moment, and we are always living in the joy of God. As King David put it: "For thou shalt eat the labour of thy hands: happy shalt thou be, and it shall be well with thee" (Tehillim 128:2).

There is a subtle teaching from Rabbe Nachman of Breslov, great-grandson of the Ba'al Shem Tov, which is fun and interesting. When the angel realized that he could not really defeat Ya'akov, he struck the "palm of his thigh." Commenting on this seemingly strange wording, Rebbe Nachman taught that when difficulties come to Am Yisrael, the solution is dancing and clapping of the hands—in other words, moving into the place of joy, because "palm" implies hand clapping and "thigh" implies dancing. When the angel struck Ya'akov on the sciatica, he weakened his defense by thwarting his capacity for joy. This gives us an idea of how the dark side often tries to neutralize our access to joy as symbolized by dancing and clapping. When we are joyous, the power of the dark side becomes minimized. Sadness and depression separate us from God, and joy helps us reconnect to God.

As Yisra'el, Ya'akov now moved about with a new level of consciousness. Having defeated the angel as "spirit of flesh and blood," he moved into a whole new consciousness of oneness with God. 'Esav, who now experienced the light of Yisra'el for the first time, was attracted to it and really wanted an ongoing relationship, but Ya'akov passed up the proposal because he knew he needed to separate from the dark side influence that 'Esav represented. After they separated, Ya'akov went to a place called Sukkot where he built spiritual homes, or *sukkot*. By waking up to the awareness that there is only God, and that within that consciousness we have complete wealth, we are able to let go of the dark side temptation of 'Esav's materialism. This in turn allows us to be *happy* with the lot in life that Hashem has assigned to each of us.

From these teachings we come to understand the next segment of this parashah pertaining to Ya'akov's experience in Shekhem, which is today called Nablus. What exactly occurred in Shekhem is questionable and highly controversial. The Torah tells us that Ya'akov's daughter Dinah went out to meet the women of Shekhem, when Shekhem himself (Shechem), the son of the local chieftain Hamor (Chamor), saw her and wanted her. What followed may be interpreted in various ways:

Leah's daughter Dinah, whom she had borne to Jacob, went out
to visit some of the local girls. She was seen by Shechem, son of
the chief of the region, Chamor the Hivite. He seduced her, slept
with her, and [then] raped her. Becoming deeply attached to
Jacob's daughter Dinah, he fell in love with the girl, and tried to
make up with her. Shechem said to his father Chamor, "Get me
this young girl as a wife."

(Bereisheet 34:1–4)

Jacob learned that his daughter Dinah had been defiled. His sons
were in the field with the livestock, and Jacob remained silent until they came home. Meanwhile, Shechem's father, Chamor, came
to Jacob to speak with him.

(Bereisheet 34:5–6)

When the sons came home, they were very upset. In the meantime, while they were seething with fury over what had happened
to their sister, Chamor came over to them and said: "My son
Shechem is deeply in love with your daughter. If you would, let
him marry her. Intermarry with us. You can give us your daughters, and we will give you ours. You will be able to live with us,
and the land will be open before you. Settle down, do business
here, and [the land] will become your property."

(Bereisheet 34:8–10)

Something intriguing was happening here. They were talking about intermarriage, a major issue in the Jewish world today. The sons of Ya'akov responded "with cunning," to make a deal with Hamor:

"We can't do that. Giving our sister to an uncircumcised man
would be a disgrace to us. The only way we can possibly agree is
if you will be like us and circumcise every male. Only then will
we give you our daughters and take your daughters for ourselves.

We will be able to live together with you and [both of us] will become a single nation."

(Bereisheet 34:14–16)

The implication was "you need to convert to Judaism." And so all the men of Shekhem agreed to do this. They were thinking about joining together with the clan of Ya'akov. However, their intent was not to join with Ya'akov out of a desire to adopt Yisra'el's spiritual path, but out of a desire for a share in the wealth that he was blessed with: "Won't their livestock, their possessions, and all their animals eventually be ours? Just let us agree to their condition and live with them" (Bereisheet 34:23). So everybody was thinking a little more politically than "Oh, we're converting to walk in the ways of God," although that is the symbolism of ritual circumcision.

On the third day following the people's collective circumcision, two of Dinah's brothers, Shim'on and Levi, singlehandedly attacked the whole town in revenge for the dishonor of their sister, because they believed that she had been raped. They slaughtered all the newly circumcised men who were now too weak to fight back.

On a metaphysical plane, we say that this was a cleansing of the self-centered judgment that characterized Shekhem. Nevertheless, it caused a lot of difficulty and it really makes people aware of a tension between Yisra'el and Ya'akov and between Ya'akov and his sons. What was that tension? The tension was somewhat connected to the roles that they played—the roles of alma d'itgalia and alma d'itkasia, which represent Ya'akov's dual role. His grandfather Avraham and his father Yitzhak were alma d'itgalia. Their role was to take the teachings of the Torah and of enlightenment to all the peoples. Ya'akov's role was meant to do that as well, but *also* to be the father specifically of the Jewish nation and thereby the awakening of all peoples.

The Torah is a blueprint for creating the Israeli nation, Am Yisrael, as well as a guidebook for deveikut/chey'rut. This inevitably created some tension. Ya'akov, in essence, divided those roles among his children. Alma d'itgalia was given to the children of Rahel, who was outgoing and reaching out to the world, and that manifested in Binyamin and Yosef (primarily Yosef). The other ten brothers, who represented the energy of Le'a, had to do with safeguarding the Torah within Am Yisrael. That was the tension between Yosef and his brothers that later manifested in Yosef being sold into slavery. It was also the tension that played out in Shim'on and Levi's attack on Shekhem, because they were alma d'itkasia, which has to do with the preservation of the sanctity of Israel. They were therefore opposed to intermarriage.

After the destruction of Shekhem, it was time to leave. Everyone in the surrounding area was terrified of these people because of how powerful they were. And Ya'akov knew he could not remain in the area, not after what had just happened. The nature of what happened to Shekhem revealed a split nature in the dynamics of Ya'akov's children. Ya'akov's son by Rahel, Yosef, understood the universality of the Torah, while his other sons were the keepers of national responsibility, guardians of the Torah. In the end, twenty-five years later, when it was time for Ya'akov to leave his body, he recounted with disappointment the actions of Shim'on and Levi, and the other brothers: "Let my soul not enter their plot; let my spirit not unite with their meeting ... for they have killed men with anger, maimed bulls with will. Cursed be their rage, for it is fierce, and their fury, for it is cruel" (Bereisheet 49:6–7). Yet he assigned them the task of upholding the Torah Way. The camps were there, the complexity was there, and there was a little tension brewing between the two camps. The key to resolving this tension was to have a broader understanding of this whole complex picture.

As he prepared to leave the region of Shekhem, Ya'akov had a vision: "God said to Jacob, 'Set out and go up to Beth El. Remain there and make an altar to [me], the God who appeared to you when you were fleeing from your brother Esau'" (Bereisheet 35:1). And so they all picked up and went. But some form of cleansing had to happen, and not just an outer cleansing. There is always an inner cleansing that needs to happen as well. In spite of the terror that had fallen on folks across the land, people still flocked to Ya'akov for the rich teachings that he brought. He had many followers. So he assembled them and asked them to surrender all of their idols and all the other things that reminded them of the life they left behind. Then he said to them: "Get rid of the idolatrous artifacts that you have. Purify yourselves and change your clothes" (Bereisheet 35:2). He demanded this even of his own people. He then buried all these items, representing idol worship, beneath an Ey'lah, a "goddess tree," situated in the region of Shekhem. Only after having cleansed his followers and his family did he lead them to Beth El, which was the Temple Mount, the site of his first vision. Once they reach Beth El, God appeared to Ya'akov and said: "'Your name is Jacob. But your name will not be only Jacob; you will also have Israel as a name.' [God thus] named him Israel." It is interesting to note here that the name Yisra'el (ישראל) is also the acronym for the names of the primary ancestors of Yisra'el: *yod* (י) for Ya'akov and Yitzhak; a *shin* (ש) for Sarah; *resh* (ר) for Rahel and Rivkah; *alef* (א) for Avraham; and *lamed* (ל) for Le'a.

Next, God said to him: "I am God Almighty. Be fruitful and increase. A nation and a community of nations will come into existence from you. Kings will be born from your loins. I will grant you the land that I gave to Abraham and Isaac. I will also give the land to your descendants who will follow you" (Bereisheet 35:11–12). The Torah then tells us that Ya'akov once again named the site of this vision Beth El, literally "house of God."

As they continued their journey, Rahel died in childbirth right near Bethlehem, and she was buried there, and Binyamin was born. Rahel was a beautiful and wonderful person on the physical plane. She represents the trials and tribulations of everyday life for most people. Life is not quite as we planned it, but is nevertheless a great adventure. After the passing of Rahel, who was his most favored wife, Ya'akov moved his bed into the tent of Rahel's handmaiden, Bilha, who was also one of his four wives, and mother to two of his sons. Reuven, the first son of Le'a, objected to this. We do not know if "he lay with her" literally, as it is told in the Torah. Quite possibly he may just seen Bilha in the nude when he went into her tent to fetch his father's bed and relocate it into his mother's tent. Regardless of what actually may have transpired, his action caused him to lose his birthright as the firstborn.

While Ya'akov was traveling, the Torah says that Rivkah's nurse died, but it was really a message that Rivkah had died. Ya'akov had not seen his mother since leaving home twenty-two years earlier. Yitzhak was too old and too blind to bury her, and according to the Midrash, the Hittites buried her. A spiritual message here is that Yitzhak had created such oneness with his neighbors that Rivkah's burial represents a testimonial to the unity consciousness created by alma d'itgalia. Ya'akov journeyed to Mamre, which was in Hebron, to visit his father Yitzhak, who was now 180 years old. Shortly thereafter, Yitzhak died, and 'Esav and Ya'akov buried him together. They had reached some kind of peace.

Then the Torah says "These are the generations of 'Esav" and lists the descendants of 'Esav. The question, of course, is why do we need to know who his descendants were as part of the Torah writ? This is because of the prophetic allusion to the future struggle between the descendants of the two brothers. Some of the descendants of 'Esav, through his son Edom, eventually became Rome, and so the struggle between Ya'akov and 'Esav, the Torah is warning, was destined to play out again. Rome almost destroyed all of Am Yisrael. The Roman empire represented all the different levels of negativity that exist, and the Torah is therefore giving us a heads-up. It is giving us a chance to identify this and immunize against it.

As we have seen, this is a very complex parashah; it represents the beginning of Am Yisrael, the split within Am Yisrael, and, more important, the divine struggle within *all* of us. Empowered by t'shukat deveikut, the divine urge, Ya'akov was able to overcome his dark side and become the enlightened being he was meant to be. May everyone be blessed with the empowerment to activate and win the struggle of Ya'akov with the light over the dark, and to become truly Yisra'el. May the victory of Yisra'el over the darkness, over the struggle with the dark angels, over each of our struggles with being a full human being, continuously happen so that we may become the enlightened divine beings we are meant to be.

Amen

VayYeshev

$\longrightarrow$

V<small>AY</small>Y<small>ESHEV</small> is a complicated parashah replete with many spiritual teachings for the unfolding of a person on the path of liberation. The first teaching involves Ya'akov's desire to settle down. He wanted to live a serene and peaceful life, but no sooner did he settle down than the tragic incident of Yosef and his brothers erupted. Ya'akov favored Yosef above all his other sons, and even wove a special coat of many colors for him. If that was not enough to kindle the flames of jealousy in the family, Yosef added fuel to the fire by sharing with his brothers his dreams. In these dreams, through various symbols, his brothers, and even his father and mother, bowed down to him, and he ruled over them. Having had enough of him, the brothers conspired to dispose of him, and Yosef ended up being sold into slavery in Egypt. To explain away his sudden absence, the brothers brought Ya'akov a bloodied strip of the colorful cloak he had gifted to Yosef and concocted a story about him being torn to shreds by wild animals.

So, just when Ya'akov thought he was retiring to live out his days in serenity, news of the tragic "death" of Yosef crashed into his plans, and the anguish at the loss of his favorite son kept him locked in grief for several decades. Righteous people want to live in serenity in this world, but the holy one, blessed be he, says to them, "Is it not enough that you will enjoy serenity in the world to come, but that you should want it in this world as well?" Yes, everyone would like serenity, but the message to the righteous is that we are never done; we cannot rest on our laurels. We must continue to struggle against the dark side within and without in order to arouse the heavenly mercy, so that all of Am Yisrael will be uplifted. This is a profound part of the message. One is never finished on the spiritual path even if one's teachers proclaim that person liberated; one is never done while in the physical body. To presume otherwise brings one into the ego of liberation, which can have a devolving or stagnating effect. A powerful attitude to have is that of Rebbe Nachman, who approached every new spiritual level as a beginner. One who is always beginning is never finishing, and that person thereby retains the joy and simple awe of the sephirah of hod (הוד—majesty) in encounters with the Divine throughout his or her life. This is a lot more fun than thinking you are someone or are somewhere.

A second lesson in this episode of Ya'akov's life is "you reap what you sow," or the Hebrew version of this: midah k'neged midah (מדה כנגד מדה—measure for measure). Ya'akov was deceived by his sons regarding Yosef, just as he had deceived his father Yitzhak, by dressing in the clothing of Gan Eden to receive the blessing intended for 'Esav. By bringing Yosef's blood-stained coat to him, his sons created an energetic rectification for his deceptive interaction with Yitzhak. Nor did the karmic consequences stop there. The ten brothers of Yosef, who were involved in his kidnapping, also reap from their actions, the ancient sages tell us, by being later reincarnated as the Ten Martyrs, great rabbis of the second century who were tortured, crucified, and burnt to death by the Romans (Midrash Mish'lei 1:19).

All of this is alluded to very subtly in the Torah, in one of only two places in the entire Torah where two dots appear over a single word. In this case, it is the word et (את), which is not exactly "the," but is a conjunction between the noun and its object. It indicates that the light (shekhinah) was present when Yosef's brothers decided to sell him. It was important that Yosef was sold into Egypt to prepare the way for Ya'akov and his family to go down into Egypt for an overall purification of Am Yisrael, so that they could receive the Torah upon leaving Egypt a few hundred years later.

On a surface level, this does not seem to make much sense. Ya'akov was punished for deceiving his father, in order to fulfill his mission of creating Am Yisrael, and Yosef and his brothers were punished by the apparent direct intervention of the angel Gabriel and the shekhinah energy (Zohar, Vol. 1, folio 184a) to bring Yosef and eventually all of Ya'akov's tribe down to Egypt, so they could be purified enough to receive the Torah. There is a powerful teaching: "Whatever God does is for the best, even though we do not understand it" (Talmud Bav'li, Berachot 60b). Moshe made this clear to us as well, in his swan song: "Hidden things may pertain to God our Lord, but that which has been revealed applies to us and our children forever. [We must therefore] keep all the words of this Torah" (Devarim 29:28). In this case, we can see the bigger picture from a historical perspective.

To reach higher levels of spiritual evolution there must be another level of purification, which in this case is exactly what is happening. Even though it may not be comfortable, we should appreciate the opportunity to burn up negative actions from the past in order to increase our spiritual evolutionary energy. It is important to see God in all that happens and not to become polarized by the drama occurring around us. This is what the sages meant when they said, "One ought to acknowledge divine blessing in bad situations as much as one in good situations" (Mishnah, Berachot 9:5).

Ya'akov's fourth son by Le'a, Yehuda (Judah), played a leading role in plotting Yosef's fate, but he did not escape retribution. He caused his father to lose a son, and in turn he lost two sons. His eldest son Er died after marrying a beautiful woman named Tamar, whom he abused by making love to her only for his own satisfaction, and refusing to grant her children for fear that she would no longer be as attractive. According to Hebrew familial law, if a man died childless, his wife automatically married the next brother in line for the purpose of establishing progeny on behalf of the deceased brother. Of course, if the widow did not wish to be married to the brother of her husband, or he did not want to be with her, either could be released from this process by a ritual known as *yee'vum* (יבום) (Devarim 25:5–10).

The next brother in line was Onen. Again, his only right to be intimate with Tamar was to give her children on behalf of his childless brother. Onen did not do this. He abused his right to be with Tamar by spilling his seed on the ground, thus using her for his own sexual pleasure alone. For this grave sin of sexual abuse of another person, he too died. Contrary to popular belief, then, the sin of Onen was not about "wasting seed," which is permitted by Jewish law in the course of mutually consensual lovemaking. Rather, his sin was about the blatant abuse of his sole purpose of being allowed intimacy with Tamar, and instead using her body for his own pleasure, alone (twelfth-century Rabbi Yeshayahu D'Itrani, *Tosefot Ri'd,* on Yevamot, folio 3b).

The next son in line to be automatically married to Tamar, under this ancient Levirate law, was Shela (Shiloh). But Yehuda was hesitant to risk the death of his third son at the hands of Tamar, whom he mistakenly presumed to be jinxed. So he said to Tamar, "Live as a widow in your father's house until my son Shelah is grown" (Bereisheet 38:11).

Shortly after Tamar was sent home, Yehuda's wife, Shu'a, died. Widowed and lonely, Yehuda was in the field burying his grief over so much loss by keeping busy shepherding his flocks. Then one day, while leading his sheep to greener pastures, he ended up near the village of Timnah, which was where Tamar lived. Tamar heard about this from her friends. She thought: "He is not letting me be with Shela because he is afraid of me. He thinks his sons died because of me. So he is never going to allow me to be with Shela." Tamar, the ancient rabbis tell us, had a prophetic vision that the messianic lineage would emerge through her and the line of Yehuda (Midrash Tanchuma, Vayyeshev, Chap. 17). So she was determined to have a child from Yehuda's loins one way or another, if not through his sons than through him directly. Hearing the news of Yehuda's approach to Timnah, she removed her widow's garb and adorned herself in the guise of a holy prostitute and loitered along the path leading into Timnah. Yehuda saw her as he approached the area. He was weary, lonely, needy, and asked her to be with him, not recognizing that she was his daughter-in-law.

"What will you give me in exchange?" she asked him.

He had no money with him, so he said, "I will send you some kid goats from my herd."

She said, "Okay, that will work if you give me some collateral to keep until you have some kid goats to pay me."

He asked, "What form of collateral do you wish?"

She said, "Your mantle, your signet ring, and your shepherd's crook."

It is no accident she asked for those items representative of Yehuda's leadership, symbols of future tribal rulers that would emerge from him, and eventually the messiah. He surrendered these items to her, and they made love. Unbeknownst to him, he impregnated Tamar; this was the line from which King David came, and eventually, perhaps in our own times, the messiah. Tamar was finally pregnant, and the messianic lineage, thwarted by Er and Onen, was freed up to continue its unfolding. Yehuda eventually married Tamar after everything was revealed, and acknowledged how wrong he was and how right she was. (Bereisheet 38:11–26).

The Zohar teaches that when a high soul enters the world, obstacles are put in the way by the dark side. Because King David came from this ancestral line, it went under the radar of the dark side, especially since this was the also the same lineage from whence the messiah will come. Thanks to the actions of Tamar, the dark side was at least temporarily outsmarted.

These are examples of how a spiritually evolved and enlightened person generally views his or her life. The view is that one is free, and that the scenario of the external world merely tests that realization in the internal world. This is part of the spiritual teaching of the story of Yosef. He was thrown into a pit with scorpions and poisonous serpents, which was a veritable death sentence. It was a miracle that he survived. He was sold into slavery to Potifar, the head of the pharaoh's guard. Yosef's role was to bring the message of God to the nations. He shared his holiness with the Egyptians and transformed Potifar's household and eventually the Egyptian nation altogether. But, in the process, he underwent many tests and trials. Potifar's wife tried to seduce him, but he withstood the temptation. With the passage of this test he moved from malchut to the higher world of yesod and became a tzaddik. Frustrated by his refusal to respond to her advances, Potifar's wife falsely accused Yosef of trying to seduce her, and he was thrown into jail for his righteous actions and further purified.

Yosef understood all was for the best and he held firmly to his spiritual awareness. He was the master of his situation. He was not a victim of his brothers, of Potifar's wife, or of being in prison. He became a holy man, and was recognized as such. He was the epitome of alma d'itgalia. His brothers disliked Yosef because he reported to his father, Ya'akov, their mistreatment of the animals and the sons of Bilhah and Zilhah (maidservants of Le'a and Rahel) as well as their infidelity with the local Kena'anite daughters. As such, Yosef represents the universal responsibility aspect of Am Yisrael, which was the work of Avraham, Yitzhak, Ya'akov, Rahel, and Yosef.

An important theme of this parashah is, therefore, the variance of Am Yisrael, the differences that manifested in the sons of Ya'akov, which would later play out through the evolution of different perspectives and practices within the one nation of Israel, each legitimate in its own right. These differences emanated from the differences in the spiritual dynamics of Le'a and Rahel. Le'a's sons (Yosef's paternal brothers) represent their mother's path of alma d'itkasia. Therefore, instead of seeing Yosef and his worldview as complementary to theirs, they saw it not only as different but opposed to theirs, and therefore as a threat, for which they felt it was okay halakhically to dispose of him. Unfortunately, this is the state of polarized reactive thinking that exists in Am Yisrael even today and in most of the world. It is unclear why this continues, as the Torah has sufficient wisdom for resolving such hurdles. What, then, is going on that we keep repeating the same mistakes our ancestors made rather than learning from them? 'Amos 2:6 states: "Thus says the Lord; For three transgressions of Yisra'el, I will turn away his punishment, but for the fourth I will not turn away his punishment: because they sold the righteous for silver, and the poor for a pair of shoes." The pair of shoes refers to the two different paths embodied by Yosef and his brothers, respectively, for the purpose of serving Am Yisrael as an expression of the shekhinah energy. The brothers sold Yosef because they were jealous, and he had a particular path different from theirs, which was to spread the Torah to all the nations, and in this case to Egypt.

Alma d'itkasia is the hidden world; alma d'itgalia is the visible world. Yosef's brothers represent alma d'itkasia in that their apparent negative actions were actually for the purpose of the preservation of Am Yisrael. That these two groups seemed to oppose each other suggests something else is going on. Until this time, Avraham, Yitzhak, and Ya'akov had been focused upon dissociation from the outer world and separation from dark and un-evolved forces. Avraham dissociated with his family, with Nimrod, and with the city of his birth. Yitzhak dissociated from Ishmael. Ya'akov dissociated from 'Esav. Each generation was characterized by a setting apart from the outer world of darkness, for the sake of God. Now it was time for berur (בירור), discerning or questioning about one's inner motivation and spiritual mission as part of, in this case, Am Yisrael. On a deeper level it was the act of self-inquiry and non-delusional clarification of the nature of reality in the Jewish path to enlightenment. Yosef was initially dissociated from his brothers, with both sets having some holy focus, as part of the inner understanding that within Am Yisrael spiritual people actually have different spiritual roles and missions. Yosef as alma d'itgalia had a role to bring the holy teachings to the world, which he did. Yosef had the strength that none of the others had, and this strength of alma d'itgalia helped him to thrive, where the others would have spiritually died. He saved his tribe, the Jewish people, because his understanding and attributes were the right ones for his mission, even though his brothers did not understand or validate their differences with him as being for the good of their tribes.

It is difficult to live successfully or evolve spiritually in this kind of polarity. Rather, it is spiritiually helpful to understand that each of us has a divine task in supporting the evolution of the light on the planet. Yosef was so strong in the power of netzach (נצח), the power of spiritual victory, that he was unaffected by all the influences surrounding him. He was tested by Potifar's wife, and was able to overcome his base desires. He maintained his holiness and is an example of what a true tzaddik is able to do. He did not experience a spiritual death of assimilation as many do when they go out into the world alone. Yosef's power was the presence of the Divine in his life, which, in turn, inspired all those whose lives he touched. Yosef also transformed Egypt on many levels. He changed the economic structure to care for the poor, introduced the purification of ritual circumcision, and generally brought Egypt to another level.

He remained who he was, whereas the sons of Le'a had other roles to play in the creation of Am Yisrael. One of these roles was creating the lineage of Yehuda, from whence came King David. In this parashah, Yehuda suggested selling Yosef into Egyptian slavery, and thus saved Yosef's life by suggesting the brothers sell him instead of murdering him. Later Yehuda became a great leader as he was transformed by his own life process and his interactions with Yosef. In this way Yehuda furthered the mission, even though he walked a different path than Yosef.

The oldest of Yosef's brothers by Le'a, Reuben, also played a role in rescuing Yosef, but he lacked the strength exercised by Yehuda. He had the idea of preventing Yosef's murder by throwing him into a pit so that he could rescue him later. Instead of returning in a timely manner to rescue Yosef, he "did the minimum" and did not return until after the brothers had sold him into slavery. Doing the minimum does not work on the spiritual path. One never knows when the extra effort will completely turn the situation around. The serious student on the spiritual path does not evolve by just getting by.

Yosef was aided in his mission, like his father Ya'akov, by being a ba'al chalomot (בעל חלומות), a master of dreams. Not only did he keep the overview that whatever God does is for the best, but he was informed and empowered by his dreams as to what was happening. These two levels of understanding helped him maintain an awakened perspective on the outer events of his life so that he did not become discouraged or depressed as his father Ya'akov had become. Even Ya'akov did not have the spiritual strength to hold perspective. When Yosef's bloodied coat was brought to him, he became depressed and was unable to prophesy for twenty-two years. He slept on the ground during this time because he was in such a state of separation from Hashem. From this we understand the devolving power of depression because it separates us from the Divine, and, as such, it is the power of Satan working on us. This is why in the Hasidic tradition, as well as in the teaching of the great Rambam, it is taught that we should do whatever healthy things possible to move out of a state of depression such as celebrate, dance, sing, and eat healthy food (Mishnah Torah, Hilchot De'ot, Chaps. 2 and 3).

Yosef's dreams were a great guidance. In the Talmudic tradition, dreams are considered one-sixtieth as strong as direct prophecy (Talmud Bav'li, Berachot 67b). In his first major and public dream, everyone in his family bowed down to him in the image of stars (brothers), and sun and moon (parents). In another dream his brothers bowed to him in the field, in the form of bushels of wheat. Kabbalistically, the field represents the holy field in which all Am Yisrael toils. When Yitzhak spoke to Ya'akov, he said, "See, my son's fragrance is like the perfume of a field blessed by God" (Bereisheet 27:27). That is the power of the field that Yosef had mastered. This is the field that spiritual awareness awakens us to.

However, there remained one important lesson for Yosef to learn about dreams: to be careful to whom one is sharing a dream, as the interpreters of the dream may create the reality of their interpretation (Midrash Eichah Rabbah 1:18). Moreover, we see what his brothers did to him in reaction to his sharing his dreams with them. Sometimes, the person with whom you share the contents of your dreams may resent or feel threatened by the dreams. One kabbalistic story makes this point clear: A person had a dream and went to twenty-two dream interpreters. Each one had a different interpretation and all the different interpretations came true.

While in prison, Yosef was asked to interpret the dreams of his cellmates, the pharaoh's butler and his baker. The butler dreamt that he was squeezing the juice out of some grapes into the pharaoh's goblet. The baker dreamt that he was carrying a basket of bread to the pharaoh and birds alighted upon his head and pecked at the bread. The grapes represented the building of the Temple. The bread represented the destruction of the Temple. The butler with the grapes was told he would be reinstated after three days, and the baker with the bread was told he would be killed. These interpretations came true, and Yosef asked the butler to remember him to the pharaoh for his divine ability. Because he asked the butler to do him this favor rather than having faith in God, Yosef spent two more years in prison, before the butler finally remembered to tell the pharaoh about him. This happened when the pharaoh had a series of prophetic dreams that none of his wizards were able to interpret.

The parashah ends with one clear integrated teaching. The spiritual path requires that we master our sexual and egocentric desires, be willing to go through our purifications with the understanding that they are spiritual gifts, and not let in the satanic energies of depression and discouragement that create a sense of separation from God. In this context, we never lose sight of our understanding of our mission from Hashem, which, as for Yosef, is our spiritual evolutionary path. With this understanding there is nothing to ever give up, as nothing is really happening (like a dream) except for our spiritual evolution back to the One. Our spiritual mission is part of this specific process, and the roles given uniquely to each one of us are for this purpose. It is important to respect, unlike Yosef's brothers, that we have different missions and roles as part of our particular evolutionary pattern. In this way, and with this understanding, we become like Yosef, our forefather, who was a master of yesod and netzach.

No matter how average we might feel, or how low our self-esteem, given these simple understandings and attitudes, each of us has the potential to become a tzaddik, like Yosef. It is through the teaching of m'aseh avot siman labanim that Yosef empowers us for our spiritual success. At the same time, we must be aware of, and be at peace with, the fact that there is never a vacation from the struggle against the dark side until we leave our bodies. My tzaddikim instructed me that I could never take a vacation until I leave the body, and that I must always uphold kedusha (holiness). The easy life that Ya'akov longed for was not an option for him either. The truth boils down to this: How can we take a vacation from service to God? Yosef's life becomes a model for us in this sense. We must manifest "our" dream, which is Hashem's inner direction to us, and to which we are given to attune as our sacred design, our holy gift, and never surrender to the trials and tribulations of the spiritual darkness. It is especially the responsibility of a spiritual teacher, to hold the light and certainty and inspiration so that we may face all trials and emerge as masters of our inner states. May we be inspired by the power of Yosef and all tzaddikim holding this certainty and inspiration as we move toward our destiny of deveikut.

Amen

Miketz

Tʜɪs parashah starts out with the deepest meaning, opening with: "Two full years passed. Then Pharaoh had a dream" (Bereisheet 41:1). Now, how does that create the deepest meaning? We need to understand what this "two full years passed" is all about. The end of two years of what? The Torah is referring to the two-year period prior to the pharaoh's prophetic dreams. Those two years are important, because they enabled a process by which Yosef would eventually be raised to the position of second to the pharaoh. It is deep because it reflects Yosef's journey into Mizrayim (מצרים)—Hebrew for Egypt. Yosef handled himself pretty well during his exile, except for this one occasion that some Torah sages posit cost him two more years of purification, when he depended on his cellmate rather than God, as discussed earlier. Otherwise, he had complete faith that God would take care of him. His tiny moment of lack of faith occurred when he asked the butler to put in a good word for him with the pharaoh. This action implied that he thought humans could take care of things outside the help of Hashem. This slight weakness of faith landed him two extra years of imprisonment.

The other side of this discussion is that faith should also be accompanied by faith-based action, as was evidenced at the Israelites' crossing of the Sea of Reeds, following their exodus from Egypt. According to the oral tradition, Moshe was unable to split the sea even with his use of the sacred seventy-two divine names. The sea did not respond until Nachshon, head of the tribe of Yehuda, dared to jump into the waters. He continued walking even as the water reached his nostrils and then it split (Midrash Bamid'bar Rabbah 13:5). As it is taught in the time of Pesach (Passover), the Hebrews needed to make the faith-based action of putting the blood of the passover lamb on their door sills and posts, so that the angel of death, who was given free rein against the firstborn, would pass over their homes. In this context, we might ask, was not Yosef's action of asking the butler also a faith-based action?

These are two wings of the bird: faith-based action and grace. It is quite possible that Yosef simply had two more years of purification, no matter *what* he did. The righteous walk on the razor's edge and have to live their lives by a higher standard. This is one of the keys to the whole meaning of deveikut. As the second-century sage Rabbi Simlai taught: "All the 613 mitzvot are condensed into one, as is written in the Book of the Prophet Habakkuk (2:4), 'The just person shall live by their faith'" (Talmud Bav'li, Makot 23b–24a). This teaching is also supported by the prophet 'Amos' teaching: "Seek me and you shall live" ('Amos 5:4). To be alive means to know God. To be fully awake in deveikut is to completely trust your whole life to God. It implies living as the complete general and personal expression of the divine will.

This intense, intimate trust and oneness with the Divine is very difficult to achieve for those who have been hurt in their lives by others. It is difficult for those who have had a damaged intimate relationship, difficult for those who have had a parent who abandoned them or hurt them, difficult for those who have had to listen to the priests or the rabbis tell them "This is the way it is" without having their own experience of the Divine in an intimate way, and, finally, difficult for those who have been simply told "Shut up and follow the rules." For those who have been hurt in relationships, to be at this level of intimacy that Habbakuk and Amos are talking about is extremely profound. The model of relationship we have with our parents, or other loved ones, has a strong affect on our ability to relate to the Divine. Fortunately, it is not the only factor affecting this relationship.

One is unable to live at this level of intimacy and still have an ego. In other words, we cannot know God and live as a separate ego. Often the people who have the most difficulty on the spiritual path are the ones who possess all the scholarly knowledge, know all the stories, know the Mishnah, know kabbalah, know the Torah, know the halakhah, ... but yet do not know God. To know God requires a deep surrender and trust. Ultimately, the only way one can have that surrender is to know there is nothing to surrender. This is why some rabbis communicate in the third person, including Rebbe Premishlander and Rebbe Zusha, because they did or do not see themselves as a separate entity. On a higher plane we do not exist as individuals, but only as a conscious emanation of God. In being separate, one is in the ego and, by definition, cannot be in the awareness of deveikut. And yet, at a different level, our face and the face of God are one, and we are the unique expression of the

Divine on the earth in our oneness. A good intellect can acquire knowledge *about* something, but what is lacking is the direct experience of knowing.

This is a very profound teaching for Yosef, because Yosef wanted to speed up the process. Our role is to work very hard, and wait for God to open that door in God's time, not ours. And of course, we have to know *when* that door is being opened. When we get too far ahead of that door being opened, because everybody says "It is more efficient, to do it this way" or "It is better to do it that way," we get an extra two years in jail. And thus we often have to keep relearning this lesson of Yosef and the teachings of Habakkuk and 'Amos, to just live by our trust in God.

One of the roles of the spiritual teacher is to help you get beyond the idea that you are doing it yourself, by the power of your own ego, by the power of your own practices. A living teacher allows one to understand and work out intimacy issues with a person who is awake and loving, and whose only desire is your elevation. Because there is so much distrust and ego in the world, it is very hard for people to be ready to have a living teacher.

There are different teachings out there about doing it on your own, doing it this way or that way, but there is a reason why God spoke to Avraham and exemplified the act of teaching. This is also why Avraham learned from the direct teaching of Shem and Eber, and why Yitzhak learned from Avraham and Sarah, and Ya'akov from Yitzhak and Rivkah, and why Yosef spent so much time with Ya'akov. In these examples, not only did the family relationship and spiritual relationship merge, but the blend forged the *kehila* (קהילה) of a living teacher, and a family of God emerged naturally. This sort of community helps people shift into that relationship of trust. We are not talking about an inauthentic surrender whereby you take on a teacher who you treat as a god; that is a form of idol worship. It is being in a trusting relationship, opening your heart to a person, as a practice for opening up to God. This is often needed to help transform a negative transference from dysfunctional parenting. It may not be possible to be liberated until your heart is opened up to God, and you see God in all people. When you are ready, the teacher will be there to help you open up your heart. This is very subtle, because at the same time, the teacher must be completely committed to the enlightenment of the student as a spiritual friend.

Unfortunately, the spiritual teacher-student relationship, as part of the spiritual path, has not only been abused in the East, but has also been abused by rabbis, priests, ministers, and gurus in a variety of ways. Nevertheless, it is still a profound way of helping people open themselves up to a personal, heart-centered relationship with the Divine. This requires surrender in general, and specific surrender to God's timing, as in the case of Yosef. We keep forgetting this and want things to happen on our own time schedule, but the truth is that everything is already happening, has already happened, and at the same time nothing has ever really happened.

Part of the issue is to know how much of an effort to make, and how much of an effort is enough. So the real effort is not necessarily the physical effort, but the subtle play of detaching from our belief that we will awaken through ego. It is only when we *transcend* the ego that we are able to see that blessings come not as a result of our actions, but blessings come from the creator by the creator's will. This is known as grace. And sometimes we just do not understand. One of the difficulties for the logical mind is the fact that spirituality does not only take place in the planes of time, space, form, and being, so it appears to be a little illogical. We are multidimensional beings who ultimately need to go beyond even our identity with being. Those who say, "That or this is not the way to grow" do not understand that there is a flow that is beyond their knowing. We do not have to understand this flow. We simply need to make an effort to be *aligned* with this flow. That is the best we can do. The more aligned we are with the flow, the more the blessings can flow to us and within us. As King Shlomo (Solomon) pointed out some three thousand years ago, it is about timing. "Everything has its time" (Ecclesiastes 3:1). In that process, we also have to understand who we are on a personal and heavenly level, and that we are unique in our process.

How different Yosef was from his brothers. His brothers who sent him down were from Le'a, and Le'a is the hidden reality. Our overall reality may be greatly influenced by the outer reality in the sense of taking on the habits of the outer world, so those committed to hidden reality need to work very hard to avoid the cultural influences of the outside world. When they caused the sale of Yosef, who was from Rahel, they thought that Yosef was going to go into spiritual oblivion. But it was just the opposite, because he was able to be in any cultural situation and survive. Remember, he came from the energy of Ya'akov as alma d'itgalia, the revealed world. His work was to influence the world, but not to be influenced *by* it. He knew how to touch, but not to blend. Even though he rose to become the second most powerful person in Egypt, just short of the pharaoh, he remained known as "the Hebrew" or "Jewish lad." This is a key thing to appreciate, that his brothers, who were in the lineage of Ya'akov's energy as alma d'itkasia, were not at that spiritual level of his lineage energy of alma d'itgalia, and so could not understand him.

At his elevation to viceroy of Egypt, Yosef was thirty-three years old. He was sold into slavery when he was seventeen, so he had been in Egypt about sixteen to seventeen years, and yet had managed to keep his integrity intact. The Egyptians knew him for who he was, "the young Hebrew lad," as Pharaoh's butler described him to the pharaoh.

What is evident here is that Yosef held tenaciously onto the mystical qualities and integrity of the attributes of his parents, and through these he was able to influence the world. In many ways, like his father and Rahel, he was exalted and guided by dreams, had mastered the occult arts, and was accompanied by angels. Yosef even *looked* like Ya'akov. He was also similar to his father in that his brothers were jealous and resentful of his status as functionally the firstborn and the carrier of the lineage, and so wanted to kill him, just like 'Esav had wanted to kill Ya'akov over the issue of the firstborn role. Furthermore, both Yosef and Ya'akov were wealthy on the physical plane. Both died in Egypt, and in both cases their bones were carried back to the land of Israel.

What is, again, remarkable about Yosef is that he was able to continually reflect that it was not he, but that it was God. His uncanny gift of interpreting dreams was by the power of the Divine, not by his personal skill. With so much power and fame placed in his lap, the temptation to presume that it was his own personal skill must have been overwhelming. When he interpreted the dream of the baker, he said this was God speaking. When he interpreted the dream of the pharaoh, he said God supplied the answer (Bereisheet 40:8 and 41:16). In this way, they were profoundly affected by the power of his interpretation. Pharaoh himself referred to Yosef as possessing the spirit of the Lord (Bereisheet 41:38). That really was a powerful acknowledgment, coming from a pharaoh and the idolatrous world in which he was living.

The eighteenth-century Rabbi Zusha, part of my rabbinic lineage, had a very interesting story that gives an insight into the way of Yosef. Rabbi Zusha envisioned he was about to die; when he went before the angels judging him, he thought: "I'm fine if they ask me why I wasn't like Avraham, Moshe, and others, because I wasn't supposed to be them. But I'm trembling, because what if they ask me why I wasn't like Zusha."

Each person has to be his or her unique self as the expression of Hashem. That is one of the teachings of Yosef's life. He was his authentic self and never tried to be an Egyptian. In foreign countries, people often want you to be like them, rather than be your truth, which is another key to relationships. It is the key to understanding Eros, or seeing inside the essence of people or situations and honoring and celebrating that essence with them. When you know that, then you are on the path to liberation because you are able to see everyone as a spark of the flame of the Divine.

The role of the teacher is to bring forth this spark. The way of the tzaddik is neither to repress one's own spark or that of anyone else. That is why Yosef was so respected by the Egyptians and the pharaoh, because he talked about God and he was just "this Jewish lad" in a land where people had low regard for his people. The term the Egyptians used for Yosef was *ivri* (Hebrew), meaning "boundary crosser." The deeper meaning of this term is the implication that the whole world is on one side, and Avraham and Yosef are on the other side, alone, opposing it. Not that there are really sides, but we are talking about the idea of one's expression. That is because Yosef came from alma d'itgalia, the revealed world, and the sons of Le'a, who could not imagine surviving in Egypt, came from alma d'itkasia, the hidden world.

Once we understand these profound enlightenment teachings, we realize the need for surrender; the need to know that we are but an emanation of God. Surrender means allowing that emanation to take place without holding any preconception or position of how it should be. This experience is enabled by and developed from our interaction with a tzaddik (a spiritual teacher), and is vital for working out issues of intimacy, fear, and pain, particularly when we have all the losses, misery, and control situations of abusive previous relationships. When we project them onto the spiritual teacher as part of healing those issues and wounds, we have the enhanced possibilty that we may get to a place where we can truly experience the Divine and teach from that place.

These lessons come to us at every level. When I was an American football player in college, I played on the starting team as a sophomore and did not really speak (for two years) to the coach. It was only when I became captain in my senior year that I would speak to the coach. This was not because I did not like the coach (I really respected and liked him), but because I had to be quiet and follow before I could lead or teach. In my experience with one of my tzaddikim, there was a big sign on the wall: "Those Who Want to Lead Must Learn to Follow." In order to wake up, you have to first surrender, and then God's grace touches you and puts you in a place of real spiritual leadership. These are very deep lessons, and very hard for people to get, because it means one needs to go beyond ego and need for control and to control others. It means one must go beyond the temptation to become an instant guru.

People talk a lot these days about how "we are all equal." We are, indeed, all equal. We are all great souls, and everybody has his or her role to play. In the context of different roles and different levels of awareness that we bring into the world of malchut, however, on another level we are *not* equal. When people theorize from the little knowledge they have absorbed from the world of atzilut (divine emanation) that "We are all equal, and we should all make decisions equally," they are misinterpreting what they have heard from that realm for their own egocentric needs in the world of assiyah (action). We indeed are multidimensional beings, and part of the spiritual evolutionary process is to learn how to walk between the b'limah and the mah. Yosef's brothers could not see this, and even Ya'akov himself could not see that they would all be bowing to Yosef, that Yosef's dreams were prophetic. We indeed are all equal on the higher planes, but on the physical plane we are given different roles that may not seem equal, but are roles given to us for our spiritual evolution.

Yosef became the tzaddik of the next generation. He was above his brothers as his dreams had prophesied. He was the carrier of the lineage of that time. One of his tasks was to create the space to save his family and prepare for their purification so they could receive the written Torah. Yosef explained this to his guilt-ridden brothers in the next parashah, when he revealed himself to them:

"Now don't worry or feel guilty because you sold me. Look! God has sent me ahead of you to save lives! There has been a famine in the area for two years, and for another five years there will be no plowing or harvest. God has sent me ahead of you to ensure that you survive in the land and to keep you alive through such extraordinary means. Now it is not you who sent me here, but God. He has made me Pharaoh's vizier, director of his entire government, and dictator of all Egypt."

(Bereisheet 45:5–8)

Yosef knew the big picture. Yosef knew he had to go through a certain amount of purification and surrender to his life circumstances. These incredible tests and tribulations prepared him spiritually for the next step. And then he slipped for a moment and got another two years in jail, just because he asked somebody to do him a favor, rather than trusting in God. These trials perhaps may seem harsh, but they are incredible teachings. Here he was at thirty-three, finally prepared. Pharaoh had the dreams, which Yosef, as the voice of God, interpreted. Pharaoh recognized Yosef's spiritual greatness and elevated him to second in command of all of Egypt. He was ready for this jump from jail to second in power over all of Egypt in a split moment.

With all the great sages of Egypt, why could no one could understand and interpret the pharaoh's dreams? How hard was it to interpret the meaning of a dream about seven fat cows being eaten by seven lean cows, or seven fat ears of corn being eaten by seven lean ones? Perhaps Hashem was creating blindness in them so that it would be Yosef who had the opportunity to do so. Moreover, we might note here that the River Nile was considered a god to the Egyptians back then. It was a source of agricultural wealth. For thousands of years, it overflowed its banks and allowed people to irrigate far and wide. That is how it became a god. For Yosef, the Hebrew, to now come and declare that the god the Nile was going to stop being their source should have been heretical. But for Yosef, it was just a powerful river, and he could see right through the issue. He was in a different paradigm. He knew that God was not nature, but that God was *in* nature. His interpretation was a direct teaching that there was only one God, and nature was just an emanation of that God, and would do whatever God "wants." "There is a higher power," he brazenly declared by his bold interpretation. This was the antithesis of the Egyptian way of life. This was why he could make such a radical interpretation.

A deeper teaching from this takes us back into the meaning of enlightenment and really the Jewish-kabbalistic teaching for the world. That teaching is that we are not limited to our lower nature. We are not limited to our horoscopes; not only that, it is our spiritual responsibility to be open to the possibility that we can transcend nature, because for liberation to take place we *must* transcend nature. This is a completely different and profound mindset in terms of the meaning of Yosef's life as his teachings.

As we go a little further, there is another piece to this. Later in the parashah, Yosef's brothers were sent to Egypt to get food. He recognized them, and they did not recognize him, partly because they could not imagine that he had not only survived, but that he was now second in command to the pharaoh! He gave them a really hard time, not because he was mean-spirited, but because he was their teacher, and he was trying to burn off the negative energy that they created by selling him into slavery, which in their mind was certain spiritual death. They were forced now to face difficulties such as being accused of espionage and then of theft, and put in jail for three days. They understood that it had to do with the way they had treated Yosef. They revealed, through Yosef's questioning, that they had a younger brother, Binyamin (Yosef's brother by Rahel). Yosef told them, "Don't come back here without your younger brother." They believed they were really in trouble. Yosef held Shimon hostage to guarantee their return. Shimon and Levi were very powerful together as just the two of them had destroyed Shekhem. Yosef did not want to let them be together for this reason, and imprisoned Shimon alone. When they returned with Binyamin, Yosef had a special meal for them with the table set according to their order of birth, which further confused and scared them about what was going on. They might have thought, "Who is this guy?" "And how does he know the chronological order of our ages?" Yosef further set them up by putting his divining cup in Binyamin's bag when they left. Then he sent out his warriors to capture Binyamin and accused his younger brother of stealing the cup. This created now a possible tikkun for Yehuda, who was the one who had suggested that they sell Yosef into slavery. Yehuda finally had to stand up and take action to defend his brother, which he had failed to do earlier for Yosef. He said, "Look, you can't take the young lad! It would kill his father, who has already lost another young son. Take me instead!" This was a significant scenario. This is what a spiritual teacher or tzaddik often does, creating situations that allow people to grow and wake up spiritually, and to face their dark side. When they understood what was going on, Reuven said to the brothers, "I told you so."

Yehuda's action is another great spiritual teaching. To do teshuva (תשובה— returning toward God) requires us to get to the source of why we did an evil action to begin with. It requires then changing our patterns or behavior so that the source of our evil action no longer exists. This is fundamental to the spiritual evolutionary path. There needs to be a tremendous kavanah, or intention to change from the heart. If he had truly had the kavanah of the heart behind his intention, and if honoring his father by protecting his brother had been strong enough at the time, he would not have allowed his brothers to throw Yosef into the pit. He would have stood up and would have pulled Yosef out of the pit and taken him home. It is not really *what* we do, but *how*, or the kavanah with which we do it.

In the Jewish tradition, we have our halakhah (הלכה), which people claim to be "the rules," but in a deeper way, it is "the walk," which is the literal translation of the word. It is the walk between the b'limah and the mah, between the something and the nothing. If we do not walk that chasm with a strong kavanah (spiritual intention) that in every moment we are choosing God, and that in every moment we are surrendering to the Divine, then we are not really doing the mitzvot properly. We do not draw the energy down from the heavens, which the mitzvot are designed to do. We do not get the transformation that comes with being *lived* by the mitzvot. Without this quality of kavanah, our prayers "are with broken wings," as the Ba'al Shem Tov put it. We are, then, not operating on the high and focused level that is needed. And if we are not doing this with great love, devotion, and surrender to the Divine, then it does not mean much. In fact, he taught, it may even work against us.

These powerful spiritual teachings all come out of this parashah. We see this whole scenario unfolding as such. It seems illogical until we see the whole picture. God filled Yosef's brother's hearts with jealousy, so that they sold him into slavery. Unbeknownst to them, this was happening with the blessings of the shekhinah herself! Next, God created a famine so that Ya'akov and his family had to migrate into Egypt. Meanwhile, Yosef had prepared the way, allowing everyone to survive the famine. In this powerful process, everyone was forced to spiritually evolve.

In overview, the healing and the resolution of the split among Ya'akov's sons happened by Yosef's surrender to God through his belief that "whatever God does is for the best." Added to this are the important ingredients of kavanah (the power of spiritual intention), teshuva (spiritual purification), and the supportive role of the tzaddik. All of this is very much part of the tradition of deveikut and are foundational elements given in the Torah as a path of deveikut/chey'rut. We cannot incorporate these qualities in our life walk if our egos are too big to surrender, to open up, to face the threat of intimacy, to unfold in the awareness that it is not us but God doing it all, and we are just the unfolding of it. It is therefore important for us to overcome our ego before we can even talk about deveikut and chey'rut. May everyone be blessed that we are able to walk the path of Yosef.

Amen

VayYigash

THIS parashah is about breaking out of the world of alma d'shikra (the world of illusion, known in modern terms as "the matrix"), and it is foundational for the path of enlightenment. When Yosef, in his role as viceroy of Egypt, had demanded that Binyamin be brought to him to prove the brothers' story, Ya'akov was reluctant to send him. He had already lost one of Rahel's sons to wild animals (or so he was led to believe), and he was being asked to risk losing yet another. Yehuda offered himself as collateral, as an arev (ערב) or guarantor for Binyamin, promising his father he would take full responsibility for the safety of Binyamin. He thus gave his word to his father to be a guarantor of Binyamin. This position meant that he was essentially feeling his oneness with Binyamin, and so Binyamin and Yehuda became arey'vim zeh b'zeh (בזה זה ערבים), bonded one within the other. This revealed a much deeper sense of unity and God-merging, and that is what vayyigash means—"to become closer." Of course, what we are really talking about is becoming closer to God. As the story unfolds, Yosef had set a trap as a test for his brothers, and as a way for them to make a tikkun. He even gave Binyamin five times more food and money than the others, but this time they did not become jealous. They had realized that they were all one and it did not matter. This scenario becomes the template for the fundamental Jewish principle of kol Yisra'el arey'vim zeh b'zeh (כל ישראל ערבים זה בזה)—"All Israelites are bonded one within the other" (Talmud Bav'li, Shavu'ot 39a).

Before sending the brothers back home, Yosef "sets up" Binyamin, as mentioned earlier, concealing his divining goblet inside Binyamin's richly gifted backpack, and before they could leave Egypt, they were overcome by Yosef's henchmen who brought them back so that Binyamin could be tried for his "crime." This is where parashah VayYigash begins. Yehuda was not going to let Binyamin be imprisoned, and "approached," taking a daring step toward the highest official of Egypt, who, unbeknownst to him, was Yosef. As he offered himself in the place of Binyamin, Yehuda was immersed in enlightened greatness. This was the beginning of his kingship lineage and his energy as the seed of the Davidic kingship lineage, which will ultimately lead to the emergence of the messiah. Yehuda's impassioned speech on behalf of his younger brother Binyamin showed Yosef that there had been a real healing and a shift in consciousness, not only in Yehuda, but most likely in all the brothers. His brazen protest demonstrated that they had made their way out of the alma d'shikra.

It also became clear that Yehuda had shifted from his sense of separation with the energy of alma d'itgalia represented by Binyamin, and had increased his love, respect, and oneness with his father. It was a shift from an unconscious, reactive, separation thinking, to a more conscious, *proactive*, oneness awareness. Yehuda finally merited becoming the royal lineage, because he understood the importance of this oneness. In the Jewish way, royalty is about the ability to create and experience unity. To become a king, wrote Maimonides, requires that "his heart is the heart of the entire community of Israel" (Mishnah Torah, Hilchot Melachim 3:6). That is how deep it is. And that was, of course, why Ya'akov was able to recognize and believe that Yehuda could be his guarantor, before agreeing to let Binyamin go to Egypt. Yehuda in this moment completed much of his tikkun for being the one who suggested Yosef be sold into slavery, and he became the forerunner of the lineage of Yisra'el's kings. He was transformed. In the unfolding of our spiritual path, we continually have these options. There is often the choice in life that either elevates us or separates us. All of us are given those choices. They have a profound effect on our unfolding.

Yehuda's love and understanding deeply touched Yosef's heart and in the process came close to him (vayyigash). Yosef was so moved that he could not help but reveal his true identity to his brothers. So in that moment when they were brought before Yosef, feeling completely trapped and separate from Hashem, the illusion of alma d'shikra disappeared, and they realized there was never any danger, and that Hashem was always with them. They received that powerful teaching of "whatever God does is for the best." On another level, "And Yehuda drew near to [Yosef]" suggests that Yehuda was now vibrating on a higher level, closer to that of Yosef's. What a change from twenty-two years before, when they threw him into a pit, and Yehuda came up with the idea of selling him into slavery. Then they had said they hated him (although "hate" basically translates as "no connection with"). Now, however, Yehuda and his brothers felt their oneness connection to their brother. This unity consciousness brought Yehuda and Binyamin as one. That is why the great prophet Achiya HaShiloni (who later became the spirit teacher of the Ba'al Shem Tov) was able to prophesy concerning both Yer'va'am, the future king of the northern ten tribes, and Rach'va'am, the future king of the one southern tribe (First Kings 11:29–36), because it was really about two tribes, Yehuda and Binyamin, becoming as one.

Having exposed his true identity, Yosef immediately asked "How's my father?" to emphasize his love for his father. Then he said to his brothers, seeing that they were completely overwhelmed: "Now, don't worry or feel guilty because you sold me. Look! God has sent me ahead of you to save lives!" (Bereisheet 45:5). So many revelations come from that statement alone; it is almost the whole portion in itself. It unravels the whole mystery of why Yosef had not contacted his father all along, at least to let him know that he was alive and well. From a deeper point of view, it would cause the unification too soon, and the process of tikkun for his brothers could not happen as it did. They had to get to a place of oneness first. They had to first transform themselves if they were to transform into a real unified nation. This was the flow that Yosef was tuned in to. He was a *merkavah* (מרכבה), a "chariot." What does it mean to be a chariot? Chariots are linked to the sephirot. Avraham, Yitzhak, and Ya'akov were linked to the middle three sephirot, and, at the same time, they lived in the world of malchut. That is what it means to be a chariot. The chariots connect zeir anpin and malchut (the upper realms and the lower realms) at the same time. So when the brothers sold Yosef, they were chariots at the level of malchut alone, or the twelve signs of the zodiac.

The bondage in Egypt, which resulted from Ya'akov bringing the tribe into Egypt, was a tikkun for the same people who caused the Great Flood in Noah's time, and those involved in building the Tower of Babel, as they were to be further purified to receive the Torah. The story continued with Yosef sending his brothers back to Kena'an to fetch his father. When Ya'akov heard that Yosef was alive, he went into a dead faint; it was hard for him to believe. The words of his sons and the gifts from Yosef, however, convinced him to go down to Mizrayim to reunite with his long-lost son.

Along his journey, Ya'akov prayed at Be'ersheva and, with the power of the Ruach HaKodesh, was restored by the joyful news:

> God spoke to Israel in a night vision, and said, "Jacob! Jacob!"
> "Yes," replied Jacob. God said, "I am the Omnipotent God of your
> father. Do not be afraid to go to Egypt, for it is there that I will
> make you into a great nation. I will go to Egypt with you, and
> I will also bring you back again. Joseph will place his hands on
> your eyes."
>
> (Bereisheet 46:2–4)

God addressed all of Ya'akov's concerns, including his hope that Yosef would be with him at the time of his death, and would carry him to be buried in the land of Yisra'el. A purification had to happen now for the people. They had to go into Egypt, into Mizrayim, and face the darkness and return. This was a test, and God was already guaranteeing that it was going to happen.

On another level of this prophetic oneness, we can see the deepening alignment of the energies of Le'a (the inner teachings and preservation of the Torah Way for Am Yisrael) and the responsibility to *share* the teaching with the world as symbolized by Rahel. Even though it is temporarily lost these days, this teaching, in the spirit of m'aseh avot siman labanim, has great meaning for the redemption of the world. What we see are the subtleties of how one can get lost in the separation consciousness of alma d'shikra. Each has their downside and upside. The world of Le'a, Yehuda, and the Levites is about guarding the sanctity of the Torah within the boundaries of the nation of Yisra'el, but they do not teach Torah to the world. They confine their efforts to spreading it within the Jewish mission alone, so it creates limitation and separation from the ultimate mission, which is creating the awareness of oneness with the *whole* world, not just with the Jewish people. The way of Yosef, on the other hand, is about sharing Torah with the world, but at the risk of getting lost or assimilated in the process. In fact, the prophet Hoshea prophesied that the tribe of Efrayim (descendants of Yosef) would be assimilated into the nations of the world (Hoshea 7:8). In the process of going out and sharing, one can be affected by all the nations. One must be spiritually strong like Yosef to succeed in this outreach to the nations.

Up until our own time, 5771 (2011) at this writing, two separate ways have been playing themselves out in subtle, but very clear and disrespectful struggles. Although the way of Yosef can bring a person to assimilation, nevertheless, at the same time, building those bridges helps bring the teachings of deveikut/chey'rut to all the peoples of the world. There is a danger in the way of Le'a's children, in that they do not share with the rest of the world, and therefore appear to limit the mission. The path of Yosef is to share with the world. The path of the Levites is to share only with the exclusive inner circle. In the long run this supports the inner strength of the mission of alma d'itgalia.

In the VayYigash story, Yosef and his brothers still walked these two divergent paths, yet the path of each complemented that of the other, and they became unified. This is a great teaching. Sometimes we must hold the energy and mission for both. We see this with Moshe as well. Moshe, born of the path of alma d'itkasia as a Levite, nevertheless fulfilled his mission to share the Torah with the world. He welcomed the non-Hebrews of Egypt to walk with Yisra'el and incorporated the laws of equality for them along the way. This is mentioned more than thirty-six times throughout the Torah: "The foreigner who becomes a proselyte must be exactly like one who is native born among you. You shall love him as [you love] yourself" (VayYiKra 19:33–34, Devarim 10:19, and elsewhere).

One of the most famous sharings was with Yitro, a Midianite high priest who was also Moshe's father-in-law. Moshe was able to draw Yitro closer to the Torah, share bread with him, pray with him, and offer sacrifices with him along with the elders of Yisra'el (Shemot 18:7–12). As mentioned in an earlier chapter, Yitro was one of three advisors (Balaam, Iyyov, and Yitro) to the pharaoh concerning what to do with the Hebrews and the exodus. Iyyov got the message of the exodus even before the Jews had left. Yitro got it when the Egyptians were destroyed at the crossing of the Sea of Reeds. And Balaam *never* got it because he was too attached to his ways as Lavan, an opponent of Ya'akov. Yitro later changed his name to Reu'el, meaning "friend of God." His "conversion" influenced much of the surrounding pagan culture and brought a major shift to the world.

Moshe held both teachings simultaneously because he realized the bigger mission of Am Yisrael, the vision that would later be articulated in the prophecy of Yesha'yahu: "... for my house shall be called a house of prayer for all peoples" (Yesha'yahu 56:7). In the story of Yosef and his brothers, then, we see the unfolding of the bigger, God-directed picture where there is finally going to be a unity in the two divergent modes of perception that comprise Yisra'el. There was a unity among all the brothers. This is what needs to occur again if Israel is to become whole and bring peace to the world.

Another example of this is Aharon, brother of Moshe, who was seen as an *ohev shalom* (אוהב שלום—lover of peace) and a *rodef shalom* (רודף שלום—pursuer of peace). Aharon saw the larger picture. This merging has to happen if there is to be world peace. It has to start in Israel, with Israel taking more responsibility for integrating her own society into a sense of oneness rather than separation. That, in itself, would bring a great healing for the world. And, of course, this is a task for all of us. It is not an easy task, but it is the task before us.

The pharaoh supported Yosef's tribe in coming down to Mizrayim. The tribe was offered land in the area of Goshen that was good for raising herds. As shepherds and herdsmen living in Goshen, they would maintain a way of life separate from that of mainstream Egyptian culture and society in general, with lots of time for hitbodedut (התבודדות—contemplation and/or meditation) to maintain the inner ways and commune with Hashem.

When the two segments of Yisra'el came together they were able support each other. In that moment in time, the twelve brothers became one, Le'a and Rahel became one, and the inner Torah (holding the sanctity of the Torah for Am Yisrael) and the outer Torah (sharing it with the world as a light onto the nations) coexisted in a very positive way. Aside from Moshe, very few people were able to really hold both of these energies simultaneously. What we see, then, is that the total mission depends on the sense of oneness that allows both functions to coexist and reach out to heal the world. In that way, we will be able to teach the world through example and influence through our actions.

Another important teaching of this parashah is the potential of people to heal. Before the brothers sold Yosef into slavery they did not consider the immense pain that their action would cause their father Ya'akov. In VayYigash we see how deeply sensitive and concerned they had become around their father's pain, and the lengths they were willing to go to protect him. When Ya'akov arrived in Egypt, he blessed the pharaoh, and he shared a complaint when he was asked how old he was. He said he was 130 years old, adding "The days of my life have been few and hard. I did not live as long as my fathers did during their pilgrimage through life" (Bereisheet 47:9). With that statement and lack of appreciation of what God had done for him, with not enough understanding that what God did was for the best, and not seeing the whole picture, he complained. For some inexplicable reason Ya'akov did not understand that every obstacle had been a chance to work on himself. That complaint cost him some years off his life. He only lived another seventeen years, to be 147, instead of 180. So he lost thirty-three years off his life. However, in these seventeen more years he may have become the full enlightened Yisra'el of perfect balance and beauty that he was destined to be, a process that perhaps began in Be'ersheva before going down to Egypt, when he declared "hineini"—"I am here!"

Yisra'el may have actually been the first person to "become sick," which is a clue to yet another teaching. The Midrash makes a point that the human aging process did not exist before Ya'akov (Otzar Midrashim, Rabbeynu Hakadosh, Keta 9). People just simply died. We can think about aging in a peaceful way, however, as a blessing, because it reminds us that time is moving on, and it reminds us of our death, and therefore of the importance of maintaining our health for empowering our spiritual work.

The Ba'al Shem Tov told a story of a father who wears a scary mask for his little son, and doesn't take it off until his son sees that it his father behind it. In a sense, that is really what we are talking about. We need to see that the power of God is behind all things, and truly, truly believe that. Yisra'el truly got that understanding in the last seventeen years of his life; he is described as ful-filled during this time. It is called being satisfied with what we are given, also known as noncausal contentment. It is an important understanding because the tzaddik may be gifted with a lot of difficulty in his life. These last seventeen years may symbolize his deveikut/chey'rut stabilization. The overall message here is: When we know our oneness, we see that whatever God does is for the best. In chey'rut (enlightenment) we begin to live openly and fully with-out resistance to life, embracing all that God brings to us for our evolution, grounded in that sense of oneness with all things and all people, so that we are able to hold and maintain our internal holiness—our kedusha.

There is a certain amount of awe in this process. That is important to keep in mind. The Talmudic sages say "Everything is in the hands of God, except awe of God" (Talmud Bav'li, Berachot 33b). Now, what does that mean? The word for awe is *yir'a* (יראה), which also translates as "we will see." Only when we are in awe of God are we really able to see. When we understand the beauty of God's plan unfolding, this is enough to keep us in deep awe. That is very much part of the path of enlightenment; the awe of seeing God behind all events and in all things. In the corresponding reading of the prophets that go with this parashah, the prophet Yehezqel (Ezekiel) is told by God:

> "... take the one stick, and write upon it, For Yehuda, and for
> the children of Yisra'el his companions: then take another stick
> and write upon it, For Yosef, the stick of Efrayim, and for all the
> house of Yisra'el his companions: and join them one to the other
> to make one stick; and they shall become one in thy hand."
>
> (Yehezqel 37:15–17)

This was already prophesied in the Torah in the story of Yosef and his brothers, that there will be a synthesis of the paths of Rahel and Le'a. It is something that has to be integrated within ourselves as well, as in our life in the world. This parashah empowers us in that overall process of deveikut/chey'rut, to move from an egocentric and ethnocentric perspective to a universal perspective, while at the same time honoring our roots.

At this time on the planet, the forces of enlightenment are requiring us to integrate within ourselves. May everyone be blessed with the overview of Yosef in bringing abundance, understanding, healing, and the ability to see the oneness with all people, and to transform ourselves from separation consciousness to the unity consciousness of enlightenment. May we, by example, share our holiness with the rest of the world. May all be blessed to maintain and build the internal kedusha, and in turn be able to share this holiness with the whole world.

Amen

Vayechi

PARASHAH Vayechi begins by telling us that Ya'akov lived in the land of Miz-rayim for seventeen years, and those seventeen years were years of vayechi (ויחי). The phrase "And he lived" means that during those years he became to-tally aligned with the cosmic flow and supernal joy—seventeen years of being alive, awake, and fully in the flow. These years brought him into a more steady awareness in the consciousness of chey'rut. It was with the hineini awareness of his response to Hashem at Be'ersheva before descending into Mizrayim. His focus was on the s'hma (listening) when he met Yosef, and became recon-nected to the joy of the oneness encrypted in the sh'ma. The power of that reconnection fully activated the sephirotic quality of tiferet (Yisra'el), linking it with yesod (Yosef), thus fulfilling both their roles in bringing the light of Hashem into the kingdom of malchut.

In the process of seeing the bigger picture, in knowing that "everything God does is for the best," Ya'akov was able to wake up to the awareness of noncausal, full peace, completion, contentment, oneness, compassion, joy, and love. The last seventeen years of his life were a gift to integrate in a field of fulfillment the stabilized state of chey'rut and deveikut, liberation and divine union. Yisra'el, who represents the deep inner truth, balance, and beauty of tiferet, was a full expression of Hashem for his tribe and for the world. It is said that he was second only to Moshe in the clarity of his level of prophecy and understanding. Why is it that Moshe and Ya'akov attained such high de-grees of prophetic powers when they were outside the land of Israel? Because of the purifying fire of adversity. Maintaining one's balance and proactive state is a true test of chey'rut.

Mizrayim is where the outer and the inner ego dominate. One must be in the place of *HaMakom* (המקום), the expression of God. It is to be imperturb-able in the midst of chaos. Egypt (symbolic of the ego) is synonymous with, and is the seed of, all future chaos. To master Egypt at this time was a sign of what all people must do to be in the awareness of chey'rut. Sometimes we feel we must have the most perfect conditions. Eating only 100 percent organic food, wearing wholly organic clothes, and living in a perfectly ecological house is, of course, okay, as long as we are in equal vision, and we are really not attached to those conditions. The tendency is to get an ego attachment with the idea of perfection, developing an egocentric-control consciousness, and that is where we get into trouble. Moshe and Ya'akov were in the most difficult of conditions, and they were able to attain higher awareness even there. So the deeper view, in essence, is to go beyond the limitations of the outer conditions. The story of the patriarchs and matriarchs is one of amazing perseverance, faith, desire for deveikut, and service of Hashem through the great mission of awakening their tribes and the whole planet.

Vayechi is interesting because it is also the sephirah of malchut of Bereisheet, and the book of Bereisheet, in essence, is the seed that gives energy to the whole Torah, for the whole year. All the other four books come out of Bereisheet. Those seventeen final years of Ya'akov's life represent the *tav* (ת), the last letter in the Hebraic aleph-bet system, and the great gift that comes out of this quality of living. In some sense we can say that Egypt represents the most intense negative intelligence. It is the full extent of the negative forty-nine gates, which only Avraham, Sarah, Yisra'el, Yosef, Moshe, Aharon, and Miriam could handle. In that process of handling and transcending the challenge, they were able to become so strong that they could overcome it. This involves overcoming suffering, pain, confusion, chaos, dark forces, and the illusion of life-threatening situations as perceived in alma d'shikra. Waking up to chey'rut is not a simple task and rarely do we get through it unslimed.

Ya'akov made Yosef take an oath to bury him in the Cave of Machpelah. There are different ways to interpret this. One is that Ya'akov had already been tricked once with Lavan and Rahel, and now he did not want to take any more chances. He knew that if Yosef took an oath, it would give him even more power in convincing the pharaoh to let him leave Egypt to bury Ya'akov. However, there was also a much different level being communicated. He was to be buried with his ancestors, but that is only one superficial view. The deeper view is that Yisra'el wanted to go beyond time and space, and stay in the consciousness of the enlightened ancestors, like Avraham and Yitzhak. The land, Israel, is symbolic of going beyond the ego, so in a sense, the ancestors lived at the source, and Ya'akov was helping Yosef return to that source. Not only was Ya'akov returning, but he was really supporting Yosef in returning to his own source and being the energy of that source. Sure enough, when Yosef breathed his last, he made the Israelites swear that they would take his bones with them when they returned to the ancestral homeland (Bereisheet 50:25), which they did (Shemot 13:19).

The oral tradition is very interesting because it says that 'Esav also attended the procession of Ya'akov's burial back in Canaan. A little fight broke out, and one brother's child, Chushim son of Dan, drew his sword and cut off 'Esav's head. And so they buried the head of 'Esav alongside Ya'akov (Midrash Pirkei De'Rebbe Eliezer, Chap. 38). Interestingly, it is 'Esav's head that merited burial in this sacred cave, not his body. The body had lived a life of violence and destruction in the physical world, while the head actually had a different consciousness, inspired by Rivkah and Yitzhak. So there was a kind of healing in the end, and we see that 'Esav was not really completely dark, and that even in the darkness, there was a point of light.

In the *Book of Chronicles* of Joseph ben Gorion and in the oral tradition, there is an additional story to the burial. It is said that Zepho, son of Eliphaz, who was the son of 'Esav, quarreled with Yosef and the other brothers about the burial. A battle broke out and the forces of Yosef prevailed. Zepho and his army were taken captive, and Zepho remained in prison until Yosef left his body. At that time, Zepho escaped to what we now know as Italy. He ruled over the Caetheans in Rome and ultimately became the first ruler over Rome.

The next teaching is the blessing of the sons. This is also interesting, because it was the fourth generation in a row where the youngest gets the nod to hold the lineage over the eldest. These four generations are: Yitzhak replacing Yishma'el, Ya'akov replacing 'Esav, Yosef replacing Reuven, and now Yosef's youngest son Efrayim replacing his eldest son Menashe. The message is that being born first, or into a spiritual family, or having certain psychic-spiritual sensitivities or natural spiritual abilities is not enough for spiritual victory, netzach (נצח), on the spiritual path. The key is kavanah (כונה—spiritual intention), perseverance, and t'shukat deveikut (תשוקת דביקות—longing for divine union).

In the immediate situation with Menashe, who was the eldest, Ya'akov saw, in advance, that his progeny would become idol worshippers, which indeed was the case. Yeraboam and Achav, future kings of the separatist northern tribes, would come from Efrayim, and Yehu from Menashe. Yehu would rid the land of Ba'al worship, but continue the idolatrous practices of his predecessor Yeraboam and worship the Golden Calf that had been reconstructed in the north (Second Melakhim 10:28–29). Ya'akov chose to bless Yosef's youngest son first because he saw from his third eye that the younger son would be on a higher spiritual level. This actually happened in all four of the generations. The patriarch, in each generation, had to make the choice of who could best carry the lineage, and in this case it was Efrayim rather than Menashe. Puzzled at his father switching blessings on his sons, Yosef really did not get the whole picture of what was going on. He tried to take Ya'akov's right hand and move it back to Menashe. From this comes the message that we should not judge things by their outer appearances (Mishnah, Avot 4:20), because, mostly, it is never what it seems.

Another spiritual lesson from this lineage is that on the spiritual path there is no such thing as protocol, and there is no guarantee that just because you are the oldest or been around the longest that somehow you have the right to be the carrier of the lineage. Spiritual transformation is not rote, and the spiritual teacher or tzaddik must be in tune with the immediate circumstances and the bigger picture. In any case, the sons of Yosef themselves were both able to truly hold the energy so that Efrayim being chosen was not a negative reflection on Menashe. They both were chosen, as it is said, "as Ya'akov's own sons." They replaced the tribe of Yosef. And Ya'akov said to Yosef, "Now, the two sons who were born to you in Egypt before I came here shall be considered as mine. Ephraim and Manasseh shall be just like Reuben and Simeon to me" (Bereisheet 48:5). This blessing is what is given to the children on Shabbat to this very day. The blessing that Jewish fathers give to their sons on the eve of Shabbat is "May Elohim consider you to be like Efrayim and Menashe." And mothers bless their daughters with "May Elohim consider you to be like Sarah, Rivkah, Rahel, and Le'a." The blessing particularly honors the actual fortitude of Efrayim and Menashe, who both maintained their Jewish identity in the land of Mizrayim and focused on chey'rut. Efrayim worked in service under Yosef and Menashe studied with Yisra'el. Each became a tzaddik in his own unique way. They became the tribes that replaced Yosef himself.

One of the powerful qualities inherent in Yosef's sons was that they never bowed to the pressures of their surrounding culture, and they retained the religious passion of their ancestral faith even against the background of Egyptian paganism. They were part of alma d'itgalia. They, like Yosef, were able to hold the energy. This is not the easiest thing, and this is why in Jewish circles, we bless children that they be like Efrayim and Menashe, for these two sons did not assimilate, go different ways, or become idol worshippers. Only the strongest are able to resist the temptation to be like the crowd. This is what is required for liberation; you often have to stand alone while living in the truth, and not get caught up in the glamour and superficiality of most peoples' lives. This blessing is about being able to stand strong and not be seduced by the unconscious, "comfort zone" energies of the masses. In that sense, those who can hold the energy of lekh lekha (return to the self) benefit from the deeper meaning of the blessing. Yosef also benefited by returning to the land of Israel to bury Yisra'el/Ya'akov. It helped him blend with the deveikut/chey'rut consciousness of the liberation of the ancestors. He received the direct energetic experience of his lineage.

As we look at this a little further, we get another insight, which is basically to understand that one cannot see the face of God and remain alive, as God informed Moshe (Shemot 33:20). We have to give up all of our ego-driven, comfort-seeking, people-pleasing, co-dependent behaviors, and become dead to the illusionary world (alma d'shikra) in order to be fully alive. This is the meaning behind the Jewish sages' puzzling response to a question posed to them by Alexander the Great.

Alexander of Macedonia asked the sages of Israel, "If one wishes to live, what should he do?"

They replied, "He should die."

He then asked, "And if one wishes to die, what should he do?"

They replied, "He should live" (Talmud Bav'li, Tammid 32a).

In order to receive these insights and see the face of God, we have to be at great inner peace. That is why Ya'akov could not really do this until he gave up his depression, and then he could truly be at that level.

One of the great stories that has been passed down concerns the eighteenth-century mystic Rabbi Elimelech (a direct lineage link in my rabbinic tradition).

One day several of his disciples came to him and asked, "What do you do when you are having a bad day, and things aren't going well?"

He said, "I don't know about that; go ask my brother Zusha." He then pointed toward a corner of the study hall where Rabbi Zusha was sitting with a broken table, with just one candle, and with one of his legs elevated because of an injury.

They approached him to ask: "What do you do when you have problems? How do you keep your head up?"

He replied: "You were sent to the wrong person. I don't have any problems."

In a sense, the only way to be at peace is to be really filled with peace and understand that the rest is all alma d'shikra.

Now, Ya'akov saw the whole future, but the Torah never revealed what exactly was going on, except that there would be times of bondage and that his tribe would one day leave Egypt for freedom. In his final hours, he blessed his sons. The first three did not exactly receive a blessing: Reuven was somewhat excluded because he disrespected his father's bed. Shimon and Levi were too judgmental, especially after their uncontrolled anger at Shekhem. If they had been more empowered through a blessing, the judgment of the world would have been overwhelming.

The blessings began with Yehuda, the fourth son. Yehuda became the forerunner of the lineage of King David, of the messianic energies, and of the restoration of the Tree of Life reality. "The scepter of royalty shall not depart from Yehuda forever," Ya'akov told him, although, as prophesied later by Hoshea, "They have set up kings, but not from me" (Hoshea 8:4). Zebulun was blessed with physical sustenance to support other people on the spiritual path. Issachar was called the donkey. Well, what does it mean to be a donkey? It means he was persistent and strong on his spiritual path. He was empowered to carry a great deal of weight in his service. Asher took on the energies of Aquarius in the zodiac and the ability to overcome chaos on the personal level. His daughter Serach was the wise woman who recognized and confirmed Moshe's legitimacy centuries later (Midrash Pirkei D'Rebbe Eliezer, Chap. 47), and she was one of the ten in this lineage who were taken up to the heavens alive (Talmud Bavli, Derech Eretz Zuta, Chap. 2). She stayed on earth at least 240 years. Naphtali was about speed and balance, as a hind (female deer) returning to the source. Yosef was empowered to be able to overcome the evil eye and other levels of darkness that would try to afflict Am Yisrael. He is described as a many-branched tree, planted beside a spring whose branches give off tens of thousands of Efrayim and thousands of Menashe. He became the feeder of the foundation stone of Israel.

Ya'akov gave a blessing to Manashshe and Efrayim in Bereisheet 48:16: "May He bless the lads, and let them carry my name, along with the names of my fathers, Abraham and Isaac. May they increase in the land like fish." How do Yosef and his children have immunity from the evil eye like fish? In the teachings of the Talmud Berachot 55b, it says: "Fish in the waters are concealed by the water and thus not susceptible to the evil eye. So too, the descendants of Yosef are not susceptible to the evil eye." The evil eye is associated with the energies created by jealousy, envy, and hatred. These pollute the environment and affect the health and wellbeing of the person at which they are directed. Like the fish, immune to the evil eye because they are in their own world, unconcerned about outer negative feedback, so the righteous, including Yosef and his sons, remain consistent with their inner truth of the oneness of God, though they lived in the outer and inner ego of Egypt, a foreign land full of temptations.

Yosef was able to stay strong in the midst of all these. Even as the Egyptian viceroy with incredible power, he was clear in his way of life, which put God at the center. He was clear in his enlightenment and faith, which made him aware that everything was the will and grace of God. None of them were caught in the world of alma d'shikra (the world of illusion). In that sense, Yosef was immune in the land as the fish is immune in the water. Yosef and his sons represent strong souls, whose self-esteem does not require them to seek the endorsement of the surrounding unawake population. They remained focused on the inner truth of Ayn Zulato, the oral Torah, and their way of righteousness, which made them immune to the evil eye.

This is a wonderful blessing to have, and, as we say on Shabbat to our children: "May everyone have the strength of Yosef, Efrayim, and Manashshe in leading a God-centered life. May all be blessed like these three that they do not fall to the koach hamidameh (the power of illusion)."

Ultimately Yisra'el's blessings to his sons was one collective positive, evolutionary blessing. Even after the blessings, the brothers still were not at the highest level of oneness. They made up a story of how Ya'akov said that Yosef should forgive them, because they started worrying about Yosef, rather than trusting in God's protection and Yosef's forgiveness. Yosef reassured them, saying, "Don't be afraid. Shall I then take God's place?" (Bereisheet 50:20).

Vayechi is a perfect ending to Bereisheet, because it is about being alive. Bereisheet is the seed of the path to the true aliveness of the Torah Way of deveikut/chey'rut. It gives us the fundamentals and guidelines of a 6,000-year-old path of enlightenment, which is the ultimate aliveness as the breath of God in all creation. May we all know these truths through our direct experience and steady being. May we all become living embodiments of Avraham's teaching as encrypted in the mystical Sefer Yetzirah, which is the truth beyond time, space, form, and beingness.

Amen

The
Book
of
Shemot

Shemot

T HIS particular parashah and book need a little introduction, as the title is mistranslated as "exodus" rather than "names," the literal meaning of the word shemot (שמות). Having a name was the next phase in the enlightenment process for Am Yisrael. This will be easier to understand with the following overview.

Parashah Shemot is the first parashah of the book Shemot. It begins in Shemot 1:1 with "These are the names of Israel's sons who came to Egypt...." The opening highlights the principle that the people's liberation from bondage correlates with the significance of one's individual name as a reflection of the face and name of God. Contrast this to the denigration of living in slavery, where one is numbered and nameless. Freedom from Mizrayim, which on the inner planes is a metaphor for the ego, is a symbolic part of this liberation process.

In the book of Shemot, not only do we receive the seventy-two names of God, but we also receive the power of the name of the highest sephirah, keter, as *Eheyeh* (אהיה) and also the God name, *Yod Heh Vav Heh* (י-ה-ו-ה), also known as the Tetragrammaton. This is very important information to have because, as the ancient rabbis taught, a prayer without mention of the divine name, without the heartfelt praise of God, does not have much power (Talmud Bav'li, 12a). What we need to appreciate here, again and again, is that the Torah is a manual for enlightenment. In this context, "these are the names" appears in the present tense, not in the past tense. Enlightenment in this tradition includes the divine presence in every moment. This is the present, holding the seed of the past.

Shemot as "names" also means that we are calling upon a tremendous lineage of powerful names. We start with Avraham, Yitzhak, Ya'akov, Yosef, Moshe, and David. In the first triangle of the *Mogen David*, a symbol of enlightenment and for the protection of the people, we are given the names of Avraham, Yitzhak, and Ya'akov. These first three make up the upper triangle, which cannot be touched by the satan. The lower triangle is represented by Yosef, Moshe, and Aharon. The word shemot, or "names," also refers to the souls and the names of the twelve tribes, who reincarnated again later to receive the Torah. This lineage of names is a lineage of great enlightened beings, great tzaddikim, who came to the planet to help awaken the people. When we call upon the ancestors, as we do in the *Amidah* prayer three times each day, we are opening up another level of energies for our prayers to be effective and for our path to be empowered. The book of Shemot also presents us for the very first time with the seventy-two names that are needed to draw the grace to free the people.

In freedom from physical slavery, we gain a personal name as we end our purification as nameless slaves. Our personal name and face are one and, ultimately, are the name of God. This transition is the next step in the enlightenment process. When we have a name and face we can stand before God in what is known as *Lifnei Hashem* (לפני השם—"in front of," or "in the *face* of"). The word "face" in the Torah tradition also implies perspective. It is said that there are seventy faces to God's revealed self (Sefer HaSh'lah, Mesechet Shavuot, Perek Torah Ohr, No. 2), and seventy faces to the Torah (Midrash Bamid'bar Rabbah 13:15–16), and for enlightenment, we would naturally embrace all of them as the full experience of the One. This is implied in the phrase "Do not have any other gods before me" (Shemot 20:3). Another way of translating this is "You shall have no other gods [projected] on my face." When there are infinite faces of God with seventy as the basic number, choosing only one face, name, or perspective is considered a subtle form of idolatry. Idolatry begins with an attempt to put a particular face or definition on God.

In the inner and ongoing experience of enlightenment, one becomes free to be the expression of God in any divinely directed way. In enlightenment we are free to move in any direction. There are no boundaries (*ayn lo gevul*—גבול לו אין) in our individualized expression of the Divine as the Divine moves through us, as long as we are *mekaven ratzon Hashem* (מכון רצון השם), meaning that we become the intention of the will of God as Moshe was throughout Shemot, and as was Pinchas in BeMidbar.

The enlightened one awakens to *partzuf shalem* (פרצוף שלם), the *full* face of God, as revealed in the created world and beyond. We then naturally begin living as the inspired expression of Yah in every moment. In this awareness, you (the individualized awakened "I am") join with Am Yisrael, Torah, and God in perfect oneness. It is an expression of the many and the One of the *sh'ma*. This enlightened way of understanding is also expressed in the Zohar: "Three realms are bound one within the other: The Holy Blessed One [God], Torah, and Israel" (Zohar, Vol. 3, folio 73a). As the Rambam expressed it, "All is a singularity" (Mishnah Torah, Hilchot Yesodei HaTorah 1:7). These seventy faces are but the appearance of the different faces of the one singularity.

The power of the name, as we move out of slavery, begins with having an individual ego name, but through a process of intense *berur* (בירור—disidentification with the ego by being lived in the Great Torah Way), one enters into post-berur awareness. In my experience, the post-berur consciousness means living as the cosmic emptiness, the bitul hayesh (ביטול היש), while simultaneously expressing God's will as synchronous with our individual will, resonating through our unique body/mind/I-am complex. At this level, the divine will, as keter, expresses as our individual face, name, and will.

Implicit in this is the Torah affirmation that every human shares a unique perspective, and it does not necessarily have to be an *enlightened* perspective. Having a name is a precondition for this enlightenment process to happen. Paradoxically, through one's unique face, one is able to embrace one's original face. This *original face* is the *many* faces of God. We do so by mystically letting go of our identification with our *unique* face (which I call the personality, actually a case of mistaken identity) and surrendering to the ayin (אין—nothing). Once we are no longer identified with our personality, we are able to know our unique face, or name, for the first time. What we discover is that it is the *Self* of *All* filtered through our given unique body/mind/I-am complex.

In the great Torah Way of enlightenment, this letting go of our identification with the ego, concurrent with an emphasis on the extreme depth of humility, is exemplified most obviously by Moshe (BeMidbar 12:3). The importance of lack of pride was also strongly emphasized as a key teaching of the Ba'al Shem Tov, a great enlightened and holy rabbi. The Great Torah Way, as the sages over the ages have practiced it, reinforces an enlightenment process based on intense pre-enlightenment spiritual practices. This is emphasized by midrashic stories of the ancient sages, who were said to have meditated and prayed three times a day for three hours, meditating both one hour before and one hour following an hour of prayer (Talmud Bav'li, Berachot 32b).

An example of this intensity was the inspiring and intense personal austerities, meditation, and prayer of the Arizal (sixteenth-century Rabbi Yitzhak Luria), who spent seven years on Elephantine Isle in the Nile meditating in solitude and focusing on the Divine before his enlightenment. Undoubtedly, these seven years, along with God's grace, enabled him to reveal the unique, elevated kabbalistic teachings he shared in the last three years of his life. The intense prayer, meditations, freezing mikveh (ritual bath), and fasting rites of the Ba'al Shem Tov, practiced for years before his enlightenment, are further examples of the intense purification and mind-quieting practices of our great enlightened sages. These rituals enabled them to quiet the mind and become egoically empty vessels, in order to receive the full light of the Divine, toward their enlightenment transformation.

In this purification process, we naturally, at some point, through an act of grace, experience t'shukat deveikut (divine yearning), which drives us more and more to experience the subjective nectar of deveikut (divine union) and ultimately *neshikat elohut* (divine kiss). In this unfolding, over time, the Divine, as the body/mind complex, progressively transforms into a vehicle of luminescent light. Ultimately it builds so much light that it shatters the delusion of the mind and thus helps us transcend the mind altogether. The great ones did not try to eat, talk, or technique their way to God in any way. They simply lived and were lived *by* the Great Torah Way.

They were thereby immersed in the divine emptiness and silence (*kol demama dakah*) where, through grace, they naturally became the unique individualized expression of the Divine. In this context, they are examples of the intense spiritual life necessary before naturally becoming the unique expression of the enlightened walk between the b'limah and the ma, the nothing and the something.

The enlightenment walk in this tradition is the PaRDeS walk, as multidimensional beings, simultaneously expressing in all four worlds from the *nothing* of the world of atzilut to the *something* of our unique expression in the world of assiyah. They, and we today, live fully established both in the ayin (nothing), while emoting as a unique personal expression in the *something*. In this fire of purification, we become identified with our true self, or core identity, as the flaming spark of God and as the Self of All, because we have awakened to the resonance of God both within and without. We become, then, the unbroken singularity, living and expressing, simultaneously and synchronously, in all the worlds, from the nondual to the dual. In this enlightened context, we do not lose our individualized awakened humanity, but in truth we gain it. We begin to live as fully awake humans on every level. We become identified with what the great mystic, Rav Avraham Yitzhak Kook (one of my inspirations, the first Chief Rabbi of Israel and a vegetarian), refers to as one's essential "I," or the "I" in "I am Adonai, your God." This is the greater and deeper meaning of Shemot. It all starts and ends with the name, as all of the Torah, as a guide to enlightenment, that comprises the name of God (Zohar, Vol. 3, folio 73a).

There is also a process in Shemot called teshuvah that is very much a theme throughout the eight portions of this book of the Torah. It highlights periods when the people are open to teshuvah, which means returning to God through correcting a past dysfunctional pattern by going to the source of the pattern and repairing it back to health. Shemot is a tunnel of transformation for Am Yisrael and even for Moshe, who reached the highest levels attainable by a human in this book. The best way to understand Shemot in this stage of Am Yisrael's evolution of consciousness is in terms of time as both a circular and a linear historical spiral on the path of deveikut/chey'rut.

The Arizal, in further refining and detailing the reincarnation teachings of the Zohar, offered an important perspective on the cycles of reincarnation in the rectification process of the erev rav. The Midrash teaches that when Kayin killed Hevel, Adam and Cha'vah in their grief separated from one another and entered into intense austerities for 130 years before reuniting to conceive Seth. During their time of separation Adam mated with female demonic energies and Cha'vah with male demonic energies through unclear circumstances (Midrash Bereisheet Rabbah 24:6). In a sense, Adam and Cha'vah thereby created hybrid offspring, who were simultaneously very evolved and deeply contaminated with dark-side energies. These offspring are said to be the ancestors of today's erev rav. As with the process of all humans, the Arizal taught that these energies had to be rectified, that is, transformed into pure light. This process of rectification continued for this group of souls at the time of the Great Flood. They reincarnated as a group during the time of the Tower of Babel to be rectified yet again. Generations later they were further purged at Sodom and Gomorrah. They incarnated again in the time of Yosef, when they joined Yosef's heritage, ritually circumcised themselves, and converted to his ways, as is written in Bereisheet 41:55: "Go to Joseph. Do whatever he tells you." They eventually became intermingled with the newly settling Hebrews as Yosef's brothers and their families, and lived as Am Yisrael. Their purging continued during their 210 years of intense suffering as slaves in Egypt alongside their indigenous Am Yisrael co-religionists. By the end of their slavery in Egypt, these direct descendants of Adam and Cha'vah were purified enough to receive the Torah alongside the indigenous Am Yisrael, and became known as the ey'rev rav (ערוב רב) mentioned in Shemot 12:38 as "a great mixture [of nationalities]" (Kuntrus Ha'Ari ahl Parashah Shemot, quoted in Sefer HaSh'lah, Torah Ohr, Sefer Shemot, Parashat Bo, No. 3). This may be why Moshe was not born until Yokheved reached the age of 130, corresponding to (and a tikkun for) the 130 years that Adam and Cha'vah mated with these demonic entities (Sefer HaSh'lah, Torah Ohr, Sefer Shemot, Parashat Bo, No. 2). The additional subtle message in this teaching is that everyone who sincerely chooses has the opportunity to be redeemed.

We have a teaching that comes from the second-century sage Nachum Ish Gam'zu: *Gam zu la tova* (גם זו לטובה), literally meaning "This too is for the good." Whatever God does is for the best. This was mentioned in Bereisheet as well. We can look with disbelief and pain at the sufferings of Am Yisrael, including during the periods of the Crusades, the Spanish Inquisition, and the Holocaust (in which at least seventy of my personal family members were murdered), not to mention the centuries of relentless pogroms and massacres between these periods of mayhem. They were all tragic times, and yet they also need to be appreciated as purifications. Moshe predicted such purification as the Holocaust before the people could re-enter Israel, if they did not follow the Torah Way, and he warned them that they would be kicked out of the land (VayYiKra 18:28). The Torah teaching is that purification precedes enlightenment and happens whether or not one is ready for deveikut. This gives us an overview of what is happening throughout Shemot and through-out the history of Am Yisrael, including today.

Freedom from Egypt was good, but it had the opportunity to manifest be-cause the people had been spiritually purified through their suffering. This rectification process continued on throughout Shemot, even long after their liberation from Mizrayim. It is said in the kabbalah (e.g., Sh'lah, Mesechet Pesachim, Drush Gimmel L'Shabbos HaGadol Sh'nofel B'parashat Metzo'ra, No. 36 and in Bi'ur Ha'Hagadah, No. 12) that Moshe was the incarnation of the soul of Hevel. According to the Arizal, there were three incarnations of the soul of Kayin, which went through three different types of rectifications with Moshe (Hevel) as part of Kayin's tikkun (תיקון), or repair. The first incarnation of Kayin was the Egyptian, whom Moshe found beating a Hebrew slave, and whom Moshe then slew with the name of God. The second incarnation was Yitro, the high priest of Midian, who rectified the conflict with Hevel twofold: (1) by giving back to Hevel (Moshe) his flock of sheep, and (2) by giving Hev-el his daughter Zippora in marriage since part of the conflict had been that Hevel was born with two twin sisters (the first humans married their siblings) and Kayin was born with only one, which made him even further jealous of Hevel, beyond the sacrifice issue. The final rectification occurred later when Korach (the third incarnation of Kayin) stood up to challenge Moshe. As a result of his attack on Moshe, the earth opened up and swallowed him and his supporters (BeMidbar 16:32). This was to rectify the fact that Hevel did not stand up against his brother Kayin. Here Hevel (as Moshe) stood up to Kayin (as Korach) and defeated him. These incarnations of Kayin were somewhat rectified during this time. The power of the name and the purification of the people were thus happening continually. Slavery, as we know it today, is about the mind, not the body. Many people are enslaved in the metaphorical matrix of modern civilization and culture. Shemot is a direct guidance of how to break out of that matrix.

As we enter into the background story of Shemot, we read about a major shift in the consciousness of Egypt, which had been a haven to the Hebrews from the time of Yosef. Owing to Yosef, "the Hebrew," its survival during a severe seven-year famine, Egypt's leadership now does a complete turnabout:

> A new king, who did not know of Joseph, came into power over
> Egypt. He announced to his people, "The Israelites are becoming
> too numerous and strong for us. We must deal wisely with them.
> Otherwise, they may increase so much, that if there is war, they
> will join our enemies and fight against us, driving [us] from the
> land."
>
> (Shemot 1:8–10)

An entirely new regime had come to power that strove to regain its sense
of nationalism and Egyptian pride. The pharaoh "forgot" about Yosef and the
gifts he had brought to make Mizrayim the great and powerful state it now
was. This scenario would be repeated throughout the history of Am Yisrael,
as nations would benefit from the contributions of the Jews, and then con-
veniently write them out of their history (not to mention persecute them
and expel them). We cannot ignore the fact that the dearth of physical and
documentary evidence concerning the contributions of the Am Yisrael to our
civilization came about not as a consequence of natural erosion, but because
time and time again the records of the Jewish experience were deliberately
discarded and the very evidence of their existence destroyed by human agen-
cies (see Samuel Kurinsky, *The Glassmakers: An Odyssey of the Jews—The First
Three Thousand Years,* pp. xxii–xxiii). This is grossly typified by the Holocaust
denial syndrome and the attempts to actively undermine any archeological
findings that validate the historical existence of Am Yisrael living in Eretz
Israel, in an unbroken presence, for 3,700 years (except for the 210 years of
slavery in Egypt, approximately 3,300 years ago). Instead of seeing Am Yisrael
as an ally, the new regime saw them as a threat. Gratitude is very important
on the spiritual path. The pharaoh's lack of gratitude eventually resulted in the
destruction and humbling of the great nation of Egypt. It is always good to
be humble and grateful for all that we have been given. Everything is for our
personal elevation toward the Divine.

The pharaoh was informed by his astrologers that a boy child would be born
who would defeat him and redeem the slaves. To prevent this from happening, he instructed two midwives, Shifra (who was actually Yokheved, Moshe's
mother) and Pu'a (who might have been Miriam, Moshe's sister) (Midrash

Kohelet Rabbah 7:3), to put to death any newborn male they delivered. Of course, the midwives disobeyed and instead aided and abetted the rescue and survival of the newborns they delivered, offering one excuse or another to the pharaoh (Shemot 1:18–19). Desperate, the pharaoh commanded his people to throw all male babies into the Nile. This included Egyptian babes, since it was not known whether the redeemer of the Hebrews would be an Israelite or an Egyptian (Midrash Shemot Rabbah 1:41).

When Pharaoh's decree was issued, 'Amram and Yokheved, Moshe's parents, decided to separate and all of the Israelites followed their example, because they feared bringing children into the world only to have them thrown into the river. Their daughter Miriam, a young prophetess, however, chastised them for this decision: "Your action is far worse than that of the pharaoh. For the pharaoh's decree affects the males while your example will affect both males and females alike!" 'Amram, a leading figure among the Hebrews, accepted Miriam's admonishment and restored intimacy with his wife Yokheved, and all of the Hebrews followed suit (Midrash Shemot Rabbah 1:13).

Yokheved was also 'Amram's aunt, so it was not a completely kosher marriage. Nonetheless, the rules were different prior to the receiving of the Torah at Mount Sinai (Midrash Bereisheet Rabbah 18:5), and their marriage served to protect Moshe from satanic energies in the same way as Yehuda, who mated with his daughter-in-law Tamar, created thereby the Davidic and messianic lineage. It is taught in the mystical tradition that these "low" births avoid the destructive eye of Satan. 'Amram, according to the mystic midrashic tradition, was the reincarnation of Adam. At the age of 130 (symbolic of the amount of time Adam and Cha'vah had spent apart before conceiving Shet), Yokheved (the reincarnation of Cha'vah) conceived and birthed Moshe (the reincarnation of Hevel). Yokheved was not initially the incarnation of Cha'vah until she was spiritually ready at 130 years (Sefer HaSh'lah, Mesechet Pesachim, Perek Torah Ohr, No. 12). In mystical kabbalah, a soul may enter a person at any age to complete its spiritual mission and does not harm that person in the process. Midrash tells us that Miriam, the daughter of Yokheved, prophesied at four years old, "My mother is destined to bear a son who will deliver Israel" (Midrash Shemot Rabbah 1:22). It is also taught that Yokheved regained her youthfulness at 130 years old and had an early delivery. She was able to nurse Moshe an additional three months, which further delayed his discovery by the pharaoh's men (Midrash Shemot Rabbah 1:20). Moshe was put into the water at three months old. Miriam was five years older than he was, and watched the basket until the pharaoh's daughter Batya discovered it. Batya rescued Moshe from the Nile. It is said that Batya became a disciple of Moshe's and actually left Mizrayim with the Israelites. It is said that she was one of the ten people known in this tradition to have been taken up into heaven while yet living (Talmud Bav'li, Kalah Rabbati, Chap. 3 toward end).

The different midrashim say that baby Moshe would only nurse from his Hebrew birth mother Yokheved and not from any of the Egyptian nursemaids (Otzar HaMidrashin, Moshe, Keta Dalet). Miriam approached Batya and told her of a good nursemaid to care for him and was able to arrange that Moshe's biological mother, Yokheved, could nurse him. Having been nursed and weaned by his Hebrew birth mother, Moshe understood that he was really Jewish, though raised by the pharaoh's daughter. Not unlike in the Buddha story, he grew up sheltered in the palace until one day, at age forty, he decided to leave and observe the "outside world." He noticed an Egyptian severely beating a Hebrew and reacted by slaying the Egyptian. He possibly already knew the seventy-two names of God and killed the Egyptian using a specific combination of these names. The next day, he came upon two Hebrew men quarreling, and when he attempted to intervene, they turned and accused him of hypocrisy. In Shemot 2:14 one of them said, "Who made you our prince and judge? Do you mean to kill me as you killed the Egyptian?" Moshe was frightened. "The incident is known," he said. The word of the slain Egyptian taskmaster reached the pharaoh, who now suspected that his daughter's foster child was the very redeemer of the Hebrews he had feared years earlier. He ordered Moshe captured and executed. They tried to kill him, but were unsuccessful. Moshe fled to Midian (northwest region of modern Saudi Arabia), where he lived in exile.

It is taught in the oral tradition that prior to his arrival in Midian, Moshe first fled southward to Kush (today's Ethiopia), where he ended up helping Kushite warriors retake their capital city, which had been seized by Balaam, the black magician. After he defeated Balaam and the warriors were reunited with their families, he was elected chief of the Kushites, married the queen of

Ethiopia, and lived there for forty years. Eventually, he left and journeyed to the land of the Midianites. There, he noticed that the shepherds were harassing the seven daughters of the high priest of Midian. He came to the daughters' defense, and they took him home. The high priest of Midian recognized Moshe as a high being and gave him his daughter, Zippora, to marry. The high priest of Midian was Yitro (Reu'el) a great being who at one point was consultant to the pharaoh. Moshe decided to live with Yitro's clan and to marry Zippora. They had a son and named him Gershom, which means "stranger there." Moshe said, "For I have been a stranger in a strange land."

According to the Midrash, there was a great ancient staff embedded in the earth of Yitro's garden that no one could pull from the earth. The staff had the forty-two-letter name of God on one side and the seventy-two-letter name of God on the other side. Moshe was told that in order to marry Zippora he must pull the staff from the earth. Moshe was easily able to pull the staff from the earth and thus proved his spiritual quality (Otzar HaMidrashim, Moshe, Keta 6–7). This part of the Midrash possibly inspired the King Arthur story.

It is taught that Moshe led his flock far away into the desert, and that he came to what the ancients called the Mountain of God (*Horev*—חורב). There, Moshe experienced his mystical vision at a burning *s'neh*, or thorn bush, that grew in the sacred mountain of Elohim (Shemot 3:1, 18:5, 24:13).

Many feel that this mountain exists on the Sinai Peninsula, while a few others insist that it is located in the original Midianite region in what is today Saudi Arabia. It is presently completely fenced off by the Saudi government and inaccessible to the public. Obviously, to identify the real Mountain of God, which would further validate the exodus story, is not of interest to the Saudi government, because it would further legitimize the historical reality of Am Yisrael and the revelations of the Torah. Few have claimed to have actually visited either location. Why is this important? Why should we care? From a shamanic, energetic, magical kabbalistic, and historical lineage perspective, there are few things, if any, that are more important than finding the actual site where the direct transmission from God to Am Yisrael took place. This is the site where the Ten Commandments and the Torah were energetically transmitted and received by three million people. Native Americans, indigenous peoples from around the world, and many mystical Jewish people know that the one who controls these ancestral sites, such as the real Har Sinay and the Cave of Machpelah in Hebron, have an important influence on the children of the ancestors. If this seems an unusual insight, it helps to consider the hundred of thousands of Jews who annually visit the burial sites of their tzaddiks in Eretz Yisrael, Eastern Europe, and around the world. This goes far beyond the archeological-political struggles over proving that the Jewish physical and archeological history does or does not exist.

The Mountain of God, also known as Hashem al Tariff, located in the Sinai Peninsula, has been identified by the "Naked Archeologist," Simcha Jakobovici, using strict Torah criteria, as the "real" Mount Sinai because it fulfills all the details of identification. In a private meeting with him in Israel he outlined for me how to actually find the real Har Sinay, which I hope to do soon. The Torah criteria are:

- Har Sinay must have a high plateau at its base, which can hold approximately three million people for one year. (Hashem al Tariff has this base.)
- Har Sinay must be easily and centrally accessible for millions to reach. (Hashem al Tariff is located on the central Sinai route and sits literally at a central junction.)
- Har Sinay must have archeological evidence of previous use. (Archeologists have found that surrounding Hashem al Tariff is the largest concentration of ancient open-air sanctuaries on the Sinai Peninsula, and these have been carbon-dated back 7,000–8,000 years.)
- Har Sinay must have evidence of a stream that ran out of the top of it. (Archeologist have found evidence of an ancient stream at the top of the mountain with ancient calcifications called travertine, indicating the presence of an ancient stream.)
- Har Sinay must have powerful acoustics from the top to the bottom of the mountain. (Those visiting the site have found this to be true.)

- Har Sinay must be located within fourteen days walking distance of Elim and within eleven days walking distance of Kadesh Barnea. The approximate pace, in kilometers per day, for three million people, with sheep and goats, is 15 km/day. The third point of confluence was approximately 60 km of "goat grazing" distance from a Midianite community. This was Moshe's approximate "goat grazing perimeter based on Bedouin goat grazing studies." (Although most Midianite communities were located in Saudi Arabia, archeologists have found significant proof of a lone Midianite community on the Sinai Peninsula in a place called Timna, approximately 60 km from this holy mountain.)

There are at least ten possible "Mount Sinais," but this location is the only one that meets all the Torah criteria. For example, a visit to St. Catherine's Mount Sinai reveals that energetically, archeologically, and geologically it does not meet the qualifications for the authentic Mount Sinai. It does serve as the Mount Sinai accepted for tourism purposes, based on St. Catherine's selection of it around 300 AD as the "real" Mount Sinai. Later, the sixth-century Roman emperor, Justinian, established a monastery on the site and officially deemed the mountain the Mount Sinai of the "Old Testament" Torah parameters for the Mountain of God (see Schaff, *History of the Christian Church*, Vol. III, p. 467). Regardless of what St. Catherine thought, it still has to fulfill the actual Torah parameters.

Ironically, earlier Christian founders, like Paul of Tarsus, had clung to the ancient tradition of the Jews that Mount Sinai was located in Arabia (Galatians 4:25). The Jewish historian of the first century, Josephus, placed Mount Sinai in the region of Midian, which, again, is in modern-day Saudi Arabia (*Antiquities*, 2:264 and 3:76). This Saudi Arabian Mountain of God location is also supported by the second-century Roman/Egyptian geographer Claudius Ptolemy, who wrote: "And near this city [Midian] Moses would shepherd his flock at the mountain called Sinai, the tallest of all the mountains in the surrounding area" (*Geography*, c.a. 1460; 6:7, 27).

Shemot 3:2 says: "God's angel appeared to [Moses] in the heart of a fire, in the middle of a thorn-bush. As he looked, [Moses] realized that the bush was on fire, but was not being consumed." Shemot 3:4 says: "When God saw that [Moses] was going to investigate, He called to him from the middle of the bush. 'Moses, Moses!' He said. 'Yes [Hineini (הנני)],' replied [Moses]." Hineini means "Here I am"—even more, it means "I am totally present." It is a statement of awareness. Avraham, Yitzhak, and Ya'akov all proclaimed hineini when God called to them. In Shemot 3:5, God says: "Do not come any closer. Take your shoes off your feet. The place upon which you are standing is holy ground." This issue of holy ground is significant. The presence of God is very powerful. The priests used to go barefoot for this reason. It is a symbol of humility. Shoes represent the ego. On a practical level, humans are meant to be a bridge between heaven and earth. When we are barefoot on the earth, the tremendous amount of negative-ion energy that is built up in the earth enters our bodies, and we become connected to all life on earth. Shoes disconnect us. The high priests were barefoot so they could be more connected.

Moshe was then assigned to return to his people, Am Yisrael, and particularly to the process of freeing Am Yisrael from Egyptian slavery and being a conduit for the Torah. His assignment, which he accepted hesitantly, came from the God of Avraham, Yitzhak, and Ya'akov (Shemot 3:6). This was very overwhelming for Moshe, because he was not prepared to handle this magnitude of divine energy. In this process, as with any divine assignment, we see that Moshe had the opportunity to take a great step forward in his spiritual evolution. God said, in Shemot 3:7–8: "I have indeed seen the suffering of my people in Egypt. I have heard how they cry out because of what their slavedrivers [do], and I am aware of their pain. I have come down to rescue them from Egypt's power. I will bring them out of that land, to a good, spacious land, to a land flowing with milk and honey, the territory of the Canaanites, Hittites, Amorites, Perizzites, Hivites and Yebusites." The Gergashi, who were the seventh tribe, had migrated out of Kena'an, so they were spared from destruction and/or servitude to Am Yisrael.

The flame of the burning bush was the angel of the eternal speaking. It was possibly the archangel Mikha'el and the glory of the divine energy of the shekhinah. It is taught that the shekhinah energy had left the people when they were in Mizrayim, and now the people were ready for the return of the shekhinah energy. The fire of the angel represents the severity of gevurah (גבורה). This is why Moshe was afraid. He *felt* this severity. After God announced that he would save the people, he let Moshe know that he would be God's instrument in carrying out this work. Moshe was intimidated and the Lord assured him that he would take care of everything. Moshe then said, in Shemot 3:13–14:

> "So I will go to the Israelites and say, 'Your fathers' God sent me to you.' They will immediately ask me what His name is. What shall I say to them?' 'I Will Be Who I Will Be [(*Eheye Asher Eheye*—אהיה אשר אהיה)],' replied God to Moses. [God then] explained, 'This is what you must say to the Israelites: I Will Be [(Eheyeh, or I Am—אהיה)] sent me to you.' God then said to Moses, 'You must [then] say to the Israelites, YHWH, the God of your fathers, the God of Abraham, Isaac and Jacob, sent me to you. This is my eternal name, and this is how I am to be recalled for all generations.'"

Here God reveals the Tetragrammaton to Moshe. There are different understandings of what this means. It is a source of some spiritual confusion. Moshe was asking which of God's names he should mention to Israel. The only name that speaks of God's miracles and grace is the Tetragrammaton, the great name. This is the name of grace in all of creation. God answered, "I will ever be what I now am." The Lord said to the people "I will be." A slightly different interpretation is "As you are with me, so I am with you" (Midrash Aggadah, quoted in Ramban ahl HaTorah, Shemot 3:13). When people give charity, God opens his hands to them. Devarim (Deuteronomy) 28:12 says: "God will open His good treasury in heaven to give your land rain at precisely the right time, and to bless every thing you do. You will lend many nations, but you will not have to borrow." Iyyov (Job) 12:15 says: "Behold, he withholds the waters, and they dry up: then he sends them out, and they overwhelm the earth." These are profound teachings. People ask why charity is important; it is about creating a circuit for the full flow of energy. If people do not open their hands, God will not open the divine hands to us and establish us in grace. Eheyeh is written three times in this account to mean "I am He who has been, who is now, and who will be in the future" (Midrash Shemot Rabbah 3:12). In essence we are saying that God is the absolute truth. God is beyond time, space, form, and I Am-ness. The third mention of the Eheyeh also suggests that Moshe became the embodiment of the Tetragrammaton (Midrash Pirkei D'Rebbe Eliezer, end of Chap. 39). Moshe was instructed to tell the people Eheyeh (I Am) had sent him. Eheyeh in this context is graciousness and mercy. We understand that God is existence beyond relative reality. God is prior to the first and beyond the last. God is eternity. Another way of translating Eheyeh Asher Eheyeh is "I am the Absolute." While it is more popularly interpreted as "I am that I am," it is more accurately translated as "I am the Absolute." Moshe's task here is to explain the name and its relevance and reestablish the absolute reality for the people. In a sense, Moshe is coming to bring justice, which, in this situation, is justice within mercy. Justice must be brought to the Egyptians as an act of mercy on behalf of the suffering Israelites. Another way of interpreting Eheyeh Asher Eheyeh is therefore "I will be in judgment what I will be in mercy." There are many subtleties in this interpretation. In this context, Moshe's understanding might also be "The Absolute One has sent me to you." The Tetragrammaton is an aspect of mercy for the Hebrew people. The third use of Eheyeh then corresponds to the Tetragrammaton. Eheyeh and the Tetragrammaton imply eternal existence. The last two letters of Eheyeh (י and ה) are the first two letters of the Tetragrammaton. The names of God are all interrelated.

By identifying himself as the God of Avraham, Yitzhak, and Ya'akov, Hashem was referring to the covenant that the Divine made with these patriarchs. When we recognize the lineage, we are able to activate more of the channels. In the kabbalistic teaching, when it says, "This is my eternal name" (Shemot 3:15), it is a reference to this lineage. And when it next says *V'zeh zichri* (וזה זכרי), "and this is how I am to be recalled for all generations," the letter *vav* (ו—"and") implies a continuum. We, on this path, are all part of this profound continuum.

In Shemot 3:16, God said to Moshe, *"Pakod pakad'ti et'chem"* (פקדתי אתכם פקד)—"I have surely remembered you." God assured Moshe with these words that they would listen, because they knew that this sign was in use by Yosef and Ya'akov, as a sort of password. Ya'akov said in Bereisheet 50:24, "And God will surely remember you" (פקד יפקד אלהים אתכם). Yosef used the same words when he addressed his brothers in Bereisheet 50:25, "When God grants you [this] special providence" (פקד יפקד אלהים אתכם). It is said that Yosef used this expression twice, emphasizing that he received it as part of the lineage tradition. It is indeed part of the secret teachings. And the Israelites knew from oral tradition that the rightful person to come and announce their salvation would announce it with those exact words, "pakod pakad'ti et chem" (פקד פקדתי אתכם); this was a secret passed down. The tradition from Ya'akov to Yosef was a secret and specific way of talking about the name of God. This is something to remember in these tumultuous times—pakod pakad'ti, as in "I have surely remembered you, in announcing the return to the Holy Land, restoring a physical nation-state in 1948, and also into the future." Yosef handed this message to Levi, and Levi gave it to Ke'hat, and Ke'hat gave it to 'Amram, Moshe's father. Moshe claimed his legitimacy by saying this in addition to the holy names.

Part of being an enlightened spiritual teacher on the path is that one never stops evolving. This is certainly the case with Moshe at the burning bush, but he was still in doubt and requested a sign from God. In Shemot 4:2–4 God asked Moshe, "What is that in your hand?" Moshe replied "A staff." "Throw it on the ground," God instructed him. When Moshe threw it on the ground, it turned into a snake, and he ran away from it. God said, "Reach out and grasp its tail." So Moshe reached out and took hold of the snake and it turned back into a staff. The serpent emerging from the staff can be understood as symbolic of awakening and initiation of consciousness on the final step to deveikut/chey'rut. Some midrashic sources suggest that Moshe's initiation actually began seven days prior to his arrival at the burning bush (Midrash Shemot Rabbah 3:14). It is reasonable to think, then, that Moshe had an inner awakening of the shekhinah energy during this time, as symbolized by the staff turning into a snake. This awakening was far more rare in those times than today. Not only is the serpent a symbol of awakened consciouness, but it is said that it was also used to frighten Moshe for his gossip against the Israelite people in Shemot 4:1, when Moshe said that the people would not believe him when he went to them. The snake "trick" was a message to him that he had spoken evil by saying something negative against the Jewish people. This is *lashon hara* (לשׁון הרע), literally, "evil tongue." His presumption about the people was partially true, as the people were at the forty-ninth gate of negativity (the lowest); however, this is a powerful lineage, and one must be careful about speaking against it without respect. Not even Moshe was exempt.

What made Moshe a candidate for this major awakening? It was his destiny and his loving humility, as evidenced by his caring for his flock down to every single lost sheep. He was truly the "good shepherd." That is what drew grace to him. Moshe was also told to place his hand inside his robe next to his heart. Upon removing his hand it was white and leprous. White symbolizes purity, as it says in Isaiah 1:18: "If your sins be red, they will become white like snow." Moshe was going through major purifications during this seven-day trial, and with the burning bush and his interaction with Am Yisrael. These were part of his unique path to deveikut/chey'rut, which he successfully walked. When he returned his hand to his heart, it returned to its healthy condition. This was also a message for him and the people to return to their hearts, and thus return to God.

An overview of the story shows that Moshe demonstrated his purity from the very beginning by refusing to suckle from an Egyptian nursemaid. He demonstrated his humility in caring for the flocks of sheep. He showed his empathy by feeling the pain and suffering of the Israelites. Ultimately he showed his visionary abilities by seeing the bigger picture when he came to liberate Am Yisrael. A leader must be humble, heart-centered, pure, and visionary. Moshe was growing into all these aspects during this seven-day spiritual initiation. Moshe was spiritually transformed during this process and he continued to grow even after this was accomplished. There was more evolution in store for Moshe. At the first mention of Eheyeh, Moshe moved to the sephirah of binah (בינה), the realm of Divine Mother (אימא עלאה—literally, Great Mother or Mother of Above), the spiritual energy from which all creation emanates (Zohar, Vol. 3, folio 108b). At the mention of *Asher*,

Moshe awoke unto chokhmah, the direct apperception of the Divine. At the second mention of *Eheyeh*, Moshe moved into the level of keter, the divine will. Moshe had now mastered and become the upper three sephirotic energies of the Tree of Life. When Hashem activated the Tetragrammaton for him, Moshe was able to understand the middle six sephirotic energies—chesed, gevurah, tiferet netzach, hod, and yesod. At the third mention of Eheyeh, God said Eheyeh and "this is my name forever," Moshe had become powerfully awakened in this process. The profound teaching introduced in Bereisheet, *Maʾaseh avot siman labanim* means "The ancestors' lives are a teaching (or prophecy) for the descendants—for us." This phrase gives us an insight into one level of the meaning of Moshe's initiation. The teaching here is that we must all master the Tree of Life on our way to enlightenment as Moshe did. The prophecy is that we will all master the Tree of Life. This is a very clear outline of the importance of becoming Etz Chaim and the importance of being lived by Etz Chaim in all of its ten dimensions.

After Moshe received this message and was given his assignment, God said in Shemot 3:19–22:

> "I know in advance that the Egyptian king will not allow you to leave unless he is forced to do so. I will then display my power and demolish Egypt through all the miraculous deeds that I will perform in their land. Then [Pharaoh] will let you leave. I will give the people status among the Egyptians, and when you all finally leave, you will not go empty-handed. Every woman shall borrow articles of silver and gold, as well as clothing, from her neighbor or from the woman living with her. You shall load this on your sons and daughters, and you will thus drain Egypt [of its wealth]."

This was an interesting message Moshe was told to convey to the people. How do you borrow jewelry when you have no intention of giving it back? The message here is that everything in our lives is borrowed; even our physical bodies are borrowed. We are here in this physical body to wake up to the Divine. Whatever we have is given to us by the light. Whatever we lose is part of the burning/purging process for our transformation. An important enlightenment teaching is: You can never lose what you never had, and you cannot gain what you have already attained. In the purification process, which everyone, including Moshe, has to go through, there are three ways to purification: the first, and least demanding, is a loss of money and/or charity; the second is sickness; and the third is death. Giving away their jewelry was a way for the Egyptians to do some minor purification after more than two hundred years of oppressing the Israelites in slavery. When Avraham, Yitzhak, and Ya'akov went down into Egypt, they suffered, were purified, and as a result emerged spiritually and physically wealthier than when they had entered. It is interesting to note that the original Hebrew word usually translated as "and you will thus drain Egypt [of its wealth]" or "and thus shall you ransack Egypt" is ve'nee'tzal'tem (ונצלתם), which is grammatically rooted in the word "rescue" (הצלה), in which case it would read "And thus shall you rescue Egypt" by enabling them to purify through their surrender of wares and implements to the newly liberated slaves.

As this process of purification progressed for Moshe, he became more and more centered in the direct knowingness of the Absolute. We see here that Moshe was a different and more evolved person after this seven-day initiation. Moshe then returned to his father-in-law to humbly and respectfully ask for his permission to fulfill this enormous mission as a further purification. Shemot 4:20 says: "Moses took his wife and sons and, putting them on a donkey, set out to return to Egypt. He also took the divine staff in his hand." Why did Moshe show up with his family? Just as it is today, this was part of the path and represents a certain amount of emotional maturity, strength, and stability. It made him more believable. He then met Aharon at the Mountain of God. During this time, Moshe initiated Aharon and revealed to him the Tetragrammaton. In this process, Moshe became Aharon's tzaddik, and Aharon became Moshe's prophet, just as Moshe was the prophet of the Divine. In Shemot 4:16 God said: "He will speak to the people for you. He will be your spokesman, and you will be his guide." Shemot 4:27–31 says: "God said to Aaron, 'Go meet Moses in the desert.' [Aaron] went, and when he met [Moses] near God's Mountain, he kissed him. Moses described to Aaron everything that God had told him about his mission, as well as the miraculous proofs that He had instructed him to display."

Once they arrived back in Egypt, Moshe and Aharon brought together all the elders of the Israelites, and Aharon told them everything that God had said to Moshe. He also performed the signs before the people, and they believed. And when they heard that God was concerned about them and had seen their misery, they bowed down and worshipped. The people were ready to believe. Though they had gone down to the ultimate forty-ninth grade of negativity, the intervention came at a time when some of the people were ready to hear it because of their extreme discomfort.

Shemot 5:1–2 says: "Moses and Aaron then went to Pharaoh and said, 'This is what YHWH, God of the Hebrews, declares: Let my people leave, so they can sacrifice to me in the desert.' Pharaoh replied, 'Who is YHWH that I should obey Him and let Israel go? I do not recognize YHWH. Nor will I let Israel leave.'" The pharaoh had no concept of a personal God, but he did have knowledge of the *impersonal* God. The Torah from the time of Avraham teaches there is a personal God that intervenes in our spiritual evolution. This personal God of Avraham, Yitzhak, Ya'akov, and Moshe was simply beyond the pharaoh's comprehension. He had no understanding of a personal God that intervenes in creation and in the lives of humans for their evolution. The great visionary and evolutionary breakthrough by Avraham was his introduction of the personal God that intervenes in our lives, from the macrocosmic level (as in the Big Bang) to the microcosmic levels, in which our individual lives are specifically affected. When one knows the personal God in one's life, one's whole experience of life changes, as does the path of enlightenment. This direct knowing of a personal, intervening God keeps us from falling into the ignorance, arrogance, and separation of Kayin's way of thinking. It keeps us from thinking like the fallen angels, who saw themselves as separate from God, and who lived, and still live, in the consciousness of separation. It protects us from falling into the trap of Nimrod's atheistic, separative thinking, as expressed in his attempted assault on heaven through the construction of the Tower of Babel. It keeps us away from Pharaoh's limited thinking, as he believed himself to be a god. It keeps us from thinking like the modern pharaohs of today, who believe that their massive wealth makes them gods and therefore grants them the right to manipulate the lives of the rest of humanity with worldwide attempted control scenarios. Moshe was saying "God will intervene whether you believe it or not—it doesn't really matter." It is prophesied for our own times, that when we reach the forty-ninth gate of negativity, the messiah energy, as the neshama of the neshama of Moshe will intervene (pakod pakad'ti). In this kabbalistic Torah tradition, the soul of Moshe is Hanokh (Enoch), and the soul of Hanokh is prophesied to become the messiah. This message again and again is that we are the un-folding of a divine plan.

As the plan unfolded, God created room for doubt in Moshe's heart when the pharaoh reacted to Moshe's promise of redemption by increasing the workload of the Israelites and forcing them to find their own straw to make bricks. It was an interesting part of the path, and even Moshe questioned God at this point. However, the overview through which to understand this questioning is that all difficulties bring purification. Even in this instance, Moshe forgot the deeper truth of Etz Chaim and fell into a temporary doubt. Moshe said in Shemot 5:22–23: "O Lord, why do You mistreat Your people? Why did You send me? As soon as I came to Pharaoh to speak in Your name, he made things worse for these people. You have done nothing to help Your people." Moshe went back to Midian for six months to get clearer, and then returned again to demand that Pharaoh free the Jews. The suffering people were complaining and Pharaoh's heart had been hardened. God then said to Moshe: "Now you will begin to see what I will do to Pharaoh. He will be forced to let them go. [Not only that, but] he will be forced to drive them out of his land" (Exodus 6:1).

The first parashah of Shemot is a deep teaching that the power of the name of God can liberate, and the power of the name of God can even kill to clarify teshuva and bring about spiritual evolution. This was all for the purpose of birthing of Am Yisrael at Mount Sinai in the desert. It is a hard teaching because even Moshe had to evolve in this process. In the eighty-day process after ascending the Mountain of God, Moshe became, accord-ing to some sages, half angel. All the people were transformed through their receiving of the Torah process. This first step served to purify the people through their suffering, to build a strong leader in Moshe, and to have Moshe, Aharon, and Miriam lead the people into physical and spiritual lib-eration. May we all be blessed that we use all the powers of Shemot we have been given, again today, in the physical liberation process, as well as for our enlightenment today.

Amen

Va'Era

Va'Era begins with God's answer to Moshe, who asked, "Why is Am Yisrael now suffering from Hashem's guidance in my intervention with Pharaoh?" There was a hint of doubt in Moshe's question, which also subtly highlights a hidden way of Hashem communicating with Am Yisrael. Moshe and Aharon were told to "be gentle." There are two levels of God's expression. When Elohim speaks, it is connected with judgment. When the Tetragrammaton speaks, it is as the grace of chesed, meaning "mercy." An important subtle message, in the beginning of this parashah, is that God first spoke, and said "I Am" (אהיה). This was the merciful God who commanded Moshe and Aharon to lead Am Yisrael gently. Usually, judgment precedes mercy, but in this case, because of how lost Am Yisrael was, they needed mercy to help them move right from the beginning. The people had completely lost their way and had become submerged and immersed in the way of "Egypt," which is the way of ego, materialism, and separation from God. Am Yisrael was not ready to awaken from this state. According to the Midrash, many of the people were unready to leave their physical, mental, and spiritual slavery after the eighth miracle. One of the Mishnah stories says that at the time of the darkness plague, there were still three million Hebrew people who were not ready to leave, and all of these died during the ninth plague of darkness. Even with all the miracles and messages, they still did not understand, and those who were unready lost their chance. They were given mercy first, and then they merited judgment.

Moshe said: "The people don't want to listen to me. They will say, 'I don't have time. I'm working hard.'" This is generally and often people's response to the spiritual path. We hold regular meditations, but people respond: "Oh, I'm working too hard to come to meditation and prayer. I just can't seem to make it." This is the work of the ego. Satan, manifest as the ego, convinced the people to disregard Moshe, and, of course, Pharaoh did the same. This is the resistance to the light. People were constantly becoming distracted by their lives, and this lack of singlemindedness keeps people from waking up. People are still slaves to their "work" today just as they were then, and the issues are the same. People remain slaves partially because they choose to be enslaved by their work. There is never enough busyness to ease a mind that is scared of experiencing the Divine in one's life. There are so many people who have even had the bliss of s'micha m'shefa (Hanihah), which is the gentle chesed way from Hashem, to help us wake up and have a direct experience of the Divine. Even then they cannot hold it because they cannot overcome their conscious or unconscious fear! They go back to their world and continue to organize their life and awareness to avoid progressing in their spiritual evolution. What that means is very clear: If you have not had a direct experience, or do not understand the experience of the divine kiss, it is very hard to remain motivated. The Great Torah Way helps to keep us on track by keeping God at the center of our lives. So when the grace of the divine awareness happens, we are more ready to receive it and nurture its growth. The antidote answer is a Torah lifestyle that constantly focuses on experiencing the transcendent dancing in the immanent world. It is not "either/or," but rather a blend. Focus on God, be awake in all that one has to do, and the divine unfolding will take place. There is nothing to master except our tendency to deviate from the Torah Way, which ultimately leads us into awakening to the light. The Egyptians, as well as the Hebrews, really needed the ten plagues (the gevurah way) to awaken them to the truth, because they had become so lost in their egocentric lives that they needed stronger medicine.

God replied, revealing a much bigger picture, in Shemot 6:1–8:

> "Now you will begin to see what I will do to Pharaoh. He will be forced to let them go. [Not only that, but] he will be forced to drive them out of his land. I am YHWH. I revealed myself to Abraham, Isaac and Jacob as God Almighty [*El Shaddai*] and did not allow them to know me by my name YHWH. I also made my covenant with them, [promising] to give them the land of Canaan, the land of their pilgrimage, where they lived as foreigners. I have also heard the groaning of the Israelites, whom the Egyptians are holding as slaves, and I have remembered my covenant.

Therefore say to the Israelites [in my name], 'I am God. I will take you away from your forced labor in Egypt and free you from their slavery. I will liberate you with a demonstration of my power. And with great acts of judgment. I will take you to myself as a nation, and I will be to you as a God. You will know that I am God your Lord, the One who is bringing you out from under the Egyptian subjugation. I will bring you to the land regarding which I raised my hand, [swearing] that I would give it to Abraham, Isaac and Jacob. I will give it to you as an inheritance. I am God.'"

This was a very clear message that God was fulfilling the prophecy that Ya'akov passed on to Yosef. It is the message of "pakod pakad'ti et chem." The people needed only to be patient. It was also a teaching reconnecting Am Yisrael to its great enlightenment lineage and its power at a new level of enlightenment understanding. The evolution of consciousness and levels of enlightenment are themes that first appeared in parashah Noah. These are the teachings of "walking with God" and "walking before God." With Moshe's revelations and the Torah at Har Sinay, Am Yisrael took another step in the enlightenment lineage evolution.

It is taught that Avraham, Yitzak, and Ya'akov were given the name of God as El Shaddai, and that they did not ask for the *Great Name*. It is taught that Moshe, as part of the next enlightenment step, asked for the Great Name of God. It is a Torah teaching that there is an evolution of levels of enlightenment that even the greatest of the lineage could assimilate. It was enough (*dai*) for the patriarchs to recognize the existence of God's presence in the world as a personal, intervening, immanent God, for the first time in history. The gift of the name El Shaddai, meaning *victory*, was symbolized through God's continual miraculous intervention in all their lives. At the same time, these great beings could only handle a certain amount of the new level of energy beyond Noah. Any more shefa and their vessels would have shattered. Moshe represents the next evolutionary level of enlightenment energy, as evidenced by his ability to see through a clearer prophetic lens.

In the Midrash, it is said that when Moshe traveled forward in time to the second century CE to experience Rabbi Akiba, he, in turn, was not able to understand Rabbi Akiba's interpretation and transmission of Moshe's own teachings (Midrash Bamid'bar Rabbah 19:4). Moshe was being told that he would be the fulfillment of the covenantal promises God made to Avraham, Yitzhak, and Ya'akov, if he could be patient and trusting enough to stand back and watch it happen. Symbolically, the revelation of the Tetragrammaton to Moshe, in this public way, revealed a profound upgrade of the enlightenment consciousness available on the planet. The Tetragrammaton and Torah were revealed so that the awareness of the Divine could be experienced today through Torah study, as well as through historical liberation intervention miracles, such as the exodus, as well as the personal miracles of the patriarchs. The revelation of the Torah at Har Sinay made the teachings of deveikut/ chey'rut available to humanity. It is no accident that the Torah was revealed in the no-man's land of the desert, symbolizing that it was available to all of humanity, if they so chose, as exemplified by Yitro (Midrash Tanchuma, Bamid'bar, Chap. 6). It opened the pathway for the prophecies of Yesha'yahu (Isaiah 11:9—"the earth shall be full of the knowledge of the Lord") and of Yermeyahu (Jeremiah 31:33—"they shall all know me, from the least of them to the greatest of them"). These are prophecies that everyone will eventually wake up to the absolute reality of YHWH.

It is a clear Torah evolutionary principle that enlightenment is given in each generation according to the capacity that each generation may assimilate it, so that each successive generation would be available for the next level of enlightenment. The Torah transmission at Har Sinay represented and still represents the highest enlightenment teachings yet available on the living planet: "Bereisheet bara." It is my feeling that from this historical point, we began to "walk before me and be perfect" (Bereisheet 17:1). Few today have awakened to the full meaning of "Bereisheet bara." Ah! ... but *we* will in *our* generation.

As already pointed out, Moshe was initiated to an even greater revelation of God than were Avraham, Yitzhak, Ya'akov, and Yosef. As part of this, aside from the evolutionary deepening of the meaning of deveikut/chey'rut, Moshe had to lead and awaken an entire people, whereas the forefathers and the foremothers were more concerned with themselves and their individual families, while introducing these teachings to the world. Moshe needed a lot more divine light to "get the job done." What was also challenging for Moshe was that he was telling people it was time to leave, meaning it was time to wake up and be free, to move into the Torah-elevated experience of enlightenment! The people said, "Well … right." He got a really cool reception from most of the people, but not all of the people.

Then, right in the middle of this parashah message, the Torah recounts Moshe's lineage. Lineage is very important. When we look at this Torah path of deveikut/chey'rut, we are looking at the power of 3,400 years of lineage. In each generation we are able to reach a little higher level because we have the light of the lineage behind us, as well as our added light. The explicit Torah teaching is that we are empowered by our lineage. The Torah is also clear that it is our duty to expand the enlightenment awareness in each generation. Parashahs Noah and Va'Era both tell us that there is an evolution in consciousness that we are invited to awaken to in each generation. The Torah is teaching us to look both backward and forward simultaneously. We honor our enlightenment lineage by looking backward, and we honor our ancestors, and the Torah, by looking forward, no matter how much resistance we might come up against.

The importance of lineage is present throughout the Torah on several levels. For example, Aharon married Elisheva. Elisheva was Nachshon's sister (Shemot 6:23), and Nachshon was the first person to run into the Sea of Reeds before it even parted (Midrash Bamid'bar Rabbah 13:5). When we consider entering into a relationship, we consider our potential mate's lineage, because the family we come from *does* affect our worldview. It is better to enter into a relationship with someone with whom you share a lineage. There exists both a family lineage and a spiritual lineage. It makes life much easier in terms of a successful relationship.

Another question that this parashah brings up is the role of miracles in our spiritual evolution and our freedom to choose. In this parashah, God literally overruled and bent the laws of nature for the survival and the next step in Am Yisrael's evolution. This was so that God's gift of Torah could be brought to the world. Clearly, miracles serve as a wake-up call for the evolution of consciousness, but people do not necessarily transform by witnessing a miracle. They can be a little blown away, they can be a little surprised, they can be a little in awe, … but then they tend to forget. The bottom line and the teaching of the Torah is that we have to change ourselves. The real miracle is not flying in the air, walking on water, or parting the sea. The real miracle is to walk on the earth as a full Torah-aware human being, in resonance with all of creation, as the merging of the heavens and the earth. For example, to become healthy, we simply have to follow the laws of nature that God has given us. The Bereisheet 1:29 diet, a plant-source-only, live-food cuisine, was given to us by God to follow as we evolve toward it in our consciousness. The Ten Speakings are guidelines to help us awaken and live holy lives as we evolve into them in our consciousness. In other words, the real necessary miracle is to learn to live the Great Torah Way. This is basically up to us. It seems that at this time in history, only if Am Yisrael is in dire need will God invoke miracles, instead of using them as a general way to impress people. Miracles do not really get people to turn inside toward their own light to experience the wonder of Torah evolution. The path of Torah is to turn inside, to experience and awaken to your our own light of God within. It is about waking up to the light of Hashem that we are. Miracles, which have us depending on an outer person or source, can at some level, even undermine our experience of our own divinity, in a way that our inner light, the immanent light as opposed to the transcendent light, becomes somewhat dimmed.

That is why the journey of Am Yisrael in the desert was just a stopping point on their way to the Promised Land. Am Yisrael needed some external miracles for us to pay attention, but that was it. We then needed the forty years in the desert with the "miracles" of following Hashem to help us transform by our own hard work and faith. A further reason not to focus on miracles, psychic healings, and so forth, is because people get seductively comfortable with them, and do not want to take responsibility for their own growth. In later parashahs, we see the struggles the people had after the spies were sent. It was as if they were saying, "Well, do we want to give up this miracle womb yeshiva of the desert, where manna is falling from the sky, water is coming from rocks, and our clothes never wear out?" The real test of the forty-year walkabout was: Were we willing to surrender and do the hard work on the physical and inner planes to really manifest our inner light? This is one of the great questions about the role of a tzaddik in one's life, and the best relationship with the tzaddik for one to maximize the spiritual life? A certain amount of communion with the tzaddik is spiritually strengthening, but too much dependence can be weakening. The people were faced with a strange dynamic. Their special life in the desert was clearly guided by the transcendent light, by the cloud by day and the pillar of fire by night. However, they were afraid to enter the Promised Land, where the light of divine immanence would ultimately eclipse the light of divine transcendence of the miraculous desert.

The mystery of the miracles revealed in this parashah is also related to the teachings of the plagues. These plagues were a teaching for the Egyptians, Moshe, and all the people. The ten plagues represent the activation of the ten sephirotic energies, along with our ability to learn from them. Am Yisrael had reached the forty-ninth gate of negativity, and they needed a refresher course in cosmic truth. Each plague was a wake-up call for them as well as for the pharaoh. Pharaoh's objections to Moshe's request from God were as follows:

- A personal God did not exist.
- There was no God of Am Israel.
- This God had no power over Pharaoh.

Therefore, from Pharaoh's perspective, there was no reason for him to let Am Yisrael go. Because of Pharaoh's egocentric lack of spiritual understanding, the first nine plagues, on one level, were about his getting the message from God about who was in charge. This issue of who is in charge goes back before the pharaoh. It was present with the fallen angels and their rebellion against heaven, and their continued attempt to undermine creation and evolution. It was core to the Kayin and Hevel conflict, wherein Kayin insisted that man was independent from God and in charge. It was present with the antediluvian population and the technologies that separated them from God. It was present with Nimrod at the Tower of Babel, who tried to use antediluvian technologies to attack the heavens. It was again present in this situation with Moshe and the pharaoh. The Torah teaches that God personally intervenes with acts of grace in our lives and the evolution of the planet on a regular basis. Pharaoh was being taught an important message in humility as well as in this cosmic reality. The Egyptians did, in fact, acknowledge God's existence, but as a transcendental rather than immanent deity. Their god existed in the heavens, but not on the earth. Moshe went to Pharaoh (someone he grew up with) and presented him with a totally outrageous viewpoint from Pharaoh's limited understanding. Pharaoh was in resistance. During the first five plagues Pharaoh's stiff neck was his own choice. The first five plagues were an intense purification and an opportunity to awaken to the cosmic teaching being offered in a relatively gentle way. For the first five plagues Pharaoh was dealing with his ego. He was given the opportunity to make redemption for his dealings with Am Yisrael, and for his lack of understanding. Unfortunately, most of us on the Great Torah Way to enlightenment need to learn the divine cosmic principles the hard way, like Pharaoh. During the second five plagues, he became trapped in his egocentric position and no longer had choice.

The first three plagues were the blood, the frogs, and the lice. It is said in some of the Midrash that Pharaoh would bathe in the blood of the infants he had killed for his skin condition. He was, in essence, doing human sacrifice. The river turning to blood and the death of the firstborn were a partial redemption for these activities. By the second five plagues, Pharaoh had gone too far and justice required that his avenue of repentance be withheld so that he could be purified. As part of this transformation process for Pharaoh, the Lord said to Moshe in Shemot 7:1: "Observe! I will be making you like a god to Pharaoh, and your brother Aaron will be your prophet." Moshe acted as a divine equalizer and a divine teacher to Pharaoh, but it was a hard way of teaching. In Shemot 7:4–5 God said: "This is why Pharaoh will not pay attention to you. But then I will display my power against Egypt, and with great acts of judgment, I will bring forth from Egypt my armies—my people, the Israelites. When I display my power and bring the Israelites out from among them, Egypt will know that I am God."

Before the cycle of teaching miracles began, the stage for teachings and potential repentance was set and in that unconscious context Pharaoh challenged Moshe to show a miracle. Aharon threw down his rod, and it became a serpent. The magicians of Egypt threw down their rods, and they also became snakes, but Aharon's snake devoured their snakes. This was the first clear statement that Moshe's immanent God was superior to Pharaoh's magic. There was also a deeper miracle within a "magic" miracle. It was a double miracle in that Aharon's staff swallowed the staffs of the Egyptians. This represented not only overcoming nature, but also the use of magic in nature. From the beginning, Pharaoh and his magicians were shown that the Divine was in charge at a higher level than magic, and it must have been difficult for them to ignore. But Pharaoh and Pharaoh's magicians were in denial about what they had seen, so they needed more "cosmic medicine."

To activate the first plague, God told Moshe to meet Pharaoh in the early morning at the Nile where he was defecating. This had some subtlety in that the Egyptians believed the pharaoh to be a god; however, gods do not defecate. Moshe caught the pharaoh "with his pants down" in the early morning, defecating at the riverside. From the beginning, there was no way for the pharaoh (who represents the ego) to win. The first plague happened in front of a portion of the people and Pharaoh himself. It represented the purification of malchut. Aharon touched the river with his rod, and it became blood. A reason Moshe did not touch the river was because that was where he had been rescued and protected by the river. So shamanically, he had to honor those energies of the Nile. All liquid in Egypt, no matter the container, turned to blood, but nothing happened to the water of the Hebrews in Goshen. Blood represents the life force, and by turning the river and waters to blood, God was striking at the heart of the Egyptian life force. It represented the sephirah of malchut. Psychically and physically this weakened the Egyptians. The Nile was a primary god for the Egyptians, and turning it to blood was a powerful statement about the power of Hashem. The Egyptian magicians were also able to accomplish turning water to blood through the dark arts and the power of demons. In the world of alma d'shikra (world of illusion), Pharaoh's heart was hardened, because Moshe was not showing them anything "new." This plague went on for seven days. Moshe then went back to Pharaoh and warned him to let the people go, or frogs would invade Egypt. Like many of us in the spiritual unfolding process, the pharaoh refused to listen, which resulted in an intensifying of the spiritual teachings to help him listen more clearly. The pharaoh, symbolic of the ego, was a "slow learner" who refused to surrender to the greater truth.

The next plague was activated and frogs came from everywhere. Shemot 8:2–3 says: "Aaron held his hand out over the waters of Egypt, and the frogs emerged, covering Egypt. The master symbolists were able to produce the same effect with their hidden arts, making frogs emerge on Egyptian land." The frogs were everywhere. They even jumped into the fires and resurrected themselves after they were burnt. The frog plague represents the purification of yesod, the foundation of the Tree of Life. The frog energy also is said to have taught King David, when he was proud of his praise of God. God said: "Listen to the frog. Does it ever stop praising me?" David was humbled when he realized that the frog never stops singing God's praise. According to the teachings of the sages, the frogs are also a symbol of the Torah scholars. It is even said in the Talmud that at the time of Daniel, Chanania, Mishael, and Azaria, they looked at the power of the frogs willing to do God's will by jumping into ovens, so that when they were threatened by Nebuchadnezzar's furnaces, they chose to enter the furnace instead of bowing down to the king. The croaking of the frogs was said to have driven the Egyptians mad, in the same way that the Torah scholars offended the forces of darkness. The frogs never cease from praising God. The sound of the constant praising of God symbolizes the sound of the Torah scholars learning the Torah. Because frogs are not pretty, they teach us to look at the inner qualities of a person instead, and to value a person's inner qualities rather than the outer shell. In Shemot 8:4–5, Pharaoh pleaded with Moshe: "Pray to God! Let Him get the frogs away from me and my people. I will let the people leave and sacrifice to God." "Try and test me," replied Moses. "Exactly when shall I pray for you, your officials and your people? The frogs will [immediately] depart from you and your homes, remaining only in the Nile." The magicians in their delusionary denial credited the plague of frogs with bad astrology rather than Hashem. They claimed that Moshe was timing the plague with natural occurrences. Moshe made a wise move, in that he allowed Pharaoh to choose the time that the frogs would depart. This made it very clear that this was God's doing and not some astrological phenomenon. Again God's presence was proved in a not-so-subtle way. In Shemot 8:11, however, Pharaoh broke his promise after the frogs were removed. "When Pharaoh saw that there had been a respite, he hardened his heart and would not listen to them, just as God had predicted." This often happens in our spiritual life: we make a promise to God, and then change our mind or forget about it when our prayer is fulfilled. In other words, like Pharaoh (the ego), when we receive the reprieve of a judgment against us, we often forget that we were given a reprieve and return to our old ways of living. We do not receive the full rectification and continue the behavior again and again. But we do not need plagues in our lives if we pay attention and do not forget when we receive respite. If we forget, God intensifies the judgment, as happened with the pharaoh and the plagues.

In Shemot 8:12–14 the Lord told Moshe:

> "Tell Aaron to hold out his staff and strike the dust of the earth. It will turn into lice all over Egypt." They did this. Aaron held out his hand with his staff, and struck the dust of the earth. The lice appeared, attacking man and beast. Throughout all Egypt, the dust had turned into lice. The master symbolists tried to produce lice with their hidden arts, but they could not. Meanwhile, the lice were attacking men and beast alike.

God was playing with the Egyptians. There is a teaching that demons cannot rule over anything smaller than a kernel of rice; while another teaching says they have no power over anything less than the size of a lentil. The demons had no power over small things, but rather only larger things, so the magicians were being forced to acknowledge the presence of Hashem in these miracles. The third plague was the purification of hod. It was proof that God had dominion over the large and small dimensions. This was beyond what the magicians could do. Aharon raised the lice from the dust of the ground with his rod. The magicians admitted in Shemot 8:15: "'It is the finger of God,' said the master symbolists to Pharaoh. It was the purification of hod. But Pharaoh remained obstinate and would not listen." The magicians created some doubt, but did not fully credit Hashem with the plague. The lice infested the Egyptians and their animals, but they did not enter Goshen, the residence of Am Yisrael, thus making the point again that God was personal. Pharaoh asked that the plague cease. Moshe agreed, and Pharaoh said he would let the people go. But Pharaoh's heart became hardened again. His ego took over, and he would not let the people go.

God was making another point to Moshe: "I revealed myself to Abraham, Isaac and Jacob as God Almighty [El Shaddai] and did not allow them to know me by my name YHWH" (Shemot 6:3). This was important because

Moshe was now telling the people that God is the Eternal One. It was a new identification of God and clarity of the cosmic depth of God for the people. Some of the Midrash teachings suggest that the patriarchs also knew the name YHWH, but that they did not know it through prophecy. We can infer that they actually did know the name, but that they had attained it in a different and perhaps intuitive way, choosing to keep it secret from the public, while handing it down privately from person to person. So when Moshe mentioned it to the counsel of elders, headed by Asher's daughter Serach, she was able to identify Moshe as the one who would be sent by Hashem as the liberator. But the energetic depth of YHWH may not have been available to the patriarchs in a conscious way. In a sense, they may have just known about it subconsciously. The energy that came through them (the patriarchs) was the divine presence. It came to them more through the energy of gevurah. Moshe's understanding yielded the quality of *mercy*. He was actively using the Tetragrammaton and the name of God as the Eternal, which the people were not ready to do.

The next plague was of wild beasts and correlated with netzach. The message was made clear that there was a personalized God of the Hebrews, as the wild beasts only attacked the Egyptians and only went into their homes. They did not touch the Hebrews. Moshe returned to Pharaoh and warned him in Shemot 9:2–4:

> "For if you refuse to let them leave, and continue holding them,
> God's power will be directed against your livestock in the field.
> The horses, donkeys, camels, cattle and sheep [will die from] a
> very serious epidemic. God will [again] make a miraculous dis-
> tinction, [this time] between Israel's livestock and that of Egypt.
> Not a single [animal] belonging to the Israelites will die."

To prove the point, the Lord designated "tomorrow" as the day that this would occur. This plague represents a purification of chesed on the Tree of Life. The pharaoh and the people still did not understand, and the pestilence killed all the domestic animals, but none of those of the Hebrews.

For the next plague, the Lord asked Moshe and Aharon to take a handful of soot and throw it up into the heavens. The soot became a pox on the

Egyptians. They broke out in blisters and boils, but Pharaoh's ego continued to grow. The purification of gevurah was the plague of boils. He refused to let the Israelites go again. Shemot 9:13–16 says:

> God told Moses to get up early in the morning and confront Pha-
> raoh, saying to him the name of God, Lord of the Hebrews, "Let
> my people leave and serve me. This time, I am prepared to send
> all my catastrophes against your very heart. [They will strike]
> your officials and your people, so that you will know that there is
> none like me in all the world. I could have unleashed my power,
> killing you and your people with the epidemic [sent against the
> animals], and you would have been obliterated from the world.
> The only reason I let you survive was to show you my strength,
> so that my name will be discussed all over the world."

And with that the fiery hail was forecast. The plague of hail was the purification of tiferet. This hail was both fire and ice never seen before in Egypt. Because their lives were at stake they were informed of what was coming so that they could prepare for it. The hail descended and the fire and thunder descended, overwhelming the people. But they were still resisting the force of the Divine. It was becoming obvious that this was beyond nature. Everything left in the fields was destroyed, but again this did not happen in Goshen. Shemot 9:27–28 says: "Pharaoh sent word and summoned Moses and Aaron. He said to them, 'This time I am guilty! God is Just! It is I and my people who are in the wrong! Pray to God. There has been enough of this supernatural thunder and hail. I will let you leave. You will not be delayed again.'" Moshe was again willing to stop the plague and in Shemot 9:29 Moshe said: "When I go out of the city, I will spread my hands [in prayer] to God. The thunder will then stop, and there will not be any more hail. You will then know that the whole world belongs to God." In the midst of this, the Egyptians received some grace. Shemot 9:31–32 says: "The flax and barley have been destroyed, since the barley was ripe, and the flax had formed stalks. But the wheat and spelt have not been destroyed, since they are late in sprouting." There was a window of grace, if Pharaoh was willing to wake up. Pharaoh claimed that he would let them go, but as soon as the hail and thunder ceased, he again hardened his heart. This is like many people today who, when they leave the hospital, forget why they had to go there to begin with. Bad habits, and resistance to Hashem, die hard.

Va'Era ends with the plague of the fiery hail. Pharaoh again acted out and refused to let the people go. Va'Era teaches that the eternal, supreme, and personal God was, and is, real. This was specifically taught to the Egyptians, as well as to Am Yisrael, who were at the forty-ninth gate of negativity. We may summarize the teaching of the plagues of Va'Era as follows: The first three plagues verified God's existence and shifted reality to a larger perspective. The Egyptians and the Hebrews were so overwhelmed with the plagues that they had to accept the powerful presence of God in the world. The second three plagues showed that this was the eternal, personal God, and that this was the God of Am Yisrael. This was beyond Pharaoh's imagination and conceptualization, as he could not accept both a transcendent and immanent God. This forced the Egyptians, as idol worshippers, to acknowledge a personal God that could side with a particular nation.

One other deep conversation needing acknowledgment is the question of free will. The reading says, in a very interesting way "I will make Pharaoh obstinate" (Shemot 7:3). Well, then, what choice did Pharaoh have? It *also* says "[God] said to Abram, 'Know for sure that your descendants will be foreigners in a land that is not theirs for 400 years. They will be enslaved and oppressed" (Bereisheet 15:13). So, where was the choice here? Was there any free will? This parashah speaks very directly to this. Rashi resolves this by saying that Pharaoh had the choice in the first five plagues, and then after that he got into such a hole that he lost his power of choice. This also happens with addictions. We can get addicted to sugar; how many people know and have had the experience of "If I can just stay away from the first bite, I'm okay, but after the first bite it's all over." Or, you choose to play with heroin, and you get addicted. By the time you get addicted, it is very hard to break it, and you need outside intervention to break free. In this context, what choice did Pharaoh have, and what choice did Am Yisrael have? Bereisheet 15:13 says: "Know for sure that your descendants will be foreigners in a land that is not theirs for 400 years. They will be enslaved and oppressed." This was what God told Avraham. Where was choice in this statement? The choice is how *we* perceive the world. Do we perceive the world as Pharaoh, as a personal godless world, where ego reigns as pharaoh consciousness. This is what we see in most of the Western world, regardless of what religions people profess; it matters little, the choice is still materialism and the god money. Do we see we always have a choice to see that God is behind all things, from the smallest to greatest. We can choose to see God working behind all things, and all things being the expression of God. This is where choice begins. Yet, there is a *play* here. As a metaphor in the discussion of free will, we have a movie theater with a series of movies we can choose. God gives us the movie theater and ten or fifteen different movies, and it is our choice to pick which movie we want. If Pharaoh had simply said "I recognize there's a personal, immanent God," things would have been different.

At this point in history teachings did exist about the one God, as Omenhotep (Akhenaten) had taught the one God about eighty years earlier, but he lost out to the traditional Egyptian way. However, he had been a pharaoh who taught the one God, and supposedly he even shared some of that teaching with Moshe. (These are stories. We cannot prove this, but there was some teaching going on and a clear struggle in Egypt over the idea of one God.) So, could Pharaoh have just said, "Oh, yeah, it's God speaking, so I'll let you go … see you later"? He had a choice at the first five plagues. After that, even with his advisors telling him to let the people go, his ego had taken over, and he no longer had a choice. At every moment, as it teaches in the kabbalah, we have choice. At every moment, a new creation is being made, and we have a choice. Our choice is bringing either order or chaos into the world and into our lives. And so, as the Rashi, the twelfth-century Spanish commentator, taught, "Pharaoh hardened his own heart." And because we have freedom of choice, we are accountable for the results that we create from our choices. We have a choice, for example, that we either see a world filled with God, or a godless world. That determines the second point, which is, as we make choices based on the understanding of God's presence in the world, we are able to make wiser and more meaningful choices than if we see it as a godless world. In this conscious context we then walk through every moment seeing that it *as* a miracle—the miracle of God's creation.

May we all be blessed to see that we are living in the *active* miracle of God's creation. May we all awaken into the knowledge of the intervention of the personal God in our lives. May we all be blessed that we need not go through ten plagues in our lives to begin to awaken. May we realize that God is in control and always has been. May we begin to see that God personally and repeatedly intervenes in our lives for our spiritual evolution.

Amen

Bo

~~~~~~~~

SHEMOT 10:7 says: "Pharaoh's officials said to him, 'How long will this [man] continue to be a menace to us? Let the men go, and let them serve God their Lord. Don't you yet realize that Egypt is being destroyed?'" Pharaoh was now willing to free the people, but he set conditions. He asked, "Exactly who will be going?" To which Moshe replied: "Young and old alike will go. We will go with our sons and our daughters, with our sheep and cattle. It is a festival to God for [all of] us." This was necessary because Am Yisrael is one and shall not be separated. Pharaoh could not egoistically let go, so the next plague, the purification of binah, was given. Moshe stretched out his hands and locusts came to the land of Mizrayim and ate every plant of the land that had not been destroyed by the hail. An east wind brought the locusts. Again, Goshen, where the Hebrews lived, was protected, and again, Pharaoh summoned Moshe and Aharon and admitted he had sinned and asked for forgiveness. The plague came to a halt and all the locusts were removed.

The lesson of parashah Bo transcends the story that will be told, but the statement that communicates the essence is to be found later in parashah Yitro during the revelation at Mount Sinai: "I am God your Lord, who brought you out of Egypt, from the place of slavery" (Shemot 20:2). According to the Zohar, this statement is considered the foundation of Torah, all of the "commandments," and the complete path of Israel (Zohar, Vol. 3, folio 84b). In truth, it is the key to understanding the path of deveikut/chey'rut, and is a component of that path.

We have been talking all along about hard work. The other wing to hard work is grace, as in the grace of God that is needed for deveikut/chey'rut. You cannot technique your way to God. You can live the Way of the Torah, but it is an act of grace that takes one to deveikut/chey'rut. YHWH (יהוה) is the name of God as grace reverberating in our DNA. This is played out in this parashah, because it was complete grace that brought the people out of Egypt. Am Yisrael had almost reached the fiftieth gate of negativity, known as "the gate of spiritual suicide and obliteration." Many had actually reached the fiftieth gate. At this point, the Jews, based simply on merit alone, were unworthy of being freed from bondage. Why, then, did they get liberated? What happened?

The answer takes us back to the power of YHWH, the Tetragrammaton, as grace. Each name of God represents a specific quality of God's manifestation in creation. Elohim (אלהים) is the quality of God that manifests in nature, boundaries, principles, regulations, judgment, law, order, justice, and the law of cause and effect, also known as karma, or "measure for measure." Because of this, Elohim could not rescue the people, because there was no grace in Elohim. It is YHWH, the name of God as grace, who came to the rescue, establishing the power of God as a compassionate sustainer, a God who extends beingness, sustaining our existence in every moment. We are unified with Yah as the rays of the sun are unified with the sun itself. The power of YHWH transcends the laws of nature, and therefore overcomes nature and becomes the miracle-working force that transcends time and space. Although it is commonly misunderstood, it is clear the Torah teaches that the primary name of God, as the Eternal One, is YHWH, and the essential attribute of God in the Torah is love, compassion, and grace. Elohim works with time and space and the laws of nature. That is what is embodied in this story.

This same understanding is also communicated in the Song of Songs: "The voice of my beloved! Behold, he comes leaping upon the mountains, skipping upon the hills" (Shir Hashirim 2:8). Nothing can stand in the way of God's love. God's love transcends all barriers. Even though the justice aspect of God emanates as Elohim, a more powerful emanation is love, compassion, and grace.

> The highest of all the heavenly realms is the realm of Love. And therein does the Holy Blessed One dwell, for the Holy Blessed One is always enrobed in Love. And the Holy Blessed One does not ever separate Itself from Love. As is written: "And a river flowed forth from Eden" [Bereisheet 2:10]. Indeed, it flows forth continuously, and bonds with the universe in Love.
>
> (Zohar, Vol. 5, folio 267b)

There is one very important piece we need to explore carefully as we look at the original account of the passover story, of the great drama of the Hebrew exodus from Egypt. At first glance, it seems like a strange story. First, on the tenth day of the month of Nisan (ניסן), each family was to tie a lamb in front of the house for four days. On the fourteenth day, at mid-afternoon, they were supposed to slaughter the lamb. Then they were to collect the blood and paint the doorways, so that when the angel of death arrived to take the firstborn of Egypt, in the final plague, he would know which homes were occupied by Jews, as if God would not know who was Jewish or Egyptian. Third, the ceremonial Passover meal actually began before the people were passed over, before they actually left Egypt—that is how confident the people were. We were celebrating our freedom from bondage before we were freed. This is the correct understanding, because from the perspective of chey'rut, you are free as soon as you fully comprehend that you are free. There is nothing to obtain; you merely awaken to who you are.

So, why was the lamb left in the yard for four days? It was because one of the main gods of the Egyptians was a lamb. They put a lamb on display for four days and then slaughtered it. This was a strong public statement that Am Yisrael did not accept the Egyptian gods. They put these Egyptian gods right in their front doors to symbolically demonstrate that they did not accept them. Part of the spiritual warfare of those times was to defeat the energies (gods) of the people one was struggling against. Slaughtering the lamb was actively symbolic of defeating the Egyptian gods. It was a complete symbolic non-acceptance of the Egyptian lifestyle. The sacrificing of the lamb also represented the Egyptian way, which was the desire to receive for self, alone. This was the ego, which had to be sacrificed. Additionally, Nisan is the month of Aries, the moon of the ram. There was much power given to Aries, so leaving in this month made a strong statement that Am Yisrael was not limited in its evolution by its astrology. Pharaoh even told Moshe, at some point before the locust plague, that he could not let everybody go because his astrologers had said that the planet Rahu was against the Hebrew people and that they would not do well. Moshe said, "Forget it. Our God is going to help us transcend any astrology that you may be warning us against."

In essence, Egypt represents ego. Before Hashem could take us out of Egypt, we had to be willing to take Egypt out of ourselves. To be able to receive God's grace, Am Yisrael had to show self-motivated effort and willingness to come meet God by performing this ceremony. Those people, who were unready, according to various midrashic sources, were eighty percent of the Hebrews (more than three million). They died during the plague of darkness, This was the purification of chokmah. Those who died were the ones who had passed through the fiftieth gate. Only twenty percent of the people, those who were no farther than the forty-ninth gate, were ready to leave Egypt and rectify themselves.

The beginning of spiritual evolution requires an act of faith. First the Jewish people had to remove from themselves the mindset of Egypt. There also needed to be a paradigm shift before the people could begin the journey to freedom. The Jews chose to participate in the act of God's grace by declaring themselves, for the entire world to see, worthy of redemption. This is a key teaching. God always is shining grace on us, but do we accept the grace? Smearing the blood on the doors was a way of opening us up to grace and of demonstrating our readiness to receive grace.

Another key kabbalistic teaching is that once the angel of death is given permission, it does not discriminate between the righteous and the wicked, so it is important for the righteous to know they are not exempt from these forces and to learn to "get out of the way." Another teaching is that nighttime is the domain of the dark forces, so it is good to be inside at that time. As it says in Tehillim (Psalms) 104:20, "Thou makest darkness, and it is night; when all the beasts of the forest do creep forth." Today, as then, repeating the name of YHWH draws grace to you, as is written, "Wherever I allow my name to be mentioned, I will come to you and bless you" (Shemot 20:21). This is easier than smearing blood on the doorway and having to do physical sacrifices, but the principle is the same.

Bo is a lesson in acknowledging God's unconditional love for each of us. This unconditional love is the foundation for the whole Torah Way. If we cannot resonate with the idea that God loves us enough to redeem us, even when we are not worthy by our actions, we simply are not able to understand the power of the name YHWH. Being the frequency of YHWH in every moment of our lives draws the grace that brings compassion and love that transforms and transcends the power of judgment against us.

As we look at the whole pattern of the plagues, we get a deeper understanding of what the pharaoh was struggling with. As mentioned before, he believed that: (1) there was no such thing as an immanent God; (2) there was no such thing as the God of Israel (a God who is personally intervening in our lives to support the evolution of our consciousness individually and for all of Am Yisrael); and (3) most arrogantly of all, God had no power over the pharaoh. The plagues addressed these three issues the hard way for the pharaoh. The first three plagues showed that God existed, everywhere from the macrocosmos to the microcosmos. They had lice everywhere in their lives. Frogs were everywhere, and blood was everywhere. The second three plagues made the point that, yes indeed, there was a God of Israel, and this God of Israel, who set the people free, was a God who was saying clearly "Israel is my son, my firstborn" (Shemot 4:22), and that the people of Israel would receive and have received preferential treatment, or providence.

One may question: "We've suffered through the Crusades, the Inquisition, and been through the Holocaust—how is this preferential treatment?" Unfortunately, preferential treatment does not mean there is no purification required for not living the Torah Way. That said, Am Yisrael, against unbelievable odds, has survived as a people. Throughout thousands of years, during which other great civilizations have disappeared, Am Yisrael still thrives. This is where preferential treatment comes in. This will become the tragedy of the Palestinians and the Arab world if they do not acknowledge that this whole scenario will be played out again as it was in Egypt. This is unfortunate, but for reasons beyond my understanding, it appears that we are going in that direction.

The first seven plagues can be considered the seven lower sephirot. It spoke specifically to these two issues: (1) that there is a God, and (2) that the God of Israel indeed gives preferential treatment to Am Yisrael, in spite of missing the mark so much. The last three plagues helped the pharaoh learn that there is a God who is omnipotent far beyond the power of a pharaoh. For him to begin to understand that, he needed the eighth plague of the locusts, which destroyed all the food that was left. It represented binah, the sacred feminine, which Pharaoh was not acknowledging. When he did not comprehend at that level, when he still said "I'll let you go but I won't let your animals go," Moshe said "No, that won't do." The symbolism is that all of Israel was one soul, including all the animals with which we share a collective soul. God blew breath into all of us. So, after the locusts came the plague of darkness, which corresponds to the sephirah of chokhmah. The darkness was very individualized again; all of Egypt was in a cloud of darkness, except for the Hebrews, who had light. But, even then, there were three days of darkness, when eighty percent of the Hebrews died. Once these people were buried, and Pharaoh still would not let the people go, the tenth of Nisan came, and the whole process finished out with the final plague. The tenth plague was keter, the purifying of all ten sephirotic energies. The ten plagues correspond to the ten times God said in the creation story "it was good," and so are linked to the creation energy. The seed of Israel had become so tarnished that it needed complete purification before the ten utterances could be given. Israel was purified at a seed level. In levels of incarnations it represented the souls made by Adam and nonhuman spirit energies that were purified in the flood, at the Tower of Babel, at Sodom and Gomorroh, for 210 years in Egyptian slavery, and through the energies of the ten plagues that again purified the k'lipot (קליפות), the husks, from the ten sephirotic energies, so that Am Yisrael would be ready to receive the Ten Speakings (often mistranslated as "the Ten Commandments"). The lower seven sephirot represent the human body, and the upper three represent the head and the higher vision, the seed level from which our thoughts and our consciousness emanate (Sefer HaSh'lah, Toldot Adam, Bayt YHWH, No. 22).

The people were also instructed to leave nothing behind during their exodus, because the pharaoh wanted to retain or hold on to something physical from the Israelites as a way to control them. The dark side always wants to hold on to the light so that it can keep draining it of its brilliance. We had to separate completely and entirely, so that there would be nothing for him to hold on to.

Moshe, at the time of the darkness plague, told the people that they needed to "borrow" all the gold and silver of the Egyptians. There are two messages here. One is that it was repayment for the 210 years of slavery Am Yisrael suffered. The second message is more important, which is that as we break out of alma d'shikra (עלמא דשקרא—the world of illusion), we understand that all we think we have is actually borrowed, and we cannot lose what we never had.

In the plague of the death of the firstborn, equivalent to keter, all negativity was washed away. A particular energy here was cleared for the Egyptians, too, because Pharaoh had killed so many of the boy children, and now the energetic return (*midah keneged midah*—מדה כנגד מדה) was coming back to him. The overall message is that the ten plagues were given to us by God as grace to help both Am Yisrael and the Egyptians overcome the results of their negative actions. The displaying of the blood on the doorposts to protect against the plague of the slaying of the firstborn has transformed into the mezuzah (מזוזה). The mezuzah can be seen as a symbolic remnant of those times. The tenth plague occurred at midnight. This is the moment when kabbalists feel God goes into the Garden of Eden to communicate with righteous people (Zohar, Vol. 1, folio 92b), and it is often the time kabbalists wake up to study. In the haftorah of Bo, the corresponding reading from the Books of the Prophets, the prophet Yirmeyahu tells us that there is nothing to be afraid of (Yirmeyahu 46:27–28). Indeed, there is nothing to be afraid of as long as we stay connected to the light of God. It is through the light that the grace comes.

In the moments before we left Egypt, we were also told to bake our bread as simply as possible, without *chametz* (חמץ—additives or leavening). The absence of chametz is an important part of the Passover ceremony; it is a code, symbolizing ego, because ego gets puffed up. And like the lamb rite, it represents the energy of receiving for self, alone. If we are going to leave Egypt, which represents egocentric and ethnocentric thinking, we have to leave behind our personal Egypt, or the chametz, which is our desire to receive for self, alone.

It was also at this time that God directed the Hebrew nation to honor the new moon. This is symbolically significant in that slaves do not really think about time, because their time is not theirs. They are kept captive in machine time. Now they are being reintroduced to the divine time of the planets, sun, and moon. By linking to the divine time, they are able to break out of the matrix of slavery and machine time, and thus are able to connect with God through the cycles of nature, and therefore deepen their connection with the Divine.

Near the end of this parashah, we talk about the redemption of the firstborn. This is a very subtle concept. They were talking about the firstborn son. If we do not work well with the firstborn son, and the tremendous energy that a firstborn brings into the world, this energy may be transformed into a negative energy. So the redemption of the firstborn is a consciousness or a ceremony that really supports all of us in creating a focus on God as the center of all creation. From a spiritual evolutionary point of view, the idea of the firstborn can also be understood as a new beginning, which is the mitzvot energy of teshuva. New beginnings happen when we go back to the source of the imbalance and make the internal correction so that missing-the-mark energy does not happen again. In this way we can be in a constant evolution of new beginnings. We always have the opportunity for a rebirth, and we have the ability to become the firstborn in every moment.

This teaching of Bo is waking up to the core Torah Way of not just believing in God as Elohim, as creator, but also as YHWH, a personal God, an immanent God of grace, or zeir anpin (זעיר אנפין), tiferet. YHWH is the God beyond the heavens and the earth, beyond Elohim, who personally guides our spiritual evolution back to the source, which is the Eternal One prior to time space, and being. This is the message of deveikut/chey'rut.

Parashah Bo is about the grace that overcomes judgment. As we work on our bodies and minds in a way that purifies the k'lipot, so that all of our vessels can hold the Or Yashar (אור ישר—descending light) and the *Or Ganuz* (אור גנוז—concealed light), and we can better receive and hold the grace. Part of receiving and holding grace is remembering and being grateful for the continual grace that we did receive from the beginning of the Big Bang through the Ruach Elohim at $10^{-35\text{th}}$ second (that's 10 to the minus thirty-fifth of a second), preventing us from being absorbed into the black hole. On Shabbat, with the *kiddish*, we remember the continual intervention of YHWH in our lives, from the act of creation through the exodus, and in every moment of our lives. Shemot 13:9 says: "[These words] must also be a sign on your arm and a reminder in the center of your head. God's Torah will then be on your tongue. It was with a show of strength that God brought you out of Egypt."

Although it benefits us to be in awe of this all the time, wearing the phylacteries (tefilin) is a particular time to remember this continual act of grace. In this context exodus was a divine impulse of liberating light that continuously reverberates in every moment of our lives. God personally intervenes in our life both then and now with a *netuyah* (an "outstretched arm"), and a *yad chazakah* (a "strong arm"). The arm of YHWH is always reaching out to us to pull us out of the confusion of alma d'shikra and *alma peruda* (world of duality), in which we continually become enmeshed in a way that puts us to sleep to the ultimate truth and meaning of why we are put here on the earth—deveikut/chey'rut. The Torah Way is given to us to help us transform our crude body-mind-soul into the kedusha of the divine light of YHWH reflected through our physical body-mind-soul. In that way, the Torah revelation will be in our mouth as a reflection of the truth of God reverberating in our hearts.

Today, as in the chronological time of Egypt, the geological, political, and social turmoil of the plagues are upon the whole planet to wake us up from all our distractions and attachments so that we may truly return to God as the living presence of the Divine in every moment of our lives. We have the opportunity to not let our "hearts become hardened" and to return to the way of God. The words of Yirmeyahu (Jeremiah) 5:20–23 are an ancient and present teaching:

> Declare this in the house of Ya'aqov, and publish it in Yehuda,
> saying, Hear now this, O foolish people, and without under-
> standing; who have eyes, and see not; who have ears, and hear
> not: Do you not fear me? Says the Lord: will you not tremble
> at my presence, who have placed the sand for the bound of the
> sea by a perpetual decreee, that it cannot pass it: and though its
> waves toss themselves, yet can they not prevail; though they roar,
> yet can they not pass over it? But this people has a revolting and
> a rebellious heart; they are revolted and gone.

Although in Kohelet (Ecclesiastes) 1:9, King Solomon teaches "That which has been, it is that which shall be; and that which has been done is that which shall be done; and there is nothing new under the sun," this time we can awaken from our materialistic stupor and return to the source and awaken to deveikut/chey'rut, experienced as prior-to-consciousness, and expressed as divine love and experience of unity with all on the planet. The outstretched and strong arm of God is calling us and is willing to pluck us out of the Egyptian-matrix-egocentric world and return us to the divine presence. Now, as then, it is our choice to free ourselves with God's grace, from our pharaohic, egocentric worlds. Parashah Bo is about the possibility of doing it as a collective humanity beyond the twenty percent.

May we all be blessed that we chose to live in the Torah Way of deveikut/chey'rut and fulfill our ultimate destiny as the awakened love- and light-filled children of God. It is our time.

Amen

BeShalach

THIS parashah highlights another aspect of the Torah Way of deveikut/chey'rut as emunah (vbunt—faith). Without faith, nothing really happens in the spiritual world. The ancient rabbis narrowed the 613 mitzvot down to essentially one mitzvah and that mitzvah is stated in Habbakuk 2:4: "The just shall live by his faith." Or, as also mentioned in 'Amos 5:4: "Seek me [God] and you shall live." This is the essence of the Torah, as articulated in the Talmud (Makot 23b–24a). The entire Torah, then, is summed up in Habbakuk's statement about faith. The Zohar, too, considers faith extremely important: "The person who walks in the ways of the Torah, walks with faith that nothing harmful of this world can affect him" (Zohar, Vol. 1, 201b). Faith brings about redemption, and that's what we see in this parashah. The first act of faith was following the Cloud of Glory (Anan HaKavod—ענן הכבוד) during the day and Pillar of Fire (Amud Ha'Esh—עמוד האש) during the night. Shemot 13:21 says, "God [the Eternal One] went before them by day … [and] by night." In some of the midrashic sources, "the Eternal One" includes as well the Celestial Court (Midrash Shemot Rabbah 19:6; Zohar, Vol. 2, folio 46a). In this context, the Eternal One went before them by day and the Celestial Court (which may have been the archangel Mikha'el) went by night. In the time to come, however (messianic times), only the Tetragrammaton will go before us (Midrash Shemot Rabbah 19:6), and, as it says in Tehillim 139:11–12, "the light be night about me, even the darkness is not dark for thee, but the night shines like the day: the darkness and the light are both alike to thee." What King David was describing is a stage in the deveikut/chey'rut process, a steady experience in which one experiences the continual influx of the light, whether awake or "asleep." For the awakened ones, the internal messianic times are here now, as David described.

Incredible Light Energy of That

Half asleep and fully awake
The energetic body filled with indescribable, blazing light
Explodes through the total being
With a delectable fullness
Of Joy,
Of Peace,
Of Contentment,
Of Love,
Occurring without reason or cause,
the natural human state
Existing as the matrix of beingness within
As phenomenon and prior,
In the silence of the night,
In the silence of meditation,
Rises like a thousand blazing suns
And settles down,
But never sets in the activity of the day.
It is always background and often foreground
To an underlying matrix
Of ecstatic noncausal well-being, peace, love, beauty, content-
    ment, and joy
Emanating twenty-four and seven,
Residing as infinite light of Divine Presence
Uplifting this one as the One in every moment of every action
Blazing forth as the nothing of awareness
In the silence of the Divine Presence
In the stillness of the mind and body
As the day unfolds through the night
Half asleep and fully awake
The ecstasy of the Divine Self
Is beyond cause, comprehension, and I am.
It is Yah's permanent Grace to everyone
Incredible Light Energy of That
The Light of I am That is all that ever was, is, and will be.

When the Egyptian army caught up with Am Yisrael, this cloud (Amud Ha'anan or Anan HaKavod) moved as a cloud of protection and darkness that separated the Hebrews from the Egyptian camp. In front of it was the Pillar of Fire, which also was situated between the two camps, giving enough light so that the Hebrews could begin walking across the Yam Suf (Sea of Reeds). What was going on was an outright miracle that the Egyptians seemed to ignore as a warning; even in the morning, when the cloud went before to lead the people, the Pillar of Fire remained between the two camps, causing further chaos and destruction among the Egyptians. Yet their egocentric focus was so great that they could not see the hand of Hashem in this process and stop their pursuit. The spiritual teaching here is, how many times are we like the Egyptians? How many times do we ignore the divine warnings in our lives and proceed onward into the most difficult purifications because of it? It becomes clear: The pharaoh's heart continued to harden beyond reason, which suggests that when these things happen they are much needed purifications. In these circumstances, it is best to accept the purifications with appreciation that whatever God does is for the best. The Amud Ha'anan/Anan HaKavod may also symbolize the central column of the Tree of Life, which is always protecting us by elevating our consciousness. We may also consider that this cloud of glory of Hashem may create a veil of protection for us when called upon even now.

When the people first left, the Torah tells us that God "made the people take a roundabout path, by way of the desert to the Sea of Reeds" (Shemot 13:18). Instead of going north and traveling along the coast, away from the desert, which would appear to have made life easier, God took them south, putting them in a position vulnerable to the pharaoh. So, the very first moves required a certain amount of faith. Pharaoh's scouts saw this route and interpreted it at its lowest octave. They believed that God and the Hebrews had gotten confused in the desert. Because God had hardened Pharaoh's heart, the decision was made to attack and recapture them. In deeper reality, the people of faith were not lost and knew that their direction, in the historical continuum of their individual and tribal purpose, was not only their personal deveikut/chey'rut process, but also the establishment of the *Beit HaMikdash* (בית המקדש) on the Temple Mount. It is not unusual that people critically judge those on the spiritual path, when they do seemingly illogical things, and the Egyptians were not going to let go of the Hebrews easily. On the spiritual path, we will continually find people clinging to people of light as friends, yet choosing not to take the spiritual path actively themselves. They want the energy of the closeness, but without the intention of developing spiritually enough to live in the energy. This is a useful principle to understand as we all evolve on the spiritual path, because this happens at every level. It is most difficult in a family situation. There are a variety of ways to ameliorate the situation, and it all can work especially in relationships where the person who has the resistance to God does not actively try to block or undermine the spiritual evolution of the one who is more intensely involved. The pharaoh, however, was intent on actively blocking Israel's spiritual evolution and mission. God hardened his heart so that he would pay the consequences immediately. Another way of understanding "hardening of the heart" is that God was actually gifting him with an enormous opportunity to shift his consciousness from evil to good. But in order for the degree of that shift to match the degree of the wrongness from which it needed to shift, God had to intensify the challenge, to harden his heart, as a test of the truth of his conviction.

The Hebrews reached the edge of the Yam Suf, the Sea of Reeds (Red Sea is a mistranslation), and when they looked behind them, they saw Pharaoh and his army chasing them. They panicked. Now, there were 600,000 able-bodied men and close to three million people altogether, including women, children, and elders. Pharaoh had 6,000 warriors and chariots at best. However, the Hebrews, because of their slave mentality, panicked and lost their newly born, miracle-based faith. Mingled among them were the ey'rev rav, the mixed multitudes, who continually fostered the energy of doubt, hate, and rebellion against the truth and against the leadership of Moshe, Aharon, and Miriam. These were the people who would later worship the Golden Calf, which ultimately thwarted the opportunity, not only for the Hebrews, but also the entire world, to activate the messianic times with the full receiving of the Torah. The first opportunity for the advent of the messianic times was with Adam and Eve, but that was thwarted by the serpent as an agent of the dark side. The second opportunity was at the foot of Mount Sinai, and was sabotaged by the ey'rev rav and the Golden Calf incident. We are now living in the third opportunity for the messianic times to manifest.

The ey'rev rav said in Shemot 14:11–12: "Weren't there enough graves in Egypt? Why did you have to bring us out here to die in the desert? How could you do such a thing to us, bringing us out of Egypt? Didn't we tell you in Egypt to leave us alone and let us work for the Egyptians? It would have been better to be slaves in Egypt than to die [here] in the desert!" The slave mentality was so deep in the people. This was partially why the miracle at the Yam Suf had to happen. Moshe attempted to reassure them: "God will fight for you, but you must remain silent" (Shemot 14:14). The splitting of the Yam Suf was more than a miracle of physical rescue. It was a miracle that lifted the people up from the negative forty-ninth gate to the positive fiftieth gate of consciousness. It was a direct movement to the highest level of consciousness, which some of the people were ready for.

This brings up the issue of the ey'rev rav (mixed multitude), whom Hashem advised Moshe not to take with him, but out of Moshe's love for everyone, he wanted to share this momentous spiritual opportunity with all (Midrash Tanchuma, Ki Tissa, Chap. 21). Learning from Moshe's experience, we need to be cautious about how much ey'rev rav energy we allow into our midst, in supporting people in their personal and group journeys to deveikut/ chey'rut. Too much involvement with ey'rev rav consciousness is more likely to unbalance or block the energy of the group consciousness evolution.

As the Egyptian army approached, the pressure was now on Moshe, and he called out to God for help. God said to Moshe in Shemot 14:15: "Why are you crying out to me? Speak to the Israelites, and let them start moving." It is pretty clear that Moshe had the seventy-two names of God at this point, which are encoded in verses 19, 20, and 21 of Chapter 14 of this parashah. The seventy-two names carry a tremendous amount of power, and God said in Shemot 14:16: "Raise your staff and extend your hand over the sea. You will split the sea." So Moses did as Hashem advised, but the sea did not part right away. According to the oral tradition, it parted only after Nachshon, son of Aminadav, leader of the tribe of Yehudah, walked into the sea and continued walking until the waters reached his nostrils (Midrash Bamid'bar Rabbah 13:4). Incidentally, Nachshon was indirectly related to Moshe through his sister Elisheva, who was married to Aharon (Shemot 6:23). This incident makes a powerful point that even with Moshe's use of the seventy-two divine names, the people had to have faith to create this change in consciousness, and Nachshon had this faith and did what was necessary.

Faith and action go hand in hand. Right action is an expression of faith. Blind faith misses the point that grace and hard work are two wings of the same bird. An unfortunate example of this is a true story that happened in the 1980s. The Russian River in Sonoma County, California, had become a raging flood and a group of people decided that instead of doing the appropriate thing in flow with the situation (which was to get out of the way), they would meditate and pray for God's intervention while situated on a boat dock in the river. The raging river eventually washed away the boat dock, and they all drowned. If they had been in wise faith, they would have acted by appreciating the grace they had to be able to leave the area. This could also be said about the choices of those who could have left Europe before the Holocaust, but who chose, instead, to stay because of their faith. The correct decision is not always clear, but it is best to act with wise faith on the spiritual path and not confuse blind faith with being spiritual. We may also use the power of faith when Hashem guides us to solve a situation through our actions as co-creators with the Divine here on earth.

As the Israelites crossed the Yam Suf, the waters returned upon the pursuing Egyptians and they were all killed. There is an oral tradition that God spared the pharaoh so that he might wander the earth telling of the wonders he had witnessed (Midrash Pirkei D'Rebbe Eliezer, Chap. 43). The splitting of the sea and passing through it can be considered yet another mikveh of purification for the Egyptians, for excessive actions against Am Yisrael, and for casting Hebrew newborn males into the Nile River. For the Hebrews, it meant the final purification phase, before they received the Torah, from the time of Adam and Cha'vah, to the flood (a gigantic hot and cold mikveh purification for the whole world), to the Tower of Babel, to the firestorm of Sodom and Gomorrah, to the 210-year purification in Egypt, which also included their purification from the sexual licentiousness of the previous cycles, and now, passing through the mikveh of the Yam Suf as the final purification phase, they became free from all desires, especially sexual desires—a powerful step in the enlightenment process.

In celebrating this great miracle of being saved, and this great purification, Moshe led the people in song, following which his sister, Miriam, led the women in a second round of dance and song accompanied by drum. This was a powerful dance and song and contained a powerful statement: "My strength and song is God" (Shemot 15:2). This was about faith. This dancing and singing was celebrating the splitting of the sea. Called "The Song of the Sea," this song goes right to the point: "My strength and song is *Yah* (יה) and this is my deliverance; this [Yah] is my God, I will enshrine Him [Yah] my father's God, I will exalt Him [Yah]." It is interesting that in this part of the song, it only uses the first two letters of the Tetragrammaton. This is one of only two instances in the entire Torah that the two-lettered name of Yah is used. It is associated with the statement later in this parashah that the hand is upon the throne of Yah (Shemot 17:16). It implies that Hashem swore that the throne will not be perfect nor will the great name be complete until the seed of 'Amalek is entirely blotted out. Yah refers to the attribute of justice and, as it says in Yesha'yahu (Isaiah) 26:4, "the Lord God [Yah] is an eternal Rock." The tribe of 'Amalek, whom the Hebrews encounter at the end of the parashah, symbolically represents the element of doubt on the spiritual path. On the physical level they attacked the Hebrews from a distant place, from which they were not threatened by the travels of the Hebrews, while all the other people on their route were in awe and terror of God. They were descendants of 'Esav (Bereisheet 36:12) and had no fear of God. In BeShalach, the prayer of Moshe accompanied by his upraised hands defeated them. Centuries later, the first Hebrew king, Sha'ul, had the opportunity to unify the name by destroying 'Amalek, but he had false chesed, or mercy, and did not complete the assignment to eliminate them entirely. He spared their king (First Shemu'el 15:9). 'Amalek appeared again later in Persia through the clan of Haman and his ten sons, who plotted to exterminate the entire Jewish population but were defeated, ironically, by two descendants of Sha'ul, Ester and Mordekhay. In more recent times, 'Amalek reared his (or its) ugly head again in the form of Hitler and his inner circle, who, like Haman's sons, were hanged. It is taught that Hitler and his key staff consciously understood their association with Haman and his ten sons, which they actually acknowledged at their execution.

On the spiritual path we have so many powerful injunctions against killing, such as what King Sha'ul experienced, but if King Sha'ul had followed God's command, there may not have been a Hitler. If we choose out of compassion to let a rapist out of prison before he is rehabilitated, and he rapes or kills more women, have we made the right decision? Would nonviolence, which worked for the civil rights movement in the 1960s, have worked against Hitler? These difficult questions are part of the spiritual path and help us to evolve, but challenge our liberal belief systems. At the level of chey'rut, we are not able to hold any position except the will of Hashem in the moment, and thus are able to move in any direction like the prophet Shemu'el did in response to Sha'ul's false, egocentric mercy. He energetically removed him from the throne in time and replaced him with David, whose chesed consciousness was properly placed. During David's exile by his son Avshalom, one of Sha'ul's relatives, Shim'i, cursed David as he fled and threw stones at him and his men. When David's loyal warriors reacted by asking permission to kill him for insulting David, "the anointed of God," he, in his right mercy, declined their request (Second Shemu'el 16:5–12). As a result, Shim'i lived long enough to have children, from which eventually came Mordekhay and Ester, who are described as descendants of Shim'i (Ester 2:5). Thus, in the end, David's rightfully placed mercy repaired the breach that had been created by Sha'ul's misappropriated mercy. We must be open, as articulated in the wise teachings of King Shlomo, that there is a time and place for everything and for us to have the intuitive wisdom to make the right decision in the right moment (Kohelet 3:1).

Moshe had faith, while the people lacked faith. Nevertheless, they continued to move south into the desert as guided by God through Moshe. They were definitely taking a route that did not appear practical from the physical perspective, but from a spiritual perspective, it provided a series of tests that the people needed to go through to awaken. The journey became the teacher. The splitting of the Yam Suf helped free the people from imprisonment in the slave consciousness they inherited in Mizrayim. They were not completely cleansed of it, so they were given three days without water, because water, according to the Zohar, is symbolic of consciousness (Zohar, Vol. 2, folio 60a). They come to Marah, where they finally found water, but the waters were bitter and they could not drink them. Now God showed them the healing ways of homeopathy. He threw a bitter-tasting tree into the water (Midrash Vayikra Rabbah 27:6), and the water turned sweet. This is the first example of biblical homeopathy—like heals like. Following this they were given the path of holistic health in Shemot 15:26: "If you obey God your Lord and do what is upright in His eyes, carefully heeding all His commandments and keeping all His decrees, then I will not strike you with any of the sicknesses that I brought on Egypt. I am the God who heals you." It is fundamental to the support of spiritual life to have a healthy body, for as our sages have taught, when the body is healthy it gives space and strength for the power to meditate on the Divine. In the words of the twelfth-century Rabbi Moshe ibn Maimon (Rambam/Maimonides), who was also chief physician to Saladin, sultan of Egypt:

> One ought to place upon one's heart that one's body and organs need to be whole and strong in order that their soul be in a good place of knowing God, for it is impossible for one to access insight and wisdom when one's body is hungry and sick, or one's organs are hurting.
>
> (Mishnah Torah, Hilchot De'ot 3:3).

From Marah, they continued to Elim, still heading south and moving toward the desert of Seen. In Elim there were twelve pools of water and seventy palm trees—these are key holy numbers. Then they moved further on into the wilderness of Seen. By the fifteenth day of the second month out of Egypt, the people had run out of the matzah, which had lasted sixty-one meals, as a silent miracle, and had maintained them for much longer than their supplies. They had also eaten many of their livestock. Again "the people" began getting upset because they did not have bread. According to the Zohar, whenever the Torah uses the term "the people," it refers to the ey'rev rav on every level, and when it uses the term "children of Israel," it refers to the holy ones of Israel and the Levites (Zohar, Vol. 2, folio 45b). In Shemot 16:3, they brought their complaint to Moshe: "If only we had died by God's hand in Egypt! There at least we could sit by pots of meat and eat our fill of bread!" The ey'rev rav stirred up rebellion among the people whenever they had an opportunity. In their lack of faith they said in Shemot 16:3: "But you had to bring us out to this desert, to kill the entire community by starvation!" Lack of faith and doubt are important undermining factors on the spiritual path and need to be continually addressed in thoughtful ways, as exemplified by the children of Israel, on the other hand, who remained quiet and knew these were purifications and spiritual tests they were being given. The ey'rev rav of all types, including the religious ey'rev rav within Am Yisrael itself, manifest even today in a variety of frankly negative forms—self-righteous liberals, extreme-right conservatives, overzealous fundamentalists, anti-religious secularists, and politically radical atheists. Because their clever statements can be confusing today, as they were 3,400 years ago, the B'nei Yisrael should be careful to whom they listen and by whom they are influenced.

They were now ready for another teaching, which was the answer to their complaints. And so, God brought down the manna from the heavens, and tested them with certain rules regarding the gathering and eating of the manna. Initially, some of the ey'ev rav did not have the faith necessary to follow these rules, but after more than forty years of having their food come from heaven, without having to grow or hunt for it, they eventually began to understand the importance of their daily bread arriving in this form. It was a daily gift and reminder of the divine providence in their lives. The manna did not come in a form they could recognize; they did not get bagels, and they did not get matzah or leavened bread. What they received was manna! This was a very important teaching about food, in that all of our sustenance comes from God. Food is a love note from God. Each morning they were reminded of the glory of the Eternal One in their lives. The quality of the nourishment in manna correlated with how much they appreciated God, and how much they blessed the food. This was perhaps the first blatant Torah message that God is in the food, and when we bless the food, we activate the divine energy in the food. We are also thereby turning the blessed food into an antenna for God's presence, grace, love, and vitality. Blessing the food plugs us into the source of all life-force and nutrition. When you do not bless the food, you only get nutrition for the body alone, which is not the same thing. When we bless our food, however, we open up and activate the "on" switch, and the food becomes a vehicle for the transmission of God's life-giving force to enter the world and to enter us. In order to taste divine love in our food, we need to bless it and prepare it with love. This blessing then activates the taste buds of our soul. In blessing, we acknowledge Hashem as the source of all. Now we have been introduced to the importance of blessing food, and the whole understanding at that level. It is also important to bless the food and the source of the food *after* the meal. This creates a re-energizing cycle to the heavenly food chain in which the angels are intermediaries. It kindles the Or Hozer (אור חוזר—the reflective light) and rouses the mayim nukvin (מים נוקבין—the waters of the feminine) to rise toward the heavens, which then activates the descending energy in future food as the Or Yashar (אור ישר—the directed light and downward flowing light) and the blessings of mayim de'kurin (מים דכורין—the waters of the masculine).

One of the other guidelines for gathering manna was not to gather more than you need. However, people still gathered more than they needed, they kept it overnight, and it rotted. From the perspective of *din* (judgment), one begins to wonder when they were going to get it? Practically speaking, it often takes people a while to truly "get it," so we should look upon these lapses through the eyes of chesed (mercy). As we extend this into modern life, the same spiritual problems exist today. People have tremendous problems concerning their eating habits and especially overeating, although we have now added anorexia nervosa, the food imbalance of *under*eating. Eighty-two percent of Type 2 diabetics in the U.S. are overweight, forty-eight percent are obese, and thirty to forty percent of Americans are overweight in general. On a causal level, overeating and overweight can best be understood as "there is never enough food to feed a hungry soul." On a visual level, how many rabbis, and Am Yisrael in general, are overweight? Hashem's teaching of not to take more food than you need, as well as the basic Torah teaching to take care of your health, is being violated when we create these unhealthy conditions. Excess food and improper or excessive sexuality are the two major desires that must be mastered as part of our spiritual evolution and the preparation for the messianic times. In ancient times as well as now, the mastery of sexual and food desires, which at the higher levels has to do with creating holiness in sexuality and in food, were considered spiritual preconditions for receiving the Torah. The sexuality test for Am Yisrael comes later in BeMidbar in parashah Balak.

God now added yet another food/greed test, by mandating that on Friday there would be a double portion of manna, and no gathering was to be allowed on Saturday, because it is Shabbat! Still, some people went out to gather on Saturday, but there was no manna to be found. When were they going to listen and have faith? Although the B'nei Israel did not do these things, the people (ey'rev rav) did not have enough faith, violated Shabbat, and again flunked the test. In modern psychological terms, it was a divine behavior modification program that God was putting the people through while they were in the desert, because some of them had become so negatively influenced by the ey'rev rav and were too slow to truly understand what the big message was … and still is.

The spiritual testing continued as they traveled through the wilderness of Seen and ran out of water. Again the ey'rev rav were upset and started murmuring. They still did not have faith. In Shemot 17:2–7:

> The people began to quarrel with Moses. "Give us water to drink!" they exclaimed. "Why are you quarreling with me?" asked Moses. "Are you trying to test God?" The people began to suffer thirst because [of the lack] of water, and they began demonstrating against Moses. "Why did you bring us out of Egypt?" demanded [the leader]. "Do you want to make me, my children and my livestock die of thirst?" Moses cried out to God. "What shall I do for this people?" he said. "Before long they will stone me!" God said to Moses, "March in front of the people along with the elders of Israel. Take in your hand the staff with which you struck the Nile, and go. I will stand before you there on the rock at Horeb. You must strike the rock, and water will come out of it for the people to drink." Moses did this in the presence of the elders of Israel. [Moses] named the place Testing-and-Argument [Massa U'Merivah] because the people had argued and had tested God. They had asked, "Is God with us or not?"

The result was that water gushed forth and the people were again temporarily satisfied. However, the connection of faith and miracles is a subtle spiritual topic. Miracles may have an immediate effect, but the deeper and more permanent effect for faith is one's inner experience of the Divine. One can know the Torah literature backwards and forwards, but without the inner experience of the Divine, faith and real understanding of the divine mystery are limited. To know Hashem requires a synergy of mystical heart and intellectual mind. Just mind alone is not enough and in a subtle way can amplify egocentric pride and separate us from the Divine.

The people's lack of faith culminated in attracting an attack by the Amalekites, the first tribe to assail the Hebrews. They came from a distant place, as pointed out before, so they were not at all practically affected by the migration of the Hebrews through the land and had no obvious cause to do battle with them. 'Amalek is the code word for "doubt" on the spiritual path. During the ensuing battle with 'Amalek, Aharon and Hur helped Moshe to hold his arms up, with the staff of God in his hand, because as long as he kept his arms high and held his staff up, the Hebrews were winning. Eventually, the Hebrews were victorious and they defeated 'Amalek. But Moshe knew better; he knew that 'Amalek had only been "weakened" (Shemot 17:13), not totally defeated. He knew that the Amalekites would continue to be a thorn in the side of Israel, and he said, "God shall be at war with Amalek for all generations." It was not going to be so easy, and at that time God said in Shemot 17:14, "I will totally obliterate the memory of Amalek from under the heavens." In other words, "I will blot out all doubt." Following the battle, Moshe built an altar there, and named it *Adonai Nissi* (יהוה נסי), "YHWH is my banner," because, he said, "The hand is on God's throne. God shall be at war with Amalek for all generations" (Shemot 17:15–16). In other words, the grace will come to us from generation to generation to defeat 'Amalek in every paradigm.

In summary, one of the greatest teachings of the kabbalah and Torah is the importance of emunah (אמונה—faith) for bringing forth spiritual redemption. It was played out in the crossing of the Yam Suf, which is metaphorically made of our negative energies, or the k'lipot, of our lives, as well as negative thought forms and beliefs. It was played out in the journey in the desert. And so today through the energy of m'aseh l'avot simian labinim and with the grace-drawing power of our spiritual teshuva and purification, all the k'lipot can be washed away. Then we will be able to enter the fiftieth gate of holiness, and, through grace, awaken to deveikut/chey'rut. May everybody be blessed that, through faith and through the "going forward," (our good works in the world), we are able to cross the Yam Suf in our lives and awaken to our oneness with God.

Amen

Yitro

⟨⟩⟩

THIS parashah starts with "Moses' father-in-law, Jethro, sheik of Midian, heard...." The question is, "What did Yitro hear?" As we look more deeply into the issue of Yitro, we begin to understand that this lesson is one of the most important parts of the spiritual path. It is about listening, or being willing to listen. What brought him to hear? And why is this parashah named after Yitro, Moshe's Midianite father-in-law, when it is about receiving the Torah and the Ten Speakings? What caused him to join Am Yisrael, when everyone else in the world did not? And, after all that was going on, why didn't everyone come?

We can start with the question: What does it mean to truly listen? In so many instances the Torah speaks of listening: "Jethro heard" (Shemot 18:1); "Now listen to me. I will give you advice, and God will be with you" (Shemot 18:19); "Moses took his father-in-law's advice" (Shemot 18:24); "Now if you obey me and keep my covenant, you shall be my special treasure among all nations" (Shemot 19:5); "All the people answered as one and said, 'All that God has spoken, we will do'" (Shemot 19:8); "They [the people] replied, 'We will do and obey all that God has declared (naaseh v' nishshma—נעשה ונשמע)'" (Shemot 24:7). It is not like we will question, or we will contemplate it, or we will think about it, or we will do it if it fits our concept of how it should be, or if it is convenient for us. It is simply, you speak to us and we will listen, which means we will act on it; we will follow it.

It is said in the Midrash, that God went to all the different nations to offer them the Torah, and they all had one objection or another (Midrash Pesikta Rabbati 21:2). But Am Yisrael said, "We will do, and we will hear" (na'aseh v'nishma). This means they were ready to become the will of Hashem unfolding. This is also what distinguishes Yitro. He was committed to the spiritual path as a high priest, when not everybody was. That is why, most of the time, people cannot hear spiritual teachers. Many people are not in touch with the difference between how they are behaving and who they are meant to be. The

Torah and related kabbalistic teachings emphasize again and again that we come into the world to know God, to do tikkun ha'olam (תיקון העולם—heal the planet) and ultimately to heal, or make tikkun ha'nefesh (תיקון הנפש), which is about self-correction. Most people do not really make these improvements voluntarily and have to learn the hard way through life's challenges. It is a much higher vibration and easier way to be proactive in these experiences toward our transformation.

What is it that Yitro heard? On one level, he heard of the miraculous splitting of the Yam Suf (Sea of Reeds), and God's explicit role in the victory over 'Amalek. Now, the splitting of the Yam Suf was a very clear miracle, but the second miracle was perhaps more powerful. There were many miracles going on at that time. Yitro saw that in the war against 'Amalek, the people of Israel's victory depended upon Moshe keeping his hands raised in prayer. That was the second miracle. At that point, Yitro understood that there must be spiritual power guiding the Israelites, and he knew that in order to connect with that essence, he needed to go out to the desert and be with these people.

So why in the desert? What was going on in the desert? Why not receive the revelatory experience of the Ten Speakings in the Land of Israel? The Midrash explains that one needs to render oneself totally open and empty, like the desert, in order to truly understand the Torah (Midrash Bamid'bar Rabbah 1:7). Rashi writes: "Your heart should not be divided against the place. You should never say, 'In this place I can worship God, but in another place it would not be possible.'" The Torah was given not in a special place, but in the wilderness, so that the people would know to live by the guidance of the Torah everywhere they were. It was in this context that Yitro understood and heard, because of spiritual understanding, that if this was the way things were, then it would not be enough to receive the Torah in his own house, but he must go out on the road and receive the Torah there also. Only then would he be able to be on that path and on the path of full awakening. Yitro realized that to become a part of the Way of the Torah, and to fully wake up, he must leave his home and his country as Avraham had done, and go out into the wilderness: "Lekh lekha" (לך לך). This is another reason why he was honored; he was willing to receive and then to shift from "receive for self, alone" to "receive in order to share."

The willingness to receive is a precondition for the Torah as it leads to chey'rut and deveikut. It began with Avraham, who was willing to receive the message, and, again, go out into the wilderness into the uncertain, the unknown, and the unpredictable. This is the dedication one needs—being able to give up our comforts of home, country, identity, self-concept, belief system, cultural traditions (that sometimes we call religions), and to go into the world of the unknown. In the unknown, God is no longer in a box. In the unknown, God is the living expression of all creation. And so this section is named after Yitro, to honor the fact that Yitro was open, as a living example of the Torah Way to chey'rut and deveikut.

The second important piece is that we tend to think of the Jewish people as the only people who were chosen to receive. Really, God created everyone, and everyone is chosen in his or her own particular way. The question is: Are we willing to receive the messages of God in our lives? The fact that Yitro was the first to receive, and be open to this, again demonstrates that the Torah belongs to everyone, and it was therefore given in the desert because the desert does not belong to anyone in particular but to all (Midrash Bamid'bar Rabbah 1:7). The Torah is a guideline for deveikut (God-merging), in all ways, for all peoples. Everyone who chooses to be chosen is chosen; and everyone who chooses not to hear is not chosen. We are chosen in different ways, also. We are chosen in the sense that everyone in the whole world is chosen to know God, and we all have different paths, in a sense, to knowing that oneness. The criterion is to be open and to have an empty cup that is ready to be filled by God, rather than have our cups full with all our beliefs, concepts, and ideas of how it should be. That is why Yitro was honored the way he was. This is why we have the sh'ma, which says, "Hear, O Israel, Adonai is Our God, Adonai is One." Are we ready to hear that God is One? We can say it a thousand times; but are we ready to hear it in our direct experience?

Before Moshe went up the mountain to speak with God, Yitro did another interesting thing. He spoke to Moshe and essentially said, "You know, you need to reorganize the way you are administrating justice and create a whole new judicial system, in which you only see the difficult cases, while relegating the less difficult ones to the tribal elders." Now, Moshe was almost ready to receive God. He had been preparing three days like everyone else. Why did he stop and listen to this Midianite high priest? He fully listened, honoring his father-in-law in every respect. The meta-message of this little story is that before we are ready to listen to God, we have to be able to listen to each other. We have to feel the oneness with each other! Our relationship with God begins with our relationship with others. Indeed, "Hear, O Israel" implies that by listening to our fellow human beings and honoring the spark of God in them, we will be open to the flame of God in our own lives. This is the essence of all relationships, with God or with fellow human beings, to listen and hear the essence of the truth. Ultimately, it includes the ability to listen to ourselves as well. This was perhaps why God led us in a cloud, because when we see something so vividly, it is almost hard to listen because we are so affected by the vision. The pictures speak to our subconscious minds in a way that most words can only begin to do. It is said that the Hebrews saw a vision, and they saw the words. The message, which is so deeply missed in the world (in the Jewish world and beyond), is that we need to learn to see each other outside of our boxes. We need to learn to see each other in the context of understanding that we are all sparks of God, and to see this in all people, outside egocentrism and ethnocentrism, and into the mystical oneness of who we are. It is interesting that throughout the entire Torah, we are never commanded to listen. It says, "If you will listen ...," because the listening has to come from us. That is what Yitro did, and that was what Moshe exemplified when he listened to Yitro and adopted the counsel of his father-in-law before even going up the mountain to receive the counsel of God!

For many people, one of the greatest miracles of history, such as what happened at the Yam Suf, does not make a difference because they were not really ready to see or listen, though they may have been overwhelmed in the moment by a particular miracle. It is a time of great awakening, but like the Canaanites, many do not choose to give up their idol worship and child sacrifices to be part of things. To be chosen, it is a precondition that we choose to want to deepen our understanding and experience of the deep mystery. First we must reaffirm our relationship with each other as one people without all of our boundaries, concepts, and limitations, and only then can we access the experience of the Divine in ourselves and in each other.

The actual giving of the Torah was the connection of the oneness of who we are. At that point, Israel became Am Yisrael, the nation of Israel. There are two parts to the giving of the Torah: *Kabbalat HaTorah* (קבלת התורה), which was the actual receiving of the Torah, and *Ma'amad Har Sinay* (מעמד הר סיני), the whole experience of the direct encounter with the Divine at Sinay. Why were they different? The difference is that Ma'amad Har Sinay describes the process of individual Hebrews becoming a nation as Am Yisrael, with the reception of the Torah as part of that transformation. In the outer experience of the Eternal One, we spontaneously became one soul, which became a national identity and reality consensus. We actually met God face to face; we did not hear it through a prophet. We experienced the direct apperception of the Divine. The first two Speakings were given to all of us; and in the first two Speakings, we were born as a nation. The key here that makes this unique is that the whole nation had the collective awakening experience of oneness with God. That is what made us, at that moment, a special nation as Am Yisrael. At that point, the Torah became a guide for our primary purpose in life and in the world, which was, and is, to know God fully and to support the whole world in also knowing God, if interested. This tangible meeting and realization, and the statement "the whole nation saw the voices," further deepens this idea. Amazingly, in a process of forty-nine days, they were transformed from being slaves to being privileged to experiencing one of the highest states of human awareness: the direct apperception of the Divine. Some of the midrashic teachings imply that the experience was so strong that even the babies in the wombs felt it, and so strong that the whole of Am Yisrael actually left their bodies (temporarily died), and God had to resurrect them (Midrash Shemot Rabbah 29:4). Some sages suggest that the fiery flames and trembling of the mountain, accompanied by dangerously high voltage, and the increasingly powerful, land-piercing sound of the shofar, may have combined to create an interdimensional rift that enabled a full extraterrestrial, interdimensional communication to take place.

We became an empowered nation when we met God. We remain a nation that has met Hashem, even though, for most of us, our internal ancestral memories have grown dim. This is our path—to know God and to merge with God in the living everyday awareness of our lives, and to share with the rest of the world in a way that these teachings can be received. From this perspective, we see that the Eternal One started the process with the three patriarchs, prepared and purified this tribe to the maximum it could receive, and used the defeat of Pharaoh and Egypt (the strongest political force in the world at that time) to publicize the existence of the Divine so that people would, at least, notice what had happened. The intended purpose of it all was to upgrade the consciousness of humanity. People had been prepared for a thousand generations, at the end of which, they were finally ready to receive the Torah. The first part of prophecy had been fulfilled. Our work has been given to us. Our work is to be lived by love. Our work is to be lived by Hashem. Our work is to be lived by chey'rut and deveikut. Kabbalat HaTorah and Ma'amad Har Sinay are the foundations of the Torah Way as the living Torah as an expression of the Divine. They are all based on the ability to simply create a quiet mind, so that we can listen with an open mind, and so that we may transcend the mind altogether.

Parashah Yitro is also about the reception of the Torah, and again, we look at Yitro, who was open and receptive to a better way of life. We understand that this parashah was named after Yitro, because he was willing to put spiritual transformation at the center of his life. This means to put God at the very center of our lives, as the only criterion by which we guide our lives. There is no dating when the Torah was received, and although it was a single historical event, without an actual date, we can place ourselves in the consciousness of receiving it each Shabbat, each day, and each moment, when we are open to the light of Hashem within ourselves and everyone else.

Part of what Am Yisrael (it is not clear if the ey'rev rav were actually part of Kabbalat HaTorah) received was a three-column approach. We have a receiving, left-side column and a sharing, right-side column. The third column, the central column, is the power of restriction, or control, of the ego, which means we are able to share when we need to share, and we are able to receive when we need to receive. These three columns are actually the Tree of Life (Etz Chaim). That is what makes this system unique versus a more dualistic system such as the Yin-Yang and other dualistic systems.

The receiving of the Ten Speakings/Utterances (also known as the Ten Commandments) is the core of this parashah. The world has had to go through the rather poor translations of the Torah, from Hebrew to Greek to Latin to English, so there is bound to have been a loss of energy and accuracy in the transmission. One such misinterpretation is calling the Ten Utterances or Speakings the Ten Commandments. In Hebrew they are also known as *asseret ha'dib'rot* (עשרת הדברות), literally meaning "ten of the resonances." In the Zohar they are called the ten *ey'tzot* (עצות), or "suggestions" (Zohar, Vol. 2, folio 82b). None of these translations of the original Hebrew say, or in any way imply, the meaning to be "commandments." They are intended as guidelines, suggestions, and teachings. People already had, from the time of Noah, the seven Noahide laws, which were transmitted to Avraham from Eber, who received it from his great grandfather, Shem, Noah's son, also known as Malkizedek. However, they did not seem to catch hold. Having laws, which are an external experience, did not really work. So, what was different between the Ten Speakings and the seven Noahide teachings? The difference was, we had a new context. The Ten Speakings are about the relationship between God and ourselves; this is particularly true for the first five. The last five are about our relationship with other humans. In a sense, the first five Speakings/Utterances/Resonances are about the quality of divine energy in our relationship with each other as human beings. It is dependent on our internal God experience, which becomes our guide. In the Ten Speakings, Resonances, or Utterances, Shemot 20:3, it does not read, "Do not have any other gods before me." It really says, "You should have no other gods upon my face." What does that mean? In a sense, "face" is a term for intimacy, for knowing. When you see someone's face, you know that person. It means that we do not add onto the seventy faces of God any limiting definitions or images. It also means that we do not limit it to a one-face interpretation, when there are seventy faces or aspects of the Divine as the full face, because that, too, puts God in a box. One of the great teachings we get from Yesha'yahu (Isaiah) is: "For my thoughts are not your thoughts, neither are your ways my ways, says the Lord. For as the heavens are higher than the earth, so are my ways higher than your ways, and my thoughts than your thoughts" (Yesha'yahu 55:8–9). We cannot put God in a box and say "This is knowing God." In fact, even the word "God" is a mistranslation. It really, in this context, is Elohim, which is a plural term that implies "all powers of God." The classical use of the term "Eternal One" for YHWH is also a major mistranslation. Another level of mistranslation is to talk about God as a "God of vengeance." This is inaccurate. In the

Hebrew original it reads "God who is master over vengeance," because God is not subject to human emotions and reactions such as revenge and grudges (Yirmeyahu 3:12). Rather, God is the lord over vengeance and anger. God is the lord over jealousy (Midrash Tehillim 94:1).

The meta-communcation of this first utterance also suggests that we need grace to awaken to enlightenment, because we are so enslaved to our ego. Our job is to do the work to become a superconductor of the Divine as much as we can through our prayers, meditations, and acts of service to draw the grace of God because we cannot technique our way to enlightenment. Tehillim 81:10 says "There should be no strange god to you," meaning that God will never be a stranger to you. "The lip of truth shall be established forever" (Mishle 12:19). Tehillim 145:18 says "The Lord is near to all of those that call upon him … to all that call upon him with truth." If we do not perceive God everywhere, it means we do not see God anywhere. Proverbs 16:8 says "See the name of God everywhere." This is the deep enlightened meaning. As it teaches in the Zohar, there is no existence except in the existence of God—Ayn Zulato. Devarim 4:39 says: "Realize it today and ponder it in your heart: God is the Supreme Being in heaven above and on the earth beneath. There is no other."

The very first Speaking is "I am God your Lord, who brought you out of Egypt, from the place of slavery" (Shemot 20:2). This is saying: (1) "I am a cosmic God"; (2) "I am a special God that personally takes care of all Am Yisrael and all people"; and (3) "I am a God that helped you as a tribe transcend Mizrayim externally and the ego internally." It is not just the idea of God in the abstract sense. This is both a transcendent and immanent God, who not only guides all creation and actually intervenes in every instant and in big moments like the Big Bang and the exodus, but in all people all the time to bring them to deveikut/chey'rut over cycles of lifetimes.

According to the kabbalah, the Ten Utterances correspond to the ten sephirot of the Tree of Life. The very first Speaking has the sephirah of keter (כתר—divine will) concealed within it. It implies the existence of a personal creator of whose will we can choose to be the cooperative expression. It is an immanent God who is personally connected, in a sense, to Am Yisrael as the firstborn and to all people, and personally connected in a way that helps us overcome our egos in the process of deveikut/chey'rut.

The second Utterance is chokhmah (חכמה), which is about idol worship, or giving power to any source other than God. This could be money, power, fame, or it could be gold idols that are still in existence today (we call it currency), or silver idols, or wooden idols. It also included, in those times, the worship of astronomical bodies (sun, moon, stars, and planets), the worship of angels (very common today), and the worship of demons and spirits prevalent among the dark forces and among people who do not understand channeling. Idol worship is anything to which we give away our sense of power. It is antithetical to the knowing that the word of God is our ultimate source of power. It also includes creating any limiting conceptions of God by focusing on only one of the seventy faces as the "true" face.

"Have no gods before me" means, from an enlightenment context, to see God in all things. The presence of God is dancing everywhere. It implies we should not limit ourselves to one face of God and ignore the other primary sixty-nine faces and spend time egoically fighting that we are the only ones to "have the right face." In enlightenment we see and appreciate all the faces of God instead of focusing on one exclusive face. *"Baruch shem k'vod ...,"* as in Yirmeyahu 10:10, "The Lord God is true." The teaching here in the level of exiting Egypt, we go inside to free ourselves from the ego so that the truth of God is all that exists in our life (Bamid'bar Rabbah 13:15–16), and for enlightenment, we would naturally embrace all of them as the full experience of the One. This is implied in the phrase "Do not have any other gods before me" (Shemot 20:3). Another way of translating this is "You shall have no other gods [projected] on my face." When there are infinite faces of God with seventy as the basic number, choosing only one face, name, or perspective is considered a subtle form of idolatry. Idolatry begins with an attempt to put a particular face or definition on God. This teaching means to see God in all things, but not to specifically worship any form as God. For example, we may be in awe of the hand of God in nature (known as panentheism), but we do not worship nature as God (called pantheism and idol worship).

In the inner and ongoing experience of enlightenment, one becomes free to be the expression of God in any divinely directed way. In enlightenment we are free to move in any direction. There are no boundaries (*ayn lo gevul*—גבול אין לו) in our individualized expression of the Divine as the Divine moves

through us, as long as we are *mekaven ratzon Hashem* (מכוון רצון השם), meaning that we become the intention of the will of God as Moshe was throughout
Shemot, and as was Pinchas in BeMidbar

The third Utterance, which is associated with binah (בינה), is not to use the
name of God in vain. When we use different names of God, they have angelic
names associated with them, such as the forty-two-letter name encrypted in
the first-century prayer *Ana B'koach*. We have to be very careful about that.
We should be living totally in the name of God in every moment, in every
breath; at the same time, we do not want to trivialize it and deprive ourselves
of its true power.

"Do not take the name of God in vain" is also about maintaining the awe
and fear of God, which is the one quality we have of our own volition. In our
lives we are in the fear and awe of God and therefore there is no room to take
the name of God unnecessarily or to take an oath in God's name. The constant
awe of God is expressed in Tehillim 19:10: "The fear of God is pure. It endures
forever." If something endures forever, we know that it is real and absolute. Tir
Avos 2:17 says "All your deeds shall be for the sake of heaven," and when all our
deeds are for the sake of heaven, we will never take the name of God in vain.

The fourth Utterance, chesed (חסד), is about honoring, observing, and
remembering Shabbat. At its most fundamental enlightenment approach it
means having a quiet mind so that we can be amplified receptors of the Divine. In that context we naturally are not involved in the thirty-nine types of
work described as forbidden on the Shabbat. This refers to the word *zachor*
(זכור—"remember") and we rest in the noncausal bliss of the divine love of
deveikut. It is to remember the act of creation as it emerged from the nothing
prior to consciousness; it is remembering the divine spark within each of us. If
our awareness is limited, then we have to "keep" (*shamor*) the Shabbat, which
includes the avoidance of the thirty-nine categories of work (*melachah*—אכה-
מל) in the consciousness of *yir'at Hashem* (יראת השם—fear or awe of God).
This shamor of Shabbat forms an external container that makes it easier to experience the inner (zachor) Shabbat that is more about *ahavat Hashem* (השם
אהבת—love of God).

Shabbat is a time to become refreshed with a renewed spirit of Hashem
in our lives. It is a time to remember the truth and source of our cosmic

consciousness as the breath of God, which can take us beyond time, space, and being. Shabbat in this context helps us to understand that we are immortal souls, and to know our ultimate, unending oneness with the Eternal One. In that process of our remembrance, all that we do becomes holy; at least one day a week we keep that remembrance. It is also the remembrance of the first Shabbat and of the act of creation as the initial example of God's continual intervention in order to evolve consciousness on the planet. The receiving of Shabbat is continuous as is the cosmic creation of it. It is taught by the sages that there are two Shabbats: the seventh day of the week and the remaining six days. It is taught that when we celebrate both, we are in deveikut/chey'rut.

"Remember the Sabbath to keep it holy" guides us to experience Shabbat itself as a day of enlightenment. It's a time when we create a quiet mind, which automatically takes us beyond work. Shabbat creates, when we take it as a holy ceremony, rather than a ritual, a holy environment that transforms our consciousness into the One. Literally, that holy environment of Shabbat upgrades the psychospiritual effects and upgrades the epigenetic memory of our DNA to bring even this expression into the resonance of the enlightenment awareness. It is taught that when we have two Shabbats in a row (the day of Shabbat and the following six days), we indeed become enlightened.

This awareness is the foundation of the second five Utterances, because if we are remembering God all the time, every day is Shabbat, and we act with a certain amount of holiness. Obviously, we do not have to be told not to murder or steal. By being lived by the first five teachings, the second five become naturally internalized. This is the key to understanding what these Ten Utterances/Speakings are about. They are a guideline (not "commandments," as they have been mistranslated), for how to evolve spiritually and how to live our lives in the most holy way that forms the foundation for awakening to deveikut/chey'rut.

The fifth Utterance corresponds to gevurah (גבורה), and is about "honoring your mother and your father," which has a lot to do with honoring our ancestors and lineage and thus respecting them as guides on the spiritual path. It is to remember the God of Avraham, of Yitzhak, and of Ya'akov. In this context, we may connect to *ma'aseh tzaddikim* (מעשה צדיקים—the works of the righteous) and to ma'aseh avot siman labanim as powerful prophetic cycles and spiritual tests and transformations that are part of this lineage. Every word of a tzaddik, no matter how trivial it may seem, can create a powerful result. This is the hidden meaning of ma'aseh tzaddikim.

On another level of enlightenment perspective this means the merging of the heavens and earth within us, *shvikud oshehinte*. The Torah tradition as we understand it in the kabbalah is that enlightenment is associated with the merging of the inner and outer male and female uniting within ourselves. This is Abba and Imma becoming one. At that point of awareness there is total enlightenment integration.

The sixth Speaking is associated with the sephirah of tiferet (תפארת). It does not really say, "Do not murder"—that whole idea is a little bit backwards. In Hebrew, it does not really work as a commandment. More accurately, it reads "You will not murder," versus "you may not or must not." The implication is that you will not murder if you are observing and living the way of the first five Speakings, because you will not be prone to committing murder, sexual abuse, theft, and slander. You will be in the oneness, and so the consciousness that results is … you will not murder.

"Don't commit murder" on a deeper level means that one should do nothing that takes us away from God. When we move away from God in our consciousness, we create a murder of our soul. As we are in awe of God, so we should be in awe and respect to the spark of God within us. This teaching also implies the impurity associated with, and serious damage associated with, trying to directly or indirectly murder another's soul with our actions or words. This is also a result of violating the ninth teachings and using lashon hara to murder someone's soul.

The seventh Speaking is associated with netzach (נצח). It is often translated "Don't commit adultery," which is not an accurate translation. The Utterance more literally reads "You will not commit sexual abuse" of any kind, and it has to do with the wrong use of the sexual impulse. This certainly includes adultery, but is a wider prohibition. Although considered a capital offense, adultery was difficult to prove, since Jewish law required two witnesses to have actually seen a full intercourse event and have warned the couple of the potential consequences of the sexual intercourse before it took place (Talmud Bav'li, Sanhedrin 80b). It is doubtful that anyone was ever executed for adultery in Jewish history. It may be that the best way to understand the "death penalty" is that threats of harsh punishment in the Torah are more about emphasizing the severity of a particular transgression. In Jewish law, or halakhah, for example, technically a single woman having sex with a married man does not constitute adultery for either party, since a man was permitted more than one wife or sexual partner in biblical times (Talmud Bav'li, Yevamot 5a). However, in modern rabbinical teachings since the tenth century it has generally not been accepted, and, from a family therapy point of view, triangular relationships almost always damage relationship intimacy and can be disastrous to the married relationship, so in no way am I, as a rabbi, family therapist, psychiatrist, and holistic physican, recommending this sort of activity. Nonmarital sex, in general, is not prohibited in Judaism, as it is in Christianity (Talmud Bav'li, Sanhedrin 21a). However, when done in secrecy, without the knowledge of others one is intimate with, or in unequal power relationships such as a teacher-student relationship, it creates *g'neyvay daat,* a "stealing of the mind," and thus violates the eighth Utterance (Talmud Bav'li Tosefta Baba Kama 7:3). Although it may be consensual, it is not "informed consent," and thus also violates the seventh Utterance as such actions become a subtle form of sexual abuse.

The prohibition against adultery is more classically against committing sexual abuse, which extends to incest. In Jewish law, sex with a child or a parent is a severe crime. It is not accepted. However, it is allowed with an uncle, niece, or cousin, and of course in earlier times, prior to the giving of the Torah, our people sometimes did marry some of those relatives later forbidden by the Torah, such as Ya'akov marrying two sisters simultaneously, or Yehudah marrying his daughter-in-law Tamar, or 'Amram marrying Yokheved, who was his aunt, and from whom came Aharon, Miriam, and Moshe. Sex between siblings is forbidden, but it is not considered criminal. Rape, which is considered sexual abuse, not only extends to a man having sex without mutual consent with somebody out in the world, but also to forcing his wife, to whom he's legally married, to have sex against her will (Talmud Bav'li, Eruvin 100b). Also, this prohibition touches on other situations such as homosexuality. Whereas Christianity forbids all homosexual activity, Judaism technically forbids male homosexual acts that include sodomy, but not other homosexual acts (Talmud Bav'li, Sanhedrin 54a–56a and Sotah 26b; Maimonides's Pirush HaRambam ahl HaMishnayot, Sanhedrin, Chap. 7). Lesbianism has never been forbidden (Pirush HaRambam ahl HaMishnayot, Sanhedrin, Chap. 7; Talmud Bav'li, Sanhedrin 54a and Yevamot 76a). Though such sexual activities might not have been well accepted and considered lewd, they were not forbidden. Bestiality (sex with an animal) was also forbidden.

The eighth Speaking, which is associated with hod (הוד), is "You will not steal." It has to do with behaving as if we deserve something that we do not, in fact, deserve, or that has not been ordained to us. It has to do with physical objects, but also with taking the light from someone.

"Do not steal" also means we should not steal from ourselves. The Torah Way of enlightenment requires that we be fully honest with ourselves. The teaching of *sinat daat* not only applies to outer relationships but also to not deceiving ourselves and falling into alma d'shikra (world of illusion). For us to go deep into the spiritual path requires that we go beyond the ego comfort zone where we fool ourselves and steal from our own mind. The deep and true Torah spiritual path involves a process of berur—self-examination of reality and our inner motivations. It means to be clear and honest with ourselves. As implied in Shemot 22:1, if we are practicing berur, we will find the thief within and overcome it.

The ninth Speaking, which corresponds with yesod (יסוד), is one of the harder ones for most people. "You will not bear false witness" includes lashon hara (לשון הרע), or gossip and slander. It results in the murder of both our souls and the one we are gossiping about.

It also implies one should not bear false witness against oneself. Don't lie to yourself. In the act of berur we lose the deceptive "I" and ego that wants to keep us in our comfort zone and move into radical honesty with ourselves about ourselves. Tehillim 32:2 says "In his spirit there is no guile." One's spirit is the desire to serve God. When we are truly in the post-berur and/or enlightened state, the desire to be the living will of Hashem is completely honest and without guile.

The tenth Speaking, which corresponds to malchut (מלכות), is "You will not covet what somebody else has," because the minute we covet what others have, we assert that God is wrong in what God has delegated to each of us. As the second-century Ben Zoma taught, "The wealthy person is the one who is happy with what they have" (Mishnah Avot 4:1). "Don't be envious of your neighbor" also implies that we understand that everything God does is for the best. Everyone is given unique gifts and strengths. This allows us to accept the events in our lives as part and supportive of our ultimate destiny, which is to know God.

The Ten Speakings or Utterances are much more sophisticated than a simple set of golden rules or commandments. They are not a dogma, which brings reward or punishment. As Martin Buber put it: "One who rejects God is not struck down by lightning, and one who elects God does not find hidden treasures. Everything seems to remain just as it was. Obviously, God does not wish to dispense either medals or prison sentences."

The Ten Speakings are a way of life that supports and guides our spiritual transformation, bringing us into the culture of deveikut/chey'rut, so that the grace of God may help us know our oneness. The word "commandment" comes out of a mindset that is really not part of the Jewish tradition that gave birth to the Ten Utterances. People who were not part of the original understanding, and may have had specific agendas for what they wanted to communicate, accepted the "commandment" mistranslation. The Torah is not "the law." Torah is a Hebrew word that literally translates literally as *guide*. On one level we are "people of the law," but on a deeper level, we are not only "people of the law," as we are sometimes disparagingly called, but we are people of God (open to the unknown) walking like Moshe up the Mountain of God into the great spiritual mystery as we are guided by the great Enlightenment Way of the Torah and the Ten Utterances/Speakings/Resonances. The Torah was given as a guide to help us know God, to help bring us closer and ultimately to merge with God. This is fundamental and a deeper teaching of this parashah.

It is taught that one may receive the Torah every Shabbat. The more we are opened to this, the more we can begin to receive the Torah in every moment. It is an endless receiving until we become lived by it in every moment. May everybody be blessed with the understanding that we are one tribe, one nation, one people, one world, and with the ability to listen and talk with one another in the context of that oneness. Through that context and that listening we become more and more one with God, and thereby realize the full teachings of the Torah. May we be all blessed with this level of understanding.

Amen

Mishpatim

IT may seem a little strange after the amazing spiritual experiences described in parashah Yitro, to be talking about justice in this next parashah, interrupting the incredible narrative of divine revelation that has just unfolded, but parashah Mishpatim is actually the next teaching of this very same narrative. It gives us a very important message, that we are to walk between the b'limah and the mah, the nothing and the something. We are guided to know the divine revelation of parashah Yitro of the absolute truth, which is the b'limah (divine nothing) and yet be, at the same time, grounded in bringing the sacred into our everyday actions, into the mah. This is both the mystery and practical reality of the Torah Way. In this way, we learn that every action starts with the love and inspiration of God in the realm of b'limah, so that we might fill every moment of our lives with the presence of God on the plane of the mah (something). Mishpatim is an explicit way of articulating this liberation teaching.

On a surface level, Mishpatim appears to be more mundane, but it is the essence of what it means to be a good person and to live in virtue and holiness, as the foundation for living in deveikut/chey'rut (spiritual liberation). We do not simply jump from spiritual experiences into liberation. It takes building a foundation of holiness, leading us to the highest virtue: to live continuously in the ecstatic divine presence of God experienced as the continuous noncausal spiritual joy, peace, contentment, oneness, compassion, and love. Whereas in Yitro we experienced a collective ecstatic revelation of God, in Mishpatim we were taught how to create kedusha as a foundation for living in the virtue of God at every moment. By living in the radical virtue of Hashem we become freed from the pain of emptiness and misery of evil in our lives, and we see, through the desperate emptiness of a world where particularly our young people are fascinated and seduced by media focus on zombies, vampires, and the dark occult in general. In this secular, atheistic world, evil has a sexy, seductive, and lively illusion to it, which is but a thin veneer, covering up an empty, hollow, desperately sad heart and soul. And in glamorizing living in this twilight zone between the living and the dead, virtue became contracted and minimized to mean duty, obligation, and responsibility, rather than living at the highest level of virtue as a fully God-activated simcha (שמחה—spiritually joyful) human being, who is really the one having all the fun.

It is the human condition and gift to be given a hollow emptiness in our soul as well as the opportunity and motivation to access the light of God that is hidden in the darkness of this hollow emptiness. The Sinai revelation gave us a taste of this delicious light at the bottom of our soul, and Mishpatim gives us part of the means to access it on a regular basis. The yetzer tov (טוב יצר—impulse toward good) guides us toward living to access this soul light of God in deeper and deeper ways. The yetzer hara (יצר הרע—impulse toward evil), in its contrary way, leads us to desperately avoid the pain of this empti- ness and "lack" at the center of our soul by any means other than turning to God. It leads to acts of destruction and violence against ourselves and oth- ers, including meaningless sex, drugs, alcohol, rape, terrorism, and other evil acts of domination, self-destruction, and cruelty to others. We do anything to avoid feeling the pain of our emptiness and incompleteness in a desperate, temporary effort to feel alive. These wanton actions further separate us from the light of God, within, and move us deeper and deeper into evil actions to "feel alive." We become like zombies struggling to feel alive. We become like vampires feeding on another's life force in order to feel real and energized. Unfortunately, whether consciously or not, this is becoming more and more the world situation today. Mishpatim, in this context, gives us a way to begin to fill this emptiness with the light of Hashem and to avoid desecrating our- selves with evil actions.

An additional gift that helps us move toward God to fill the emptiness is the *na'aseh v'neshima* (נעשה ונשמע) of Shemot 24:7. Our response to God at Sinai was "We will do and obey all that God has declared." It was a promise of Am Yisrael to keep the Torah before even studying it. It is taught that this response revealed a secret given to the angels. It was a statement of the existence of the direct knowing found in the world of atzilut that we have within ourselves, as do the angels. This direct knowing naturally guides us in serving God and becoming the living Torah. So, not only the written Torah and mitzvot were revealed at Har Sinay, but the light of our own divine essential nature was also revealed. Once we make contact with this essence at the source of our soul, we lose the fear of our emptiness, because we intuitively know that underneath that empty hole is the ecstatic light of God. It is the gift of this knowledge that helps us not to succumb to the counsel of the yetzer hara directing us toward evil actions as a solution to the pain of our emptiness.

On the p'shat level, Mishpatim opens with the proper treatment of the *eved ivri* (the indentured slave), but on a deeper level, it addresses the essential life choice that we all must make either consciously or unconsciously. We must choose or not choose devotion to God and the path to deveikut/chey'rut as the central theme in our lives, or instead live our lives as a slave to the "matrix." These choices are reflected in Shemot 21:3, where it says "he shall leave …" and in Shemot 21:6, where the slave protested and said "I do not want to go free." In other words, "Am I ready to free myself from the slavery of the ego and all its desires, materialized in time, space, and I Am-ness keeping me enslaved?" or "Am I not ready to move out of my egocentric comfort zone?" It may seem like an obvious choice, but it would be good to remember that according to the Midrash, eighty percent of the Hebrews did not want to leave the slavery of Egypt and died during the plague of darkness (spiritual ignorance). Many of those who did leave soon changed their minds and wanted to return to the comfort of Egypt. So God kept Am Yisrael in the desert for forty years until a new generation grew up that was ready to fight for their freedom. Hashem was gracious enough to give us the Shabbat as a weekly cycle of seven to be a constant reminder to leave behind all of our tendencies toward slavery for at least one day a week, and to remember the purpose of life.

A core theme of Mishpatim is the natural cosmic law of cause and effect, that there is a consequence attached to all we do. This is the meaning of Shemot 21:23–25, addressing liability for harming someone: "However, if there is a fatal injury [to the woman], then he must pay full compensation for her life. Full compensation must be paid for the loss of an eye, a tooth, a hand or a foot. Full compensation must [also] be paid for a burn, a wound, or a bruise." While this has been misinterpreted as revenge, it is not revenge in any manner; it actually implies restitution (Talmud Bav'li, Baba Kama 83b).

A simple reading a few lines later, in Shemot 21:26, makes this more clear: "If a person strikes his male or female slave in the eye and blinds it, he shall set [the slave] free in compensation for his eye." Those who interpret "eye for an eye" as revenge have chosen to read this deep teaching of the law of cause and effect in a most negative, superficial, and Torah-undermining way. It is an explicit statement of the law of cause and effect. Every action has a consequence. The action of consequence is a great act of grace because it allows us to clear the negative energies we have created by our actions. Mishpatim outlines the subtle understandings of how this works as a guiding principle for creating justice on the plane of human interaction. It is a deep Torah teaching that there are no victims, and there is no one being punished. There is only the cosmic principle of the law of cause and effect unfolding as a gift in our lives, even though, at times, it may not be experienced as a gift. The best way to understand it as a gift is to apply the teaching "Whatever God does is for the best" (Talmud Bav'li, Berachot 60b). It is a gift because every time we experience the consequences of our actions, it is the clearing of energy that we have accumulated. The more energy we clear, the freer we are to experience the Divine in our lives. It is also a gift, if we view it that way, because it creates an awe-filled worldview in which we become grateful for all that comes our way in life, and so it is easier to retain our state of simcha, or spiritual joy.

Once, while flying back from Israel, I reached to get something from the overhead compartment, and, because of a tear in my rotator cuff, lost control of my bag. It fell on the head and shoulder of a Haredi (ultra-Orthodox) man. We looked at each other for a moment, and then he said "I guess I deserved that." Because we had the same understanding we both shared a good laugh. Instead of a negative situation arising, in a mutual understanding of this principle, we had an uplifting moment. All events happening in the world, to a people, to a nation, or to an individual person, work on the same principle. This principle is active over lifetimes, and so it even affects our destiny. Sometimes we get a warning such as in the Deuteronomic parashahs of Ki-Tavo, Netzavim, and Ha'azinu of how to behave to avoid being kicked out of the land, and of the terrible consequences that will follow us throughout history even 3,400 years later, with the effect of our actions climaxing in the Holocaust as the predicted purification, before we could return to the land as we did in 1948. Moshe told us what would happen if we as a people chose to act in a certain way, and it happened. It has happened all throughout our history, since the beginnings of the exile. When our prophets forewarn us, it is generally worth listening. A wise person is one who understands the ramifications of his or her actions.

As difficult as it is to say, we are not victims (and that includes ninety-five percent of my father's family, who died in the Holocaust). To take the position of victim does not give us the opportunity to evolve from that clearly disastrous situation and to, instead, change our ways, and return to the path of the Torah. The halakhah is not the law. It is a way of experiencing the Divine as the walk in our everyday lives, so that all we do is elevated in holiness. These laws are wisdom to protect us from consequences that we may not like. The other misconception is that the results of our actions are punishments. They are not punishments; the unpleasant results are ways of the Divine of balancing the energy, so that we may continue our spiritual evolution and learn from the results of our actions. Another way of understanding this cosmic law is that we reap what we sow. We have had our cosmic experiences, and now what is our walk? Our walk leads us into being awakened people. The cosmic experience is the seed from which full awakening grows. Mishpatim follows the cosmic, collective, divine revelation of God, shared by all of Am Yisrael, because the next step is to bring this awareness into every aspect of our so-called mundane realms in ways that sanctify the mundane, so that we experience and imbue the Divine in all our actions. With that in mind, we get a better understanding that this is not physical law, but rather cosmic law. This law helps us win the battle with the yetzer hara (יצר הרע—negative side), which delights in inciting us to do actions that bring negative results. In Mishle (Proverbs) 16:32, King Solomon delineated the strength that comes from winning this internal struggle when he said: "He that rules his spirit [is better] than one who captures a city." Essentially linked to this is the idea that if our morality is not completely natural in our hearts, based upon our sense of oneness with one another (through atzilut reality understanding), then we must invoke self-control. This self-restraint is the middle column and gives us spiritual growth. This is how we can live in the world. The kabbalists have taught us to develop a number of spiritual understandings for these simple rules. However, this is not about sophisticated understandings or rules. It is about how to live as a mensch in the world. It is about how to live as a heart-centered, loving person guided in full love and sincerity in the world. This is not blind obeisance such as slavery; rather, it is complete and conscientious devotion to the Divine. All other forms of slavery take us away from keeping the Divine at the center of our lives.

A positive result of living in this God-centered way is health: "You will then serve God your Lord, and he will bless your bread and your water. I will banish sickness from among you" (Shemot 23:25). This passage is exciting because it says that when you are spiritually healthy and tuned into the Divine, you will be free from disease. This is clear in every world and in every culture; you are what you eat, and what you eat affects your mind and your spirituality. This teaches that when food and drink are pure and healthy (in other words, free of pesticides, herbicides, microwaves, X-rays, or genetic modifications), they do not cause sickness but will nurture and heal you. Furthermore, there will not be any "miscarrying womb[s] and dry breasts" (Hoshea 9:14). It is a general prescription for health that when you eat healthy, whole food, you will be healthy. If you eat junk food, even if it is kosher, you will have poor health and an unclear mind. An unclear mind cannot elevate the spirit to know God. When people are unhealthy, the rate of infertility increases, as we are seeing in our modern times. When the passage says "I will make you live out full lives," it is indicative of longevity and freedom from pandemics. When we fulfill the mitzvot, the resulting positive energy will be naturally healing in everything we do. The water, food, and air will be of a high frequency to bring us health and wellbeing.

Another useful teaching is Shemot 23:29–30, which helps people understand the slow and gentle process of healing and spiritual unfolding:

> "I will not drive them out in a single year, however, lest the land
> become depopulated, and the wild animals become too many
> for you [to contend with]. I will drive [the inhabitants] out little
> by little, giving you a chance to increase and [fully] occupy the
> land."

When we understand this teaching as the internal process of physical and mental purification of our negative thoughts and bodily toxins, we are given the way in which healing on all levels of body, mind, and spirit happens. If it occurs too much too quickly, the system may get overwhelmed with a massive detox effect, and one can actually die. There are multiple stories of such happenings among the Hasidim of the 1700s. Steady and consistent is the way of developing kedusha until the final shattering of the mind takes place, and we rise above the mind through the grace of God to deveikut/chey'rut. Patience and perseverance are key qualities on the great Torah path of enlightenment.

Another fundamental quality needed for deveikut/chey'rut is surrender to the flow of the Divine. When Moshe shared the teachings he received from Hashem with the seventy elders, his brother Aharon, and his sons Nadav and Avihu, and then with the people, the collective response was "We will keep every word that God has spoken" (נעשה ונשמע—na'aseh v'neshema) (Shemot 24:1–3). This is the great statement of surrender to the Divine. The ability to do without egotistically questioning is fundamental for higher spiritual evolution. This is not an invitation for a psychotic person to follow delusions and bring harm to oneself or others. This is about spiritually mature people, such as the seventy elders, Moshe, Aaron, Nadav, and Avihu, operating at the highest level of spiritual evolvement and discrimination, being capable of transcending the egocentric limitations of the mind. This is why, although everyone can benefit from a tzaddik, the most powerful benefit comes to one who is spiritually mature enough to merit a *tzaddik gamur* (צדיק גמור—liberated tzaddik). In other words, we are not talking about mindless surrender.

Once they were in this state of surrender and deveikut, Moshe, Aharon, Nadav, Avihu, and the seventy elders spiritually ascended and had a collective vision of the God of Israel. It is important to note that they all had the same vision.

> They saw a vision of the God of Israel, and under His feet was something like a sapphire brick, like the essence of a clear [blue] sky. [God] did not unleash His power against the leaders of the Israelites. They had a vision of the Divine, and they ate and drank.
>
> (Shemot 24:9–11)

They made offerings and ate the offerings. This vision brought them noncausal joy, love, peace, bliss, and contentment. These are the true human emotions. They were eating out of that great joy. There are several other ways to interpret the eating and drinking response to such a potent revelatory experience. One perspective is the practice of avodah b'gashminut, which means experiencing Hashem in every aspect of life including sexuality, eating of food, and all mundane matters. Of course, as in the eastern Tantric traditions, unless they happen spontaneously, as in this case with the seventy-four elders, it is a tricky practice that can lead to, and be an excuse for, hedonism, overeating, and ruining one's health and spiritual state in the illusion of l'shem shamayim—"for the sake of Heaven." A heavy, overweight, unhealthy body violates the Torah teaching of maintaining one's health as a way of protecting one's soul. A full belly rarely creates a quiet mind, empty enough to receive the divine presence. This leads us to a second interpretation. Perhaps they needed to ground themselves with food and drink because the energy of the vision was so great. This is not atypical of people who have such powerful meditation experiences.

Once I had a spontaneous vision, similar to that of the seventy-four elders, while praying and meditating. During this vision I saw an emerald-sapphire stone under the blazing feet of God, and the throne of God filled with white light absent of a specific form. At that time, however, I did not make the connection with this historical shared Torah vision event. Ascending to the world of beriah (the pure mind) and having this experience was so energetically profound, however, that I could neither eat nor drink nor move after coming out of meditation, and it remains a part of my inner teachings. The seventy elders and Nadav and Avihu had a deep level of awakening in their vision, where they saw God on a throne. This is the level of the world of beriah. They were able to hold the vision and tongues of fire appeared over their heads, and they began to prophesy. The tongues of fire represent the activated shekhinah energy; it was a collective s'micha m'shefa. This spread down even into the camp.

Two in the camp, El'dad and May'dad, began to prophesy, because the people and the seventy elders were able to hold more light and so they received more light. They were called atzilim (אצילים), meaning "those who emanate," because after this vision the spirit of God radiated from them. At the same time, it is important not to confuse a vision with a deeper understanding.

Although they beheld a vision of God, they had not broken through into an eternal steady awareness such as that of Moshe. They had an elevated vision from which they came down. They were filled with a great light, and the Ruach HaKodesh was awakened within them. They were spiritually elevated. But it is clear that these elders had yet to integrate this experience. In just under forty days they lost the tongues of fire, as nether Aharon, Hur, or the other elders had the spiritual strength and wisdom to stop the building of the Golden Calf. They had been spiritually empowered so that Moshe could ascend the mountain, but they could not hold energy of that magnitude for long, and eventually Aharon enabled the great disaster that followed. They beheld God, but they did not enter into the eternal, permanent awareness that Moshe had. Moshe walked with the eternal in his everyday life, whether on top of the Holy Mountain or at its foot.

Following this activating event, Shemot 24:12–13 says:

> God said to Moses, "Come up to me, to the mountain, and re-main there. I will give you the stone tablets, the Torah and the commandment that I have written for [the people's] instruc-tion." Moses and his aid Joshua set out. Moses went up on God's Mountain. He said to the elders, "Wait for us here until we return to you. Aaron and Chur will remain with you. Whoever has a problem can go to them."

Continuing, in Shemot 24:15–18:

> As soon as Moses reached the mountain top, the cloud covered the mountain. God's glory rested on Mount Sinai, and it was cov-ered by the cloud for six days. On the seventh day, He called to Moses from the midst of the cloud. To the Israelites, the appear-ance of God's glory on the mountain top was like a devouring flame. Moses went into the cloud, and climbed to the mountain top. Moses was to remain on the mountain for forty days and forty nights.

At some point in our spiritual unfolding we are given the opportunity to choose if we are willing to fearlessly walk up the mountain into the unknown, disappearing into the cloud of nothing, or staying in the comfort zone of the Golden Calf, resigned to keeping God and ourselves in a box. At some point in this process, Moshe was transformed into being half angel and half human. May we all be blessed with the spiritual courage and awareness of Moshe.

Amen

Terumah

THIS is an interesting parashah because it starts out by describing the flow of energy between the Divine and us. The first line of the parashah relays the message that we need to receive in order to share. Although the Torah is describing the construction of an outer mishkan (מִשְׁכָּן—the sacred space for the in-dwelling of the Divine), the deeper spiritual message is to make an inner mikdash (מִקְדָשׁ—a holy sanctuary) within ourselves, thus sanctifying ourselves and our society. The mikdash is the holy sanctuary within us where the spark of Hashem dwells and where it may fill our whole being when our life becomes the terumah (heave offering). This is the lesson of any offering.

The parashah begins: "God spoke to Moses, saying: Speak to the Israelites and have them bring me an offering. Take my offering from everyone whose heart impels them to give." A little later, in Shemot 25:8, the instruction continues: "They shall make me a sanctuary, and I will dwell among them." This expresses the energetics. In the play of energy, we are "tuned-in" if we are able to give back a portion of what we have received as an offering. In the same way, the purpose of building the mishkan is not to retreat from the world, but rather to activate consciousness in the world, and to create a more conscious humanity.

An offering is not just to other people; it is to God. Everything comes from heaven, and if we are going to build a tabernacle, the materials must come from heaven from a mystical point of view. In the play of energy, we are acting in cosmic harmony, if we are able to give back as an offering a portion of what we have received. The deeper teaching is that all service is only for God. Although our work in giving charity and service supports institutions, individuals, families, and tribes across the earth, service and charity at the deepest level is for our own purification and spiritual development.

Making our life as an offering is for our highest purpose—to know Hashem. That is why beggars at the Wailing Wall understand that they are doing a service for the person giving them charity, and they will brazenly tell you so. The prophet Yermiyahu knew this when he tried to find a suitable beggar to give charity to so that he could prevent the destruction of the first Temple. Our charitable acts support institutions and works on earth, but ultimately they are for God, who desires that we care for one another. Metaphorically, this is akin to the yearning of the female for the male—or the yearning for God, which is described in biblical romantic terms as a male-female interaction metaphor.

This cycle energizes the higher planes of zeir anpin, the face of the masculine tiferet (beauty) energy in relationship to the mayim nukvin (feminine waters or energies). The mayim de'kurin (masculine waters or energies) then descend onto the earth plane and reactivate the feminine energies of the earth and all of creation on it, including the humans. Those who actively participate in this divine cycle through their mitzvot and other offerings are then further filled with light and the energetics of the Divine. This downward flow completes the circuit and generates energy.

When we look at this entire flow, we see that offering a "thank you" positively connects us. This upward flowing energy also creates protection on the physical plane. The terumah must be given selflessly, for the love of Hashem or as an expression of our oneness. This cycle is only activated when the offerings come naturally from the heart and are not consciously or unconsciously an egotistically motivated business deal to gain money ("donate to the church now and you will get five-fold back"), or to get one's name on a plaque or a building. In the flow of the offering to God, all offerings are an act of giving (which is a masculine act), but although the terumah is an offering, it is considered feminine since the act of giving opens up the channels for receiving. The terumah offerings correspond to the feminine energies as the partzufim (faces) and represent the mystical secret of Or Hozer (returning light). The light descends upon us, and then we reflect it back to the Divine. The light is a giving and an ascending arc, which is feminine.

Mayim nukvin, the feminine ascending waters, represent the energies of Le'a and Rahel, which represent the two *hehs* (ה and ה) of the Tetragrammaton. The upper heh, *imma* (אמא—mother), is the sephirah of binah (בינה—insight and understanding). The sephirotic face of binah is the matriarch Le'a.

The lower heh is called Rahel. These are the "wives" of zeir anpin, and comprise the sephirah of tiferet.

The upper heh is unified with yod (י), *abba* (אבא—father), and is related to the sephirah of chokhmah (חכמה). This represents the secret of *yih'yeh* (יהיה), or "will be." It is said that on the day when the messiah comes, God yih'yeh (will be) one, and his name one (Zekharya 14:9). When we look at this whole flow, we see how we are plugged into the Divine by offering a "thank you." When this circuitry is activated, it creates a protection on the physical plane and kindles the desire of the feminine for the masculine. When the male energy wishes to attract the female, he gives to her. This descent of above to below is the shefa (שפע—divine flux), which flows from imma (sacred mother) down to the sephirah of malchut (מלכות), the face of the matriarch Rahel, called mayim de'kurin or masculine waters. It is also known as Or Yashar (אור ישר), or directed light. The female must then return this energy back to maintain this interest. This is the offering of the feminine waters. This is the arousal from the lower levels of malchut (Zohar, Vol. 1, folio 17b). This completes the circuit and generates energy. This cycle of giving and receiving is the key to understanding this parashah and the Torah energetics. The spiritual dynamics of this cycle are key to basic kabbalistic understanding of how we are supported energetically on the earth plane.

An additional metaphor inherent in the construction of the mishkan is that they are constructing this sacred energy carrier in the wilderness. The wilderness is representative of our daily encounter with the chaos of unconsciousness in our everyday lives and in the world around us.

The three levels of the terumah offerings for the building of the mishkan are: prayer, Torah study, and acts of loving kindness manifesting on the physical plane as service and charity (*shey'rut*—שירות; *tzedakah*—צדקה), such as the offering of the half-shekel (Shemot 30:13). These three pillars are avenues to help us to best express our service, and, according to the first-century BCE sage Shim'on HaTzadik, are the very foundations upon which all of existence hinges (Mishnah Avot 1:2).

Prayer activates consciousness. Prayer activates our kavanah (כונה—intention) and emunah (אמונה—faith), and our ability to connect with the Torah as the outer mind of Hashem. As the experience of prayer becomes more deeply heartfelt, and the fire of Hashem inflames our hearts with love, we begin to connect to the Torah as the *inner* heart of Hashem. Merely knowing about the Torah does not seriously help us access the inner Torah. The inner Torah may be accessed through *tefilah* (prayer) and hitbodedut (meditation), which connect us with the heart of Hashem and the living fire of Hashem in our lives. This is deep terumah.

The second terumah offering is Torah study, which is a foundation of our relationship with God, humanity, and the living planet. It also explains our reason and purpose for being here. The Torah reveals this as deveikut/chey'rut (divine union/liberation). The word Torah in its original translation from Hebrew does not mean "the law," but "the guide." It guides us to be lived by the mitzvot and is the blueprint for both deveikut and chey'rut as the ultimate purpose of life. This does not exclude, in the beginning, the importance of the fundamentals of kedusha (holiness) such as the mitzvot. The mitzvot help us to create a basic morality for righteous living, and for becoming a good human being, or mensch. They are also vital foundations for going deeper into the Torah.

The third offering is service to Hashem. This includes prayer and Torah study as well. Each of us has a unique service, which prayer and Torah study begin to clarify for us. That is why this terumah is described as "my heave offering" or *terumatti* (תרומתי); it is the recognition that our whole egotistical structure as the body/mind/I-am complex is given to us as a tool for service. We can more easily access our specific service with prayer and meditation. This third form of offering is then the activation of the sephirah of chesed (חסד—kindness), the energy of service toward uplifting the world. These are the mitzvot that have a positive impact upon the world. These three pillars—Torah, prayer, and service—help us to fulfill the entire energetic system.

The goal of the mishkan is not to retreat from the world, but rather to activate consciousness in the world and to create a more conscious Adamic human. By continually living in kabbalat Torah (קבלת תורה—receiving of the Torah), we have the wondrous opportunity to be in an ongoing eternal meeting with the Divine. Our prayers are the daily moment-to-moment sacrifices that continually activate the mikdash.

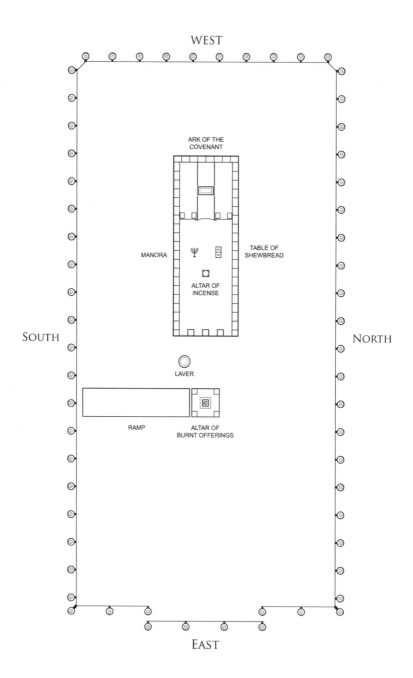

WEST

SOUTH

NORTH

EAST

ARK OF THE
COVENANT

MANORA

TABLE OF
SHEWBREAD

ALTAR OF
INCENSE

LAVER

RAMP

ALTAR OF
BURNT OFFERINGS

The Tabernacle and Enclosure

When we build holy sanctuaries within ourselves, the divine will comes and dwells within them. The point of tefilah (תפילה—prayer), Torah study, and service is to build and activate our innermost sanctuaries so that the shekhinah energy will dwell in these holy places.

When the mikdash within us unfolds, we begin to understand why the *Aron Ha'Brit* (ארון הברית), or Ark of the Covenant, was created. The Ark consisted of three boxes, one layered within the other. The inner and outer layers were gold, while the middle layer was made of wood. It was a capacitor and a superconductor, but metaphorically it represents the need for a golden soul and an exterior representing the connection with the Divine through the holiness of all our actions. The wood of the Ark was *atzai shittim* (עצי שטים), or acacia wood. The Hebraic name for this wood, shittim, is related to the word for foolishness, *shtut* (שטות). It helps us to understand the evil inclination. As this deeper understanding of the Ark of the Covenant unfolds, we see that by creating a consecrated holy place, all our acts are consecrated, and we enter into a constant state of prayer. The mikdash is about being acutely aware that we are in this constant state of prayer. Therefore we are constructing this mikdash in the wilderness of chaos, or the unconscious world.

Am Yisrael had just been given its identity at Mount Sinai through the medium of Ma'amad Har Sinay (מעמד הר סיני—standing at Mount Sinai). However powerful this was, it was a single event. The Ark, however, designed to remain always portable, offered the opportunity for an energetic matrix, which became an ongoing connection with the Divine. It was the opportunity to be in the eternal meeting with the Divine always, once we realized we are in a constant state of prayer. The Divine dwells within us, fired by our constant state of prayer, service, and holy action. This ongoing state of prayer, which is amplified by the mikdash, was the next foundation following the great revelation at Sinai. The prayers were a substitute for the daily sacrifices that were done in the mikdash. As many of our sages have taught, in the act of prayer, one should imagine standing within the Holy of Holies. By building holy sanctuaries within ourselves, the Divine will come and dwell within them. A purpose of tefilah is to build innermost sanctuaries so that God will dwell in the holy places that we create deep within ourselves. When looking at the details of this teaching, we see that when they built this tabernacle, God said, "They shall make me a sanctuary, and I will dwell among them" (Shemot 25:8). It does not say "so that I may dwell within *it*." The importance of building a tabernacle inside each and every one of us, so that the Divine will be revealed within us, is crucial to the enlightenment way of the Torah. What does it mean to build a tabernacle within ourselves? It does not mean we build a little box and swallow it. It means that we become like the Ark, which is composed of gold on the inside, gold on the outside, and wood in between.

From the Talmud, we learn that the Ark was the same size as the door of the Temple. You would think they would have known not to do this, but a miracle occurred and the Ark became smaller and was thus able to fit through the doorway (Midrash Shemot Rabbah 8:1). The meta-communication here is that if we are going to connect to the mishkan, we must make ourselves smaller and humbler. When King Solomon built the temple, he was criticized for making narrow windows on the inside and large windows on the outside. But the purpose was not to let light *in*, but to shine light *out* into the world (Midrash Tanchuma, Baha'alotcha, Chap. 2). This is the essence of the three *terumot*. We are guided to become a channel of light unto others. We study the Torah, we pray, but our actions must reveal the light. This is the three-column approach.

The tabernacle we build in our hearts is to serve all for all generations. The mishkan, after all, was the predecessor to the temple. Now that we do not have the outer temple, we are invited as a matter of spiritual survival to build an inner temple. This was the original plan. Our inner temple is constantly being built up or torn down within us. Terumah is a spiritual offering, which manifests on the outer plane as charity.

The Ark's design was as golden within as it was without. One of the most important energies of the Ark, however, was what was on top of it. Here was sculpted the image of the cherubim (כרובים), two angels spreading their wings out toward one another. Shemot 25:18–22 reports the instructions from God for the Ark's top design:

> "Make two golden cherubs, hammering them out from the two
> ends of the cover. One cherub shall be on one end, and one on
> the other. Make the cherubs from [the same piece of gold] as the
> cover itself, on its two ends. The cherubs shall spread their wings

upward so that their wings shield the cover. The cherubs shall face one another, but their faces shall [also be inclined downward] toward the cover. Place the cover on top of the ark [after] you place into the ark the testimony that I will give you. I will commune with you there, speaking to you from above the ark-cover, from between the two cherubs that are on the Ark of Testimony. [In this manner] I will give you instructions for the Israelites."

The cherubim have much symbolism. The angels support our prayers. The two angels facing one another express harmony. When the people did the will of God, the angels would face each other, but when there was misalignment, they would turn back to back (Talmud Bav'li, Baba Batra 90a). They were said to have been living energies dancing the expression of Hashem as a minor miracle. They faced each other also as male and female (Yehezqel 1:9, 3:13, and 10:20; Zohar, Vol. 3, folio 59a), representing the intimate embrace of Am Yisrael (the feminine) with the Divine as Ayn Sof (אֵין סוֹף—the masculine). These angels also represent Adam and Cha'vah, as they were created together. In Talmudic times the term used was do'partzufim ("two faces") (Talmud Bav'li, Berachot 61a)—two hermaphroditic twins embracing one another, symbolic of Adam and Cha'vah who were created as a singular hermaphroditic human (Bereisheet 5:2). On a deep level, this symbolizes a quality of balance between male and female, the arena in which God communicates with us. From a kabbalistic view, these are all symbols of the amalgamation of male and female in which the Divine becomes most clearly revealed.

The wings of the cherubim represented the mitzvot and the divine names and attributes expressed in love and awe. It is important not to be bogged down by guilt but to spread our wings and do good deeds not out of a sense of owing. In our relationships, we activate the divine energy within when we lovingly embrace each other as cherubim and fly up to Hashem. These angels facing each other express not only divine harmony, but also a conduit for bringing down the shefa (divine downward flowing energy) and prophecy. It was taught that the space between the two cherubim was the optimal space to commune with Hashem: "Any place where there is no feminine and masculine together, is no place worthy of beholding the Face of the shekhinah" (Zohar, Vol. 3, folio

59a). The masculine cherubim represented the Divine and the feminine represented the shekhinah as Am Yisrael. These were two halves or hermaphrodite twins embracing, symbolizing the ultimate merging and rectification of Adam and Cha'vah back into their essential oneness. They are symbolic of the definition of a full human being as the merging and unification of the incomplete individual male and female. The dance of the cherubim symbolizes an integrated balance between male and female, in which we can more fully receive the Divine in our lives, as the image of God (Bereisheet 1:27).

It is significant that the two cherubim embracing as Eros were situated at the very center of the Holy of Holies. Because the cherubim are at the very center of the Ark, we have to acknowledge Eros as a central part of the mystical Jewish path of deveikut/chey'rut. This path is activated and amplified when the two cherubim merge in holy Eros. When we understand that at the center of the Holy of Holies is Eros, we are able to come to terms, on the highest level, that Eros was not originally exclusively about sexuality. Rather, sexuality overtook Eros when Eros was exiled, following the fall of the first Temple. The original meaning of Eros is the experience of the ecstasy of merging with the Divine in every moment and in every situation. It is living for, and eventually as, the ecstatic, erotic experience of the Divine at the core of our lives. Divine love dwells at the heart of Eros no less than at the center of the Ark. In this context, the Torah Way to deveikut/chey'rut is divine love. It is no accident that the Torah says in Shemot 25:22, talking about the space between the cherubim: "I will commune with you there, speaking to you from above the ark-cover, from between the two cherubs that are on the Ark of Testimony." Thus, the transmission point with the Divine is located in the very space between the two cherubim making love.

It is, at least, a subtle undermining of the greatness of the Torah as a way to deveikut/chey'rut, when people limit the meaning of the Torah and Am Yisrael, by calling us People of the Law (as implied when they say "People of the Book"). Although Torah study may self-limit itself to focus on intellectual meaning and law in that context, our sages have pointed to love as the full expression and meaning of the Torah Way.

The law, stiff with formality, is a cry for creativity, a call for nobility concealed in the form of the commandments. It is not
designed to be a yoke, a curb, a straight jacket for human action.
Above all, the Torah asks for love.... All observance is training in
the art of love. To forget that love is the purpose of all mitzvot is
to vitiate their meaning.

> (Rabbi Abraham Joshua Heschel
> in *God in Search of Man*, p. 307)

There is no love like the love [inherent in] Torah.
> (Talmud Bav'li, Avot D'Rebbe Natan 28:1)

Hillel expresses this clearly in his response to a challenge to define the Torah teachings to a standing-on-one-foot definition before mounting a horse
as "What is disconcerting for you, do it not unto another" (Talmud Bav'li,
Shabbat 31a). This classic statement is based on the Torah's injunction "You
must love your neighbor as [you love] yourself" (VayYiKra 19:18), which the
second-century Rabbi Akiva held as the most fundamental principle of the
entire Torah (Midrash Bereisheet Rabbah 24:7). Divine love is the core essence
of the great Torah Way as it leads us to the divine merging of deveikut/chey'rut.

In the tabernacle there was a table with twelve loaves of bread. These represented the twelve constellations of the zodiac, whose power we symbolically transcended by consuming them. It symbolized us receiving grace in a
way that could help us transcend our astrological patterns. On the table was
the seven-branched menorah (מנורה), or candelabra, representing the human
form from which we ascend. We are like the candelabra in that we only give
off light when we are lit by Torah study, prayer, and divine service in chesed.
Our walk in the world has the power to turn these lights on.

There were eleven coverings on the tabernacle. Ten of these symbolized
the sephirot on the Tree of Life. The eleventh was an offering to Satan. Usually
through our negative actions we give more to Satan than is necessary. Satan
deserves one sprout, not a bowl of them. The walls of the tabernacle gave a
clear line between the black and the white. Are we holy or not? The Holy of
Holies was within the tabernacle itself, which reminded us of the levels of

holiness within ourselves and the different opportunities to connect with the light. The outer level was the altar, which represented our sacrifices or mitzvot kindling the lights of the candelabra.

A perimeter around the tabernacle symbolized holy space and the creation of such. We must be very careful concerning which influences we bring into our space. The care with whom we associate is important because we are affected by our associations. We need to learn from the stories of Avraham separating from Lot and of Ya'akov separating from 'Esav.

Although we study Torah and pray, the deeper teachings are that our actions reveal the light. This is part of the teachings of the three-column approach mentioned above. The mishkan (tabernacle) we build in our hearts is to serve all for all generations. At this point in history we do not seem to merit an outer temple, but are guided to build such a strong inner temple that we will collectively *draw forth* the outer temple and the messianic times that will accompany it. Our inner temple is constantly being built up or torn down within us. Terumah is a spiritual offering whose meaning is to constantly rebuild our inner temple.

It is interesting to note that all the measurements of the Ark ended in halves. This is an interesting spiritual message that suggests that in the process of our spiritual evolution we are never complete. Even if we are acknowledged to be in steady deveikut/chey'rut, there is always more. We are never done. One of the worst egotistical mistakes of highly evolved people is to think they are complete. The attitude of always being a beginner keeps us childlike in all aspects of our lives. The Torah is there to remind us that no matter how many times we study it, there is always a new insight and spiritual teaching waiting to be revealed. The half coin terumah symbolizes a baseline teaching of the spiritual path as the two wings of the spiritual bird: one wing is the three parts of terumah, or self-effort, and the other wing is the power of the grace of Hashem. Together, they make a full gold coin and create a golden way of life.

May we all be blessed that all the branches on our candelabra be fully lit, and that we act in the consciousness of the Holy of Holies within us. May our cherubim face each other always, and may our Torah culture of life and enlightenment illuminate the world.

Amen

Tetzaveh

THIS parashah delves deeply into spiritual subtleties. It talks a lot about the sacred garments of the kohain (priest or shaman). The clothing represented the vibration rate of the priest. If he did not have a certain vibration rate, the frequency of the Holy of Holies would kill him. His clothing, his state of purification, and the purification of his mind all had to be at a certain frequency. This inspires great awe for the divine process. In this context the priestly clothing, having to be blessed by Moshe, was a critical part of the ritual service. The service of a kohain, if he was not wearing the prescribed clothing, was considered invalid. Part of the ordination of the kohain actually involved his becoming enrobed in the ceremonial clothing. Not only did these clothes represent the purified frequency of the kohain, and help to maintain that frequency, they also represented the quality of the priest's thoughts and moral fiber, his midot (qualities of character).

The kohain was part of a collective human bio-computer. His ritual garments had to be worn in a particular manner, especially the breastplate (choshen), into which was sewn twelve gems, representing the twelve tribes (there were also specific letters of the Hebrew alphabet corresponding with these). The breastplate also contained a mysterious oracle referred to as Urim V'Tumim (אורים ותומים) and was tied to the chest of the kohain gadol (chief priest) with techelet, sky-blue-dyed threads of wool, representing the merging of the heavens and the earth. When he was fully dressed with these vestments, the kohain became a cosmic bio-computer. People would ask questions and the gems on the breastplate would generate answers in a way that only the kohain knew how to interpret. This special set of vestments, combined with the kohain who wore them, presented a unique way for the Divine to communicate with Am Yisrael. This gives us an overview of the significance of the breastplate. Again, the clothing represents the frequency.

The frequency was very important. Each article of clothing represented an aspect that needed to be purified. The clothing created a frequency that would purify and calm the high priest. The kohain gadol was not to have any other thoughts while working in the Holy of Holies. If his thoughts went astray, they had the potential power to destroy. When a human was amped up in this clothing, great power was available, thus requiring respect in the situation. The clothing represented *kavod tiferet* (כבוד תפארת), or the splendor of the Divine. The clothing was originally made for Aharon and blessed by Moshe.

One of the most intriguing aspects of all this is the oracle, the Urim V'Tumim. It is said that this particular article came from Moshe. The Urim V'Tumim were names of God. We speculate that the urim (literally, "illuminations") was the holy seventy-two-sectioned God name, and that the tumim (literally, "completions") was the holy forty-two-lettered God name (Zohar, Vol. 2, folio 234b). Only Moshe knew this from a direct transmission. These were inscribed on parchment and folded in a particular way and placed in the breastplate in a certain way.

The breastplate was called the breastplate of judgment or *choshen mishpat* (חשן משפט). This power was inherent in the clothing. A subtle truth here is that we as humans are cosmic, multidimensional bio-computers. We are not simply talking about our clothing, but every aspect of who we are. If our bodies are impure, and if we place irradiated, genetically engineered junk food in our system, we are unable to rise above the bio-computer mind and commune with the Divine. Basically, our system, when toxic, becomes jammed. This understanding originates with these teachings about the *kohan'im*. They had to undergo purifications. They had to ritually immerse in ritual pools, or mikvehs. This seven-day process prepared them to enter the Holy of Holies, to fully activate themselves as human bio-computers.

It was thought that the kohain's heart had to be purified to understand the meaning of the cryptic messages activated in the Urim V'Tumim. It is taught that the ability to endure this frequency was a level of Ruach HaKodesh that was lower than prophecy but higher than the *baht-kol* (בת-קול—the divine voice), which was something that was activated in the second century, after the power of prophecy had ceased and the Urim V'Tumim was unavailable. This represents increasing one's frequency when entering prayer so that we can match this frequency in our lives.

Moshe initiated Aharon and his sons and created these special garments. This involved a particular ceremony, as described in Shemot 29:20: "When you then slaughter the ram, take its blood and place some of it on the right earlobe of Aaron and his sons, as well as on their right thumbs and right big toes." This was an initiation into being the right hand of God. The ear is an extension of the brain and represents the ability to listen. The thumb and the right toe represent action and relate to the higher brain centers, namely, the pineal and pituitary glands. This ritual was then intended to activate their higher frequencies.

Following these rites, they were anointed with fresh olive oil. The burning of specific oil in the menorah (מנורה), the seven-branched ritual candelabra, preceded the amping-up of this energy. The priests do not stand between us and the Divine but rather *activate* the connection. The menorah, in the same way, was a connection to the light and the activation of this light. The focus on the pure oil is symbolic of us having a very pure heart. Only the first six drops of oil extracted from the olives could be used to symbolize this purity. The olive oil represented the sephirotic quality of binah as the level of creation. When they were anointed with oil and blood, they brought down a certain amount of light into the situation.

Tetzaveh is the only parashah in the Torah that does not mention Moshe. After the Golden Calf, Hashem wanted to destroy the people. Moshe advocated for them by saying "Take me instead." Hashem agreed to spare the people, but Moshe's name was removed from parashah Tetzaveh. This willingness to be erased from history showed his profound concern for Israel and demonstrated the degree of his humility. This is what is required of a true kohain. We must wear clothes, while knowing that we are not our clothing, and retain a certain frequency. We must take care of our bodies, while knowing that we are not our bodies. We are only Hashem. Moshe understood this. His humility came from his awareness. This humility is a requirement for anyone wishing to walk on earth as a spiritual teacher. Moshe's willingness to manifest his humility is a profound teaching for us. If we know that we are the nothing, prior to the something, then there is no need for any egocentric actions. As King Solomon said: "Vanity of vanities; all is vanity. What profit has a man off all his labour wherein he labours under the sun?" (Kohelet 1:2). Nothing matters and nothing is real. Moshe was acting from this perspective.

Each of the high priest's vestments dealt with a different kind of purification. The *ephod* (אפוד—vest) cleansed the people of idol worship. The breastplate was for burning up judgment. The *ahv'nayt* (אבנט), or tunic, helped deal with *lashon hara* (slander/gossip). The tzitzit (ציצית) were for remembering the mitzvot. The *mitz'nehfeht* (מצנפת—headdress) was for ego. The *meech'ne'sey-vahd* (מכנסי-בד), or linen kilts, were for sexual morality and purity. Ultimately, if you wish to be a high priest on the spiritual path, you must have a well-functioning bio-computer to transcend, so that you may know that you are the One. Priestly succession was a genetic phenomenon. It implies the importance of maintaining a high frequency and passing it on to our descendants. In this case, it is a father-to-son lineage. The role of the son is to be open to the seriousness of the lineage to which he is serving.

A major part of the altar rites involved the *ketoret* (קטרת), the sacred incense blend that burned perpetually. There were eleven herbs in the mix. Supposedly, a noted archeologist did find about 300 kilograms of this incense in one of his digs. Ten of these incenses represent the sephirotic energies that need to be purified. The eleventh incense is the way to defeat the satanic energy and is an offering. These incenses, along with the whole temple setting, created such a frequency that no insects or dogs could penetrate the field in the whole of Jerusalem. The ketoret was a part of that psychic and soul protection and purification.

May we all be blessed to be the frequency of Moshe, to live in the frequency of oneness, which neither takes us above or below others, but makes us all equals in the oneness. May we all be blessed on the spiritual path as high priests of our paths. May we understand the significance of all we do, including the way we dress, as a reflection of our frequency and our inner presence. May we always live, walk, talk, and dress in ways that reflect the highest frequency of love and light for the whole world.

Amen

Ki Tissa

In essence, the message of Ki Tissa is, if we cease evolving in our spiritual understanding, we will fall back to a lower level. The ego wants us to stay at the lowest level of understanding, and this parashah is subtly about the struggle to overcome "the inner Satan" expressed through the ego, versus waking up to the truth. It actually starts with Am Yisrael having reached the highest level of awareness ever in the history of humanity, with tongues of fire above their heads after having just received a direct divine revelation. The question was … Could they hold on to this profound awareness? We need to understand that the more awake a person is, the less the ego is in control, and the ego will do whatever it can to consciously or unconsciously undermine its loss of control. As the Talmud puts it, "One who is more spiritually evolved than his fellow is also that much more challenged by his impulse toward ego" (Talmud Bav'li, Sukah 52a).

This parashah is thus about the conflict between the force of consciousness and that of ego in the context of chey'rut. It starts with the counting of Am Yisrael's population of those twenty and older. Remember, the people had just come out of Egyptian slavery; slaves did not exist with a name—they had no meaning as individuals. So the counting and giving a name is why this book of the Torah is called Shemot, because it has to do with the naming, or accounting, of the people, who until now had been nameless, dispensable slaves. (It also has to do with the transmission of the seventy-two names of God.)

As mentioned earlier, the census demanded that each person twenty and older bring half a coin, which was something every person could contribute, so that everyone could feel the oneness. The wealthy were not to add to this amount, and the poor were not to offer less. Am Yisrael was to see itself as classless, and all of its constituents as equally important. Half a coin teaches us that we never see the whole picture. It also encourages an attitude on the spiritual path in which there is always more to complete, and there is no "perfect spiritual master" on the earth plane to feed our child-parent fantasies of having the perfect parent. Moreover, it represents a personal worldview, in which we can choose to see the cup either as half full or half empty.

Then they moved to washing hands and feet prior to sacred service, which had to do with the general prerequisite of creating holiness before taking any action. The hands are the organs of expression, and the feet help us to move toward God, so they both need to be purified. All the negative energies needed to be cleansed before they could enhance their awareness of the Divine within themselves. The larger message here is that, as a nation of priests, the more we purify ourselves before a ceremony, the higher the frequency of light we are able to hold and to generate. The sacred oil turns on the switch of higher energetic potential and therefore enables a higher connection, which is why oil-anointing was part of the ceremony for the initiation of a kohain/priest.

The sacred incenses, the prescribed herbs and spices, also were and are part of the vibratory upgrade. These really did exist. In March 1998, the late Wendell Jones, a professional archeologist and the real *Raiders of the Lost Ark* hero, and a team of volunteers, found a clay juglet, measuring 5 inches high, in a cave in Qumran. It contained most unusual oils. Originally, they thought it was a remnant of some balsam oil that was prescribed by the Torah. But then Jones—who had been digging in Qumran for more than twenty years and had been successful in identifying the sacred Rock of Nurturance (*ehven shetia*—אבן שתיה) in Israel—discovered in yet another cave a second bottle of oil plus 600 kilos of a reddish-brown organic substance that had been hidden for millenia. He eventually brought these spices to Israel's then highest rabbinic authorities, Rabbi Yehuda Getz and Rabbi Obadiah Yosef. They analyzed them and agreed to let Wendell "burn" them for scientific purposes. Basically, he had discovered remnants of both the incense and the oils. "The residue of the incense lingered for days in the area," he reported, and the area had changed, no longer infested with flies, moths, and aromas of other sources. After the *ketoret* (mixture of eleven sacred herbs) was burned, no sign of these insects were found anywhere, which fits with the description of the effect of the incense. The ancient rabbis reported that no flies were found in the area of the Temple, nor was a snake or scorpion ever able to harm anyone in the vicinity of the Temple (Mishnah, Avot 5:5), so this ketoret aroma was extremely powerful.

So what is it about this anointing oil and ketoret spices that makes them so powerful and important? Three thousand years ago, King Solomon wrote about the oil and incense that they "gladden the heart" (Mishle 27:9). But there is much greater significance than your heart rejoicing—that's just the end product. Their importance comes from a deeper place of understanding, connected to the classical kabbalistic concept of shevirat ha'keylim (הכלים שבירת), the shattering of the vessels. Incapable of holding the light of creation, the primeval universe exploded, shattered, for nothing can receive without also being capable of giving. In exploding, the fledgling universe gave of itself, gave forth sparks of itself in its shattering, thus readying it for receiving, for creation to be gifted.

It is said that the ketoret consisted of ten spices (corresponding to the ten sephirot of the Tree of Life) that had a nice aroma, and an eleventh spice (representing the dark force) that had a vile odor. Ground together into a single blend, they paralleled the eleven energies of tohu, the realm of chaos, and represent the complete rectification of evil. One of the spices, galbanum (חלבונה—chal'vonah in Hebrew), alludes to the elevation of evil back to its primal root in the realm of holiness, which is the whole purpose of being on the planet. "The shattering of the vessels," in the Arizal's system, refers to the sephirot of the universe of to'hu. Each vessel shattered when God allowed a little of the divine light to shine into them. In the oral tradition, only seven shattered, but the upper four did not. The eleven parallel the eleven spices, but they are only mentioned by the oral tradition. As God's light entered into each sephirah, it shattered and fell, creating the basis for physical universes, eventually crystallizing our universe. There were at least seven shatterings according to the kabbalah, but the higher ones remained intact, because they still had to be a channel to repair and fill the lower universes.

In metaphorical response to this, God had to withdraw some of the light as there was too much for the vessels to hold. It would make things too perfect and there would not be free will. By free will (an illusion of choice on the plane of assiyah, or the physical plane) we make choices of whether to move closer to God or farther away. The "choiceless choice" is part of the paradox of kabbalistic teachings. These choices affect our spiritual evolution. In order to create an environment where we could have free will, the light was withdrawn by

God constricting the God-self, so to speak, or tzim tzum, by virtue of which a space void of God presence was formed, or what we call the teheru, literally, "cleared space." Light was then shone into that hollow at a lower vibration rate so the creation of "other" could occur, and so that we could handle it.

All of this relates to the ketoret, because the sephirot of to'hu are the basis of our present universe. The shattering of the sephirot of to'hu took place in the astral plane (world of yetzirah), or higher in the heavens, and then descended into the parallel universe of the physical world. In some kabbalistic teachings, according to the Arizal, the primitive sephirot of to'hu were created in a way that they would shatter when the light entered them. In a sense, the higher consciousness of God's presence was there, but the vessels could not hold it. The vessels had consciousness, and they had a mission. Their mission was to allow for lower and lower universes to be created that would ultimately allow for a world where human beings could have the illusion of free will, which exists in alma d'shikra, the world of illusion, as this physical plane of reality. In order to do this, God's light had to be diminished, and had to pull back. The vessels had to sacrifice themselves to shatter. The vessels of possibility understood that in opening up to receive powerful positive energy, they would also have to receive some negative energy in order to create the balance intended for the physical plane of assiyah. Thus, they were inevitably created to be imperfect and flawed, because otherwise they could not fulfill their mission, which is the diminishing of God's light in order to enable the creation of lower universes, and hence the possibility for free will.

Essentially, part of the mission of the vessels of possibility was to make it clear that good *and* evil come from God. "There is nothing of the other side," the Zohar tells us, "which does not also have a spark of the divine light within it" (Zohar, Vol. 2, folios 69a–b). Sparks of light that fell, as the result of these vessels shattering, became the basis of a lower set of dimensions, in which God's existence and light became more and more unclear. In that lack of clarity, the darkness, or Satan, or ego, came into existence, which appears to overtly fight the light. The power of ketoret represents the ability to elevate and extract the holy sparks out of this physical realm of negativity. These are known as "shells" or k'lipot (קלפות). Had evil been an independent entity, we would be living in a world of duality, first of all, and humanity would not have the ability to rectify it through teshuvah. *Evil* had to be created as a fallen aspect of *good* so that one could raise it back to its source. We can thus read into the opening of Bereisheet that "the darkness on the face of the depths" is about evil coming out of good. The whole process on the planet is to elevate evil back to light, therefore redeeming it, and ourselves, for the healing of the planet (tikkun ha'olam) and of ourselves (tikkun ha'nefesh).

> Evil is powered by a capacity for its existence that is as divinely
> rooted as is the capacity for the existence of Good. The greater
> the degree of Evil, the greater the Good that that very Evil could
> become if reconfigured. No capacity, no capability, is possible
> without being empowered by the divine root of all roots. Thus,
> the greater the power drawn for wreaking evil, the greater the
> power—that very same power—for channeling goodness.
> (sixteenth-century Rabbi Yehudah Loew of Prague [Maha-
> ral] in *Netzach Yisrael,* Chap. 7, folio 45)

The ancient rabbis tell us that Moshe was taught the mystery of the ketoret by none other than the angel of death (Talmud Bav'li, Shabbat 89a), and that the ketoret therefore had the power to nullify evil decrees, even that of death. Later we see that when the plague broke out in the desert, Moshe had Aharon walk through the camp of the Israelites with the ketoret pan burning with incense (BeMidbar 17:11). And how did it get this power to overcome death and evil? It was almost homeopathic. In the original light, the dark synergy of early to'hu (chaos), the darkness could not manifest as full-fledged evil until the light itself broke into micro-levels and could separate from the darkness. That breakdown is called death and darkness, the ultimate concealer of God's light. In fact, the Hebrew word for darkness, cho'shech, actually translates as "withdrawn" or "held back," as it is the holding back, or concealment, of the light. The ketoret had, especially in the nature and number of ingredients, the power to overcome death and darkness and thus the power to completely transform all evil in ourselves and in the world into the good. In essence, the power of transforming evil, by elevating it back to its source in holiness, is suggested by the use of the ketoret. Of course, it is more than the incense that does this, but it aids in this process. This is probably why it was introduced at the very beginning of the parashah dealing with the Golden Calf incident.

The Eternal One also built in spiritual support by reminding the people to honor the Shabbat as a day of deveikut/chey'rut and the three key holidays for coming to the mikdash: Pesach (פסח), Shavuot (שבועות), and Sukkot (סוכות) (spring, summer, and autumn, respectively). They were now fully equipped for spiritual war within themselves. But unfortunately, spiritual faith and patience did not seem to be built into their protective shields. So when Moshe took longer to return than they expected, they began to lose their focus, and Aharon was not able to give them the strong leadership they needed to avoid disaster. To delay their reactions and concerns Aharon aided in conjuring the image of a Golden Calf, hoping to distract their focus away from Moshe's absence. The Midrash tells us it was the ey'rev rav, the mixed multitudes, that got some of the people to worship it. After all, it says, "This, Israel, is your god, who brought you out of Egypt" (Shemot 32:4). By saying "your god," it would appear that the declaration originated from those outside of Am Yisrael, namely the ey'rev rav (Midrash Shemot Rabbah 42:6).

It is clear that when Moshe came down the mountain he was very disappointed in Aharon for not supplying the leadership Am Yisrael needed. In his anger, he smashed the two tablets of the divine writ, realizing that the people were not ready for so direct a revelatory transmission. Shemot 32:25–26 then tells us:

> Moses realized that the people had actually been restrained.
> Aaron had restrained them, doing only a small part of what the
> outspoken ones [had demanded]. Moses stood up at the cap's
> entrance and announced, "Whoever is for God, join me!" All the
> Levites gathered around him.

They were then asked to slay those who had actually engaged in worshipping the Golden Calf, and three thousand out of the three million were killed.

This story of the Golden Calf, and the sin of the Golden Calf (chet ha'egel— חאט העגל), is a deeper story than merely the people's spiritual immaturity. As the Midrash explains, it was the subtle, dark efforts of the ey'rev rav. As they would throughout our history, they diverted the masses into putting God back into a box and turning the people away from the mystical understanding of God beyond the egocentrically comfortable form of Elohim into YHWH's formless, nondual, supernatural grace and power. Moshe's teaching represented an extraordinary leap in consciousness. It was beyond most people's understanding. Thus it was relatively easily to appeal to the contracted consciousness of the ey'rev rav in most of the people, with the exception of the Levites. The Golden Calf was an effort to replace the beyond-understanding, nondual, formless reality of God with an egocentrically familiar and comfortable dualistic form of Elohim. This was made more subtle because within YHWH is contained the energy of Elohim as an expression of YHWH. Elohim represents the law aspect of the Great Torah Way, and in that it has an important role, but the ey'rev rav wanted to stop the evolution of the people at this level, rather than supporting them toward the higher spiritual level of YHWH. In this higher level, they could walk up the mountain into the Ayn Sof, into the No-thing.

Although it is easy to point our fingers at the ey'rev rav as the problem, they reflected the aspects of the fearful, contracted desire to be egotistically comfortable that lies within each of us. They were successful only because they resonated with the ey'rev rav part of most of the people then. The energy of the ey'rev rav exists today in all religious communities in a way that keeps fear and contraction in people's hearts so that they remain ever afraid of the mystical walk into the unknown, necessary for liberation. The ey'rev rav within us finds it much easier to put faith in something that gives us the illusion that it will provide security and safety in our everyday lives. An endless variety of material illusions serve as Golden Calves of security for us. A variety of ey'rev rav teachers, in all the religious traditions, as well as in the New Age and secular worlds, support us in striving after these illusions of security, rather than turning to the Great Way of the Torah. The Torah, on the other hand, encourages and guides us into the deep unknowable mystery of Hashem and ultimately to deveikut/chey'rut, which is the ultimate purpose of life. The story of the Golden Calf in this context is a warning from the past, a very ancient revelation for our own times. We no longer have the unconscious luxury to keep worshipping the gross and subtle golden calves of our world both within and outside of our religious contexts. This parashah is a clarion call to dissolve the ey'rev rav tendencies within us and walk up the Mountain of God into the deveikut/chey'rut awareness, our ultimate destiny.

Moshe then said he would go up the Mountain of God to make atonement for their sin. Moshe, in his heroic humility based on his atzilut understanding of the truth, said to God in Shemot 32:32–35:

> "Now, if you would, please forgive their sin. If not, you can blot me out from the book that you have written." God replied to Moses, "I will blot out from my book those who have sinned against me. Now go; you still have to lead the people to [the place] that I described to you. I will send my angel before you."

The Eternal One also said to them (in Shemot 33:3), "I will not go with you," but (in Shemot 33:1), "I will send an angel ahead of you...." The angel's name is Metatron (מטטרון), and the numerical value, or gematria, of its name is equal to that of Shaddai (שדי), the Almighty and protector from death (Shemot 23:20–21). Moshe knew that angels are simply justice, and that they lack the compassion of the Eternal One. So he responded (in Shemot 33:12–13) by pleading for mercy:

> "You told me to bring these people [to the Promised Land], but you did not tell me whom you would send with me. You also said that you know me by name and that you are pleased with me. Now, if you are indeed pleased with me, allow me to know your ways, so that I will know how to [remain] pleasing to you. [Also], you must confirm that this nation is your people."

"My presence will go and lead you," replied God (Shemot 33:14). God consented to Moshe's request in Shemot 33:17. This energy of God leading the people continued up until the time that Moshe left his body, and then God did send the angel Metatron, and the angel appeared to Yehoshua in Yeriho:

> And it came to pass, when Yehoshua was by Yeriho, that he lifted up his eyes and looked, and, behold, a man stood over against him with his sword drawn in his hand: and Yehoshua went over to him, and said to him, "Art thou for us, or for our adversaries?" And he

said, "No: but I am captain of the host of the Lord, I am now come."

(Yehoshua [Joshua] 5:13–14)

Metatron then guided the people, and as he spoke to Yehoshua he said, "Put off thy shoe from off thy foot; for the place on which thou standest is holy." Obviously he was saying "This is holiness" (Yehoshua 5:15). So God completed the promise to Moshe, and Metatron later returned to lead Yehoshua and the people after they crossed the Yarden River. Am Yisrael was then guided by a redeeming angel who was of the frequency of the Great Name.

As it says in Yesha'yahu (Isaiah) 26:4, "For the Lord god is an eternal Rock." Metatron means "the guide of the road." This is a key concept, because God sent an angel to the people to do just this: keep them on the way, and ultimately, guide them in the establishment of the inner and outer sanctuaries.

Then Moshe ascended the Mountain of God again for another forty days and nights without food and water. Only this time everyone was told to stay away from the Mountain of God for Moshe was to receive a more intense transmission of light. Although the words on the second set of tablets he was now told to write were pretty much the same as those on the first, some sages feel the new set wielded a more earthly energy. The first set is known as *hit'or'rut d'le'ala* (התעוררות דלעיאלה), or arousal from a heavenly dimension, and the second set of tablets is called *hit'or'rut d'le'tata* (התעוררות דלתתא), or arousal from below, or the earth plane—a lesser energy that Am Yisrael was more likely able to handle.

Moshe asked to see a direct vision of the Divine, but although he was a higher prophet than anyone else in Hebrew history, he was only allowed to see the "back" of God (i.e., not a full vision) as the Torah teaches that no one can see God fully and live (Shemot 33:20). In the vision, Moshe was given additional acts of grace, known as the thirteen attributes of divine compassion (and this is one reason the number thirteen is considered a lucky number in this tradition). Shemot 34:6–7 states:

God passed by before [Moses] and proclaimed, "God, God, Omnipotent, merciful and kind, slow to anger, with tremendous [resources of] love and truth. He remembers deeds of love for thousands [of generations], forgiving sin, rebellion and error.

He does not clear [those who do not repent], but keeps in mind the sins of the fathers to their children and grandchildren, to the third and fourth generation."

When Moshe descended from the Mountain of God, the skin of Moshe's face shone; Moshe put a veil over his face again, until he went in to speak with God.

Moshe and the mishkan were at such a high frequency that Moshe now kept the tent of meeting outside the camp. Most likely he did this because God now refused to let the divine presence be put inside the camp, until five and a half months later when the mishkan was built.

Like everything else in the Torah, the critical and famous part of Ki Tissa, which is the sin of the Golden Calf, can be interpreted on all four levels, as it is so deeply complex. This is where the half coin comes in. We cannot understand it all, but we are going to take a deeper look. This parashah is considered the ultimate "missing the mark" event of the Jewish people, and is referred to as chet ha'egel, the sin of the Golden Calf. Many of our sages have taught that every single calamity that has befallen Am Yisrael is a form of "punishment" for this. At the lower level, this can be seen as a rejection of God and of Moshe, but was this really the case? There is an insight into this that came at the end of the reign of Shlomo (King Solomon) when Shlomo had left his body. There was a revolt by Yarov'am against Shlomo's son, the King Rehav'am. Yarov'am established a separate kingdom up north in Shekhem with ten of the tribes. He severed all ties with the southern kingdom of Yehuda, and thus of Yerushalayim, and prevented his people from making their pilgrimage to the Holy Temple in Yerushalayim during the three seasonal celebrations mentioned earlier. To do this, he set up two golden calves along the road to Yerushalayim, one in Bet El and one in the area of the tribe of Dan. Now this is amazing to think about: We had already done this once; had we not learned? But he said to his citizens: "It is too much for you to go up to Yerushalayim; behold thy gods, O Yisrae'el, who brought thee up out of the land of Mizrayim" (First Melakhim 12:28). Again, it is difficult to imagine, but we may look for an understanding of the deeper issues, because, again, the acts of Yarov'am and the Golden Calf incident are connected. Many of the people never felt that this was against the desire of the creator! On a lower level of spiritual understanding, it is possible that it came from a desire to worship God, but in a safe and conventional way, which was to put God in a box, relegating God to an image. They wanted to serve the eternal God, but only in the way they found most convenient, not in the spiritually evolved way prescribed by Hashem. We saw a hint of this when the people reacted to the direct revelatory experience at Mount Sinai: "You speak to us, and we will listen. But let God not speak with us any more, for we will die if He does" (Shemot 20:16).

Most of the people never believed that the statues actually had powers of their own, although the less evolved actually did worship the Golden Calf. They were looking for a step down of the spiritual energy. They sought a mediating force between them and the Eternal One, and so they created in their mind a representation of God, to serve as an intermediary between them and God. Aharon unintentionally fed into this delusion by announcing in Shemot 32:5, "Tomorrow, there will be a festival to God." On one level, it came out of a desire to serve and support their spirituality, but on a lower level, they may have felt, in a deluded way, that they had passed the phase of human leadership, and would now be led directly by a deity. Some Torah sages feel they were committed to going back to Moshe if he returned. So in a broad sense it was not a full rejection, but clearly it was a missing of the mark. It was not quite a full miss, but they did miss it in a disastrous way. They made a physical likeness of a particular attribute of God, which is forbidden, for it is a reflection of a lower consciousness, putting God in a box, though not a rejection of spirituality altogether.

Yarov'am, on the second round, was reminding the nation of the past Golden Calf, and awakened in them the same kind of motive to know God, to strive to know God on that lower level. This was all the workings of ego, because Yarov'am wanted to separate and fragment the nation, by trying to get them to direct religious fervor not away, but toward God on a very low, finite plane. Through the statues he was able to achieve his egocentric power desires. He convinced the ten tribes that bowing to the Golden Calf was more important than visiting the Temple. There, the God without form was the focus. There one could encounter one's true self, mirrored in the No-thing. Even today we see that religious fervor is a good thing, but only if it is directed in the right way. In the wrong way, it leads to religious intolerance and fanaticism. On the deepest level, reinforcing this religious fervor with our mortal concepts of physical and mental forms, we actually create more ego and move farther from God. The chet ha'egal was an extension of ego. It materialized in the Golden Calf, but its origin is "we want to be safe, we want to be in the mind, we cannot deal with the unknown." In that way of thinking, we are not ready to be the light of Moshe, who boldly ascended the mountain into the unknown. This is what is needed to be part of the culture of deveikut/chey'rut. On another level of insight, in every generation, the closer we are to God the more vulnerable we also become to idolatry, because of the intensity. This is because idols are very "safe" for the ego and lower the energy in a way we can more easily handle, but at the same time we risk becoming deluded by them and therefore trapped.

At every stage, God is testing us. In Ki Tissa, both Moshe and Aharon were tested. Moshe's love and humility in relationship to the people were tested, and he passed the test by standing up for them. Aharon failed his test by allowing the people to run loose and not taking a strong leadership position, and he bore the consequences. Aharon's failure is a reminder that no matter how high one is on the spiritual path, the tests become harder and more subtle. May we be blessed to understand that we are always walking the razor's edge, and that we need to be vigilant against tendencies toward impatience and anger, and alert to the sincere stumbling of the people around us, even our spiritual teachers.

Amen

VayYaKhel

‿‿‿

As a friendly reminder to the collective of Israel, Moshe gathered the children of Israel and said to them: "These are the words that God has commanded for [you] to do: You may do work during the six weekdays, but Saturday must be kept holy as a Sabbath of Sabbaths to God" (Shemot 35:1–2). This takes us again to the importance of Shabbat, for we are continually reminded of the importance of Shabbat throughout Shemot. The honoring and living of Shabbat has many implications. Shabbat is a defining day of consciousness; it is the one day of the week when we align with the oneness of creator and creation. It is a time when we enter into the deveikut/chey'rut consciousness we intend to take with us into the following week. It is taught by our sages that if we are able to properly observe two Shabbats in a row, which is the Saturday Shabbat, plus holding Shabbat consciousness for the next six days (this is the second Shabbat), we will more permanently move into deveikut/chey'rut.

On Shabbat we create a spaceless space and timeless time that are indeed sacred. It is a consciousness space where we can receive the divine presence. In a sense, we are creating a divine tzim tzum (contraction) and then a tehiru (vacuum), so that the light of the Divine can come into us on Shabbat. Work, in that context, is therefore defined as anything that keeps us from becoming totally receptive to the Divine. The essence of Shabbat is about creating a quiet mind to receive the divine influx.

Thirty-nine categories of work (*avot melachot*—אבות מלאכות) forbidden on the Sabbath were taught to Moshe on Mount Sinai. They are derived from the Torah's description of thirty-nine categories of labor involved in the construction of the mishkan and all of its implements. Because, following these detailed descriptions, God said "You must still keep my sabbaths" (Shemot 31:12), it is implied that when Sabbath comes, all of these types of work involved in creating the mishkan (of which there were thirty-nine) must cease.

Shabbat observance should not only be done on a surface level, but on an inner level as well. If we are excessively concerned about mechanically fulfilling all the mitzvot, our minds may be so filled with that "observance work" that there is a danger of losing the quiet mind needed to receive God. Instead, our mind may become preoccupied with "Am I doing this right, am I doing that right," and we end up only creating Shabbat on the physical plane. Shabbat is on the plane of spirit. Our Shabbat preparation is about creating a quiet mind and a quiet spirit, totally open to receive the presence of the Divine. Only thus can Shabbat truly be active in our lives.

The difference between the Shabbat day and a festival (חג—*chag*) day is that on festivals we invoke the holiness into them by preparing for them and sanctifying them. Shabbat is holy on its own, as it is said, "Keep the Sabbath as something sacred to you" (Shemot 31:14). There is no special commandment or holiness to be created; we simply need to refrain from working, by virtue of which we allow for an empty mind. In other words, "Be still and know I am." That is the essence of Shabbat. When we have succeeded in living two Shabbats in a row in this consciousness we do not really separate Shabbat from the rest of the week, because the week is filled with the whole energy of Shabbat.

On Shabbat we invoke the shekhinah energy and the activating and honoring of all creation as the expression of God. In this way, the energy of Shabbat stays with us for the ensuing six days of the week. It is even taught that some of the energy of Shabbat lasts through Wednesday, and from Wednesday onward we receive holiness (kedushah—קדושה) from the Shabbat that is coming. This is one of the secrets taught by the second-century mystical master, Rabbi Shimon bar Yochai: "If only the Jewish people would properly keep two Shabbats in a row, they would be redeemed immediately" (Talmud Bav'li, Shabbat 118b). The first Shabbat is, of course, the traditional Shabbat, and the second Shabbat is keeping Shabbat consciousness throughout the other six days. The idea is to bring holiness into all the weekdays. This is the meaning of the two Shabbats suggested by Rabbi Shimon. We are talking about a high state of deveikut. Shabbat in this context deepens the connection of our soul to heaven. This, in turn, affects how we perceive the world and brings a higher frequency into the world, which uplifts and heals the whole world.

Torah is about awakening to our direct union with God, because what we are talking about is being the expression of Shabbat, rather than "observing Shabbat." The mystery of Shabbat is to become the experience of Shabbat.

Shabbat is grounded in stillness. It is *binaht halev* (בינת הלב), the wisdom of the heart, which is what connects us to Shabbat. Shabbat is a proactive way to cleanse ourselves of the impure actions from the previous week so that they do not accumulate. Shabbat gradually helps us purify undesirable character traits. In this context, Shabbat is not given to everybody; we must merit it. It is a day when we free ourselves from the chief idol of the world—money— along with the idols of technical civilization, which we allow to divide us from Hashem. Shabbat, in that way, is a day of peace between humanity and nature. "Work" is, then, any kind of disturbance between humanity and nature, or of the unity between men and women. On Shabbat we let go of the disease of separateness activated by Golden Calves so we can experience our oneness with all of humanity and with God.

Shabbat is often called the consciousness, or wellspring, of the world to come (*me'ein olam ha'ba*—מעין עולם הבא). In the Torah tradition, it is not the act of not working, which is the supreme value of Shabbat, but refreshing the soul (rest), in which the purpose is simply to be a complete human being filled with the joy of Hashem. On Shabbat, we move from the work of creation to the divine mystery of creation. We are no longer in a manipulative relationship with the world. To work on Shabbat is to think that one is self-employed rather than serving Hashem. Shabbat is based on true freedom on every level. In this way we identify with higher consciousness and not ego.

On Shabbat our taskless task is to live as a full human being. The real *oneg* (עונג), or pleasure, of Shabbat is to experience the natural noncausal joy, peace, contentment, love, compassion, and oneness of our natural human state. On Shabbat the attachment to ego can be washed away in the downpour of holiness. It is a time to balance our human doings with our human beingness. During the week we have a *birurim* (בירורים—discernment) consciousness, focused more on sorting out worldly reality. On Shabbat we go to the higher definition of birurim—letting go of self-delusionary reality and, in its place, allowing for the experience of absolute reality, of Ayn Sof (אין סוף). It means aligning our inner motivation with the divine will, in which there is only the will of God happening without the bewildering interruption of ego. In postberur consciousness we merge with the name of God itself. This is a high level of Shabbat consciousness. We begin then to live in achdut (אחדות), the cosmic unity in which we experience our oneness with God and experience God in all of creation. Each Shabbat is a teshuvah (תשובה), a return to God. It is a renewal of our eternal covenant with Hashem.

On Shabbat we try to do nothing that creates fragmentation for self, others, and the cosmos. Shabbat is about accomplishing nothing on the physical plane. It may even take us as high as the consciousness of the Ayn Sof prior to time, space, and being. On Shabbat we have the unique opportunity to engage our neshama ye'teirah (נשמה יתירה), our amplified soul, through which we are better able to reconnect to our holy rhythm. In this way, Shabbat becomes part of the art of living, as the consciousness of Shabbat is to be totally human on the highest plane. Shabbat is a taste of unity and enlightenment consciousness. It is a time in which we touch our own immortality. To remember Shabbat is to remember the truth of who we are. It is about being in an awareness of God in the moment. When we are able to be in this consciousness we become Shabbat; we become the experience of Shabbat as total unity.

On Shabbat, by quieting our minds, we open up a vortex between the heavens and earth that helps us to access the deeper and greater soul essence of who we are. This is the deeper meaning behind the concept of the neshama ye'teirah, the extra, or amplified, soul consciousness that is accessible to us on Shabbat. It is not that an additional soul comes in, but the higher parts of our soul are more easily experienced.

A key way to understand Shabbat is to be the experience of Shabbat. Shabbat is about deepening and expanding our experience of the light. Every seven days we have the opportunity to keep enhancing and reinforcing Shabbat awareness. Our sages teach that to observe the mitzvah of Shabbat is akin to observing all of the mitzvot of the entire Torah (Midrash Shemot Rabbah 25:12). In this context, Shabbat connects us to the first Shabbat of creation and also to the leaving of Egypt, both of which required a divine intervention for the continuation of the evolution of consciousness. In this way, we begin to understand that human history, as described in Bereisheet, is a series of divine interventions and cycles in which, at least, the seventh part of that cycle, Shabbat, is one of balance and peace.

In parashah VayYaKhel, Moshe said to the nation: "Collect among yourselves an elevated offering to God. If a person feels like giving an offering to

God, he can bring any of the following: gold, silver, copper, sky-blue [wool], dark red [wool], [wool died with] the crimson worm, fine linen" (Shemot 35:5–6). Here he asked for a love offering. It was an offering not because they thought they should give, but because they truly felt in spirit that this is what they wanted to do. "Each person who was ready to volunteer then came forward. [Also] each one who wanted to give brought a donation to God for the making of the communion tent, all its necessities, and the sacred vestments. The men accompanied the women" (Shemot 35:21–22). "Every skilled woman put her hand to spinning.... Highly skilled women volunteers also spun the goats' wool" (Shemot 35:25–26). Both men and women were equally involved in the offering to God.

And then Moshe said to the children of Israel: "Bezalel shall thus do all that God commanded, along with Oholi'av and every other skilled individual, to whom God has granted the wisdom and understanding to know how to do all the work necessary for the sacred task." What is the message here? God can make anyone skillful and deep if that person is filled with the spirit. As it turns out, Bezalel was twelve years old at the time, and his work partner was another boy, Oholi'av, the son of Ahisamakh from the tribe of Dan. It is a clear teaching that God inspired them both. "Moses summoned Bezalel, Oholi'av, and all the other skilled individuals upon whom God had bestowed a natural talent, all who volunteered to dedicate themselves to completing the task" (Shemot 36:2–3). The wisdom referred to here is that which comes from really knowing we are there to serve God. "All the most talented craftsmen worked on the tabernacle itself, which consisted of ten tapestries made of twined linen, together with sky-blue, dark-red and crimson wool, brocaded with cherubs" (Shemot 36:8).

We begin to get more of a sense of what this process is about. A talmudic rendition of the event goes like this:

> When the Holy One said to Moses, "Go and tell Bezalel to make
> me a Tabernacle and an ark and the vessels," Moses reversed
> the order, not thinking correctly, and he said to Bezalel "Make
> an ark, vessels, and the Tabernacle." Bezalel said to him, "Our
> Teacher, Moses! As a rule, a builder first builds a house and then

brings vessels into it. But you say make an ark, vessels, and Tabernacle. Where shall I put the vessels that I am to make? Could it be that the Holy Blessed One told you to make a Tabernacle, an Ark, and then a vessel?"

(Talmud Bav'li, Berachot 55a)

This was a twelve-year-old boy speaking to Moshe, who was eighty and had just split the Yam Suf (Sea of Reeds), but he was speaking in truth, and not from ego, so Moshe listened to him. Moshe replied to Bezalel, "You must have been in the shadow of God as God was speaking to me." Sure enough, the word bezal'el means "in the shadow of God." The depth of these people in these times is quite interesting. The Talmud explains that while Yesha'yahu looked through a foggy lens, Moshe looked through a space of clear glass. This is the difference between Moshe and the rest of the prophets. They could see God, but not with the luminosity of having God speak directly through them (Talmud Bav'li, Yevamot 49b).

The term kavanot (כונות) means sacred meditation and acts of divine unification that are specific to each commandment. However, they are worthless unless they are activated. In other words, only in this physical world, where the teachings can be physically observed, can there be revelations of God, because these acts help to unveil the presence of God in our lives. Bezalel means the shadow of God, and that has to do with the idea of a world in which clouds obscure the "sun" of God. This is the world of action, and it is a way and opportunity, through sacrifice and service, in which we are able to connect with God in a wholly different way. When God says to the people "Make me a dwelling-place, and I will dwell within them," it means that the dwelling place of the mishkan is a way to activate the energy, and from that dwelling-place, it goes out in essence as a transmitter that activates the divine awareness in all the people. That is why it says "within them" instead of "within him" or "within it," because the Holy One vibrates as a message of light within all the people of the world, not just the Jewish people, and it is God's desire to be revealed in this world. That is one thing we must keep in mind as we begin to get a deeper understanding of what is going on in this parashah.

God instructed Moses to take a count (of the warriors) for the mishkan, and asked everybody to help. It is a tradition that you "do not count Am Yisrael" directly. The reason for this is that a leader may want a tally because population is indicative of power—military power. The Jews, however, have been relatively few in number throughout their history. Nor did God elect them for their sacred task because of their vast numbers: "You are among the smallest of all nations" (Devarim 7:7). This rings true also with the mathematics of the power of the spiritually awakened: True, you have to have a certain amount, whether it is the square root of one percent, or one percent, but the power of God dwells within the people. The result is that the strength of a spiritual force is not in its numbers, but in its connection to the Divine.

There is a little story about King David, who wanted to take a census of his warriors. He acted against the advice of Yoav, the chief of staff, in doing so. After taking the census he realized he had sinned, and repented. The prophet Gad came to him, and gave him three options: seven years of famine, defeat in battle for three months, or three days of pestilence in the land. David chose the last. During the plague that immediately came, 77,000 people died. Finally God stopped the plague (Second Shemu'el, Chap. 24). David's error was in misunderstanding and underappreciating where the power of Am Yisrael came from. The power of Am Yisrael is not in numbers, but in its connection with God. That is the truth for all spiritual people on the planet. Our power is not with numbers, but in the spirit of God: "Not by might and not by power, but by my spirit, says the Lord of hosts" (Zekharya 4:6).

The half-shekel coins involved in Moshe's census were donated to the service of the mishkan as a way of counting the warriors. In this way, each warrior felt himself a partner in the people's spiritual unfolding, rather than merely a number. In essence, the meaning here is that the "down-home," grassroots people are the foundation of Am Yisrael and the world. For when God says "Build me a sanctuary and I will dwell amongst them," it means in the heart of all beings.

It is very symbolic that the coins contributed by the warriors were used to build the foundation of the mishkan walls. They melted the coins down and created silver bricks, which held up the walls. The symbolism of using the gifted coins as a way of taking a census is that the people, the spiritual people, are the foundation for God's earthly existence. The temple is built upon the people, and all the spiritual people are, in essence, the house of God. The building of the mishkan thus represents our ability to be of service to God, and creates a vibratory center that vibrates outward, bringing everyone into alignment with God. This is the greatest service to the world. When we build it we are not saying that God only dwells in the mishkan. Rather, on the surface, it is about creating a space that amplifies the vibration of God. On a deeper level, all the details of all the work that went into it, how it was built and what was woven, are, in a sense, guidelines for how we must build a living mishkan within ourselves. This is the key to spiritual life. It is about how we lead our lives in the world, how we create our own sacred space within ourselves, and how we create a sacred space within our homes. All of this serves to activate the light of God within ourselves. The purpose of the mishkan within oneself is to infuse every moment, every breath, with the scintillating divine presence of God. When we activate the mishkan within ourselves, we activate the light of our soul, and become whole in a very deep way.

There were exact specifications for the building of the mishkan—exact details, exact parameters. It is said that, "When Moses saw that all the work had been done exactly as God had ordered, he blessed [all the workers]" (Shemot 39:43). When we work with that awareness of exactness, it takes us into a deeper connection with the Divine. Details do make a difference. We often believe that details are insignificant, but they are vital, and that is the point we are making here. It is about the details, not the individual details in an obsessive way, but seeing every detail as part of a larger vibratory expression of activating the light of God within ourselves.

Moshe blessed the people for their excellent execution of the details, lauding them for their devotion to the details. This represents a complete surrender to the Divine. Then, when this happens, the Torah says, "The cloud covered the communion tent, and God's glory filled the Tabernacle" (Shemot 40:34). The teaching here is that when the Jewish people succeeded in experiencing God in the process of the details, then in essence, it meant that we could then experience the presence of God in every detail. If we can do this we have then mastered the subtle art of experiencing God in the world. Therefore, the Ba'al Shem Tov talked about the importance of yechudim (יחודים),

mantric unification meditations, because it was an active practice of experiencing the unity of Hashem in the world. He taught that yechudim are seven times more important than studying the Torah (*Tziv'ot Yivash*). However, he did not say *not* to study the Torah.

Once the glory of God filled the tent, Moshe could not enter (Shemot 40:35). As God stepped back to allow us our own sacred space, so must we step back to allow for God's sacred space and refrain from judgments of God's actions or seeming inactions.

The book of Shemot is, in essence, about the birth of the spiritual and physical Am Yisrael. The Torah narrates how it was nurtured through the continual process of meeting God, through the meeting in Sinai, through everyday revelations, through the halakhah, and through the building and creation of the mishkan. As the Zohar teaches, God, the expression of the Torah, and Israel are all one entity (Zohar, Vol. 2, folio 126a).

Shemot unfolds in a very interesting way. It opens with the enslavement of the Hebrews and how we learned through suffering, and concludes with how we can live our lives in a way that we are continually experiencing God in the world and in ourselves. This is the deepest level of freedom. That is the meaning of the mishkan, because it is really a metaphor for building the inner mishkan. This concept is referred to by our ancient sages as *mikdash me'at* (מקדש מעט), the microcosmic sanctuary—the act of becoming a living sanctuary of God.

There is a balance, certainly played out among the most religious and more mystical people. There is *k'lal* (כלל)—the beautiful ideas, dreams, and, in a sense, the essence of what Jewish spiritual life is about, and *p'rat* (פרט)—the details involved in manifesting those ideas. The danger is that we can get caught up in all the details, as pointed out by Rav Kook, and miss out on the essence. It is the essence that needs to be infused into everyday life through the detail. The *k'lalim*, which are the basic deep essential and spiritual principles, and *p'ratim*, the details, need to be brought together in a workable way. Rav Kook, the first Chief Rabbi of Israel (and a vegetarian), suggests in some of his writings that we have lost touch with the k'lalim, the deeper underlying principles, because we have gotten so wrapped up in the p'ratim, in the details. We have lost sight of the forest because of the trees. Now it is time to get back to emphasizing the wonderment of the essence and the spiritual teachings, which are universal teachings that take us to the presence of God. However, the k'lalim need to be played out through the p'ratim, the details, in a conscious way. The balance we are seeking is between the inspiration inherent in the k'lalim, and the practicalities of the p'ratim, so that we might bring the presence of God into our everyday life, in every moment. The presence of God is what is important. It is deep Torah Way.

When we look at every detail involved in the construction of the mishkan, we discover yet another lesson in the importance of detail. Every person is a detail in the collective mishkan of Israel. That helps us move away from labels of "secular," "spiritual," "reform," "conservative," "orthodox," "ultra-orthodox," and so on, because we are all "a detail in the mishkan." We are all "hanging out in the courtyard of the mishkan" together. This is why Moshe blessed all the people, because, in essence, the true mishkan is that we are all one in viewing and in creating mishkan, in every moment, as our lives are, in a sense, a mobile mishkan of the spirit of the people. That is why we have God communicating to Aharon through the stones on his breastplate, which also had the names of the tribes inscribed there in the mosaic. The mishkan is about building bridges and building the Ark within the people. It is about actually l'hitpallel (להתפלל), which means basking in the light of our prayers, as opposed to repeating them as automatic sayings, because they have real intense meanings for us. The purpose of building the internal mishkan, the purpose of Shabbat, and the purpose of everything we do is to be in the presence of the Divine and to continually enhance our connection with the light.

Another subtle teaching here is that the great zeal and excitement of the people surrounding the building of the mishkan may have been the result of their recent experience of the Golden Calf. Obviously, they now wanted to move away from that wrong direction. It is taught that in that process the ey'rev rav, the mixed multitudes, developed a subtle hatred and some of the Midrash says that they were therefore not allowed into the mishkan, for fear that they would take the vibration of their hatred into it. As we know, for almost forty days, there was no energy of death, and everyone was invited into the presence of God. After the Golden Calf incident, the ey'rev rav became filled with the energy of hatred and death, and were banned from the tabernacle in order to keep the energy of hatred and death from entering it. So, to build an inner and outer mishkan, our hearts need to be filled with love, and we need to remove the ey'rev rav of our own thoughts and of the negative energy of hatred, which connect us to death. Hatred is a misunderstanding that some people use to justify their egocentricity, which causes separation from God, and is a form of idol worship, because in hatred one is investing energy into something separate from oneself. When we are in hatred of something, we are really having negative energy toward it. There is "God 'hating' 'Esav," for example (Mal'akhi 1:3). Did God actually hate 'Esav? Not really, not in the sense of how we use that term today. The word used there for hate, *sin'ah* (שנאה), means something totally different in Torah context. Sin'ah implies a feeling of separation from, as 'Esav had separated himself from God. So when it says, "And God saw that Leah was שנואה 'unloved' [by Ya'akov]" (Bereisheet 29:31), it does not mean that Ya'akov hated Le'a in the way we understand that word in its English rendition. Rather, Ya'akov felt closer to Rahel than to Le'a, which made Le'a feel separate from him. Hatred in the way we know it in the English vernacular is given an entirely different word in the Hebrew, *s'tam* (שטם), which is found in only two places in the entire Torah, and in both places it implies a hatred of the sort that leads to causing harm by violence and outright persecution. The two appearances of this rare term for hatred are in the Torah's account of 'Esav's hatred of Ya'akov (וישטום), described in Bereisheet 27:41, and of the brothers of Yosef hating him and seeking to harm him or kill him (וישטמהו), described in Bereisheet 49:23. This quality of hatred is different from sin'ah, for in those two instances it was clear that persecution, and even death, was intended. That is the meaning of hatred as we know it today. So we cannot and do not want to fall into the consciousness of ey'rev rav, which says that it is okay to hate (in our modern meaning as a feeling of violence and closed-heartedness with the energy of idol worship). We should not hate people who disagree with us. We can look very closely and see how all the different nations use their scriptures to justify their ego-based hating. We can see the way the Koran has been used to justify hating the Jewish people, even killing them, and how certain ultra-orthodox (Jewish) circles justify hating people by their misunderstanding of the meaning behind the word sin'ah, taking it literally as we use it today to hate people actually, physically, and egocentrically. This is not what we are talking about. Hate, in the Torah sense, means something completely different. It means that which separates us. In this context, the ey'rev rav is not allowed in the inner temple. You cannot be in the mishkan if your heart is filled with hate, and not filled with the love of God.

What we see again is the importance of relating with a pure heart. The people gave with a pure heart, which became for them both a teaching and a purification. It was made possible not merely by their giving alone, but by their giving with a pure heart, and out of love. They gave charity and performed service with a pure heart.

In its design, the Holy of Holies was separated from the rest of the Temple. In a sense, we can feel deep inside ourselves that there is an empty space filled with light that radiates in all of us. In that empty space, we are the entire tabernacle and the Holy of Holies is the heart of God that dwells within us, for "the Holy of Holies dwells within the heart" (Tikuney Zohar, folio 137a). The curtains in the tabernacle represent the veil of ignorance, the concealment of the light, and as we continue to connect with the light, we are able to lift the curtain and have the direct experience. The eleven coverings of the tabernacle, and the eleven sacred incenses, represent one more than ten. The eleventh has to do with overcoming Satan by making a subtle offering to nullify Satan. The walls of the tabernacle give us boundaries in which we can more actively live our lives in ways that create holiness. The Ark itself is described as being covered "inside and out" with gold. It is a teaching that we must be the golden light of God within and without to really be the holiness. We cannot say one thing and do another, or feel something else in our hearts (Talmud Bav'li, Baba Mezia 49a).

As we are building the inner mishkan, this is what we are talking about: We have our boundaries, we take care of them, we acknowledge all the details of our life as being infused with the presence of God. We acknowledge our relationships as being infused with the light of God. And we, in a sense, become golden like the Ark, inside and out.

Outside of the Ark were the twelve loaves of gold. Some people feel this is a metaphor for the manna. They rubbed *levana* (לבנה—frankincense) on it, to create a frequency to activate consciousness. The twelve loaves also represent the twelve signs of the zodiac. By eating the twelve loaves on Shabbat with holy intent, we overcome the energy of our destinies as outlined in the stars. We can draw grace to rise above Elohim, to a higher octave of our potential. The candelabra represents the light of God. It was lit every day to activate the God light for the entire world. The altar itself is significant as it symbolizes the meaning and intention of the sacrifices we make in our own lives, to burn up the "animal" of our ego.

The cherubim, previously discussed, represent a process of continual divine revelation. As King Solomon said, "In all thy ways acknowledge him" (Mishle 3:6). The dedication of the mishkan is mentioned three separate times in the Torah because of its importance: once in Shemot, once in the book of VayYiKra, and once in the book of BeMidbar. The purpose of the inner mishkan as well as the outer mishkan, or Beit HaMikdash, was to be a way to continually connect with God and bring the people into alignment with the Divine, and each dedication spoke to a different aspect of Am Yisrael. In essence, the outer temple, as it reflects the inner temple, was a perfect way for Am Yisrael to meet God face-to-face throughout history.

Three festivals took place that all of Am Yisrael would attend at the Holy Temple. It was a special time, because it was said that they would roll back the curtain that separated the Holy of Holies from the rest of the temple. When the curtains were rolled back it was like the heart of God being exposed. What is in the heart of God in the moment is symbolized by the cherubim in the play of divine Eros atop the Ark, and represents the eternal marriage of Hashem with Am Yisrael. When the people saw the cherubim they experienced the expression of God's love for them; the people saw and felt that they were loved by God, as Moshe had emphasized to them earlier (Devarim 7:8). The divine Eros of the cherubim also mimics the love of man and woman in sacred relationship. It is the truth of Eros, which is God loving God's self as manifested in all aspects of life. With the creation of the mishkan we had then the willingness of the Divine to return to the midst of Am Yisrael.

Shemot records the birth of a spiritual people. It was Moshe's responsibility as a servant of God to direct the building of the mishkan. It would serve as an eternal meeting between Am Yisrael and God, not only on the outer plane, which is no longer presently available, but also on the inner plane. The detailed instructions involved in building the outer mishkan contained the energy for building the inner mishkan. It helps us to see and experience the dance of the cherubim in our own hearts, and to feel the expression of God, and the experience of God, in our own hearts. As the Book of Shemot nears to closing, we are left with a complete design and way to connect with the Divine on the outer planes and, most important, on the inner planes of our own hearts. We have thus the opportunity to become the dance of the cherubim making love to God, and God making love to us. In Shemot, the eternal connection with God is activated in our own hearts and in the hearts of Am Yisrael. This is the great gift from God through Moshe for activating the spirit of God in the spirit of the people.

This particular book, Shemot, is about Moshe, who under Hashem's power and guidance began his career with the people as slaves and liberated them out of slavery, and then helped to further liberate those who were ready from their internal slavery. It established the light of God on a concentrated physical level in an outer form of the mishkan to help people reconnect to the light of God on the inner plane. Now Am Yisrael, as a spiritual and physical nation, was ready to serve all of creation and become "a light unto the nations" (Yesha'yahu 42:6), as it became in the times of King David and King Solomon. May we again be a light to the nations as we were in those earlier times.

Amen

PeKudey

~~~

THIS parashah starts with Shemot 38:21: "These are the accounts of the Tabernacle" (the Tabernacle of Testimony). It describes Moshe's efforts in finishing the mishkan. The whole mishkan is called the Tabernacle of Testimony, also known as the Tent of Meeting, while the tabernacle refers more directly to the ten curtains and the items associated with these curtains located closer to the center of the mishkan. The immediate focus is on Moshe's completion of the Tabernacle of Testimony (the precursor to the first Temple) as a physical place for the energy of the Divine to reside on earth. Moshe, who was not a kohain, nonetheless acted as the high priest, the kohain gadol, for the first seven days, until Aharon and his sons were fully initiated as priests. Moshe was put in charge of assembling the tabernacle, and on the eighth day of the preparations it was filled with the divine presence, veiled in the midst of the Anan HaKavod, the Cloud of Glory, which covered the Tabernacle of Testimony. The Anan HaKavod did not even let Moshe enter without permission. God's eternal presence was again established in the camp of Am Yisrael following the Golden Calf disaster.

The book of Shemot and the parashah of PeKudey end with Shemot 40:38: "God's cloud would then remain on the Tabernacle by day, and fire was in it by night. This was visible to the entire family of Israel, in all their travels." The Anan HaKavod hovering over the Tabernacle of Testimony was analogous to the cloud over the Mountain of God, which Moshe was also not allowed to enter without invitation. In other words, the Anan HaKavod over the Tabernacle of Testimony was meant to be with Am Yisrael throughout their remaining thirty-eight years in the desert. On a deeper level, it was to remain with Am Yisrael even beyond those times, if we chose to hold the energy until the total mission of this cycle was completed and the messianic times arrived.

The Book of Shemot describes the liberation of the people from Egypt after they endured their last major purification necessary to complete the prophecy that the Torah would be given after two thousand cycles from the time of Adam and Cha'vah (Talmud Bav'li, Sanhedrin 97a). The highlight of

Shemot was the receiving of the Torah in what appears to be an interdimensional transmission by God to all of Am Yisrael initially, with the rest of the transmission to follow through Moshe. It describes the first and only time in history, so far, where millions of people as a whole nation of every age and class, including children in the womb, had a direct experience of Hashem. A key principle in this great tradition and lineage of deveikut/chey'rut is that meeting God should be a way of life, not a one-time encounter. This principle was well expressed by King David: *"shiviti Hashem l'neg'dee ta'mid,"* or "I have set the Lord always before me" (Tehillim 16:8).

Shemot not only describes the exodus of Am Yisrael from the external Egypt and the receiving of the Torah, but also a continuing process of maintaining the internal progression of freeing themselves from their internal Egypt with the establishment of the Tabernacle of Testimony, which, in turn, served as an antenna for the physical energy on the outer plane. The teaching of Shemot 25:8, "They shall make me a sanctuary, and I will dwell among them," is an invitation for the opportunity of experiencing Hashem in our inner sanctuary by experiencing the light of the Divine within, through being lived by the Ten Speakings, prayer, meditation, mitzvot, the observance and experience of Shabbat awareness, and creating yechudim, in every moment and in every situation. In the creation of the Tabernacle of Testimony, we also have the initiation of the Levites and the kohan'im, the priesthood, to support the people in maintaining and developing this energy.

In the overall exodus event, there was the historical public experience in the ten plagues and the defeat of Egypt, the strongest power on the planet at the time. There was also born the awareness of the existence of: (1) a transcendent and immanent God; (2) a personal God who actively participates in the unfolding of human spiritual consciousness on the planet earth, as well as in the heavens; and (3) a God of grace who is greater than all natural forces or empires on the planet.

Shemot describes the birth of Am Yisrael on all levels, as one collective soul, melded into oneness at Har Sinay. Shemot gives the preconditions necessary for spreading the teachings about this one intangible God throughout the world. May we all be blessed that we can contribute to the spreading of God awareness, on every level of our society, and in every person's heart across the world.

Amen

The
Book
of
VayYiKra

VayYiKra

$\sim\!\!\!\sim\!\!\!\sim$

Vᴀʏʏɪᴋʀᴀ (Leviticus) is the first parashah of the book of VayYiKra, the third book of the Torah. On the p'shat, or literal, level, it appears that this parashah is all about how to sacrifice animals, but this is apparent only at the most primitive level of understanding. The essence of the book of VayYiKra is intense devotion to the Divine. It is the first time the Torah speaks outwardly of linking to the light of the Divine as our source. So this portion, VayYiKra, and this whole third book of the Torah, also called VayYiKra, is about spiritual devotion to the One. It is also about appreciating ourselves as divine emanations. As we do this, we are able to meditate so that we merit experiencing holiness with clarity, rather than see it through the distorted lens of the ego and its misperceptions. In other words, VayYiKra is about burning up spiritual darkness so that we can truly dance in the truth. To do this almost everyone needs to go through internal sacrifice as a potent form of devotion.

According to kabbalistic teachings, even the animals sacrificed at that time consciously lined up to be sacrificed, because they knew that the process was part of their tikkun, or correction. The good news for vegetarians and vegans is that today the sacrifices are internal. We sacrifice by how we choose to face the obstacles we encounter, whether with consciousness or with ego. The challenge and purification process today is to be present and to be open to all that is. VayYiKra supports us with the energy and strength necessary for us to evolve spiritually. Throughout the Torah, there is a tremendous focus on sacrifice as a key part of the purification process involved in waking up. However, there is more to VayYiKra than simply sacrifice. Devotion to the Divine is another key message in VayYiKra.

As we explore a little further, we come to understand that VayYiKra is focused on the task of Am Yisrael in the world. This third book, VayYiKra, is also referred to as *Torat Kohan'im* (תורת כהנים), or guide for the kohan'im (priests). It may seem that there is therefore not a connection or relevance here to the collective, to the people in general, but, in fact, you cannot separate the two because the Temple (בית המקדש—Beit HaMikdash) was a receiver and an energy transmitter of the light, channeling the light to all of the people. It was an amplifier. This does not mean that the people could not get the light directly, or to increase one's light one had no alternative but to go to the temple. It means that the mishkan, and then later the Beit HaMikdash, acted as an amplifier of divine light, as discussed earlier.

There are many areas that the kohan'im had to address, beyond judgment. One was ritual purity and impurity, called *taharah* (purity) and *tumah* (impurity). Purity therefore related to all of Am Yisrael because it had to do with kedusha, which was a responsibility of the kohan'im to be aware of, as well as to hold the awareness that Am Yisrael was to be a kingdom of priests and a holy nation (Shemot 19:6). On one level, therefore, everyone is a kohain. Whatever task was assigned to the kohan'im, in the framework of Am Yisrael, was consequently relevant to the nation and the world. As a nation of priests, from the Jewish perspective, the responsibility was to show the meaning of holiness to the rest of the world. This is still a major task. If Israel is somehow to get beyond all of the difficulties that it faces in the Middle East and in the world, she needs the guidance of VayYiKra to do this.

VayYiKra's spiritual power comes from devotion to God and the holiness and purity that come from that devotion. The very first role assigned to the kohan'im was to enhance world peace (BeMidbar 6:23–26). This was a different kind of peace than merely a lack of war. It was about improving the conditions of all people. It was about learning to live peacefully with people who have different ideas and viewpoints, and bringing everybody together. It was about seeing that everything and everyone has a particular purpose, and respecting that. Harmony does not necessarily come from a process focusing solely on being equal (a relative viewpoint), but on acknowledging that we all have our different roles, and that we all have a right to exist in our different roles. That is the way Aharon, the first kohain gadol, worked. He promoted shalom (שלום), which comes from the word shalem (שלם), or complete. He worked to hear the different sides, to validate everyone, and to find a way to honor everybody's position (Midrash Pirkei D'Rebbe Eliezer, Chap. 17). This was not based on the theory of compromise. It focused, rather, on how people could become clear on their actual position and find unity with the position of the other.

We understand in this whole process, as it refers to all of Am Yisrael, that kedusha was not reserved for rabbis and priests, but was the responsibility of the entire nation, of all Am Yisrael. For us to do this today, we need to be clear about our own nature as individuals and as a nation. The Judaic priesthood was not a personal, self-serving station, but was (and still is) meant to be a national way of life for the Jewish people, as a kingdom of priests and a holy nation (Shemot 19:6), to be a light unto the nations (Yesha'yahu 49:6)—a light that says all are chosen in their own particular way. This is not easy, but it was the path of Aharon and the path of the Jewish priesthood.

The major emphasis of the whole book of VayYiKra is addressed in this first parashah of VayYiKra, namely, the laws surrounding the kohan'im, and particularly Aharon. It discusses the service to God as a responsibility for everyone, and the role of kohan'im in terms of assessing between pure and impure blood, guilt and innocence, and leprous symptoms versus impure marks. As peacemakers, they had the task of settling disputes that arose among the people, particularly around the issues of civil law and complicated laws related to ritual purity and impurity. Why were the kohan'im chosen, and not the judges? Because, again, the kohan'im were the lovers and pursuers of peace; that was their function. Aharon is described as the one who loved peace and pursued peace (Talmud, Bav'li, Avot D'Rebbe Natan 12:6).

Shalem means complete, and shalom is, therefore, a state of being wherein one experiences no lack. In a state of true shalom, everything is allowed to exist, and appears in the right relationship to the other. From a Torah perspective, it is not about everybody being the same or everybody being equal. Rather, it is a way to create very clear boundaries and to define appropriate places for all. Each person brought to the collective individual skills and distinct qualities. Disputes were not resolved by forcing the compromise; they were resolved by encouraging each side to recognize their own position in relevance to the other. In this system, different from a court system, no one came out guilty or compromised. Instead, they found a place for everyone to live together in harmony. The priest developed the ability to make true peace in the world and to demonstrate the relevance of purity and impurity in leading one's life. The task of Am Yisrael today is to fit everything into its rightful place. The first-century BCE Rabbi Hillel the Elder used to say: "Be among the students of Aharon. Love shalom and pursue shalom. Love people and bring them closer to the Torah" (Mishnah, Avot 1:12).

As we are able to fit the pieces of human complexity into a single whole, we develop love for each individual and his or her personal expertise. Each is an important part of the greater whole. In this process, it is important to unconditionally love one's neighbor without constantly worrying about that person's spiritual accomplishments. Through this approach we open the door, by showing others their place in the comprehensive whole, to come close to the Torah. This is obviously not the easiest thing to do in our world today, but it is the essence of sacrifice and the inner priesthood, and is thus beyond the idea of animal sacrifice. It is about sacrificing our ego for the sake of the Divine. The ego is the animal that is being sacrificed.

A particular and interesting relationship with the angels emerges in understanding this parashah, because there was a flow of cosmic energy that was activated when all of this was performed in an appropriate, harmonious way. This is a key to the very opening of the parashah, "And God called to Moses," which the sages held as an expression of endearment (Midrash Torat Kohanim 1:7), an expression of tenderness and affection also used by the angels. One angel will call to another, as it says in Yesha'yahu 6:3, *"Kadosh, kadosh, kadosh adonai tz'vayot. Baruch shem k'vod malchuto l'olam va'ed"* ("Holy Holy Holy is the Lord of Hosts. The whole world is filled with Divine glory."). This is a calling that we all feel. It unites the energy of the heavens and the earth.

When God tested Avraham by asking for the ultimate sacrifice that could be proposed to a parent (the sacrifice of his son, Yitzhak), he passed the test and was stopped short of the final step of the sacrifice. Instead, he took the ram that got caught in the thicket nearby and offered it as a burnt offering "in the place of his son" (Bereisheet 22:13). This model was true for all animal sacrifices, in that they were always in place of a person. On a surface level, the whole point of animal sacrifice was that it was a step up from human sacrifice. While that was certainly true, the very first animal sacrifices were done long before people were doing human sacrifices. The first animal sacrifice recorded is that of Hevel, second son of Adam and Cha'vah. He and his brother Kayin were offering sacrifices as a way of expressing their devotion to the Divine. Kayin was a land farmer. He grew vegetables, but he did not sacrifice from the best of his produce. He was not fully in a complete devotion surrendered state to the Divine. Hevel was a shepherd of flocks, and when he offered up an animal in sacrifice, he offered from the best of his herd (Bereisheet 4:4), and was in a state of complete surrender. This is why, the oral tradition tells us, Hevel's sacrifice was chosen and Kayin's was not (Midrash Bereisheet Rabbah 22:5).

After the fall of the second Temple, prayer replaced animal sacrifice (Talmud Bav'li, Berachot 26b). Fasting, too, was and is a form of sacrifice, because in a fast we are literally sacrificing our fat, and, if we become a little dehydrated, we are also sacrificing our blood, as our blood volume then decreases. This is particularly true with the way they fasted in ancient times, either by dry fasting or water fasting. There was a certain suffering in the way people did these fasts. It is said that in offering our fat through ritual fasting, we burn away our sins, because we are not only giving of our fat and blood, but even of our very strength and power. There are many ways to view all the individual kinds of suffering that people go through. If we take suffering the right way, as a gift from the Divine, then that suffering becomes a true sacrifice. The sufferings of the Jewish people, although not necessarily conscious and voluntary, have also been a kind of sacrifice and purification. When we perceive our own suffering of trials and tribulations as a way of God calling to us, then it becomes as the *kri'ah* (קריאה) way in which God called to Moshe, an expressions of tenderness, affection, and love from the creator. This is a whole different way of looking at what we perceive as difficulties. They are opportunities for us to burn up our missing-the-mark, also known as sin. As we do that through ritual, through fasting, through intense prayer, and intense meditation, as well as through service (*sherirut*) and charity (*tzadaka*), we burn up the negative actions and thought forms by which we live and perceive our lives. Such sufferings, the ancient rabbis tell us, are referred to as "loving sufferings" or *ye'surin shel ahavah* (יסורין של אהבה) (Talmud Bav'li, Berachot 5a). The noted eighteenth-century sage, Rabbi Shimshon Rafael Hirsch, summed it up:

> The evil and challenges that come our way which God at times seems in our eyes to tolerate, actually serves to ennoble us and strengthen our moral fiber. The wrong which we must sometimes

endure is part of that training course of suffering that will refine us—a training that God reserves primarily for those who by their choices and actions in life have demonstrated their capacity to learn and to grow from it. This is why suffering is not given to the wicked as often as it is given to the righteous.

(S. R. Hirsch in *The Psalms*, Vol. 2, pp. 167–169)

It is taught in the Zohar that people's good actions empower angels to receive from each other (Tikunei Zohar 39a). The angels, then, are better able to receive from one another when people perform charity or perform acts of kindness for one another, or even when they sing sacred songs (Zohar, Vol. 2, folio 18b). Simply listening to the difficulties empowers the angels if you are truly moved by the difficulties, and if you go through your own thoughts of repentance from that place, and if your heart is open. When one person learns the Torah from another, receives a favor or money or something else from another, the angels then are also empowered to receive from one another. By our positive thoughts and actions, we start off a whole cosmic cascade. It is the same as when we bless food, we are blessing the angelic forces that stand behind the food, therefore empowering the whole cosmic hierarchy. That is why it is important to bless our food before the meal and to also give thanks after the meal.

It is said in the Midrash that when Moshe was in heaven and received the Torah, he heard the ministering angels praising God, saying *"Baruch shem k'vod malkhuto l'olam va'ed"* (ברוך שם כבוד מלכותו לעולם ועד)—"Blessed is the name of the one whose glorious kingdom is for all eternity."). When Moshe came down he taught this to the people (Midrash Devarim Rabbah 24:7), and we recite it to this day as part of the sh'ma. In a sense, we received from the angels an extremely important part of the sh'ma prayer. In return, the angels receive from us the "calling," which is of course the way God called to Moshe, the *keri'ah* calling to return to God, the call to receive from one another. This calling is empowered by the Jewish people's and all peoples' ability to receive from one another. In that calling is also contained the pain of the people—our own personal pain, but not the pain of the angels. So in a sense, that calling, which is God's ability to call to us as God called to Moshe, or our ability to hear and receive each other, is all part of the sacrifice necessary to bring peace and harmony into the world. It is a sacrifice that needs to happen now, today.

The first word of this parashah, VayYiKra (ויקרא—"And he [God] called [to Moshe]") has been transmitted down the ages with a small א (aleph) at the end of the word, as in ויקרא. Many times we are called by God through dreams, through direct visions, through meditation, but we do not always hear. To be able to hear we need to transcend our egos, and the small aleph helps us hear and respond to those callings.

As we penetrate deeper into the meaning of the word "sacrifice," which is known as korban (קרבן—literally, "the act of drawing near"), we understand that the root of that is korov, which may be interpreted in two ways. One is to be close to God, because the aim of the sacrifices, or korbanot, is to be closer to God. But it also is about war, and what we are warring with is the ego. This is the key understanding here. Primarily, what brings us closer to God is to war on our egocentric negativity. This is a deeper way of understanding korban. When we do sacrifices, which today are personal sacrifices, or even in those ancient days of animal sacrifices, we are connecting with the spiritual energy behind the sacrifice. When they sacrificed an animal in ancient times, they were calling upon the divine creator energy that was prior to the manifestation of that animal.

That opened connection with the Divine is what activates the light flowing to us. None of the sacrifices were or are anything "for God," meaning for anything that God "needs":

> "Listen, my people, and I will speak; O Israel, and I will confront you. I am Elohim, your God. I am not criticizing you regarding your sacrifices, and your offerings that are before me always. I claim no bulls from your property, and no he-goats from your corrals. For after all, all the beasts of the forest, the animals grazing on the thousands of mountains—they are all mine. I know all of the birds of all the mountains, and the creatures of the fields; they are all with me. If I were hungry, I would not tell you, for the earth and all that fills her is mine. Do I eat the flesh of your sacrificial bulls, or drink the blood of your sacrificial goats? Sacrifice

to Elohim your gratitude; and pay onto the upper realms with the fulfillment of your vows. And call to me in the day of trouble. I will then rescue you. And that is how you can honor me."

(Psalms 50:7–15)

Sacrifice is clearly a way for us to connect with the divine consciousness, whether with prayer or action. In the ancient way of sacrificing a cow, an ox, a ram, a goat, or whatever, these kosher animals represent the three poles—positive, negative, and neutral—that allow a complete energetic circuit to occur. When they sacrificed, the people had to connect with the animal's internal energies, and that connected them to a certain level of being. A kosher animal with split hooves that chews cud contains the energy force literally of an atom that has the three columns of the Tree of Life. It is a complete circuitry of energy. God does not need our sacrifices.

Hashem is complete and absolute. Sacrifices are for our benefit in order to create a certain level of light and understanding, and to bring ourselves closer to God. Bereisheet alludes to a darker and rarely discussed dynamic in animal sacrifice. Those performing the sacrifice, if knowledgeable, were able to capture the nefesh (נפש) energy (the universal energetic currency) of the animal to build their own nefesh. This included the symbolic offering of the goat to the dark force of Azazel (עזאזל) (VayYiKra 16:7–10). The dark forces and demons live off of and compete for this nefesh. According to the vegan philosophical understanding, whatever we do to animals eventually will be done to us.

It is widely documented that Hitler and his SS were deeply ensconced in the black arts and, in this context, were likely consciously involved in the slaughter of six million Jewish souls as an act of ritual human sacrifice. As if this was not enough, their war continued to sacrifice approximately 54 million people, all told. His sponsors, from the very beginning before he rose to power, were the Thule Society, a very dark organization, then based in Bavaria. We should not be so naïve as to think that these demonically driven energies have disappeared and that human sacrifice, the agenda of which is to rob humans of their nefesh (which is more powerful than animal nefesh), is not still happening today. We are somewhat protected from these dark forces on a personal way by living a sincere Torah life of mitzvot, in which the power of our nefesh and light is so strong that these forces cannot penetrate our fields of light. Moreover, we are guided on how to get out of the way, as some did in the time of Holocaust. Unfortunately, not everyone listened to the warnings, and even today not many listen to the whispers of God and the divine angelic helpers involved in the battle with the Sit'ra Ach'ra (סטרא אחרא—the "other side"), here on the physical plane. This is the meaning behind the sacrifices on the higher heavenly levels of understanding.

At a lower level, we have the explanation of the Midrash, that the purpose of the sacrificial rites was to prevent the people from falling back into idolatry—at least they would be sacrificing to God rather than to idols (Midrash Vayikra Rabbah 22:8). The twelfth-century Rabbi Moshe ibn Maimon (Maimonides, or Rambam), who also subscribed to this understanding, admitted, however, that the true meanings behind the sacrifices was *ne'elam* (נעלם), a hidden secret beyond our grasp (Mishnah Torah, Hilchot Me'ilah 8:8). Yet, as we have seen through the lenses of the kabbalah, and the deeper meaning of sacrifice we have explored from the viewpoint of deveikut/chey'rut, it may not be so hidden, after all. Sacrifice on this deeper level, we have seen, is about connecting to the light. It may also activate the "calling" principle among the angels—"As above so below, and as below so above" (Zohar, Vol. 1, folio 39b). It is also being open to what is, and appreciating that whatever God gives us is a gift of the fire of purification to rectify where we have missed the mark and to offer us an opportunity to move closer to the Divine. This is the real meaning of sacrifice.

Maimonides even went so far to say that, according to the sages, the world exists for the purpose of korbanot (Mishnah Torah, Hilchot Me'ilah 8:8). This world is certainly a place for the gift of the fire of purification, which requires us to be willing to sacrifice. When enough purification is done, then we enter into the world of holiness, and ultimately deveikut/chey'rut. In that sense, sacrifice is part of the deveikut/chey'rut spiritual evolution, as long as we understand we are not sacrificing someone else (like an animal), but that it is our own ego that we are sacrificing. The sacrifice is always to YHWH, the Tetragrammaton energy of grace, the energy of tiferet, and not to Elohim, the energy of judgment (Zohar, Vol. 3, folio 110a). Prayer is one way of sacrificing without the temple rites, but truly being open to "All There Is" in our lives is the ultimate way of being a living sacrifice.

The symbolic gesture of animal sacrifice helps us to get a better insight into all this, because part of us is egocentric, impulsive, and animalistic, in that we need to eat, sleep, and take care of our physical needs as limited beings. However, there is another spiritual part of us striving to identify with consciousness and become one with consciousness.

This reality has no limits; it is beyond the physical. At another level, then, sacrifice—which is burning up ego in the realm of time and space—is not just about offering up the animal within us, but also the physical world around us. In this process, we begin to understand what this world is about. The world is the cosmic energy, the emanation of the Divine, and our role in it is to be devoted to That and be one with That. We often get so immersed in the world of duality (alma d'peruda—עלמא דפרודא) that we think that this is what the world is about. The kabbalah teaches that this is all an illusion—a divine illusion, but still an illusion. Even though we talk about being "co-creators" and at some level part of Elohim, we are indeed. But we must, at the same time, be aware that from a kabbalistic, atzilutic perspective, the world is an illusion, and all is one with no illusion of free will. Paradoxically, this lineage is about connecting to the light in the world of assiyah (עשיה) and knowing Hashem in every moment. The extent of the control we have is how we choose to experience what is happening in the world. It is therefore important to understand and appreciate one of our basic teachings, best articulated by the second-century mystic, Rabbi Akiva: "Ideally, one should train oneself to affirm that 'whatever God does is done for the best'" (Talmud Bav'li, Berachot 60b). We need to be aware of how we are run by our ego desires, and that is what we are offering up when we are sacrificing. Are we willing to let our animal desires rule us? Or will we choose to sacrifice them so that we can become clear enough for the attainment of higher consciousness? The sacrifices, which are the burning of ego and of our identification with time and space, help us bring our lives back into perspective.

Prayer, too, is not about praying "for God," as if God needs our prayers. God does not need our prayers. God does not need our sacrifices. *We* need them! God has created this whole game on the world of assiyah so that we can wake up. Prayer is about tapping in to our purpose and aligning with God. This is why the real meaning of sacrifice is, as the first-century Rabbi Gamliel put it, "Do [God's] will as if it were your own will" (*asei rizono kir'itzoncha*—עֲשֵׂה רְצוֹנוֹ כִרְצוֹנֶךָ), which is about becoming one with the will of God (Mishnah, Avot 2:4). The act of sacrifice is giving up all the stuff that the illusory ego wants, that keeps us from being in touch with the divine will. The gift, or intent, of sacrifice allows us to reconnect with the meaning of life, which is to go beyond the Elohim understanding that says "I'm a partner with God," to where there is no "I am" and we are simply one with God. It is at this level that the korbanot make a difference.

Contrary to what "modern secular" people say, that we do not have a need for sacrifice anymore, we do have a need for sacrifice, namely, the sacrifice of the ego, which helps us to wake up. We are asked to sacrifice our tendency to avoid the results of our actions, and to sacrifice our resistance to receiving the gifts of God, which are not always comfortable.

On the literal, or p'shat, level, the animals involved in the ritual offerings of the ancient altar have important symbolic meanings:

- Cattle offerings represented the energy of death. They helped the people to remove the fear of death and the energy of death from their lives.
- Sheep and goat offerings were more symbolic of the ego, and helped the people to burn up the energy of ego in their lives. They helped them escape the bondage of their desires.
- Bird offerings were more specifically intended to help the people cleanse from their selfish behavior, to help them let go of their comfort-zone mentalities. The birds' ability to fly, and therefore defy the gravity of the ego—and of our narcissism, and of our comfort zone—gave the power to transcend the limits of the three-dimensional body-mind identification.
- Food offerings gave the people the strength to do their work. Here we need to understand the circuitry again. Within all plants there is a soul. The soul within the plants cannot manifest without our help. Once we eat them, they become

part of us. Our actions, whether positive or negative, become
connected to the souls and the energies of the food we
consume. Therefore, if you take foods that are very *kedusha,*
they will help elevate our soul actions, and in that sense, we
help elevate the souls of the plants. This a kabbalistic teaching.

- In ancient times, salt was included in all offerings. The
  numerical value, or gematria, for the Hebrew word for salt,
  meh'lach (מלח), is 78, which is exactly three times the gematria
  for the Tetragrammaton (יהוה = 26, and 3 x 26 = 78). Salt is
  considered inanimate, so it helps us elevate the souls that
  are trapped in the *do'mem* (דומם), or rock people, spirits
  incarnated in the rocks.

I in no way support the eating of animals, and have lived quite healthfully
on a plant-source diet since 1973. But, in ancient times, as now, there was, and
is, a teaching that we may help to elevate the souls of animals by eating them
while reciting certain specific prayers for their elevation. The authentic Torah teaching on this ritual is that the flesh food must be authentically kosher
(factory-farmed "kosher" has been challenged in a variety of investigations to
be too cruel and crude to be called kosher) and the person doing the ritual
should be a Torah scholar. These conditions certainly limit who can halakhically do this ritual and how it is to be done. Having animals as pets can also
elevate and rectify the soul trapped within the animal. Also, by the same principle, we elevate the souls of plants when we eat them. We can also elevate the
souls trapped in the do'mem, the rock people, through eating organic raw salt.
This takes us to a deeper understanding, which is that one of our functions in
this world is to elevate and transform souls, even those of the rock people, and
to welcome their wisdom into us. Our ancient sages knew this, as did the Native Americans, as evidenced in their inipi (sweatlodge) ceremony, intended
as an opportunity to receive and elevate the rock people.

Peace offerings are also mentioned in VayYiKra. As we pointed out, this
was a primary task of the kohan'im, in bringing peace to themselves, to Am
Yisrael, and to all the peoples of the world. When that happens, then there will
be peace in the world.

There were also sin offerings, to purify missing-the-mark, or sin. Sin offerings were executed with animals. If one did not possess an animal, it was accomplished with a sprinkle of flour (VayYiKra 5:11), because, again, this was about not about anything that God needed. It was for the sake of the people. Today, we do not have to burn an animal; we just have to live attentively in this world, and the results of our actions will naturally burn up our sins (חטא—chet). The sin offering works most powerfully when we are conscious that whatever God does is for the best, and that all the difficulties we face in our lives are for our own spiritual awakening as a gift from God.

Sacrifices reflect what we are ready to purify. This is part of the old saying "God gives us what we can handle." If we choose to offer less than our capacity, it is as though we have not given at all. That is why Kayin's sacrifice was not accepted. He was not fully present, and he was not fully surrendered to the process of waking up on the planet. What matters most is the effort and the consciousness that we invest, taught the second-century Ben Hayhay, not the amounts and frequency (Mishnah, Avot 5:23). Or, as the sages of Yavneh taught, "Whether one does a lot, or whether one does a little, it matters not, as long as one's intention is directed to [God]" (Talmud Bav'li, Berachot 17a).

Whether we miss the mark intentionally or unintentionally does not matter. When we understand this, we better understand the things that happen to us. For example, we receive a certain amount of money each year, and our daily bread is allotted to us, each according to our divine destiny. Sometimes, however, we have not been ready to receive what has been allotted to us, and when we are ready, we ask to receive what has already been given. If we are living in alma d'shikra (עלמא דשקרא), the world of illusion, then we think we have created the money. If we act dishonestly to get more, the money we are supposed to receive will not come, and we will receive less than what we deserve, less than was supposed to come in the first place. As the Talmud says: "Before you ask God for what you want, thank God for what you have" (Talmud Bav'li, Berachot 30b). Or as the second-century Ben Zoma taught: "Who is the wealthy one? The one who is satisfied with what they have" (Mishnah, Avot 4:1). Stealing, too, or making a clever business deal that takes advantage of someone else, is a way of trying to circumvent the laws of the universe, and when we do any of that, then "what we desire is not given to us, and what we already have is taken from us" (Talmud Bav'li, Sotah 9a).

This brings us back again to VayYiKra's most significant insight. The results of all our actions are consumed in the fires of consciousness.

The message of Yesha'yahu 44:21–23, which is the haftorah (corresponding reading from the prophets) for this parashah, is the promise:

> "Remember these, O Ya'akov and Yisra'el. Thou art my servant. I
> have formed thee; thou art my own servant. O Israel, thou shall
> not be forgotten by me. I have blotted out as a thick cloud thy
> transgressions, and as a cloud thy sins. Return to me, for I have
> redeemed thee. Sing, oh Heavens, for the Lord has done it: Shout,
> you lower parts of the Earth, break forth into singing, you moun-
> tains; O forest, and every tree in it; for the Lord has redeemed
> Ya'akov, and has glorified Himself through Israel."

Devotion and surrender, as experienced through sacrifice and the willingness to be purified, are at the core of this parashah! God is always going to take care of us by providing us with the opportunity to draw closer through purification. The advantage of being in this world is that we always have a chance to make a tikkun, or correction or attunement, and reconnect more deeply with the Divine. May we all be blessed that we are able to joyfully make these tikkunim. May we always remember that that opportunity is there for us if we choose to take it! May we all be blessed that we choose to take it, and be willing to make any sacrifice necessary for our spiritual evolution.

Amen

Tzav

⟜⟶

Parashah Tzav is read on Shabbat HaGadol (שבת הגדול), the Great Sabbath, which precedes Passover, or Pesach (פסח). From the culture and perspective of deveikut/chey'rut, this Shabbat is very important and clarifies the spiritual path intended by the Torah. To understand this, we have to get a feeling for the symbols involved here, because this is about awakening. It also teaches us about God as a perpetually intervening influence on the evolution of consciousness on the planet. Passover itself clearly has many levels of understanding. It is not just about the political liberation of the people; it is the process of spiritual liberation.

One of the questions has to do with our relationship with God in a devotional sense (which is one of subtle separation). We begin to see the difference when we have the direct, heart, and personal connection versus an impersonal connection. Maimonides, the great twelfth-century rabbi and physician, made the point that humanity's poor self-esteem led it into idolatry. From Maimonides's perspective, the ancients could not believe they merited a personal relationship with God. Therefore, they could not really have the love connection. Because of this, they sought more personal help from what they honored as "servants of God," such as the sun and the moon. This created intermediary relationships between them and God. That is why the Torah says: "Do not have any other gods before Me. Do not represent [such gods] by any carved statue or picture of anything in the heaven above, on the earth below, or in the water below the land" (Shemot 20:3–4). They believed their lives were so unimportant that they were guided by the power of the stars, because God could not possibly care about them in a personal way.

In the period of Enosh (thirty-fifth century BCE), he and the wise of his day made a serious error in assumption. They reasoned that, because God had created the celestial bodies to minister to our earth and honored them by placing them in the heavens, therefore, they were God's servants and deserved to be honored by mortals. They argued that just as a chieftain wishes his servants to be honored for his sake, so does God wish for us to honor the planets and stars. They therefore began to build temples to the stars and offer sacrifices to them. They also worshipped them and prostrated themselves to them, and by these deeds they hoped to win God's favor. This is how the institution of idolatry was born. Years later, however, false prophets arose and preached that God had commanded the worship of some image or star by bringing offerings and also by erecting edifices of various imagery. Moreover, their priests invented certain rituals, which they promised would bring prosperity, and, at the same time, forbade certain acts, which they believed would bring ill fortune. Later, further falsifiers claimed that a star or angel appeared to them personally and demanded to be worshipped through certain acts. In the course of time, God was forgotten altogether, and only God's "servants" were remembered and worshipped as gods themselves. The name and awareness of God vanished from the mouths of the multitudes, who knew only their temples and the images of wood and stone, which they had been taught to revere since infancy. Their priests and learned men continuously preached that there was no God except for the stars, in whose likeness the idols had been made. The true God, however, remained unknown then except to a few individuals, such as Chanokh, Methushelah, Noach, Shem, and Eber. And thus the world continued until the birth of Avraham our father, pillar of our world (Rambam, Mishnah Torah, Hilchot Avodat Kochavim 1:1).

The Pesach story is a totally different message. It is intensely about a personal love relationship with God: "Keep the Festival of Matzahs" (Shemot 23:15). The sages said that anyone who disgraces the Pesach is considered as if they performed idolatry (Talmud Bav'li, Pesachim 118a) because the celebration of Pesach is a statement that God loves us, personally takes care of us, and guides our individual journey. For this reason alone, we do not need any idols to act as intermediaries.

One of the profound messages in the Great Torah Way is that God's love and care for us is unconditional. When the Temple existed, all the tribes would come to the Temple three times a year: on Pesach, Shavuot, and Sukkot. We know that God exists everywhere, so why would an individual person or a whole culture need a temple? The Temple was akin to a super amplifier and transmitter of the divine experience. Even today, people spend time with the tzaddik, or spiritual teacher, to have that direct amplification and to intensify their personal connection to the Divine. That is also what happens when there is s'micha m'shefa (סמיכה משפע—initiation by divine grace). S'micha m'shefa intensifies that personal connection, so that God is more readily experienced.

On the Temple Mount, the Eros of God is more intensely experienced during those three times a year, when people were guided to make the pilgrimage to the Beit HaMikdash. It did not require any real preparation, although the Shabbat HaGadol prepared them on a certain level. Pesach is a time when the energy of the Divine pours out on to the earth if we are ready to receive it. The ceremony of Pesach is a vehicle for receiving that energy. The Torah refers to each of the three festivals as a *moed* (מועד), which in Hebrew means "to meet." The Mishkan that we carried in the desert was called *ohel moed* (אוהל מועד— "communion tent") (Shemot 28:43), a special place to experience God. Pesach is a place in time to meet God.

The Torah often calls the festival *mikra kodesh* (מקרא קודש), "a sacred holiday" (VayYiKra 23:7), because these special times of meeting bring out the manifestation of our holiness and godliness. These festivals of God have more importance today, because we no longer have the significantly more open and powerful communications system with the Divine that we had at the time of the first Temple. Then, we had the Ark of the Covenant, the vestments of the high priest, and the high priest himself (the kohain gadol), who was trained to act as a bio-human-interdimensional communications system. Their disappearance as an integrated divine transmission communication device and amplifier not only weakened Am Yisrael, but, at least for a period of time, decreased and, according to most of the sages, ended the functioning of the prophets and their powers (Talmud Bav'li, Baba Batra 12a). In other words, prophecy in its first-Temple form disappeared following the disappearance of the original vestments of the kohain gadol and Ark of the Covenant.

What has not disappeared, however, is the awareness in the Torah teachings that the human species exists as the walk between the b'limah and the mah. As multidimensional beings, we live simultaneously in both the heavens (astral planes and higher) and the earth. The Torah addresses these truths directly and specifically throughout the book of VayYiKra. From this perspective, the primordial intent of the Torah is as a guidebook to return to deveikut and chey'rut as the highest level of human purpose and existence. Second to that, and a partial precursor to the first, is that as mystical human beings activated by our kabbalistic studies, we all have access to the flows of inter-dimensional communication activated by the Ruach HaKodesh (Holy Spirit of the shekhinah expression of the Divine on the earth). We have examples of this in the prophetic visions of Daniel, who lived after the fall of the first Temple, as well as other Children of the Ascent (*B'nei Aliyah*—בני עליה), such as the Ba'al Shem Tov in more recent times. Beings like these have and are us-ing the powers of the Ruach HaKodesh to rebuild the divine "heaven to earth/earth to heaven" communication system, one person at a time. The practice of aliyah, ascension, was first activated and made public by Chanokh (Enoch) who made a permanent aliyah. Prior to that we had Adam who was already ascended at the very Adamic beginning on earth. The power of m'aseh avot siman labanim principle is still with us. We all have the capacity to ascend directly. The B'nei Aliyah are powerful links in the chain of authentic Torah tradition known as *mesorah* (מסורה). These beings, and perhaps others as well, can see angels and also ascend, walk in the heavens with our ancestors, and possibly touch the throne of God. We are not forgetting that the moral teachings and basic kabbalistic philosophy of the Torah are the basic founda-tions that all of this builds on. It does not mean that God is not with us all the time. It does not mean that we are not in the Presence all the time. It is just that in the Temple, on these three particular meeting times, the energetics are designed for more intensity.

Parashah Tzav talks about the meal offerings, and specifically orders: "Aar-on and his descendants shall then eat the rest of [the offering]. It must be eaten as unleavened bread in a holy place.... It shall not be baked as leav-ened bread [חמץ—*chametz*]" (VayYiKra 6:9, 10) because leaven, particularly during Pesach, is seen as the ego and negativity that has to be released. So, there is a general prohibition of offering chametz during this time. The Zohar considered the concept of chametz as symbolic of the evil inclination, or the swelling of the ego (Zohar, Vol. 1, folio 226b). That is why we burn the cha-metz on the eve of Pesach and abstain from eating anything with chametz for the duration of Pesach (Shemot 13:7). This is interesting because on Shavuot, which commemorates the receiving of the Torah, we actually offer up loaves of baked bread laden with chametz (VayYiKra 23:17). We do this on Shabbat, too (VayYiKra 24:5–8). The leavened bread deliberately and ritually offered on these occasions has to do with acknowledging that on Shavuot and on Shabbat we are infusing the world of duality (alma d'peruda) with the spirit of the shekhinah in the most powerful way for the week (Zohar, Vol. 2, folio 183b).

It may be confusing, but when we understand the symbolism it makes perfect sense. We will now look at Pesach to help us understand this symbolism. First, Am Yisrael was told a week before they departed that they needed to prepare. Clearly, it was not a big surprise, and they certainly could have baked bread, but instead they had matzah, composed simply of flour and water, with no additional fermenting ingredients. This is because the matzah symbolizes the willingness to take advantage of the window of opportunity to move freely and lightly into deveikut awareness without being weighed down or held back by extra "fluff," or chametz. There are different cycles in our life, and we have to know the right time to "go for it!" Without that knowledge, without that intuitive feeling, we often miss the opening and its message. Pesach is a festival that creates the opportunity for each of us to let go, to leave our own Egypt behind, and to know. Pesach is the initiation of the awakening process. In a sense, s'micha m'shefa starts the awakening process, and that is the matzah. If we miss that, it lingers, rises like yeasted flour, and becomes chametz. That is why we do not eat chametz at this time. Matzah represents the promise of reaching our full potential! That is what Pesach is about. It is the moment when Am Yisrael was born into a new beginning!

The second peak of this awakening process is Shavuot, which is when Am Yisrael received the Torah. The central theme here is achievement. Shavuot occurs fifty days later. We capitalize on the window of opportunity and allow it to reach its full potential. So, when we make a sacrifice, which, in this case, is the Temple of our own consciousness, we are tapping into a moment of raw potential. The Temple Mount, known as *Har Ha'Bayit* (הר הבית), represents a window of opportunity, where we have a chance to return home, because Har Ha'Bayit literally means "the hill that is home." It is a process that allows us to do teshuva (תשובה) and to return home. The matzah represents the activation of our potential not yet realized, as does s'micha m'shefa. At this deeper level, chametz on Shavuot represents having arrived, and having a full and steady awakening to the Truth as deveikut/chey'rut.

There are different levels of freedom. The message of matzah is that freedom is not the goal, because it is given to us! The question is "Freedom for what purpose?" The awakening of the shekhinah energy, as the activated Ruach HaKodesh, is the freedom to merge with God as deveikut/chey'rut. To know Shavuot is to serve and become One with God. However, timing is important. This is why God gave us, as one of the first mitzvot, Rosh Chodesh (ראש חדש), the new moon celebration, the cycle and gift of time (Shemot 12:2). As slaves, time was not ours. In freedom, time is ours. Torah, in this portion, is telling us that the only time is *now*. This is why we eat matzah on Pesach and not on Yom Kippur. It is on Pesach that we woke up. We touched into the higher consciousness. We pulled out of the slavery of the mind, and began to identify with consciousness of Hashem, as who we are. Pesach represents the first taste of consciousness, and the ability to see our potential. On Yom Kippur and Shavuot, we are already flying with the angels and beyond.

It is in this context that we begin to appreciate the deeper meaning of the kohain gadol, as a bio-mystical communications amplifier with God. And that is what this parashah is about: the kohan'im and their particular role in the whole picture. An important part of this role was the *sh'lomim* (שלמים), the peace offering that brought shalom. From the perspective of Aharonic peace, each player was given a role: the altar had a role, the kohan'im had a role, and the bringer of the sacrifice had a role. This is why the mishkan was dedicated three times, to enable each to play his or her roles individually. The first time is in Shemot, in which the mishkan represents the eternal meeting between Am Yisrael and God; then it is mentioned here in Tzav; and the mishkan will be mentioned a third time in BeMidbar. For each time, it has a different purpose. In Tzav, we see that Aharon and his sons were inducted into divine service in the mishkan. We must realize that although we are talking about the kohan'im, we are also talking about Am Yisrael being a nation of priests, readied by the "official" priesthood toward a state of holiness that must be developed in the process of becoming one with God and a light unto the nations. This intent was specifically built into the kohanic system, into the whole process of the mishkan, with a joint purpose of radiating peace to the world. The sacrifices, which, on one level, burned up our own egocentric, narcissistic tendencies, also brought peace to the people, peace to the world, and peace in the flow between Am Yisrael and God.

We have to be clear, as previously discussed, that the sacrifices were never for God's benefit, but were for us to burn up our impurities, so that we could come ever closer to and merge with God. They helped us come closer to God as we burned up what separated us from God. In this Aharonic peace that brought peace to the world, peace is a state of completion, where everything has a place and purpose. Peace is attained when all the elements exist in their proper place, and none of them tries to be other than what it is meant to be. Every piece has its own integrated role. In this level of peace, everyone is included, from the inanimate to the talkers. All are important. The sacrifice could not take place if all the elements were not in place. The shalom of the Beit HaMikdash was the ability to develop each individual character as part of the greater whole, part of the divine cosmic design. These sacrifices teach that when each individual is at peace, knowing his or her relationship to the greater whole, then the nation can be elevated, and from that, true peace in the world can take place.

Shabbat HaGadol is about creating closeness with God. At that time, while the Jews were still in Egypt, there was great concern, because God saw that if they did not awaken, the Jewish people would not merit redemption. In order to prevent this from happening, according to the midrashic teachings, God gave two commandments involving blood: the blood of the paschal lamb, and the blood of circumcision. As it says in Yehezqel 16:6: "And when I passed by thee, and saw thee weltering in thy blood, I said to thee, In thy blood live!" From this teaching, we learn that by the time Am Yisrael was redeemed, they had acquired a merit through their observance of these two "blood commandments," the paschal lamb and ritual circumcision. The Shabbat before Passover is called Shabbat HaGadol, "The Great Sabbath," because it is in memory of this crucial moment and movement toward deveikut/chey'rut.

As we move a little deeper into Tzav, we get the specifics of the Temple priests. Before we do this, we would benefit to understand the depth of consciousness that we are operating from on Shabbat HaGadol. It says in the Midrash, "In the future, God will take the sun out of His pouch, and the tzaddikim will be healed by it, and the wicked will be harmed by it" (Midrash Bereisheet Rabbah 78:5). This is referring to the light of the creator. If we are able to repair and build the vessels through the Way of the Torah, we can hold this light. If not, it can burn us up. Part of being able to hold the light is being able to hold the will of God as it plays through us. This is not always comfortable. If, at the end of our lives, we consider our greatest accomplishment to be "everybody loved me," we have a somewhat distorted understanding, because we did everything to appease people. Torah life is about learning to act from the truth.

In other words, the mystic is not concerned about being loved. The mystic is concerned only about being the Truth, which is being in alignment with the light. That is why it is written about angels that their feet are straight (Yehezqel 1:7); and we should seek to be like the angels. Angels move straight ahead. They do not look to the right or to the left, and they are not affected by what is said or thought about them by others. Nothing stops an angel. It means, in this whole process, as a nation of priests, that we have to do what is in truth, the best that we perceive it, rather than being guided by social and economic pressures. In other words, we have to live as though we are not running for political office.

This parashah discusses changing clothing. This refers to changing consciousness. We dress particularly in holy ceremonies because those garments are vested with a certain consciousness, which helps reverberate and affect our consciousness. It is not about changing our physical clothes; it is about shifting consciousness through our clothes. This applies to going to a certain location when you meditate, or going to the Temple, or whatever supports your shift in consciousness to the highest level.

"Tzav" means command, or instruct. All our actions, in this way, are commanded by our desire to deepen our connection with the Divine. The very first offering mentioned here is the burnt offering. It needs to remain burning on the altar for twenty-four hours. It symbolizes the destruction of our personal agendas. The wording for "shall remain burning" is *mok'dah* (מוקדה). In the Torah scrolls, as transmitted for thousands of years, the מ in mok'dah is a very small מ, as in מוקדה. The numerical value of מ itself is 40, the number of days Moshe spent on the mountain and the age generally when the soul is more able to be elevated (Mishnah, Avot 5:21); it was also the number of years Moshe lived in Egypt, and the number of years he lived in the desert of Midian before returning to Egypt to redeem the Israelites. The מ is also symbolic of the womb (and is even shaped like a womb), and thus refers to the bridge between the upper and lower worlds. It is a narrow bridge that can only be crossed if we understand that there is only the Ayn Sof (אין סוף), and that out of Ayn Sof comes creation. This is the source of everything.

The next offering is the meal offering. The meal sacrifice, or *mincha,* helps us transform those worlds into the right side. This meal offering helps us make the positive side stronger. In the process of this shift in consciousness, when there is no longer a Temple and there is no longer a Temple priest, we become the priests of our own consciousness. Our job is to act and move as consciously as possible and in every action create peace, which includes inner peace, as well as outer peace of order.

The sin offerings help us burn off the negative results of our actions. The guilt offering is really not about guilt as we define it, but about teshuva (תשובה). It is about helping us return to the source, and to burn up the dysfunctional character traits, or midot, that were the motivating energy behind actions that missed the mark. As priests today, as in the time of old, we become channels to help people reconnect into the light. It is our role to find people with whom we can share the light. Our job, as it was of the kohan'im in ancient times, is to channel the light onto the planet so that people may act in the consciousness of tikkun and transform themselves.

The specific practices of the priests involved: (1) changing clothes or, in other words, shifting consciousness, but also wearing special clothes; (2) initiation by blood, which was applied on the tip of the right ear, the right thumb, and the right big toe, all of which have to do with activating da'at (דעת—third-eye intuitive energies); and (3) preparatory seclusion for seven days, or a cycle of seven that could be seven months, or even seven years, in order to purify themselves.

The role of the high priest was to create an inner and outer Temple for Am Yisrael and for themselves, and then to share that holiness as an inspiration for all. In that way, they were able to do tikkun ha'nefesh (תיקון הנפש—fine-tuning of the personal soul), and tikkun olam (תיקון עולם—fine-tuning and fixing of the world at large).

The initiation energy takes us to the haftorah of Tzav, or the corresponding reading from the book of the Prophets, Yirmeyahu (Jeremiah), Chapter 7:21–23:

> "For I did not speak to your fathers, nor command them in the day that I brought them out of the land of Mizrayim, concerning burnt offerings or sacrifices: but this thing I commanded them, saying, Obey my voice, and I will be your God, and you shall be my people: and walk in all the ways that I have commanded you, that it may be well with you."

We need to understand that what we are given in the Torah, and all these holidays and all these cycles, is intended to help us walk in these "ways"! Then Yirmeyahu goes further:

> "But they did not hearken, nor incline their ear, but walked in the counsels and in the imagination of their evil heart, and went backward, and not forward. From the day that your fathers came forth out of the land of Mizrayim to this day I have sent to you all my servants the prophets, sending them from morning till night. Yet they did not hearken to me, nor incline their ear, but stiffened their neck: they did worse than their fathers."
>
> (Yirmeyahu 7:24–26)

The concluding teaching of the Torah Way of deveikut/chey'rut, which appears near the beginning of Tzav, is VayYiKra 6:5–6, which is a flame of truth that spreads throughout this parashah as well as the rest of the Torah: "Ve ha ha'esh al ha'mizbeach tukad bo' lo' tichbeh" ("The fire of the altar shall be ignited with [the remains of the offerings]"). Each morning, the priest shall kindle wood on them. On [the wood] he shall then arrange burnt offerings and burn the choice parts of the peace offerings. Thus, there shall be a constant fire kept burning on the altar, without being extinguished." It is also mentioned here that "the kohain shall put kindling wood on the fire every morning." An eternal flame needs human support. The Mishnah tells us that there is an eternal light, a miraculous heavenly fire constantly keeping the altar fire burning so that they did not need a kohain or anyone else to keep it going.

There is a natural eternal fire of the Divine in our own hearts, but it gets very dim if we do not live the Torah Way, which keeps it blazing. In this way we become the priest who puts the kindling on the fire of our own hearts. On another level, we have an external miracle of the eternal fire from the heavens, but by adding the wood each day we create a subtle paradox: Is it pure miracle, or does the fire burn from the physical kindling wood? In fact, it is the play between the b'limah and the mah, both realms in which we walk simultaneously. Seeing it solely as miraculous would eventually desensitize us to the wondrousness of God's works, and seeing it only as natural would dim our vision from seeing it as coming from God. On the outer level, this paradox calls us to be co-creators with Hashem.

The *ner ta'mid* (נר תמיד), or eternal flame, represents the symbolic heart and soul of Am Yisrael that shines when we distinguish between the absolute reality and the temporal reality. It is brightened when we respond proactively in the face of doubt or in our encounters with challenges such as that of Esther, when she was trying to decide what to do. Her uncle and mentor, Mordechai, told her: "For if thou dost at all remain silent at this time, then shall relief and deliverance arise to the Jews from elsewhere; but thou and thy father's house shall perish: and who knows whether thou art not come to royal estate for such a time as this?" (Esther 4:14). Our choice to put kindling on our spiritual light is our choice make the effort to be the high priest putting the kindling on the fire of Hashem in our heart and in this world, as an inspiration to others.

The Torah Way to deveikut/chey'rut requires endless perseverance in maintaining and further increasing the light. Are we willing to live as a flame of God in this world? We have to be open to God's direction, if we are going to wake up on the path and keep the fire going to stay awake. May we be blessed that we are ready to change our ways, so that we may dwell in the consciousness of the One. May everybody be blessed that we are able to know the merging of the One; that we are able to burn the chametz of our lives so that we may partake anew in the awareness of spiritual life, and again to identify with consciousness rather than the ego.

Amen

Shemini

THIS parashah opens about a year after the Golden Calf incident. The people had completed the Tabernacle and had gone through seven days of an initiation ceremony for the Tabernacle, the kohan'im, and the kohain gadol. The priests, as noted earlier, were very much an integral part of the Tabernacle, and served as total bio-human amplifiers of the divine energy on the earth plane. Moshe had acted as the first kohain gadol for seven days, setting up the Tabernacle and initiating the priests. The Tabernacle itself, however, had not yet been activated by the presence of the Divine. This happened on the day of Shemini, the eighth and final day. But first it required action from below, so to speak, from the creation realm, through the sacrificial rites involving specific offerings.

Aharon was asked to offer a calf as a sin offering, or korban chatat and a ram as a burnt offering. The Jewish people, through the elders, offer up a goat as a sin offering, and a calf and a lamb for an olah (עוֹלָה), or burnt offering. The calf was for Aharon's sin offering, and the goat was for the people. The difference between a burnt offering and a sin offering needs to be clarified. A sin offering means atonement for a wrongful action. An olah, a burnt offering, is for intentions and desires that could have led to an action but did not. Aharon was told to bring a calf to demonstrate that he had been forgiven for his part in the sin of the Golden Calf. The Jewish people brought a calf as part of the initiation of the Tabernacle because their involvement in building the Golden Calf could be healed through building the Tabernacle. The two offerings were brought in different contexts: for Aharon it was a sin offering; for the people it was a burnt offering. What was the difference? After all, Shemot 32:24 tells us that it was never Aharon's intent to build a Golden Calf. According to the Zohar, he had innocently thrown the gold he collected from the men into the fire, and a calf came out through the magical powers of two of Pharaoh's sorcerers present among the ey'rev rav, the mixed multitudes that left Egypt among the Israelites (Tikunei Zohar, folio 142a). The chet (חָאט) that Aharon created with the Golden Calf was therefore neither intentional nor was it a completed action on his part, so why did he need to bring a sin offering? The answer is that he probably did not need to bring a sin offering. But as a leader, he felt deeply responsible, and bringing the offering would remove blame from the people, relieve them of the bulk of their guilt and redirect it to himself instead. This was in line with the special characteristics of our Torah leaders throughout history.

The offering of the Jewish people was the olah, because it was much less for any action on their part than for desires and intention that could have led to an action. Their desire, of course, was to have an intermediary to lean on, to have some help through an alternative source, rather than trusting in God. But they simply did not possess the consciousness to relate to the abstract in that way. So, that is why they brought an olah.

After the offerings were given, Aharon gave the priestly blessings for the first time:

> Aaron lifted his hands toward the people and blessed them. He then descended from [the altar where he] had prepared the sin offering, the burnt offering, and the peace offerings. Moses and Aaron went into the Communion Tent, and when they came out, they blessed the people. God's glory was then revealed to all the people. Fire came forth from before God and consumed the burnt offering and the choice parts on the altar. When the people saw this, they raised their voices in praise and threw themselves on their faces.
>
> (VayYiKra 9:22–24)

This was an intense time of redemption, and people were, at best, in shock at seeing the fire come out of nowhere and burn up the offerings. At that point, one of the midrashim tells us, Aharon's two eldest sons, Nadav and Avihu, felt that that this heavenly fire was going to burn up all the people as well, because they felt it was the fire of purification for the sin of the Golden Calf. Immediately after that, "Aaron's sons, Nadav and Avihu, each took his fire pan, placed fire on it, and then incense on it. They offered it before God, [but it was] unauthorized fire, which [God] had not instructed them [to offer]. Fire came forth from before God, and it consumed them, so that they died before God" (VayYiKra 10:1–2).

This is an extraordinarily profound and uncomfortable message. What is being said here, and why did this happen? The strange fire was a fire lit it by their own hands, rather than using the fire from the Divine. It was their own human-made fire. But what made this fire "unauthorized" was that it was not made from the supernal fire, and God had not commanded such worship. There are different explanations for the meaning of this. Some people feel that they were in an inebriated state, and they made what they thought was a wise decision to protect the people without consulting their teachers. They were standing next to their uncle Moshe and father Aharon, who were their teachers. We have to understand a little more about this because it is much deeper than it appears. It is not as if they were being insolent. These people were considered very high in consciousness. So, what exactly did they do that got them burnt up?

First, they saw the descent of fire and they recognized that this fire emanated from the supernal place of judgment, and their concern was that this judgment would pass through the camp, burning everybody. So, they ran to offer incense to appease the force of the judgment of Elohim. This action itself showed a significant lack of understanding, because the supernal forces of judgment are not something you want to take head-on without the direction of your teachers. Even though they had good intentions, to save the people, they really misunderstood what was going on. Implicit in their lack of understanding was their doubt regarding the capacity of Moshe and Aharon to understand what they were doing. They did not honor the divine process and acted without divine direction. They therefore acted out of ego, and in that way they created a strange fire that was out of order with the divine guidance. Part of the spiritual lesson was that their actions lacked self-discipline in relation to divine service. Because they were not in *bitul* (ביטול—emptying of the Self, which allows one to be aligned with the divine will), they acted from ego and not divine will. Nadav and Avihu were watched very closely by the masses of the people, because they were the successors to the high priesthood, and the people would follow whatever they modeled.

If everybody did whatever they thought was "spiritual," without seeing the whole picture, we would have metaphysical chaos. In a sense, we see that their error was acting presumptuously though their intention was pure. Acting presumptuously means acting with arrogance. This strange fire they offered came from dishonoring the tradition and lineage wisdom of their elders, who needed to be consulted first to better comprehend what was going on in the bigger picture. For this reason, their offering was both ritually and spiritually impure.

Where does this presumption originate? Presumption in general happens when people are so egocentrically full of themselves that there is no room for God. Their cup is too full, and they assume they know through their intellectual power, rather than through their intuitive power and alignment with the divine will. This was actually a major part of the problem. The second layer of the problem was the fact that they tried to appease the potential threat through their offering via the laws of nature, which is an emanation of the God of judgment.

Again, the spiritual teaching here is the principle of bitul. To deeply serve the Divine, we must be in a state of emptiness, however holy we may think we are, so that the Divine, and not our ego, will guide us. Today, as then, there is a tendency in our society to interpret and act from our ego and not from divine direction. This is a dangerous and slippery-slope attitude. We see this in many social and religious movements today. Inherent in this spiritual egotistical attitude is a lack of significant awe for the Divine. This is not a problem when we are talking about chey'rut and deveikut (in whatever the tradition) intellectually, as if we actually know something. It becomes a potential problem when we are at the same time also deeply immersed in spiritual practices which, if we are not respectful and in serious awe, can burn us up.

On the serious spiritual path, there are many dead bodies along the way (not necessarily physically dead, but those who have become spiritually dead or lost in this lifetime). Activating the Tabernacle is not for brilliant thinkers or talkers and other people playing at spirituality. Moshe and Aharon were offering themselves on the altar of God by emptying themselves of ego and walking into the fire of Yah. It is pointed out many times in serious, non-theoretical kabbalah work that people do indeed get burnt up, and they should not attempt any serious kabbalistic work until they are spiritually mature, significantly purified, and under the guidance of others who have passed the trials of fire. We find this warning, for example, in the writings of the sixteenth-century kabbalah master, Rabbi Chaim Vital:

> Those who seek to enter the Orchard should know that it is a very harmful, dangerous space to visit. Therefore, first make certain that in your daily life you pursue peace and harmony in all of your relationships ... Also steer clear of conceit and self-aggrandizement, especially when it comes to doing the sacred work. For it is in the course of performing the sacred work that we become most prone to conceit and feelings of superiority.
>
> (Rabbi Chaim Vital's introduction to *Etz Chayyim*)

They say that when the master Rabbi Yisrael Ba'al Shem Tov was but a young teenager, around fourteen, he was indirectly recognized by the renowned mystic Rabbi Adam Ba'al Shem. (Ba'al Shem, by the way, was a very rare title. It means "Master of the [Divine] Name.") Before he died, Rabbi Adam felt he could not entrust the mystery of the divine names to anyone other than the outlandish young Yisrael, whom he had never met, and who lived hundreds of miles away, worked odd jobs, and slept in the local synagogue. Rabbi Adam did not even feel his own son, Reb Aharon, worthy of this transmission and instructed him to find young Yisrael and give him the scroll on which he had encrypted this wisdom. When Reb Aharon finally located the young Yisrael, he begged him to share some of the mysteries with him, and to actually conjure a powerful angelic force so that Reb Aharon could ask some deep questions and perhaps get some deep answers. Yisrael tried to warn the elder of the dangers involved, but the elder remained adamant in his request until the teenager gave in and performed the prescribed ritual. As the ritual reached its crescendo, Rabbi Aharon could not hold the energy a moment longer and was burned up by the presence of the angelic force and died. This is an example of this sort of thing happening.

We receive five major teachings from the profound incident involving Nadav and Avihu:

- Goodness accompanied by egocentric intention alone, and thus not aligned with the bigger picture, can be spiritually disastrous.

- Not honoring one's elders, and deciding halakhah in front of one's teacher without permission, creates an energetic break with the lineage (see Talmud Yerushalmi, Shevi'it 16a).
- Doing ceremony while in a state of inebriation, whether on alcohol or other drugs, can result in serious imbalance.
- Being in a state of ego rather than bitul, while presuming that one is doing the will of God, can be disastrous for spiritual life. The exception to this is the rare case of a tzaddik, who is in such a steady state of deveikut that the individualized expression or word is the will of God.
- Insufficient awe and respect for the divine energies jeopardizes one's spiritual position within.

As part of this discussion, it helps to understand the concept of order, because Nadav and Avihu violated order in three ways: (1) The role of the kohain in creating peace was to always be aware of the correct position of all the separate parts, and to be able to arrange the individual components in a harmonious order. To do this, the kohain had to be fully conscious of the complete universal order, otherwise his function as a kohain would be compromised. Nadav and Avihu reversed that order. (2) Nobody had asked them to take any action, and they did so on their own anyway, without honoring Moshe and Aharon by checking with them first. (3) Because they were inebriated, their ability to hold the order was also compromised. The normative sequence is intellect, emotions, and then action. Action is an accumulation of thought process. After drinking wine emotions rule actions, so that the ability for self-control is impaired and gives way to impulse. The order was then reversed, and they could not function as kohan'im.

In that moment, they forfeited their rights and protection as priests and were liable for severe consequences. Acting on impulse, they did not realize how they were dishonoring the lineage flow: Moshe received the Torah and passed it to Yehoshua, who passed it to the elders, then to prophets, then to the Great Assembly, and so on, in a specific chain of transmission (Mishnah, Avot 1:1). Nadav and Avihu disrupted that order. They disregarded Moshe's role as a receiver and transmitter of the Torah. This tells us how important it is to be paying attention to the whole picture, and that one has to develop inner qualities or midot as part of that awareness.

Rav Chaim Vital, in his book *Sha'arei Kedusha: Guide to Achieving Ruach HaKodesh*, says the most important thing is the preparation to hold the energy, which we call *mussar* (מוסר). Mussar is about rectifying and elevating midot, our character. The teaching of Rav Chaim Vital is that the proper personality development or refinement of character is essential for any type of spiritual awakening or holiness. It helps to protect us from repeating the fates of Nadav and Avihu.

In order to approach the holy, we have to be properly and humbly prepared. We cannot afford to be inebriated. We have to be sober, alert, focused, surrendered, and devoted, and to act in the proper time and order. In other words, we must be willing to align with God in a state of bitul, not to dictate to God or decide on behalf of God. They attempted to dictate. It was as though they were going to reverse the process that was going on without even checking out first what that process was about. Unfortunately, this is typical in so many people today who have become disconnected from their source and become expert at saying the "right" things that keep others happily nestled in their comfort zones. Nadav and Avihu are not the first examples of "disorderly conduct" and lack of awe in the Torah. We see it with Kayin (Cain) and Hevel (Abel). When Kayin did not get his way, he killed his brother, Hevel.

There is a certain amount of surrender involved in the spiritual path. We cannot go to the teacher and say: "Only tell me what I'm willing to hear. Don't give me any feedback that requires me to really change myself or which takes me out of my comfort zone." It does not work that way. Although we certainly try it in different ways, it simply does not take us to where we need to go. To know God, we have to get beyond our spiritual narcissism. Otherwise we are just playing at spirituality as the popular thing to do. Unless one is willing to offer oneself on the cosmic fire of the Divine, one does not have to worry about these problems, because one does not then go deep enough to be close enough to the cosmic fire to get burned. In this case, talking a good game is actually safer, but it does not really create the preconditions or kavanah (intention) for liberation. It is also much safer to simply focus on basic morality and on simply becoming a *mensch*, a good person. This by itself, too, is a good thing.

Following the deaths of Nadav and Avihu, God commanded Aharon and his two remaining sons, El'azar and Itamar, not to become intoxicated when they were working in the Tabernacle. The Torah message here is that we should not be intoxicated by any "substances" when we are connecting with the light, because we need to honor that the light of God is what elevates us, not any artificial supplementation. When we go to other substances, even though we may get "high" from it, it is a form of idol worship, because we are giving power to something other than God. Also, drugs of any sort that alter brain function make it much easier for entities to come into us, because the drugs and alcohol not only disrupt our judgment, but lower our protective shields against the dark forces.

The third section in Shemini involves the laws of *kashrut* (כשרות). Kashrut is about what it means to be "kosher" (כשר), which is to create holiness in how we eat, how much we eat, and what animals we are permitted to eat, if we are unable to keep to the diet of Bereisheet 1:29. It is also about not cooking or eating meat and milk together (blending death with life).

The act of eating meat can be a ceremony of releasing and elevating a soul who has reincarnated as an animal. One of the subtle kabbalistic teachings is that certain souls regress to animal incarnation because of their actions in a previous life. By incarnating as a kosher animal they have the opportunity to be elevated back to human incarnation when people eat them with a specific ceremony to release their soul. Identifying which foods are kosher gives us a code through which we can know which foods are more likely to contain souls that need to be elevated through eating. And then we can meditate more on those foods. Unfortunately, the traditional teaching is that one needs to be a devout Torah scholar to be able to do this correctly.

Another important factor is that the animals need to be raised in a humane way and killed in an appropriate humane kosher way. Kosher, after all, literally means "prepare," as in ritually and humanely preparing the soul of the animal to be released from its body as opposed to traumatically ripping the soul of the animal from its body. Therefore, nonkosher is called *treif* (טרף), which literally means "ripped." The problem today, however, is twofold: (1) few people are dedicated Torah scholars, meaning not just intellectually but spiritually, in the context of deveikut/chey'rut consciousness; and (2) the *shechita* (שחיטה),

the rituals around how animals are killed for consumption, is often not authentically kosher. In too many cases, the animals, while technically killed in a traditional kosher way, are coming from factory farms that create cruel and unholy, soulless situations for the animals, which would therefore disqualify them from being kosher for consumption. It is very rare these days to find a Torah scholar doing the humane ritual slaughter, and of animals that have been raised in an appropriately humane and *truly* kosher manner.

Why were animals slaughtered at all? Why were the people told to separate meat and milk? There is a great story in the Talmud about the redactor of the Mishnah, the third-century Rabbi Yehudah Hanassi. One day he was sitting under a tree teaching his disciples when a little calf ran up to him and hid under his robe. The calf had run away from a nearby slaughterhouse. The rabbi said to the calf: "Go back to be slaughtered; it is for this that you have been created." At that moment, a divine decree was made against him because he had not shown pity on the creature. As a result, he became very ill and suffered for many years, until one day he showed pity on a family of young rats and was healed (Talmud Bav'li, Baba Mezia 85a; Midrash Bereisheet Rabbah 33:3). Judaism does permit us to eat meat if the animal has been raised and slaughtered properly. Of course, again, in most cases animals are not raised humanely and slaughtered properly. You can go to the major kosher slaughterhouses and see how the animals are treated miserably. In most cases, these slaughterhouses are mass production plants devoid of the consciousness of holiness that is necessary for the proper preparation for the release of the animal's soul. None of these holy observances happen in these places because the sheer number of animals being slaughtered each hour (due to extreme consumer demands) exceeds the time reasonably required for performing the rituals with holiness and sacredness. The animals, even in most "kosher" slaughterhouses, suffer immensely and unnecessarily.

A deeper message in Rabbi Yehuda Hanassi's misunderstanding was when he incorrectly said to the calf, "For this you were created." The Talmud teaches us that contrary to his declaration, animals were not created for human consumption. The first man and woman, Adam and Cha'vah, ate a plant-source-only diet of fruit, vegetables, nuts, and seeds (the diet recommended in Bereisheet 1:29). But during the time of Noah, after the worldwide mikveh of the Great Flood, God allowed humans to eat meat as a temporary dispensation (Bereisheet 9:3). There does not even exist a specific prayer for eating meat as there is for wine, bread, fruit, and vegetables. The teaching here is clearly that eating meat is *not* a Torah ideal. In fact, in the time of Moshe, eating an animal outside the complex rituals connected to the sacred altar was considered tantamount to "spilt blood," a term often used for murder (VayYiKra 17:3–4).

The ideal for humanity is to eat a plant-source-only diet. One reason for the meat-eating concession was that humanity was showing an inclination toward aggression and cruelty at the time of Noah. Bereisheet 9:3 sublimated the human lust for meat. The rabbinic thinking on this is that there is indeed something cruel and vicious about meat-eating, but that it is also a way of releasing aggression. The resolution of the paradox between the ideal and the pathway to that ideal is that until people arrive at a higher state of consciousness, it is better to satisfy humanity's need for aggressive expression by allowing them to eat certain animals rather than harming other people. As the ancient rabbis put it, "The Torah speaks in ways intended to counter the evil impulse" (Talmud Bav'li, Kidushin 21b). In this context, Bereisheet 9:3's provision is much like the provision made in Devarim 21:11. In this provision the Torah harnessed the passions of the Jewish warrior in the heat of battle, by allowing him to take a female captive he found attractive. However, he had to take her home and marry her with all the honors and responsibilities of Jewish husbands to their wives. This was a concession, of course, not an order, and was preferred to the random rape in the field so common in warfare even in our own times.

These concessions help people move toward the Torah ideal step by step. When people come to understand that eating meat and ingesting death may actually create more cruelty and aggression in a person's mind, as well as sickness and disease, if one's consciousness is not ready to be elevated, then the desire to eat meat will fade away. This has not happened yet, as we see in the Jewish tradition, where eating meat is often a part of enjoying Shabbat. Eating meat has gone from being allowable as a concession to being woven into the tradition as a truth. In a sense, as the Talmud says, "God created the evil inclination, and also created the Torah as its antidote" (Talmud Bav'li, Kidushin 30b). The laws of kashrut, then, even when they are followed to the letter, still tend to create a psychological atmosphere of unease and complication for the spiritually sensitive person. In other words, eating meat is not ideal, just as marrying a captive is not ideal. Although meat eating is allowed, it is important to note that Judaism is second only to Hinduism in India regarding its percentage of vegetarians. It is no accident that the first Chief Rabbi of Israel, Avraham Yitzchak Kook, was a vegetarian and wrote some beautiful statements about it in relation to the Torah Way.

As we go further into the parashah, VayYiKra 11:2–3 says: "Of all the animals in the world, these are the ones that you may eat: Among mammals, you may eat [any one] that has true hooves that are cloven and that brings up its cud." What is the hidden message about a cleft hoof and chewing cud? The code suggests two things. However, before we explain this, we must discuss the three types of mitzvot that make up the Torah: *mishpatim* (משפטים), *ey'dot* (עדת), and *chukim* (חקים) (Devarim 4:45). Mishpatim are those laws whose meanings are obviously very clear, such as those regarding theft and adultery. Ey'dot are those mitzvot that we would probably never do on our own, but there is logic to them, such as those regarding Shabbat and the cyclical festivals. Chukim are those ritual laws that seem completely incomprehensible, such as the Red Cow ceremony or the kosher laws. We do not really understand them, but we try to understand them and fulfill them anyway. This is probably what the prophet Havaqquq (Habakkuk) meant when he wrote *"v'tzaddik b'emunato yich'yeh"*—"but the just shall live by his faith" (Habakkuk 2:4).

We will still try to discover the meaning behind the chukim. In the case of the kosher laws, we may have enough understanding to categorize them as part of the mishpatim. It takes deeper insight, however, to comprehend why the people were only permitted to eat of specific animals, and why they were not allowed to mix milk and meat. To explore this properly, we have to look at the spiritual reasons behind not eating meat. From one perspective, eating meat creates within us this tension in which we have both an active physical side and a dormant, unmanifested side yearning for God and higher purpose. From another perspective, eating meat brings us to the issue of death. Judaism takes the impact of our contact with death very seriously. Every time we come into contact with death, we are asked to pause and consider the implications. Every time you eat meat, you are coming in contact with death. When a family member dies, we have a seven-day grieving process. When women menstruate, we have the laws of *nidah* (נדה), since the breakdown of the uterine lining represents a loss of a potential life that might have been. The same applies to men, if they lose semen in wet dreams, or if they ejaculate a bloody emission instead of life-potential semen, in which case they have the laws of *tzav* (זב). These are all contacts with death. The Jewish approach suggests that contact with death deserves one taking time to think about it. Therefore, in those states of being one did not approach the communal altar, but were instead accorded a period of sacred solitude, which is actually the literal meaning of the word nidah (solitude), often mistranslated as menstrual. Then, once one resolved the matter and made peace with it, they immersed in a mikveh, because the mikveh represents life, the birth waters of the womb. This is all death giving way to life and taharah (טהרה—purity), and purification overcoming the tumah (טומאה—impurity) of death. Therefore, when we eat meat, we are eating death, because an animal had to die for us to eat it. Dead flesh itself is a strong symbol of our own mortality. We do not see people taking mikvehs after eating meat, but it probably is not a bad idea to do so, to erase the energy of death one has just taken into their system.

Because the edict that allowed us to eat meat was given right after the flood, it suggests that the meaning of the flood may have been related to it. One general interpretation is that in antediluvian times we functioned on such a low level of consciousness that we were better off eating meat as a way of dealing with our violence than suppressing it. But, if we are to eat meat, kashrut suggests that we should consider what quality of meat we ingest. This is why the meat that the Torah specifies as permissible comes from herbivores as opposed to predatory animals, so that we are not also taking in the energy of the death that the predatory animals collected by killing other animals. This is a mystical explanation. Animals that chew their cud, on the other hand, are eating grass, and they have an entirely different digestive system. Also, a split hoof is less likely to be used as a weapon than a full hoof or claws. And as for mixing meat with milk, we do not wish to integrate meat, which represents death and cruelty, with milk, which traditionally represented compassion and life. Milk used to represent compassion and life. These days it does not represent this at all, because of the way milking cows are treated, but 3,400 years ago it did mean that. The image of a baby suckling at its mother's breast is an image of nurturance and sweetness. We do not mix milk with meat because we want to keep mercy and life separate from cruelty and death.

The kashrut way helps to support character change and deepens self-awareness. That is why this parashah ends with the powerful statement of VayYiKra 11:44–47:

> "Do not make yourselves disgusting [by eating] any small crea-
> ture that breeds. Do not defile yourselves with them, because it
> will make you spiritually insensitive. For I am God your Lord,
> and since I am holy, you must [also] make yourselves holy and
> remain sanctified. Therefore, do not defile your souls [by eating]
> any small animal that lives on the land. I am God, and I brought
> you out of Egypt to be your God. Therefore, since I am holy,
> you must [also] remain holy. This then is the law concerning
> mammals, birds, aquatic creatures and lower forms of terrestrial
> animals. [With this law, you will be able] to distinguish between
> the unclean and the clean, between edible animals and animals
> which may not be eaten."

We are being encouraged to sanctify ourselves to be holy like God, and part of the sanctification process is to eat those foods that are considered holy by the laws of kashrut. We lose that holiness when we eat and drink for bodily pleasures alone, rather than for energy needed to deepen our spiritual work. In this way of understanding, kashrut is not only about what we eat, but also about eating in holiness. This includes eating the minimum deemed to be sufficient, rather than overeating and becoming obese. This too is part of the kashrut practice of holy eating. It means that the optimal spiritual diet is not living to eat, or eating to live, but eating to enhance our communion with the Divine. The meaning of kashrut can thus be expanded to the intention of creating holiness in every aspect of our lives.

A message from God, as I interpret it, is: "I am the Lord, your God. To know me requires transforming yourself into the consciousness of Holiness." May we all be blessed with the ever-expanding consciousness of holiness in our lives!

Amen

Tazria

T AZRIA is about the choice of creating life or death. It opens up with life, with the ritual laws around birthing, and moves into the consequences of distorting that life gift, the spiritual disease of metzorah (מצורע), akin to leprosy and affecting the body, clothing, and the home, and having seven levels of imbalance. Mainly, metzorah is associated with the energetic results of slander and gossip, but may extend into the consequences of murder, vain oaths, incest, arrogance, robbery, and envy. In general, it is associated with the second set of the asseret hadib'rot (עשרת הדברות), or the Ten Speakings (commonly mistranslated as the "Ten Commandments"). This spiritual disease reveals publicly the impact of our consciousness upon our environment and our physical bodies.

The world we live in is affected by our very individual and personal perception of reality. When the ancestor Ya'akov hesitated to descend into Egypt to see his son Yosef, God told him not to worry about taking such an arduous journey at his very advanced age, because "Joseph will place his hands on your eyes" (Bereisheet 46:4). What did this mean? It was a reference to death. The colors and shapes of the world dwell within the eyes, so to transition from one world into the next, the eyes must be closed. In order to transition into the world of unity, we must let go of our dualistic perceptions. This is a zoharic way of perceiving the question this parashah raises (Zohar, Vol. 3, folio 169a). The Zohar is not saying that the world is an illusion, but that reality shifts with perception and affects the world around us.

Our perception is in the domain of free will. It is also the place where we realize, in faith, that everything God does is for the best, or else we succumb to the appearance of chaos. If we perceive God's presence behind all things, we will interpret all events as beneficial to our spiritual uplifting.

In this context, we see God in everyone and in everything. This moves us away from the place of slander and gossip. Refraining from slander and gossip requires a certain amount of discipline. Spirituality without discipline is merely a hobby. Walking our talk between the b'limah and the mah—the flame between the something and the nothing—is part of the Great Torah Way. The teaching on the mitzvot, the daily prayers, and anything connecting us to the Divine, helps us to maintain this discipline. If a ritual becomes rote, it loses its power and becomes weak and disrespectful (Yesha'yahu 29:13). Rituals and ceremonies must be sincere to invoke the Divine.

The parashah of Tazria is about the effects of our actions as manifestations of our thought upon our physical world. We can live in a world in which we celebrate the divine presence in thought and word and deed—or we can live in a world where the shekhinah remains in exile. Tehillim 119 says "I am a stranger on the earth." And further states: "You are my witnesses; I am God." In other words, God is in the world in proportion to how aware we are of God in the world. As the master Rebbe Mendel of Kotzk (1787–1859) replied when asked where God is: "God is wherever you let God in." For God to be in the world, we must be God's witnesses. This understanding is a key to deveikut/chey'rut. A cornerstone of deveikut/chey'rut is taharah, or purity. Taharah is a way of life that is about always connecting with God as the center of our universe and continually drawing closer to God consciousness. Tehillim 16:8 says *"Shiviti Hashem l'neg'dee ta'mid"* (שויתי השם לנגדי תמיד)—"I keep the name of God in front of me always"), which is another way to focus our vision on the Divine in our lives.

As noted earlier, the disease introduced in Tazria is referred to as a kind of leprosy and is said to be the result of gossip or tale-bearing. It would initially appear as a rash or a skin eruption. A person with this condition would then go to the kohain, and he would determine whether the person was metzorah (leper) or pure. Our mind causes us problems in so many ways. The Ba'al Shem Tov pointed out that we often misread God's messages to us. Part of getting a clear message is to always be aware that the shadow in the world around us is our own shadow. "He who is constantly chastising others," the Talmud warns, "probably sees in them his own faults" (Talmud Bav'li, Kidushin 70a). It would be harder to gossip or slander if we simply saw our own reflection in all circumstances. In this way, the outer world is our constant teacher as the emanation of the divine play around us. The great twelfth-century physician Maimonides wrote that ideally we should never have to go to a physician, if only we would meticulously follow the Torah's teachings regarding the proper maintenance of body and soul (Mishnah Torah, Hilchot De'ot 4:20). But of course neither can we just sit and let life run us over when things go awry. Sometimes we have to take action and not depend upon the promises of the ideal. When the five kings captured Avraham's nephew, Lot, for example, Avraham gathered an army of warriors to go rescue him. He did not sit idly by and wait for miracles. While grace is important, we must also act with common sense.

If people thought they had leprosy, they would remove themselves from society and seclude themselves in nature for a period of seven days. This would allow them to contemplate their behavior and examine their life. Seven is an earth number, and symbolizes the cycle of Shabbat (six cycles of creation, culminating in the seventh). All these things demonstrate the correlation of Torah rites with nature. These seven days were for purification and regaining equilibrium. The seven-day cycle makes the point that we cannot really know our inner condition with a glance; it is best to give things time to unfold. Rambam used the term "the straight path" for all areas of our life journey. This is the path of balance, or the middle road (Mishnah Torah, Hilchot De'ot 1:4). This is the balance of chesed and gevurah. The seven days of seclusion allowed one to view mistakes made on the higher plane.

It is very much a part of our faith to believe that if we do our part, the rest will happen in a way that elevates us spiritually. This kind of consciousness beckons for *hitlahavut* (התלהבות), a "burning, ecstatic" frame of mind directed in service and partnership with God. The third-century Rabbi Chanina taught that, "everything is in the hands of God except *yir'at shamayim*" (שמים יראת—"awe of God") (Talmud Bav'li, Berachot 33b). It is my experience in supporting many people in the Great Torah Way of deveikut/chey'rut that in addition to awe of God, we also have the free will choice to consider acting on another essential question: Do we choose life, or death? "Life" is living in the awareness of taharah, which is moving ever closer to life in God. "Death" in this context is the consciousness of tumah, in which we feel disconnected from God.

Another teaching in Tazria is that if we are *am k'shei oref* (עם קשה עורף— "a stiff-necked people"), Hashem will often send us some type of difficulty such as ill health/metzorah, or family or business problems, to get us to pay attention. One must then go to the kohain for a diagnosis and thereby indirectly seek help from an outside source. This is why a spiritual teacher-tzaddik is so important for those who are ready, as these types of problems give us an opportunity to see if we are ready for a teacher. This entire cycle is to help people come back into balance. We are like the moon, waxing and waning. Like the heavenly beings who are constantly *ratzo v'shov* (רצוא ושוב) (Ezekiel 1:14), we, too, are constantly coming and going, separating and connecting to the light, dying to egocentric activities and being reborn into light and spiritual re-emergence. All of the difficult situations in our lives can be used toward our personal betterment if we choose to be conscious of the fact that they are gifts of wake-up calls. This is all part of the path of deveikut/chey'rut, to use every situation to support our awakening.

May we all be blessed that we have enough conscious power to choose to shift our direction toward the light, and choose to call upon a spiritual teacher who can help us do this.

Amen

Metzorah

THIS is a very interesting parashah, which has to do with living in community. These people, we have to understand, were living and traveling in a mobile "yeshiva" out in the desert. And it was fairly "magical": Their clothing and shoes did not wear out, food was delivered to them by airmail, seas and rivers split before them, water followed them everywhere (the Well of Miriam), and so many other miraculous events happened for them, daily, during their forty-year wilderness trek.

One of the many things they had to deal with as a huge community in transit, was lashon hara (לושן הרע), meaning "evil tongue," as in slander and gossip. Journeying moment to moment, exposed to the divine light, there were often spiritual consequences to otherwise physical actions or behaviors. The consequence for slander was metzorah (מצורע). Metzorah itself, while it implies a spiritual form of leprosy as discussed earlier, is a variation of the word mei'tzir, which means "to extend beyond boundary," as in making up rumors, or otherwise mixing into issues that are beyond one's business. People infected with tendencies toward rumor mongering and gossip risked being stricken with leprosy, which did to them what they had done to others: exposed their private life to the public. Because gossip and slander were so undermining and damaging for a conscious community, the leper had to be isolated from the community in an enforced state of seclusion. This appeared to be the most effective way to deal with an individual's addiction to evil speech. The temptation of evil speech, lashon hara, is very strong in most people. Even if we are speaking of others with good reason, it often turns to defamatory gossip. The result is that we weaken our connection with the Divine in that process. Evil speech does not mean simply "gossip." It also means idle words, unnecessary speech, and speech that is true but has no purpose. In other words, you may say something true, but, in fact, is so out of context that it acts as a way of creating negativity or hurting someone.

Once we really understand the importance of each word we speak, and we begin to take responsibility for every utterance that leaves our mouths, we become much more conscious about how we speak about and to each other. As Rav Kook writes: "Senseless words gain their strength from a weak and ineffectual spirit. When one speaks them, they give rise to an ugly force, defiles the soul, and the air of the world is clouded" (Orot Hakodesh, Vol 3. p. 279). When people have elevated their soul, they feel the tremendous power of speech. They begin to recognize the value of words, and the value of prayer and of blessings. They begin to understand how their words influence the world, and truly how their words become actions that influence the world.

People often cannot stop gossiping because their ego is so big that they cannot receive feedback concerning their behavior or have any insight about it. They continue on and on with their evil actions and evil speech. In the Am Yisrael community, ultimately, they would develop leprosy, which was in a sense an unusual rash, a severe skin outbreak. This in turn would force them to seek the diagnosis of the local kohain to determine if this was a natural phenomenon or a spiritual consequence. If it turned out to be the latter, the individual was sent outside the boundaries of the community for a seven-day period of seclusion. The kohain was chosen rather than a physician because it was not seen as a physical disease, but a spiritual imbalance. Sometimes the ego was so big that the individual was not willing to change, so the tzo'ra'at would not diminish after the seven-day period and that person would have to remain in seclusion longer. Some of these people were so trapped in their egocentric belief systems that they constantly redefined reality in a way that justified their actions. This form of self-delusion often resulted in a misuse of words and a misuse of meaning.

Once the people settled in the Promised Land, such individuals were sometimes *blessed* with the plague of tzo'ra'at first appearing on the walls of their homes! This was a blessing in that it was a compassionate wake-up call from God. Then, if they did not change their ways, it would extend to their clothes. And finally, if there was still no shift in behavior, it would go on to their bodies. If they paid attention, however, the correct action was simply to disassemble their house, and then they would often discover a treasure where the people, who had abandoned the house before them, may have hidden a fortune. Metaphorically interpreted, the house represents the physical body and the hidden treasure represents the soul. When one is willing to truly work on oneself, and face ego tendencies, he or she will discover the treasure of the soul in the process of disassembling old patterns (the body-ego). These people will then be able to continue on their spiritual life journey in a good way. If some cannot take responsibility for their actions, and prefer to cover them up with biblical quotes or New Age psychobabble, or with gossip about others, then the disease becomes too strong for the community. For the community to survive, these people have to be asked to leave the community, no differently than in ancient times.

This is all very difficult because we live in a self-deluded society that often uses "love is everything" to justify and/or excuse all actions. Nevertheless, we need to acknowledge that some behaviors threaten the wellbeing of the community, and some people's egos are too big for them to change their behavior early enough to avoid damage to others. And so, this ancient example is a message of how to deal with it. And, in the bigger picture, it was and is the most loving solution for everyone concerned, including the person who was infected with lashon hara to begin with.

How does one give loving feedback? If the feedback is unloving, sin is created, so it is very difficult and tricky. The Torah teaches "You must admonish your neighbor, and not bear sin because of him" (VayYiKra 19:17). Well, how do you do that? How do you give feedback with love? For example, you can choose not to give any feedback at all and be like King David, whose son Avshalom never received a negative or critical word from his father in his whole life. The result was that Avshalom felt free to lead a rebellion against his father that almost crumpled the kingdom of Yehuda. So what do we do? The answer is, we must truly care about the person, and our words should be coated with concern and care. For this reason we must be like the leprosy. We must approach the person with tact, first a little bit on the walls, then a little bit on the clothes, and then on the body. In other words, God admonished the people with gradual warnings. One approach that I often use is to talk in a circular way that gives little hints here and little hints there. If the person still does not hear me, it is only then that I tell him or her directly. It is much more pleasant and enjoyable to give the clues and have the recipients themselves get it. The clues and/or the direct telling, if necessary, have to be given with love. This was modeled three thousand years ago by the prophet Natan. He was sent by God to wake up King David after the Bat Sheba/Uriyya scandal. David could not see what he had done wrong, and so Natan approached him with a tale, a metaphor, something external to David that offered him ample room to gradually see for himself the implications of his actions (Second Shemu'el 12:1–13).

Another point arises in this complex understanding. Criticism is gevurah, and we could not exist in the world if gevurah ruled. On the other hand, chesed is endless loving, and endless loving would create chaos in the world. This would be like being in the movie theater, and turning on all the lights and adding spotlights. It would be too bright for the film to be seen. Likewise, you would not see the play of the world. On one level, our world is a movie. It is a movie that is there for our spiritual growth. Although it appears to be real, it is not real. The play of our lives is a divine gift that gives us lessons we draw on as we learn more evolved ways to face our challenges, and ways that help us elevate ourselves spiritually. In our movie metaphor we see that there needs to be enough dimming of the lights (gevurah) so we can see the boundaries of the images on the screen. The New Age concept of "love is everything and God is only love" creates an imbalance that does not let us see the complexity of the picture. The danger in this thinking is that chesed is allowed to shine so brightly that we cannot see the "movie" and get the lessons. On the deepest level, it is through gevurah as contraction (tzimtzum) that the creation of the world took place. Likewise, there needs to be a little bit of gevurah to constrict the light enough so that you can see the movie, and participate fully and consciously in your life play. When there is a proper balance between gevurah and chesed, we have tiferet, which is beauty. Tiferet is the harmony that is created by the balance of chesed and gevurah in the joy of our lives.

This is a primary spiritual task. Decisions in this context often appear paradoxical to those who do not have full information. For example, to make a choice of chesed in a place where someone has blatantly broken a community rule or repeatedly violated the community way of life, is to still grant them yet another chance and another, which may, for one person or situation, be the best choice and for another may be a poor choice.

Sometimes, however, a person whose ego is so big that he or she cannot hear feedback might turn it all back on you. In such instances, the individual refuses to accept any accountability for his or her actions, and instead covers them up with a variety of biblical quotes or New Age talk. The resulting plague becomes too severe; the leprosy, the tzo'ra'at, begins to infect the community too deeply and, as explained before, the individual must be asked to leave for the survival of the community.

These gevurah choices often make us much stronger and much healthier, as individuals and as a community, because at some point the outer plague has been eliminated and this is not activating the intra-psychic plague of the community. These are often deep, paradoxical, and complicated issues, which is why they are so powerful for developing spiritual wisdom. Metzorah is also related to two Hebrew words meaning "to bring out the bad" (l'ho'tzee hara—להוציא הרע).

Lashon hara really comes from the place of big ego, and it creates a language that supports one's ego. It is all about receiving for self, alone. At its extreme, it can be understood as the characteristic of a narcissistic personality. Metzorah is a deep understanding of how to work in community, modeled by how these issues were dealt with during the time of Moshe. These are issues we are still dealing with in our own times, and so the Torah gives us ancient insight into grappling with problems that exist today.

It is taught that when one indulges in lashon hara, he or she not only sins against society and individuals, he or she also sins against God. When you insult God's people and God's nation, it is an insult to the Divine itself. So, the third part of the healing is this: It is not just enough to return to society and change one's ways, but one really needs to return to God as well. This is what we talk about as taharah. From tumah, the "impurity state of being full, and thus void of space for God," to taharah, "the purity state of being clear, and thus creating a sacred space for God." This is what brings total peace, shalom.

Shalom is achieved when one knows his or her place in relationship to community and to other people, and also in relationship to the One. The work of the spiritual teacher, or tzaddik, is to help teach the person afflicted with tzo'ra'at to make peace with the people of the community, to make peace with all individuals, to make peace with oneself, and to make peace with the

Divine. When that peace is achieved, we have taharah, which is purity. This is a very deep teaching, and it is the essence of a healthy community, the essence for healthy life, and essential for evolving spiritually.

The final teaching in parashah Metzorah is from VayYiKra 15:31: "You [Moses and Aaron] must warn the Israelites about their impurity, so that their impurity not cause them to die if they defile the tabernacle that I have placed among them." A more clear translation is "that they shall not die as a result of their impurities." Perhaps at no other time in history are these words divine music to the ears as they are today. It means that at any point in our lives we may reverse the process of separation from Hashem. In the Torah Way context it means that sincere teshuvah and returning to the Torah Way we can purify any spiritual impurity that we were either born with, or that we created by our own actions in this lifetime. Teshuvah done in the deepest way means to return to the time of the creation of our negative action, such as lashon hara, and heal the pattern that created it to begin with, and commit to not reactivate that negative pattern the rest of your life. This can be done for this lifetime or even for tumah created in past lifetimes. One of the biggest difficulties in doing this is the guilt syndrome, which the yetzer hara uses to keep us separated and alienated from God. This profound Torah teaching of VayYiKra 15:31, however, allows us to completely defeat the yetzer hara by sincere inner cleansing and action.

Fulfilling the ultimate mitzvot and purpose of life (knowing Hashem) requires the deepest level of soul-searching purity. To awaken at the level of deveikut/chey'rut we are being asked to maintain purity or taharah on every level of our lives. The more profound the spiritual purpose, the more intense is the level of taharah that is required. For example, the kohain gadol had to live at a higher level of taharah than the average kohain, and the average kohain than the Levite. The more profound the spiritual goal, the higher the level of ritual purity it requires. This applies not only to the individual, but also to Am Yisrael, if Am Yisrael is to heal its national soul.

Many feel it is "unfair" that the world holds Am Yisrael to a double standard, with much higher expectations of Israel and its army. But Devarim 23:15 asks just that of us: "God your Lord makes His presence known in your camp, so as to deliver you and grant you victory over your enemy. Your camp must therefore be holy." To create an enlightened person and nation requires a more intense level of purity. Part of this process includes the practice of mitz-vot, mikveh, and offering through ceremony, prayer (תפילה—tefilah), repeat-ing the name God (הגיה—higiyah), and meditation (התבדדות—hitbodedut).

Taharah includes purifying the day (*teharat yoma*—יומא טהרת) and the person or nation (*teharat gavra*—גברא טהרת). The mikveh helps us to purify and heal the day or time. In a more comprehensive way, it involves the way we live our lives. For example, Avraham was described in Bereisheet 24:1 as "well advanced in years," which implies that his years and days were fully focused on God and thus well spent. As we approach the messianic times, this more intense level of taharah includes our diet, which implies no longer eating flesh food, and returning instead to the original cuisine of Gan Eden (עדן גן) as expressed in Bereisheet 1:29. When we eat flesh food we eat death, which is the ultimate tumah. We then take in the fear, pain, trauma, and victim-consciousness of the animal, and it manifests in us as misery, anxiety, depres-sion, diseases of our modern times, and an unconscious willingness to allow ourselves to become enslaved. On the other hand, the enlightenment cuisine, helps our subtle spiritual vessels, and full body, become a superconductor of the Divine and thus helps our body, mind, and spirit to rise up to the fre-quency of the Divine, which we are meant and promised to be. In this way we become the ultimate offering and thus become *tahor gavra* (fully physically purified) and all our previous chets, our missing-the-mark choices, become transformed into merits (Midrash Shemot Rabbah 31:1). Further supporting the teaching of the power of personal transformation via a full immersion in a Torah lifestyle, we are taught that the place of a serious Ba'al Teshuvah, in heaven, is higher than that of a person who was born into holy circumstances, and who has led a completely righteous life (Talmud Bav'li, Berachot 34b).

May we all be blessed to fully and joyfully understand, and maturely use, the power of "they shall not die as a result of their impurities."

Amen

Acharey Mot

THIS parashah begins with the aftermath of the death of Aharon's sons, Nadav and Avihu. The message revealed here is:

> God spoke to Moses right after the death of Aaron's two sons,
> who brought an [unauthorized] offering before God and died.
> God said to Moses: Speak to your brother Aaron, and let him not
> enter the [inner] sanctuary that is beyond the partition conceal-
> ing the Ark, so that he may not die, since I appear over the Ark
> cover in a cloud.
>
> (VayYiKra 16:1–2)

This was a message about how one was to approach the Ark of the Covenant or the inner sanctum of the Mishkan. It was a message that Yah gave to the kohan'im and to the nation, using Aharon's two sons as an example. No one was to enter this sacred space just because he or she felt like it. No one was to approach at an unappointed time or in a chemically altered state of consciousness, such as being inebriated. First, one had to purify oneself, and become mentally and spiritually prepared to be fully present and alert so that one may resonate with the divine energy.

There is an additional interpretation of the deaths of Nadav and Avihu, gathered from the Midrash. Following the demise of Aharon's sons, the Torah tells us that Moshe reminded Aharon that they had been warned earlier: "This is exactly what God meant when he said, 'I will be sanctified through those close to me, and I will thus be glorified'" (VayYiKra 10:3). The Midrash adds that Moshe then said to Aharon: "My brother, when I learned that God would dedicate the mishkan with the death of a great man, I assumed that this would be either you or I. Now I see that your sons were greater than both of us" (Midrash VayYiKra Rabbah 12:3). Nadav and Avihu were selected. This was how Moshe comforted Aharon, and Aharon responded with silence.

On one hand, Aharon understood that the death of his two oldest sons was a direct result of his not leading the people away from the sin of the Golden Calf while Moshe was up on the mountain. On the other hand, he also knew that a greater plan was unfolding here, and that whatever God did was for the best. This was a teaching to the community as to how one should approach Hashem and the Ark at all times. One does best to approach the Divine in awe and reverence in alignment with the lineage teachings and free of anything that obscures consciousness. This means to approach without the use of mind-altering drugs. In the "approach," we would not want to open ourselves up to encounters other than with the divine presence flowing through every moment of our lives. The Torah Way of deveikut/chey'rut is not confined only to ceremonial times; it requires this state of awareness in every moment.

Aharon was also warned not to approach Hashem through the Tabernacle at any times other than prescribed times such as Yom Kippur, and only with the proper kavanah and reverence. The message here is that the spiritual walk at this level of intensity is not something to play with or simply talk about; it is an intense walking on the razor's edge.

Aharon was then told how to perform the intense purification rites in preparation for the God-aware ceremony of Yom Kippur. Aharon was open to repentance as an example of one willing to take responsibility for his role in the Golden Calf disaster. As a kohain gadol, he changed his clothes four times during this ritual. This is a metaphor of what we all must do. There is a fabled teaching that helps us to understand this more clearly:

There was once a poor beggar, who dressed in rags because he had no money to buy clothes. A tailor decided to help him. He took his measurements, and told the beggar to return in a few hours. When the beggar returned and tried on his clothes, he immediately began yelling angrily at the tailor: "Look what you've done! You just wanted to make fun of me! These clothes don't fit, they are too small."

Patiently, the tailor asked him to calm down. He said, "The new clothes will certainly fit, but first you must take off the old ones."

In order to purify and elevate ourselves, we must first remove our old clothes. Our "old clothes" are a metaphor for the egocentric fragments that compel us to receive for self, alone. If we do not remove them, the light cannot penetrate into our consciousness, because we are still covered in old clothes. In this context, this parashah is about healing on the heavenly levels for our actions on the earthly plane.

Aharon was told to sacrifice two goats. One, depending on how the lot fell, was a sacrifice to God. The other was to absorb the negativity of the people and the land and was offered to Azazel, a leader of the fallen angels who supported the dark side. In the two-goat ceremony, good was separated from evil. The goat was sacrificed to the devil, Azazel, by bringing it deep into the wilderness and releasing it. This sacrificial rite helped to open the doors to connect to the light. We must be very careful in dealing with the dark side. This scapegoat can actually touch us on the soul level and burn us up. Although we cannot avoid the dark side in our lives, we must learn to only so much as touch it, but never to blend with it. A kabbalistic teaching in this regard is that by giving an offering to the dark side, it is an appeasement that satisfies it so that it does not attempt to take everything. This was the original meaning of the ten-percent offering. After that, anything more than this goes to God. This approach can be traced back to other indigenous peoples such as the Mayans, who made small offerings to the dark side for identical reasons.

According to some schools in the oral tradition, Nadav and Avihu did not intentionally sin because there was no clear guidance at this point. They were tzaddikim at a very high level, and their sacrifice was atonement for all. The souls of Nadav and Avihu were offered to save the souls of all the people. It is said that they both reincarnated later as Pinchas, who again saved the people at a later point in the Torah narrative. As tzaddikim they took on the sins of this generation, and suffered and died for them. In our tradition, the leading tzaddik of the generation takes on the sins of that generation through his or her suffering or the actual loss of his or her life (Talmud Bav'li, Mo'ed Katan 28a). In this tradition it is taught that a messiah comes in each generation, but only gets activated if the people of the time are ready. So far, no generation seems ready since the time of Moshe (the messiah for his own generation), but perhaps in our time we will become a generation ready to receive the grace of Hashem.

What is the meaning of blood in the Jewish tradition? The people were told not to make offerings in the wilderness outside the altar or to drink the blood of animals. God did not want the people to take on the spirit of the animals. When you drink the blood of an animal, you ingest its spirit. When this is done in the wilds, far from the altar, that spirit is released into the one eating it, and the blood may bring demonic energy along with it. The people were being taught how to safely work with the dark occult forces in everyday life. In later Torah times, people could not be part of the Sanhedrin unless they were trained in the occult, so that they could protect the people (Talmud Bav'li, Menachot 65a). Unfortunately, and to a large extent, this has been lost today.

The Torah's injunction against blood also provides us with an interesting physiological insight. The blood is the carrier of the spirit in that it holds the nefesh, or lower soul life force energy, of the organism from which the blood has been spilt. In eating meat, it is impossible not to ingest some blood, as residual blood remains in the small arterioles and capillaries that cannot become blood-free, even when the animal is killed in a kosher way. Drinking or eating blood is forbidden, because it infuses us with the soul essence of the animal. Given a technical physiological approach to this issue, people really should not eat meat at all if they do not want to take the animal energies, emotions, and spirit into themselves, in addition to potential demonic energies that may surround the spilt blood. This is part of the hidden teaching of Bereisheet 1:29.

It is no accident that in the great liberation traditions around the world, vegetarianism is recommended, as it was and is in Judaism. There is one exception to this. Some animals carry the reincarnated souls of humans who, because of their actions in a prior lifetime, devolved into an animal body. In certain kabbalistic traditions, consuming a bite of kosher animal flesh was a way to elevate a human soul trapped in the animal form, but only when done consciously and with specific prayers. As pointed out before, this can only be done by a trained Torah scholar and with properly kosher animals ritually slaughtered. There is some question today whether this is at all possible with the shocking revelations of scandalous practices in major kosher slaughterhouses, and also whether animals are raised in humane conditions prior to their slaughter. The cruel and soulless environments of factory farms are not to be considered kosher even if the animals are slaughtered in a ritually correct manner.

There are different kinds of sins that people tend to commit, and they are addressed in this parashah. While it is obvious that one should not steal or murder, there is ultimately no free will on the higher planes of the world of atzilut, which is the plane of direct apperception of God. A teaching of the Ten Speakings is that negative activity does not work because there is a returning consequence for all negative actions (*midah k'neged midah*). The more we act in ways that are not aligned with divine will, the less we are connected to the light. The Ten Speakings highlight the actions that separate us from God. On a deeper level, the more we are aligned with the experiential singularity of the Ten Speakings, and especially the first five Speakings, the more our lives synchronize with the natural way of life prescribed by the Torah.

This parashah also includes warnings against sexual abuse and perversions, which in a broader sense, is what the word usually translated as "adultery" in the Ten Speakings really means. The teaching for Am Yisrael is painfully clear: The various forms of sexual abuse, listed in detail in VayYi-Kra 18:6–29, ritually practiced by the seven Canaanite tribes we were told to remove from the land, are more than illicit; they are acts of perversion and distortion.

> "Do not let yourselves be defiled by any of these acts. It was as a result of them that the nations that I am driving away before you became defiled. The land became defiled, and when I directed my providence at the sin committed there, the land vomited out its inhabitants. You [however,] must keep my decrees and laws, and not become involved in any of these disgusting perversions—neither the native born nor any foreigner who settles among you. The people who lived in the land before you did all these disgusting perversions and defiled the land. But [you shall not cause] the land to vomit you out when you defile it, as it vomited out the nation that was there before you. Thus, whenever anyone does any of these disgusting perversions, [all] the people involved shall be cut off [spiritually] from the midst of their people. Keep my charge, and do not follow any of the perverted customs that were kept before you [arrived], so that you not be defiled by them. I am God your Lord."
>
> (VayYiKra 18:24–30)

Because these seven Canaanite nations were particularly singled out for their perverted actions, and not other nations living in the land, there is a significant suggestion that these nations were following what is known generally as the left-hand path to God, which is based on a whole variety of what the Torah would consider sexual and other types of perversions. The lesson here is loud and clear: The use of drugs and alcohol (not including moderate use of ceremonial wine or grape juice), which alter consciousness and are often part of the left-hand path, are antithetical to the Torah Way. The warning in the previous parashah to keep away from these things "so that they shall not die for their impurities," is an invitation to do teshuva and change one's ways. In this context, every member of Am Yisrael has an important responsibility to act in accordance with these warnings and instructions, so that we are not kicked out of the Holy Land—literally. The lessons are also there to help us control and focus our sexual impulses toward elevating the experience of the Divine in our lives. In this way, we experience the eros of the Divine in every moment as central to the path of deveikut/chey'rut, which is the land of liberation, rather than squander our sexual energies on perversions.

It is no accident that this parashah opens with the death of Nadav and Avihu and the warning to Aharon of how to approach the Divine without getting literally or spiritually killed. The message of this parashah is particularly important in our secular, relativistic world, where we have created the ability to convince ourselves with our egocentrically justified talk that all actions are okay and will not interfere with the enlightenment process. This parashah gives enlightenment teachings that the spiritual and New Age liberals do not like to hear, namely, that there are many dead bodies along the way to liberation, and how important it is to move and act in awe as well as in love, as we walk the authentic spiritual path. I have not heard of anyone in any enlightenment tradition who has become truly enlightened on the left-hand path. On the contrary, those who have tried either were damaged or died (blocked from liberation, or literally died) along the way.

May we be blessed that we constantly remember the importance and power of our choices and actions to bring us either closer or farther away from the Divine. May we feel connected to God in our hearts, and may our right actions continue to reconnect us to the feeling of unity with the Divine.

Amen

Kedoshim

This parashah begins with the passage from VayYiKra 19:2–3: "You must be holy, since I am God your Lord [and] I am holy." The meaning of holiness (קדושה—kedusha) has many messages that help us go deeper into spiritual life. At the very least, living according to the Ten Speakings creates a morality that minimizes chaos in our personal lives and in the community. However, the Torah wants us to be more than "moral"; it wants us to transcend into the oneness, which comes from holiness and is a precondition to oneness (deveikut). Holiness is a calling for something deeper to happen. In this context, it is theoretically possible to be moral and simultaneously unholy. While morality is important, it is based more on interpretations of the Ten Speakings that come from social consensus, in particular. Cultures and subcultures often hotly debate their varying renditions of the Ten Speakings. On the moral level, one acts out of social restraint, which is subject to the relative nature of social whims. Of course it gets even more relative when people are operating outside the guidance of the Ten Speakings. During the Holocaust, for example, it was moral, according to social standards established by Germany and other anti-Semitic countries in the region, to imprison and execute the Jews, and to execute anyone protecting them. This morality is obviously culturally relative.

Holiness is a reflection of a higher standard. Morality is more connected with the cultural flow, while holiness may require standing up for and living in the absolute truth, even when it goes against the standards of culture and society. In a peculiar way, holiness is also a form of selfishness. Holy selfishness is based on a deeper living and understanding of the Ten Speakings, in that we take care of ourselves by taking care of the other, with whom we are one. One who is living in kedusha (holiness) refrains from exploiting others—not because of any set of rules mandated by the Ten Speakings, but because of the inner understanding that we are all one as a reflection of the Divine.

Kedusha is an expression of the divine Self, or spark of the Divine, that is in all of us who are part of the Adamic race. If we simply "follow" the Ten

Speakings and the mitzvot, we are being moral. But when we act as sparks of the Divine, and manifest our actions as natural expressions of the will of God within us, we operate on the plane of holiness. Holiness emerges from divine awareness without consideration of reward or punishment. This is what the second-century Ben Azzai meant when he taught that "the reward of a mitzvah is a mitzvah" (Mishnah, Avot 4:2).

This is an important teaching. When God says, "You must be holy, since I am God your Lord [and] I am holy" (VayYiKra 11:45), God is speaking to us on this level.

Many of the great tzaddikim were not particularly liked or appreciated in their time because they led their lives according to the will of the Divine as it moved through them. But often, after they died, they and their teachings were celebrated. The great, liberated eighteenth-century tzaddik, Moshe Chaim Luzzato, was disliked during his life. Some of his books were even burned and considered dangerous, but today he is loved and appreciated, more than two centuries after his death. The most wondrous and holy sage of recent times, the Ba'al Shem Tov, was attacked by many for his revelations. Today he is revered by a vast majority of even the descendants of those who opposed him. The liberated tzaddik cares nothing for the opinions of his contemporaries. The tzaddik operates as a holy channel for the divine will. Often tzaddikim are not fully appreciated by the society at large until they are physically unavailable; this is true of many blessings in our lives. We tend to appreciate them after we have lost them. Holiness includes appreciating others in our lives. If we are unappreciative of others, others will be unappreciative of us. The danger in unholy spiritual living is the tendency to perform the mitzvot for purposes of self-aggrandizement, or so that others will notice us and think highly of us. The tzaddik does not live this way. Every time we think about what we will get in return, we miss out on holiness, and the positive energies of our mitzvot slip through our hands.

The times in which we are now living may be very close to the messianic times. A story about the enlightened Rabbi Menachim Mendel of Vitebsk supports these teachings: Once a shofar was heard sounding in the distance, and the townspeople asked the rabbi if the messiah was coming, because it is written that when the messiah comes a great shofar will be heard from the Mount of Olives (Yesha'yahu 27:13). The rabbi walked out of his house, looked around, sniffed the air, and said: "No, the messiah is not coming. His smell isn't in the air." The people were confused and asked, "Why did you have to leave your house to figure this out?" He responded, "Because the messiah is already in my home."

For some of us, it does not matter what goes on externally, because the messiah has already returned to our hearts. When we connect with the eternal truth of who we really are, then every act becomes an act of holiness. Because God is holy, we naturally express holiness as God's light, if we choose to live and eat in a way that illuminates the world. This is a prerequisite to the mitzvah of "You must love your neighbor as [you love] yourself" (VayYiKra 19:18). One cannot love one's neighbor unless one knows oneself as the soul beyond the ego. In the context of pre-messianic times, one of our most important roles is to understand and awaken to our actual immortality. We would therefore do well to understand that we are an expression of the truth of the Divine.

Another teaching in this regard is *"Acharei-mot kedoshim"* (מות קדשים אחרי), which is the name of this parashah when combined with the previous one on the occasional Shabbat when both are read together. Literally, this combined title means "After death, they are holy." Many tzaddikim continue to teach after leaving their physical bodies. Moshe, Eliyahu, and Avraham are examples of this. Many of the great tzaddikim, like the Ba'al Shem Tov, become in a certain way more alive after their deaths. A verse in the Torah says, "Among you, there shall not be found anyone … who attempts to communicate with the dead" (Devarim 18:11). On a more esoteric level, this teaching refers to the tzaddikim, in that after they have left their physical bodies they are still very much alive. Although we are not to seek out the advice of ghosts, nevertheless, because the tzaddikim are connected to their immortality, we can consult with them both directly and indirectly.

There are many stories about rabbis whose physical bodies died but are preserved. When the Nazis dug up the body of the eighteenth-century holy master Rabbi Elimelech of Lizhensk, they found it to be perfectly preserved, and light shone from his eyes. When the Nazis tried to dig up the Ba'al Shem Tov's body, they were unnerved because his body, also, had not decomposed after 200 years, and light radiated from his eyes. It is said that Eliyahu is the only prophet left in the world, but that only the holy may connect with him. He appeared as a teacher for tzaddikim such as the Ba'al Shem Tov and for others in other times when he was needed.

The parashah also teaches that we should not mix wool and linen. Although there is no readily logical p'shat explanation for this mitzvah (and thus it falls into the category of a chok, meaning that it has no direct reason that we are capable of understanding), there is yet significant symbolism in this practice. On a variety of levels it symbolizes the importance of not intermingling different energies. This can be interpreted as a subtle reference to it not being beneficial to spend boundless time with negative people, even if one is trying to be proactive with them. It helps us to understand that those serving the light are still affected by the energy of those ey'rev rav people who are attracted to the light, but remain burdened by much egocentric and/or dark energy. This is the practical meaning of "and I have separated you out from among the nations to be mine" (VayYiKra 20:26). This spiritual teaching is found throughout the Torah, because it is so essential for the success of the long-term netzach energy needed for the spiritual victory of deveikut/chey'rut, which, again, is the highest purpose of Am Yisrael, and so that we may become a luminous light to ourselves and to all the nations. It is not unusual for spiritual teachers to get "slimed" in their efforts to elevate the ey'rev rav. This is just part of the service. We have to be willing to take on some temporary negativity as part of this service, as well as other spiritual challenges that the service creates.

There are things that disconnect us from the light, and there are things that connect us to the light. The more connected to the light we become, the more radiant we are, and the easier it is to do this type of service and burn off the "slime" through the fire of our light. This mitzvah may then apply to a future time when it will make clearer sense. One such possibility is a kabbalistic mystical teaching that in messianic times there will be a radical DNA change in animals, as well as in humans, so that the animals will attain a state of awareness similar to our present human awareness. It also suggests in Bereisheet 1:30, "For every beast of the field, every bird of the sky, and every thing that walks the land, that has in it a living soul, all plant vegetation shall be food." This implies that even the carnivorous animals will become vegetarian.

The Torah's injunction against weaving wool and linen into a single fabric can be understood on a surface plane as well. Linen is the highest-frequency natural fiber there is, and it should not be associated with wool, which, from a high moral and animal-welfare perspective is a form of theft from the sheep and an example of the oppression of the weak at the hands of the dominant. By not using linen and wool together for private use, we are respecting the rights of the animal and the higher kedusha frequency of the linen. We are avoiding this blend, so that linen should not be combined with the lower frequency of the slightly impure, "stolen" wool. This is why the only exception to this rule was the sacred vestments of the kohain gadol, because the otherwise forbidden blend is being used for divine purpose, and the negative ramifications become overridden by the principle of "Love God your Lord with all your heart, with all your soul, and with all your might" (Devarim 6:5). Moreover, the kohain gadol had to embody all of the beings of the planet whenever he entered the sacred space of the One who unifies all, and thus was clothed in stone beings (the stones on the breastplate), plant beings (linen), and animal beings (wool).

"Do not act on the basis of omens" (VayYiKra 19:26). Another translation of this verse is "You shall not use enchantment." Enchantment is the use of occult mechanics to affect people's minds against their will, which is also known as "black magic." This is another moral teaching that concerns the unethical practice of imposing a stronger mind over the mind of another and overriding the sovereignty of another person's psyche, especially for selfish purposes. This is the classical definition of black magic. This is what is commonly practiced today through subliminal messages being flashed in advertising, television, and the media in general. It is also filtered into our minds through propaganda and distorted news information such as what we see with anti-Semitism, as well as other common venues like political speeches. Because this form of "enchantment" is so common, we have become desensitized victims of it. The Torah serves as a warning to wake up to these abuses and label them as what they are. The teaching of the stronger overriding the will of the weaker is a significant Torah teaching, applying both to human-human interactions as well as human-animal interactions. Some people feel that the way we treat animals eventually becomes the exploitative and impure way we also treat other humans. The tzaddik, King Solomon taught some 2,900 years ago, is the one who "regards the life of his beast" (Mishle 12:10).

VayYiKra 19:26 reiterates the teaching "Do not eat on blood." On one important level, the kosher laws reflect a subtle Torah principle, which is to direct people away from where they are. And so, if the majority are not able to follow the Torah ideal, such as the diet of Bereisheet 1:29, then the Torah seeks to create a practice that helps people move toward that ideal. The deveikut/chey'rut celebrates God at the center of everything in our lives. With this awareness, a mitzvah is fulfilled because of the knowledge that all actions come from the source. Holiness is not about having faith or having a belief system; it is about the quality of God consciousness in our actions. It is not determined by social convention or by people trying to impose their codependent needs on you by defining holiness as that which meets their codependent patterns and agendas. Kedusha demands strong integrity in every action. Holiness is not about sanctifying our will or desires; it is about sanctifying our actions. Holiness does not belong to the few; it is the living responsibility of everyone.

The chosen people were chosen to create holiness on the earth and to be an inspiration to all the nations. Holiness does not mean superiority. It is a reflection of a specific focus and a particular mission that one has. Kedusha is the God-awareness present in how we live our mission. Each of us has the same potential and the same responsibility in this way. This parashah speaks to our divine potential to achieve kedusha, and emphasizes what a foundational and important role of the Torah Way holiness plays in our journey toward deveikut/chey'rut. Kedusha is developed through building our midot (character). It is not only the platform from which we leap into the joy of deveikut, but it is also the way of life that helps to repair our broken vessels so that we can hold the higher and more intense light of the Divine. In this inner experience of kedusha, we emanate our deep love for (and our sense of oneness with) all people and all creatures of the planet and beyond. With this understanding, we can fully become the expression of VayYiKra 19:17–18: "Do not hate your brother in your heart. You must admonish your neighbor, and not bear sin because of him…. You must love your neighbor as [you love] yourself. I am God."

May we be blessed to always walk in the lifestyle of kedusha so that we might respond to God's will of "You shall be holy to me, for I, God, am holy, and I have separated you out from among the nations to be mine" (VayYiKra 20:26).

Amen

Emor

〜〜〜

THIS parashah takes us into a deeper realm of deveikut/chey'rut, in which there is only the One as the sole focus of our existence. Emor (אמור) means "speak," as in "speak the truth." The parashah deals with the issue of kedusha, holiness, with regard to the kohan'im, the priests, who in those times were the shamans and the spiritual teachers for Am Yisrael. It thus also addresses the role and responsibilities of spiritual teachers in our society today. For the kohan'im in the ancient times, kedusha was primarily ritualistic. They were limited in their choice of whom they could marry, and they were subject to a variety of ritual injunctions around death.

At the simplest level of meaning, kedusha, in the first-Temple times and earlier, was defined by one's perisha (פרישה), meaning "separation from forbidden things." In Bereisheet (the creation story), we gain some insight into what perisha really means. Our sages tell us that Hashem had created and destroyed many universes before bringing this one into existence (Midrash Kohelet Rabbah 3:14). One of the forces that had been created in these previous universes was the force of darkness, which we also can call "evil." Bereisheet 1:2 implies this evil as the "darkness on the face of the depths." In this context, evil is not merely the absence of light; it is the force of evil, which was clearly a creation of God, as is pointed out in Yesha'yahu (Isaiah) 45:7. It was from out of this darkness that God said "'There shall be light,' and light came into existence" (Bereisheet 1:3). Once the light emerged, we had the polarity of light and darkness, the light being the force of good and the darkness being the force of evil. The idea of light and dark is key to understanding the meaning of kedusha and the meaning of perisha. In Bereisheet 1:4, God separated the light from the darkness. And so kedusha, light, or holiness, means to separate oneself from darkness, from tumah, or uncleanliness.

This primordial separation of kedusha and tumah in the act of creation became chaotic and unbalanced, a drama that repeated itself again when Adam and Cha'vah ate of the forbidden fruit of good and evil, and actively blended the forces of good and evil inside themselves. In that action the primordial separation of perisha, the separation of light from dark, became reversed. Since everything God does is for the best, did they really sin? Is not this the way of humanity on the planet, a way that has even become part of our spiritual path? Our spiritual work involves creating kedusha in our lives by overcoming our tendency toward duality, so that we become the light and separate ourselves from darkness in our actions and thoughts.

The Torah, as a handbook for deveikut/chey'rut, gives us some clues of how to live our lives as the multidimensional walk between the b'limah and the mah. In this manner, we can better distinguish between the temporal reality (known as the three-dimensional world), which brings us into darkness if we get too attached to it, and the light of the absolute reality. When we make that distinction, we separate the light and darkness in every moment. This is the meaning of holiness. Tikkun, which is about fine-tuning, as in tikkun ha'nefesh and tikkun ha'olam (the healing of ourselves and the healing of the planet), is about separating the light from the dark and finding a balance. For the past 5,771 years, from the time of Adam and Cha'vah, humans have been struggling in this state of imbalance, where light and darkness are merged. Yet, it is the human path to be able to distinguish within that fusion the ultimate reality of Ayn Zulato (אין זולתו)—"there is nothing other than God." This is the sod (סוד), or mystery understanding, of the Torah Way versus the culture of death. The culture of death, on the other hand, is but a limited vision of temporal reality, in which exploitation of the planet, animals, and people, is seen as the path to the illusion of an ultimate goal. The Essene Teacher of Righteousness, put it beautifully: "Dost thou forsake the Eternal for that which dieth in an hour?" That is the essential confusion and question in our world. In modern language, we can say that when our minds identify with ego, which is time, space, and being, we are not identifying with the truth. We only attain chey'rut consciousness when we no longer identify with ego, with time, space, and being. When we identify with the prior-to-consciousness qualities of deveikut and chey'rut in a consistent manner (maybe not 100 percent of the time, but significantly more than fifty percent of the time), we enter the relative stage of self-realization or enlightenment.

God laid down for Adam and Cha'vah and all humanity that they (we) should walk the long but powerful path of perisha, separating the light from the dark, so that we would identify solely with the light. In that process, darkness loses its power and its roots on the planet. In the larger context, when enough people are able to live more and more in this way, we create the preconditions for the messianic times. We will be able to receive and become the messianic energy, and therefore, draw the messiah.

Adam and Cha'vah ate of the Tree of Knowledge of Good and Evil, and it became part of who they (we) were, and thus became part of our spiritual path and struggle. The kabbalistic teachings make it clear that both good and evil are from Hashem as emanations of the One, and that ultimately the forces of darkness challenge us to rise to ever-new heights of consciousness as we develop the strength to choose good over evil. In this context, they are a gift to us.

In Jewish mythology, we are told that each of us is born with a good angel and a bad angel, each vying for our attention and obeisance, and constantly challenging us to make choices between living in the energy of yetzer hara (dark forces) or yetzer tov (forces of light and goodness). As part of the game plan, Am Yisrael was given the holy Torah as a support and guidebook for how we can overcome this inherent disposition and rectify ourselves. This is what tikkun is all about. In this context, we understand halakhah anew. The 613 teachings unleash the powerful spiritual energies from the heavens, which then descend through the channels opened by living the path of the mitzvot. These energies emanate from the spark of the Divine dwelling within the observance of the mitzvot. This indwelling spark is known as the shekhinah, and is the source of what we call kedusha. Kedusha can then be understood as the divine light manifesting in our universe. The more kedusha created, the more light is able to separate from the darkness; and the more we are able to restore the primordial state of this separation that existed at the beginning of the Big Bang.

As we expand kedusha in our own lives, the "spiritual equilibrium" between the light and the dark of the universe becomes restored. The observance of the mitzvot brings spiritual light, and thus healing to the world. Concretely, the more we observe the mitzvot, the sooner the primordial balance is restored.

Regarding tikkun for the world, we now understand the importance of kedusha on the cosmic level. We also see clearly the additional layer of responsibility applied to the role of the kohain in biblical times, since he was supposed to be a living embodiment and example of the frequency of kedusha. It was expected of him to inspire the entire Jewish people to be priests unto the nations and carriers of the frequency of kedusha. There are two layers: what is expected of the people, and what is expected of the kohan'im, or, in our own times, the tzaddikim.

One of the secrets of tikkun, in kabbalistic terms, is mayim nukvin (נוקבין מים), or "feminine waters," which we have referred to in earlier parashahs. Mayim nukvin refers to the deep desires for spiritual change in the hearts of the seekers, or the Torah-observant person. When there is an offering on the altar, this purity of heart and desire of soul is offered up as spiritual sacrifice. This is the key for what was mentioned several parashahs before: the role of everyone, in every moment, to create holiness in every act, by being fully present in mind, body, and spirit. Only then does every act become dedicated as an authentic sacrifice to God, thereby bringing more light onto the planet. We are thus challenged in every moment to be in a state of complete surrender to the divine will.

Moshe's blessing to the kohan'im was "They shall [therefore] teach your law to Jacob, and your Torah to Israel" (Devarim 33:10). The role of the kohan'im was transferred down, after the destruction of the first Temple, to Yirmeyahu (Jeremiah), and Yehezqel (Ezekiel), who were also guardians of the prophetic traditions. Eliyahu Hanavi, at least according to the Midrash, was also a kohain (Midrash Mishlei 9:3). The role of these great spiritual teachers, whether we call them kohan'im, nevi'im (prophets), or tzaddikim, is to shine the primordial light, released on Day One, to the entire world. They are to inspire all peoples, not just Jews, to do teshuva—to return to God, and thus be worthy of the light. They are simply to be servants of the people, of their students, to inspire them to be fully alive in the truth of the Divine.

We can actually say that kohan'im, nevi'im, and tzaddikim are indeed angels, because the word for angels in Hebrew, mal'achim (מלאכים), literally translates as "messengers," as in messengers of God, and that is what they are. The role of the spiritual teacher is then to completely surrender in service to the people. Historically, it is believed that because of the sins of the people, the Temple and the priests were taken away. Traditionally, the kohain was a Jewish male, but in these times, and even in those times, there were great female teachers as well. In other words, any person who wishes to live a kohain degree of commitment can fulfill this role by earning it. The second-century Rabbi Meir included non-Jewish people as well: "Even a non-Jew who is devoted to Torah is like a kohain gadol" (Talmud Bav'li, Baba Kama 38a). All of Am Yisrael, and every other nation for that matter, has an obligation to shine the light of God by its actions in the world. This is what is meant by kedusha.

As we evolve in our spiritual awareness, a stricter standard of life is expected of us by holiness, a standard with which not everyone is particularly comfortable. As you begin to let go of your ego, the standard naturally gets higher, because as you go deeper, the path grows narrower, so there is more ego burning to do. We cannot do the same things we did as teenagers or in early phases of our spiritual life. The role of the tzaddikim is to keep inspiring themselves and the people to higher and higher levels of kedusha. On the surface level of p'shat, our parashah focuses on the roles of the kohan'im, who are being asked to maintain a higher level of taharah, of ritual purity, than the rest of Am Yisrael. Since the destruction of the Temple, the role of the kohain gadol and the kohan'im has diminished and essentially disappeared. The only thing left in this culture that was considered holy was the Torah, which cannot become tumah (Talmud Bav'li, Berachot 22a). So, after the fall of the Temple, there was a tremendous focus on study and relationship with Torah as a way of maintaining and building holiness. Prayer had become the new form of sacrifice so that everyone benefitted from living at the level of taharah that the kohan'im were instructed to live by. A particularly positive side to all this is that we all have the choice to take on the role of the priests, and more fully have the potential to become a nation of priests.

The early followers of the Chassidic movement, under the mystical, brilliant insights of the Ba'al Shem Tov, attempted to restore the earlier paths existing before the fall of the first Temple. Their hope was that Judaism would no longer be confined only to Torah study, but would become reconnected to a much richer and fuller, heart-centered tradition. The Chassidim reintroduced the emotional factor to divine service, and the religious intensity that emerged out of connecting the intellect with the emotions. However, in this shift, they also opened themselves to the possibility of imbalance.

At the same time that you bring the heart energy in, and open yourself to potentials of higher levels of connection with God, you also become much more vulnerable to other energies slipping into the heart place. In that sense, we become more open to paradox. The teaching of the Ba'al Shem Tov in *Tzava'at Harivash* was that meditation, prayer, yechudim, and merging with God were seven times more important than Torah study alone. This radical approach to kedusha did not exactly meet with universal approval among the Torah scholars of the times (the eighteenth century). There was some theoretical basis for this opposition, namely, that when you open your heart to God and work with intellect, there is an increased possibility of imbalance. The deeper one goes on the spiritual path, the more one needs to walk the razor's edge with as much focused consciousness as one can generate. The potential of spiritual evolution is greater when we step out of the box, but the risks are also greater. Nonetheless, deveikut/chey'rut asks that we leave our egocentric comfort zones and walk up the mountain into the unknown, as Moshe did. This is why the tzaddikim often lived (and still do live) lives of exceptional, intense purity and balance. This is to counterbalance the risks of emotional imbalance.

As we have discussed, the role of the kohan'im was gradually transferred to the later prophets, the *mekubalim* (kabbalists), and the tzaddikim who studied, knew, and lived kabbalah. VayYiKra 21:6 says: "They must be holy to their god, and not profane their God's name. Since they present God's fire offerings, the food offering for their God, they must remain holy."

What were they really offering? They were offering their souls to God through service. Although there are some general ideas of kedusha, there may also be sincere areas of confusion. For example, the ancient sages were in disagreement concerning the process around assigning the dates for the three sacred festivals. Rabbi Akiva was of the opinion that the people determined the timing of the three festivals, basing his position on VayYiKra 23:2, 23:4, and 23:37, where the same phrase is repeated three times, corresponding to all three cycles: "There are special times that you must celebrate as sacred holidays to God." This, he insisted, also implies that the Jewish people determined the festival dates even if they (1) erred inadvertently, (2) erred deliberately, or (3) erred by being misled (Sifra, Emor, Parashta 2 and 3). When we make the blessing "Blessed are you, God, king of the universe, who has sanctified us with your commandments," it is a reminder that we need to trust ourselves, even over rabbinical commandments or interpretations. This can be interpreted as a heretical teaching, but in actuality it is a statement that our true soul energy is what generates the divine commandments.

Rabbi Safra Shapiria wrote: "In the name of his holiness, my Teacher, my Grandfather, the Rebbe of Magol Nitze, we have learned the following: 'Whatever kavanot (meditative intentions) a Jew decides upon for his use in the worship of God, those kavanot become the proper and appropriate ones.'" His teaching is clear. If a person cannot integrate into his worship the kavanot specified by the Arizal, then, if his thoughts nonetheless come from his heart and soul to God, they become the proper and appropriate thoughts, each in accordance with her or his individual level of knowing desire. This returns us to the initial understanding of kedusha. It is the level to which we nullify ourselves before God. The more we feel the nothing of ourselves before God, the more Divine. When you are coming from an empty place in which only God exists, then everything that comes from you is divine, and divine teachings and actions begin to flow through you. The whole point of kedusha is to be so aware and so empty that the Divine moves through you in every moment creating more and more light. This is a teaching about bitul (ביטול), the nullification of ego, and implies a shift from identifying with ego to identifying with consciousness. Bitul brings us closer to God until all our actions become God's commandments expressed through our individual body-mind-I am complex.

This parashah also discusses the cycle of the holidays, or more appropriately, holy days, and each one has a particular meaning, when it says "These are God's festivals that you must celebrate as sacred holidays at their appropriate times" (VayYiKra 23:4). A comedian once said, "I tried being an atheist, but I gave it up because there were no holidays." As a play on words, a holiday is really a "holy day." It is not an escape to Hawaii or some island retreat. It is a time to bring paradise to us, into our everyday life. It is a time to bring the celestial into the terrestrial. In Hebrew, we refer to it as moed (מיעד), which means a date, or meeting. A holiday, in a sense, is a love date with God. Do we need a date with God? God is with us at every moment; we all know that. But it is easy to forget that God's presence is present, and so we have special times when we can tune in to that. The holidays help us to be aware that God's love is with us all the time and inspires us with kedusha. Each holiday is a time to remember and celebrate our timeless love of God, for God, as God, with God, from God, and as receiving God, which covers both the dual and the nondual levels of understanding.

The idea of holidays makes us more aware of the concept of time. When we are slaves, we are not allowed the privilege of time, which is ours when we have freedom. The holiday of Passover is therefore about freedom within time. Of course, the ultimate freedom is beyond time, but we must first go from slavery, where we are stuck out of time, out of control, and move into time, specifically the holy time of the cycles of the stars and planetary bodies. When we align ourselves this way, we align ourselves with the expression and guidance of the Divine. And so, holy time is a way to connect with God's guidance through the stars. The Gregorian time reckoning of the twenty-four-hour day and sixty-minute hour creates a slight disorientation from holy time's flow. It brings us into machine, or "matrix," time and away from holy time. Machine time again turns us into slaves as economic units.

The Torah includes both circular and linear time. Circular time is an understanding of the cycles of the holidays according to the cosmic influxes that are flowing onto the planet with each holy day. For example, Rosh Hashanah is the spiritual new year of the yearly cycle. It is a time for receiving the energetic influx of Libra (Tishrei) with its qualities of justice and judgment, as well as celebrating and receiving, anew, the energetics of the birth of the Adamic race onto the planet. There is also the Torah's linear history. When these are combined together we experience time as a spiral that includes the principle of ma'aseh avot siman labanim, as it plays out in present time. As we evolve into enlightenment (deveikut/chey'rut), which takes us beyond time and, at the same time, synchronizes us with time, we honor and live in this spiraling cycle. Shabbat, the most important of these spiraling cycles, is both a time when we are able to transcend time and see the beauty of God's presence in every moment, and a time to be lived by God in every moment of spiral time.

Pesach is about going beyond the slavery of the ego, which means things, ideas, and codependent behaviors, many of which start from childhood and continue being projected on the people around us, even our teachers. Pesach is about the quality of life. The *Omer* (עוֹמֶר), a seven-week-long barley offering ritual between Pesach and Shavuot, is about the purification of our seven lower sephirotic qualities over the course of forty-nine days, in preparation to receive the Torah on Shavuot. We have seven weeks in which each of these seven phases may be sanctified on seven different levels. So we are counting the weeks, and we are counting the days. In essence, seven qualities of each of the seven sephirot are thereby sanctified, and we, in turn, become holier during this time of the Omer. This is why the Torah calls the Passover festival a Shabbat. Generally, most of the Jewish festivals are holy because the Jewish people sanctify them, making them holy. God, on the other hand, sanctifies the Sabbath (Bereisheet 2:3 and Shemot 20:11). Through our sanctifications in the counting of the Omer, the Passover festival is called a Shabbat.

As we look at the lessons of Omer at another level, we go back to the lesson of Rabbi Akiva, who taught that the most fundamental principle of the Torah is to "love your neighbor as yourself" (Talmud Yerushalmi, Nedarim 30b). This principle is also the essence of the holy days of the counting of the Omer, in that each day is a phase that brings us more holiness, which, in turn, draws us closer to one another in love and respect.

Following the Omer is Rosh Hashanah, which is about quality of life for the coming year. It is a celebration of the beginning of the new yearly cycle. It is also a time when we immerse ourselves in processes of purification, it being the seventh month, and seven representing purification. Once we have purified ourselves, we are ready for the next festival, Yom Kippur, which comes right before the harvest festival of Sukkot. Accordingly, by the time we get to Yom Kippur, we have attained the power to harvest the light. This light, which elevates us in awareness, is strongest on Yom Kippur. It takes us to the upper sephirotic energy of binah. Sukkot, the third festival (in the seventh month), is the light of mercy. It gives us the opportunity to surround ourselves in the light. It is also a time, again, to harvest what we have planted. It represents the light around our internal potentials, individually and collectively. On *Shemini Atzeret* and *Simchat Torah*, which follow immediately after Sukkot, all of the work of the holidays that we have done becomes unified into a concentrated awareness of the truth that lasts through the year.

VayYiKra 24:7 then mentions the ritual of the twelve loaves used in the Tabernacle. These sacred breads represent the twelve tribes of Israel as well as the zodiac. The ritual symbolized the purification of the people's actions, so that whatever was negative will not bare fruit. On those twelve loaves were applied a little bit of holy aromatherapy, a small drop of frankincense on each one.

This parashah's focus on death is another way of understanding the lessons of separation and holidays, because death reminds us that our physical bodies are here today and gone tomorrow. Given the very long history of our planet, we might say that we are here as weekend visitors. The role of the spiritual teacher in the lives of people who are unaware, who say "Well, since we're only here for a weekend, let's just have a big party," is to remind them that we have a higher purpose. Even though we appear to be here only for a tiny fraction of cosmic time, we will keep recycling until we awaken. One reason the priests are told to avoid contact with death is because they did not want their thoughts to become deluded. On contact with a corpse, we begin to think that we are just a physical body, and we are only here for a weekend. Contact with death can confuse people in this way and create doubt. Of course, the doubt only comes from holding on to our egocentric interpretations of how our lives are supposed to unfold, rather than remembering that whatever God does is for the best.

Another way in which contact with death decreases spiritual energy is the sense of powerlessness that one might experience when confronted with death. On the other hand, we can turn it around by using our contact with death to remind us that we have a limited time on the planet, and, therefore, we need to invest more and more energy into the single purpose of life, to know Hashem. The sadness or depression that may come from exposure to death may also undermine our connection with God. Joy takes us to God on the highest octave of service where it morphs into noncausal joy, while depression drops us to a level of separation.

This parashah also recounts the tragic story of the young man who cursed God's name. The son of a Jewish mother and an Egyptian father, he became angry and abused the name of God. In that moment his sense of connection with the One stopped and he became dead, symbolically. Connected with this, we have the seemingly famous and sorely misunderstood adage, as previously discussed, "an eye for an eye and a tooth for a tooth" (VayYiKra 24:20–21). This statement has been grossly misinterpreted as being about revenge. This is the fool's way of interpreting it, because, in truth, we are talking about the universal laws of cause and effect. It is a profoundly misunderstood statement as part of people's efforts to misconstrue the deeper Torah, or to use the Torah to justify revenge. Revenge has nothing to do with us. The cosmos takes care of balancing things; it is not our responsibility. It is basically saying that divine justice will be done, whether in this lifetime or another lifetime. It is saying that when you create an energy moving in a certain direction, you experience the results of the energy moving in that direction. Something is going to happen. Therefore, the ancient rabbis defined this statement as the need for restitution, as in "the value of an eye for an eye," and so on. After all, what good does it do to punish someone who knocked out an eye by knocking out his eye too? In the meantime, no one wins, and we have two one-eyed people meandering about. It is more important for the perpetrator to pay the doctor bills of his victim and any resulting loss of income, than to have his eye plucked out. And what if the perpetrator is blind? What would be the point in knocking out his eye? Or if he is lame, what would be the point in cutting off his limb? (Talmud Bav'li, Baba Kama 83b–84a). Again, it was never intended as a statement of revenge. God is going to take care of the results of any action.

All of this is played out in the story of the man who blasphemed the name of God. The oral tradition gives an interesting background to this incident and to the "measure for measure" involved. This was not the son of a Jewish woman who happened to fall in love with a nice Egyptian man, who then left Egypt with her people. Jewish women did not sleep with Egyptian men during their time in Egypt; they kept their whole sexuality very separate during that period. The Egyptian father in this story was a taskmaster back in Egypt prior to the exodus. He had become attracted to one of the Jewish women on his shift, and one day, when everybody had left for work, he broke into her home and had sex with her. Soon thereafter, Moshe came upon the scene of an Egyptian beating on a Hebrew, as we read about in the Torah (Shemot

2:11–12). In actuality, the oral tradition tells us, this was the taskmaster beating on the husband of the woman he had just slept with. It was in this context that Moshe slew the Egyptian with one of the seventy-two God names. Moshe knew, by way of the Ruach HaKodesh, that the Egyptian had forced himself on the wife of the man he was now beating, and so he killed him on account of his having raped the woman and on account of his beating on her husband (Midrash Tanchuma, Shemot, No. 9 and Midrash Vayikra Rabbah 32:4). According to another oral tradition, the Egyptian taskmaster was also one the incarnations of Kayin, just as Moshe was one of the incarnations of Hevel, and that healing between the two occurred when Moshe sent his [Kayin's] soul flying, through the sacred name.

The woman, forced by the taskmaster, became pregnant from that incident and eventually gave birth to the young man who now, in a fit of anger, cursed the God name. This young man, in other words, was the offspring of this spiritually invalid connection. As a result, he blasphemed the Divine and was cut off. This story is an interesting lesson about how things get rebalanced in different ways somewhere down the line. The action of the Egyptian taskmaster resulted in being "cut off from the generation"—that is, he ended up with no one to carry on his name, no progeny, since his one and only son was now also "cut off from life." The second-century kabbalistic master, Rabbi Shimon bar Yochai, said that anyone who reads the Torah literally is a fool (Zohar, Vol. 1, folio 27b).

So, whether the young man was actually killed, or not, as a result of his action is not the point at all. In that moment when he was caught up in his anger, he lost his contact with the Divine and, therefore, became spiritually dead. Looking at the story this way gives us a deeper understanding. Anger itself is a form of idol worship (Zohar, Vol. 3, folio 179a), because, in that moment, we give our power over to something other than God.

Going back to the lessons of the Omer, the thirty-third day of the counting of the Omer later became a day of special celebration (*Lag B'Omer*), but only because it was the day a great tragedy, due to anger, ceased. For weeks up until that day, thousands of Rabbi Akiva's students had died from a plague. The Talmud suggests the reason for this was that they were not seeing God in each other, and they therefore did not behave respectfully toward one another

(Talmud Bav'li, Yevamot 62b). They created a state of anger, separating them from the truth. It is also said that the Holy Temple was destroyed because of "hatred for no reason" (Talmud Bav'li, Yoma 9b). Now, the good news is that it can be rebuilt because of "love for no reason"!

The seeds of our actions do not necessarily get worked out the same day. Sometimes they get worked out forty years later. That is also the way of "satan." *Satan* is a Hebrew word meaning "obstruct." There is no person with a red tail and horns, but rather a force of darkness that tries to delude us, and either blocks or elevates our evolution, depending on how we respond to the teachings inherent in the situations that come our way. Our lessons are often complicated, because our actions are often separated from the results. It is not always as simple as when you overeat and then get sick, as an instant result. It is more common that we overeat and indulge in sugar, and twenty years later we develop diabetes. In the moment, we tend to separate the action from the result. That is how we get sucked into repeating out-of-balance actions, because we do not see the results immediately. Sometimes we do, but most of the time we do not. It all comes back to creating holiness in the mundane, in the everyday actions of our lives. There is no word for "vacation" in Hebrew. *Chofesh* (חפש), the modern Hebrew word for vacation, does not exactly mean vacation; chofesh means freedom. Change the vowels, and you get *chee'pays*, which means "seek." If you want to create holiness in every moment, you should do so, and never really take a vacation from that. You have to keep seeking out the meaning encrypted in every moment, in every circumstance. We have Shabbat, for example. We get a break every seven days, but we never really get a break from creating holiness in every moment. Satan takes no vacation. There are no breaks here. So in response, we would do well to live that in every moment, and remember that every thought and every action can be holy, can be sanctified.

How we perform an action is more important than the action itself. The more kedusha we create, the greater opportunity we have to share the light. We also have more responsibility and more constraints when we do this. One of the hardest things for people to understand about spiritual teachers (and clearly, this applies to anyone who is seriously involved with and committed to the great chey'rut way of the Torah) is that the more elevated we become, the more responsibility we have, and the more cautious we have to be about every word we utter (Mishnah, Avot 1:11). At different levels, then, we have different responsibilities and different restrictions. Even the animals, as pointed out in this parashah, had to be 100 percent pure and unblemished to be eligible for sacrifice. A physical defect showed that something was also amiss on the spiritual level. When we think about that son who desecrated God's name, we understand that God does not care if we desecrate or sanctify the name, as God is not punishing anyone here. It is really about nourishing the God within us. We diminish the spark of light within us when we do things that create separation, and we then become tarnished. On the other hand, we shine when we are in deveikut. It is not for God's sake that we should not be negative or live primarily in reactive duality. It is for our own sakes (Midrash Tanchuma, Shemini, No. 7).

In summary, this parashah is a practical part of the Torah teachings, which build the vessels of light. It helps us understand that we, as spiritual people in whose lives God is central, are lived by God, lived by love, and lived by deveikut/chey'rut. Moreover, we are supported by the process of sanctifying every action. In this way, we identify with consciousness instead of ego. In this way, we create more and more light. We not only transform ourselves into beings of light, but also create a web of light that supports the coming of the messianic age. May we all be blessed by increasing our ability to live in and build kedusha.

Amen

BeHar Sinay

B<small>EHAR</small> Sinay is one of the most socially and spiritually conscious parashahs, as well as one of the most harmonizing for society and for the ecology. It begins with VayYiKra 25:2–4: "When you come to the land that I am giving you, the land must be given a rest period, a sabbath to God. For six years you may plant your fields, prune your vineyards, and harvest your crops, but the seventh year is a sabbath of sabbaths for the land." Continuing in VayYiKra 25:8–10:

> "You shall count seven sabbatical years, that is, seven times seven years. The period of the seven sabbatical cycles shall thus be forty-nine years. Then, on the tenth day of the seventh month, you shall make a proclamation with the ram's horn. This proclamation with the ram's horn is thus to be made on Yom Kippur. You shall sanctify the fiftieth year, declaring emancipation [of slaves] all over the world. This is your jubilee year, when each man shall return to his hereditary property and to his family."

This was very profound on a p'shat level, because it was a plan meant to maintain a highly conscious social order that does not create human slavery. This is a social document supporting the development of consciousness that would bring world peace if honored. On the surface level, the people were given a Shabbat that, when honored, would give the land an ecologically beneficial rest. However, connected with this was a reminder that the people did not own the land; it belonged to God. At the end of every fifty years, during jubilee, all land was returned back to the original tribal owners and everything began again. This profound social document is almost incomprehensible in today's world of capitalism. It was designed to equalize the social order. People who did poorly could begin again and were not trapped in slavery. People who did well must also reset their circumstances, which prevented monopolies and prevented skillful people from misusing their abilities to enslave and dominate others. It taught them that they did not own the land and, indirectly, taught the Torah principle hishta'vut, non-attachment. It prevented exploitation of resources and people. BeHar Sinay shows how to create harmony on all levels of society and with the ecology of world.

This parashah is called BeHar Sinay because Har Sinay is a humble mountain. It is small and humble relative to the mountains surrounding it. It was taught that when the mountains were vying for where the Ten Speakings would be received, Mount Sinai was chosen because of its humility. This social document was designed to spiritually help to manifest humility among all the people. Shabbat is for us to come into our attunement with the Divine on a periodic basis as it occurs every seven days. Shabbat reminds us of who we are and of our connection with the Divine. It is a sanctuary in time that allows us to go beyond time. By occurring every seven days, Shabbat is a built-in reminder to create an empty mind. It reinforces the individual awakening process. During *Sh'mittah,* which occurred every seven years, all farming activity on the land stopped for one year, which enabled the land to regenerate. This allowed the people of Am Yisrael to return to a more natural state with time to study Torah and pray more intensively for one whole year. Every seven years, the Sh'mittah created the space for Am Yisrael to deeply connect as a nation. It reminded them that they did not own anything, but that they were here, in the land, sharing it. In that unity, all of Israel returned to a more natural and conscious state. Agriculture stopped, debts were cancelled, and everyone had an opportunity to focus on the Divine to awaken their spirits. Finally they had *Yovel,* the year of jubilee, occurring every fifty years, which restored the holiness, or kedusha, of an entire generation. At Yovel, every fifty years, they could heal a whole generation of imbalance.

Economic slavery was cleared. It was a time to return to the Divine and to return to the original state of consciousness. It was no accident that Yovel began on Yom Kippur. Paradoxically, they had an opportunity to connect with their generation and commit to a higher level of kedusha for the following generation. Shabbat, Sh'mittah, and Yovel were given to periodically help the people reconnect with their holy true nature as Divine presence. This was a clear way to understand their apperception of deep beauty and teaching. I am in awe of this process. This is a plan for the whole world, as the Torah teaching and principles support the evolution of spiritual consciousness in each generation.

Constantly focusing on worldly pursuits entraps us and enslaves us. When we step back from mundane work and focus on these cycles, we have an opportunity to connect to the truth on multidimensional levels. The earth plane represents malchut. Every seven years we can disconnect from the earth plane and increase our opportunity to connect to higher planes. Every fifty years there is such a shift that we are able to connect to the mystical plane of creation in binah, the divine mother. For example, to make people industrial units to be economically exploited is not the Torah Way. The sovereignty of land and its inhabitants, in the Torah teachings, should never be viewed as economic units to be exploited. This is the underlying deeper message of the three levels of the Shabbats. These cycles give us a continual option to choose between life and death. These three cycles give us a chance to choose between the Torah culture of life and enlightenment (deveikut/chey'rut) over the satanic culture of death, which sees the land and its inhabitants as nothing more than soulless economic units to be exploited. This is a clear commentary on today's trends, and the efforts and threats of the New World Order to destroy all people, animal, and national sovereignties. This effort against the spiritual sovereignty teachings of the Torah has been going on since the time of Babel and Nimrod, who was the world's first dictator. He attempted to have Avraham, who was the first Jew, acting as a spiritual revolutionary for the right of sovereignty, burnt in the fire. Nimrod, the hunter of souls, had attempted to establish himself as god and ruler of all people. This was 4,000 years ago—it did not work then, and it will not work today, for it is against God's ultimate plan, which is the freedom and enlightenment of all peoples of the world. The efforts to destroy sovereignty may function temporarily to serve as a wake-up call, but they will not succeed in the long run. Avraham defeated Nimrod spiritually, then, and Avraham's grandson, 'Esav, killed Nimrod physically. The principle of ma'asheh avot siman labanim will again prevail in our times as well.

The Levites were not to have any possessions. Their job was to connect primarily with the Divine. Today our opportunity as modern kohan'im and Levites is to live connected to the light and maintain a balance by knowing the truth. The jubilee year and the Sh'mittah (sabbatical year) were times when humanity's non-Torah economic slavery activities and habits could be remedied in the forgiveness of all loans. Associated with this was the concept of *ribit*, which is the prohibition against taking interest on loans. The concept of usury is not only immoral, but leads to slavery and misery of people. In our present contemporary times, it has become easier to see how our entire economic system is based on enslaving people and nations. This activity will not survive in the world, as divine intervention will move society toward a higher level by returning to the way of the Torah. The Torah is very clear about the need for a more humble and just society where people care for each other and love one another as themselves, as it says in VayYiKra 19:18: "You must love your neighbor as [you love] yourself. I am God." The result of ignoring ribit is enslaving debt, known as *shmittat kesafim*. Canceling debts heals the planet and the economy. If these principles were really lived in Israel, she would certainly be a light to the nations; and she would become be a boon to the world.

As we look at this profound document, another statement brings us deeper understanding. VayYiKra 25:21–23 says:

> "I will send you such a blessing in the sixth year that the land will
> yield enough for three years. While you plant during the eighth
> year, you will eat from the old crop and will continue to eat from
> it until the harvest of the ninth year comes in. The land must not
> be sold permanently, because the land is mine and you are but
> aliens and my tenants."

What is being said here is that God will perform a miracle every seven years. The crops will produce three times their yield. It is taught that this will only be done in the land of Israel, but it is talking about a miracle. It is an opportunity to play things out on malchut and learn to respect sovereignty and take care of each other and learn to live in proper harmony and balance. We have these three ways of doing it. VayYiKra 25:35–38 says:

> "When your brother becomes impoverished and loses the ability
> to support himself in the community, you must come to his aid.
> Help him survive, whether he is a proselyte or a native [Israelite].

Do not take advance [interest] from him. Fear your God, and let your brother live alongside you. Do not make him pay advance interest for your money, and do not give him food for which he will have to pay accrued interest. I am God your lord, who brought you out of Egypt to give you the land of Canaan, [and] to be a God for you."

This truly describes a just society where everyone is taken care of and there are no metaphorical or literal slaves. The reason the Torah Way is superior to socialism and communism is that these social and economic systems do not have a process of bringing consciousness and God awareness to people beyond politics. For example, they do not have a process for helping people to understand what the Native Americans have always known: We don't own the land; we are merely caretakers of the land. Sh'mittah and Yovel were designed to eliminate all forms of slavery and social injustice. That is why it says in VayYiKra 25:23: "Since the land is mine, no land shall be sold permanently. You are foreigners and resident aliens as far as I am concerned." This is a very clear statement: There is only the Divine dancing in the illusion of us as individual separations. The only reality is God. We end with that teaching in a quote. VayYiKra 25:55 says: "[All this] because the Israelites are [actually] my slaves. They are my slaves because I brought them out of Egypt. I am God your Lord." The message here is clear: "Wake up!" These Torah teachings are built into the social system to prevent people from falling asleep on a periodic basis, so that we remember that there is only God. We live here as the servants or the play of God upon the planet for the spiritual evolution of our individual souls. Even the living planet is nothing more than an expression of the Divine.

May we all be blessed that we remember this divine truth. Hopefully we will not need the three seven-cycle system to remind us to remember Ayn Zulato.

Amen

Bechuko-thai

Bechuko-thai literally means "in my decrees," and opens with "If you follow my laws and are careful to keep my commandments, …" the land will thrive in balance and there will peace. This promise follows VayYiKra 25:55–26:8, where it explicitly says, "[All this] is because the Israelites are [actually] my slaves. They are my slaves because I brought them out of Egypt." Both passages are core teachings of the Torah Way to deveikut/chey'rut, to live as the expression of keter, the will of God. At its highest level, this means knowing Hashem from the inside out. It means to be as servants to the God will, who will follow the divine decrees and laws. It also means that we will work at becoming empty egoless vessels for the fullest manifestation of the will of Hashem, as it flows through us in our own unique expression of the Torah mitzvah way. To be that expression requires us to be lived by being the will of God. It asks us to know God, rather than to know about God and the Way of the Torah.

These teachings give us the foundation for understanding the Ba'al Shem Tov's liberated lessons. He taught that meditation was seven times more important than Torah studies. In other words, the yechudim of kabbalistic meditation gift us with the direct experience of merging our hearts with the Divine to create an experience of God-merging. By so doing, we open ourselves up to be lived by keter from the inside out as the ancient Essenes did, as opposed to the way of Jerusalem, where the focus was to understand from the outside in.

How is this to be done? How are we to become the will of God expressing itself in our unique way? The secret is to create the inner conditions by which we merge our hearts with the Divine. Then, ultimately through bitul, we become the single heart of Hashem expressing. This deveikut state is facilitated by meditation, prayer, repetition of the name of God, devotional chanting and singing of the name, as in *"shiviti Hashem l'neg'dee ta'mid"*—keeping the name of God before us at all times (Tehillim 16:8). In this way, our awareness of Hashem remains constant at the inner center of our universe. It is through this way of life that we become the will of God expressing. We start as the servant on the Way of the Torah, and eventually disappear into Hashem. This is the deepest level of understanding this parashah's guidance.

The Torah promises to give us abundance on every level when we follow the ways of God:

> "[Or] make yourselves false gods. Do not raise up a stone idol or a sacred pillar for yourselves. Do not place a kneeling stone in your land so that you can prostrate yourselves on it. I am God your Lord. Keep my Sabbaths and revere my sanctuary, I am God. If you follow my laws and are careful to keep my commandments, I will provide you with rain at the right time, so that the land will bear its crops and the trees of the field will provide fruit. [You will have so much that] your threshing season will last until your grape harvest, and your grape harvest will last until the time you plant. You will have your fill of food, and [you will] live securely in the land. I will grant peace in the land so that you will sleep without fear. I will rid the land of dangerous animals, and the sword will not pass through your land. You will chase away your enemies, and they will fall before your sword. Five of you will be able to chase away a hundred, and a hundred of you will defeat ten thousand, as your enemies fall before your sword."
>
> (VayYiKra 26:1–8)

God was clearly saying that if Am Yisrael will live in the way that has been outlined for them, they will create such positive energy that they will have peace, abundance, happiness, and safety. Their energetic field will be so strong that five will chase away one hundred and one hundred will chase away ten thousand. Incidentally this particular energetic principle is what a lot of peace meditations are based on. It is the principle that a small group creating an energetic field collectively will create an energetic field equal to the square of the number of people working separately. A hundred people meditating will affect 10,000 people. These principles actually work. They have been experimentally proven. God does not lie. If we create positive energy, it aligns us with the earth and effects the environment in a variety of positive ways. This is an ancient Hebrew shamanic teaching most commonly connected with drought and rain in Israel. An example of this is that when people around the world meditate for peace on the equinox and solstice, they literally decrease the average number of sunspots by thirty-six percent during those specific times. In other words, when we send out strong group positive energy, we affect not only the earth, but also at least the whole solar system, including the sun. Are we willing to listen to the potential level of the power of the light? Are we willing to be that light to the nations we are prophesied to be?

This section specifically gives the promise of enlightenment. "I will keep My sanctuary in your midst, and not grow tired of you. I will make My presence felt among you. Thus, I will be a God to you, and you will be a nation [dedicated] to Me. I am God your Lord. I brought you out from Egypt, where you were slaves. I broke the bands of your yoke, and led you forth with your heads held high." (VayYiKra 26:11-13) Walking with "heads held high" is a metaphor for experiencing God face to face. After we have been freed from the slavery of the mind/ego (symbolized by Egyptian slavery), we live in direct apperception of the Divine. The promises, "I will make My presence felt among you" and "I will keep My sanctuary in your midst," imply that the presence and consciousness of God will be active amongst the people. This is a statement of collective enlightenment. God not only promises peace, agricultural prosperity, good weather, great enjoyment of food, abundant procreation, national security, protection from war and predatory beasts, but also Am Yisrael's enlightenment. All we have to do is follow the great way of the Torah as God's way.

The blessings and curses in this parashah are telling us that we have choices, and that we are responsible for the outcome of those choices. We cannot blame others and evolve spiritually. This does not mean, however, that we are not affected by those around us. This is why God spoke to the whole nation of Israel. Ultimately, each one of us must make a decision to align with the culture of life and liberation as the Way of Torah, or we choose by our actions to align with the culture of death.

The curses hold a variety of clear statements and have actually been happening for centuries. Simply put, we are talking about cause and effect. The natural causes and effects determine what happens to us on a basic level unless the higher principle of grace intervenes. However, because of the many blessings received, and our closeness as the servants of God, the result of failure to obey will fall upon our heads sevenfold. When one is close to the fire, one gets more of the illumination of the light, but it is also easier to get burned. This is cause and effect in an amplified way.

Am Yisrael receives immense blessings and benefits, but because Am Yisrael is so close to the fire, it is easier to get burned. Negative actions cause negative reactions. The decrees and laws help us to avoid negative causes and effects. The curses are a reminder and warning of what the results will be. They give us a glimpse into the potential future. It is a blessing to have the ability to see the results of our actions beforehand, so that we can avoid acting unconsciously. This parashah is then saying "Your actions have consequences, and this is what they look like." This is a blessing, for it gives us a chance to look down the road to see the clear results of our actions. The blessing gifts us with ample space and time to save ourselves from unnecessary hardship. It also allows us to take full accountability for our actions, as uncomfortable as it may seem. The ninety-eight curses in this context are not punishments. They are an effort to forewarn us about the potential consequences of our actions. If we follow the guidance, we will see the positive results of our actions, such as peace in the land and rain for our fields. The fruit of our actions will blossom. And if we do not act appropriately, the curses will seed and grow worse and worse, in the same way it worsened for Pharaoh, until we get it. And that means we can always change mid-flight.

This natural law of cause and effect, operating in the world of Elohim, helps support our spiritual development. If we can live in the awareness of the impartial law of cause and effect, we can see that God is never punishing us. Rather, we are punishing ourselves through the consequences of our negative actions. When we act poorly, we do not have inner peace. The land is negatively affected by our negative frequency. Our frequency affects our food as well. When we act inappropriately we "will eat and not be satisfied," because we put negative energy into our food.

The third set of curses is about the destructive animals attacking us. An old teaching says that carnivorous animals were never meant to hurt humans except if humans are acting in evil ways. If humans are choosing blessings, then evil beasts will not roam the land. Symbolically, then, an evil beast is the result of our actions. Our beastly enemies that overwhelm us are the thoughts of our minds. By our proper actions, we draw so much light within that our thoughts will be stilled, and we will be able to commune with the Divine. This is why in Yesha'yahu it says that one day the lion will eat straw like cattle (Yesha'yahu 11:7). When everyone is acting in harmony, the lions will not attack humans, because we are not creating evil actions. As taught by our sages, the dangerous beasts only prey on humans because of their sins (Talmud Bav'li, Shabbat 33a).

Rabbi Uri of Strelisk (eighteenth century) was traveling by coach with several of his disciples when suddenly the horses came to an abrupt halt, and the driver spotted a huge bear charging angrily toward them. Rabbi Uri stepped calmly out of the coach and walked straight toward the charging bear, staring into her eyes as he walked. The bear slowed down, stopped, stared back for a while, and then walked off into the woods. When the disciples cheered the rabbi and proclaimed the incident a miracle, Rabbi Uri said to them: "It is no miracle. Rather, anyone who walks the walk of balance and harmony has no cause to fear otherwise dangerous animals."

The same applies to tragedy in general, that living disharmoniously breeds tragedy and discontent (Talmud Bav'li, Avot D'Rebbe Natan 38:1, and on). In the words of the sixteenth-century kabbalistic master Rabbi Yehudah Loew of Prague:

> For God created everything in a perfect arrangement, and tragedy is outside of that perfect arrangement. Thus, when there is sin, which is out of harmony with the perfection of the arrangement of the order of the universe, there is tragedy, which, too, is outside the arrangement of the order of the universe.
>
> (Sifrei HaMaHaRaL, Derech Chaim, Chap. 5, folio 241)

The fourth set of curses are about plagues. If enough people play out negativity, they create plagues of consciousness, and eventually literal physical plagues as well. The fifth set of curses is holocaust. The root of the twentieth-century Holocaust is hatred. To avoid such a plague or a holocaust, we must go to the source of the problem, which is our individual and national consciousness, and correct it, or do a tikkun. We must remember this causal root of tragedy and choose the way of blessings to prevent it from happening again.

Then we will have learned something valuable and will no longer abide in victim consciousness. We must return to the Torah Way to prevent a holocaust from happening again.

These things are ultimately for our spiritual benefit, and while they are at times very uncomfortable, they will, oddly enough, still not necessarily succeed in getting our attention, unless we are ready to recognize their inherent gift. These are important teachings to consider. God says "If you walk in my statutes …," meaning that we need to engrave on our hearts God's words so that our actions are guided by those words. In our every action we have the opportunity to choose the "blessings" and become beings of light, as well as the light unto the nations that we were meant to be. The warnings of the curses, we have seen, are a wake-up call. They awaken us out of our stupors and encourage us by "divine behavior modification" to follow the Great Way of the Torah, which is ultimately a much easier way to live.

We have a promise from God that if we walk in the ways of the Torah, we will have abundance, peace, tranquility, and ultimately liberation, as oneness with God and as the "image of God." This is what we are offered. So, what keeps us from accepting this way? It is the ever-distracting power of Satan. The power of Satan in our lives is the ego, and it is the main reason we do not follow the Great Torah Way. This is humanity's greatest weakness. We are exceedingly susceptible to the egocentric sense of separation. From a symptomatic perspective, ego is the cause of our inability to discern our divine purpose in life from our egocentric expression. Satan is always trying to get us to build up our ego and ignore the Way of the Torah. Satan loves holocausts. The ego says "more is better." This is the problem with money, power, sexual domination, and supremacy over others, the very wrongs that Sh'mittah and Yovel are intended to prevent. From a nondual kabbalistic way of understanding, Satan is an expression of God's will, divinely assigned to challenge us with temptation, so that we can have the choice and opportunity to overcome temptation, and thereby build character and evolve spiritually.

Ultimately, all the harsh consequences described in this parashah result from forgetting our purpose for being on the planet, which is deveikut/chey'rut. That is our only purpose. What complicates this is that we are given an ego with which to operate in the world and to fulfill our divine purpose. But the fulfillment of our divine purpose is not as important as passing the spiritual tests involved in simply living in the world. It is therefore important that we understand all of our life circumstances as spiritual tests that will either elevate us or bring us down. According to how we respond to these life circumstances, we will either become spiritually empowered and draw closer to the Divine, or spiritually weakened and distanced from the Divine.

With this understanding in mind, we return to the importance of personal responsibility. When enough people in a nation make the right kinds of choices that elevate their spirit and increase light, then they indeed become "a light to the nations." On the other hand, when we identify with the ego, instead of realizing that it is merely a means in the world, not an end in itself, problems arise. If you were given a car to act as your transportation vehicle, it would be silly to identify with the car as who you are. Yet this happens all the time in the world. Your car becomes your status symbol. It becomes an object of pride and obviously ego. In the same way, people become confused about money. Some say it is the root of evil, which it certainly could be. Money, in a spiritual way, however, is an energetic currency, but it is certainly not the highest energetic currency. The highest life force currency is the nefesh, as explained in Bereisheet. Money is an extension of ego. It can be used to uplift or to create downfall.

Our entrapment in ego may progress first as the expression of God through our identification with I Am-ness, then to "I think, therefore I am," and finally to "I have, therefore I am." By the time we have arrived at the place of "I have, therefore I am," the ego has completely taken over. It is the greatest degeneration of our true nature. This is the primary egocentric confusion. Money, as energy, may be a supportive vehicle for our spiritual tasks, but gathering money and power usually gets confused as the primary purpose, rather than as a supportive energy for helping us to fulfill our main task, to know God. As we recite in our daily prayers, "Blessing source are you, Adonai our God, sovereign of the universe, who provides for me what it is I need" (Talmud Bav'li, Berachot 60b). Our secondary task is to elevate ourselves spiritually by how we fulfill our spiritual mission in the world. The second-century rabbi, Ben

Zoma, taught that "the truly wealthy person is the one who is satisfied with what he or she has" (Mishnah, Avot 4:1).

How do we reverse the egocentric, satanic, self-destructive process that obstructs our path to the Torah Way? We do this through the act of teshuva. Teshuva means to return, to go back, to acknowledge the source of the imbalance in our lives and make corrections. Through this action, we become transformed and are less likely to repeat our mistakes. We are given the lesson of teshuva at the end of this parashah, the finale of the book of VayYiKra. Teshuva, after all, is what brings us freedom. We are then free to move toward creating more light in our lives. We are free from the slavery of the ego. We begin our return to the Divine. Teshuva is the great gift that allows us to become light beings and to rise above our ideas, feelings, thoughts, passions, and opinions, which lead us away from God. Teshuva returns us to a state of bitul (emptiness), in which we become one with God. In Bechuko-thai we learn that, when we submit to the yetzer hara (the dark forces without and within), we bring on ourselves sickness, poverty, and death. VayYiKra 15:31 offers us an alternative option, "that their impurity not cause them to die." In other words, we have the option to turn things around if we are sincere and exert effort to discover the source of our ego imbalances and choose to destroy this inner enemy.

As the last parashah in VayYiKra, Bechuko-thai is about how to live in shalom and shalem within ourselves and the world in a way that creates tikkun ha'nefesh and tikkun ha'olam. The model of the kohain gadol is the path that we all would do well to take. It is the path of holiness that aligns us with the way of the Torah, which brings positive results to our actions. The divine promise of VayYiKra 26:3, 4, and 14 is summarized: "If you follow my law I will give you rain and abundance ... but if you don't follow the Torah Way, I will give you misery." We have a choice. Hillel the Elder (first century BCE) said, "If I am not for myself who will be for me" (Mishnah, Avot 1:14). This means that if we do not take responsibility for our actions and instead blame others (if we do not acknowledge our choices to move toward or away from God and choose rather to make excuses and to rationalize our actions), we will continue to remain ignorant and project out into the world what is happening within us. We cannot blame our environment, our culture, our humanity, our astrology, or our genetics.

Many people today are talking about the great calamities looming ahead. These calamities are a projection from our own inner calamities. It is best to look at and destroy the causes of the inner calamities. The second-century kabbalah master Rabbi Shimon bar Yochai put it this way: "More severe are the calamities that befall one's inner personal life than the calamities predicted in the prophecies regarding Armageddon" (Talmud Bav'li, Berachot 7b). It is our egocentric imbalances that need to be resolved within us. This purification, if done internally, does not necessarily have to happen externally. When the outer calamity is avoided, the inner calamity will have kedusha.

Excuses are partial truths, but ultimately we have the power of good and evil in our lives, and we have the power to choose the way of holiness. "If you walk in my ways," said God (which means acting responsibly in every moment and owning our actions), "then your life and your land will dance in the great peace of liberation, of deveikut, of God-merging."

May every person in this world dance in peace and holiness and enjoy noncausal joy, noncausal bliss, noncausal contentment, noncausal peace, noncausal compassion, and the oneness of the Divine.

Amen

The
Book
of
BeMidbar

BeMidbar

Tʜɪs parashah very profoundly captures the essence of spiritual life. It is the key to understanding the book of BeMidbar, because we are speaking of the desert, which is what the word bemidbar means. The parashah begins in a very powerful way: "God spoke to Moses in the Sinai Desert" (BeMidbar Sinay). The wilderness has different meanings. One of the most powerful meanings is the silence—in essence, the emptiness. Unless one can make oneself hefker (הפקר), open and ownerless like a wilderness, it is very difficult to imbibe the deeper wisdom of the Torah (Midrash Pesik'ta D'Rav Kahana 12:20). The desert implies an empty mind, and where there is emptiness, we are most available to experience deveikut. When there is true emptiness, all of creation and all of God's presence can be experienced. The emptiness is present all the time, but the silence is only experienced when we decrease the noise of the mind (Talmud Bav'li, Chagigah 13b). In other words, to know the Divine, we must be like the wilderness … completely open, empty, and ownerless. To understand it on that level is to have particular appreciation for the opening statement of this parashah. When there is ego, we have preconceptions that block the mind. The ego then owns the mind. So, to optimize the receptiveness of the vehicle of the word of God to the will of God, we have to be like the wilderness … open, empty, and egoless. To be in this consciousness we have to be in humility, surrender, and a place of inner peace. That is the state that Moshe was in. So, the wilderness is not only a physical location like Sinai, but the wilderness is a state of mind. That is the deepest message of BeMidbar.

It is said that Mount Sinai was picked because it was the most humble of mountains (Midrash Bamidbar Rabbah 13:3). Moshe received the Torah from Sinai—why not one of the large mountains, such as Everest? Because Sinai was like a little hill compared to its neighboring mountains; to give the Torah there emphasizes the value of humility. Humility is a prerequisite to accessing the awareness of chey'rut (liberation) and the deep Torah understanding. Mount Sinai and the Desert of Sinai both represent humility, nothingness, surrender, the emptiness of the mind, and, therefore, the best place to acquire true humility. Associated with true humility is hishta'vut, which is equal vision. Equal vision is seeing God in all things equally, wherein one is neither above nor below the other.

The desert has other important meanings. In the Sinai, the Hebrews were leaving captivity and mental slavery, and had to empty their minds of all the conscious and unconscious habits of slavery. The heaviest slavery was the slavery of the ego—the desire to receive exclusively for self, alone. In the process of slavery Am Yisrael had become covered by k'lipot (קליפות), the ego shells that block us from experiencing the light of the Divine, always emanating from within us. Going into the desert (of the self) means to be removed from the ego of receiving for self, alone. It means opening to experiencing the oneness of who we really are. The advantage of slavery is that we do not have to take responsibility for our lives (which, in reality, is a large spiritual disadvantage). We are the victims of slavery, and therefore create a mindset of "What do I have to do with this or that? It's not my fault!" The symbolism of the desert means we have to take responsibility for who we are. We have to leave the slavery of blaming other people. We are accountable. It is in that accountability that we are able to bring shalem, or completeness, and kedusha, or holiness, to the world. The process of throwing off the thought forms of slavery, which do indeed separate us from Hashem, is called teshuva. It is teshuva that allows us to return to God awareness. Entering the desert in humility, in openness, with, in essence, the "beginner's mind," we are able to connect to the complete divine presence within ourselves, and everything is able to turn and return to the divine sanctity of the way life is meant to be.

Interestingly, the word bemidbar (במדבר—"in the desert") has the same gematria, or numerical value, 248, as the name of our ancestor Avraham (אברהם). The Torah gives us the tools to begin to become aware of the light within, and gifts us with 248 positive instructions ("Thou Shalts"). Avraham was, and is, the chariot for the sephirah of chesed, which expresses his kindness, sharing, and mercy. The acts of kindness, sharing, and mercy help open us up to the light within, and burn off the k'lipot of receiving for self, alone. Avraham is the essence of receiving in order to share, and he is the essence of chesed. The metaphor of Avraham's tent being open in all four directions is a metaphor of how the mind has to be open to receive from any direction with no preconceptions, as these create resistance to life's gifts.

In the process of bemidbar, we moved from the egocentric consciousness of the Egyptian enslavement, which was to receive for self, alone, to the kedusha approach of receiving in order to share, which was Avraham's essence. Sharing is not always comfortable, however. The story of ninety-nine-year-old Avraham sitting in front of his tent on a blazing hot day makes this point. It was the third day following his ritual circumcision, which is often the most painful and most uncomfortable period, especially for an adult. He then had a revelation of the Divine, and he saw three strangers approaching. He did not necessarily know they were angels, but he saw the three strangers and came out of his divine revelation, because hosting strangers is more important than even divine revelation! In sharing, you, in a sense, mimic the ancient Talmudic teaching that we are to behave like God, who always shares and cares and tends to the needs of creation (Talmud Bav'li, Sotah 14a). In that way, we are always sharing. So Avraham was living in this consciousness of "receiving in order to share." Now Avraham was not comfortable, but nevertheless, leaving the revelation of the Divine, beyond body and mind, and receiving these three strangers, on the third day following his circumcision, was indeed moving out of the comfort zone. Sharing beyond our comfort zones tests how serious we are about sharing. The more we desire to give, the kavanah, or intention, of giving, even if it is uncomfortable, deeply activates our inner light.

The Torah was not given within the boundaries of the land of Am Yisrael. The Torah was given in the desert because there are no boundaries there. It is open to all. This teaches us that everyone has a right to the teachings of the Torah (Midrash Tanchuma, Vayak'hel, Chap. 8). It also implies that everyone is welcome to connect with the Torah because it is not a specified possession of only Israel. In the tradition of Am Yisrael, those seeking inner revelations, like the Essenes, the Rishonim, the desert fathers, and the ancient kabbalists, would retreat into the desert. Kabbalists loved going into the abandoned desert. In a place where there was nothing, they could feel they had nothing. They would also go to the desert because it was there they felt Satan was the strongest. Therefore, this was the place to build one's personal altar, to bring light to places where there was none. In the emptiness of the desert, bemidbar, we have the opportunity to bring the greatest light and to burn up the forces of negativity. So the kabbalists used to meditate in the desert to destroy the forces of Satan in his own territory, and to confront Satan where he was the strongest.

In truth we are talking about the desert of our own k'lipot. There a tremendous amount of spiritual growth takes place. There great transformation takes place, because there we face and transform the k'lipot into mirrors of light.

In this parashah, YHWH tells Moshe to count the people. Now, God knows how many people there are. So what is the meaning of the directive to "count the people" (BeMidbar 1:2)? Each person who was counted was accountable, but also each was given the light that he or she needed to be accountable. The very first opening line here lays out the deeper spiritual meaning from the point of view of liberation: our minds must become as the desert—empty, humble, in hishta'vut, and open to all, that is, with no resistance to life in any way. In the life of the desert we are encouraged to maintain the mitzvot, the Torah way of life, and build our light body, our light sanctuary (our inner mikdash) in the very face of Satan, demonstrating that the power of light is greater than the power of darkness. The more light we create, the more we become the frequency of the Divine.

The desert is also about purification. It is no wonder we call it *negev* (נגב), Hebrew for cleansing, for wiping the slate clean. As we purify on the physical, emotional, mental, and spiritual levels, the light body within us, which is always there, becomes activated and enhanced. The more light there is, the deeper the connection we have with the Divine. From the light body, the door to the divine presence opens up, and we are able enter deeply into the truth of who we, and be open to the experience of deveikut, which is always there waiting for us to receive it and to become it.

The minute Moshe counted the people, they moved out of the thought forms of slavery, because every individual counted, every individual had meaning, and all people, through their distinct way of life, had the opportunity to increase their light and to increase both the personal and collective light body. In essence, everybody received a blessing because counting is a way of measuring the life force. The point of counting, when people live the spiritual life outlined in the Torah, is the generation of increased light, which, in turn, increases the light force. The innate characteristic of light is to remove chaos.

As we develop the light through our experience of the desert mind, the bemidbar mind, we are able to create more light and thus diminish the chaos. This is, of course, the principle of prayer, which is to become our prayer (l'hitpallel—להתפלל). In l'hitpallel, there is emptiness in the act of being the prayer. This takes us back to bitul hayesh (ביטול היש), which, again, is about experiencing our emptiness. This is the meaning of the desert; this was the deep enlightenment teaching of the Ba'al Shem Tov as well. As we read in the book of Iyyov (Job), "But where shall wisdom be found?" (Iyyov 28:12). When we understand that we are nothing, then all of the Divine can enter into us; this is the bemidbar experience. It is essential, not only to the liberation process, but in the truth of the state of deveikut/chey'rut as well, because it allows the mind to remain quiet so that we feel our emptiness at all times.

We are hollow vessels that allow us to be simply at one with the Divine in every moment. As we look at bitul hayesh, the nothingness, as well as the quote from Job, we see that basically an empty mind is fundamental to the enlightenment process, in which nothing is moving except the emptiness of the Divine within. This is the essence. In the silence of Moshe's liberated mind, he was able to receive the Torah. By his own admittance, he was not a man of words (Shemot 4:10). We too must have the consciousness of bemidbar to engage in a deeper deveikut/chey'rut process.

The Levites were not counted along with everyone else, because they were seen as having their own unique relationship with God, one that was slightly different from the rest of the Israelites who had to be counted. This takes us to another understanding of the depth of parashah BeMidbar. All the Israelites, except the Levites, were counted from the age of twenty and older who were fit for service (BeMidbar 1:3). The Levites, however, were counted from the age of one month (BeMidbar 3:15). This was because the Levites were specifically elected as servants of God. They represented the firstborn sacrifice that God demanded (Shemot 13:15; BeMidbar 3:12), and their lives were consecrated to God from the minute of their survival as newborns. (In the Jewish tradition, survival of a newborn is affirmed after one month of post-natal age. During the first month there's some question as to whether the baby is going to survive, and after one month, there is a sense that, yes, the child has made it onto the planet.)

The Levites were numbered according to their families from the age of one month on, and the rest of the tribes were numbered by twenty and up, as that was the age for going off to war. This was a message to the nation of Israel that we exist as both body and soul. The soul aspect is from the very beginning, and the general metaphor for this is the Levite. We also have a body that we must care for and grow into. The metaphor for the body is the warrior, our ability to do battle in this complicated world, to strive against all obstacles to know God, and to work through our ego complexes, our k'lipot. The body is also our vehicle for serving God in the world. When used properly, in this context, the body and the body-mind complex become vehicles for drawing closer and closer to the Divine. If used improperly, the body becomes a vehicle for separating ourselves from God. The Levite tribe is then a metaphor for the soul aspect that guides the body of Am Yisrael.

How the Levites were chosen to carry the energy of the firstborn and became the sanctified ones needs to be clarified. While a few of the firstborn of Israel participated in the Golden Calf disaster, none of the Levites did. The Levites were substituted as the exclusive firstborn of Israel offering to Hashem and were thus sanctified. Before the time of the Golden Calf, all the firstborn sons of Israel were considered kohan'im (priests). But after the Golden Calf, according to midrashic teachings, the angel of death, or negativity touched everyone. Only the Levites, who did not participate in the sin of the Golden Calf, remained as the firstborn offering (Midrash Shemot Rabbah 31:8).

We all have, in a sense, the potential to be Levites, but we get caught up with golden calves in our lives, and we lose that privilege. Even though the Levites were elevated, they still needed the blessing of the light, because no matter how high we are, we still need that connection. The Levites numbered 22,000 and all the firstborn of Israel numbered 22,273. The 273 extra were redeemed with a five-shekel offering. If we do not hold the energy spiritually, we will get replaced by those who do. We are either going deeper on the spiritual path or going backward.

The Levites took on the role of the soul of Am Yisrael. The nation of Israel survives on the strengths of two aspects: the soul and the body. A nation must have an infrastructure, an economic structure, and a political system, and it must be able to defend itself. But that is not enough. Throughout history many nations have come and gone (for example, the Babylonians, Egyptians, Romans, and Greeks); they did not have the spiritual strength connected to God. The blessing of Israel is *Am Yisrael chai* (עָם יִשְׂרָאֵל חַי—the Jewish people will live forever). It is all based on this one thing! "You will be a kingdom of priests and a holy nation to me" (Shemot 19:6). This is the message of both this parashah and the entire book of BeMidbar. Although we cannot say that this is happening today in Israel, we may still maintain that the roles of other nations are not the same as that of Israel, because according to our shamanic roots, we are "God's chosen people," elected to bring light to the nations. We are to be a model for the world, in combining the task of a king (the secular world) with that of a priest. That is why it says "A kingdom of priests and a holy nation." To live up to this calling is, of course, very difficult and challenging. Yet Israel must succeed at this in order to manifest her ultimate national destiny and fulfill her reason for existing and surviving all these thousands of years in spite of global attempts to destroy her. All those who tried to destroy Israel have vanished into the pages of history books. Israel's window of opportunity to become what she was meant to be is right now. Israel needs to hold the light also in relationship to the Palestinians, to the Arab world, and to the whole world. This is a time of severe testing for Israel.

We have to appreciate that Judaism is not only a religion and a complete path to deveikut/chey'rut, but it is the basis of the nation of Israel as well. Today, many in Israel do not understand the Torah as the expression of Hashem, as the basis of the soul, and the true banner and purpose of Israel. The only other time that this has ever happened successfully, that a nation's soul energy has become an explicitly national energy (aside from Kings David and Solomon), was when King Ashok brought Buddhism into India, and his reign brought a Golden Age to India. This could be the destiny of Israel too. So, the body, which is all the Israeli people, except for the Levites, is the national vitality. All of Israel must be imbued with kedusha, holiness, whether it is in prayer or deciding foreign policy. This is a very deep and very difficult thing. Just as we exist as body and soul individually, so does our national collective exist as body and soul. The body is the political side and the soul is the spiritual side. The Levites did not go to war; that was not their task. Their task was to hold the spiritual energy and to contribute to the spiritual side of Am

Yisrael. One of Israel's roles, as a nation, is to fuse these two in complex, difficult, and dark inner and outer worlds.

Another teaching of this parashah involves the four camps in the desert. There were four camps of the Israelites, and four camps of the Levites organized around the Ark. The particular way that these camps were structured helped the people to rise above the forces of nature, because the four camps represent the four elements—air, earth, water, and fire—and each camp had a flag to help overcome the potential negativity of each of those forces. These forces are also known as the *ar'ba ruchot* (ארבע רוחות—the four winds, or spirits), and are described as the energies of the four directions. They each had attributes, colors, and animals to go with them. In the north is *tsafon* (צפון), meaning "the place of concealment." North is also considered kabbalistically a place where Satan can penetrate us; it can be a place of judgment through which Satan may entrap us if we are not paying attention (Zohar, Vol. 3, folio 250a). We do the best we can by walking the steady four-legged path of the ox or bull, the animal of the north, which is also that of a full human being, a mensch, performing the mitzvot and living according to the Torah Way. The steadiness of the ox helps to protect us from the inner tendencies of Satan manifesting as egocentric energies. The color associated with the north is red, and the associated angel is Gavriel, the power of the name of and word of Hashem. In the west is *ma'arav* (מערב), meaning "from the place of blending" and "the place of sunset." The color is black and the animal is the human. The west is about "lack" in a certain way, or darkness, which stimulates the bringing forth of the light, and about healing on all different levels. The angel associated with the west is Rafael. In the South is negev (נגב), meaning "place of cleansing," or *da'rom* (דרום), meaning "place of rising." The animal is the lion, and the color is white. It is also the place of compassion and leadership. Michael is the angel. Finally, in the east is *miz'rach* (מזרח), meaning "from the place of shining"; another term for the east is kehdem, meaning "the place of beginning." That is represented by the color yellow, for the place of shining. The animal is the eagle, which flies so high with an inspired overview to see that the sun never sets or rises and that there is no death for the soul. The angel of the east is Uriel (Zohar, Vol. 3, folio 154b).

Each camp also had a specific way in which the tribes were organized. The camp in the east, *rachamim*, had to do with grace, and with the tribes of Yehuda (kingship), Yissachar (Torah), and Zevulun (wealth). Rachamim also had to do with three of the months: Nissan (Aries), Iyar (Taurus), and Sivan (Gemini). The east represented the yod (י) of the Tetragrammaton, and the season of spring. The second camp, in the south, represented the energy of chesed, or mercy. It was represented by the tribes of Reuven (teshuva—cleansing), Shimon (honor that comes from cleansing), and Gad (strength). They, in turn, were associated with Tammuz (Cancer), Av (Leo), and Elul (Virgo). It was the first hey (ה) of the Tetragrammaton and represented the season of summer. The third camp was the west. It represented malchut, the physical world. The corresponding tribes were Ephraim and Menashe (considered half tribes); Ephraim represented hot and cold, and Menashe symbolized snow. The third tribe in the west was Benyamin, representing the shekhinah. The associated months were Tishrei (Libra), Cheshvan (Scorpio), and Kislev (Sagittarius). This camp represented the vav (ו) of the Tetragrammaton and the season of fall. Rafael is the angel, representing the earth element. The fourth camp was the north. It represented *din*, or judgment. The tribes were Dan (darkness), Asher (light), and Naphtali (blessing). The associated months were Tevet (Capricorn), Shevat (Aquarius), and Adar (Pisces). It was the final hey (ה) in the Tetragrammaton, and represented winter.

A useful teaching we derive from all this is expressed in Kohelet (Ecclesiastes) 3:1: "To everything there is a season, and a time to every purpose under the heaven." Everything is organized in a cosmic design. These archetypical energies are there to help us work through a full yearly cycle in all directions and through all the seasons, and by way of all the astrological signs. This kind of spiritual work involves mastering as part of our unfolding. As we face all these tendencies in the cosmic circle, we must be willing to not only look at the light that we have, but also to do teshuva, which is in the south; but it is really for the whole circle. This requires our willingness to face all those elements within ourselves as part of the enlightenment process, so that we are the spiritual Torah warriors who can face and liberate all the k'lipot within ourselves.

In BeMidbar, we see how Hashem has arranged all these interactive forces as a cosmic design. It helps us understand how we are influenced by and can move with these seasons and these times for doing what we are doing. The key tribe representing the east is the tribe of Yehuda. That is where the sun comes up, where the light comes from, and so, it is, in a sense, the source of positive traits that help us open up to the light. The south is the place of the quietness, the bemidbar, where everything is manifested after we have done our work. The sun sets in the west, a place where we must look at our darkness and at the healing that is to be done. That is perhaps why the angel of the west is Rafael, the keeper of healing, since when we make the breakthrough in the place of the west, we have the most powerful teshuva, and transformation, taking place, because the light emerges from out of the dark places (Zohar, Vol. 3, folio 47b).

In the north is the place of concealment. The Levites in this constellation formed the inner circle of the four directions. Their role was the bridge between the upper and lower worlds. The kohan'im were the priests; they were at the upper levels of this. They were in the east. In the inner circle were three families from the tribe of Levi: Kehath, Gershon, and Merari, and they each had different roles. The family of Kehath was the most elevated of the Levites. They took care of the Ark and the physical tools of the Tabernacle, and they had the job of healing and of touching the Ark when it had to be moved. They had this job because it is said they cared the most (Midrash Bamidbar Rabbah 5:1). It matters not how bright we are nor how much we know, but how much we care and our kavanah. So, Kehath was a prime example of this.

The three families of Levites each had a directional placement. The Kehath family was in the south, the Gershonites were to the west, the family of Merari was to the north, and Moshe, Aharon, and the kohan'im were in the east. They formed a circle within a circle. One interpretation of this formation is that everyone has a role, just as every tribe and every Levite family had a role to play. The message here is not to be someone else, but to live your role. In living our role, we have the best way to heal ourselves of our k'lipot and manifest the full light of who we are. The power of bemidbar, the emptiness of the mind, the humility and surrender of the desert of the wilderness, best empowers us to do this.

There is an additional pattern to why Israel has been able to outlast the four beasts that have tried to dominate Am Yisrael—the Babylonian, the Persian, the Greek, and the Roman beast (which morphed into the Holy Roman Empire, or the Church)—and what some people now include as the Muslim world. The Christian and Muslim world are the feet and toes of a mix of iron and clay of Nebuchadnezzar's dream vision described in the Book of Daniel (2:34). Am Yisrael is nurtured by the elixir of life of the living Torah, and has a divine mission. It is hard to talk about this, but when you look at the destiny, and you look at the assignment, they are the firstborn. There is a certain advantage as a firstborn, and maybe that has to do with a certain everlastingness. At the very core of the collective soul of Israel is divinity. When we understand this, we have the principle of "Am Yisrael chai," that the people of Israel will last forever. This seems illogical, and certainly people have attempted to eliminate Am Yisrael, all the way through the Hitler era and certainly the stated public intention of some of the Persian, Muslim, and Arab leaders today. But all these empires have collapsed—the Egyptian, Babylonian, Persian, Greek, Roman, and Nazi. Somehow, no matter how small its population, Am Yisrael has survived. Why this survival against all reasonable odds? Because, as it says in Shemot 19:6, "You will be a kingdom of priests and a holy nation to me." And what we see here is the combination of the priesthood (symbolic of the soul), represented by the Levites, and the holiness of Am Yisrael (the body). Its job was, and is, to connect with the Divine.

The Torah is teaching something that needs to be listened to at a deep level and followed in the State of Israel. We must elevate the consciousness of national affairs to be a revelation of the Divine, inspired by the energy in the Beit HaMikdash, and in that way, the task of the king and that of the priest become as one synergy of not only Am Yisrael, but the whole world. The statement "You shall be for me a kingdom of priests and a holy nation" is not really about two separate things. The role of the priests and the people focusing on the Torah is to bring everyone into the vibration of the highest level of Torah wisdom. This in turn would bring us back into the desert consciousness of the Torah Way that is ultimately meant for everyone and communicated in a way so that we can culturally assimilate the core teachings.

The wisdom of the Torah is bitul hayesh, to be completely empty so we are always experiencing the revelation of the Divine in every instant of our physical, emotional, mental, and soul experience. That is the deeper meaning of "a kingdom of priests and a holy nation"; it is to be a nation that truly understands not only its oneness with each other, but also its oneness with all people. When that oneness happens in consciousness, then we have the meaning of true peace. True peace is not a negotiated peace. In true peace, there is only the One; there is no duality and we are experiencing the oneness of our human connection and the oneness of the Divine and all of creation. It is the dispassionate-passionate hishta'vut of equanimity in every moment. It is, in a sense, shiviti Hashem le'neg'dee ta'mid, which is the great teaching in Tehillim 16:8: "I have set the Lord always before me." It is the experience of hishta'vut, equanimity, that no matter what happens, it is beyond praise or blame; it is all the same, for we then experience God in all things because we are coming from the place of emptiness, from the bemidbar, where there are no preconceptions of how it is supposed to be. It teaches us that God is everywhere, that whatever God does is for the best, and that everything God does is a teaching for us. It is from the emptiness that we are then able to be living in complete emunah (faith) and yechudim (unifications), merging with the light in every situation. It is this profound way of life that brings us to apperceiving the teaching and inner experience of Vayikra 19:18: "You must love your neighbor as [you love] yourself. I am God." This is the natural consequence of living the Torah Way.

Shiviti means "equal to me," because I realize that God is before me at all times and that brings me to the way of life of yechudim. For this we need to live the essence of bemidbar. We need an empty mind to be in the place of shiviti Hashem le'neg'dee ta'mid (keep the name of Hashem in front of you always).

The Torah Way is the balance between self-effort and grace. We cannot technique ourselves to God. We cannot create formulas and hope that they will make us enlightened. We cannot simply follow mitzvot and know Hashem. Rather, we can only arrive at these experiences through the Torah Way of alignment with the forces of nature and alignment with the physical and spiritual laws. This is another level of what BeMidbar is about. We must be empty to surrender to the divine unfolding within us and to the Divine as it expresses outside of us. We then become naturally aligned with the Divine as it unfolds for who we are, individually and collectively. In this way we prepare ourselves to be a vehicle for receiving grace. Grace in the kabbalah is associated with *Ey'ma Ila'ah*, the great grandmother (Tikunai Zohar, folio 120a). The mysterious grace of Ey'ma Ila'ah is needed for deveikut/chey'rut. It is the shift that comes from grace that allows us to be in that permanent awareness of oneness with God. To be bemidbar as the empty mind, humility, and surrender, creates the conditions that allow us to awaken beyond the mind into the place of oneness. This is the deep secret of bemidbar! It is the pathless path to enlightenment.

May we be blessed that we find the truth and light of Hashem within ourselves so that we can follow it, and draw the grace that allows us the permanent awareness of deveikut/chey'rut. May everyone be blessed with a direct experience of bitul hayesh and the continual awareness of shiviti Hashem le'neg'dee ta'mid, and may we see and appreciate the joy and beauty of the Divine in all things, including ourselves.

Amen

Naso

NASO, a verb for the action of carrying or raising up, refers to the purpose of the Torah and of the work of the kohan'im, to raise up the people. The time of Naso usually falls just before, or sometimes just after, the festival of Shavuot, which commemorates the historical receiving of the Torah on Mount Sinai. In a sense, Shavuot celebrates the marriage ceremony that then took place between the people and the Divine, with the Torah being the ketuba, or ritual marriage contract. There is a certain power that connects us with this energy of Shavuot that we can draw on for the whole year. It has to do with the power of Torah study at the deepest level, which goes significantly beyond the current traditional scholarly study of the Torah.

An interesting story about the Maggid of Mezerich makes this point clear. His wife always wanted him to meet the Ba'al Shem Tov. The Maggid did not really feel that was necessary because he felt he knew everything. (The Maggid had read every spiritual book there was.) But his wise wife prevailed, and he went to meet him. It took him a month of walking in the snow, and when he finally met the Ba'al Shem Tov, the first thing the Ba'al Shem Tov did was share with him a story that seemed very trivial. The Maggid could not understand why he was being told this story. The next day, the same thing happened. The Ba'al Shem Tov told him something light and seemingly mundane. At that point, the Maggid, convinced his wife was wrong, was about to take his leave, but then decided to first share his disappointment with the Ba'al Shem Tov. The Ba'al Shem Tov listened, and then asked him to read and explain a portion of the Torah. When the Maggid was finished, the Ba'al Shem Tov explained the same portion, but every time he pronounced the name of an angel, the angel manifested. He spoke the name "Michael," and Michael appeared. He mentioned the name "Uriel," and Uriel appeared. And so it continued, on and on. The Maggid then understood that although one can have the knowledge and scholarly explanations of all the books, it is not the same as knowing the truth.

Faith in the existence of God is the underlying message of the entire Torah. Complete certainty that the light of the Torah, as God, is within us and everywhere in creation is the foundation of Torah study on the deeper levels. The Torah and the kabbalistic teachings make it clear that: (1) there is only God, (2) that God is singular, (3) that all of creation is rooted in God, and (4) that the duality we experience is an illusion of alma d'peruda. There is no reality outside of the existence of God.

This brings us to a Torah understanding and lifestyle that includes several fundamental teachings:

- Free will is an illusion, as all that exists is divine providence, down to the most minute detailed happening in the world of creation.
- Whatever happens (or whatever God does) is for the best.
- Everything is holy and radiates as God everywhere; it makes no difference whether we pray in a temple, the beach, or a field of grasses, or whether we consider something positive or negative, holy or unholy.
- All worldly activities, while living in an awareness of deveikut, become equal to Torah study, mitzvot, prayer, and meditation.
- Every spoken word or thought is a message from God if properly reflected on; ultimately, there is no difference between the words of the Torah and an "idle comment" on the street.
- All actions by people toward you or around you are a message from God.
- All world events and activities are made possible by God.

These radical teachings are among the more esoteric and ancient Torah teachings more recently re-emphasized by the Ba'al Shem Tov; he stated in Tzava'at Harivash that meditation is seven times stronger than Torah study. These are also the teachings of liberation as I experience them in this and other traditions. These seven points reflect one key attitude and understanding that enhances spiritual life: living in intense, awe-filled deveikut (a God-merged state) in every moment, at all times. Repeating the name of God with each breath (even when asleep, meditating, or praying), seeing all creation as the living Torah of God expressed in every moment, and classical Torah study are all prerequisites that help to access this God-merged awareness of deveikut. Deveikut is, then, the constant remembrance of God in every moment.

For most people, deveikut happens over time as an ever increasing, repeated experience of Ruach HaKodesh (רוח הקודש), gifting them with an internal ecstasy in a particular moment. Having this experience occasionally like an artist or musician, or in a moment of inspired scriptural reading or ecstatic dance, is an awakened momentary encounter with deveikut, but should not be mistaken for the unbroken awareness of full deveikut. In full deveikut, we become filled with noncausal love, awe, contentment, peace, ecstasy, oneness, and compassion. There is a constant awareness of the light of God in every moment, whether awake or asleep. We experience God in all possibilities. These are the inner qualities of full deveikut/chey'rut liberation. Another way of saying this is to jump into the fire of God in our own hearts, in the play of the shekhinah in creation, and in the source prior to the nothing of all creation. Start by staying close to the fire the best you can until you are consumed into the fire; at that point it does not take much effort and it is too difficult to not surrender.

Naso is the largest portion of the Torah, and therefore gives us even more energy and a greater connection to the divine as it uplifts us. One of the beautiful qualities about studying the Torah is that it is endless; there are always fresh new insights that shine forth. There is a nice story relating to the idea of study, learning, and being a continual student of the truth. A young man went off into the woods and lived in isolation for fourteen years studying the Torah. When he returned, he felt he completely comprehended it and did not require a master, or the like. However, his uncle insisted that he meet Reb Zusha. When he came to Reb Zusha, the elderly rabbi greeted the young man and declared, "Anyone who thinks of himself as 'I am he' will not see the true word of God." The young man immediately understood. Anyone who is filled with pride or ego cannot truly experience the light of the Divine. He then became a student of Reb Zusha. So, the real student of Torah never calls himself a kabbalist or a Torah scholar, but at best merely a student of Torah or a student of kabbalah. In this way, we are always open to the light coming through to us.

In the Zohar's discussion of Naso, it talks about a great gathering that occurred in the second century when Rabbi Shimon bar Yochai emerged from a cave radiant with light. What was that light? It was, in essence, the light of the absolute truth, the light of immortality, and the endless light of the divine presence. The reception of the Torah is not only a giving and a saying, but, in essence, also includes the reception of a teacher. Moshe received and taught the whole Torah, but most everyone received only the divine "commandments." At that point, before even receiving, the people were in such a state that they declared, na'aseh v'nishma (נעשה ונשמע—"we will do, and we will hear"). Still, there was only so much they could receive. This illustrates a very important point. In the vision of Yehezqel, for example, one of the most unique highlights of his vision is that it moved! Yehezqel's vision moved as a chariot of fire with the moving *chayot* (animal like—חיות) different faces. Metaphorically, this teaches us that God's presence does not settle in one place, but God's radiance emanates, filling the whole creation as God's poetry in motion. This was particularly important regarding Yehezqel's vision, because, in his time, the Jewish people were in captivity outside the land of Israel. Today we are still in spiritual captivity both outside and within Israel. It helps to be aware that God's radiance is coming from everywhere, wherever we are open to the radiance. That is the deep teaching in all the spiritual work, but particularly in the Torah. The Torah must be taken into our very essence—into our blood, flesh, and bone—raising our very vibration rate. That might be how we got the idea that there are 613 mitzvot in the Torah. We did not arrive at that number because we actually sat down and counted them. We came to that number because we knew that the Divine fills every bone and sinew in our bodies every day of the year. At that time, they felt there were 248 bones in the human body, and 365 days in the yearly cycle (totaling at 613).

The haftorah for the second day of Shavuot is a reading from Habakkuk 2:20 through 3:19. It opens with "But the Lord is in his holy temple: let all the earth keep silence before him." It is through silence that we create the space for the constant experience of God and for the great wisdom to come. When great wisdom continually comes to us, we are able to continually open up to the radiance. The key again is about teaching. We say that the giving of the Torah was not just a saying, but a spiritual, experiential teaching. Solomon's Shir Hashirim (5:6) says "My soul went out when he spoke." The Ba'al Shem

Tov explained that "Part of the soul of the speaker leaves at the time of speaking and goes into the students." Torah teachings from the heart are not just a speech coming from the speaker, but part of the essence of the soul of the teacher that is given out. This is why even though some of the energy is communicated via DVDs and books, it is most powerfully communicated in person, soul to soul. In that way, we understood that in the Ten Speakings, when it says "I am the Lord, your God," it does not say *ani* (אני), but rather *anochi* (אנכי)—"I, my soul" have written and given these words. Anochi is "I, my soul." God has written and given the soul of the Divine to be revealed through the Torah. And the final piece of this understanding is, as it says in the Psalms, "Let thy steadfast love be my comfort, according to thy word to thy servant" (Tehillim 119:76). "According to thy word to thy servant" is an interesting statement because usually God does not speak directly to people in the sense of words, but in the revelation at Sinai, every individual present felt that he or she was directly and personally spoken to. In the Psalms it also says: "I will lift up my eyes to the hills from whence comes my help. My help comes from the Lord, who made heaven and earth" (Tehillim 121:1). God created the heavens and earth out of nothing. Sometimes in our lives, it appears there is no escape from a daunting situation, and yet the Divine moves to save us from out of the nothing, from out of nowhere.

There is another lesson in all this, which offers an additional perspective on Torah study. It says in the Talmud (Avodah Zarah 2b) that God lifted Mount Sinai and held it over the people like a gigantic barrel about to be dropped. Now, they had already accepted the Torah, and said "I will do and I will hear." What else was needed? God said, if you accept the Torah, everything will be well; if not, there shall be your burial. On a gross level, it appears the people were being threatened, but the Zohar offers a different interpretation. It says "Israel camped opposite the mountain" in Shemot 19:2, and "the mountain" may refer to the patriarch Ya'akov (Zohar, Vol. 2, folio 69b). After all, the initial revelation to Moshe at Sinai opens with the words "This is what you must say to the family of Jacob" (Shemot 19:3). God then shadowed the people with the mountain because God had hollowed out the mountain. In other words, you need to accept the Torah in such a way that your ancestors do not remain out of reach like mountains above you, but so that they surround you everywhere like a barrel that you can reach out and touch. There is an energy and grace that the ancestors received, which, if honored, can be drawn unto ourselves. As it says in Devarim 4:37, "It was because He loved your fathers, and chose their children after them, that [God] Himself brought you out of Egypt with His great power." So, as we get in touch with the passion and actions of our ancestors and honor our lineage, we are able to draw that same energy to us. The Torah brings the energy of the ancestors into our lives as well.

Naso is the third and final account of the preparation of the Mishkan, or sanctuary, which later would turn into the Beit HaMikdash, the Holy Temple (literally, "the house of holiness"). The first description is in the book of Shemot, where God instructed the people "They shall make me a sanctuary, and I will dwell among them" (Shemot 25:8). The second encounter is in the book of Vayikra, having to do with the laws of the kohan'im, who would be administering the Mishkan. In Naso, the Mishkan was finally completed, and was being anointed by Moshe. After he had anointed and sanctified all the sacred vessels and implements, God then said to Moshe, "Let them present their offerings for the altar's dedication, one prince each day" (BeMidbar 7:11).

At this point, Naso gives us an additional clue to the ways and teachings of the Torah, communicated here through its account of the offerings that the twelve tribal princes brought to the altar. Now, it is interesting to play with the correlation of the offerings of the twelve tribal princes and modern astrology, because clearly the twelve tribes represent the twelve zodiac energies. A natal chart's rising sign is often considered the most important sign, and each tribe had a certain offering they had to make to clear any imbalances that might result. Depending on each sign, either the sun sign's or the rising sign's qualities inspire us to make a certain correction in ourselves that purifies us to be in the Temple. Aries, generally, can be considered to make the correction of letting go of ego, learning self-control, learning patience, and thinking and analyzing before acting. Taurus invokes the correction of facing our attachments to materialism, money, and physicality, and helps us to elevate the importance of flexibility, rather than stubbornness, as a way of creating comfort and ease in life. Gemini invokes the energy of developing certainty over doubt. Certainty is a most important part of the spiritual path, and doubt is the main undermining energy. Cancer teaches us to become less emotionally based, needy, and dependent in decision-making, helping us to move beyond code-pendent relationships to interdependent relationships. Leo is about making the correction of letting go of ego, and the ability to be humble. Virgo is an opportunity to let go of the tendency of excess judgment and criticism, and to look inward to our own actions rather than the actions of others. (Please understand that this not merely about sun signs. We are talking about certain tendencies of humans that are associated particularly with the rising sign, but may come with different combinations of the planets as they move through the constellations.) Libra invokes the need to find balance in life, to create harmony in the universe in ways that do not exhaust us by demanding too much. Scorpio helps us to face the issues of self-control, and to resist the ex-treme emotions of jealousy, negativity, and holding grudges. Sagittarius helps us to be open to channeling the light and avoid dependency on others to do the work for us. Dependency on others includes such maladies as addictions to drugs and gambling. Those with a Capricorn imbalance need to break out of the limitation of their five senses, and trust their intuition over simply rely-ing on a material, mechanistic way of being in the world. Those who have a tendency for an Aquarian imbalance need to look at their desire to break rules so they can reveal their light through their new ideas and revelations. Those with Piscean potential imbalances need to watch the tendency to go with the flow, get caught up in addictions, rather than go with the truth.

Although each tribe had an inner difference, their ceremonies at the altar were exactly the same and were repeated twelve times, for the twelve tribes, for twelve days. On the twelfth day, the dedication of the Mishkan was com-pleted. The princes, in their offering, were the final participants in the dedica-tion. This has deep implications because we usually think about the Temple as the domain of the kohan'im, or priests, but that was not the case. The Beit HaMikdash belonged to the entire nation. It did not belong only to the priests, any other elite group, or the monarchy; it belonged to the whole nation. So the Beit HaMikdash was not merely connected to the spiritual aspect of people, but was physically connected to the whole of Am Yisrael, to both the spiritual and physical aspects of the nation! This is interesting because when we look at Am Yisrael then and today it had and still has a secular and spiritual polarity. These aspects need to come together for the Mishkan to be complete. Only the singularity exists. All these divisions obscure the singularity of God. The Mishkan was fused with both a spiritual service and a political dimension. Later, in the Beit HaMikdash, they indeed had a Sanhedrin, as the high court. There were three courts: one at the entrance to the Temple Mount, one at the entrance to the Temple itself, and one in the office of the gate, underneath the Beit HaMikdash. Interestingly, the banks and the economic systems were also based at the Beit HaMikdash. Today we separate these, with banking being completely secular and disconnected from any moral or spiritual responsibility. (This may be why the worldwide banking system has become so corrupt and degenerate.) The banks were established on the grounds of the Beit HaMikdash, because the Temple was holy, and it was the center of the nation. The Beit HaMikdash, as the center of the nation, encompassed all that was in the nation, both the holy and the mundane.

The Beit HaMikdash was also the site of specific functions and ceremonies involving the monarchy. The king had a special place in the Beit HaMikdash designated for special ceremonies, such as *HaKhel* (הקהל) at the conclusion of Sh'mittah (שמיטה), which was on Sukkot. The king would do a special public reading from the Torah at that time, and he would teach the people. This demonstrated that the king ran the nation, but on certain times the king and the kohain gadol would switch places, and the king would become the spiritual teacher. In that way, the HaKhel ceremony is significant in that it had the king reading and teaching the Torah. The king, we see, was also responsible for the spiritual welfare of the nation. At the highest level of the leadership of a nation there is no separation between the roles of the divine leader and the politician. Of course, that only works when the king is in a holy state of being, or when the rabbis and the politicians live in a holy way. This is not what is happening in the world today.

The United States established separation of church and state, and Israel is moving more clearly in that direction. There are reasons for this: primarily, that today there are no holy monarchs or political leaders. We do not have, as in the times of King David and King Solomon, people who totally dedicated their lives to God and to God's people, and therefore ran their nation in a holy way.

Today economics and political power in government are designed primarily for the benefit of the wealthy. If economics were coming from a holy way of consciousness, it would upgrade the entire world—protecting the living planet, protecting the ecology, protecting and nurturing the lives of all the people, feeding the hungry, and ridding our cities of deadly pollution. We could, indeed, very simply, if we were so spiritually inclined, design a world economy that would choose to do all this.

The Beit HaMikdash was not just a Temple. It was an integral part of the national make up of the people, through which the heavens and the earth were fused. The Torah is saying that the optimal government is one that is run by people who are in constant communion with the divine as deveikut/ chey'rut liberation. Until we have that, no system of government or way of life will ever be a sufficient source of light to be steadily satisfying to individuals, or the general population.

In Naso, we also have a discussion of the responsibilities of the Levites (the sons of Kehath who carried the Ark and the sacred implements; the sons of Gershon who were responsible for covering the Tabernacle in order to filter the light that radiated from it, and tone it down or up, depending on how well the people could handle it; and the sons of Merari who were in charge of the posting beams, or the foundation). This suggests that there is foundational light, as well, that needs to be looked after when we are considering the total spiritual practice. Naso points out again the importance of purifying the camps, and asking people with physical diseases and impurities, which were seen as indications of spiritual impurity, to stay outside the camp until they were healed. It is important to consider whom we associate with and how we affect others if we are in a negative state.

Naso also introduces us to the laws of *sotah,* a ritual designed to free a woman accused of adultery from carrying the stigma of suspicion. Literally, sotah implies the act of going astray. If a man suspected that his wife had "gone astray" and was having sex with another man, her guilt or innocence was brought to the forefront through this special ritual of trial by water. Contrary to barbarous witch-drowning rituals of the Church, which required a miracle to save the accused woman from drowning, the sotah ceremony required a miracle to kill the accused woman—not only her alone, but her lover as well. Also, if the accused woman's husband too was guilty of sexual misconduct, the waters would not have an affect on her (Talmud Bav'li, Sotah

47a–b). The water was contained in a basin and into it was dipped a parchment with the Tetragrammaton. The woman was then given the option of either confessing her guilt (if she was indeed guilty, of course), or drinking from the truth waters that contained the God name, YHWH. After drinking it, if she were guilty, it would be made known, as her thighs would miraculously begin to sag, and she would be rendered infertile the rest of her life. If she was guilty but admitted it, she did not need to drink of the ritual waters and was released, and she had to separate from both her husband and her lover. There was no capital punishment for a couple involved in adultery unless there had been two qualified witnesses who had warned them beforehand of the severity of their crime, and who had actually witnessed them then having full intercourse (Talmud Bav'li, Sanhedrin 80b), not just "making out" (Talmud Bav'li, Sanhedrin 54a–56a). The incident of the near stoning of the adulteress in the New Testament is, therefore, clearly a fiction invented by Gospel writers to further their agenda of discrediting Jews and Judaism. If the accused was innocent, she would walk away healthier and more beautiful than she ever was, and very fertile. This archaic ceremony may only rarely have happened, and there is some question as to whether they ever really did this. But it does make the point that doubts between people are more destructive than knowing the truth, and in this way, using the power of God to remove doubt and free someone of social stigmas is very helpful. The sotah, on a deeper level, was a way to protect the wife against the unfounded jealousy of the husband or to improve the marriage relationship. It was a desperate way to improve *shalom bayit* (שלום בית—domestic tranquility) in situations of suspicion. It is said that Hannah, mother of the great prophet Shemu'el, was so desperate for a child that she even went so far as "threatening" God that she would become a sotah.

Naso also discusses a group of people called the Nazirites, who thought that they could somehow be closer to God by the spiritual practice of not cutting their hair and not drinking anything from a grape, and avoiding tumah (טומאה), or ritual impurities, as if there were a formula, a technique, for moving closer to God. It is safer to say that there are no physical techniques, such as "you can do A, B, and C and attain chey'rut." Rather, one attains chey'rut (true liberation) simply by being lived by love, and by making the purpose of

life to be in deveikut. It is about intending all of our actions toward harmony
with ourselves, with those around us, and with the universe, and avoiding
bringing chaos. It is a Torah Way of life that opens us up to the experience
of the light of the Divine within ourselves. The other teaching hidden in the
Nazirite discussion is *ha'roeh et ha'nolad* (הרואה הנולד). This is the realization that whatever is happening to us, in our lives or to others around us, is
a teaching for us, and that, even though we may not experience it that way
in the moment, we have faith that in the end, it will all make sense. As the
second-century Rabbi Shimon taught: "What is the way toward deveikut that
one ought to pursue? *Ha'roeh et ha'nolad*—the one who sees beyond the moment toward the greater plan of God" (Mishnah Avot 2:9).

The teaching inherent with the lesson of the Nazir is that he or she avoid
all tumah (impurities). It is a preventive approach for protecting our spiritual wellbeing. It can be called "putting a fence around the Torah" to protect
against creating tumah and chaos in our lives. At the same time, there is a
Torah teaching that no one is stable in the Torah until he or she has made the
first mistake. The message of the Nazir is to put real kavanah into not missing
the mark. A teaching of the Ba'al Shem Tov was that whatever is happening
in our lives is a teaching from the Divine, and we should be alert to the hidden messages that are encrypted in the events in our lives and in the events of
the lives of others. This is perhaps why the Nazir Torah comes after the sotah
discussion, which is to suggest that we should learn from the mis-actions of
others and try even harder to live the Torah Way.

> God spoke to Moses telling him to speak to Aaron and his sons,
> saying: "This is how you must bless the Israelites. Say to them:
> 'May God bless you and keep watch over you. May God make
> His presence enlighten you and grant you grace. May God direct
> His providence toward you and grant you peace.' [The priests]
> will thus link my name with the Israelites and I will bless them."
>
> (BeMidbar 6:22–27)

To walk as a blessing before God, among the people, and to bless them
through one's life, actions, and word is the Avrahamic teaching. It is the Great

Way of the Torah, in which we become a blessing to ourselves, our family, our tribe, and the world. As we dedicate the Mishkan, for the third time in Naso, it connects us with the immortal truth of who we are, and how subtle and difficult it is to have this view that our physical, emotional, mental, and spiritual selves all come from the divine emanation, and to know in our actions that all the world is nothing other than this divine emanation. At a very deep level, it begins to open us up to understand that the Jewish way of seeing God in all things is a very sophisticated understanding of the teaching of deveikut. It also highlights the power of the male and female interaction as a celebration of the divine in relationship, as demonstrated by the two cherubim on the ark. Sexuality and Eros (celebrating the Divine in all of life) are included in the Torah Way, because the sexual act, as it is practiced by kabbalists on the eve of Shabbat, is an act of merging the worlds of male and female into the oneness. It can be the merging of the Tetragrammaton, the yod heh (יה), which is the b'limah (בלי מה), or nothing, into the something, the mah (מה), which is the vav heh (וה).

These are deep teachings that reveal the Way of the Torah as a way of complete liberation in the midst of the world. May we be blessed that we know this way as the walk of the Torah in our lives and see everything in life as the living Torah unfolding.

Amen

BeHa'alotekha

BEHA'ALOTEKHA means "when you raise up [the flames]." This refers to the lights of the menorah (מנורה), the candelabra that burned in the Mishkan. The menorah's light represents the illumination that brings revelation. We do not create the light when we kindle the flames of the menorah, but we create the capacity to reveal the divine energy, to reveal the hidden.

In our society, we have a funny value system based on the philosophy of Déscartes: "I think, therefore I am." He had the horse before the cart. The Jewish perspective would be: "I am, therefore I think." Although the rational mind has been honored as a source of wisdom, in our present society it has become a source of disease. The rational mind creates disease not only because we cannot easily shut it off, but also because the rational mind creates limitation. In BeHa'alotekha, the act of waking up and becoming liberated is about freeing ourselves from the bondage of the mind. We begin to experience the awareness of the absolute in the sephirah (ספירה) of chokhmah (חכמה). This gives us the experience of the concealed (נסתר—nistar). The term that hints at that is known as olam habah (עולם הבא—literally, the world to come). It is the totality of the life force on all levels, both hidden and revealed. It is the unrevealed world that reveals itself in a way that shows us the truth. When Aharon would kindle the light of the menorah, he was revealing the presence of olam habah. It is the awareness of the experience of enlightenment, not in the next lifetime or in another world, but right now, revealing the unrevealed world to come, now, in this world. Lighting the menorah in BeHa'alotekha symbolizes the revealing of the unrevealed world at the beginning of each day. This was the responsibility of the kohan'im. This is the deep meaning of Aharon's lighting the menorah. It is the revealing of olam habah, the world to come, while we are in olam ha'zeh (עולם הזה), this world.

There is an important statement here about the importance of consistency in one's devotion. To the Levites there is an implication that the daily lighting of the inner lights, symbolized by lighting the outer lights of the menorah, is the source of light for all of Am Yisrael. This is alluded to in BeMidbar 8:2: "When you light the lamps, the seven lamps shall illuminate the menorah." Today, without the Temple service, it is inherent on all of us to be as the Levites, activating the light for everyone by the light force of our daily lives and daily actions, no matter how small. What is important is not just the intensity, but the steadiness of our spiritual service (עבודת השם—*avodat Hashem*).

The secret of the the menorah is that it contains one of the prime messages and understandings for enlightenment. The Lord spoke to Moshe directly, as previously noted, telling him to speak to Aharon. Moshe essentially told Aharon, "When you raise up the flames, the seven flames shall give light toward the face of the menorah." This one sentence is loaded with the deeper meaning of the menorah. The sages taught that the menorah is the essence symbol of the wisdom and enlightenment path of the Torah (Baba Batra 25b). Part of that wisdom expressed by the seven branches of the menorah is that the Torah is the common source of all wisdom symbolized by the "face or base," but there also exist different approaches to the common wisdom symbolized by the seven lamps arising out of the common base. It recognizes the unique sovereignty of each individual and the importance of each one following the lamp (individual path) in the larger Torah context to which they are uniquely drawn. Thus is a person's unique path of deveikut/chey'rut aligned with the Torah as the base of the lamp or overall path of light and wisdom. This is why the lamps face the center of the menorah, symbolizing unity within apparent diversity. This is also why the menorah was to be made from a single piece of gold, *mikshah zahav*. The Torah reveals the underlying unity of all forms of Torah wisdom no matter how apparently diverse they may appear to one looking from the outside.

The menorah, of course, is the seven lamps branching out of a single base. Kabbalistically, it symbolizes the powers of the seven lower sephirot, the power to move between the upper and lower worlds, and the power of healing. The menorah represents the seven-day Sabbath cycle with Shabbat being the central lamp. The three lamps before represent Wednesday through Friday as the days being filled with the new shabbat energy, and the three lamps after represent Sunday through Tuesday as the post shabbat energy carrying through the week. Even though the kohain gadol would pray for everybody regarding everything, when the ancient Commonwealth of Israel existed, the princes remained important because they operated in a spiritual way. They represented the fusion needed for a complete State of Israel. In this way, God assured Aharon that he had a particular merit over the rest of the tribes. Even though the other tribes bonded politics, economics, and the land with God, their reign was limited. The Divine spoke to Aharon, essentially saying in BeMidbar 8:19 and 8:22: "Your reign of the spirit will last forever. Am Yisrael will survive because what you have and what you represent is eternal. The spirit of the Jewish people will live forever." This is important, because the divine power of the Torah, which represents the spirit of Am Yisrael, is what did indeed sustain Am Yisrael through the millennia of their exile, the *galut* (גלות), and will continue to support all Jews who are in exile as the different governments and countries hold their sway. The Torah remains with us always to give meaning to Am Yisrael.

In the first Temple, the Torah was placed in the south side. The south side represents the light. The menorah and the lighting of the lights was in the south and given to the priesthood to maintain, and it was associated with knowledge and wisdom. Aharon and the Levites were given this responsibility, immediately after the tribal princes completed their offerings, to balance the energies of the two powers, that of the Levites and of the princes of the tribes. This configuration, which included the Levites, makes the statement that the eternal spirit of Am Yisrael is not dependent on having a physical land, army, government, or even the most holy temple.

The Maccabees, who emerged later, represented an attempt to heal the Jewish community in the land of Israel by rededicating the Beit HaMikdash after it had been desecrated by the Greco-Assyrians. They were temporarily able to fuse politics and divinity. The lights of Hanukah, the eight-branched menorah, were chosen to represent their struggle and this fusion. The lighting of the lights therefore involves all these levels. However, the sacrifices that were dependent on the Temple, and which the princes participated in, only existed as long as the Beit HaMikdash existed. The candles and the menorah, however, exist forever! In this overall process, the Levites were chosen as the first-born and sanctified to bless B'nei Yisrael forever. The message is that we have within us the ability to bless each other forever, independent of any external structure, time, or situation. It is a broader repetition of Avraham walking before Hashem as a blessing to the world. This is a critical role for each of us, to live beyond all structure so that we might preserve the awareness of the spirit of God in all the people.

After Moshe told Aharon to light the menorah, the Torah recounts "Aaron did that." Why would Aharon not do so? What is this Torah statement referring to? On one level it is referring to the fact that even when Moshe told the people to do something, the negative side, called the ego, could very easily convince them that their personal wisdom knows better, and that they could change the orders. This is one of the powers of the negative side—its ability to convince us that we know everything. Moshe had to deal with the fact that the people had witnessed miracles galore—from the ten plagues, to the splitting of the Sea of Reeds, to the giving of the manna—and yet there was still constant tension between him and the people, because of their egos.

The symbolism of the princes' offerings is also significant in the spiritual-social-political context model of Am Yisrael. The princes themselves represent the political, economic, and military aspirations of Am Yisrael, and their strength, as they brought their sacrifices to the Beit HaMikdash, lay in their capacity to fuse all the elements within the nation in a way that would support their legitimate role as part of the Temple energetics. The highest functioning energy of the State of Israel was enabled only when all those elements were fused harmoniously. Yet, in the process, the Levites were separated out from Am Yisrael as a thirteenth tribe. This was rectified when Hashem directed Am Yisrael to bless and support the sanctification of the Levites for being taken by Hashem as the firstborn offering. In this context, although they were treated separately, Hashem honored the sacred and separate balancing role they played for Am Yisrael.

The Levites represented only one part of Jewish affairs, as the divine side. As a Levite by birth, I take it to heart that I am a firstborn offering, and this requires a serious kavanah in committing myself to the Great Torah path of deveikut/chey'rut—to give myself as an offering to God on every level. When we become an offering to God, we put God in the center of our lives on every level. The Divine is our main reference for how we make life decisions. This awareness, however, created a subtle, functional, and important division between Am Yisrael and the Levites, so that the Levites could best provide and sustain their function as the keepers of the light for Am Yisrael.

It is indeed difficult for most people to maintain their light and share it in the realm of alma d'shikra (עלמא דשקרא—the world of illusion). Therefore, whether we are Levites or not, those of us who have consecrated ourselves to God as an offering need to hold on to the oneness that we share with all, while at the same time keep ourselves a little separate, so that we do not assimilate into the main-stream consciousness and lose our ability to keep and generate the light. This is particularly important in these present times, when there is so much resistance to the spiritual in the world. There is today an ever downward-spiraling conscious and active creation of an atheistic secular paradigm with science as the new God, and with the spiritual, mystical, and religious delegitimized as superstitious.

As the parashah progresses, we enter into another issue: the difficulty in surrendering to God. When people travel away from home, the first thing they like to do is complain about the food. This appears to be no different for Am Yisrael in the desert, and particularly the ey'rev rav. First they complained in general, and that is when a fire came down from God (BeMidbar 11:1). Then they began complaining specifically about the food situation: "Who's going to give us some meat to eat?" "Meat" did not mean red meat, as the complain-ers clarified: "We fondly remember the fish that we could eat in Egypt at no cost, along with cucumbers, melons, leeks, onions and garlic. But now our spirits are dried up, with nothing but the manna before our eyes" (BeMid-bar 11:4–6). It was too much for Moshe to listen to this nonsense when they had been given everything—liberation, freedom, and miracles to save them. Moshe spoke to YHWH and said, in BeMidbar 11:11–15:

> "Why are you treating me so badly? Don't you like me any more? Why do you place such a burden upon me? Was I [the woman] who was pregnant with this nation [in my belly]? Did I give birth to them? But you told me that I must carry them in my bosom, as a nurse carries an infant [until we come] to the land that you swore to their ancestors. Where can I get enough meat to give all these people? They are whining to me to give them some meat to eat. I cannot be responsible for this entire nation! It's too hard for

me! If you are going to do this to me, just do me a favor and kill me! Don't let me see myself get into such a terrible predicament!"

In response to Moshe's lament, Yah tells him to ease his burden of leadership by delegating authority. Moshe is now told to gather the seventy elders, whom Hashem then initiates with spiritual energy, so that they might better support Moshe. Of course, again, it was only good as long as the elders stayed awake and did not let their egos get in the way. In the midst of these uplifting energies, the Lord, through Moshe, said to the people:

> "Prepare yourselves for tomorrow, for you will then have meat to eat. You have been whining in God's ears, saying, 'Who's going to give us some meat to eat? It was better for us in Egypt!' Now God is going to give you meat, and you will have to eat it. You will eat it not for one day, not for two days, not for five days, not for ten days, and not for twenty days. But for a full month [you will eat it] until it is coming out of your nose and making you nauseated. This is because you rejected God [now that He] is among you, and you whined before Him, 'Why did we ever leave Egypt?'"
>
> (BeMidbar 11:18–20)

This message has multiple levels. God was trying to help the people return to the food menu outlined in Bereisheet 1:29, a live-food, plant-source-only diet with the all-nourishing manna, which was optimal for their physical and spiritual health and for the living planet. But the people were unable to hold this energy. What followed sometimes happens in people who go back to a meat diet; they actually get sick eating the meat, but here it is worse and many die as part of a lesson from the Divine. In this context, this was a Torah teaching on meat eating. BeMidbar 11:33 continues:

> The meat was still between their teeth when [the people] began to die. God's anger was displayed against the people, and He struck them with an extremely severe plague. [Moses] named the place "Graves of Craving" [קברות התאוה—*Kivroth HaTaavah*] since it was in that place where they buried the people who had these cravings.

And so, even though there is a debate about vegetarianism, it is very clear that the original dictate of the Torah in Bereisheet 1:29 explains why the people were given the manna over any other food source. As mentioned earlier in our discussion of Noah, humans, in his time, were given a dispensation and were permitted to eat meat, but this was because of the physical and moral situation then, not as a directive to eat meat.

The message in this story is that God was trying (through the manna) to bring the people back to a higher level of nutrition for spiritual evolution that was distant from the degenerative habits of Egypt (the ego). Many of the great rabbinical sages, such as the twelfth-century physician and rabbi, Moses Maimonides, made the statement that the eating of meat was allowed only until people were spiritually ready to embrace the higher octave of not killing brother and sister animals, and to refrain from lusting and hoarding the planet's rich resources, a problem far greater today than in Torah times and even in the era of Maimonides. He also stressed that the sages of Israel instructed us to minimize the consumption of meat as much as we can, since they correlated eating meat with giving in to unhealthy lusting (Mishnah Torah, Hilchot De'ot 5:10).

But Torah wisdom is always ahead of the times and is practical for any given moment. Its emphasis on a meatless diet remains practical and healthy, because we now know that a meat-centered diet requires up to twenty-nine times more energy, ten times more water, and much more land and food. For example, the grain needed to feed 100 cows can easily feed 2,000 people! But until people are more spiritually mature, there will continue to be meat eating. It is no accident that the first Chief Rabbi of Eretz Yisrael, Rav Kook, as well as the former Chief Rabbi of Ireland and the Chief Rabbi of Haifa, were all vegetarians. And when the messiah comes, it is prophesied that he will not be eating meat. The messiah will be a vegetarian, and so will all the animals, including the wolf and the lion, the bear and the leopard (Yesha'yahu 11:6–7). Until that time, we need to be patient and understanding. Gradually, the world is being forced to give up a meat-centered diet as the planet's resources dwindle and the general toxicity of pesticides and radiation is more concentrated the higher we go up the food chain. Some research suggests that radiation alone is thirty times more concentrated in beef than in vegetables. The eating of all types of flesh food also creates poor health, because a high-flesh-food diet is a major contributor to two to four times more cancer, up to four times more heart disease, and two to four times more diabetes. These chronic degenerative diseases are the major leading causes of death in the world today. In that meat eating is associated with more toxicity and chronic disease, it violates the Torah teachings of *pikuach ha'nefesh* and *sh'mirat haguf*, to preserve health and protect life. More of us are also realizing that eating meat promotes cruelty to the animal world and therefore violates the teachings of *t'sa'ar ba'alei chaim*. It disrupts and destroys the ecology and therefore violates the teaching of *bal tashchit* (avoiding waste, especially of food). A meat-centered world lifestyle is directly connected to forty to sixty million people starving to death each year and therefore violates the principle of tzedakah, to feed the hungry. Ultimately, eating flesh food makes it harder for us to be in a state of peace because of the vibration of death and cruelty it carries and which we then ingest into our bodies and minds and therefore disrupts shalom and creates tumah. Meat eating also undermines the teaching of *v'nishmartem meod l'nafshotechem*, to be extremely protective of your nefesh. The overall result of a plant-source-only diet of Bereisheet 1:29 is Kal Yisrael, preserving community. On one level, a meat-centered diet outside of the Beit HaMikdash can be considered a *chilul Hashem,* a desecration of God's name because of the destruction of life and spirit, while a plant-source-only diet could be considered a *kiddush Hashem,* a blessing and santification of God's name.

This does not mean that we cannot, if qualified, do the mitzvah of raising up a soul who has incarnated in an animal by taking a bite of meat, as kabbalists and Torah scholars have done in the past. But, as pointed out before, to merit to merit doing this, one must be a devout Torah scholar and have fully kosher meat, which is hard to find because of factory farming practices. It is my opinion, and that of other rabbis, that an animal raised in the soulless, cruel method of factory farming cannot really be considered kosher even if it is killed in an impeccable kosher manner, because for an animal to be considered kosher it may not be treated in a cruel and soulless manner during any stage of its life, let alone during the process of ritual slaughter. Also, doing this specific ceremony, when consciously used on rare occasions, is not the same thing as having flesh food as a regular part of your diet.

Another teaching in BeHa'alotekha has to do with prophecy and activating the Ruach HaKodesh. As mentioned earlier, God decided to activate the Ruach HaKodesh in the seventy elders, to form the first Sanhedrin with Moshe as its head. In essence, the job of the Sanhedrin was to help guide the people. When the spirit of God came down upon the people they were awakened and the Ruach HaKodesh was activated. We could say it was a group haniha or s'micha m'shefa (סמיכה משפע—initiation by the divine flux). Shortly thereafter two people outside the Sanhedrin also received the power of prophecy and began prophesying in the camp. Their names were Eldad and Medad, and the spirit was said to have rested upon them as well. BeMidbar 11:26–29 says: "They spoke prophetically in the camp. A young man ran to tell Moses. 'Eldad and Medad are speaking prophecy in the camp!' he announced. Joshua son of Nun, Moses' chosen attendant, spoke up. 'My lord Moses,' he said. 'Stop them!'" Moshe then said something really beautiful: "Are you jealous for my sake? I only wish that all of God's people would have the gift of prophecy! Let God grant His spirit to them [all]!"

As we evolve spiritually, some people have a misunderstanding about the whole idea of evolution. It is important that we do support everybody in the personal evolution, because then the whole world wakes up. It is a win-win for everyone. There is a tendency, perhaps in every group or religion, to idolize one person who is the "holy person," and see everyone else is an impostor, or at least not "the one." It becomes such an ego projection that people are willing to kill to assert that they are correct and the others will go to hell. Today there are many holy people out there, and they are helping to wake up more holy people in the world today. This is a powerful way to change the consciousness of the world and be a light to the nations. Moshe told Yehoshua clearly, "I would like everybody in the world to be this way" (BeMidbar 11:29). In fact, each of the seventy elders in the Sanhedrin was responsible for praying for one of the seventy non-Israelite nations, and had to master all seventy languages (Talmud Bav'li, Sanhedrin 70a), because the task, again, was to help wake up everyone, not only Am Yisrael.

Prophecy is often misunderstood, but in those times, in those contexts, prophecy meant a great deal. It meant to hear from God. Although, with the exception of Moshe, all the prophets had to hear through a veil of some sort, Moshe heard directly (Zohar, Vol. 3, folio 191a). In the Jewish tradition, our holy sages have said that prophecy stopped with the passing of Haggay, Zekharya, and Mal'akhi (Talmud Bav'li, Baba Batra 14b). What has not ceased is power of the Ruach HaKodesh, which continued to filter through a different venue known as the *baht ko'l* (בת קול), the "daughter of the voice" (Talmud Bav'li, Tosefta Sotah 13:4). It is almost the same as prophecy, but not quite. The Ruach HaKodesh is the reception of divine inspiration. The only difference between it and prophecy is that when one receives a message that is directly from Hashem for the people, it is prophecy. You often read about the prophets saying, "Thus says Hashem: 'Speak to....'" Ruach HaKodesh is, in a sense, the divine wisdom and enlightenment that comes through us in matters of spirit in a more general way. In the rabbinical tradition, we talk about how we can listen to music that is divinely inspired, or see art that is divinely inspired, and clearly, many of these artists will tell you they were divinely inspired! The Ruach HaKodesh may come through all types of peoples and in all walks of life, but usually it comes through more consistently in people of a high level of spiritual attainment in very personal and creative ways. With the prophet, however, God was instructing him or her to deliver a very specific message to a specific person or people, often a moral message about waking up. Examples in the Jewish tradition of the Ruach HaKodesh inspiration include: King David and the Psalms; and Rabbi Yehuda Hanassi, of the tribe of Judah, who had the divine inspiration after the destruction of the second Temple to write down the oral tradition. Up until the time he did so, writing down the oral Torah was considered an offense (Talmud Bav'li, Gittin 60b). Yet he felt inspired to write it down for the need of the collective, and he completed the foundation of the oral Torah, which we call the Mishnah (משנה). Other inspired books such as Proverbs, Job, and Daniel are also considered examples of the Ruach HaKodesh. What is beautiful about all this, and what is also sometimes hard for people to understand, is that sometimes the Ruach HaKodesh comes through in ways that seem contradictory. But the answer lies in Mishle 14:28: "In the multitude of people is the king's glory." That is really the answer that Moshe was giving to Yehoshua—the more people are inspired, the greater the glory of Hashem. And so, when Hashem took of the spirit He had bestowed upon Moshe, and poured it onto the seventy elders, thus creating the first Sanhedrin, other people too began to prophesy.

Although the Ruach HaKodesh can stream down upon anyone, "whether Gentile or Israelite, whether man or woman, whether slave or maidservant" (Midrash Tana D'bei Eliyahu Rabbah 10:1), not everybody is going to come up with the same answers, because the *ruach* (רוח—wind) of God plays through the instrument of each person differently. Although the general principles stay the same, it is in that diversity that we achieve greater understanding, because different people receive different and sometimes paradoxical messages. Each message is inspired uniquely to different people according to their level of consciousness. In this way, people of all different levels of awareness are addressed.

From a Jewish point of view, the Ruach HaKodesh often expresses an expanded understanding of both the Torah and the Jewish national soul (*knesset Yisrael*—כנסת ישראל). Each of the tribes therefore had their own inspired understanding of how they were to live. In today's context this is expressed through the various sects within Judaism. We have the unique expressions of the Ashkenazim (European), of the Sephardim (Iberian), and the Temanim (Yemenite). In this context, tolerance and understanding of the mystery of the varied expression of the Ruach HaKodesh is a lot more functional and spiritually unifying than intolerance, prejudice, and arguing over differences in insight. A positive example of how to work with these differences was demonstrated in the sixteenth century when Rabbi Yosef Caro (who was Sephardic) wrote the *Shulchan Aruch,* and Rabbi Moshe Isserles (who was Ashkenazic) wrote the *Hagaʾot* (הגהות), the "further studies" of the Shulchan Aruch replete with sometimes differing opinions. Often these two sages respectfully disagreed with one another, but that was okay, because it is important to respect the different ways when they come from a sincere place. The opinions of both nonetheless are combined into a single book we call the Shulchan Aruch, literally, "The Set Table." A table is usually set with more than one plate, and more than one dish. Fifteen hundred years earlier, when the students of Shamai and Hillel argued because each was convinced that he was right, a heavenly voice declared, "Both, the opinions of these and the opinions of those are the words of the Living God!" (Talmud Bav'li, Eruvin 13b).

It would be great if we could truly understand and live in that quality of tolerance, because judgment is one of the traps on the spiritual path and is a trap that Miriam and Aharon also fell into, when they began to criticize Moshe regarding his relationship with a Kushite woman. BeMidbar 12:1 says "Miriam and Aaron began speaking against Moses because of the dark-skinned woman he had married." Some say the Kushite woman referred to was his wife Zipporah, who "was as beautiful as a Kushite," and Miriam was concerned that he was not spending enough time in intimacy with her (Midrash Tanchuma, Tzav, Chap. 13). Another tradition maintains that during the "lost years of Moshe"—the period between his flight from Egypt and his arrival at the well in Midian—he had wandered through Ethiopia and had married a widowed Kushite queen after helping her people regain their kingdom from the black occult magician Balaam (Otzar Hamidrashim, Moshe, Keta 6).

No one really knows exactly what this incident was about, but it is secondary to the larger message. "They [then went on to] say, 'Is it to Moses exclusively that God speaks? Doesn't He also speak to us?'" (BeMidbar 12:2–3). YHWH, in response to their arrogance, came down in a pillar of the cloud, stood at the door of the tent, summoned Aharon and Miriam, and said:

> "Listen carefully to my words. If someone among you experiences divine prophecy, then when I make myself known to him in a vision, I will speak to him in a dream. This is not true of my servant Moses, who is like a trusted servant throughout my house. With him I speak face to face, in a vision not containing allegory, so that he sees a true picture of God. How can you not be afraid to speak against my servant Moses?" God displayed anger against them and departed. When the cloud left its place over the tent, Miriam was leprous, white like snow.
>
> (BeMidbar 12:6–10)

Aharon pleaded with Moshe, "Please do something here." And Moshe did. In BeMidbar 12:13, Moshe prayed "el na re'fa na lah" (אל נא רפא נא לה)—"O God, please heal her!") and she was healed. But first she spent seven days outside the camp to purify from her lack of respect for Moshe.

The message in this story answers the earlier question about everyone prophesying. It is wonderful that everybody received the Ruach HaKodesh and that everybody woke up. It is wonderful that some people received prophecy. But we need to learn from this story that the quality of each person's prophecy differs from that of another, and is unique to that person alone. It also helps to understand that Ruach HaKodesh, and prophecy, and deveikut/chey'rut are not the same thing. Enlightenment is being almost constantly in a state of Ruach HaKodesh and prophecy is a specific time of heightened Ruach HaKodesh with a specific message from God to the people. You can be a prophet, but still be a student, as was the case with Miriam and Aharon. This is an example of why those who have access to the Ruach HaKodesh should still remain respectful of our enlightened teachers and tzaddikim. Miriam and Aharon, even though they were among the highest, did not show respect for Moshe, who was a great enlightened tzaddik at the very least, as well as the greatest prophet in the lineage. Even at their level, Miriam and Aharon had to bear the consequences. This is the double-edged sword: We wake people up, we turn them on to God, but the power of that connection can cause us to become deluded. One's teacher continues to play a guiding role even for the enlightened student, who has far less experience in the state of liberation. The *tzaddik gamur* (enlightened spiritual teacher) can help one not fall into the trap of the ego of enlightenment. In the evolution of spiritual conscioiusness, we are never done, so humility is always a protective strategy, as well as a good way to live. The danger is that not infrequently newly enlightened people do not necessarily know how to handle the energy of liberation. It takes years and years of experience, tutelage, and continued evolution to be able to handle the power of the spiritual in a way that one's newly "enlightened" ego does not get in the way. These two teachings together are powerful lessons about what happens in spirituality on the higher planes.

Another great lesson in BeHa'alotekha is the teaching of the second Pesach (פסח שני). There were some people who had been busy tending to the dead and were, therefore, ritually unprepared for the Pesach rites. It is unclear whether they were taking care of the bodies of Aharon's two sons at the time or carrying the bones of Yosef, but the fact was that there were some people doing holy work that required contact with death, and they were going to miss out on the sacred rites of Pesach. In BeMidbar 9:8, Moshe told the people to wait until he tuned in and learned what Yah had to say about this. And so was born the mitzvah of *Pesach Sheni,* the second Pesach. Nothing is lost, and there is always a way to fix and make up what seems to have been missed. We have the opportunity to repair our mistakes and missed opportunities of the past. In other words, there is always a second chance for us, no matter what has gone on. The message of Pesach Sheni is that there is always a way to fix or make up what has been lost for the sincere student.

It is inherent in the Torah teachings that there is always a second opportunity, or more, to do teshuvah. It is taught that one of the most important actions we have to do, to bring the coming of the messiah, is personal and collective teshuvah. In most cases this is far beyond second chances. Judaism, however, emphasizes that there is always time and opportunity to return to God. To think less than that is a delusion of the dark side that separates us from the Divine. This understanding is fundamental to the Torah Way. So, this story is about a second chance, because Pesach is in a sense about redemption from Egypt. There is nothing in this world that exists without a will for it to exist. All that we want comes into existence because of that. This is the mysterious power of *ratzon* (רצון), the desire or will. Likewise, the return to Israel in our own times was a function of 2,000 years of Jewish willpower to return to the homeland. The power of Israel's willingness to exist is key to the historically momentous event of the restoration of our ancient homeland. If we start to get complacent, however, it could be lost, because the Arabs, too, have a very strong will.

This mitzvah of Pesach Sheni was created by the intense desire of just a few people who wanted to experience Pesach but could not, due to specific circumstances beyond their control. The Pesach Sheni itself is the ultimate second chance after being stuck for 210 years in Egypt and moving into extreme negativity, so the intent of this mitzvah is not about our immediate situation, but about directing our consciousness toward where we know we need to be. That is the meaning of l'hitpallel, again—to "be our prayer." Pesach Sheni is the essence of the potential that allows us to be involved in l'hitpallel. It is about the intense desire to be aligned with God that overcomes any immediate missed opportunities. This was a mitzvah that came as a result of people who really wanted to do this and be part of the whole Passover experience. It is the desire to know God in a bigger way that allows us to go beyond surrendering to a particular situation. The ultimate Passover Sheni is the will to fully know Hashem.

The messages in this parashah are profound. It establishes the Levites as the carriers of the eternal aspect of Am Yisrael. It strongly establishes the importance of the eternal aspect of community, in that the love of God is critical for the enduring existence of Am Yisrael. And that the Torah is a carrier and generator of this God force and has an important role in the sustaining of Israel over the time of its galut. The parashah also establishes the importance of the menorah, the importance of kindling those flames each morning to keep the light in its radiance always, burning continually in the south as a reaffirmation of the eternal human spirit. We are also reminded of the guidelines around prophecy, remaining humble before God, even after we have experienced an awakening of the Ruach HaKodesh. We are reminded that this awakening and periodic activation does not mean we are enlightened. In this parashah, we see once more the humility of Moshe, whose dream it was that everyone would prophesy, and who was humbly willing to share of his Ruach HaKodesh, not only with the seventy elders, but with whoever else desired it and was ready for it, such as Eldad and Medad. We also witness his humility in the way he remained silent and did not react when Miriam and Aharon gave in to their egos and judged him from a place of feeling they were equal to him.

All of this is about understanding the subtlety of the spiritual path, and how much we have to work to be steady in the awakened state, when the power of Ruach HaKodesh is awakened within us. This parashah also reestablishes Hashem's Torah teachings that the plant-source-only diet is the highest Torah ideal and one that best facilitates our spiritual evolution and our journey back to God. We always get a second chance, yet we should try not to need a second chance.

We are also taught in BeHa'alotekha the importance of community. We are all basically connected as one soul, and we all have different roles. The ultimate community is one that can fuse the social, political, economic, and spiritual. But the eternal heart of that community remains the spiritual, represented by the Levites. May we all be blessed that we keep the eternal light of the spirit alive within us so we may survive the galut of the soul, the galut of our nation, the galut of the separation from God. And may we be blessed that in the awakening, we move beyond the song of the individual soul, beyond the song of the nation, beyond the song of the earth, to the song of all the multiple levels of creation, and understand our oneness with all these levels as an emanation of the Divine.

Amen

Sh'lach

God spoke to Moses, saying, 'Send out men for yourself to explore the Canaanite territory that I am about to give the Israelites. Send out one man for each patriarchal tribe. Each one shall be a person of high rank'" (BeMidbar 13:1–2). This clearly states that the Israelites were told from the very beginning that the land was given to them. In that case, why did they need to send scouts to see if the land was good? Leaders from each tribe were sent for this purpose. They were not common people; they were the princes, with a great deal of spiritual awareness and rank among the people as is stated in BeMidbar 13:3. They were the tzaddikim of the time. BeMidbar 13:16 says, "[However,] Moses gave Hoshea son of Nun the [new] name Joshua (Yehoshua)." Going into the land was an apparent challenge to Am Yisrael, so changing Hoshea's name to Yehoshua (Joshua), meaning "God will help," gave him increased spiritual energy to meet the challenge.

There are several levels of challenge in this parashah; one of them was the task of going into the highly spiritually charged energy of Eretz Yisrael. According to the oral tradition, one of the scouts, Kalev ben Yefuneh, actually stopped at the Cave of Machpelah in Hebron, the burial site of the early ancestors, in order to gain more spiritual energy to fortify himself against the attitude of the other scouts as well as his own tendencies toward anxiety as he entered the land. In this way, Yehoshua and Kalev could be elevated to the energy of the Tree of Life (עץ חיים—Etz Chaim), which the land of Israel represented.

In BeMidbar 13:20, the spies were briefed by Moshe to scout out the Land of Canaan: "Does [the land] have trees or not? Make a special effort to bring [back] some of the land's fruits." Why did they need to see if there were trees? Even in the desert there are trees. This was fertile land. The question being asked on a deeper level was, "Was the Tree of Life energy there?" There are other energetic trees around, too, such as the Tree of Knowledge (עץ הדעת— Etz Ha'Da'at), the tree of duality, doubt, and uncertainty. That was the tree that

Adam and Cha'vah had eaten from. Moshe asked them to discover which of the two was the predominant tree (energy) in Eretz Yisrael. The Tree of Life represents the realm of certainty and the mystical spiritual realm of the Torah. The realm of zeir anpin is the sublime awareness of Etz Chaim, and it was one from which one may fall if one is not careful.

According to my internal experience, there is also what I call Etz Ayin (עץ אין), the Tree of Nothing, which is beyond Tree of Life consciousness and is awareness prior to creation. It is a *chiddush* (new inspirational insight). Etz Ayin offers a more permanent and steady certainty and awareness of God. Kalev was possibly connecting with the deep ayin of certainty from the awareness of the ancestors. In this awareness he would have been able to leave behind the illusion of free will. At the level of Etz Ayin, the world of atzilut-keter (אצילות–כתר), there is no illusion of free will; there is only the service of the Divine, as the divine will unfolding. What was really being asked of the scouts, in other words, was whether the land is holding the energy of Etz Ha'Da'at or Etz Chaim. The phrase "fruit of the land" is, then, not simply referring to the material fruit, but is also symbolic of the spiritual fruit. The fruit of the land was bigger than ordinary fruit and had a more intense energy to it. The fruit of the land was and is truly spiritual consciousness.

Moshe warned the scouts not to connect too closely with the land during their mission as it might affect their judgment. Nonetheless, these twelve tourists began to feel the land and to experience the spiritual intensity of the land, which, in turn, may have raised concern and fear. Their perceptions may have activated a spiritual issue, their desire for and resistance for God. This is a common spiritual dilemma in almost all people. People say "I want God, I want God," but as they begin to go deeper they become afraid that they will disappear into the unknown and not come back, or that they might just move too far out of their egocentric comfort zones. They actually become afraid for their ego's survival. I have raised this question with literally thousands of spiritually focused people and all have at some point admitted this fear. I know about this awe and fear from a direct experience in 1972, when, while attending a lecture on the Torah, I began to see angels appear. I thought "I must be crazy!" But then the lecturer, without any input from me, turned toward the angels and greeted them by name. There were thirty to forty people in the room, and only the lecturer and I could see the angels. They were beings of light shining intensely. They were not human in form except for their faces. After that experience I felt yir'at shamayim (יראת שמים—fear and awe of the heavenly realms) for about an hour. Still, I decided not to run away, but to overcome the fear and plunge into this new realm of spiritual life. Not everyone makes that decision to move forward, but everyone is at some point confronted with that choice. We all have desire for and resistance to God. The resistance does not arise until the desire begins to manifest through other realms, and we begin to get a stronger awareness of the divine presence. It is a decision that almost everyone on the spiritual path is faced with, and so it is good to be forewarned.

At a higher level, we see that the ten spies were unable to go beyond their resistance to this light pouring in at a higher frequency in Eretz Yisrael. Only Yehoshua, now named and empowered for a higher vibration, and Kalev, who had taken in the energies of the ancestors as they traveled from the south in Hebron, were able to be at this frequency. Only these two received the blessing to enter the land forty years later. The ten spies were intellectually and fearfully seduced by their own egocentric desire to receive for self, alone. They chose to maintain their comfort zone in the desert with negative interpretations of Eretz Yisrael. As the princes of the tribes, they were placed in a central place of responsibility and meaning, but moving into Eretz Yisrael threatened their egocentric comfort zones. As many Torah scholars learn, it is safer and easier to study in the yeshiva, and it is more challenging to take divine awareness and maintain it in the world, where work, responsibility, and finances must be addressed. Being in the world also requires sharing instead of receiving for self, alone. Entering the Promised Land meant leaving the wonder and comfort zone of the desert journey with the food air-dropped in and the water flowing steadily from the ground. On entering Eretz Yisrael, they were going to have to leave their comfort zone and work for everything. Entering Eretz Yisrael would require shifting away from the comfort of receiving for self, to receiving in order to share, to become tzaddikim at the highest level. They may have also feared their own inability to move up to such a high level.

Israel was not just promised to Am Yisrael; it was truly given to them. Were they ready to receive it? The raw energy of Jerusalem is powerful. Today, when this energy is too much for a person, it may result in what we call the

Jerusalem psychosis. This may happen to people who are unable to ground the energy by sharing or are just too mentally unstable. In my role as a psychiatrist, I have literally had to send people out of the land, back to their homes in Europe or the U.S., when this was happening to them. We must appreciate that these people in the BeMidbar story were about to enter Israel, a place of very deep and powerful energy for which not everyone was fully ready. The spies represented an egocentric agenda, as part of the resistance. To go into God, one must cease identifying with the ego. The ten princes could not let go of their egocentric identities, and therefore could neither connect with Etz Chaim nor truly enter the land.

Entering Yisrael requires serious preparation if we are going to be open to the intense holiness of the land. Unfortunately, there are few real ceremonies today that initiate and bond us to the land and open us to its energetics with the intensity of love and awe that it merits. So, when I made aliyah (immigrated to Israel), I created my own spiritual initiation into the land. I meditated and prayed for seventy-two hours without food and water in the Negev Desert in a semi-cave near Arad, unsheltered from the sun most of the day, high up in a cliff. At night I began to hear, in this very isolated place, the noise of shepherds and their herds as if Avraham, Yitzhak, and Ya'akov were shepherding there. At one point, a luminous figure appeared, and identified himself as Avraham. The figure only stayed for thirty seconds and silently communicated the energy of Avraham and the energetics of his lineage. He transmitted the energy of receiving in order to share (the energy of chesed) to me and opened a profound connection to the ancestral spiritual desert energy of the *avot* (desert fathers/patriarchs). The aliyah ceremony became a rebirth ceremony. After that, while talking with a local archeologist, I subsequently learned that this very area where I stayed was among the actual routes that the patriarchs had walked while herding their flocks. My sojourn in the Judean Desert brought me to the desert of the mind, a completely quiet mind, opened to receive the divine presence and able to be inflamed with the divine fire teachings of this awesome Holy Land lineage. Needless to say, it was a powerful aliyah initiation.

Without the ability to release and share the truth, we cannot maintain the emptiness and receive the flame of God, which burns up the world of illusion (alma d'shikra) within us.

Ten of the twelve spies were simply not ready. When they returned and delivered a negative, fearful report, the people fell into intense resistance and actually wanted to stone Moshe and Aharon and return to Egypt. Although these ten spies were tribal princes, they were spiritually the ey'rev rav, and they created the typical confusion and weakening of faith and perspective in the people that led them to temporarily rebel against God's directive to enter the land. We see this today as well with the modern-day ey'rev rav and their undermining commentaries on the Middle East, which ignores the flow of authentic prophecy and creates confusion and lack of faith in God's plan unfolding. They do this by focusing in a disjointed, microscopic view of each isolated conflict, disconnected from the whole. The way of Avraham is the faith-based overview of the deep uncomplicated truth. It is being guided by the direct knowledge of God, the deeper experience of which takes one to the noncausal oneness, compassion, love, peace, contentment, and inner joy as the will of God unfolding. The ey'rev rav do not really understand this, and act more like Korach who, as we will see later, undermined Moshe directly with his clever pseudo-moralistic and legalistic mindset.

Am Yisrael had seen plenty of miracles. They witnessed the ten plagues, which activated and purified their own individual Tree of Life. They saw the defeat of the mighty Pharaoh and the otherwise impregnable Egypt. They saw manna fall from the heavens and water rise from the earth. They witnessed the laws of nature reversed. However, they did not develop their inner essence, because they were living in the outer miracle. Going from the desert filled with miracles into Eretz Yisrael, where the miracles would cease, was a big challenge that would require inner strength to detach from their comfort zones. Nevertheless, the spies introduced a fair question: At what point does one know that he or she is ready? When I became a medical doctor I began working with clients because it was the natural flow after a certain amount of preparation. In the same way, the ten princes were given the opportunity to trust that it was time to enter Eretz Yisrael.

In BeMidbar 13:2 God says, "Send out men for yourself to explore the Canaanite territory that I am about to give the Israelites." God made it very clear that the people already had the land; it had already been given to them, but the people did not have the inner strength to receive it. The spies suffered from a subtle imbalance summarized as "a person is led in the direction they wish to go" (Talmud Bav'li, Makot 10b). This is the way the mind works. Without living the Torah way, we can create the illusion of our own reality, rather than live in the reality through which God is guiding us. This is the ego, which leads to Satan. Satan is leading us, and we can clearly see the illusion of Satan-powered egocentric energy that led these ten into perceiving a reality that was not only inaccurate, but also resulted in their death. They were spiritually cut off from the Divine.

In BeMidbar 13:27, it was the spies themselves who called it the land of milk and honey, but they were unwilling to receive the milk and honey. It was too much energy for them, and they felt they had too much to lose by moving up to this next level. They were asked to go beyond the ease and simplicity of the roaming desert yeshiva and instead to live in the Eros of God's presence in every situation and in every moment. They chose to see the land as one that "consumes its inhabitants." They were afraid that they would be lost in the physical world. They were not ready to be in this state of continual Eros, seeing God and the dance of the Divine in all things. They were not ready to enter the land with an empty mind. Their overall lack of confidence, lack of connection with the Divine, and egocentric fears were the real problem. They could not truly speak with the simplicity and power of Kalev in BeMidbar 13:30 when he said: "We must go forth and occupy the land. We can do it!" He was in a state of faith prior to being in direct certainty. BeMidbar 13:27 says, "We came to the land where you sent us, and it is indeed flowing with milk and honey, as you can see from its fruit."

The ten doubters then spread negative reports about the land and its inhabitants—about the land devouring its inhabitants, and Amalek being there, which is a symbol of doubt born out of doubt. BeMidbar 13:32 recounts:

> They began to speak badly about the land that they had explored.
> They told the Israelites, "The land that we crossed to explore is
> a land that consumes its inhabitants. All the men we saw there
> were huge! While we were there, we saw the titans. They were
> sons of the giant, who descended from the [original] titans."

By spreading this evil report, the spies caused great negativity, as described in BeMidbar 14:2: "All the Israelites complained to Moses and Aaron." In the desire-resist paradigm of spiritual life, they communicated their own resistance to the Divine and to the higher state of the unknown of Eretz Yisrael, and thus activated this resistance to Hashem in Am Yisrael. The people were not able to overcome their resistance to Hashem, which manifested as their fear of the difficulties they thought lay waiting for them in the Eretz Yisrael. They focused instead on their imagined hardships that they would have to face to win the land spiritually and militarily, rather than the joy, love, and peace of being the expression of the divine will and the higher consciousness that comes from that. This is common in the unfolding of the spiritual path and why it is so much more beneficial to focus on the light and love that is generated from a true spiritual path rather than the illusionary or potential hardships involved in getting there. As I experienced in a seventy-two-hour desert fast, without food and water, there appears to be harshness from a certain perspective, but deeper than that was, and is, an incredible noncausal love, oneness, peace, contentment, ecstasy, compassion of the Divine, and the power of the ancestors, which took me beyond any physical discomforts. Without the power of our ancestors, focusing on the seventy-two hours in the Negev Desert without any food and water might have been discouraging or difficult.

Although the Lord wanted again to wipe out the people for their resistance, Hashem responded with restating some of the thirteen acts of divine compassion. Behind the harshness of gevurah is always the compassion of chesed. Moshe says in BeMidbar 14:18–24:

> "God is slow to anger, great in love, and forgiving of sin and rebellion. He does not clear [those who do not repent], but keeps in mind the sins of the fathers for their children, grandchildren, and great-grandchildren. With your great love, forgive the sin of this nation, just as you have forgiven them from [the time they left] Egypt until now." God said, "I will grant forgiveness as you have requested. But as I am Life, and as God's glory fills all the world, [I will punish] all the people who saw my glory and the miracles that I did in Egypt and the desert, but still tried to test me these ten times by not obeying me. They will therefore not

see the land that I swore to their ancestors. All those who provoked me will not see it. The only exception will be my servant
Caleb, since he showed a different spirit and followed me whole-
heartedly. I will bring him to the land that he explored, and his
descendants will possess it."

It was no accident that the people of Kalev of the tribe of Yehudah were
given the region Hebron to inhabit.

It is no accident that the very day of the spies' negative report and the
resulting resistance and mourning of Am Yisrael was the ninth of Av. Their
actions created the foundation of the worst day in the history of Am Yisrael.
The ninth of Av as it occurs historically includes the fall of the first and second Temple, the expulsion from Spain, the Inquisition, and the beginning of
the Holocaust. It also has the potential to be the most intense day of positive
spiritual life. But it is up to us to transform it into such a time.

Part of the mistake the spies made was viewing Torah study as disconnected from the evolution of Am Yisrael. They really were not willing to combine
the spiritual with life in the physical world; however, Am Yisrael and Eretz
Yisrael are linked and require both to come to fruition. At some level, we must
wake up to the kabbalistic, shamanic understanding that to every people there
is a specific land assigned to them by the Divine. God had chosen this land for
Am Yisrael, and the interaction between Am Yisrael and the intense spiritual
energy of the land would bring one another to fruition. The ancestors built the
energy for the land. Any Native American will vouch for this understanding.
A quote from Crazy Horse at the Crazy Horse Memorial makes this principle
clear: "My land is where my dead are buried." Today we see the Hopis and the
Navaho fighting over their ancestral lands and striving to keep corporations
seeking uranium and oil off their lands so they do no further damage to the
energy of the land and consequently to the energy of the people.

Zekharya 8:12 says, "For there shall be the seed of peace; the vine shall
give her fruit, and the ground shall yield its increase, and the heavens shall
give their dew; and I will cause the remnant of this people to possess all these
things." Conquering nations do not separate people from their land unless
they are trying to destroy them. The U.S. attempted to separate the Native

Americans from their land by placing them on reservations located far from their natural homelands. The Babylonians, the Persians, the Greeks, and Romans all took Am Yisrael away from their land in an attempt to destroy them. The Persians, however, were willing to let them return to build their second Temple. Anyone with any kabbalistic, Torah, and historical understanding knows that Am Yisrael was, and is, the people of this particular land we today call Eretz Yisrael, and that our people have been living there for an unbroken period of 4,000 years, except for 210 years of enslavement in Egypt. Every organic seed reflects the energy of the land and tells us the history of the people. This is why Hebron is so incredibly important. It is the tombs of our ancestors. We cannot divorce Am Yisrael from Eretz Yisrael. To recover the land cannot be a military venture only, but we must understand the connection of the core essence of Am Yisrael and the *midas* (spiritual life in the life of Yisrael). It is essential that we comprehend the importance of Eretz Yisrael as spiritually and shamanically blended with Am Yisrael. The land needs to be regained by both military might and living the Torah Way of life. This includes treating all the strangers who support the existence, life, and growth of Am Yisrael in Eretz Yisrael in a just way.

The Amalekites and Canaanites were in the area through which the camp of Am Yisrael had to pass, and the ten tribal princes died the night after their report of a mysterious disease referred to only as "the plague." The people were then told that none of them, from ages twenty and older, would come into the Promised Land, except for Kalev and Yehoshua. In a desperate attempt to reverse the decree and redeem themselves, the people decided to fight the Canaanites and enter the land. But Moshe said to the people, in Be-Midbar 14:41: "Why are you going against God's word?" It won't work!" In essence, he was saying: "The Torah is not with you; I am not with you; God is not with you." This was a clear message that the next step to clear the negative energy was to do teshuvah, to look at their reaction the day before and change the egoic pattern that caused it. Instead they chose yet another egocentric approach of resistance to God, although it emotionally seemed correct. This is a lesson for how to handle what appears to be a negative situation. Do teshuvah before moving on. Instead, they went to fight anyway, and many of them were killed. They were also being taught a very basic rule for entering the land;

Torah justice shall be for everyone—for Am Yisrael and for all the strangers in the land. BeMidbar 15:15–16 says, "There shall thus be one Torah and one law for you and for the proselyte who joins you." As we gain control of Eretz Yisrael, we must treat each stranger in the land with the same love and compassion that the Torah says to treat ourselves, for it is written there "It is an eternal law for future generations."

The people were also told to give thanks every time they ate the bread of the land. It is a tradition to offer a part of our food each time we eat, to prevent us from falling into solely receiving for self, alone. Another section in this parashah recounts an incident in which a person was found publicly gathering wood on the Shabbat. He was brought before Moshe, who commanded that he be stoned. They did so, and he died. It is said in the oral tradition that this person felt that people had to see the seriousness of breaking the Shabbat, and that he offered himself as an example. He was not being thoughtless, but rather was giving his life as a lesson for keeping the Shabbat. Other traditions have it that he was forewarned about the prohibition of gathering wood on the Shabbat, but he chose to do so anyway (Talmud Bav'li, Sanhedrin 41a).

Yet another gift of ritual was given in this parashah so that Am Yisrael remember the spiritual aspects of its essence. BeMidbar 15:37–40 says:

> God spoke to Moses, telling him to speak to the Israelites and have them make tassels on the corners of their garments for all generations. They shall include a twist of sky-blue wool in the corner tassels. These shall be your tassels, and when you see them, you shall remember all of God's commandments so as to keep them. "You will then not stray after your heart and eyes, which [in the past] have led you to immorality. You thus remember and keep all my commandments, and be holy to your God. I am God your Lord, who brought you out of Egypt to be your God. I am God your Lord."

This warning is a teaching that ends the parashah and tells us that in order to maintain and expand our consciousness in Eretz Yisrael, and transform ourselves into beings of light, the Divine is offering us the tzitzit to wear so that we may be aware of the divine presence at all times. The sky-blue techelet serve as an open antenna to increase our own light and protect us by the miracles of the Divine from all dark forces and entities that may wish to penetrate our field.

May we all be blessed that we can follow the Torah Way and enter Eretz Yisrael consciously by connecting with the Tree of Life (Etz Chaim) and so that we may enter with complete, irreversible certainty into the presence of God in our lives, and so that we may be spiritually empowered to enter Eretz Yisrael, to live at the highest level of spiritual intensity available to us, and to share this energy thoughtfully and compassionately with all people.

Amen

Korach

ALTHOUGH the English translation does not make it clear, in Hebrew this parashah opens up with the word "vayikach" (ויקח), meaning "And he [Korach] took." This is the complete explanation of the whole parashah. In it, we are dealing with Moshe's and Aharon's cousin, Korach, the son of Yitz'har and great-grandson of Levi, as was Moshe. They had a common grandfather, Kehoth. Amram, who was the father of Moshe, Aharon, and Miriam, was Yitz'har's brother. Korach was, in essence the first cousin of Moshe, Miriam, and Aharon.

A major family issue was going on here, and it almost directly exposed Korach as a prototype of the spiritual ey'rev rav (someone born Jewish, but acting with the ey'rev rav mentality). As part of the ey'rev rav archetype, he was basically an egocentric fraud. The immediate driving force behind Korach's egocentric action was that he was very upset that Elizaphan had been made prince over his family. Korach claimed "My father is one of the four brothers." Amram was the first, and he took a double portion for himself, as Aharon became the kohain gadol, and Moshe became the leader. Next in line should have received the next assignment, and since his father was the second brother, he felt that he should have been appointed prince, instead of Uzziel's son Elizaphan, who was the fourth brother (Midrash Tanchuma, Korach, Chap. 1). In a sense, he is saying "Therefore, I reject all that Moshe has done."

That is the way the ego of the ey'rev rav works. He turned whatever the family issue was into a national debate to undermine Moshe and the Torah. He completely lost perspective in a not too unreasonable argument that he had. It helps to appreciate that Korach was no lightweight. He was a Torah scholar, and he was extremely wealthy. According to the Talmud, he had found much wealth that was hidden by Yosef in Egypt. He used his wealth to reach a high level of esteem among the people of Israel, but as we see often happening in people with wealth, they get caught up in "I have, therefore I am," and move forward into "I have, therefore I want more." In this case, he wanted more. He wanted to be a priest and or prince as well! This is what we see in him and in many people who are dominated by ego.

As students, it is important to "take," but then there is a transition, which is to "take" in order to share. Korach never made that shift in the energetics of moving from left pole (receiving for self, alone) to right pole (receiving in order to share), and then ultimately becoming the central pole of the three columns of the Tree of Life. Korach never shifted from being a taker, and Korach's wife, according to the Talmud, was pushing him into becoming an even bigger taker, while the wife of O'n, one of Korach's cohorts, tried to talk her man out of getting involved with Korach's "cause" (Talmud Bav'li, Sanhedrin 110a). According to the Talmud Korach's wife said: "Look, Moses has all the money. He is building a tabernacle, but he just wants the money for himself, and he's given all the goodies to his brother Aharon." What does this tell us? The people around us affect us. As we look at this story, we are looking at Korach, Dathan and Aviram (the sons of Eliav), and O'n (son of Peleth). They are of the tribe of Reuven, and Reuven's tribe was situated adjacent to Korach's tent (Midrash Bamidbar Rabbah 3:12). We are affected by the people around us in a variety of interesting ways.

Korach then shows up with 250 people, mostly from the tribe of Reuven, who himself was a displaced firstborn, replaced by Judah. Thus, Korach's followers also represented the replaced firstborn of Israel, replaced once again, this time, by the Levites. Korach used his intellect (which is the way ego works) in an ultimate attempt to be destructive to the deeper spiritual purpose of Am Yisrael. He said to Moshe in BeMidbar 16:3: "You have gone too far! All the people in the community are holy, and God is with them. Why are you setting yourselves above God's congregation?" Moshe saw right through this liberal, political misuse of words, which sounded correct theoretically, but was confusing and deeply misleading, undermining, and not at all related to the actual reality of God's clear direction that Moshe had been chosen to be the leader, as the most evolved of Am Yisrael. In the guise of the "idea" of democracy, he attempted to undermine the necessary reality of spiritual hierarchy and order of Am Yisrael for his own dark egocentric needs and agenda. Enlightened leaders like Moshe, appointed by God, are not democratically elected. Applying political ideas to the path of enlightenment is, at best, ludicrous. If Korach were even sincere about his democratic principles, then he would have complained earlier about being part of the Levites, who were set aside as the firstborn, and given up his high status. This logical, politically correct position, if you look at the small picture, smells correct to the uninformed egocentric thinking of the masses, but it seriously undermines the focus on the bigger picture of God's will unfolding, and, in the short run, it gives the impression that Korach is some sort of prophetic, heroic figure concerned with the welfare of the people. This is the classic manipulative and psychospiritual deceptive way of the ey'rev rav.

Moshe, who carried the big picture of God's will unfolding, saw right through the manipulative façade of the ey'rev rav, and fell on his face as a sign of humility. He then was guided by the Divine to set up a deadly test to end this egocentric rebellion that was attempting to undermine Am Yisrael.

There is a theoretical logic and small-truth perspective to both Korach's family issues and his attempt to undermine Moshe, and, if he would have been sincere about it, then it could have turned into an educational debate, based on the Torah principle of *l'shem shemayim*, which means "for the name [or sake] of Heaven." Every sincere argument that is for the sake of heaven is valid, because it brings unity to where there is *machloket* or discord. But Korach's argument, and his style and approach, were not about unity. In a sense, it was about trying to destroy the soul of Am Yisrael and the importance of Moshe and Aharon in the whole picture.

As explained in the Torah, and throughout all the Hebraic scriptures, when people become divided over different opinions, they are both wrong. *Divided* is the key word. When Korach felt conflicted and only believed that he was right (because he was identified with his ego), and believed there was only one answer, that is when the problem arose. Contrast that with the struggles of Hillel and Shamai, for example. They were able to get to a place of understanding that their conflict was an argument for the sake of heaven, and they could both be right and continue to disagree with one another while still honoring and loving each other. Korach, on the other hand, could not see that the left pole was one part of a unified whole; and that is where the breakdown happened. He was caught up in ego rather than identifying with consciousness. Moshe spoke from the higher reality, seeing the whole picture. Korach took the course of a delusional reality and chose a clever ego approach. This is contrary to the position of Aharon, as the position of peace and sharing. That is the problem here: his argument was not machloket for the sake of heaven, but for the sake of ego. That puts it in a totally different setting, because he was only thinking about his own benefit, and he did not create a space for the other to exist and have a voice. Korach could not simply say, "Hey, I have a legitimate complaint about my not being considered a tribal prince." He wanted a destructive national debate, and he wanted to be the victim, as part of his effort to undermine Moshe and Aharon's importance as leaders altogether. While speaking out against hierarchy, he simultaneously wanted the rank of prince without earning it. This is like having a football team, and all the players demanding the quarterback position. It will not work. The ego wants to be quarterback, but anybody with any wisdom knows the importance of having a complete team for proper function. Korach undermined the whole team of Am Yisrael. Everybody has a role. Everybody has a divine mission, and that is what makes the whole social spiritual process function and evolve. The Levites had their mission to spend their time studying and holding the spiritual energy. The twelve princes and the twelve tribes had their mission to do the other levels of work. Ultimately, together they made a whole, and Korach undermined this basic principle of wholeness and harmony in the spiritual hierarchy of Am Yisrael; it was not designed to operate as a political democracy.

Korach created a very interesting contradiction. Most people could see through it, but obviously many people, because of their egocentric agendas and liberal thinking patterns, did not see it. Obviously, the 250 people who were with him, including Aviram, Dathan, and O'n, did not! Korach further attempted to undermine the Torah teachings of the Divine by asking some tricky "innocent" questions, in an attempt to further undermine Moshe. According to the Midrash, Korach approached Moshe with an obscure halachic question, "If you have a talit (a shawl) that is made up entirely of blue dye, the techelet, do we still need to have a thread of techelet on the tzitzit itself?" Moshe replied, "Yes, you still have to have that." The point is that the thread of techelet energetically gives holiness to the entire talit. Then Korach had all his people dress in blue, and they disregarded that. They were in deliberate cynical rebellion; they were not in for the sake of unity, which is the whole point of machloket, or arguments, l'shem shemayim. He then posed another question, "If a house is full of holy books, is it exempt from having a mezuzah?" Moshe answered that one still needed a mezuzah. And Korach retorted: "Well, a Torah has 275 sections, but yet it does not exempt a house from having a mezuzah which only contains a few verses of a single section of the Torah? How is it that the two passages from the Torah inscribed on the mezuzah (the first two phrases of the shema) are more powerful than the Torah itself?" Moshe answered that it did not matter whether or not the house was full of books (Midrash Bamidbar Rabbah 18:3). Because it is the kedusha, holiness, from the mezuzah that adds kedusha to the entire house. In essence, Moshe was saying that the mezuzah instructions are the direct word of Hashem. A deeper interpretation is that the Torah as Hashem's guidebook for holiness, and ultimately liberation is about aligning with the mystic divine heart energy, which transcends the mind, and is not about logic, which limits the mind.

Korach used his logic to further his goals of receiving for self, alone. At some level, Aharon too had started at the left column, which is to receive for self, alone, but because he valued giving and creating peace, he moved, under the energetics of Avraham, into right-column consciousness. That is where the priesthood is eternally established. However, Korach just wanted to be part of the priesthood without earning it, without transcending his consciousness from receiving for self, alone, into the higher consciousness.

Moshe and Aharon prayed and tried to give Korach and his people some time to reconsider and wake up from their conscious or unconscious negativity. Finally, Moshe said, "Okay, come tomorrow and give the offering." Now, they should have been careful about this because they had just seen what happened to Nadav and Abihu, who had given an inappropriate offering. Instead, Aviram and Dathan completely flouted and challenged Moshe's authority. They were looking to create a war and to create division and difficulty with the claim that it was "for the love of Am Yisrael."

This whole Korach anti-spiritual, evolutionary scenario is played out in every generation, and it is no different today in today's spiritual test-crises. Not even the "I love Am Yisrael" rhetoric has changed and, as a result, many people's spiritual evolution is being undermined. Korach and his cohorts were actually calling Moshe a liar, because he had not yet brought them to the Promised Land (BeMidbar 16:14). They did not understand that they were getting there, but in God's timing.

Moshe was hurt by their words. He prayed that God would not receive any of their offerings: "I did not take a single donkey from them!" In other words, these people were complaining against a leader who had not taken or asked anything from anyone. He had done only what God desires of all of us, which is to walk humbly with God (Mikha 6:8).

The power of gevurah was unleashed here. Moshe knew quite well the consequences of a rejected offering. If they were going to do an offering that would not be accepted, they would be burned up. And this is exactly what happened. Korach and his followers accepted the dare, and they approached with their offerings. Moshe then warned the people to stay away from Korach and his ey'rev rav followers, and to move away from the tents of these people, and not to touch anything that was theirs, because they were about to witness a trial by Spirit that would demonstrate once and for all that Moshe did not elect himself, but that he had been elected by God. Moshe barely finished speaking when the earth opened up underneath Korach, Dathan, Aviram, and O'n, and gobbled them up, along with their families and their tents. At the same time, a fire shot out from the Mishkan and consumed their 250 followers.

This story teaches us that egocentric behavior eventually draws the fire of gevurah. But it is not only about the consequences of egocentric actions and consciousness. Everyone has a divine assignment. It is never a good idea to envy someone else's assignment. It is hard enough to do our own. All of life is a divine mission, and Korach did not understand this. He was really more concerned about (and "consumed" by) "I have." Because he had so much wealth, he became a slave to his ego, whose slogan was "I want more, because the more I have, the more I am." He was envious of his cousins, and missed the point that it is not about who we are on planet Earth, or how much we accomplish on the planet Earth, but who we are deep inside our soul of souls. The real question is "What is the consciousness with which we are living?" God's question to Adam and Cha'vah was not "What have you done? What have you achieved?" but "Where are you?"

Two thousand years ago, the Torah sages of Yavneh put it this way:

I am a creation, and my friend is also a creation; my work is in the village and his work is in the field; he rises up in the morning to do his work, and I rise up in the morning to do my work; as he does not interfere with my work, likewise do I not interfere with his work; and lest you say, 'I do more and he does less', we have learned that it matters not whether one does more or whether one does less, as long as one's heart is directed to [God].

(Talmud Bav'li, Berachot 17a)

What really matters in all of our discussions and all of our actions, and even in how we choose to eat our food, is "Are our intentions for the sake of heaven?" Everyone has a life mission, a "calling," and we have to remember who is calling. If it is the ego calling in this process, then we miss the point. If we remember it is God who is calling, and that we are consciousness, then we are on the way to fulfill our mission.

All missions count as equal. In that sense, Korach was right—we are all equal, but we all are given different assignments. In a football team, the guard blocks, the quarterback passes and calls the signals. All of us have different roles, and we need to be at peace with the role we are given over time; otherwise, the whole thing breaks down. That, in essence, on just the hierarchical level, was being jeopardized by Korach. What he was doing was going to destroy and cause great chaos in Am Yisrael. By his action and intention, he was not going to create a pseudo-good sounding "democratic model." The lesson of Korach's fiasco is that one person's assignment bringing him or her greater spiritual awareness, may be another person's poison. Once we start to understand this, our spiritual function in life gets smoother and happier. We are all given what we need for our spiritual evolution, and it is best to avoid egocentrically envying and being jealous of other people.

As we move a little deeper into this theme, we see that it is not just about Korach and his need to feed his ego. On a deeper level, why did Korach get swallowed up by the earth? That question takes us toward a more metaphysical understanding of the event. From a kabbalistic perspective, Korach's ey'rev rav energy actually incarnated in him as one of the incarnations of Kayin

(Cain). Moshe, as we know, was an incarnation of Hevel (Abel) (Zohar, Vol. 1, folio 28b). They were carrying out the same argument again, where Hevel (Moshe) was being attacked by Kayin (Korach), with Kayin attempting to destroy him. He was also attempting to kill or destroy Moshe's spiritual gift and mission, as a channel of God to bring forth the Torah and the three-column system. Korach was using his intelligence powered by his ego as his main weapon. The Egyptian (ego) position was that there is only the left column: receive for self, alone. Korach was saying "There is only one column here, which is to receive for self, alone." This was the Egyptian system Am Yisrael had just left. It did not allow for the three-column system to exist. It basically very innocently declared that we need to just be at the Ayn Sof (אין סוף) level, where we are only receiving, because that is what happens at the level of Ayn Sof. It is kind of like when we say "We are all one," but we do not really mean it, and people use it to justify wrong actions or behavior. Or they talk about how it is all about "love," but they are not really acting lovingly, but using the word as a form of manipulation. Korach was basically saying "We are all equal, and everything is fine." And in a limited way he was correct, we are all equal under God; we are each given a mission, equally. But God creates a mission for everybody, and we have to have the understanding and humility to know that each of us has a different mission, which on the superficial level of this incarnation appears to be a hierarchy. It is actually the outflowing of the cosmic order designed to help us become liberated. So, Korach was specifically trying to undermine the three-column system by misusing ideas of political democracy in a "politically correct" way to disconnect Am Yisrael from the cosmic order needed for our divine evolution back to deveikut/chey'rut.

Another part of the Hevel and Kayin argument was that Hevel, according to the Midrash, saw God as the source of human action and creation whereas Kayin saw technology, logic, and science as the source of all things, and that humans were essentially separate from God. These are radically different worldviews and teachings, which are blatantly a source of conflict today as well. Korach was also speaking lashon hara by saying to Moshe "You are taking it all for yourself," which of course was not true. Moshe was a tzaddik gadol, and had taken nothing from anyone. At that level, there is only one column, the middle column, which is connected to receiving for self, alone, in order to share; it is the central column which is the path of enlightenment with merging of *dakar* (דכר) and *nukva* (נוקבא), the sacred masculine and feminine. The middle column contains only light. Moshe, as a tzaddik, was already in that place of light. Korach, on the other hand, was taking the ego (Egyptian) route to the light, which is perhaps why Egypt was essentially destroyed. The Egyptian symbolic ego position was that there is only one principle: "We are here to take." This is the battle cry of the ego, undermining the process of spiritual evolution. Korach tried to create a deluded state of mind in Am Yisrael and bring them back into the egocentric state of the Egyptians, who were living in that mindset, and from whom Am Yisrael was in the process of distancing themselves spiritually. Moshe and Korach were playing all this out at a very deep level: Hevel/Moshe represented the right column, and Kayin/Korach the left column, or the negative pole. Therefore, the offerings of Korach and his 250 followers were not accepted just like Kayin's offering was not accepted.

Yitro, Moshe's father-in-law, was also said to be an incarnation of Kayin, but he was able to complete his tikkun and sever himself from Kayin energy, and to accept Moshe's greatness and to work it out within the Hevel incarnation of Moshe (Zohar, Vol. 1, folio 28b). Korach, however, was unable to do this, and the earth swallowed him up. The earth was chosen for this task because the earth, at one level, is the "negative" pole, meaning it just receives everything from the Divine. Now, at another level, the earth gives back by carrying and nurturing all of physical creation, but at one level it is only receiving. Korach was only receiving, and so he was swallowed up because he was not able to master the energy, to receive in order to share. He was only capable of "swallowing," and so it is energetically just that he, in turn, was swallowed.

One would think that Am Yisrael and the ey'rev rav would understand what was going on, but they did not. Korach and the whole group were swallowed alive. Immediately after that, the remaining ey'rev rav complained that Moshe had killed the "God's people" (BeMidbar 17:6). This resulted in a plague that broke out among the people. Moshe, again, being in the position of sharing, told Aharon: "Take the fire pan and place on it some fire from the altar. Offer incense and take it quickly to the community to make atonement for them." They were thus able to stop the plague. This not only teaches about Moshe's humility, but also the power of incense as a tool to prevent plagues, as well as the power of prayer to prevent plagues. Still, the people did not quite understand, so Moshe tried to bring the peoples' awareness to a higher level. God instructed him to gather the twelve tribal leaders and Aharon, and collect their scepters, their tribal staffs. By this trial, whoever staff sprouted, or did something else unusual, it was a sign from God that that person was the truly appointed leader. Two days later, almonds and flowers grew out of Aharon's staff. Again, God intervened to tell the people "Wake up, pay attention!" This is not about ego; it is about seeing through alma d'shikra and beyond the dualistic events of the world, in order to become liberated spiritually and fulfill Am Yisrael's collective mission of becoming a light unto the nations.

To summarize, there are certain spiritual principles that we need to honor as part of evolving on the path of kedusha and deveikut/chey'rut:

- We are here to identify with consciousness, and not with ego and the play of the dualistic world. This means that although we have a left pole, which is receiving for self, alone, and we want the left pole to be as strong as possible in order to draw down spiritual energy and grace, which is good, but we also need to make sure it connects to the right pole, which is about receiving in order to share. This is an important cosmic principle that Korach, as the archetype of the ey'rev rav, was trying to invalidate. Without this movement of energy through the middle pole to the right pole, we do not transmute it into receiving in order to share, and the result is the destructive difficulty that Korach created in his attempt to undermine the spiritual evolution of Am Yisrael. This same story is happening today with a new crop of ey'rev rav.

- Everyone has a divine mission. We are all equal as a spark of the Divine, but all the divine missions are different. One person's mission that elevates him or her could be a poison to somebody else. In this context, we understand that groups, nations, and so on need a certain level of hierarchy to achieve their mission. Even though there exists the illusion of a spiritual hierarchy, as well as a governing hierarchy, on the planet, we must always keep in mind that everyone (each at their unique level of spiritual evolution) is essentially equal, because we all evolve to God, merging at our own individual pace. A God-based spiritual hierarchy of spiritually mature people can more easily move people from chaos into order and God-merging. For Am Yisrael, the divine order of both sets (spiritual and governing) working together was established with the intention of elevating everyone.

- All holy intentions notwithstanding, there is always the danger of getting trapped in spiritual ego, as evidenced by Korach, who was at a high level of intellectual Torah scholarship. As I have said elsewhere, there are many dead bodies along the way to deveikut. In the case of Korach and his followers, it is a literal teaching.

- It is important to have a humble relationship with a personal tzaddik to support one along the way and prevent one from getting stuck and possibly spiritually or literally killed in the web of the spiritual ego. Korach and his followers were severely spiritually immature, and stricken with egocentric resistance to the divinely assigned role of Moshe as a tzaddik gadol for Am Yisrael.

- Not everyone is spiritually mature enough to have a tzaddik and benefit from the teaching and wisdom, but it is important to respect and honor the tzaddikim even if one is not yet spiritually ready for them.

May we all be blessed to have the awareness and the humility to rejoice in the divine mission that we are given, which is to know God as well as fulfill the particulars of our personal mission. May we all be spiritually mature enough to find and benefit from a tzaddik in our spiritual unfolding so that we do not end up like Korach. May we all be blessed that we are able to intensely receive, and have the ability to transmute that intense capacity, bringing therefore peace to the planet and ourselves.

Amen

Chukat

PARASHAH Chukat makes it very clear that we cannot know the mysteries of the Divine. As stated by King Solomon, who knew almost all the mysteries, "All this have I proved by wisdom: I said, I will be wise; but it is far from me" (Kohelet 7:23). The limited human mind cannot really fathom all the great mysteries of that which is beyond the mind.

This does not mean that we should not try to know the mysteries. This is where we get into the different ways of interpreting. For example, some people say "It is all about faith," and there is a good case for that. Indeed, parashah Chukat makes the point that faith is the most important ingredient in spiritual life. This is made clear in the Torah's description of the parah adumah (אדומה פרה), the "red heifer" ritual—a mystery that remains beyond any attempt at logical reasoning. We are also told in this parashah that when the people rebelled following the death of Aharon, God responded to their complaining by summoning poisonous snakes to bite them. The people quickly regretted their actions and pleaded with Moshe to save them from the snakes. Moshe was instructed by God to fashion the image of a snake out of copper, and affix it onto a wooden post, and whoever looked up at the image survived the bites.

Soon thereafter, the people were attacked by the armies of O'g and Sichon, two of the last remaining giants descended from the fallen angels, the nephilim (נפילים) (Bereisheet 6:4; Devarim 3:10), who survived the Great Flood of Noah's time (Midrash Devarim Rabbah 11:10). Having lost Aharon, who was the defense system of Israel, they had to muster all of their faith in doing battle against these two giants and their mighty armies.

Faith is also needed in studying the mysteries of our ancient way, such as that of the red cow ritual mentioned earlier. Some people say that faith means "Don't question this, just do it." On a higher level, we have to look at some of the great teachers, like Moses Maimonides and Rashi. They expended a great deal of time and energy trying to figure out "What does parah adumah mean?" Yet, we have to follow the instructions of the red cow ritual; we have to have faith that there is meaning to it. At the same time, it is our responsibility to do our spiritual work in grappling with it. We must struggle as hard as we can to understand the ways of God, and to understand that we cannot fully understand. But we can certainly draw lessons from it, and perhaps even several little bits of conclusions. But we may not understand the whole thing.

Korach is an example of that. On one level, Korach's questions were a setup. "Do we really have to follow this? I mean, if we make everything blue isn't that good enough? If we have holy books, isn't that enough to protect the room?" They were literal questions and, of course, his desire was not an argument for the sake of God (which is looked upon as a good thing), but for the sake of himself—to make himself right and Moshe wrong. Not only that, but he wanted to make the Torah wrong, and the hierarchy of the spiritual group wrong. In his eyes, Moshe, Aharon, and Yehoshua were all wrong. Korach did not ask to gain knowledge, but to undermine.

Korach was giving a variety of messages. He chose belief alone, which was where his questions were going. For him, belief was enough. Korach was saying "I understand all the spiritual reasons of why we do certain things and not others, and I don't want any help." But he missed the point. He was coming from the negative pole of self, alone. In self, alone, it is either me or it is nothing; it is all God's responsibility. Neither is the right answer in the larger context. We are light beings, and the work that must be done goes beyond faith. The work that must be done is to transform ourselves into radiant bodies of light. Without doing that work, only a limited light can be revealed.

So, when the lesson of Chukat starts out with "The following is declared to be the Torah's decree as commanded by God," is it just saying that we need to follow the instructions and not ask any questions, or is it saying something else? Moreover, is it a law of the Torah that we must ask why things are happening to us, and that we must take responsibility for doing spiritual work? Must we do everything to build the light, which then further connects our heart to the Divine?

A really interesting story showing the mystery of faith and the laws of cause and effect is one of a desperate mother who came to New York from Israel to raise money for a liver transplant for her son. She was in a taxicab. She had raised $50,000 over a period of months from incredibly hard work, and begging on the streets for her son. She fell asleep in the taxicab because she was so exhausted. When they arrived at her destination the taxi driver woke her up, and she paid him the fare and left. She did not have a bank, so she was carrying everything in her purse, and it suddenly occurred to her that she had left her purse in the taxi! The woman was beyond herself with grief and shock as she had no way of knowing which taxi it was, and she barely spoke English. But she had faith. And so, she composed herself and did a deep kabbalistic prayer with all her heart and all her faith, and went to bed. The next morning she received a call from the cab driver, saying, "I found your purse, and I think you want it back." Of course, she was ecstatic.

She said, "Why did you call me, and not take the money?"

He said, "You know, my mother told me it was very important to be nice to the Jews. I don't want a reward, I just want a blessing."

She blessed him that he should have a long, healthy, and peaceful life. He thanked her and went on his way. The next day he became very, very ill. He was not able to go to work (he was a part-time taxi driver who happened to work at the Twin Towers). This day was September 11, so her blessing saved his life. So we know a little of how this works. At one level there is a mystery, and there is also not so much a mystery (when you share and give and do good works, good things happen), often, but not always. So this is the paradox of this whole thing.

How does the red heifer ritual fit into this? The red heifer is an essential, unresolved paradox. As it says in the Torah, the person who did this ceremony, however pure he might be, became impure and must take a mikveh and wash his clothes afterwards. And the person for whom the ceremony was performed, who had been impure, became pure. What does this mean? At one level, the kabbalah teaches that whoever thinks of himself as pure is really impure, and whoever thinks of himself as impure has the potential to become pure.

We need to explore the concepts of taharah (טהרה—purity) and tumah (טומאה—impurity). Impurity implies contact with death. And taharah is purity, in the sense of clearing all negativity that accompanies this encounter. The red heifer on another level also connects the people to the restoration of energy to a short-circuited negative pole. In this context, it is significant that it follows the parashah Korach, and on one level it is the remedy for Korach.

It reestablished the three columns of energy of Etz Chaim, which Korach with his one-pole view was attempting to disrupt.

Another aspect of the red heifer was that it was an ox, which represented the greatest pull of the negative pole. It is also the light that was best able to reconnect, repair, and reactivate the full three-column circuitry and remove the tumah of Korach. Red also symbolizes the purification of the blood, or soul energy of the people before the messiah can enter the Temple Mount.

Another part of this parashah recounts the passing of Moshe's older sister, Miriam, who had been a key energetic part of the leadership of Am Yisrael (Mikha 6:4). The people became very upset over her death. One reason for this, aside from her spiritual importance, was that when she was alive the "Well of Miriam" followed Am Yisrael during their journey in the desert, providing them with water (Midrash Tanchuma, Bamidbar, Chap. 2). When she left her body, the well disappeared and they were out of water (BeMidbar 20:2). Because of their lack of faith, the people immediately began to complain, and at some level it may have pushed Moshe over his limit, as they were demanding that he create water for them out of thin air. God then said, "Speak to the cliff in their presence, and it will give forth its water." Instead, Moshe gathered everyone around the rock and declared: "Listen now, you rebels! Shall we produce water for you from this cliff?" With that he struck the rock twice with his staff, perhaps in anger and frustration, and water gushed forth. But then God said: "You did not have enough faith in me to sanctify me in the presence of the Israelites! Therefore, you shall not bring this assembly to the land that I have given you" (BeMidbar 20:12).

There are a few ways to interpret this:

- Moshe just blew it as a human being.
- Moshe knew that the people were not ready to go into the Land of Israel at the messianic consciousness, which he would bring. It is said that if he had entered Eretz Yisrael, it would have brought the messiah. Moshe would have become the messiah (Zohar, Vol. 1, folio 27a), and he did not feel the people were ready for that to happen, so he could not enter.

- Miriam had been functioning as malchut. So when Miriam
  left her body, or possibly ascended, Moshe had to take on her
  function as well, which shifted the energy. As malchut, she
  was drawing her devotion and yearning from the earth up,
  reaching to the heavens. Moshe's work was to bring down
  the light of God. With her gone, he had to come down from
  that high position and relate to the people differently to get
  them to increase their yearning for God. So by making this
  error and having to repent for that, it allowed him to not be so
  perfect so that he could come down to their level and inspire
  them from the earthly point as well.

The key spiritual focus of Chukat is faith. There are many levels of faith
and many ways not to show faith as has been well demonstrated by Am Yisrael during their forty years in the desert. They lacked faith in God, faith in
Moshe, faith in the Promised Land, and faith in themselves. Chukat raised
another level of faith, as it asked us to have faith in the mystery of the red
heifer paradox, which is beyond our rational understanding. The subtleness
of the issue of faith takes us beyond the basics of our faith that there is a God.
It takes us to an essential level of faith needed for the enlightenment process,
a quality of faith needed for the complete surrender to the unfolding (and the
timing of the unfolding) of the shekhinah energy within us.

Throughout our history, the issue of surrender to the timing and unfolding
of the shekhinah energy in our lives, in general, has been a difficult struggle,
which has resulted in a variety of tragic consequences. Even great sages such
as the three rabbis R. Ben Azzai, R. Ben Zoma, and R. Ben Avuya stumbled
amid these struggles while journeying in the mystery realm of PaRDeS (Talmud
Bav'li, Chagigah 14b). Later, rabbis such as Joseph Dela Renino felt it was time
to defeat Satan and thus he led his followers into destruction; and like the son of
Rabbi Adam Ba'al Shem, who pressured the Ba'al Shem Tov to invoke a certain
angelic being, which resulted in his death. In all these cases, these people came
to an early demise. In each case, these rabbis did not have faith in the timing of
God's shekhinah energy for the evolution of their enlightenment, and rushed
too eagerly and prematurely into the spiritual energy of divine merging.

The quality of faith Chukat teaches us requires a profound surrender to and respect for the unfolding of the sacred energy within ourselves. The best way to be open and surrendered to this movement of the Divine within is not have any particular intention, especially about enlightenment. All directed intention builds ego, and it is ego that gets us in spiritual trouble. "A man cannot have a vision of me and still exist" (Shemot 33:20). This is referring to the importance of sincere surrendered humility. This quality is essential for the evolution of human consciousness. This is why Moshe was considered the most humble man (BeMidbar 12:3). It is ego that makes us overestimate when we are ready for the next level of spiritual experience and development such as merging with the One. Desire for the One is not the same as creating an intention to merge with the One at a particular point in time. Divine desire is motivational, but not directional. This is different than having an intention in a particular ceremony, which is needed for the directionality of the flow of the ceremony. Rather, it means letting your life be lived by holiness, by love, and by enlightenment without a particular intention, yet guided by the halakhah (הלכה—practice), kedusha (קדושה—holiness), and by ahavat Hashem (השם אהבת—love for the Divine). It means living in a way that allows for and draws grace to spontaneously happen, rather trying to egocentrically force experiences in our spiritual life. It is living with surrendered wonderment to the unfolding of the divine in our lives, and being at peace with what we receive rather than desiring what others have spiritually received. Spiritually living, in this way, activates a certain inner peace and patience that sustains us on the spiritual path. It is having faith that the unfolding of Hashem's grace in our lives is exactly what we need.

The mystery of Chukat, from an enlightenment point of view, is living with the internal paradox of a burning desire for the divine and at the same time not creating an egocentric-driven, time-oriented intent. It is a metaphor for the red heifer, the ritual making impure the person doing the ceremony, and making pure the person for whom the ceremony is being performed. It is this egocentric intent that can lead to our deadly downfall as "I" makes us impure. The secret to Chukat on the spiritual plane is then to let God guide us and make us pure, and not to be led by our ego, which tends to be influenced by the dark side and tends to mislead us. There is no "enlightened one"; there is only enlightenment. Enlightenment is given to us as an act of grace. We cannot technique our way to God. We paradoxically cannot earn grace. By its very definition, grace is an act of the divine beyond our comprehension as with the divine intervention of the exodus. This is the mystery of Chukat; it is beyond logic, reason, and linearity. This is the secret of Chukat and the Great Torah Way. Our job is to keep showing up, create and live with as much kedusha as possible, and live in the readiness to receive grace however and whenever it appears in our lives. The final step to the One is beyond our control; it is in the hands of God as grace.

May we all be blessed with the peace and contentment of this understanding. Amen

Balak

Tʜɪs is a powerful parashah, because it includes the story of Balak, king of Moab, and Balaam, the prophet of Midian. On a certain level, Balaam was considered the twin soul of Moshe. The Midrash makes it clear that in Israel there has never been a prophet like Moshe, but among the nations of the world, there was one, and that was Balaam (Midrash Bamidbar Rabbah 14:19). What was the difference? Moshe was righteous, and Balaam was wicked. The light and the dark can have equal levels of power. What does it have to do with us? There is a Moshe and a Balaam in each of us. It is important to understand how Balaam fell, so we can learn about how to prevent falling in our own lives.

One of the greatest modern mythic stories is told in the *Star Wars* series, which insightfully traces how someone with power, intuition, and intelligence fell to the dark side; this, of course, is Anakin Skywalker, who became Darth Vader. Why did he fall to the dark side? First, he did not listen to God. Next, he did not listen to his teacher, Obi-Wan Kenobi—even in the end, when Obi-Wan was on the high ground and warned "Don't do it!" Still, Anakin ignored him, lost his legs, and nearly died. Finally, he did not have communion with his peers, the other Jedi knights, or communion with his wife. In fact, he lied to his wife about his situation. And he further fell when the dark side created doubt, the main component that further nurtured his downfall. He also had certain personal weaknesses such as an egocentric craving for power. His entire context was an urge toward power and domination, rather than an urge to serve God. He also had a certain amount of self-righteousness in that craving. The Jedi did not have an effective way of dealing with his shadow side, and thus Obi-Wan Kenobi could not help Anakin integrate his dark side. He only told him to suppress it. However, something that is suppressed long enough tends to come out in unbalanced ways. The result was that without getting the teaching he needed, without trusting his teacher, without having a relationship with his people and with his wife, Anakin's ego inflated without limit, and so did his craving for power. While attempting to undo a previous pattern (trying to rescue his mother by rescuing his wife at childbirth), he became an easy prey for the dark side.

Let us examine closely how Balaam himself fell. After hearing how his neighbors, the Amorites, were defeated in battle by the Israelites, and how even O'g the giant was killed, Moab's King Balak feared the Israelites as they approached his territory. Even though the Israelites did not provoke him, and were instructed by God not to war against him (Devarim 2:9), he, nevertheless, began to scheme their destruction by means other than war, since war was ineffective against them. He sent word to neighboring Midian, where Balaam was a renowned prophet and sorcerer, and requested that Balaam use his powers to destroy Israel by cursing them. Balaam's reply to Balak's messengers was: "Go home! God refuses to let me go with you. [They are a blessed nation]." When the messengers reported back to Balak, Balak tried again by dispatching messengers of higher stature than the previous ones. This time, because of his own ego and his desire for the riches and power promised him by Balak, Balaam hesitated to call the whole thing off and instead told the second group of messengers to spend the night, and he would see whether God had changed His mind. He was more concerned about his own ego and honor than about the will of God. He did not have anyone else to consult with; he had God, yes, but he would not listen to his teacher, which was God.

In essence, one of the conditions that we may fall into when we do not have feedback from community is that we hear only what we want to hear and see only what we want to see. So, Balaam denied his basic intuition and the message from God. He saddled his donkey and journeyed to meet with Balak, who was waiting for him to curse Am Yisrael. Along the way, an angel of God blocked his path, and even though he could not see the angel, his donkey saw it! While Balaam was a prophet and could see the future, when it concerned him personally, his ego eclipsed his perception.

The spiritual message is that if we can be open to what is really happening around us, we can find the answers to our questions from what we hear and see and from the immediate feedback, coming from all levels of our social community. Most of the time, the only reason questions persist is because we are afraid of the answers. I find that happening all of the time. If we are caught in our desire to receive for self, alone, as were Anakin Skywalker and Balaam, we become distanced and blocked from the truth. This is what happens when people are only thinking about themselves; the world becomes like a mirror, where we see nothing but our own reflection. We see only what people can give us, or what we can take from them. The lesson is that it is important to be able to see and hear feedback from the people around us. Anakin Skywalker could not do this; he could not even see and hear feedback from his wife. If we listen to this feedback, we go a long way toward avoiding a Balaam disaster in our lives.

Balaam was asked by Balak to give the Israelites the evil eye, which he really could not do, because they were blessed. He was told clearly by God that he could not do anything other than what God would tell him to do. I want to explore the concept of the "evil eye." We are given things, not necessarily because we deserve them, but because of what we may perhaps do in the future. When we are judged by others, it awakens the judgment over us, and may cause us to lose what we have. Therefore, it is important not to assume that nothing bad can happen to a person who is righteous and sharing. All of us are judged, and whatever we do not necessarily deserve can be taken away from us. One of our only protections is to not judge others. Then judgment is not drawn into the world, either for others or for ourselves. If we are able to hold ourselves back from judging others, then the evil eye can have no control over us. Now this does not mean that whatever we, or others do, is fine; it means we need to be discriminating when it comes to judging. That is different from judging somebody wrongly. You can also choose to say, "This not what I want to do, this is not what I want to be associated with, it doesn't really feel right to me." This is different from judgment, which is saying, "You're wrong, I'm right; I'm one up on you." It is helpful to be clear in one's life between the ongoing discrimination between actions that either takes us closer to Hashem or away from Hashem, and the destructive forces of judgment.

Balaam had his own agenda. Even though God had given him a clear message not to go, he misunderstood and kept pushing until God finally said, "Okay, go, but only with the condition that you speak only the words that I will put in your mouth." It was at this point that an angel appeared with a sword in his hand blocking his way, a clear statement by God that Balaam should have chosen to not go to Balak. Again, though, God gave him a subtle dispensation, cautioning Balaam to say only the words He put in his mouth. But Balaam did not see the bigger picture, namely, not to go, which would have saved his life. He understood in part, thinking, "It's okay to go as long as I only say what God tells me."

So, Balak and Balaam gathered and made an offering to invoke power against Am Yisrael. The dark side uses the same occult dynamics as the light, but for egocentric and destructive reasons. However, under the direction of God, Balaam blessed the Israelites instead of cursing them! He could not transform the light force into negativity because there was a protective shield around Am Yisrael, based on the power of Moshe, the elders, the kohan'im, the Levites, and the righteous of the people. He simply could not penetrate the righteousness that emanated from them. This shows that the more positivity and righteousness we create by living in the Great Torah Way, the harder it is to penetrate the shield. The efforts of the dark occult are still happening today, as exemplified by the immense dark occult power generated by the Nazis, which Am Yisrael was not collectively prepared for, as well as the dark occult forces generated today to weaken Am Yisrael spiritually and thus politically.

Because Balak and Balaam were energetically blocked the first time, they made a second attempt. Instead of trying to curse the people, they went to a location where they could only see a portion of the people. They thought that if they could attack only a few people at a time, they would eventually infiltrate the rest. But again, the curses became a blessing. They were trying to create fragmentation and discord, but they failed.

In a third attempt, Balaam tried not to curse, but to bless, and the power of that blessing, at least temporarily, transformed his negative traits. That gives us an idea of how powerful blessing and positivity can be. As Balaam connected to the light, he started to see the future, and he prophesied how all nations will rise up and fall. Balak was very upset about this, but Balaam ignored him. Unfortunately, however, his consciousness did not permanently transform, because he came up with another idea to undermine Am Yisrael. He thought that if he could not defeat them through cursing, perhaps appealing to their lustful desires would work, and they would self-destruct! And so,

Balaam arranged to sexually tempt Am Yisrael with the young ladies of the Midianites, who would only have sexual intercourse with them if they performed the disgusting idol worship rituals to Ba'al Pe'or, thus causing them to give up their own spiritual heritage.

We are constantly challenged in our spiritual evolution by the temptation to give in to the lusts of our desires. The loving and clever support of our community is extremely important at these times. They help us to not become egocentrically self-deluded by intellectual rationalization or New Age licentiousness. Equally important is creating the proper balance between enjoying and being nourished by uplifting, sustainable spiritual pleasures and excessive suppression, which may create subtle or obvious spiritual damage. Too many have become dry, rigid, and contracted on the Torah Way, or most any spiritual path, by becoming too strict with themselves. This can undermine our long-term spiritual efforts and create a variety of gevurah/judgment imbalances and violence to self and others. On the other hand, succumbing to outright lusts that damage or disconnect us from the Torah Way may result in spiritual or literal death, such as what happened to the men of Am Yisrael. Their actions resulted in a plague that killed 24,000 people (perhaps this is the same 24,000 people who died in the plague with Rabbi Akiba, because they failed to treat each other with human dignity).

How do we find the best balance that both nourishes and sustains us? We need to remember always that the ways of the Torah are *metuka* (sweetness) and simcha (spiritual joy), essential to the spiritual path, and for opening up and maintaining the spiritual connection. If the way one is walking the Torah path is not fun and nourishing for the soul, then one might do well to question if one is in spiritual balance. Feedback from one's spiritual community, spiritual elders, and spouse is therefore certainly important.

As the Midianite and Moabite women were seducing Yisraelite men into worshipping false gods in return for sexual pleasure, a tribal leader named Zimri, head of the tribe of Shimon, took his lover, a Midianite princess named Koz'bee, and had intercourse with her right in front of Moshe and the people! No one acted, until Pinchas, Aharon's grandson, at the risk of his own life, became inspired into the role of a spiritual teacher and, taking a spear in hand, killed the couple.

Again, Zimri was the head of the tribe of Shimon. He was considered a spiritually evolved leader, and yet he fell into the trap of lust. The Torah warns us again and again that no matter who we are, if we let our desires and lusts to receive for self, alone, rule us in the areas of sex, power, money, or anything, it is very easy to fall. When Pinchas killed both Zimri and Koz'bee, the plague stopped. There may be a time, which we call the messianic time, when we are so linked into the One that any negativity can be overcome. But we are not there yet, so, no matter how evolved we might be in the Torah Way, we still need to be self-vigilant.

There is another message here, which is the power of individuals within Am Yisrael to uphold all the people, and it is the power of Aharon, of Moshe, of Miriam, and later Yehoshua. Not everyone is created equal, and those who have deep spiritual understanding or deep intellectual skills should not take advantage of them to receive only for self, alone, or for their own glory. On the contrary, they must become the servants of the people, and this is how the western way is very different from the eastern guru system, which can often be abused. Of course, it may be abused in the west as well, but the essence is different. The tzaddik is the servant of the people, which puts the tzaddik in a very different position with a very different quality of responsibility.

In this story, Balak, the king of Moab, was frightened by the huge mass of Am Yisrael approaching his borders. Instead of fighting them on the physical plane, he recognized that their strength was in their words and sought to attack them through speech. He also tried to use Balaam to curse them. But instead, Balaam's prayers were very powerful, as he was told he could only bless them. One of his blessings, of course, was something that we later adopted for use in our own prayers: "How good are your tents, Jacob, your tabernacles, Israel" (BeMidbar 24:5). Another important blessing was "Jacob [is like] the dust; who can count his [hordes]? Who can number the seed of Israel?" (BeMidbar 23:10). Is this a curse, or a blessing? Is it our lot to always live in solitude, even national loneliness, or to always be separate and different? We know about this as individuals. Most people on the spiritual path feel this loneliness and separation. Of course, at a certain level, we feel the oneness with all things and with all people, but I am not speaking about this elevated level. We are clearly seen as separate and we clearly live separately, from the Bereisheet 1:29 cuisine, to whatever the whole Torah lifestyle asks of us. Nonetheless, it is a blessing, because it is linked to excellence. This is excellence on a national level as well as on an individual level. In a certain way, Israel is incapable of fusing with any other nation, and does remain separate. So when people try to force the Jews to stop doing Shabbat or *b'rit milah* (ברית מילה—ritual circumcision), or to practice idolatry, the Jews prefer to die. That is why we had Masada, where 600 men, women, and children committed suicide rather than become slaves and prostitutes to the Romans.

Balaam understood that the Jewish people needed to remain separate in order to preserve a lifestyle rooted entirely in the Torah. Where they tried or were forced to assimilate, they lost their spiritual uniqueness and power, and this was detrimental to their ability to carry out their God-given task. This, of course, is one of the most important struggles on the spiritual path as well. We are all born originals, yet most people die as copies. The whole world wants the spiritually unique and intensely God-focused person to be like them, which is why we hear "Can't you just be normal?" What I teach at the Tree of Life is "awakened normality." Comprehensive awareness is threatening to people because, when they examine it, inherently it rocks their boats. So, we remain separate in our dress, our diet, and our ethical codes. Am Yisrael has remained separate throughout history, from its exile in Egypt to the modern era. This has allowed us to survive the influence of the cultures of other nations, even when they conquered us. Balaam gave us a blessing and a prophecy of this atop a mountain in Moab more than three thousand years ago. So we need not feel bad about feeling so separate.

This separation is not because we have a bad attitude, but it is for a higher purpose. Am Yisrael had the important, difficult, and unpopular task to be an elite nation, as the firstborn, whose goal was to relate the glory of the Divine. As Yesha'yahu (Isaiah) said in Isaiah 43:7, "For I have created him for my glory." God created us to this glory as a national entity, for the whole world. I cannot say that is actually happening at this time in history, but that is the task. It must be expressed through the people, through the land, through the economy, and through all actions. At the highest level, Am Yisrael must be an expression of the Beit HaMikdash.

We may ask the questions "Why does God need to choose a nation? Why can't God just elevate the entire world?" The answer is the same one that Korach received: Only a focused elite with a focused will and intention (keter) is capable of elevating the entire world, and only a chosen nation has the power to inject spirituality into the other nations. This is one purpose of the Torah. It is to develop a focused elite, who do not see themselves from the eyes of ethnocentrism, but who feel the connection of the oneness on the higher plane. This elect group must still operate from the separate position to have a strong enough vibration, willpower, intention, kavanah, to shift the consciousness of the world. At the same time, because Israel is not yet there, they must develop in Yisrael a strong enough intention by the minority to again shift the consciousness of the State of Israel, so that it can shift the consciousness of the world. The drama of Palestinians and Israelis is one of the stages on which most of this can take place in a very good way. It is an incredible opportunity. Balaam and the other prophets put it very clearly: "I'll make you a light unto the nations to be a light unto the Gentiles." But, they also said that before you can influence the world you have to have a spiritually functional nation. Then, and only then, can you be a light to the world. Balaam's blessing was clearly a blessing: We are to be a separate nation. It is a blessing that will give us the collective willpower to fulfill our task in creation, namely, that of relating God's glory to the world. Does that mean no other person or nation does this? It means that this is the task that Am Yisrael collectively has been given, and it is not easy. Each nation, each people, has been given a different task; this is the one that we have been given.

When we assimilate and become like everyone else, which the secular forces of the world would prefer (and are pressing for now and more so in the future), we lose our spiritual individuality, strength, respect, and recognition among the nations. This is a double-edged sword, particularly in the world today, where there is so much pressure to become a "normal" nation, so that we will become liked, appreciated, and accepted. The corporate world would prefer, under corporate globalism, that everybody dress the same, act the same, and eat the same foods. This is presently happening all over the world. Indigenous people are learning that McDonald's is now their indigenous food. This is a disastrous way to go, because each indigenous people has its own gift to give, which it cannot offer if it becomes just another shopping mall for corporate globalism. When we reject our special qualities, we are rejecting God and our cosmic God-given role. If we do not fulfill our task, we miss part of the point of why we are here on the planet.

Am Yisrael is unique. It has a chosen mission, and with it of course comes purpose and responsibility. In essence, it is servitude on a national level, not as slaves or lower-class citizens, but as people with a universal mission of becoming a light unto the nations. To fulfill this we must be a light unto ourselves as well. Each of us, operating as separate individuals, must inspire the rest to embrace a collective understanding, to create a nation that is a light unto the world. It is not an easy task, but somehow I believe that we can do this. This is the blessing of Balaam.

Our consciousness has the capacity to affect the wellbeing of others, whether positively or negatively. A small group of people, holding an intention, by nature of their being, can influence the greater whole to change. This has been proven from dozens of disciplines. Simply put, all life is interdependent and interconnected. Implicit in this is an entirely new understanding of the world. We are spiritual beings. We are involved in the process of shifting consciousness as our own transcendence unfolds. To the degree that we support the paradigm of life, and the wisdom that understands the interdependence and interconnectedness of all life, we nurture and support the very best within us.

It is the nature and intention of our souls that the parashah of Balak discusses. We are to strive toward recognizing, as Balaam did, the interconnectedness and interdependence of all forms of consciousness, from the plants to the single-celled to the human beings. This is applicable to kabbalah's four worlds: the *domem*, the still beings, the rock people; *tzo'mey'ach*, the sprouting beings, plants, trees; the *chay*, the animal beings; and *m'da'ber*, the speaking beings, or humans. Each group perceives the world very differently.

The dynamics of this cosmic interdependence and interconnectedness is becoming more and more vivid. In my youth, we did not even grow up with televisions, much less internet access. Consciousness has shifted the whole world in this process. Before the civil rights movement in the United States, black people could not drink at the same water fountain as white people. Although women's right to vote was won in the early 1900s, the shift in consciousness around women's rights has happened mostly in the last thirty years. Doctors, at a point in my lifetime, were still claiming that X-rays and smoking were safe. Somewhere along the line, people began to question. The paradigms went into conflict, and ultimately the shift in consciousness began. The sixties shifted the consciousness of the world. Again and again, as Margaret Mead has pointed out, a small group of focused people holding an intention, by nature of their being, can influence the greater whole to change toward a higher, evolutionary octave. Time is irrelevant, because time and space are only parameters of the much higher expression of the Divine, as the divine will. It is about willpower. Kavanah (כונה), or intention, is the power of consciousness focused by will. As nonlocal spiritual beings, we affect each other intimately. Balaam understood this on a national level. As we take this deeper, we understand it on a personal level, on the level of kehila (קהלה) and community of how we affect each other, and simply on the level of *shey'lot u'teshuvo't* (שאלות ותשובות), or questions and answers. The role of a spiritual teacher/tzaddik is to inspire us with the certainty of the Divine within us. He or she inspires in us the certainty that we can be liberated, that the light is within us, and that we simply need to find it.

An inspired collective of people creates a spiritual support system that inspires other people to open up to that. Even a small group of spiritual people can ultimately inspire a whole nation to transform spiritually. And that nation, acting in an inspired way, can inspire the whole world to wake up! May this blessing come true in our lifetimes.

Amen

Pinchas

This profound parashah helps us understand the deeper subtleties of the spiritual path. The opening of the story is simple in a certain way, having to do with the Moabites, ruled by King Balak, who, under the advice of Balaam, wanted to penetrate the energetic shield, the spiritual strength, of Am Yisrael. The Moabites and Midianites realized they could not defeat the Israelites in battle, so they tried to defeat them in the bedroom. The women of Moab and the women of Midian (particularly the daughters of Midian) came into the Israelite camp with the intent to seduce the Israelite men. Moreover, they intended to introduce the men to Midianite idol worship. In fact, after they seduced the men, they refused to sleep with them until they bowed to Ba'al Pe'or. It is important to understand that this was not just a sexual undermining, but a lesson in how the dark occult, symbolized by the direction of Balaam, who was a master of the dark force, uses sexual activity to undermine the light. As taught in the mystical wisdom of the kabbalah, and required in the training of the ancient sages, before a rabbi could assume leadership in the Sanhedrin, he had to understand the ways of the dark occult and how to nullify them (Talmud Bav'li, Sanhedrin 17a). This not only included how to nullify shedim (demons) and dybukim (disembodied negative entities), but also awareness of larger dark forces on the planet, such as the nephilim (fallen angels). The release of sexual fluids is energetic (nefesh) food for these dark forces if intercourse is done in lustful ways, rather than for the love of God. Loss of nefesh energy, in turn, weakens the energy of the light force. The use of mind-altering drugs also makes people more susceptible to being controlled by the dark side, and often leads to violence. This happened earlier to Aharon's two sons, Nadav and Avihu, who were consumed by a heavenly fire when they made their offerings in an inebriated state.

As mentioned in the previous parashah, among the women of Moab and Midian sent to seduce the Israelite men was a Midianite princess named Koz'bee, daughter of Tzur. According to the Midrash, she was sent to seduce

Moshe to completely undermine the energy of Am Yisrael and was misled by Zimri, who told her that he ranked higher than Moshe since he was of the second tribe (Shimon), while Moshe was of the third (Levi), and he too was surrounded by so many people, being a tribal chieftain (Midrash Shemot Rabbah 33:5). She connected with Zimri very deeply; some midrashim suggest that they saw each other as soulmates! This sexual seduction strategy worked so well that the whole Israelite consciousness was threatened with destruction. In fact, by the end, 24,000 men who were involved in this lustful sexual behavior and consequent idol worship died in a plague. Every level of society was affected, all the way up to Prince Zimri of the tribe of Shimon. The dark occult worked well through the power of sexual seduction in those times, and continues to work with equal potency today. The death of these 24,000 men, and of Zimri and Koz'bee, is a harsh warning not to be fooled by or succumb to these energetically delegitimizing dark occult tactics.

The leading prince from the tribe of Shimon, Zimri ben Salou, took the Midianite princess and began to have intercourse with her right in front of Moshe, the whole Am Yisrael, and in front of the Beit HaMikdash. To make things even worse, he mocked Moshe. According to the aforementioned Midrash, he said: "What do you say, Moshe, is she forbidden, or permitted? If you say she is forbidden, then who allowed you to marry the daughter of Yitro, Priest of Midian?" Zimri's use of disconnected left-brain logic was spoken like a true spiritual ey'rev rav. He was both mocking and disrespectful to Moshe as the God-appointed mortal leader of Am Yisrael, and dishonored the energy of the Beit HaMikdash. Like the spiritual ey'rev rav that he was, he spoke out of context and was also inaccurate because he did not acknowledge the overall energetics of Moshe's marriage, as Moshe had converted Yitro, the high priest of Midian, and his whole family, including Moshe's wife Zippora, to the Great Way of the Torah. Zippora had not seduced Moshe to worship Ba'al Pe'or or any other false deity. Zimri's attempt to humiliate Moshe is called a *chilul Hashem b'fe'her'siya* (חילול השם בפהרסיא), a desecration of the divine name in public. It actually merited the death sentence. Indeed, the sentence was swiftly carried out by Aharon's grandson, Pinchas, who was, at that moment, absolutely divinely inspired by his love for God. He forgot all about asking permission. He did not check with his grand-uncle, Moshe, and decided to take it all on himself to slay Zimri and Koz'bee. It was not merely a question of illicit sexual union, but more the sin of chilul Hashem b'fe'her'siya that activated his God-guided actions. At a deeper level, just before that moment of decision, it is suggested in the Zohar that Pinchas also took on the soul energies of Nadav and Avihu (Zohar, Vol. 3, folio 217a), Aharon's two sons, who were Pinchas's uncles and who were very high souls, in spite of the fact that they had been consumed by a heavenly fire because of an inappropriate offering. In this context, he was empowered by their soul energies, and his action helped to redeem their souls.

As alluded to earlier, according to the holy writings of the Arizal, Zimri had recognized Koz'bee as his soulmate. He was doing what he believed Hashem wanted him to do, except that he did it totally out of context, insulting Moshe and the Beit HaMikdash. The message here is paradoxical. There are other problems when you look at this, such as "Thou shalt not murder." Can we just go around murdering people without a fair hearing because God inspires us to do so? This level of explanation could, therefore, be a justification for the continual murderous actions of terrorism as a general policy. Part of the answer to this comes from a section in *Olat Riya* by Rabbi Abraham Isaac Kook:

> The only valid zealousness is that which is totally devoted to God. Therefore, God came and informed everybody that Pinchas's nature was identical with that of his grandfather, Aharon, who was good to all and pursued peace. Pinchas was far from being a murderer, since his intentions were all directed toward God.... We have to purify zealousness that it will always remain only out the love of God. Generally, it is impossible, and therefore there must be self-analysis to ensure it does not become the zealousness for another human being, which is destructive, but zealousness only for God, which brings with it a covenant of peace.... The love of God at its highest level turns into divine zealousness in its purest forms. It is expressed in the character of Eliyahu, and Pinchas is Eliyahu, the zealot who is the pinnacle of love for God.
>
> (Orot HaKodesh 3:244)

The incident of the seduction of the Israelites is not simply a sexual matter; there is a bigger picture. The moment Pinchas executed these two leaders, the plague that had broken out, and had already killed 24,000 people, stopped. Pinchas did the right action with the right intention. In doing so, he maintained Moshe's honor, uplifted the consciousness of the whole Israeli people, and saved the rest of the people from the plague. In that inspired moment, his action defeated the dark forces activated by Balaam that were undermining, weakening, and compromising all of Am Yisrael.

Pinchas was of the family of the priesthood; most likely he was trained from birth in the ancient prophetic ways of the integrated mind, enabling him to be intuitively and naturally connected to the greater reality of an integrated being walking in all four worlds, using both sides of his brain as a single integrated consciousness. This is different from a generalized religious, egocentric policy of terrorism, separation, and hate, which are not remotely related to any path toward liberation. This was a one-time God-motivated spontaneous action that prevented the downfall of Am Yisrael on multiple levels and defeated a specific dark occult action. Pinchas saw a deeper multidimensional truth, and in the intensity of the moment, he let go of the blindness of our conditioned consciousness of the world of assiyah.

Pinchas was rewarded for his inspired, yet balanced, right-left brained action, with a blessing (BeMidbar 25:12). For his restoration of the sacred balance, he was granted the "blessing of shalom" (peace). The Hebrew word shalom means a lot more than mere peace when it is traced to its root word, shalem. Shalem actually means completion and balance. The action of Pinchas restored the spiritual balance for Am Yisrael and for the universe. He balanced the play of both the hidden forces and revealed forces. More than not being put on trial for murder, he was rewarded to serve as a priestly inspiration to maintain this sacred spiritual balance. Upon the passing of his father, the high priest El'azar (an act not reported in the biblical record), Pinchas became the high priest and served in that function for decades. Some of the oral tradition suggested that not only did he live for a long time, but also that he actually never died. Rather, he changed his name to Eliyahu and became the great prophet Eliyahu (Elijah), as they both had such strong zeal for God. These epic figures, or single figure, Pinchas/Eliyahu, through their/his radical actions, saved the collective soul of Am Yisrael at least twice.

Another level of what was going on is also important. The people had become very weakened by this dark occult action. The names Balaam and Balak can be transmuted to "Amalek," the quintessential enemy of Am Yisrael. The "aam" (עַם) in "Balaam" and "lak" (לְק) in "Balak" become "Amalek" (עֲמָלֵק). Amalek is associated with doubt, confusion, and uncertainty—the scourge of spiritual people on all paths of enlightenment. These thoughtforms may undermine and defeat all liberation efforts on every level. They have the power to defeat everyone on the spiritual path. It is interesting that with Pinchas's action, the plague subsided, but it did not end. We still are facing that plague today. It is doubt and uncertainty that creates the plague. Pinchas's action reactivated the energy of certainty, necessary for the people to strengthen themselves and get back on the spiritual track. Uncertainty is the enemy of all humans on the spiritual path. Uncertainty is the cause of the plague of unconsciousness. Uncertainty keeps us in the realm of the Tree of Knowledge of Good and Evil, the realm of duality. Pinchas, in this moment, moved into the realm of spiritual certainty, the realm of Tree of Life consciousness. He woke up to the consciousness of the Tree of Life and went beyond polarity. What Pinchas reactivated was the world of certainty, and thus he restored the energetic awareness and energetic shield to Am Yisrael.

Most of us live in this world of duality, the world of uncertainty, the world of the Heisenberg Principle. This is the physical world. Our primary existence, however, is actually beyond the realm of the physical. We are multidimensional beings who live in all four worlds simultaneously, and we are only partly in the physical world of assiyah. Part of us primarily abides in the worlds of certainty. Certainty is part of the spiritual mystery that helps us become one with God. It includes the right-brained way of the God-inspired heart. It is *binaht ha'lev* (בִּינַת הלֵב), the wisdom of the heart. Pinchas's action takes us back to the essential kabbalistic teaching—the world on the physical plane is the world of illusion, the world of uncertainty—and instead elevates us beyond the world of illusion to the worlds of binah and chokhmah.

In the very moment that he took on the souls of Nadav and Avihu, Pinchas's transformation took us beyond the uncertainty of the physical world to the certainty of the higher realms. This was a great transformation that he reactivated for the people. That is why God intervened so that he would not be judged as a murderer, but as a savior of the people. In that way, Pinchas became a chariot, as Yosef did. They both were chariots of the Etz Chaim. A yod (י) was therefore added to his name, which represents the additional consciousness energy of who he was, just like the hey (ה) of Avraham was added to Abram (Zohar Vol. 3, folio 213b). This is a most deep meaning of parashah Pinchas, which is the ability to transcend the three-dimensional world of illusion, and inspire the people of Israel back to the higher realms.

Part of that chilul Hashem that occurred was that Zimri seriously missed the mark, not only because he was a tribal leader and therefore responsible for the physical wellbeing of the tribe, but also because as a tribal prince, he was also responsible for his tribe's spiritual welfare. Instead of encouraging his people to adhere to the commandments and follow Moshe, Zimri led them into doubt, confusion, and uncertainty. By so doing, he redirected them away from Moshe and the Beit HaMikdash, worsening things by belittling Moshe in the presence of the people in order to justify his own egocentric actions. He acted in a way that created a plague that threatened to destroy the entire nation. Pinchas, son of El'azar and grandson of Aharon, was God-motivated to do what he did.

Pinchas received a special award for saving the people and reconnecting the people to Tree of Life consciousness. BeMidbar 25:10–13 says:

> God spoke to Moses, saying, "Pinchas (a son of Eleazar and grandson of Aaron the priest) was the one who zealously took up my cause among the Israelites and turned my anger away from them, so that I did not destroy them in my demand for exclusive worship. Therefore, tell him that I have given him my covenant of peace. This shall imply a covenant of eternal priesthood to him and his descendants after him. It is [given to him] because he zealously took up God's cause and made atonement for the Israelites."

Pinchas was not originally considered a kohain, though he was one of El'azar's children, because he was not old enough at the time that the kohan'im were created. This divine intervention showed that the priesthood could be achieved not only through lineage, but earned through personal action and example. It shows us that an ordinary person can change status through a sincere desire to do God's bidding. The Rambam (Maimonides) explained the law surrounding the tribe of Levi and concluded the chapter with the following remark about this whole issue:

> This applies not only to the tribe of Levi, but to every person who desires this [God-Merged] level. He stands before God to serve Him, to know God. If he is honest, and rejects the regular business of life, he becomes sanctified. God becomes his lot, and he will receive what he needs in this world, in a similar fashion to the Kohain and Levite.
>
> (Mishnah Torah, Hilchot Sh'mittah Veyovel 3:13)

So, Pinchas, by making certain sacrifices and taking big risks based on his love for the Divine, elevated his whole lineage.

One of the things we have to be very careful about in looking at this whole issue of the zealot, is how dangerous it can be if it is misunderstood. The story of Pinchas is often used as justification for all types of religious zeal, which is often not about the love of God, but more the love of ego and the love of a personal or political agenda. Pinchas did commit an act of murder, and under Torah law his zeal was no justification for his behavior. If Hashem had not intervened directly in that moment and not awarded Pinchas with the brit shalom (ברית שלום—covenant of peace), Pinchas would have possibly been charged with murder. The point is that Pinchas's zealous action was an exception. His murder of Zimri and Koz'bee was defined as "a unique act at a unique time." The Jewish zealot is not one who sheds blood, but one who is truly committed to God. Devarim 6:5 says, "Love God your Lord with all your heart, with all your soul, and with all your might." This means that the name of God should become love through your actions. This is a key to understanding the meaning of "zealot." Being a zealot does not give a person permission to go around killing in the name of God. That is about as dangerous an interpretation as possible, and has led people into great disaster. Those people who are truly God-fearing must tune into the fact that their zealousness must be for God only, and that every action must start with love. It is very important to remember that zealousness is authentic only if it is exercised for the sake of heaven, such as in the case of Pinchas and Eliyahu. It is important not to act out of anger, but only out of love for God. That is the big message here in Pinchas. It should not in any way be misunderstood that zealous religious violence is desirable in the eyes of God. This is the thinking of narrow left-brained (half-brained) fanatics who are not acting from the wisdom of the heart. Pinchas's intuitive, inspired action was to reconnect to the integrated oneness of the Great Torah Way of enlightenment, free of the compromising forces of darkness.

Mal'akhi the prophet predicted (Mal'akhi 3:23) that Eliyahu (believed to be a reincarnation of Pinchas) (Midrash Pirkei D'Rebbe Eliezer, end of Chap. 28) will come again in the end of days to accomplish this, to restore the hearts of the fathers (the ancients before the fall in Eden) to the sons (those who fell) and the hearts of the sons (those who fell) to their fathers (those who did not fall). Eliyahu/Pinchas in this context is an inspiring role model of reconnection to the natural way of the living Torah, which helps to restore the people to the enlightened way of God.

Parashah Pinchas also includes the passing on of the spiritual leadership of Am Yisrael from Moshe to Yehoshua through the power of s'micha m'shefa (סמיכה משפע). Interestingly enough, it was not passed on to Moshe's two sons, Gershom or Eli'ezer, thus making it clear that leadership is not a question of physical inheritance. The public transmission of the spiritual energy to Yehoshua was timely, because Moshe was not allowed into the land, and it was then close to his time to leave his body and the planet. He publicly transferred the energy to Yehoshua. In effect, part of Moshe's soul went into Yehoshua in the process of this transfer. The teaching here is that the soul energy of the teacher may go into the student when the student is ready to receive. This is an important teaching on the Great Torah Way of enlightenment and the power of lineage transmission.

This parashah also recounts the story of the five daughters of Tzelaf'chad, which bears an interesting teaching about the love of Eretz Yisrael and Moshe's honoring of the women. The daughters' names were Machlah, No'ah, Chaglah,

Milkah, and Tirtzah. After hearing Moshe expound the laws of inheritance, namely, that the Land of Israel shall be divided up among the male heads of each tribal household, these women felt it unfair to them because their father was dead and they had no brothers. What would have gone to their father was then destined for their uncles! And so they came before Moshe, before the tribal princes, the high priest, and before the entire congregation, and explained their situation. Their father had died in the desert, and he had not been among the rebellious cohorts of Korach.

The story of the daughters of Tzelaf'chad seems to be about the laws and the principle of individual inheritance, and changing from the tribal lineage of son-to-son, the real issue was their absolute desire, their zealousness, to be part of the Land of Israel, and to inherit a portion of the Land of Israel. Moshe honored the validity of their case and consulted God, who told Moshe that they were absolutely right! And, in their case, the inheritance of land (that would have gone to their father) ought to be assigned to them. Their sincerity about being part of Eretz Yisrael is surely a deciding factor, which changes the laws on the spot. This section shows that women, under certain conditions, would be able to inherit land, if there were no men in the family. Hashem says to Moshe in BeMidbar 27:7–9:

> "The daughters of Tzelafchad have a just claim. Give them a
> hereditary portion of land alongside their father's brothers. Let
> their father's hereditary property thus pass over to them. Speak
> to the Israelites and tell them that if a man dies and has no son,
> his hereditary property shall pass over to his daughter. If he has
> no daughter, then his hereditary property shall be given to his
> brothers."

It is a really beautiful statement supporting the rights of women and lauding their desire for Eretz Yisrael, which was probably unique in that region at that time. In the book of Yehoshua, we see that later, after the Israelites had taken back Eretz Yisrael, Yehoshua honored this change in the law and awarded land to the five sisters (Yehoshua 17:4).

The teaching of the five daughters connects us back to Pinchas, in that we can see on one level how Pinchas was clearly right, but on the superficial level we can say maybe he was not totally right, because he did not understand that Koz'bee was Zimri's soulmate. As the Vilna of Gaon, in his book *Even Shelei-mah*, says: "If you make the right decision for the wrong reasons, it will end up being the wrong decision. But if you make the wrong decision for the right reasons, it will end up being the right decision." So, most of all, make sure your motivations for your decisions are right; then things will surely work out right. This seemed to be the case for both Pinchas and the five sisters.

Moshe is told to count the people again. In this context, after their un-dermining encounter with the forces of darkness of Balak and Balaam (a collective Amalek), there arose the need to help each person strengthen and restore connection to the light. This counting even included the Levites, be-cause Korach, being a Levite, had contaminated them as well. The fact is that no matter who we are, we are affected by the people around us, and we have to keep purifying while on the spiritual path. We should not have the delu-sion that we are above it all. No matter who we are or at what level we operate, we can be negatively affected by the people around us, because we are, in essence, all one.

This parashah also explores all the ways that we connect to the light through the different ceremonies, including the daily prayer in the morning. It is taught that in the morning there is an entity called *tolah* that comes into being to destroy the world. At the same time, a positive tolah wakes up the energy of mercy. Through our daily prayers, which are sacrifices, this negative entity is destroyed. One thing we need to understand, if we do not understand it already, is that the darkness never rests. We can nullify or overcome it if we maintain a constant light. The darkness is working always, and if we work always, the darkness cannot touch us, cannot penetrate us. The importance of the actions of Pinchas is that he reactivated the light where the darkness had begun to penetrate. This is why Shabbat is so important. This parashah moves us from the daily prayer, to the importance of Shabbat, which, again, is always about bringing people back to the wholeness and nondual aware-ness of the Tree of Life, and to disconnect us from the physical dual world of the Tree of Knowledge of Good and Evil. It also includes the new-moon ceremony, which gives us a chance to take control of the month using the proper kavanot. It includes Passover, which is the celebration of physical and spiritual liberation. And it guides us from Passover to Shavuot, when we receive the revelation of the Great Torah Way of enlightenment that takes us to the truth of the One and gives us the total guideline for deveikut and chey'rut. We are reconnected to Rosh Hashanah, when we are cleansed from the results of our actions throughout the year, and then Yom Kippur, when we celebrate that cleansing and feel our oneness with all, and we receive Yah's energy of love. We then move to Sukkot, when we harvest that feeling. And finally we complete the cycle with Shemini Atzeret and Simchat Torah, which connect us with the energy of bliss, wholeness, and peace throughout rest of the year. In the counting, we also include the importance of the holidays as helping us reconnect and stay aligned with the Torah Way of enlightenment.

At the end of this parashah, we are recovered from the attack of the dark occult and all have become reconnected to the light. The message of parashah Pinchas is that we must be completely relentless on the spiritual path, and to use all the tools and teachings of the Great Torah Way to support ourselves on the path.

May we all receive grace through our relentless openness to the light. May we all be blessed with the power and persistence of netzach, because we are always becoming and living as a receptacle of the living light and love of Yah. May we all forever lose our worldly blindness as Pinchas did, and forever apperceive and live the divine truth.

Amen

Mattot

AT the beginning of this parashah, Moshe addressed the heads of the tribes of the children of Israel. In BeMidbar 30:3 he said: "If a man makes a vow to god, or makes an oath to obligate himself, he must not break his word. He must do all that he expressed verbally." Here there is something subtle for us to look at. Why does this start with a verse saying that God spoke to Moshe? Moshe is not the same as the other prophets who would say "So says God." This subtlety in phrasing shows us that Moshe's prophecy is superior. He says "This is the word of God."

We can elucidate on this further by looking at the sephirah of binah (understanding), also called the world of mi (מי), meaning "who" in Hebrew. This sephirah is always open to questions because the answers can never be known. It is far beyond the boundaries of our comprehension, just as Hashem is beyond time, space, and being.

The sephirah malchut (מלכות—sovereignty) is also called the world of mah (מה), or "what." We try to penetrate into the world of beyond, into the world of atzilut (אצילות). We do not really know what is happening on the physical plane, the world of malchut. If we are to restore the sephirah of malchut to its original perfection, we must know that it is unknowable. Malchut, as assiyah, is unknowable because it is the reflection of three planes that are beyond our perception. We must operate in this way, with a sense of humility and meekness. To know it, as a mystery, as an enlightened person, is to become a manifestation of the revelation of ko'ach mah (כח מה), meaning "the power of what." The Hebrew word for wisdom is chokhmah (חכמה), meaning direct knowing or direct apperception of the truth. The letters that make up chokhmah (cheth [ח], chaf [כ], mem [מ], and hey [ה]) may be rearranged to spell ko'ach mah. By realizing that we know nothing in atzilut, or in the physical plane, we become a living revelation of the sephirah chokhmah, or ko'ach mah, the power of what. This is the revelation of supernal chokhmah, which is situated nearly at the top of the Tree of Life, beyond the zeir anpin (זעיר אנפין), the seven lower sephirotic energies.

Additionally, within each sephirah, including malchut, the entire Tree of Life is repeated. In the lower chokhmah, within malchut, in the world of mah, we have the taking of that energy. Chokhmah translates in the lower world of malchut as the "wisdom of sovereignty." This is currently threatened by the global economics of the one-world government. As we go further into the parashah, we will understand how the Jewish way puts an emphasis on sovereignty in relation to the bigger picture. Whereas communism says the state is everything, the Jewish way emphasizes the sacred dynamic between individual sovereignty and the function of the state.

A humorous account illustrating this follows the election of the first Israeli president, David ben Gurion, who is quoted as saying to President Harry Truman: "You're the president of 200 million people. I am a person trying to lead 400,000 presidents!"

As history plays out, this dynamic will eventually reveal itself in prophecy as Israel stands up against the world. You must maintain your sovereignty if you are going to be liberated as sovereignty as malchut is the foundation of Etz Chaim which is the foundation of deveikut/chey'rut. You cannot be a free slave. You cannot be stuck in the matrix and be liberated/enlightened. It is not possible. This principle of individual sovereignty creating state sovereignty is parallel to the importance of a number of enlightened of Am Yisrael being a precondition for the manifestation of Am Yisrael being a light to the nations.

It is extremely important to understand the power of what. King David, as the symbol of malchut, talked about another principle that is important in understanding malchut, namely, shekhinah (שכינה), otherwise known as divine revelation. As we learn in the Talmud, whenever King David was inspired to write one of his Psalms, he would begin and end it in the same happy tone. This is the feeling that occurs when the unknowable quality of mah is revealed. It is spiritually inspiring.

Atop the Tree of Life are the two supernal sephirotic energies of chokhmah (wisdom) and binah (understanding). Both reverberate at the lower levels as wisdom and understanding in malchut. Sovereignty can only be perfected when the meaning of mah is revealed, which is to know the unknowingness of life.

This is why David begins some Psalms with "To David, a Psalm" and others with "A Psalm of David." When David began with the phrase "To

David, a Psalm," it meant that the Ruach HaKodesh (divine inspiration) rested upon him before he composed. If he began with the phrase "A Psalm of David," it meant that David began his composition before the activation of the Ruach HaKodesh. In the former case, the Psalm would begin and end in the same way.

When David was inspired to compose a Psalm, he called it "an awakening from below." Here the end was the same as the beginning. When the tone was happy (i.e., "I sing," "Hallelujah," and so on), then it is clear. When he was happy, he was inspired.

This may also explain why our sages, bless their memory, say that Yirmeyahu wrote the book of Ekha (Lamentations) before the destruction of the Temple. Ekha could not have been written after the Temple's fall because he would have been mourning. He would not have been able to access inspiration.

In the Jewish tradition, one cannot access Ruach HaKodesh in depression. It says in the Talmud "the divine presence rests upon a person only through simcha" (Talmud Bav'li, Shabbat 30b).

The Torah hints that Moshe was greater than the other prophets because he began in BeMidbar 30:2 with the statement "This is the word" instead of "God spoke." This is a little hint that the God word just came through in that very moment. Hashem spoke as "an awakening from below." This gives us an idea of the power and subtlety of words.

BeMidbar 30:3 says, "If a man makes a vow to God … he must do all that he expressed verbally." The parashah introduces us to the power of words in the concept of *neder* (נדר), or vow. Usually vows are considered to be a proclamation of abstinence, but it may also mean anything that one is committing oneself to do. It crosses over into the word "oath," which takes us into a course of action. For this reason, the power of our words is extremely important. We must pay attention to what comes out of our mouth. This is why in the Jewish tradition, when we make a statement concerning what we intend to do, we say "*b'li neder*" (בלי נדר), meaning "without a vow," so that our words do not have the force of a vow. This is important because our words create. Abracadabra actually means "I create what I speak." A vow has a greater power of creation.

This is a deeper understanding of why the Torah holds us to our words, whether we are serious or joking. To understand this more clearly, we have to do so on the level of the *mekubalim* (מקובלים), kabbalists, and what our rabbis call *chakhamim* (חכמים), or wise ones. We have to go back to Bereisheet and ask "How did creation start?" It says there that God spoke, and what he spoke came into being. Now, God is not physical. He has no mouth. What did he speak?

Words are made of letters, and letters are images of sounds. In the Hebrew tradition, every letter has a shape and every shape has a sound. God spoke sounds, and these sounds gave rise to creation. These sounds manifested as the twenty-two letters of the Hebrew alphabet. They are images of thoughts. Thought and sound give rise to being. It is clear throughout kabbalistic literature that the Hebrew letters are to be respected. This is the secret of the first part of this parashah. The sounds and the shapes create energies. When these letters, sounds, and shapes are combined in particular ways, they form supernal chants, also known as *shey'mot kodashim* (שמות קדושים—holy names). We have, for example, the forty-two-letter name, and the seventy-two names of God. The powers inherent in these names can have a profound effect, depending on how we use them. It is said that Moshe was given the seventy-two names of God so that he could energetically set up the parting of the Red Sea.

The mekubalim claimed that a powerful way to create deveikut (God-merging) is to mimic the divine attributes and manifest them here on earth. One of these divine attributes is the power of creation. This is implied in the story of the sons of Ya'akov. Before they went down to Egypt for food supplies during a major famine in Canaan, they are said to have been able to create animals to eat using the power of the word. Ya'akov forbade them to do this, but they understood the secret codes by which Hashem created the universe.

This is sacred and guarded Torah knowledge. Unlike the sons of Ya'akov, we are not to use it in a self-serving way. We have many examples of this. In the latter part of the sixteenth century, the Maharal of Prague (Rabbi Yehudah Loew) created a golem to protect the Jews of Prague from their enemies. According to some academics, this later inspired Mary Shelley to create the story of Frankenstein (Albert J. Lavalley in *The Endurance of Frankenstein: Essays on Mary Shelley's Novel,* edited by George Levine and U. C. Knoepflmacher, University of California Press, 1979, p. 252). The Ba'al Shem Tov was able to stand on a belt and cross water when mobs were trying to kill him. He also had the power to heal. He could time-travel in his horse and buggy. These people understood the power of words, but they used them in the service of Hashem.

In the deeper teachings about the power of words, it is possible to manipulate the power within sound and thought. This can take us beyond the world of the Elohim into what appears to be supernatural, but is actually scientifically based upon string theory.

We are simply saying that sound can act to change physical matter. We know that a musical note can shatter glass by affecting it first on a subatomic level to create a new reality. Superstring theory basically says that subatomic particles are a form of superstring frequencies, which make the subatomic particles bond together to form patterns. This is how these superstrings create a vibration. When these are activated, sound is formed and a pattern is created. What makes the superstrings vibrate in a certain way? The kabbalists will tell you it is the power of thought and how well that thought is focused. It is in this understanding that we have the merging of science and spirituality.

This is a warning to pay attention to our words. The sounds we make are the words that come out of our mouths. Our words count. The measure of the character of a person is how he or she uses words. Words are connected to our thoughts. This is why I say "Always begin your thoughts with the love of God." If we start our thoughts with negativity, our words create damage in the world and destruction in the universe.

According to kabbalah, we are creating a new universe in every moment. In every moment we have a choice: Are we creating a universe of order that helps us become more aware of our unity with God, or are we creating a universe of chaos that creates a feeling of separation from God? It is all about awareness. God is always present, within and without. Whether we feel unity or separation has to do with the power of our words.

A word can thus be an agent for healing or a weapon for destruction. We joke about abracadabra, but as I pointed out earlier this word is actually Hebrew and its meaning comes from *a'bra* (אברא), "I create," plus *ca* (כ), "as," plus *dab'ra* (דברא), "I speak." We create what we speak ... abracadabra. This is not fantasy. The power of our vows and oaths is very important. Every word we speak is either a vow or an oath. When we do not keep our word, we are destroying a part of the universe. In kabbalah this is considered a spiritual crime. What we say should be said thoughtfully. When we perform an action or a mitzvah, it is important to align our thoughts with that action. This is why I begin every prayer with *"l'shem yichud kudsha brich hu u'shechintei"*—"for the sake of the unity of the holy one, blessed be he and his shekhinah." This is spoken before I give any teachings. By this process we bond with Hashem in every moment.

And this is also why I end the teachings with "Amen," which is invoking, acknowledging, and bringing the power of divine grace "above" this world into this world. It is merging YHWH with Adonai to create 91. YHWH (numerical value of 26) plus Adonai (numerical value of 65) equals Amen (numerical value of 91). As we go deeper into the vows, it is important to hold the understanding of words.

Why did Moshe speak only to the sages about the ordinance of vows? In the interpretation of the rabbis, the heads of the tribes held a special power in being able to work with the vows above the heads of the people. It was the power to release people from their vows, especially if they had made them in thoughtless ways. This power is not detailed in the Torah. According to the oral Torah it was declared to Moshe on Sinai. Many of the teachings that we have today have come through the oral Torah.

The Torah treats the freeing of a vow or oath as if it were a secret of the Torah, to be revealed only to those fit to hear it. Therefore, it is only alluded to in the Torah.

There are a variety of religious vows—free-will offerings, certain areas of abstinence, burnt offering vows, meal offering vows, drink offerings, peace offerings. But there are also what we call secular offerings. As it says very clearly in BeMidbar 30:3, "he must do all that he expressed verbally." If a person vows a vow (*yider* or *neder*), then he is very committed.

You cannot make a vow to simply follow what is already in the Torah. For example, you cannot say "I'm not going to eat *n'veilah* (an animal that has died of a natural death or was not properly slaughtered), or *treifah* (an animal suffering from disease even if properly slaughtered). They are already forbidden. That is not really a vow or an oath.

We have the power to forbid ourselves that which is already permitted to us. It has nothing to do with that which is already forbidden. An oath can be a support to that which we are already doing. Shevuoth (oaths) are not the same as nedarim (vows). A vow has no object, whereas an oath is only able to render forbidden that which was previously permitted. Vows do not apply to all matters in the commandments, such as that to we already committed ourselves at Mount Sinai, so you cannot take a vow to fulfill the original vow.

Rambam wrote, "Vows are like vowing by the life of the king, and oaths are swearing by the king himself." A husband or a father has the ability to nullify a vow that affects the soul of his wife or daughter (or if it affects the relationship) if he acts immediately upon hearing it. All vows are considered to be eternal. Oaths are not as strong as vows. You cannot take a vow or an oath against what is asked for in the Torah. Vows have an object.

When you say "I vow not to drink wine," it becomes forbidden to you. The vow becomes invested with sanctity. An obligation created by a vow takes effect upon property as well. Ordinary vows have no beginning or end, and this is more like an oath. A vow is about action, but only upon matters of abstinence. An oath is different; you can say "I swear to eat this loaf," and that would be a valid oath. A vow takes effect upon the object. So if you declare "The bread is konam (forbidden bread)," it is akin to saying "I won't eat this loaf." Or if you take a vow that you will eat a loaf, it is not an oath since you did not specify exactly which loaf. If you say "I shall eat this loaf," that is an oath. It is a subtle difference.

Vows are heavier statements pertaining more to spiritual matters. When you say "I undertake upon myself to bring a peace offering," that is an obligation made, and you are going to do it. You have applied an oath to an object. If you say "I'm going to offer a piece of pie upon the altar," that is not an oath, since there is no such offering.

Vows are mostly about abstaining. Oaths are more about a positive action. It is easy to confuse the two. An oath would be "I swear to eat the loaf"—you are promising an action here. A vow, on the other hand, is about an object—"I won't eat this loaf" is a vow. These are deep and complex issues, but the point, again, is the power of words.

As we move into the next chapter, Moshe called upon a thousand men from each tribe to take revenge upon the Midianites for deliberately undermining the spiritual energy of Am Yisrael and weakening Am Yisrael. He only called upon 12,000 warriors, although the Midianites constituted a much larger population, and their cities were fortified. One of the reasons for this was that many of the Israelite men had sinned and fornicated with the women sent by the Midianites. They were therefore not fit to execute the vengeance of the Eternal. Only those who were righteous were sent.

Moshe was a little vague. He only said to execute the vengeance of the Eternal upon Midian. You would think it would be the same as it was with Amalek, to eradicate the entire people. Moshe sent Pinchas to be the high priest in charge, and the army spared the women and children. Moshe became angry with his generals about this, but he did spare the virgin women. This seems brutal by today's standards, but if we look at the genocide going on in the world today, it is not that extraordinary.

Why did the Midianites have to be slaughtered? The war with Midian and Balaam occurred because they tried to lead the people astray with idolatry fueled by harlotry. Midian (מדין) represents *dimyon* (דמין), the world of illusion. The war was symbolic of how to deal with the world of illusion. There is power in imagination. Kabbalah teaches that no one ever sins unless a foolish spirit (רוח שטות—*ruach sh'tut*) enters that person. It is said that God created the world to have a dwelling in the lower realm (דירה בתחתונים—*dirah b'tachtonim*). Kabbalah teaches that this lower world is also called the alma d'shikra—the world of illusion. What is the illusion of the physical world? It is that God is not present in our physical lives. This is the spirit of foolishness. The word for sin is chet (חאט), which means to miss the mark or create distance.

This is why we can consider the yetzer hara (יצר הרע), the evil inclination, as a *ko'ach hamidameh* (כח המדמה) or the power of illusion. The Midianites represented the power of illusion. People have this need to get into the world of illusion and believe that nothing really counts. The truth is that everything counts. We are either moving toward or away from God. We are either creating chaos or the order that makes us aware of the unity.

We are often seduced in this world of illusion. We think about it. We are curious about it. We think it doesn't matter, and that our actions do not count. This is how we get into trouble. This is how we miss the mark. The antidote is to be found in a very clear statement made by David some 3,000 years ago:

shiviti Hashem l'neg'dee ta'mid (שויתי השם לנגדי תמיד—"I place God in front of me always") (Tehillim 16:8). We must always be conscious of the presence of the Divine in every moment, and, if we do so, we are no longer in the world of illusion, because God's presence is always with us. We then become liberated from the land of dimyon, which is symbolized by Midian. We become immune from the allure of the illusion of breaking a negative mitzvah, and thus missing the mark. We are no longer attracted by that energy.

This takes us to a very clear place. When the Jewish commanders returned, they were amazed that none of the 12,000 soldiers were killed or lost. They were not deluded to think they were great commanders. They knew that Hashem was directly responsible for their success. They were not in the world of illusion. They made offerings to Hashem from what they had taken in the war. This tells us that spiritual life is about netzach. When we create the burning desire for the Divine, when the flame of God in our heart is activated by netzach, it burns away all of our impurities. Shiviti Hashem l'neg'dee ta'mid is absolutely how to live our lives, so that we are not seduced into the world of Midian.

In the battle against the Midianites, one thousand men from each tribe was all that was needed because the people were completely aligned. The tribe of Levi was sent to battle, too, but they were not counted in the census. Nonetheless, it was important to include them as well because it was a spiritual war and had to do with tribal identity.

A secret understanding of this is as follows: Until now, the word *shay'vet* (שבט) was used for the name of the tribes. Shay'vet means "war club." Here, however, the tribes are described as *mateh* (מטה), which translates simply as "staff," as in something to lean on. Shay'vet is a club, a weapon of war used for violence and control, and mateh is a staff or a scepter, representing some level of leadership. Each tribe has a leadership role as mateh to support and lead the people in its different ways.

There is a difference between a one-world government, as we have seen under the Nazis and the Communists, where the individual is nothing and the state is everything, and Judaism, which, in context, is in harmony both with the nation and honoring of the individual. It is very important that there is always a place for the sovereignty of the individual, for the unique expression of chokhmah (wisdom) and binah (understanding). In the book of BeMidbar,

God creates a place for each tribe and within each tribe for each individual, and for each individual and tribe within the nation.

It is somewhat confusing as to why the book of BeMidbar, which means desert, has been translated as Numbers. What does a number imply? In Egypt they reduced all slaves to a number. The Nazis did the same thing. Judaism says that a human being should never be a number. It was a Biblical prohibition to number the people for that reason. Each human being is the collective expression of the divine.

Likewise, Shemot is the Hebrew name for the book of Exodus. But Shemot does not mean "leaving," as exodus does. Shemot means "naming." The difference between naming and numbering is that when you are a slave, you are given a number, but when you are free, you are given a name. You have a name, and you have a face. That face is the face of God. Your name is the name of God. That is the meaning of Shemot. It is unclear why these English translations were done in this way.

There is a balance between the individual and the state. In a theocracy, the individual has sovereignty. The rights and identity of the individual have to be respected in the context of alignment and service. The word mateh connotes "sovereignty." It connotes the unity between the individual and God. This then is expressed in the Torah's description of the Jewish people as a nation of priests bringing light to the world.

Now we understand what this war was about. Israel was defending the name of God. They were responding to another nation that had explicitly sought to undermine and weaken that connection with God. This is why in BeMidbar 31:49, they point out that not a single man was lost in the battle.

The next thing that happened in the parashah was that the tribes of Gad and Reuven asked if they could stay on the east side of the Yardan River, because they perceived the land there was better for cattle grazing and that was more their focus. Gad had been born from Zilpah, Le'a's handmaiden. Reuven was Le'a's firstborn son. There was some misunderstanding with this request. They were accused of being like the spies who had returned with negative reports, afraid to go into the land of Canaan. They maintained that they were happy to fight alongside the other tribes, but that they simply wanted to build their towns on the east side of the Yardan River. It was important that they contribute to the campaign, to balance the tribal energies.

Moshe gave them land east of the Yardan to set up villages for their families and fields for their cows. Eight paternal families from the tribe of Manashe also joined them; these were mostly the Machirites and the Gileadites, representing one-tenth of the people of the Manashites. They took their inheritance in the land of Bashan, and nine parts of the people remained to settle in the land of Israel. They were given all of Bashan.

Instead of going into the Promised Land, why did Reuven and Gad want to stay on the east side of the Yardan? Perhaps they were not prepared to live at that level of liberation. Manashe was the firstborn of Yosef. He differed from his brother Ephraim in that he represented the unawake consciousness of Dinah, Ya'akov's only daughter, who later became pregnant with Asnath. Asnath later became married to Yosef and bore him his two sons.

The cattle these tribes speak about in their quest for the land east of the Yardan represent a level of consciousness that is more animalistic. These people were not able to relate as closely with the shekhinah energy that was so strong in the land of Israel. This is the all-encompassing energy; the intelligence of the universe and the indwelling presence of the Divine. They wanted to try and maintain contact with the shekhinah from outside the land of Israel, but it was a deluded form of the energy.

It is said that these two tribes, Gad and Reuven, and a tenth of the tribe of Manashe, were still deep in "matrix-robotic" consciousness. They were closer to cattle and instinctive consciousness. They didn't have their vessels developed enough to hold the energy. So they made a choice more appropriate for where they were spiritually.

Rav Kook writes: "It is impossible to identify the particular sanctity of the land of Israel, to explain its surest nature in a rational, human way. It derives from the divine spirit, the arrest of an entire nation, on the sanctified nature of the Jewish collective soul" (*Orot*, p. 9). Some of the tribes were not ready to hold this energy.

Ein Iyah, Berehut, Chap. 6, says, "The love of the land of Israel is the basis of the Torah, as it brings the Jewish people and the whole world into a state of excellence."

The symbolism of Reuven and Gad exemplifies this. They were more focused on their cattle than on their spiritual evolution. They were more focused on materialism than on their spiritual evolution. They therefore settled on what was known as *Ever HaYarden* (עבר הירדן—"the other side of the Jordan"). This is the land of Amon. That is what they were given.

There is a subtler teaching here. Second Shemu'el 7:23 says, "And what one nation in the earth is like thy people, like Yisra'el...." Comments the Zohar: "In the land they are one people." They are only called one nation when they are in the land of Israel (Zohar, Vol. 3, folio 93b). This is important energetically, and it gives us some insight into why there is so much resistance in the world to Israel reconnecting to its land, and why so many modern Israelis say "It is too difficult to live here; we need to immigrate someplace else." It is only in Eretz Yisrael, in our natural habitat, that we can say "It is one people."

Reuven and Gad decided to settle outside of Eretz Yisrael proper; they had a weakening effect. The elevation of the world is compromised in this process. From a shamanic perspective this story is critical. That is the beauty of *d'var Torah* (דבר תורה—lessons from the Torah). They make the word of God come to life, because, as mentioned at the beginning of this book, the Torah is a "guidebook to enlightenment." From this perspective, we see that when the Israelites were freed from Egyptian slavery, they were merely freed from the matrix. Only when they took the vow of the commandments were the preconditions filled for them to be individual manifestations of the Divine.

The people of Am Yisrael were and are to be channels for the divine presence in the world. We are not talking about the relevance of an individual nation, and that other nations cannot be channels for the divine. We are talking about a nation having this particular dharma. There are people all over the planet acting as channels for the divine presence in the world. When we understand this correctly in the context of the Torah as a guidebook for enlightenment, we realize that it is truly about deveikut (God-merging). We have to understand that it's not about changing something; it is about being the divine expression we are meant to be as liberated, God-merged beings.

That requires lekh lekha (לך לך), knowing who you are by walking to the Self. It requires knowing our root as neshama (נשמה)—the God breath that is our soul, and vibrating with her as an individualized soul. It requires knowing our divine purpose, our service, and our oneness in the world.

The struggle we see playing out in Mattot is not about submitting to an external force. It means true service in complete alignment with the Divine as the acknowledged source of our life, and being an expression of that divine presence in the world. It means understanding that Hashem is the source of all being, all life force. Our role, according to our personality and our individuality, is to be a vehicle for expressing the divine love, wisdom, understanding, kindness, justice, compassion, beauty, truth, peace, and the ten sephirotic energies in a variety of ways. Avraham was told "Walk before me and be whole." In other words, live as a blessing to the world. Live as an expression of the divine in the world. The mitzvoth are ways to express divine presence in the world, and to deepen our alignment with the divine. They are not laws or behavioral patterns that we do without connecting our thought with our action. When we are not living this, we create separation. Our act of separation, of missing the mark, creates a karmic reverberation. It is not a punishment, but a way of undoing that. We are not rewarded for doing good deeds or service, but in the process of service we can feel the merging *leshem yichud* (לשם יחוד—for the sake of unification with God) in every moment. It is experiencing the frequency of God within us. That is what the kingdom of heaven within is all about.

What the children of Gad and Reuven and a tenth of Menashe were choosing was to live in the culture of death—*tar'but ha'mavet* (תרבות המות). People make that choice all the time. We have options. The Torah helps us to make good choices.

Moshe was also teaching that all Israelites are responsible for one another (*"kol Yisrael areivim zeh la'zeh"*—כל ישראל ערבים זה לזה) (Talmud Bav'li, Shavuot 39a). That is why all the tribes had to participate in retaking the land that was promised to them, whether or not they were going to settle there. The book of BeMidbar, "in the desert," is then about building a unified nation focused around the Mishkan (the tabernacle), which is the frequency of the Divine made physical.

We see today, as in those times with Gad and Reuven and Menashe, that we have separations in Israel. We have the *kedoshim* (קדושים), the holy ones, and the *chiloni* (חלוני), the secular. This is a false polarity. People are in that place because they are in ego. This is why the destruction of the Temple occurred. People were in the state of baseless hatred (שנאת חנם —*sinat chinam*). Both "sides" need to recognize that we all have different opinions. They are forgetting that every human being is created in the image of the Divine, not physically, but as the divine frequency, as the spark of the Divine.

We all have the self-responsibility to be a walking expression of the Divine—thus automatically coming into harmony by not looking at divisions and separations. This explains why Moshe was so sensitized by these tribes wanting to separate out. Soon we will understand, one way or another, that we truly are all one, as we move from the culture of death to the culture of life. May all be blessed that we walk before God as a blessing to the planet, and may all know our wholeness.

Amen

Mas'e

Numbers (which we also know as BeMidbar) 33:2 says: "Moses recorded their stops along the way at God's command. These were their stops along the way." Subtleties aside, I think that the very first level of understanding this is that there were forty-two forays, which are associated with the mystical forty-two-letter name of Yah. This sacred and powerful name was later encrypted by the first-century Rabbi Nechuniah ben Hakanah into a prayer for protection at one level, and for activating the shekhinah energy at another level. Now, why would you want to activate the shekhinah energy when you go into the desert? The people were on a journey, and the journey was into the unknown. Whenever we have a holy intention, and in this case it was to merge with the Divine in the process of the journey, the dark side is always there to uplift us, but also to make it as difficult as possible. The leshem yichud prayer alluded to earlier helps protect us, as does the cryptic prayer of Rabbi Nechuniah, the ana b'ko'ach (אנא בכח).

The people faced many challenges along their desert journey. The greatest challenge, which followed them from the Golden Calf incident to the struggle in Mattot with the daughters of Moab and Midian, was "beware that your heart may be seduced and you turn to worship other gods." The sages explain that when a person is not busy with spirituality, he is busy with idol worship. So, it is about temptation, and realizing that our tendency and our temptation is to begin worshipping the god of the material plane, which, for most Americans and the rest of western civilization, is money, of course, and sex.

This parashah, Mas'e, summarizes the Israelites' journey in the desert. In the Zohar, walking is a metaphor for elevating consciousness. As we travel from place to place, we elevate the sparks there, especially if negativity is present. So, on one level they were elevating the sparks of the various places they passed through, but they were also elevating the sparks within themselves. Regardless of where we journey, we can elevate our walk through the ana b'ko'ach, with its forty-two stops. The Israelites have a fresh start at each site. There are three themes involved in all this. The first concerns the actual boundary of the land they were designated. The second concerns the manner in which they traveled. The third is about the process of the journey. The boundaries outline the energetics of the land of Israel; it goes way beyond Jerusalem. There is a tremendous amount of light within those very specific boundaries. So, the boundaries connect us to the light of that land. As partially discussed previously, it is very interesting and important to understand the formation of the traveling, because even the description of the camp is a metaphor. As it says, "Each person shall camp according to his family, surrounding the sanctuary." To the east was the flag of Yehuda, which is the tribe of kings. With him was the tribe of Yissachar, the tribe of Torah study, and Zevulun, the tribe of wealth dedicated to supporting Torah study. In the south was the tribe of Reuven, and with him were the tribes of Shimon and Gad. In the middle was the tribe of Levi, in the middle and, in essence, the core, because there are two circles—the outer circle, which protected the Torah, and the inner circle (the tribe of Levi and the kohan'im), which gave (spiritual) protection to the outer circle. The banner of Ephraim was in the west, along with the tribes of Menashe and Benyamin. The banner of Dan was in the north, and with them were Asher and Naphtali. Each tribe had a color and a stone represented on the breastplate of the high priest. Each tribe had an important position in relation to the center, the nucleus of the people, the mishkan.

The configuration of the camp was also honoring of the sanctity of the four "winds" or directions. The Zohar tells us that the human was created from soils contributed from all four directions and their respective qualities (Zohar, Vol. 1, folio 140b). The east, being the source of light, is the place of new beginnings; the west, being the source of hot and cold weather, is the place of birth and death; the south, being the domain of dew and rain, is the place of cleansing; and the north, being the domain from which the darkness comes, is the place of mystery. Being a place of darkness, we call on the animal of the north, the eagle (Midrash Bamid'bar Rabbah 2:9), to help us rise above it.

In every instance, Yehuda would be the first to set up camp, the first to travel, the first to bring sacrifices, and the first to go to war. In the south was Reuven, who was about teshuva, penance, which is good for the world; with him was the tribe of Gad, who were strong, and the tribe of Shimon, who were powerful warriors. Reuven, Gad, and Shimon came after Yehuda, as the teshuva came after the Torah. In the middle, again, was the mishkan, which, as stated earlier, was the source and key to all of Yisrael. Following them came Ephraim, Benyamin, and Menashe; they came after Torah and teshuva, because it was fitting that one should have strength in order to learn Torah and subdue the evil inclination. Dan darkened the world through idol worship during the reign of Yer'vo'am, and therefore they dwelt in the north, the seat of darkness; but then, with Dan was Asher, who lit the darkness, and Naphtali, who was imbued with blessings to nullify that. And these three traveled last, because anyone who practices idolatry regresses and needs to be purified, and therefore goes last.

The whole camp was a reflection of God's world, on not only the physical plane, but also on the angelic plane. To the right is Michael; in front is Gabriel, corresponding to Yehuda, the lion. Uriel is to the left, and Rafael is behind, corresponding to Ephraim. So the camp, in essence, was the counterpart to the heavenly court. Michael was to his right, with Reuven, and Uriel to the left, which was the north, corresponding to Dan. (Please note that the angels and animals connected with the different directions varies with the particular system.)

Am Yisrael comprised two segments: the tribe of Levi, who were the Levi'im and the kohan'im, and the rest of the tribes. The tribe of Levi focused on matters of spirit; they were ritual facilitators, and representatives of God in the world. The rest of the tribes were more political, national, and financial in focus. It was their responsibility to reveal God through national, earthly affairs. The nation of Israel is formed through the merger of the two, of both body and spirit. The spirit gives life and meaning to the body, and the body carries the spirit, and is its means of expression in the earthly realm.

If the camp of Israel is to survive in our own times, it will require a combination of both religious and national ideas. In those times, they did fuse the spirit with the physical, and this is also why they were successful. They worked together. This is why the kohain gadol had the stones of all the tribes sewn into his breastplate, to take in their vibration and to upgrade the vibration. The purpose of the kohain gadol was to elevate the spiritual health of the entire nation, and that is, at one level, how to walk through the world, from a spiritual point of view. The walk is from the b'limah to the mah, from the nothing to the something. The camp of Israel represented both the b'li mah and the mah as they walked in consciousness, and expanded in consciousness through their journey.

There is another level, which is more deeply about the spiritual, in the sense that the walking and the forty-two stopping places were points of purification having to do with elevating the world to the level of atzilut.

Through this, particularly with the death of everyone older than twenty, during those forty years, Israel went through a nullification process. In our modern terms, we can call it dissolving our identity with the ego. The metaphor that is so powerful in this is watching the germination of any seed we plant. The tree's branches, leaves, and fruits cannot be separated from the seed, although they are much larger, and before the new tree can be revealed, the seed itself must cease to be. This is the message of transformation: Our identity with the ego, our negative thought forms, must all be dissolved. Our mind must be fractured, and come again into service of consciousness, rather than service of the ego. And in that process of purification, that process of giving birth, we are able then to wake up.

Another helpful metaphor is that of a mother giving birth. Through the birth pains, she is giving up of herself so that new birth may take place and new consciousness may come into the world. For all peoples, including the Jewish people, we need to merit that light by undergoing a nullification of our identity with the ego. All the tribulations that were mentioned in these forty-two forays were, in essence, birth pains leading to the birthing and revealing of the divine light. This explains the strange wording in the Torah's description of that forty-year desert journey: "The Israelites would thus move on at God's bidding, and at God's bidding they would remain in one place for as long as the cloud remained on the Tabernacle" (BeMidbar 9:18). God's bidding is a metaphor for the sephirah of malchut (sovereignty), by which God is revealed in our world as we walk between b'limah and mah. Again, the forty-two sites where the Israelites stopped were, in essence, revelations of the messianic light, revealing malchut at the level of the sovereignty of heaven.

In the process of making this journey, we often could not see the whole picture, and that is why it is called "journeying according to their forays." But upon arriving at the eastern shores of the Yarden River, with the journey near-ly completed,Moshe prepared to leave his body and began to summarize the entire experience, gifting the people with the whole picture. At this point, the tribulations were over for the moment, and the whole nation of Israel could see the result of their forays at "God's bidding," and they were now ready to enter the Promised Land.

Liberation requires our ability to endure the journey and the pains in-volved, knowing that, in the end, all will be revealed, and the messianic times will issue forth from the mouth of God, in the name of God. Unfortunately, we do not always see the whole picture, and we get lost along the way. There are many dead bodies on the journey to liberation, as people tend to end up worshipping their own egos. And so, when we read this parashah on the Sab-bath, we read afterwards from the prophecy of Yirmeyahu (Jeremiah, Chap. 2):

> Moreover the word of the Lord came to me, saying, God and
> crying the ears of Yerushalayim, saying, Thus says the Lord; I
> remember in thy favor, the devotion of thy youth, thy love as a
> bride, when thou didst go after me in the wilderness, in a land
> that was not sown. Israel is holy to the Lord, the first fruits of his
> increase: all that devour him shall be held guilty; evil shall come
> upon them, says the Lord. Hear the word of the Lord, O house
> of Ya'akov, and all the families of the house of Yisra'el. Thus says
> the Lord, What iniquity have your fathers found in me, that they
> have gone far from me, and have walked after vanity, and are be-
> come themselves worthless?
>
> (Yirmeyahu 2:1–5)

This is the most subtle aspect of the walk into the unknown, because as we accumulate more light, we can become deluded and blinded by that very light to the subtle workings of our own ego that keep us in idol worship, which is about worshipping the extensions of our own ego as idols. And we then cry out: "Where is the Lord who brought us up out of the land of Mizrayim, who led us through the wilderness, through a land of deserts and of pits, thorough a land of drought, and of the shadow of death, through a land that no man passed through, and where no man dwelt?" (Yirmeyahu 2:6).

The subtleties of the unfolding of liberation, and the gift of enlightenment itself, are also highlighted in Yirmeyahu's prophecy: "And I brought you into a plentiful country, to eat its fruit and its bounty" (Yirmeyahu 2:7). But even then, it is easy to get lost:

> But when you entered, you defiled my land, and made my heritage an abomination. The priest said not, Where is the Lord? And they that handle the Torah knew me not: the rulers also transgressed against me, and the prophets prophesied by the Ba'al, and walked after things that do not profit. Wherefore I will yet plead with you, says the Lord, and with your children's children will I plead. For pass over the isles of Kittiyyim, and see; and send to Qedar, and consider diligently, and see if there has been such a thing. Has a nation changed their gods, even though they are not gods? But my people have changed its glory for that which does not profit. Be astonished, O heavens, at this, and be horribly afraid, be greatly appalled, says the Lord. For my people have committed two evils; they have forsaken me the fountain of living waters, and have hewn them out cisterns, broken cisterns, that can hold no water. Is Yisra'el a servant? Is he a homeborn slave? Why is he become a prey?
>
> (Yirmeyahu 2:7–14)

But nobody understood. They received no correction. "In vain have I smitten your children; they received no correction: your own sword has devoured your prophets, like a destroying lion. O generation, see the world of the Lord. Have I been a wilderness to Yisra'el? A land of darkness? Why do my people say, We are free; we will come no more to thee?" (Yirmeyahu 2:30–31).

Even when we finally begin to wake up and see more of the light, we risk giving into the delusion that it belongs to us. "Can a maid forget her ornaments, or a bride her attire? Yet my people have forgotten me days without number. How well thou dost direct thy path to seek love!" (Yirmeyahu 2:32–33).

This is the great sadness. This would mean yet more dead bodies along the way to liberation. Is it surprising, then, that the parashah continues with laws around unintentional murder? Suddenly, we are instructed to build villages of shelter for those who might have killed someone by accident, so that they would have a safe haven to flee to, out of reach of vengeance-seeking relatives of the deceased. Why are we being told this now? Well, in the context of liberation, we can understand why, because when unintentional murder happens, it means that Satan is somehow involved. The high priest was in charge of forming a protective shield around the people to keep Satan out. This is why those fleeing to any of these special villages were not allowed to leave them until the reigning high priest died, because the high priest was considered responsible!

But now we are all high priests, and we are responsible for each other along the spiritual path. So if people do leave their body, or in a sense get stuck in their ego, so that they become as if dead, we as a collective of high priests are responsible. This also explains why Moshe was against tribal intermarriage. We need to find soulmates from our own tribes. I am not necessarily talking about the particular Jewish tribal subculture within Am Yisrael we were born into. I am talking about the tribe of the Torah culture of liberation, which transcends being limited to only Ashkenazi or Sephardi cultures, and about how important it is not to bring certain people into our lives who are not connected in their hearts to the level of deep Torah understanding, though they may be from the particular Am Yisrael subculture we were raised in. It is important to associate with those who share the meaning of the Torah culture of enlightenment, which is deveikut, to know and merge with God, to cleave to God, and to delight in the unfolding and aliveness of Yah at all times, at every moment!

The Shabbat when this parashah is read often coincides with the blessing of the new moon sliver of Rosh Chodesh (ראש חודש). When that happens, we read from the story of David and Yonatan (Jonathon). It is a very beautiful story because it talks about love, the love between David and Yonatan, the son of King Saul. Yonatan would probably have been the successor to his father's throne had the prophet Shemu'el not been instructed by God to anoint David. And although he was the potential successor, and knew full well that David would become the king in his stead, Yonatan nevertheless loved David without any jealousy. To me, that is a message, that to truly feel love for another person, we give up our selfish desires. To have a successful relationship with God, or with anybody, we must be willing to sacrifice our boundaries, and sacrifice our attachment to the ego, so we can experience the oneness.

All told, this becomes a very profound parashah, because it talks about the spiritual path on so many levels, and the process of deveikut—waking up to the Divine, and all the dangers along the way. It even gives us the prayers to help protect us, ana b'ko'ach and leshem yichud. It also gifts us with the consciousness necessary for true sacrifice, to know (although we do not necessarily know it in the moment) that all of our sacrifices are creating nullification. And in that emptiness blossoms forth the Etz Chaim, the Tree of Life. May we all be blessed with the willingness to sacrifice our attachment with our egos, our belief systems, and our egocentric and ethnocentric ways of being, that we may truly know the oneness of the Divine.

Amen

The
Book
of
Devarim

Devarim

In the book of Devarim, of which the parashah Devarim is the first section, the Torah offers Am Yisrael a second chance to bring things into harmony. Moshe, through devarim (דברים), or words, offers a circular rebuke (to'cha'chah). It is a gentle rebuke. Many of the Hassidic stories work this way. They do not approach a person head-on. For example, the location where this is taking place is called Tophel and Lavan. The second-century Rabbi Shimon bar Yochai said:

> I have explored all forty-two journey sites and found no such places as Tophel or Lavan. Rather, this is Moshe's way of subtly alluding to the complaints of the people, as *tophel* (תפל) is related to the word *taphlu* (תפלו), meaning "they complained." What did they complain about? About lavan (לבן), alluding to the manna, whose color was white.
>
> (Midrash Devarim Rabbah 1:9)

Thus "Tophel and Lavan" is a veiled reference to complaints about the manna. This alludes to the principle that the tzaddik cannot give strong medicine, but must rather be gentle with administering chastisement. It helps people get in touch with their internal balance and to resist the yetzer hara, the tendencies to act in unrighteous ways. That is the key to understanding what Moshe was doing here.

Devarim is primarily Moshe's farewell address. He started by gently rebuking the people so that they would wake up. He did this out of love. He talked about mussar (מוסר—ethics). The book of Devarim is considered an ethical guidebook for the people. Intellectual understanding of the Torah is not enough. There must be a deeper connection, because, as the eleventh-century Rabbi Shlomo Yitzchaki taught: "In order to study Torah properly), Hashem requires your heart to be in it'" (Rashi on Talmud Bav'li, Sanhedrin 106b). The people did not and still have not been able to grasp this principle.

In Devarim, Moshe connected certain moral messages (mussar) that have been taught throughout the Torah. The first book of the Torah, Bereisheet, talked about the merging of the heavens and the earth. Devarim, the last book of the Torah, means "words," and words connect us to the world of action and physicality. It is here that Moshe patiently shared wisdom with the people before he left his body, and before they were ready to enter the Promised Land.

Moshe gave his Devarim message in 1180 BC, but they had been living in the land since 1677 BC, or earlier, except for the 210-year interval when they were slaves in Egypt. Some short-memoried, politically biased historians, however, would have us believe Am Yisrael did not start living in the Promised Land until 1948. Even George Washington in the 1700s spoke of the importance of Am Yisrael returning to their promised or indigenous lands. It is historically possible (especially on King David's mother's side) that part of Am Yisrael may have been living on the land since 10,000 BC. In other words, there is a long indigenous tribal history of parts of Am Yisrael on this land for as many as 12,000 years. It may be worth noting, in the confusion of the current conflict over Israel, that it was really in 1677 BC that Avraham settled in the land of Canaan. This amounts to more than 3,688 years ago. They moved there and were specifically given this land according to the Torah. They were told what land they could have, and what land they could not have. It was very explicit. There were not a lot of options in where they were led, as was made clear in Moshe's talk. He was told by God that Mount Se'ir belonged to 'Esav and his descendants, and the Land of Moab belonged to the descendants of Avraham's nephew, Lot: "Do not attack Moab and do not provoke them to fight. I will not give you their land as an inheritance, since I have already given Ar to Lot's descendants as their heritage" (Devarim 2:9).

Now we understand some of the subtlety of why the people were told to war against part of the Midianite kingdom for what they did, but not to attack the people of Moab, even though it was Moab who had instigated the conflict. This was because Ruth, the great grandmother of King David, was to come forth from the Moabites, and by her merit, everyone was spared. A good teaching here is that even if a whole family is negative, one person can be a beacon of light. This happens frequently. We often encounter groups of people in which only one person holds and shares the light, and this person can positively affect everybody else. Grace will always overcome the natural law of numbers as well as physical and systemized injustice, as these are not based on cosmic truths. Things do not have to be the way they are. The world does not have to be this way, where forces continuously validate oppression and undermine the sovereignty needed for the spiritual evolution of the people. This is a great message of Devarim, that no matter how poorly we behave, if we change our way, we will be able to merge into the One. We will be able to celebrate mass enlightenment, which is the cosmic plan for us all. We will be able to experience the noncausal joy, bliss, peace, compassion, oneness, and love of deveikut.

In Moshe's recounting of these wars along the way, we see how the Israelites were not granted a blanket license to go to war with just anyone who stood in their way. God was very specific about who to fight and who not to fight. He was explicit about the boundaries of their land and what land belonged to others. They were not simply invading the land; they were directed to retrieve land that in earlier times had been taken by others. Devarim 3:21–22 says: "At that time, I gave instructions to Joshua, saying, 'Your own eyes have seen all that God your Lord has done to these two kings. God will do the same to all the kingdoms [in the land] to which you will be crossing. Do not fear them, since God your Lord is the One who will be fighting for you.'"

In Devarim 1:7–8 Moshe directed the people:

> "Turn around and head toward the Amorite highlands and all its neighboring territories in the Aravah, the hill country, the lands and all its neighboring territories in the Aravah, the hill country, the lowlands, the Negev, the seashore, the Canaanite territory, and Lebanon, as far as the Euphrates River. See! I have placed the land before you. Come, occupy the land that God swore He would give to your fathers, Abraham, Isaac and Jacob, and to their descendants after them."

From 1180 BC to the present, Am Yisrael has lived on this land. Over two thousand years ago they lost control of the land to the Greeks, then to the Romans, then to the Christians, then to the Muslims, and finally a portion of it was returned to them in 1948. It is unfortunate that people forget these historical facts in current political discussions.

In his final speech to the nation of Am Yisrael, Moshe gave them a message to help them overcome their fears and face the future. He also gave them a series of very strong warnings about what might happen if they did not follow the teachings. If they were to stray from the path of the Torah, from the ways of the ancestors, they would lose the land, because it is living the power of the teachings that would make them *undefeatable*. He realized, at some level, that if Am Yisrael could absorb the deep messages of the entire Torah, they would be unconquerable in any situation. If they could live by the Torah, they would be able to survive the death of Moshe, and reintegrate with Eretz Yisrael (the land of Yisrael), and the land, symbolically, would awaken them to deveikut. They could then weather the storms of history. Moshe taught the essential lessons of the Torah that Am Yisrael needed to hear for their salvation. In that sense, the Torah is both Am Yisrael's national and tribal autobiography, and a manual for enlightenment.

One of the principles that was, and is, most important is the merging of the heavens and earth, which was stated strongly in Bereisheet. The other message from Bereisheet is the sense of universal oneness. Moshe reminded the people that they were a group of people who met with Yah regularly! He discussed the role of the tribe of Levi, to inspire order and divine harmony in the world, as discussed in the book of VayYiKra. He discussed the role of the majority of Am Yisrael, whose tribal princes were also entrusted with connecting the people with the spiritual world. Together, the two constituted the nation of Am Yisrael. The task was not to conquer the land physically, but to conquer it on all levels, internally and externally, and become one, physically and spiritually, with the frequency of Eretz Yisrael. In a sense, as we review the Torah journey in Devarim, we begin to understand that Devarim ends the first chapter in the history of Am Yisrael, and is obviously not the last.

In this first parashah of the book of Devarim, Moshe focused entirely on the exodus from Egypt and the journey to the Promised Land, the land of liberation. What we see historically from the time of Adam and Cha'vah, when Cha'vah slept with the fallen seraphim and gave birth to Kayin, is that a split manifested between heaven and earth. Kayin, who felt man was in control, killed Hevel who felt God was in the center of life and in ultimate control. Following his exile, Kayin created cities and technologies. The split grew more severe with the generation of the flood, where they corrupted, by their life-styles and technology, the deep meaning of love, marriage, and the relationships between people with each other and with the Divine.

On one level, this parashah is talking about relationships. In marriage we have the opportunity to fuse the spiritual and physical; the act of love is both a physical act and a more sublime spiritual event healing the heavens. In love-making, we are both merging with God and creating new life, and thus we become partners with God. The generation of Babel had totally corrupted this, and the split worsened still more. It only began to be resolved with Avraham and Sarah, and their calling to lekh lekha, to return to the sanctity of the Divine that dwells in the Self. "Avraham" means "father of many," which implies that he mended the rift by fathering many nations over many generations. "I have lifted my hand to God Most High, possessor of heaven and earth!" he declared (Bereisheet 14:22). Thus he mended the gap between the spiritual and physical, and established the essential work of Am Yisrael, which was, and is, to fuse heaven and earth and to demonstrate to the world that it is possible. He also gifted us with the enlightenment teaching of lekh lekha or "go to your true Self."

Many people claim Avraham as their father, and they are correct, as he was the father of many nations, including those of the Arab world and the descendants of the many sons he sent to the East with gifts (Bereisheet 25:6) of occult mysteries (Talmud Bav'li, Sanhedrin 91a). But specifically, in his role as the father of Am Yisrael, he began to awaken the peoples of the world to their divine nature and the importance of the personal aspect of God in their lives. There already existed teachings of knowing the impersonal one God, but he brought the understanding of a personal God of grace that personally intervenes in our lives for the evolution of consciousness. Avraham taught that God is creator and ruler over heaven and earth. He also began to mend the gap between the spiritual and the physical by invoking the spiritual into the physical world. That has been the essence of Avraham's legacy: to fuse heaven and earth on this earthly plane and in that way to walk before God as a blessing on the earth for all peoples.

The continued personal intervention of God is therefore the very first message of Moshe in Devarim, as he rebuked the people for the times they rebelled against God. They complained about the manna. The spies returned from the land of Israel and gave a false report. He expressed that God had led them here; God would fight for them as He did in Egypt. Their lack of faith undermined the process, and so they had to spend forty years in the desert while those who lacked faith died out, except for Kalev and Yehoshua. Moshe, Miriam, and Aharon also survived the forty years, but had to leave their physical roles before Am Yisrael could enter the Promised Land. Because of their lack of faith, appreciation, and understanding, it was not until the whole generation had died off that God began to speak to Moshe directly again. Until the time of the spies, Hashem spoke directly with Moshe, but during the forty years, it was indirectly in a more prophetic sense. Now, in Devarim, Moshe was again in direct communication with the Divine. Even in the relationship between Moshe and the Divine during the forty years, the oneness was limited because of the people's actions. Heaven and earth can only be linked when the entire nation strives toward this ideal. There must be a certain percentage of people with that awareness, which is the walk between the b'limah and the mah, between the nothing and the something, between heaven and earth. Am Yisrael had to be ready and fully conscious of their collective role.

Through Moshe's speech, the Torah offered us a second chance. The people reviewed the story of the exodus. By looking back and examining this story we can learn how to live our lives differently. This is important because if we do not change the way we are going, we will end up where we are going. If we do not change our consciousness, then we will keep living lives in which heaven and earth are fractured instead of unified. Devarim gives us a chance to change our direction. Moshe was saying "Please listen to what is going on."

In this context, Devarim teaches us the importance of perseverance. Moshe continued to attempt to instill the awareness that heaven and earth are one. Devarim gives us the opportunity to move into a new state of consciousness, where consciousness controls the ego instead of the other way around. Moshe was saying: "Before you enter the land, build up your light energy. See the unity, then we can revolutionize our lives." But this requires a change in our spiritual development, as we shift to a higher level of consciousness.

Devarim is usually read on the Shabbat known as *Shabbat Ha'zon*, the Shabbat of Vision. It included the vision of Isaiah ben Amotz, wherein he saw that the Temple would be destroyed on the ninth day of the Hebraic month of Av, a day of national mourning we call *Tisha B'Av* (תשעה באב). This date has always been the worst date for the Jewish people, but there is another side to this. When we change our consciousness, when we are no longer in duality, but see the unity of heaven and earth, then Tisha B'Av morphs from a day of mourning to a day of celebration and becomes the date on which the messiah will be born, according to the teaching of the great kabbalist Rav Isaac Luria (based on Zekharya 8:19 and Midrash Eichah Zuta, Chap. 28). The most intense energy of judgment for the year occurs during this time. It helps to raise the question of what life is about. To'cha'chah is a reminder about returning to the point of life. This cycle of energy goes from the seventeenth of Tammuz to the ninth of Av. This is a time of introspection and the opportunity to change one's direction. The seventeenth of Tammuz was the day that the Ten Speakings were brought down. The timing was perfect, except that the people were not ready to receive them. The sephirah of tiferet represents the heart, but it is also the sephirah of divine justice. It often seems to be paradoxical and this paradox best helps us to understand the evolution of consciousness. The innocent are cleared and the guilty receive their *midah k'neged midah* (כנגד מדה מדה), their "measure for measure."

Before the destruction of the first Temple by Babylon (today's Iraq), on the seventeenth of Tammuz they stopped making offerings. They stopped merging the heavens and the earth. An important part of the teachings of Devarim is that we must do everything that we can to continue to bring the heavens into the earthly plane. It was on the seventeenth of Tammuz that the pagan Greeks destroyed the oldest, most authoritative scroll of the Torah, and replaced it with a graven image. On the seventeenth of Tammuz, the Romans, in 70 AD, breached the walls of Jerusalem. It took them three weeks to battle their way to the Temple. They killed at least a hundred thousand people on their way; some estimate it was a blood bath of one million. For these reasons the seventeenth of Tammuz is a day of fasting from sunrise to sunset. Twenty-one days later, the ninth of Av is the most intense time of negative energy and imbalance, but also potentially the most auspicious time for positive energy, as it is the time when some say the messiah will be born (Talmud Yerushalmi, Berachot 2:4). This is also the date when the spies returned from Canaan with a negative report (Talmud Bav'li, Sotah 35b). The first Temple was destroyed on this date in 586 BC. The second Temple was destroyed on this date in 70 AD. Later a Roman emperor declared that a pagan temple should be built in that space, also on this date. This is also a period of fasting for twenty-four hours and no bathing, adorning, marital intimacy, or even the wearing of leather shoes. It is a very intense day.

When we put it all together, on the seventeenth of Tammuz, Am Yisrael blemished the supernal heart in tiferet, and twenty-one days later they blemished the supernal mind of binah. It is a hard three weeks, to say the least. They blemished the months of Tammuz and Av, which are ruled by shekhinah. Tammuz and Av correspond respectively to netzach and hod. It is said that Tammuz and Av are the eyes of the shekhinah, and when Israel sinned by its godless actions that caused the fall of the first and second Temples, it was as if the shekhinah was blinded. During this twenty-one-day cycle, music is not to be played, new clothing should not be worn, and marriages should not be held. It is a time of mourning for Am Yisrael and self-reflection, where we can repair our broken hearts and realign our imbalanced minds.

We have the option during those three solemn weeks to focus on mourning the past, but it is more important to reconnect to the divine will as the present and future unfolds, and to be aligned with it so we do not cause any more destruction that again could get us removed from Eretz Yisrael. It is an opportunity to change our actions in the present. It is a powerful time to renew our covenant with the Divine, and fulfill the mitzvot for our elevation, or we will continue making a bigger and bigger mess. The most profound way to do teshuva is to understand the mistakes of the past and not repeat those mistakes in the future by changing the seeds of the egocentric consciousness, which led to those mistakes. This requires some very serious self-reflection.

As we look upon this whole adventure, it is upon us to turn our mourning into a spiritual transformation, and to look deeply into our lives. It is a time to draw the light into our very bones and our immune systems. We need this transformation so that we do not succumb to the dark side. In Devarim, Moshe was chastising the people out of his deep love for them. This was an antidote to the chaos of the darkness that the people had back then and are still engaging with in our own times.

Moshe had waited forty years before he addressed the people, because the people were not ready to hear him. Now he felt they were capable of hearing. There is a Talmudic principle that says do not speak to people about something they are unwilling to hear (Talmud Bav'li, Yevamot 65b), but in this case, his speaking to them was a vote of his faith in the people. He was encouraging the people to change their lives.

There is a kabbalistic teaching that one should wait a week, or at least three days, to respond to someone who is out of balance, so that the person will not be reactive. In this case, Moshe waited for forty years! Why did he wait forty years? He waited because of another principle: If something doesn't help, it hurts. There is a great story illustrating this subtle common sense:

Once a poor man, a student, came to his rabbi and said he needed some money for his daughter's wedding, for which he had promised a dowry and now had nothing to offer. The rabbi took him to the local miser in town, and they just sat there. The miser was surprised to see them. He offered them food and drink, but they declined everything. They just sat in silence for a while, then got up and left. The next morning, the miser came to the teacher and asked "What's going on?" The teacher refused to say anything. The next morning, the miser came again.

This time, the teacher said, "Look, I'll tell you the answer, but only on one condition: you must do whatever I ask you to do." The miser agreed, and then the teacher told him about the man who needed money for the dowry, and he asked him to give him all the money he needed for a dowry.

"So, why did you come into my house and just sit there silently?! Why didn't you ask me at that time?"

The teacher said, "I wanted to ask you, but in the Talmud it says, we should not speak to a person about anything which that person is not ready to hear, and you were not ready to listen at that time."

In other words, it is important to say nothing when people are not ready to hear. This is a very profound thing, and it is difficult, often, as a teacher, to not share everything, but there is great truth to this. This is why Moshe had waited forty years, at which point he felt that the people were finally spiritually mature enough to hear him and be open to exploring their mistakes in the hope that they would learn from them.

Another important lesson in this parashah is Moshe telling the people all the mistakes that they had made, and how they would have to pay for them. The most severe was the issue with the spies. Am Yisrael was ready to go right into the land, but because the scouts did not have faith that they could overcome any difficulties, they came back with a personal agenda and a report of doubt, except for Kalev and Yehoshua. That resulted in a forty-year delay so people could become more spiritually developed. During this time, for thirty-eight years, God stopped speaking directly to Moshe, although God would speak with him in dreams. It was only after all the people twenty years and older had died that God resumed speaking with Moshe directly. There is a very important message here. The leader is part of the nation, and the nation is part of the leader. The leader will be subtly influenced by the limited consciousness of the majority of the people. So it was with Moshe, but the message was to teach us that the divine presence resides on the prophets *for the sake of the spiritual evolution of* Am Yisrael, and not for the individual sake of the prophets. It was not a punishment for Moshe. He, as a leader, no matter how high his awareness was, could not divorce himself from the limited consciousness of the people he led. The overall message of this parashah, and part of the Torah teaching, is that heaven and earth can only be linked on the highest level when the entire nation strives toward the idea of merging them. The whole nation had to create a situation where the leader could be empowered energetically to communicate with God. To fuse the heaven and earth means to bring the messiah in that very moment. The entire nation had to be ready and fully conscious in order for this to happen.

There is another great message of parashah Devarim. Shortly before Moshe was about to leave his physical role as the leader of Am Yisrael, he defeated two powerful giants that went out to meet Yisrael in battle as they approached Canaan. One of them was O'g, King of Bashan, who dwelt in Ashtarat and Edrei in the Land of Moab. The other was Sichon, King of Emori, who dwelt in Cheshbon. Moshe's victory over these two giants was a profound message to the people, because these were the very giants that the spies had seen, and Moshe showed the people that they could overcome any obstacle. He proved that they could win against all odds if they were aligned with the Divine. This, of course, was the message of David and Goliath. It is a message that is relevant today.

It is interesting to note that in recounting the events of the past forty years, Moshe began with the incident involving the spies and the doubt that they spread to the people. The principle here is that in an instant a wrong perception can bring even the most elevated people into chaos and confusion. That is what happened with the spies to such an extent that even Moshe himself lost his ability to directly communicate with the Divine. This Devarim talk was about making the decision to go in the right direction and in a deeper way. What was going on during this whole time? It seems the people had lost their connection to God, but in truth, God was, and is, always with the people. Devarim 1:31 says, "In the desert, you [also] saw that God your Lord carried you along the road you traveled to this place, just as a man carries his son." Tehillim 23:4 says, "Even though I walk through the valley of the shadow of death, I will fear no evil: for thou art with me." Tehillim 127:1 says, "Unless the Lord builds the house, they who build it labor in vain," which means always invoke God in everything you are doing. We have to do the labor, but we invite the Divine to empower it. The teaching of the sages is that when we are given a mission from God, God joins us in our mission. If we are not aware of the divine presence in that mission it is very hard to succeed, and it is not much fun. That happened again and again during the forty years in the desert. This is another message of merging heaven and earth, which means always to invite the Divine into the mission, every day.

There is a story told in almost every tradition about a man who dreamed that he was looking at his whole life's journey. Sometimes he saw there were two sets of footprints, which he construed as belonging to him and to the Divine. Sometimes he saw only one set of footprints. This was during the most difficult times. He complained to the Divine: "God, you always promised you'd come with me. Why did you disappear during the most difficult times?" Hashem responded: "I don't think you've got it quite right. When you saw a single set of footprints, that is when I was carrying you." As a cornerstone of Devarim, it is an important awareness that God has always been with us. Because we are unaware of it, we do not invoke that divine energy into our lives, and we do not fuse the heavens and the earth.

One of the reasons we are taught to pray to the Divine is that it actually sparks our lives with God consciousness. This is the most important part of prayer. One of the great delusions that the dark side, the Sit'ra Ach'ra, tries to fool us with is that God is judging us from a separate place. This is false, because no matter how far off the mark we have been, Yah is always rooting for us to get up and keep going. There is another story in which a child asks her father "Where is God?" The father responds, "Wherever you let God in." Part of holiness (kedusha) is to realize that the Divine created our life, has always been a part of our life, and will always be a part of our life. Our job is to be aware of that. True deveikut is simply waking up to that truth.

Moshe was setting the table for people to get it on this level. He taught: "God has always been with us, so what is the problem? The problem was every time you doubted that God was with us, you had to suffer to get the point of what was going on." That was the essence of the first level in Bereisheet. This is how we heal the division that Adam and Cha'vah created in their sense of separation from God. God spoke to them and said, "Where are you?" (איכה—*Ayecha*), meaning "What is your state of consciousness?" That was what Moshe was talking about in this parashah.

This brings us to the essence of what Moshe was teaching "You shall rebuke your friend." It means if you see someone who is really out of context—not honoring the merging of heaven and earth, not honoring the teachings of the Torah—that is given to us so that we can become closer to the Divine in our awareness; it empowers us to call them on it in a holy way. This is a mitzvah called to'cha'chah. The key to to'cha'chah is to share it with someone in a way he or she can hear it, and to share it in love and in support of that person's spiritual life. Usually when people have missed the mark, the ego has them so convinced that they are doing the right thing that they cannot see they have missed the mark until they *get the lesson from the results*. A great way to support people is to help them get that context, even though they may not hear it fully the first time. The to'cha'chah mitzvah is an obligation to uplift your neighbor in this way.

Devarim starts (Chapter 1:1) with "These are the words that Moses spoke to all Israel on the east bank of the Jordan, in the desert, [and] in the Aravah, near Suf, in the vicinity of Paran, Tofel, Lavan, Chatzeroth and Di Zahav." The people were preparing for the huge transition into the Promised Land.

Another level of understanding Devarim is that Moshe's review of all the events of the forty-year walkabout in the desert gives us a chance to relive the past events of our lives with a new awareness, therefore giving people in general and ourselves in particular fresh insight into how to live in a spiritually evolutionary way. In that way, we can extract the evolutionary energy of perseverance from Devarim, as we move toward the light. Moving toward the light, by itself, is only half of it. We are asked to walk the path of Moshe; of moving toward the light with everyone else, and creating the fusion of heaven and earth. This is a great, yet challenging part of the Great Torah Way. It is one thing to achieve individual salvation; it is another thing to be responsible for national and world salvation. The effort we create as we move toward the light is free of negativity, only when our intent is solely to merge in pure deveikut. With this new shift in consciousness, we can change everything. Devarim is, therefore, about inspiring ourselves to live at the highest octave of consciousness, as we learn from our imbalances, and endeavor to correct them, and then go even deeper.

The first Temple fell because the nation distanced itself from God, reducing divine service to rote practice of sacrificial rites and lip service to justice and charity. The second Temple fell for similar reasons, with the additional sin of causeless hatred. In both instances, the people were asleep. They were so focused on following the rules of God that they could not see the light of God, the light of love. To rectify the sin of noncausal hatred, it is good to meditate on loving for no reason, with the energy of noncausal love. This will create the preconditions for the emergence of the third Temple for the whole world.

In Devarim 1:16–17 Moshe said:

> "I then gave your judges instructions, saying, 'Listen [to every dispute] among your brethren, and judge honestly between each man and his brother, [even] where a proselyte [is concerned]. Do not give anyone special consideration when rendering judgment. Listen to the great and small alike, and do not be impressed by any man, since judgment belongs to God. If any case is too difficult, bring it to me, and I will hear it.'"

Moshe explained "I had to appoint judges," because he would not be available at all times, but the judges had to see things objectively, without personal bias. Everyone was to be treated justly. This must be rectified in the present time in Yisrael, if we are really going to stay on the land of Eretz Yisrael in holiness, which, of course, is the only way you can stay on the land.

Moshe then reviewed all the different places they were and recounted everything. Devarim 2:7 says: "God your Lord is blessing you in everything you do. He knows your way in this great desert, and for these forty years, God your Lord has been with you, so that you lacked nothing." This was the point: God is always walking with us. Whether we are aware of this, or not, goes according to our consciousness, but the reality is that God is always there.

Again, the entire book of Devarim is Moshe's farewell speech, which lasts for thirty-six days from the first of the Hebrew month of Shevat until the sixth day of Adar. Some people feel that this fifth book of the Torah is "mishnah Torah," or a review of the Torah. The first principle in Devarim is to know our oneness with God and how to return to that. This relates to the importance of rebuking your neighbors when they are out of balance, as pointed out previously as the mitzvah of to'cha'chah.

As explained at the beginning of this chapter, Devarim means words. Maimonides taught us that it is a mitzvah to give people feedback for incongruous behavior, so that they may return to the good way. He wrote "and you shall rebuke or give reproof to your colleague" (Mishnah Torah, Hilchot De'ot 6:67). "You need to let him know." It is our obligation to rebuke if people can hear it. It still is a difficult thing to do in a sensitive, thoughtful way. In this context, the goal of to'cha'chah is not rehabilitation, but, rather, connecting at the heart with people so they know they are a part of the community. It requires knowing the balance between chesed and gevurah and not throwing rocks at people who do not understand, thereby further alienating them. To'cha'chah requires the wisdom to hold that balance and make the world a more ethical, loving, and spiritual place. It is how to become a humble and holy person—a mensch. Before we can have an opinion, we must have some knowledge and maturity. To'cha'chah is about how to create a healthy relationship with the people in your kehilah or your group or community.

In this context Moshe was expressing to this new generation, how much he cared. This process is about giving feedback and, by doing so, expressing confidence in the person we are speaking with. He hoped they would change in their actions toward the world. To'cha'chah implies the belief that someone can change. Maimonides's teaching was that if to'cha'chah is not given, it can lead to further relationship division and even the extreme of hatred. It is important to give to'cha'chah appropriately to help build and preserve relationship, and to help a person evolve spiritually.

May we all be blessed that we do not need to'cha'chah, but if we do need it, that we receive it with humility, and that if we need to give it, may we give it with the consciousness and love of Moshe for the elevation of all peoples and individuals.

Amen

Va'EthChanan

"Va'EthChanan El Hashem" means "And I pleaded with God." Moshe was requesting to enter the Promised Land. Did he really need to do this? Did a person who was half angel need this? Not necessarily, but God granted him by vision the experience of being on the land. While this was happening, through his plea, Moshe spoke indirectly to the tribes of Gad, Reuven, and part of Menashe about idolatry. He talked about setting up three cities of refuge on the east side of the Yarden River, where they had chosen to settle. This was thirty-nine years after the spies returned with a negative report. He was addressing these people who were not willing to enter the Promised Land, because of greener economic pastures outside of the land of Eretz Yisrael. He was also acknowledging that these tribes were not ready to enter the high-vibration land. These tribes were merely looking for a good place to pasture, while the purpose of Am Yisrael was, and is, bigger than that. Being assigned a specific part of the earth became more complicated because the Jewish people were forbidden to conquer their cousins, the children of Edom, Amon, and Moab, who eventually surrounded these tribes and further brought down their spiritual vibration. He acknowledged their compromise for a more lucrative environment, but informed them that the east bank resonated at a lower frequency than the Promised Land. Moshe told them they would be influenced by the idolatry surrounding them, and that eventually they would abandon the Torah and God's laws and return to idolatry.

This issue repeated itself as recently as 1897, when Theodore Herzl established the first Zionist Congress in Basel, Switzerland. While he was secular, he still activated the dream of return to the Holy Land. There was much anti-Semitism in Europe at the time, exhibited most notably the infamous Dreyfus Affair, and, in this context, Herzl recognized that France and Germany were potentially dangerous lands for the Jews, and the Jews needed to find their own home. They were offered a few options for relocation: Grant's Island in upstate New York, near Niagara Falls; a place in Uganda near Lake Victoria.

Everyone knew that this was not their land, so these locations were not acceptable, but for convenience, ease, politics, and economics, the Jews of Europe chose to not return to Israel at that time. As history unfolded, World War II and the Holocaust came, and people were then unable to return to Israel altogether. Under the White Paper in 1939, Jewish immigration into Palestine was limited by the British to 15,000 people per year. This was minimal, when millions of people were being murdered under the Nazis and could not leave Europe at all.

People have choices. The Land of Israel is not something to wait to return to, when it is too late to have a choice. Through Moshe, God demonstrated that there was more to living in the land than just a place to pasture cows. Every seed in Eretz Yisrael contains the consciousness of thousands of years of understanding and wisdom. Moshe wanted them to see the land and to understand that their connection to the land was through the mitzvot as outlined in the Torah. Every indigenous people is assigned to its piece of land, and Moshe understood this, and in pleading his case, he was speaking indirectly to these two-and-one-half tribes and to all the rest of the tribes of the sacredness of the land for Am Yisrael. In Devarim 7:1, he said, "When God your Lord brings you to the land you are entering, so that you can occupy it, He will uproot many nations before you—the Hittites, Girgashites, Amorites, Canaanites, Perizites, Hivites and Yebusites—seven nations more numerous and powerful than you are." He made it clear that, even against huge odds and the fact that they were far outnumbered, God had assigned them this land for their optimal spiritual development.

Moshe also warned them of the awesome responsibility of living on this sacred soil, and the severe consequences of not living the right way. Yet he reminded them also that God is compassionate and patient, and that they could always turn things around if they were sincere about it. In Devarim 4:29–31, Moshe stated:

"Then you will begin to seek God your Lord, and if you pursue
Him with all your heart and soul, you will eventually find Him.
When you are in distress and all these things have happened to
you, you will finally return to God your Lord and obey Him. God

your Lord is a merciful power, and He will not abandon you or destroy you; He will not forget the oath he made upholding your fathers' covenant."

For Moshe, Eretz Yisrael was not an external entity, but an integral part of Am Yisrael, and bound to her inner life. In this context, as in all shamanic understandings, it was not possible to rationally explain the holiness of the land and how it meant the merging of heaven and earth. From a shamanic point of view, every people belongs to a specific location for their highest spiritual evolutionary capacity. Italians are for Italy; the French are for France; the Irish are for Ireland; and the Jews are for Israel. Each people must rise to the frequency of their specific geographical location.

This is also an interesting parashah because the whole of Devarim comes down to one word that is repeated seven times in the book of Devarim, r'ei (ראה), "look," as in pay attention. The other word that is repeated seven times is sh'ma (שמע), "listen." This parashah is more about looking than listening, because Moshe, in the previous parashah of Devarim, chastised the people for all the mistakes they made in the desert, what we call to'cha'chah (תוכחה), which is to show love through reproaching. Moshe was rebuking the people so they would wake up and pay attention. He was doing it with love, because he cared, and he knew he was not going to be there to help them through the next steps of going onto the land, since he had been told he could not go onto the land. The term "look" is then more of a mystical understanding of this parashah. Rather than seeing it as just Moshe being negative and reprimanding the people for all the hardship they had given him, he was saying, "Look, I really care about you, and because I am not going into the land, I am making it the best I can so that you should be successful." He was exemplifying a person who truly cares about his brothers and sisters.

This parashah is a continuation of Moshe's rebuke. But there is one other very important piece here: that Moshe again asked God to let him come into the land. Why was he asking so much for this? There is something deeper about Eretz Yisrael than can be understood by simply thinking, "Moshe, you made a mistake by hitting the rock instead of speaking to it, and you are going to be punished." Moshe seems to have had a deep attachment to the land, and perhaps it was an attachment that kept him from another level of enlighten-ment, that kept him from being totally free. Eretz Yisrael represents the merg-ing of heaven and earth on the physical plane for the Jewish soul in a way that helps to facilitate internal merging, as part of enlightenment. His attachment to experiencing that merging on the physical plane, rather than to be satisfied with the deeper inner merging of his enlightenment, suggests a subtle lack of understanding the bigger picture. In the overall scheme of things, Hashem was helping Moshe to face and overcome the attachment to the physical that was blocking him from furthering his spiritual evolution. Moshe was too humble to understand that on a higher plane, in the bigger picture, he was already in the Promised Land. This brings us back to Bereisheet, where the main theme was the importance of the fusing of heaven and earth, and the consequences that arise in the absence of this fusion.

Now, at another level, the people were certainly getting a message from the incident of the rock that even someone as great as Moshe cannot really escape the results of his actions. In the Midrash, Moshe was again pleading with God, "If I cannot go in as a leader, then let me just go in as a regular person."

God said, "No. Once a king, you cannot be an ordinary subject."

Moshe said, "If I cannot enter as a king or as a subject, then let me enter through the tunnels." (Apparently there were underground tunnels that lead into the Promised Land.) That was rejected, too.

"Well, at least my bones ...," and that was rejected, too.

"Then perhaps as a bird? An animal?"

Finally God said, "That's enough. Let it go." (Midrash Devarim Rabbah 2:16 and 11:10; Yalkot Shimoni , Va'etchanan, No. 821)

Devarim 3:26 says: "But God had turned Himself against me because of you, and He would not listen to me. God said to me, 'Enough! Do not speak to me any more about this! Climb to the top of the cliff, and gaze to the west, north, south, and east. Let your eyes feast on it, since you will not cross the Jordan.'" So Moshe surrendered. Moshe changed his perspective, and created the space to train the leaders to enter the land of Israel and be lights. Often this parashah is read on *Shabbat Nachamu* (נחמו), the Sabbath of Consola-tion. *Nachamah* (נחמה) is the comfort associated with Shabbat. Moshe re-ceived this comfort in shifting his consciousness and stepping back from the urgency of his desire to enter the land. Though he did not understand it, he accepted God's will and released his desire. He understood that his role was to pass on the essence of the Torah to the next generation. The people were able to flourish without the intense dependence on one leader. It may have been that if Moshe had entered the Promised Land, all of Israel would have become enlightened and the messianic era would have dawned. However, the people were not ready for this.

What was this intense desire that Moshe had? On some level, it had to do with the kedusha (קדושה), the sanctity, of Eretz Yisrael. Perhaps it also had to do with the mitzvot that can only be done there. But did Moses really need to perform these? We see from his desperation that our common understanding of the mitzvot is topsy-turvy. They do not create holiness in and of themselves. Rather, they are a result of the holiness of the land. The mitzvot are dependent on the land, not the other way around. That is why Moshe wanted to enter the land. He understood that the mitzvot were interconnected with the land. Another lesson here is that we need to personally pay attention to what we create in our lives, so that we do not create repercussions that keep us from the Promised Land, internally.

Moshe now revealed the specialness of the land in a whole different way: "This isn't like Egypt, where you can plant your seed and the Nile will irrigate. This is a land full of mountains and valleys that receive the water from the rains alone, which means it is totally dependent on God." In that context, we have a land where God is always watching. "The eyes of God your Lord are on it at all times, from the beginning of the year until the end of the year" (Devarim 11:12). If the people were deserving of rain, they would receive it at its appointed time. If rain did not come, it would be a sign that all was not well with the land. In other words, Moshe understood that in Eretz Yisrael, there would be a continuous interaction between the heavens and earth, and that is what makes the land so holy. So, in Eretz Yisrael, for Am Yisrael, the heavens and the earth meet in a way that is unlike the rest of the world; it is a place where people have the opportunity to fuse the spiritual with the physical. So, the people were being given this gift, which they needed in order to make the fusion. Did Moshe really need this particular gift? As we saw, Moshe was already half angel. When the voice spoke out of the fire, and the first two of the commandments (Utterances) came through, the people backed off and said: "Wait, this is a little much for us, and we can't do this. Can you step in for us, and be the intermediary?" At that point, Moshe took on what would happen, which meant he became half-angel, half-man, and went into the mountain. When he returned, he was so filled with light that the people could not come near him. It was a transformation beyond the effects of going into Eretz Yisrael. Perhaps he did not exactly need to go into Eretz Yisrael, except to fulfill his love and his need to lead the people into the land.

Another part of this message was that ultimately, on the level of chey'rut, one must walk into the Promised Land oneself. The spiritual teacher cannot take you all the way. The teacher can take you to the border, but grace must carry you across. The teacher can, as Moshe did for Am Yisrael, prepare you, and exhort you to pay attention, but ultimately, the walk between the b'limah and mah, with you as the spark of light between the nothing and the something, can only be made by you. The teacher can guide it and direct it, but only you can walk the walk. That, in a metaphorical sense, is why Moshe could not take Am Yisrael into the Promised Land.

On the more literal level, Moshe reminded the people that it was because of the incident at the rock that he was not being allowed into the land. As told in the book of BeMidbar, Moshe made the chet (חאט—sin), and he missed the mark. He was told: "Take the staff, and you and Aaron assemble the community. Speak to the cliff in their presence, and it will give forth its water" (BeMidbar 20:8). It was an important opportunity, for the people would see the deep connection, dependence, and linkage among God, the heavens, and earth as a result of this action. The people would say something like: "This rock can neither speak nor hear, and has no need for sustenance from the Almighty, yet fulfills God's word. How much more so should we fulfill God's desire!" (Otzar Midrashim, Keta 26). But Moshe did not communicate the message appropriately. He struck the rock twice, because he was angry with the people, and a lot of water gushed forth anyway. This took care of Am Yisrael on the physical plane, but created an imbalance because Moshe, in plain sight of the people, did not follow the will of God and did not communicate the proper respect and understanding related to the action. "Also on my account was God disappointed, because of all of you," he said, in recounting the incident. The sages tell us that he was referring to how they had gotten him so upset that he called them "infidels" (BeMidbar 20:10). That is why he was penalized, more for this than for having hit the rock instead of speaking to it. A spiritual leader is a guardian of the people on God's behalf, and is not to blow up at them (Midrash Devarim Rabbah 2:2).

This parashah also re-discusses the Ten Utterances and 613 mitzvot, which can be more completely followed if one lives in Eretz Yisrael. If one does not live in Eretz Yisrael, as long as one is meditating and praying in a proper way, spiritual evolution still happens, because we connect through our prayer. This gives us the inner understanding of how to proceed as a people even without a holy temple or a homeland. We do this by making our life priority to know God as the primary reason we are on the planet. In this context, the proper kavanah for prayer and mitzvah is the experience of the union of the heavens and the earth. It connects us with the teaching from the Zohar that says "Hashem, Torah, and Israel are One." In the name of grace we have been given the spiritual DNA of the Divine. This is not about those living in Israel or away. It is about the difference between people who want to connect with the light through their spiritual work and transformation, and those who really are not interested. Anyone who chooses to connect through efforts and grace will connect to Hashem and will be transformed. This gives us the inner understanding to be able to evolve spiritually as a people, even without a holy temple or a homeland, by holding the priority of knowing God as the sole purpose of life.

At Sinai, although the Ten Utterances were obviously important, what was also extremely important, but which seems to get overlooked, was the fact that the nation of Am Yisrael reached immortality for thirty-nine-and-three-quarters days. This occurred while Moshe was up on the mountain, until they created the Golden Calf, which sabotaged the full attainment of this gift. One of the subtle challenges on the Great Torah Way to chey'rut is the constant choice of desiring or resisting the Divine. Their resistance won out and they could not hold this ultimate purpose of Am Yisrael as immortality in the awareness of deveikut/chey'rut. The inner resistance was activated by the outer negativity of the ey'rev rav, who served as an agent for the Sit'ra Ach'ra and caused the people to lose their crowns of glory. In other words, the message was not only about accepting to live by the Ten Utterances (which also represent the energies of Etz Chaim), but that it is also important to be aware that we have the power to create or destroy our own spiritual transformation and attainment. We can move in both directions on the spiritual path, so we are always walking the razor's edge.

The first Utterance of the Ten Utterances (a manual for creating the kedusha that helps us connect to immortality) is the belief and knowingness of the existence of the creator. Being in that awareness creates an optimal state. This is keter, which is alignment with the will of God. The second Utterance is chokhmah, which is about idol worship—telling us to not believe in any other gods but the One. The common idols today are money, power, fame, security, sex, and ego, along with the futile attempt to see whatever light is within them as the main source of light. This also includes the egocentric belief that out of the seventy faces of God, the "correct" face is only that which a particular group believes in. It is this form of idol worship that is prevalent today both among the major religions and between the sub-groups of each religion. Idols symbolize the temptation to egocentrically place one's trust in anything other than the light of God. In Devarim 4:10–15, Moshe said:

> "… the day you stood before God your Lord at Horeb. It was then that God said to me, 'Congregate the people for me, and I will let them hear my words. This will teach them to be in awe of me as long as they live on earth, and they will also teach their children.' You approached and stood at the foot of the mountain. The mountain was burning with a fire reaching the heart of heaven, with darkness, cloud, and mist. Then God spoke to you out of the fire. You heard the sound of words, but saw no image; there was only a voice. He announced to you His covenant, instructing you to keep the Ten Commandments, and He wrote them on two stone tablets. At that time, God commanded me to teach you rules and laws, so that you will keep them in the land which you are crossing [the Jordan] to occupy. Watch yourselves very carefully, since you did not see any image on the day that God spoke to you out of the fire at Horeb. You shall therefore not become

corrupt and make a statue depicting any symbol. [Do not make] any male or female image."

The third Utterance, binah, is not take the name of God in vain. We have to be aware that when we use the name of God, it has to be used appropriately, and not in a trivial way. The fourth Utterance is about Shabbat, which represents the energy of chesed. Shabbat includes awakening to the immortality consciousness of deveikut/chey'rut. "Remember the Shabbat and keep it holy," we are told. By keeping our minds empty except for the frequency of Hashem, we automatically do no work and thus can receive all the energetic influx of the Divine. Shabbat is also a way of burning up the imbalanced actions of the week. It is the doorway for connecting to the One. We have to be ready to merit the Shabbat. When we are not able to practice it and live it with the consciousness of the One throughout the day, respecting the whole meaning of Shabbat and the cycle of Shabbat, we do not merit it. It is a gift for those who choose to accept the gift of the One.

The fifth Utterance, corresponding to gevurah, is "honor your father and mother," which also means honor your spiritual elders. The sixth Utterance, as tiferet, is "do not commit murder." This includes destroying others through our words and even through our business dealings. The seventh, corresponding to netzach, is "do not commit adultery." It is about trust between people on all levels of relationship and the avoidance of sexual abuse and exploitation in any form. The eighth is hod, which is "do not steal," because when we take a physical object from someone, he or she still retains the light of it, but what we are doing is upsetting the balance, because what we receive each year is determined from above. It is even worse if what we steal is something that may come to us anyway. By stealing we unbalance that flow of sustenance to ourselves. The ninth, corresponding to yesod, is about lashon hara, "do not bear false witness," which is about slandering or defaming someone. The tenth, corresponding to malchut, tells us to avoid coveting what others have. Coveting is very interesting because it implies that somehow you know better than God, or that somehow God, in one's mind, is not giving us what we need, or that He gave someone else what should have been ours. By not acknowledging the truth (that we get exactly what we need for our spiritual evolution), we fall into envy and covetousness, and thus disrupt our existence in this world of malchut.

The Ten Utterances are like a narrow bridge over which we walk through the world. The key to cross it, in a spiritual way, is to walk fearlessly in God's light. In that way, we will fulfill our destiny and our purpose for being on the planet. The sh'ma (שמע) is also repeated in this parashah. It, interestingly, has forty-two words, which connects us to the ana b'ko'ach (אנא בכח), so it is invoking all the energies of the forty-two-letter name of God. That is the kabbalistic principle—as above, so below (Tikunei Zohar, folio 40b). When we deeply reverberate in our consciousness the Sh'ma, the declaration of divine oneness, this will reverberate up to the highest worlds. When it says, "his praise is sounded in the congregation of the pious" (Tehillim 149:1), it is referring to "the meditations of the sh'ma." It implies that, when performed in the gathering of the righteous, Israel will rejoice in God's works. This is the small Israel that rises up to zeir anpin (זעיר אנפין). The power of the sh'ma causes zeir anpin to rise up and activate abba (אבא) and imma (אמא), and the *mohin* (מוחין—spiritual brains), the divine light, descends to us in our individual soul (נשמה—neshama). Zeir anpin is the essence of spiritual Israel. When we pray with deep passion, deep kavanah, we activate this downward flowing energy called Or Yashar (אור ישר), "directed light," which expands our consciousness. When we pray with kavanah, not only do we expand our own consciousness, but we activate the expansion of consciousness in all the supernal worlds.

The great wisdom is found in yir'at shamayim (יראת שמים), God-fearing, or more literally, "awe of the heavens," meaning of God. "All is ordained by God," taught the ancient sages, "except the awe of God," whether or not people will be yir'at shamayim (Talmud Bav'li, Berachot 33b). The result of having yir'at shamayim is that joy, contentment, peace, and ecstasy filter down to us through all the worlds. Although it is said in the Torah that we need only to do the sh'ma prayer twice a day, the ancient rabbis felt that it should be done four times, each time the same way, with the intention to merge the heavens and the earth. The sh'ma, which was given by Moshe to the people, is the bridge to the upper realms and the single statement of deveikut/chey'rut, that God is at the same time the many and the One. It is the essence of the Torah Way of deveikut/chey'rut, from which emanates the wisdom teaching of love.

In the haftorah reading of this parashah, Yesha'yahu 40, the teaching is that the Temple will one day be rebuilt, but we must never forget why it fell in the first place. As Yesha'yahu points out, it fell because no one was appreciating it, and no one was relating to it from a place in the truth. It is taught in the Midrash that the Babylonians were told that the Temple was just ruins anyway, because the people were not living with love. Love is the essence of the sh'ma and the Ten Utterances. They had egocentrically forgotten the Torah Way of life, which resulted in causeless animosity and conflict (שנאת חנם— sinat chinam), and they had thereby destroyed the meaning and purpose of the Temple. The ancient sages wisely put it this way: "If the youth say 'Build up the Temple,' do not listen to them. If the elders say 'Tear down the Temple,' obey them" (Talmud Bav'li, Tosefta Avodah Zarah Chap. 1). By "youth," they meant those who really do not understand that the Temple is moot if its intent is not honored. The "elders" are those who know this, and know that before we can rebuild our Temple, we need to first restore our purpose.

We end this parashah with the understanding that if we live according to the inner meaning of the Ten Utterances and the sh'ma, which is the Torah Way of deveikut/chey'rut, then we will have become the single purpose of why we are put here on the planet. If we walk this Torah Way of God, then, as a consequence, the Temple will truly be rebuilt, because it will manifest as the energetics coming from our collective soul expression as a nation, which is its purpose. May we all be blessed that this becomes the reality of Am Yisrael in our lifetime.

Amen

Ekev

~~~

THIS parashah has to do with multiple levels of meaning and focus. It includes the subtlety of the relationship between Am Yisrael and the Torah, and between Am Yisrael and the world. The Torah was given in the middle of the desert, a no-man's-land belonging to every man and every woman. It was not specific to Israel, although Am Yisrael was the only nation willing to receive it at first. Now it has been spread around the world by the children of Avraham. This implies that the inner essence of the Torah is relevant to every single person on the earth (Midrash Tanchuma, Devarim, Chap. 3). In the initial blessing for studying the Torah, we acknowledge the Torah as God's name (Zohar, Vol. 3, folio 265b). The power of the blessing requires that we resonate in spirit and kavanah with the inner nature of the Torah as the living name of God. In this way we go beyond the Torah, as information and history, and into the living power of God's name. At some level, Moshe was attempting to communicate this deeper, empowering message to Am Yisrael.

The second thing that is important here is that Moshe, having accepted the mixed multitudes (ey'rev rav) during the exodus from Mizrayim (though God had advised him against this) (Midrash Tanchuma, Ki Tissa, Chap. 22), felt that he needed to include them because the Torah was relevant to all the people. The Zohar comments, "God looked into the Torah and created the world" (Zohar, Vol. 1, folio 134a), and therefore every human being and every part of the universe is linked to the Torah.

This brings us to a whole understanding of one of the themes of the Torah: the idea of universal responsibility. Avraham was seen as the father of many nations. He taught lessons of divinity throughout the world. Symbolically, his tent was open on all four sides, demonstrating his total devotion to transmitting God's teachings in all four directions. Within this context, there are two trends in the Torah Way. We have the children of Rahel, who tend to go out into the non-Jewish society and secular Jewish world and impart the teachings to the world. Then there are the children of Le'a, who are more the inner-directed, intense-Torah-study people, keeping separate from the rest of the world and even other Jews who do not share their specific ways, but some who may be equally intense students of the Torah. We obviously see this in the ultra-orthodox and orthodox communities, in that they keep separate from each other. Those who reveal Torah to the external world, the children and energy of Rahel, operate in the realm of alma d'itgalia (עלמא דאתגליא), "the revealed world." The children of Le'a, who are connected to the inner subtleties of the Torah and are focused on the Jewish people alone, operate in the realm of alma d'itkasia (עלמא דאתכסיא), "the concealed world." Moshe was from the tribe of Levi, born of Le'a, but in his world service he crossed over to the path of alma d'itgalia, and was open to including the mixed multitudes of non-Jews who joined with the Children of Israel in their mass exodus from Egypt. In a more cosmic sense, the kabbalah and the lessons of the Torah are the teachings of the path of enlightenment for at least the western civilization. This is not the same as saying that all people should take on the Jewish customs as evolved through 3,300 years of interpretations, and evolved more specifically after the fall of the second temple in 70 AD, when the Am Yisrael became more inner-directed in order to survive.

The teachings of the Great Torah Way are a general message of enlightenment for everyone, all seventy nations, but are meant to be incorporated according to the uniqueness of each nation. The Torah in this context is about deveikut/chey'rut for all people as a roadmap of lekh lekha (return to the Self). The covenant that God made with Am Yisrael in the desert, was not the same covenant that he made with our ancestors. It is a covenant with those who are right here in this moment. Moshe's position was that we must leave the door open for anyone who wants to draw close to God. As the Midrash put it: "Why was the Torah given to us in the desert? Because just like the desert belongs to no one and is open to everyone, so the Torah is open to anyone who wishes to come and study it" (Midrash Tanchuma, Vayak'hail, Chap. 8). That is different from what the other Levites believed and actually taught. This was the positive symbolic meaning behind Moshe's inclusion of the mixed multitude. The negative part of it was that they, as the ey'rev rav, were the ones who made the Golden Calf, because they could not hold the energy, and they undermined the Levites and the other tribes.

The overall message that Moshe gave to Am Yisrael was that, if no one follows the Torah Way, it is going to lead to disaster. In Devarim 8:1, he said: "You must safeguard and keep the entire mandate that I am prescribing to you today. You will then survive, flourish, and come to occupy the land that God swore to your fathers." In Devarim 8:3 he said: "He made life difficult for you, letting you go hungry, and then He fed you the manna, which neither you nor your ancestors had ever experienced. This was to teach you that it is not by bread alone that man lives, but by all that comes out of God's mouth." Moshe was saying that by living in the spirit of the Torah Way, we will rise above the material, animalistic ego and be filled with the immortal light of God. "Safeguard the commandments of God your Lord, so that you will walk in His ways and remain in awe of Him" (Devarim 8:6). If we stay in the light of the Torah Way, we will be the recipients of much grace, and all will go well for Am Yisrael. Moshe was attempting to activate the natural link between Am Yisrael, the nations, and the Torah. He seemed to be learning that the mixed multitude was not capable of absorbing the kedusha of Har Sinay and was also rejecting him and the Ten Utterances by building the Golden Calf.

Perhaps because of his difficulties with the ey'rev rav and their sabotage of his mission, Moshe later changed his plan somewhat, focusing his efforts more and more on helping Am Yisrael receive the Torah first. Yet, in that context, the nations still had the potential and the ability to merge with Am Yisrael and reveal and activate their own hidden potentialities, because, as the prophet Zechariah predicted for the messianic era of the future: "In those days it shall come to pass that ten men out of all the languages of the nations shall take hold, and shall seize the skirt of him that is a Jew, saying, We will go with you: for we have heard that God is with you" (Zekharya 8:23). This perhaps becomes the role of Am Yisrael—to be lived by the Torah with this awareness, to spread the word of God to all the nations, so that they might receive it each in their own unique way.

There are at least two levels in understanding this. Although the final universal acceptance of the teaching of God through the Torah would only happen in the messianic time, the role of Am Yisrael will be a model of how to live by the Torah. Moshe exhorted the people, saying: "Follow this and all will be good. Follow this and you'll be abundant. Follow this and you'll be prosperous. Follow this and you'll have as many babies as you want. Follow this light of God and you will be victorious in all situations." He was also implying that when you do this, you will be a model that will inspire all the people of the world to follow the Torah. It is said that there were problems when the Christians began to take over the Roman world, and that many of the high-ranking Romans, including Nero, chose then to become Jewish instead, because they understood the depth of what was being offered. If one is with the light, great reward will come, and that reward will inspire other people to follow the Way of the Torah, which is a way to deveikut/chey'rut, our ultimate purpose on the planet. By being an enlightened people, as a nation, we would be a light unto all the nations. It is very clear that if Am Yisrael would follow the Torah Way, no one would be able to defeat its light and the power that would come from it.

In Devarim 9:1–5, Moshe said:

> "Listen, Israel, today you [are preparing to] cross the Jordan.
> When you arrive, you will drive out nations greater and more
> powerful than you, with great cities, fortified to the skies. They
> are a great nation, as tall as giants. You know that you have heard
> the expression, 'Who can stand up before a giant?' But you must
> realize today that God your Lord is the One who shall cross
> before you. He is [like] a consuming fire, and He will subjugate
> [these nations] before you, rapidly driving them out and anni-
> hilating them, as God promised you. When God repulses them
> before you, do not say to yourselves, 'It was because of my virtue
> that God brought me to occupy this land.' It was because of the
> wickedness of these nations that God is driving them out before
> you. It was not because of your virtue and basic integrity that you
> are coming to occupy their land, but because of the wickedness
> of these nations whom God is driving out before you. It is also
> because God is keeping the word that He swore to your ances-
> tors, Abraham, Isaac, and Jacob."

In Devarim 11:24–25, Moshe told the people:

"Every area upon which your feet tread shall belong to you. Your boundaries shall extend from the desert [to] Lebanon, from a tributary of the Euphrates River as far as the Mediterranean Sea. No man will stand up before you. God your Lord will place the fear and dread of you upon the entire area you tread, just as He promised you."

Many miracles were given to people: their clothes and sandals did not wear out, and food as the manna from heaven supplied their physical sustenance. Today, most of the world is not living by the Torah Way and, according to Moshe's prophecy, all of Am Yisrael and the world are suffering. Instead of being fertile and multiplying, fertility rates of couples are dramatically decreasing. By not following the Torah Way, the forces of the Sit'ra Ach'ra are empowered to pollute the public commons, disrupting the ecology, and even creating ways to decrease the world population to serve egocentric power and material desires. Plagues and chronic diseases like diabetes and cancer are rampant, and people are becoming more and more lost and alienated from the Divine. Outer miracles, without the internal vessels to hold the energy, have limited effect. The people saw the miracles, and still could not get it. So, even though the message throughout this forty-year walkabout was to look, still people looked and chose not to see. They saw the splitting of the Sea of Reeds and myriad other miracles, but they could not make the decision to have faith. You can always find fault in anything, and those who look for the light will always see the light.

It was clear from the midrashic accounts of the Golden Calf incident that the Golden Calf was misperceived by the people as more than a statue; it appeared to walk and talk, and seemed alive. Moshe was aware of the power of Satan to create entities that seem completely real, or at least wielding the power of delusion to entrap the people by making it seem real (Midrash Pirkei D'Rebbe Eliezer, Chap. 44). It may have been like the kind of delusional state some may experience with consciousness-altering drugs. Moshe responded by making a homeopathic remedy for the incident. He ground up the Golden

Calf into dust, threw it in the nearby stream, and made the people drink from it to protect them from their stupidity, counter their delusional state, and subdue their temptations. It was an antidote to the hallucinogenic state invoked by their worship of the Golden Calf.

Moshe came down the mountain after forty days, only to discover the people worshipping the Golden Calf. In reaction, he broke the tablets, and went back up again, because he had to plead for Aharon's life and all their lives, and had to spend another forty days without food and water. Devarim 9:19–21 quotes Moshe:

> "I dreaded the anger and rage that God was directing at you,
> which had threatened to destroy you. But God also listened to
> me this time. God also expressed great anger toward Aaron,
> threatening to destroy him, so, at that time, I also prayed for
> Aaron. I took the calf, the sinful thing that you had made, and I
> burned it in fire, I then pulverized it, grinding it well, until it was
> as fine as dust, and I threw the dust into the stream flowing down
> from the mountain."

In this context, Moshe acted as the tzaddik of his generation, absorbing and nullifying the results of the bad actions of his generation. Unfortunately, it was not time for him to go into Eretz Yisrael, which may have activated the messianic energy right then and there. It is taught in the mystical kabbalah circles that the soul of his soul will one day incarnate to fulfill his messianic mission (Zohar, Vol. 1, folios 25b and 27a).

The people did get another chance, and that is the important thing. They did get a second set of Ten Utterances after the first set was smashed. One of the wonderful Torah teachings is that it is considered in the kabbalah that a person who makes mistakes, but rises above them to become more holy, is considered higher than a person who has been holy throughout life without making a mistake (Zohar, Vol. 3, folio 16b). We cannot spend our time judging what happened in the past, or we may become like Lot's wife, who turned to stone by looking back. In a sense, Moshe was saying, "I am not here to shame you about what happened before. But here we are now; let us move forward into the light and remember our lessons. Hold the energy and you will be victorious in all that you do, and we will spread that light through the whole world." He talked about fearing God. This does not mean cowering before God, but, rather, being in awe of seeing and experiencing God in all things.

There is one subtlety here, because we are talking constantly about the greatness of Eretz Yisrael. From the time that the people entered the land (except for the time of King David and King Solomon), it has always been a difficult place, because of all the energy there, and it is hard to live correctly and in balance surrounded by such a high intensity of energy. That does not mean there are not many incredibly evolved people in Eretz Yisrael, because there are. But still, looking at it as a nation, the nation is having difficulty handling the energy in the highest way. If a person does not express his or her energy in a healthy way, and there is so much energy to deal with, it will come out in an unbalanced way. As previously discussed there is actually a mental imbalance that may occur to a few people in Jerusalem, aptly called the "Jerusalem syndrome." When living in Eretz Yisrael, it is best to try to live at one's highest potential. This is also true for any spiritual place: The higher the energy, the more positively or negatively it comes out, and we have to be very disciplined and thoughtful in our approach. Wherever there is a spiritual vortex, people can be elevated by it, or be thrown out of balance. In Hebrew, we call it the surrounding light, *ohr mekif* (אוֹר מַקִּיף). This is extremely important to understand.

This parashah also repeats the second part of the sh'ma, which is seventy-two words, corresponding to the seventy-two names of God, and the third part, which has fifty words, corresponding to the fifty gates of binah.

The most important thing is that people are given the light if they would choose it. As in Moshe's time, we too have the opportunity to change the desert wasteland into a Gan Eden, if we choose to, and create something from nothing. May we be blessed that although life may be difficult, yet by being with the light we can overcome all difficulties and uplift ourselves and all of humanity.

Amen

Re'eh

THIS parashah is called re'eh, one of the seventy-two names (ה-א-ר—resh, aleph, hey) to meditate on if one is lost. It helps reconnect to the Divine, to Hashem. This is really how the parashah begins; it goes right to point. Moshe said "Re'eh"—"Behold," or "See, I have set before you...." In other words, "See something!" What is it we are supposed to see? We are supposed to see more than the physical plane; we are supposed to see the spiritual meaning behind things. We are supposed to see the physical world in a spiritual context, and that makes all the difference in the world, because when we cannot see this, we cannot make the choices set before us. As Moshe said:

> "You can therefore see that I am placing before you both a bless-
> ing and a curse. The blessing [will come] if you obey the com-
> mandments of God your Lord, which I am prescribing to you
> today. The curse [will come] if you do not obey the command-
> ments of God your Lord, and you go astray from the path that
> I am prescribing for you today, following other gods [which are
> money, power, ego, or literally other gods in place of God] to
> have a novel spiritual experience. When God your Lord brings
> you to the land which you are about to occupy, you must declare
> the blessing on Mount Gerizim, and the curse on Mount Ebal."
>
> (Devarim 11:26–29)

The bottom line is that we have some choices here. We have a choice to be conscious, move toward the light, increase the light in our life, and eventually move into deveikut, or we have a choice to stay in the material world. It is a profound choice. When people ask about free will, we are speaking of this. We have the power to make a choice in our lives about what direction we are going to go, and how we are going to live. As it unfolds, the choices toward good are always the choices that the righteous, the tzaddikim, will make. The angels also will always make the choice to good. I say always, although they also can choose the dark side, but that is rare because they are closer to the Divine. The closer we are to the Divine, the more we are in the light, and the more the light makes it possible for us to see what the right choices are. That is really a very key thing about a holy person. As holy people are closer to the light, they are more likely to make the right choices, even though it may seem more difficult or it may seem strange to us. They are less likely to be fooled. So, it has great significance when we say, "What am I seeing?" In that seeing, we are able to make the proper choice of the spiritual essence behind the questions that come up for us.

An interesting story that I believe supports this lesson is about the Seer of Lublin (eighteenth century). One Friday, while he was in the synagogue praying, his wife was home rummaging through all the drawers looking for some money to buy the Shabbat candles, but there was no money to be found. She went outside, hoping someone would give her some money for the candles. Just at that moment, one of the rich people of the town happened to pass by on his way to meet with a prostitute. He recognized who she was, and saw that she was crying. He asked what the matter was, and she told him she did not have money to buy candles for Shabbat. So he gave her the money, and she blessed him in the way that only women can, which is to share the light of Shabbat; she blessed him with the light of Shabbat. Then he went off to meet his part-time girlfriend/concubine. Meanwhile, as this was happening, the holy Seer was still praying. He prayed for three hours, and his students could not understand what was taking him so long. When he was finished, of course, they wanted to know what had happened. He told them that his soul had ascended to the heavens, and he saw the forces of good and evil. He was told by the forces of light, "We are using you to help us win the battle with the darkness." But the forces of light were upset because his wife had blessed the married man going to see his lover, and she had blessed him with the light of Shabbat; they did not understand how she could do such a good thing. Then the Seer replied to the angels, "You are so straight that you do not understand that man is wicked only because he never tasted the light of Shabbat. He needs to have a chance to taste the light of Shabbat."

One of the disadvantages of being totally pure is that you can then not understand the possibility, let alone the process, of transitioning from impure, cluttered consciousness, from a place where the difference between the light and the dark is blurred. So, when the Seer of Lublin left the synagogue, he met the rich man on his way, coming back from his sexual encounter, and the rich man said, "Please, I would like to spend one Shabbat with you, because for the first time in my life I would like to feel what Shabbat really is. I am just feeling the presence of the light, and I do not know where it is coming from." He had forgotten the blessing he was given by the Seer's wife, thinking it was only because it was the Shabbat and he needed to be next to some Shabbat candles. The Seer said "Come, join us!" This rich man ended up becoming the most devoted student of the Seer of Lublin, and later actually became his successor!

If we can just once give a person the opportunity to have the touch of the light, even a little bit, he or she is often going to want more. The difference in the people who come to the Tree of Life Rejuvenation Center, between when they first come and after they have been here a while, is very dramatic, because they develop better eyes to see. As they come closer to the light, they develop the ability and the strength to keep choosing the light. This parashah, in many ways, is about netzach, the power to go beyond physical reality and keep choosing the light.

This parashah offers us insight into the deep psyche of this way of living and thinking, and formulates it as a way of moving from mere personal interests to the one collective soul of the community. In Devarim 12:6–8, Moshe told the people:

> "That shall be the place to which you must bring your burnt
> offerings and eaten sacrifices, your [special] tithes, your hand-
> delivered elevated gifts, your general and specific pledges, and
> the firstborn of your cattle and flocks. You and your families shall
> eat there before God your Lord, and you shall rejoice in all your
> endeavors, through which God your Lord shall bless you. You
> will then not be able to do everything that we are now doing,
> [where each] person does what is right in his eyes."

Although it had not yet happened in his time, Moshe was alluding to the final inheritance that the people were to have as a nation. That final inheritance was the Beit HaMikdash, the Temple.

In the forming of a nation and the forming of the one soul, there needed to be a collective place for the people to gather spiritually, so they could create the energy of the one soul. Previous to that, they had what was called *bamot* (במות)—everybody would do their own personal altar, rites, and meditations on their own. During the time when the mishkan, or the Ark, was up they were not supposed to do that. When it was down they would do it on their own. Finally, with the Beit HaMikdash, which was the building of the Temple, to be a focalizing point for the shekhinah, this final inheritance would become their gathering place, where all the sacrifices would be brought. Until then, the bamot were fine. It was permissible to do whatever one wanted. But now, all must do their public work in the place that God had chosen. The central altar (soon to be housed in the Temple) was the only place where one could offer sacrifices, and everything came out of the Temple: the money system, the food, and so on. So, when it was destroyed, perhaps it ended animal sacrifices. From the limited vegetarian point of view only, that was a very good thing, because we had reached a new evolutionary state. In this state the true sacrifice is one's personal prayer, which is the sacrifice of self and attachment with ego. However, from a larger Torah perspective, it created the exile of the shekhinah, which in a global way separated the physical p'shat world from the world of sod, or spirit, in Am Yisrael. This was a disaster. The effect of the Ark's removal from the Temple, and its vacancy from the second Temple, damaged the soul of Am Yisrael and the mediating balance between the heavens and the earth. Not only did it damage Am Yisrael on religious and spiritual levels, but it also severed the public functions from the holy functions. That has been a damage to the people, because when money, power, service, and collective thinking are separated from God, there is chaos. Since that time, without the Temple, there clearly has been more chaos.

Everything has its role and its time. During the time of the avot (אבות), our forefathers (Avraham, Yitzhak, and Ya'akov), the bamot, the personal altar, was most predominant. Later on, even in the time of the great Temple, when many operated at the level of prophecy, with the prophets hiding out in the mountains or in Qumran, it remained predominant. There was a play between the two, and I think that is where we are today, because, on one hand, as it makes it clear in VayYiKra 26:8, "A hundred of you will defeat ten thousand, as your enemies fall before your sword."

This brings us very clearly to the Peace Every Day Initiative, and to the importance of the spiritual people on the earth working collectively to change the consciousness on our planet. When Am Yisrael entered the land, and established the Temple, the national soul took preference over the individual soul. That is a little complicated, because at one level of understanding, the one-soul concept implies a high-spiritual-level national soul. It does not necessarily mean the lowest understanding that is often taught today. But it requires a delicate balance, and it is not an easy one. The balance, the Torah teaches, is for us to always be aware that the individual soul draws its life force from the collective soul, and the collective soul needs the individual for its life force. So, there is a balance between shamanically being one with the nation, and at the same time, if the nation is in spiritual chaos, being simultaneously one with the nation as your shamanic foundation, and at the same time individually penetrating to the depths, which is the heart of the nation, but not where the nation is living. In that process, as we penetrate to deveikut, that energy needs to be shared with the nation as a way of uplifting the nation. Today, it is important for the individual soul to generate so much light that, as part of the nation, it turns on the circuitry for the whole nation.

As the parashah unfolds, Moshe gave us a map of what we call anochi (אנכי), the power of seeing the difference between the good and the dark in our lives, and to make the correct choices. One of these areas of difference is about the eating of animals, specifically animal blood. At this stage, the people had been given the dispensation to eat animal flesh, but not animal blood. Why was that? The blood contains the spirit of the animal. Now, with the knowledge that the blood contains the spirit of the animal, we can rationalize from a gross shamanic point of view that, "Yeah, if I can eat a deer heart, I will get the heart energy of the deer." It is also helpful to realize that we take on all the animalistic energies of the animal we ingest. This is, of course, partly why we have the kosher laws about which animals not to eat, to protect against that. But the animals are all part of us. As Moses Cordovero said: "The creator addressed all of creation before making the human, meaning that in creating the human, the Infinite One incorporated all attributes of all animals, plants, and minerals that had been created up to that point. In each of us then are the powers of all the creatures of the earth" (Shi'ur Komah, folio 23). So, we already have it in us; shamanically, we just need to tune in to that which is in us. As we eat the animals or take animal blood, we actually have a tendency to activate those animalistic tendencies within us. At the lower shamanic levels, perhaps that is permissible, but if our purpose of life is deveikut, to know God, it may not be in our best service to eat the animals, particularly if they have been killed through terror and fear, and thus take on their energies and all their fear and terror. These are the kind of messages that Moshe was giving to the people. In a sense, kosher is just a way of minimizing the damage of eating animals, taking on their energies, and therefore becoming more animalistic. As Moshe said in Devarim 12:23:

> "Be extremely careful not to eat the blood, since the blood is
> [associated] with the spiritual nature, and when you eat flesh,
> you shall not [ingest] the spiritual nature along with it. Since
> you must not eat [the blood], you can pour it on the ground like
> water. If you do not eat it, you and your descendants will have a
> good life, since you will be doing what is morally right in God's
> eyes."

When we are talking kosher versus nonkosher, we are speaking of the importance of elevating the sparks of light as much as possible, and there are more sparks of light in the kosher. The kosher laws and the like are practices to help us move toward the Divine, not away from the Divine. The idea is to have more of the light in our lives. A kosher, or kashrut, approach is that way which extracts life force energy as nutrition from the living planet in the most holy way.

Moshe also talked about how to deal with a city where everybody turns to the dark side. You should stay away from places of negativity. More dramatically, he said you should eliminate all the people and destroy such a village, but practically speaking, it means that you should stay away from bad company, and stay away from places where the negative forces have gathered, because we are affected by the negative forces. Even in one's own family, this is important. Moshe said, in Devarim 13:7–9:

> "[This is what you must do] if your blood brother, your son, your
> daughter, your bosom wife, or your closest friend secretly tries

to act as a missionary among you, and says, 'Let us go worship a new god. Let us have a spiritual experience previously unknown by you or your fathers.' [He may be enticing you with] the gods of the nations around you, far or near, or those that are found at one end of the world or another. Do not agree with him, and do not listen to him."

What he was teaching the people is the importance of good company, chavurah. Who we associate with plays an important role. Moshe included in this a warning to avoid misleading teachers as well. He went on to say that if your teacher, even a so-called prophet, starts leading you away from God, you have to look at that also. In this context, the importance of yechidut, being in the presence of the highest truth through one's personal experience of the presence of a tzaddik gamur (a fully enlightened teacher), is a very important aspect of spiritual evolution. A classic example of this was Yehoshua's choice to remain under the personal spiritual guidance of Moshe for forty years. Moshe was giving very, very important sage advice about how to be successful on the spiritual path. The overall Torah teachings include the importance of the highest amount of light in your food, of deveikut, of good company, of prayer, and of silence (sheket), or kol demama (divine silence). These are all part of this unfolding. And, then he moved into the importance of charity and talked about tithing, and the idea of giving and loaning money to people, even if it is near the end of the six-year cycle, when all debts are forgiven, because we should care for the poor. Those who choose not to take care of the poor hamper their spiritual life.

Then he talked about the year of release, of people who had sold themselves for seven years to pay off debts, and how important it was to treat these people well and to send them on their way in a good way when their time is up. So, the importance of charity is brought up here as well.

Moshe also talked about the sacred seasonal cycles, the importance of Passover, which is to remember the actual physical liberation from Egypt, but Passover also is about liberation from the metaphorical Mizrayim, which is not a particular country, but the ego. He talked about Shavuot, which is the energy after the seven weeks of the Omer (the ritual barley offerings) are counted after Passover, and he said that this was a moment in history when we attained immortality—no death. And so that energy of the oneness, deveikut, was very high in that moment. And finally, he spoke of the energy of Sukkot, the celebration of the harvest, of what I call the "gratitude time." This is a time for gratitude for all that we have been given, and this connects us with the angel of sustenance. The more grateful we are, of course, the more we bring in God's energy.

So, in his compassionate speech, Moshe had, in essence, outlined key spiritual patterns, which were then, and are now, for the purpose of increasing the light. Once again, Moshe demonstrated to us how the Torah is an owner's manual of how to activate the greatest amount of light in our life to bring us into deveikut/chey'rut. May we also be blessed with the netzach to persevere on the Great Torah Way that Moshe shared with us.

Amen

Shof'tim

SHOF'TIM (שׁפטים) is another part of the path of liberation. At one level it is about appointing judges, and that is how the parashah starts: "Appoint yourselves judges and police for your tribes in all your settlements that God your Lord is giving you, and make sure that they administer honest judgment for the people" (Devarim 16:18). While a certain order in society must be maintained, from the liberation perspective this is really referring to destroying negative thought forms within ourselves. That is ninety-nine percent of the work. As we destroy the negative thought forms, we create the mitzvot of togetherness and connectedness. It is in this context that the Torah is given to us—not to maintain or create a religion, but to improve our wellbeing. The Torah is given to us as a guide to liberation. When we realize this, we can begin to understand that the real issues are about our inner consciousness that must be purged.

There is a beautiful story about the mysterious third brother of Rabbi Zusha and Rabbi Elimelech. Their disciples were very interested to know who this third brother was, and so they went looking for him. When they located him, they were disappointed to find that he owned a tavern and that his main job all day long was to serve vodka to everyone. But they noted one peculiar thing about him: periodically, throughout the day, he would take out a little notebook and write something down, and then put it away. Not much else was happening, so they concluded that "this is a very mundane person."

The brother offered them lodging for the night at his home because they knew his brothers the rabbis. That night, the visitors were suddenly awakened by strange sounds in the house: a thumping and a wailing, and their host's voice. Worried that he might have taken seriously ill, they broke into his room. There he stood, with his shirt off, crying. Alarmed, they asked, "What are you doing?"

He replied, "Look, during the day, whenever I have a single thought that is not harmonious, that is negative in any way, I write it down. Then, at night, before I go to bed, I ask for forgiveness. I ask for forgiveness, and I cry, and I come from my most sincere place. When I have cried enough, when I have felt the greatest amount of pain I need for that, usually the tears fall on the book and the ink fades away. Then I know that I have been forgiven."

In the third brother's efforts at teshuvah, he was clearing the four gates, which include the three columns that direct the flow of energy to the human face. He was reconnecting his energetic vehicle before he went to bed—restoring whatever may have gotten disordered during the day.

During the month of Elul (usually when this parashah is read), the energy of teshuvah is even more intense. It is specifically designed for us to review our lives, for us to look at ourselves and our actions throughout the past year, and see what changes we can make.

We hear the term "Be simple with your creator," but what does that mean? Is spiritual life that simple? Well, yes, in a way it is. You are a part of Israel when you understand that Israel implies not just the nation, the geomancy of Israel, but all the people connected with the light, who are aware of the spiritual system that connects us to the light. In essence, Shof'tim is telling us that God wants us to stay connected with the light, to love our neighbor as we love our inner self (for we are our own harshest judges), and to treat others with dignity. In essence, this is the meaning of the phrase that Moshe learned from the angels while he was atop Mount Sinai: "Baruch shem k'vod malchuto l'olam va'ed" (ברוך שם כבוד מלכותו לעולם ועד)—"Blessing source is the name that carries the glory of [God's] sovereignty forever and ever" (Midrash Devarim Rabbah 2:46–47). This is about the dance of the Divine within all things.

Every Shabbat, we read the Torah, and we discuss the Torah. Why? We do this because it helps us to stay connected to the light. It helps us to overcome the negative forces of the world, and to recharge our spiritual battery. This is what Shof'tim is truly about, and in that sense, it is simple. It is just part of the message of teshuvah: "Return to God."

In the month of Elul, we are also renewing our communication with the Divine. It is as if the gates to heaven are more open than ever! It is a time when we are able to draw the future into the past. In other words, we are able to go back into the past, understand where we have missed the mark, and move into the present and the future to live in a way that will correct that. The power of teshuvah, unleashed in the month of Elul, is the ability to completely transform one's past to good. In the Hebrew alphabet, this is the power of the letter vav (ו): to invert the past to the future. The ו literally translates as "and," the power of connecting. The vav is, in a sense, the *kaf* (כ), or open palm, coming through to us from out of the infinite and filling the reality of this world, of the finite realms.

This single light becomes the expression Adam Kadmon (אדם קדמון)— the primeval, cosmic human. Ultimately out of Adam Kadmon come the ten sephirotic energies, the four worlds, and the five "faces." Vav (ו) has the power to literally connect all of the twenty-two individual powers of creation contained within the twenty-two-letter Hebrew alphabet, from aleph (א) to tav (ת), to the light. This is important. It is the power to invert the past to the future, or the future to the past. In the Torah, the letter vav (ו) is the twenty-second letter from the beginning of the first verse in the creation account, as well as the twenty-second word. The twenty-second word begins "God said, 'There shall be light,' and light came into existence." The phenomenon of light breaking through the darkness of tzimtzum (צמצום), the primordial contraction, is the secret of time (future becoming past), which permeates space. This is the power of vav (ו) that is activated. So, during the time of Elul and of Rosh Hashanah, if you tune into the *ophanim* (אופנים—the angels), the vav (ו) becomes an important letter to activate in your consciousness.

Another instrument, another vehicle for this activation, is the sounding of the shofar (שופר), which we do throughout the month of Elul, usually around the time that we read the parashah of Judges (Shof'tim). The shofar, or horn of the ram, is symbolic of the ram whose horn was tangled in the bush near where Avraham almost sacrificed his son Yitzhak. When Avraham got the message from the angel that he should not sacrifice Yitzhak, he sacrificed the ram instead (Bereisheet 22:13). This process, on the inner plane, is about our facing din (דין), or judgment, which is the attribute associated with Yitzhak. Yitzhak, in that moment of nearly being sacrificed, reached the ultimate height of liberation, because, being thirty-seven years old at the time (Midrash Tanchuma, Va'yera, Chap. 23), he could have said, "Dad, I really don't want to be sacrificed." Instead, he was in complete surrender.

It is truly interesting and significant, that the shofar ritual was born out of the episode of the near-sacrifice of Yitzhak (Midrash Bereisheet Rabbah

56:9). The essence of both the shofar and shof'tim is our willingness to be partners with God in making decisions and transforming our character. We have outer judges and teachers who reflect back to us, but we also have the inner judge. As the eighteenth-century Rav Tzadok Ha'Kohen of Blumen pointed out: "When we were first created, Hashem literally blew the soul of life into our nostrils. In essence, then, we were the first shofar!" The blowing of the first shofar, meaning us and not the ram's horn, represents our creation, our potential, and all that we were meant to achieve. So when we blow the shofar during Elul (especially on Rosh Hashanah, the anniversary of our creation, and thus of the first shofar blowing), it represents our commitment to be part of the energetics of God, and of the path that God is laying for us for our complete liberation, for our complete deveikut.

In this context, I would suggest that shof'tim is not a negative thing, but is there to support our liberation process. What we are talking about is having that internal structure that allows us, like the third brother of Rebbe Elimelech and Rebbe Zusha, to keep challenging ourselves and "judging" ourselves, not in a negative way, but in a way that changes our midot, our character. This is what "Judges" is also about.

Now, another way of understanding it, from an external point of view, is "someone is judging me out of the honesty in his heart." It is really important not to put people down, but to judge people with righteous judgment. It takes us to what is actually essential for liberation, which is truth on the relative plane. Truth on the relative plane is "Pursue perfect honesty, so that you will live and occupy the land that God your Lord is giving you" (Devarim 16:20).

So, one reason a teacher is so important on the spiritual path is that, although we have to do a lot of the internal judgment ourselves, a tzaddik is clear enough to give us the most impartial judgments and feedback so that we can continue to evolve. This is a very important concept. It is not about being guilty, because guilt separates us from God, and judging ourselves negatively separates us from God. It is simply about seeing where the holes in our system are, where we are out of balance, where we are missing the mark.

Through our internal judgment and gaze, and externally from the tzaddik, we are able then to make the repairs (tikkun), so the light can be fully taken in. When we have people outside of us, and they give us feedback, it means that they care, because truly, if they did not care, why would they bother? We have to understand that the tzaddik will not give judgment if we are not ready to listen. It is a basic kabbalistic teaching: If we are not ready to hear the judgment, the tzaddik will not give it to us. Ultimately, Hashem is the judge, and that is why we honor Hashem, because we cannot fool Hashem. Maybe we can fool the tzaddik occasionally, and we certainly fool ourselves a lot.

There are different levels to all this, but judging yourself means you care enough about your liberation process that you at least want to invest the attention. On the other hand, over-judging yourself and others becomes an egocentric problem and actually creates contraction. When we begin to value learning where we have missed the mark, then we are able to progress on the spiritual path.

We think we are alone, but we are not alone. We have our spiritual teachers. We have God. We have our collective energies, our community. All these help us, and without them, it is very easy to fall, because without them all we have is our own ego to guide us. Then, when we become judgmental and separate, we are prone to fall. We see this in the *Star Wars* epic, in which Anakin Skywalker turned to the dark side. Instead of being liberated, he became a person with certain powers and charisma. When we speak about judges, shof'tim, we are speaking about our internal judge, our tzaddik, our community, and God. They are whom we have to stay in communion with on all the levels, and then we will be supported on the subtle and sticky path of spiritual liberation.

The parashah Shof'tim also talks about the altar, and the different kinds of altars. One of the key terms for altar is the word *mizbe'ach*. A mizbe'ach is an altar built of many stones (Devarim 27:5 and Joshua 8:31); it is different from a *matzey'vah*, which is more like a monument and usually composed of a single stone (Bereisheet 28:18 and 22). It may seem a little confusing that after Ya'akov had his dream of the ladder that went from earth to sky, he built an altar out of a single stone, a matzey'vah, rather than a mizbe'ach. But it was, after all, a marker of a sacred site, a matzey'vah, a monument to his vision, rather than an altar of sacrifice. The root of the word matzey'vah is very different from the root of the word mizbe'ach. Matzey'vah comes from the root *yatzev* (יצב), or "standing," as in the ladder Ya'akov dreamed about, embedded in the earth and reaching to the sky. Matzey'vah, therefore, is an altar that is set and stands alone, rooted in the earth and unchanging. The mizbe'ach, on the other hand, is a receptacle for *zevach* (זבח), service or sacrifice, from the root *zav* (זב), which means "flowing." So one is set, and one is flowing.

It is the flowing that we are talking about here, because we are always changing. Our ego is changing; we are eliminating dissonant energies, whereas the simple path of matzey'vah means we have somehow arrived, we are going to sit still, we are going to be a rock. In essence, we then freeze on the spiritual path. In the realm of mizbe'ach, however, we can improve our personalities, change, grow, shift, and flow. That is the key to understanding the world of mizbe'ach, which has to do with motivation to change our character, to heal. It means we are never stuck in our current illusory reality, and we have the ability to change our ego structure, to become liberated.

The matzey'vah, the monument, is one stone, and reflects only our one opinion, called our ego. The ego is satisfied with how we are, who we are, and tells us that we are okay and have no need to change. From the viewpoint of ego, we are the center of the universe, and our perspective is the only perspective that is accurate. The mizbe'ach, however, is made of many stones, because change in our character comes from the perception of many forces outside of us, different ways of seeing the world. It comes to us from our community, and from our ability to grow and make the world a better place, and also make ourselves better. So, the mizbe'ach is symbolic of an open system, versus a closed system, which allows us to evolve and transform our midot, and our body, into a vehicle of light. In the process of this transformation, we change our diets as well, along with our practices, our way of life, our patterns, and our relationship to the Zohar and the Torah, so that we are able to become a complete vehicle of light.

The three primary themes of this parashah are: (1) our internal and external judges; (2) the meaning of the shofar; and (3) lessons of the altar, namely, not to set up a matzey'vah in the place of a mizbe'ach, or next to one (i.e., do not mix flow with set unchangeability)—"Do not erect a sacred pillar" (Devarim 16:22).

The month of Elul opens up the gates to the heavens in a very particular way that allows us to ascend more than in any other month. It is also a month of cleansing. It is said that, metaphorically speaking, "the days of Elul are able to remove the foreskin of the heart," the negative k'lipot that form around the heart during the year. The month of Elul gives us the opportunity to remove this foreskin, this excess. Of course, it only happens when we are involved in the process of opening up the cosmic energetic cycle that is established in our calendar to make this happen. What keeps us from that, of course, is the problem just like we had with the Golden Calf—people shy away from change. The tendency is to feel justified and righteous in whatever we are doing, and we call this being "stiff-necked," which is a more serious problem than missing the mark. This is a little bit of what went on back then; the people had not changed their hearts. The month of Elul has to do with being able to change one's heart and open one's heart to God, which is what Moshe was eventually able to correct for the people he led.

We can make these corrections at any time. We do not have to wait for Rosh Hashanah. We can be like the third brother of Rebbe Elimelech and Rebbe Zusha, and we can do it every night! The main thing is to not have any blockage between your heart and the cosmic heart of God. Part of what shuts down our hearts is any form of hatred, which inevitably becomes violent and consuming. Hatred begins to fester, when we are judging people not for their benefit, but for the elevation of our own ego, when we are not nice, and when we are doing random acts of negativity. All of this falls into the cauldron of hatred. The Ba'al Shem Tov taught that if only one person is completely cleansed of hatred and is completely one with God, the messiah will come and the Temple will be built. During the month of Elul, we work hard at removing the deep roots of ego, as ego brings us into separation, and separation, in turn, brings us to hatred. The month of Elul is again about community, about seeing ourselves as part of one universal soul.

As we come to understand that the internal process involves judging ourselves, or using our teacher to give us feedback, so that we can purify our ego structure and evolve the midot, we see that the judges who were selected had to be agenda-free. That is the point about a spiritual teacher—not that any human can be completely agenda-free, but the spiritual teacher has the least amount of agenda. Or at least, the agenda may be our liberation (not a bad agenda!). If the judges had a personal agenda, then it is taught that they were relieved of their responsibilities. So that is a little caveat on the whole idea of judges; it only works if there is no bias.

Now, bribery alters bias. This is one reason why the Torah makes such a big point that judges cannot take bribes. There is the story of the judge who was crossing a bridge, and having a little difficulty. A stranger came by and offered him his hand. Once they crossed the bridge, the judge asked him "Where are you going?" The stranger replied, "I am involved in such-and-such case and I'm going to court." And the judge said, "I happen to be the judge for that particular case, and because of that, I have to disqualify myself, because now I have a bias, because you've helped me."

A similar story is told in the Midrash concerning the second-century Rabbi Yishmael. A man came to him to fulfill his obligation of bringing some of the first shearing of wool from his flock to the kohain (Devarim 18:4) since Rabbi Yishmael was a kohain. Later, when Rabbi Yishmael was called to judge a case, he noticed that the man was involved, and so he disqualified himself, saying "… even though the man had brought me what was already mine" (Midrash Tanchuma, Shoftim, Chap. 8). It was on such subtleties that the original judges were operating. Is this anything like judges today? The truth is, you have to be a spiritually evolved person, a very, very high being, operating within the framework of the Temple, in order to be a judge. Clearly, the judges are political today, so we are not talking about judges in light of what we have today. Rather, we are talking about spiritually evolved people who are able to operate without an agenda. One may not take bribes. Any gift that comes your way alters your judgment. That is really what we are talking about when we talk about bribes. One must be agenda-free, not even to be subtly agenda-influenced in any way.

This is why I, as a spiritual teacher, do not really like to even take contributions, unless it is absolutely necessary, and I feel it is coming from a person's heart. Sometimes it does, and sometimes it does not, but that is why, at the Tree of Life Foundation, we do not have fundraising campaigns, because we do not want any biases in terms of guiding people who are seriously involved in spiritual life. If people are not seriously involved, it is okay, we can take a little bit, but it is really not the way we are raising money. We have to earn our money. This is a subtle point about being a spiritual teacher. If a teacher begins to depend egocentrically on his or her students, or on their funding or on how many students he or she has, then that teacher starts to alter the teachings to please the students, and it becomes a popularity contest. In essence, this is a bribe. People sometimes do not understand why I am so low-key and not out in the world fundraising; this is the reason. I do not want to be in that kind of relationship, because then I cannot be in the clearest way of doing the spiritual work. Remember, the teacher, the tzaddik, has to be in a place where he is really clear, and therefore not in a place to have his judgment altered by whether a student makes a big donation, or the like. These are the important pieces here of understanding how subtle it is, and why, as I say, we minimize getting involved in fundraising, except when it appears that it might be a way for some people to burn up their karma and shift their consciousness. Sometimes giving can be the most important thing one can do to make that happen.

The parashah also talks about the kinds of sacrifices you may or may not bring: "Do not sacrifice to God your Lord any ox, sheep, or goat that has a serious blemish, since to do so before God your Lord is considered revolting" (Devarim 17:1). Sacrifice has to come from a place of honesty, a place of purity. That is why they call the opposite of this a "blemished sacrifice," and sacrificing that kind of animal was forbidden. As we open our hearts to the creator, our sacrifice must be because we want to bring ourselves closer in the process of deveikut. An ego-based desire cancels the energy of sacrifice. One cannot bribe God.

This parashah also talks about idol worship, which is another thing we may fall into. It actually includes the stone idols such as the *shiva lingam*. An idol is any thing that we relate to as bringing us energy outside of our self, anything that controls our energy. For example, hate or anger, in a sense, is idol worship because it is an energy that controls us outside of our relationship with God. Getting angry when something does not go the way we want is, again, not understanding that everything comes from God. Sex, money, power, drugs—all may become forms of idol worship. When people take a drug trip with LSD or ayahuasca (even though ayahuasca does not necessarily cause brain damage the way LSD, marijuana, and Ecstasy do), they are getting spiritual insight from something other than God. Of course, there is no such thing as "other than God," as everything is made possible by God. But it really gives you a different message. You are not earning it from the internal; you are taking something from outside of yourself that activates it, so it becomes a form of "pagan" idol worship. One may become tempted to deify these astral plane entities that are behind the drugs, like people have done with ayahuasca. It blocks your evolution, which is deveikut with the One, an internal process. Again, this is the Way of the Torah, and not the shamanic way of South America. This is a time, in the month of Elul, to take a look at that.

Shof'tim also talks about the appointment and role of a king. It is interesting because it says that Israelite kings were supposed to carry the Torah with them at all times, and they were supposed to be evolved beings. This is something that is direly missing in our world today. We really do need leaders who are actually spiritual people as well.

Next, the issue of a prophet comes up. This is a very important lesson. As Moshe said, "In your midst, God will set up for you a prophet like me from among your brethren, and it is to him that you must listen" (Devarim 18:15). And God said to Moshe: "I will set up a prophet for them from among their brethren, just as you are. I will place my word in his mouth, and he will declare to them all that I command him" (Devarim 18:18).

The role of a prophet is a difficult one, because it is not about really about "prophecy," but about upholding moral understanding, observing the righteous living of the Torah, and walking the spiritual path of the Torah. Moshe had already made it very clear: "If you go off the path, it doesn't work." One can see this in Eretz Yisrael today, where they are in great danger because there is no prophet, no spiritual leader at this moment to guide the people. Prophets like Moshe are given to us, and they are present in every generation. The role of the prophet did not end with the fall of the Temple.

All of the Ruach HaKodesh did not end with the fall of the Temple. Neither did it stop with the writing of the Torah. As Rav Kook pointed out, there are always new revelations coming through. Our work is to be tuned into the new revelations that are intricately linked with what has come before. Hashem takes care of us. Not only are we given many teachers, spiritual teachers, but prophets also may come into the world. In this context, "the world is the tzaddik." When we understand that the world is a spiritual teacher, we have that consciousness in every moment, we have that kind of refined thinking that everything is a message to help us evolve spiritually, to help us understand what is going on.

There are also many false prophets out there, using that term. These are people who really are not prepared to teach. People get a little hit of meditation or learn how to do an ayahuasca ceremony over a few years, and then, somehow, they are out there teaching and running ceremonies. It is a long process before one is ready to teach and take on that responsibility. Part of that process is burning up the ego. An aspect of this may include being initiated by a spiritual teacher, who was initiated by his or her spiritual teacher. There is often a lineage involved in a legitimate spiritual path and that is one way we are protected from charlatans.

This is not a 100 percent guarantee, but the principle is important. We have to be very careful about people who are self-assigned and self-proclaimed enlightened beings. The first questions we have to ask them are, "Who certified you? Who initiated you?" Of course, it is not as if one goes to school and gets a certificate, but when you are dealing with a lineage, you are dealing with people who have been trained by masters, and have gotten the validation from these high beings that they can be a spiritual teacher. We all are spiritual teachers, but we are specifically referring to a deeper level of teaching, like the level of the prophet. In the rabbinical tradition this lineage transmission initiation is called s'micha m'shefa

This parashah also talks about midah k'neged midah, which is all part of this judgment issue, and why we have the practices of the month of Elul. In referring to false testimony, we are told to judge the false witnesses in accordance with the sentence that would have been meted out to the innocent accused:

> "You must do the same to them as they plotted to do to their
> brother, thus removing evil from your midst. When the other
> people hear about this, they will have fear and never again do
> such an evil thing in your midst. Do not have pity in such a case,
> [since you must take] a life for a life, a tooth for a tooth, a hand
> for a hand, and a foot for a foot."
>
> (Devarim 19:19–21)

Midah k'neged midah means "measure for measure," or "as you sow, so you reap." It is not about vengeance, as it has been often interpreted by those unfamiliar with the Torah. It is about the natural laws of Elohim, which have a natural result that returns to the perpetrator. We call this return "judgment." We have different metaphors for it (e.g., an eye for an eye). But again, it is not about vengeance; this is how it is has been misunderstood by people who are more interested in vengeance and anger and wrath than in truth. Judgment is God's problem; it is not our job at a certain level. Yet, we have judges, and when judgment is done in a highly refined way, which is not really happening in our society, or almost any society today, there is a role of keeping order in the environment and the society. However, God will take care of a person's actions. When people have done something evil, it will come back at them as a part of natural cosmic Elohim law. It may happen ten or twenty years later, giving people time to change their ways. And if they do not change, the judgment manifests at the right time.

The issue of false witnesses is something so common in our society, and shows up often in the guise of gossip. When an issue comes up, try to go to the source. This is a general feedback system—two or three witnesses is a good number. I take a position that if three people tell you that something is out of balance in your life, you are wise to heed this warning. So, a very nice message on the spiritual path is that if three people give you feedback that something is out of balance, or if your spiritual teacher gives you feedback, and you want to check with other people, doing it in an appropriate way, those witnesses who come from the community can help you understand whether you are on track or not. This is a very important principle for spiritual evolution. Often we make collective decisions, though not all the time, and it is based on those kinds of issues and those kinds of principles.

Reminding us again that God is our ultimate judge, Moshe said in Devarim 20:1–4:

> "When you go to battle against your enemies, and see horses, war chariots and an army larger than yours, do not be afraid of them, since God your Lord, who brought you out of Egypt, is with you. When you approach [the place of] battle, the priest shall step forward and speak to the people. He shall say to them, 'Listen, Israel, today you are about to wage war against your enemies. Do not be faint-hearted, do not be afraid, do not panic, and do not

break ranks before them. God your Lord is the One who is going with you. He will fight for you against your enemies, and He will deliver you.'"

Here, the parashah talks about going out to war, and who can go out to war. It says one cannot go to war, for example, if one just got married and just settled down, if one just built a house or planted a field, or if one is just plain fearful. The ego puts us in a place of contentment. It is an illusion. People may say, "Now I have a nice house, money, a family." They are in a state of illusion, or they are just too afraid to face themselves. They are not eligible for liberation. That is what the Torah means. They are not eligible for the battle to cleanse the internal enemies. It does not mean you cannot have a family. It does not mean you cannot be in a relationship. It does not mean you cannot build a house. However, people become so attached to these things that they are not participating in the element of light that is coming in from all of the levels. They are not willing to face these issues and hear advice from their teacher, and are not ready for the process of liberation. This is what we are talking about, because the Torah path of enlightenment takes a tremendous amount of determination.

The ego constantly wants to delude us. The ego constantly wants us to fall asleep in the comfort zone; that is what we are talking about. The Torah takes this very clearly into consideration. Again, the Torah is not to be taken only p'shat, literally. It is to be taken as a guide for enlightenment. That is why it is hidden from those who are not ready to see it. That is why we have the Zohar, the Midrash, and other oral traditions to help us interpret it, and that is why we have teachers to help interpret it.

As we work on our selves, we create an inner peace, which, in turn, begins to create outer peace. That is an important part of it, as it says, "If they reject your peace offer and declare war, you shall lay siege to [the city]" (Devarim 20:12)—meaning that we will then overcome our egocentric limitations.

Now it also says something very ecological, and extremely important:

"When you lay siege to a city and wage war against it a long time to capture it, you must not destroy its trees, wielding an ax against any food producing tree. Do not cut down a tree in the field, unless it is being used by the men who confront you in the siege. However, if you know that a tree does not produce food, then until you have subjugated [the city], you may destroy [the tree] or cut off [what you need] to build siege machinery against the city waging war with you."

(Devarim 20:19–20)

This is a clear statement that warfare should not be allowed to disrupt or destroy the overall ecology of the land, and nowhere, including Israel, is this being honored. When we tear up the olive trees of people who have been there for hundreds of years as a way of punishing them, we are blatantly violating the Torah. We need to look at this because destroying the ecology with depleted uranium, tearing up the trees, or contaminating soil and water with all the weapons we have, is against the ecological precepts of the Torah.

So, as we look at the whole, as we look at the inner struggle, which is really what this is about on the interpretative level of sod (סוד), we also have to look at what it means on the outer level, because we live in both the world of the b'limah and the mah—the nothing and the something. The something is the world of physical reality, which is a very small part of overall reality, and the nothing is the truth of God, and the only actual reality from which all existence emanates in every moment.

Moshe was therefore talking a great deal about communion with God and about the importance of preserving this communion with the energetic circuitry of the Divine. This involves our everyday life, including laws, the courts, and the administration of "mundane" secular justice. These are the expression of God's existence in the world. The teaching again is "The world is the tzaddik." Hashem sets the laws of interaction in all walks of life. That is why the banking system and every other system came out of, and were stored within and underneath, the holy site of the Temple Mount, because it is a statement that divinity permeates what we think of as our entire "secular" existence, for us as individuals and also for what we think of as the collective national soul.

That is the intention behind Devarim 16:20: "Pursue perfect honesty, so that you will live and occupy the land that God your Lord is giving you." The external laws help to keep us in order, and in that sense the world is the tzaddik, the world is the expression of God, and the world is a way we can know

God. As difficult as it is to say, the court system in the ancient times was a symbolic opportunity to meet God in this world. The judges, who were able to work without biases or bribes, were representatives of God's justice in the world.

When we begin to understand it in this way, we understand that society does need some clarity and some guidance. In Shof'tim, we are also looking at the inner judge, the support of the tzaddik in our lives, and the support and interaction of the community as a holy feedback system that helps us evolve our midot, so that we are able to hold the energetics. May we all be blessed that we operate in the world with that consciousness and understanding. May we live every moment in ways that create harmony rather than chaos, and may we live with the moment-to-moment consciousness of the "third brother." May we be blessed that we do not judge ourselves or others, and thereby perceive ourselves or others as separate from God, because as we judge others, so we too become judged (Talmud Bav'li, Shabbat 127b).

Amen

Ki Thetze

THIS parashah speaks about the practical, about living as a human being in the world. The real spiritual test is around how we live our domestic lives, rather than our spiritual theories. It opens with "When you wage war against your enemies...." Note the Torah's use of the word "when," instead of "if." This implies that we are already engaged in war, and it outlines the applicable mitzvah so that we do not lose ourselves while at war.

There are many levels to understanding what it means to be at war. On a literal level, it could be talking about a physical war, but from the point of view of liberation, we are really talking about our struggle to remain awake as we live our daily lives. The "war" is therefore about keeping awake and not falling asleep. The war is with ourselves, with the enemy within. The war is with what we call our dark side, the yetzer hara (יצר הרע). The war is with our minds. The purpose of the war is to fill ourselves with light and dispel the inner darkness, which is why we are put on this planet. Every day requires our vigilance as if we are at war.

The yetzer hara's greatest victory is for us to go unconscious. Most of the time, people are unconscious and do not even realize that there is a constant battle going on inside of them between light and dark. We must be clear that God gave us the yetzer hara and yetzer tov (יצר טוב—the light side). The question we really need to ask is, can we remain conscious during this time, as this war is going on, and what motivates our will to keep struggling? The spiritual person is very persistent, and the more elevated you are, the more difficult the task. We have to be very clear that our job is to bring light to ourselves and to the world, and this is a spiritual war.

The month of Elul, which is commonly the time this parashah is read, requires us not only to improve the present and future here in the world of duality, but also to repair the imbalances we have created in the past. This is why we do a spiritual fast during the month of Elul, because this month-long period before Rosh Hashanah is about internal physical, emotional, mental, and spiritual cleansing. Without that, we are really not ready on Rosh Hashanah, the new year, to simply say "Oh, today I change." It takes at least a month to prepare ourselves for this. In the same way, my teachers always taught me, one must pay attention to one's own death, because if we wait until we are going to die, it is often too late to be able to prepare ourself, and then we end up taking all our imbalances with us into the next lifetime.

When Rebbe Simcha Bunim of Pesyschka was about to depart from our world, his wife stood by his bedside and broke out in tears. He asked: "Why do you cry? Do you not realize that the purpose of my entire life was so that I might know how to die?" (Histalkut Hanefesh).

Likewise, the idea is to spend this whole month cleansing and preparing, so that we can more easily do teshuva (תשובה), meaning "return to God." To return to God, we need to let go of all the things that keep us separate from God.

On the physical plane, this parashah says something very, very interesting. It is one of those subtleties in the Torah. In addressing the warriors of Am Yisreal, the Torah says when you go to war, if you spot an attractive woman among the enemy, and you cannot control yourself, you may take this woman captive, but you cannot rape her. Rather, you have to take her home with you, give her time to mourn, and then marry her and treat her as you would a nice Jewish wife, with all the privilege and honor that goes with that. You are not allowed to sell her as a slave or abuse her in any other manner. This approach toward women was revolutionary in world consciousness 3,300 years ago.

Admittedly, this is a little complicated, because why would the Torah even be open to this possibility? We have to understand that not all the Torah laws express the ideals of the Torah, but often act as ways to reach those ideals. In those times (more than 3,000 years ago), captive women were often raped by the invading armies. So, it would actually have been too dramatic a shift, especially in those times, to say, "Wow, this is not acceptable. You cannot do that." Because the people may not have been able to contain all their urges, the Torah stipulated along the following lines: If you lust for her, or you happened to have slept with her, you still have to take her home with you, and there has to be a month of mourning for her family. Then, if she converts to Judaism, and you still want her after a month, you can marry her. Additionally, she is to have her hair shaved and her traditional clothes taken away, and remain in a month of grief for this traumatic change and disruption in her life. Then, if you and she still hit it off, you are obligated to marry her in a traditional Jewish wedding ceremony.

This is a very interesting policy, because it is really saying: "If you have lust, rape is not acceptable. If you are unable to control the lust, then you are obligated to marry this lady." It was taught in those times that only the tzaddiks, the most pure of the soldiers, would go to war. So it was not common for this to happen. However, if a person could not contain himself in the heat, confusion, and intensity of battle, and he saw a "beautiful captive" (yefat to'ar—יפת תאר), there was a way to mediate the dark side so the lust could be channeled into a sacred marriage. According to the eighteenth-century Isbitzer Rebbe, Rabbi Mordechai Yosef, one first needs to distance himself from the yetzer hara and guard himself from the yetzer hara and from sin with all his might until he cannot restrain himself any further. Then, if the yetzer hara nevertheless overcomes him, and he acts on his lust, we can be certain that this is the will of Hashem. We have to be very clear: This does not mean that you can act out whatever you want and then attribute it to the will of God. This means that the Torah's instructions are intended to help people with their internal struggles, and there may be some amazing things that could happen from that, even if one loses one's battle with the yetzer hara.

The classic story, which illustrates this best, is that of the patriarch Yehuda (Judah), one of the twelve sons of Ya'akov. He was a great tzaddik, and he was drawn to make love with Tamar, his daughter-in-law, not knowing at the time who she was, because she was disguised as a prostitute in order to become impregnated by him. Interestingly, from this one exception in his life when he succumbed to the yetzer hara, came the lineage of King David (and ultimately through this will come the messiah), and it changed the course of history. So, this is an example of how God brings a spirit into people so that they act in a way that appears to be against the basic rules, but which, at the same time, is for a good reason. We never know exactly when this occurs, so we have to be very careful. In this situation, and if a situation like this is happening for you, you have to judge if this is God speaking, or lust, or what. The lesson we derive from all this is that we are instructed to serve God with both our yetzer tov (the positive urge) and our yetzer hara (the evil urge) (Talmud Bav'li, Berachot 54a). So, even the negative things that we do should be directed for the sake of heaven: "Greater is a sin committed with heavenly intent than a mitzvah performed without heavenly intent" (Talmud Bav'li, Nazeer 23b).

Still, it does not really mean that it is okay to miss the mark as long as we mean it for good, because we are talking here about a seriously extenuating circumstance wherein we are being absolutely overcome by something. What is being taught here is that the wisdom of Hashem is deeper than we can understand, and in certain circumstances we are allowed to do things like the taking of yefat to'ar, the beautiful captive woman.

Again, it is a little more complicated than this, because, at the same time, amidst the war, the rules are a little bit different. We have to remember always that the Torah makes the goal of life pretty clear, and that even the laws of the Torah itself do not always reflect the highest ideals of Judaism. Rather, the Torah expresses ways by which we might reach the ideal rather than simply stating the ideal itself. To merely state the ideal would render the Torah more a guide for angels than for humans with all of our frailties. After all, our sages remind us, the Torah was given to mortals, not to the ministering angels (Talmud Bav'li, Berachot 25b), and speaks to us in the language of humans (Talmud Bav'li, Berachot 31b).

In looking at this differently, we can think about the Torah as a system of values arranged in a specific hierarchy according to the priority in the present situation, meaning the period in which it was composed. So, sometimes certain Torah values may not be followed so perfectly for the good of the future. The trouble is that only God can decide that, so it gets a little complicated. But as the Talmud says, "God says, 'I created the evil inclination, and I created the Torah as its antidote'" (Talmud Bav'li, Kidushin 30b). Sometimes an amoral behavior may be okay, but the Torah is simply implying a basic approach to empowering people to stop doing what they otherwise might not have the power to overcome. In this way the Torah creates an allowing that keeps one connected if not able to overcome the lusts of the yetzer hara, while at the same time guides us toward the Torah ideal.

I think the best example of this is the issue of vegetarianism. Bereisheet 1:29 clearly tells us to be vegan: "The grasses of the field and fruit of the seed-bearing tree—this alone is going to be your food. Herbs and grasses. That will be your food." It is very clear on this point. Then people became meat eaters, and in the desert in Shemot the message comes again: "Here is the manna." God did not give them flesh. And again, the people could not handle it. What is happening, and what many of the rabbis teach, is that eating meat is a dispensation because people were not ready to be vegan. However, the highest way is to eat a plant-source-only cuisine. If they make rules like that, people will find themselves violating them because they cannot control their lust for meat. Now, when people did succumb to their cravings and eat meat in the desert, thousands of them died and were buried at "the graves of craving" (BeMidbar 11:34). God's message is pretty clear. The Torah therefore placed numerous restrictions around eating meat, which we call "kosher." Kosher rules dictate a special way that one has to kill the animal, has to look it in the eye, and avoid causing any trauma or pain to the animal in the process. It is very labor intensive. What is the point? The point is that then God made it as complicated as possible to keep eating meat, because it was obviously not God's preference for our diet. With the "beautiful captive woman" guideline (the yefat to'ar), we are looking at the same guiding concept.

Then the parashah goes further, and indirectly talks about divorce—that if people really do not get along, they have a right to divorce. Now, why does it say this in this section, and in this indirect way? There are two reasons for divorce. First, it is a worse sin, a worse missing of the mark, for people to hate each other (VayYiKra 19:17). So it is better to get divorced before you hate each other. Second, when your soulmate arrives, and the current marriage partner is not your soulmate, the forces of the order of nature will compel the situation so that you have to be with your soulmate, and this too often leads to having to divorce.

Discovering your soulmate takes precedence over a regular marriage, and the graceful thing is to have a divorce if you actually find your soulmate, but you have to be really clear it is your soulmate.

What the Torah is talking about here, in a very interesting way, is that the conflict generally begins at home. Now remember, we are not talking about 3,000 years ago, and we are not going out conquering people and wiping out nations and doing all these things. We are living our daily lives here and now; that, again, is the real war, right here in our everyday lives. One therefore has to look at the practical realities of relationship. One ought not to get involved with someone and sleep with them until you know that they are really the right person for you, and therefore it unfolds out of love. If it is out of lust (which is a situation of war, and that means internal war, too), then people may not be as compatible and may soon turn to fighting each other.

In this context the Torah's next teaching concerns the rebellious child. A child that would not obey his or her parents was to be seen as a dark force endangering Am Yisrael. If he was continually disciplined and still did not obey, then he must be taken to the elders, and they would have to decide what to do with him. Where does this rebellious child come from? It comes from the conflict between the parents, because their relationship was not based on love. So, you see, it is really not a good idea to engage in a relationship when there is conflict and uncertainty. Yet, relief could be granted through the rites of divorce. One still had a way to handle one's kids, because it was taught that if the parents were really out of alignment, then the kids often were rebellious, and they still provide an escape for this, too. If one must still follow one's lust, then it is necessary to understand all these difficulties and problems that may stem from this.

I think this is yet another practical way that the Torah is able to help people deal with their lust, giving them outs, so that they would have another chance to ultimately come to a higher octave in how they choose to live in the world. These are really hard messages, in a way, but, as the Talmud teaches us, the Torah relates to us as human beings, not angels. So, when the Torah implies that it is okay to eat meat, it is not commanding you to eat meat; it is but a dispensation. When the Torah implies that the warrior can act on his desire, it is not saying that this is okay, but that if he must, here is how we can work with it to make it permissible, to bring the dark force into the embrace of the light. In that way, the Torah as a spiritual path is addressing the evil inclination and our human condition and creates some degree of order where there would otherwise surely be chaos.

As we look at the Torah in its entirety, first we have the cosmic messages in the book of Bereisheet, which is about universalism and the merging of heaven and earth. In the book of Shemot, we talk about liberation, revelation, and the Mikdash, the sanctuary in the desert. In the book of VayYiKra, we discuss the laws of the priests, and that the teaching of the priests is all about peace. In BeMidbar, Moshe teaches about how each individual has a God-given place and role, and how important it is for each of us to discover that role as it concerns us individually and collectively in the overall plan. Finally, in Devarim, it is about how we play out our role in everyday life. All these pieces, you see, are clearly aligned in a deliberate order that makes sense when pieced together.

All of this occurs on the physical plane of everyday life. On the spiritual plane, however, we are already at war. War is the very essence of the pre-enlightened state. If we are conscious, we are in that battle with the unconscious dark side of ourselves. The very first step to winning this war is therefore to know that there is a war. In this context, when the Torah is speaking about a beautiful captive woman, it is not actually about lusting after a female human; rather, it represents a negative temptation. In that sense, Satan, or the dark side, will make any kind of negativity look like it is beautiful. This may be a woman, a man, a wad of dollars, or anything else that we desire. Once we understand this, we must be constantly vigilant in our spiritual life. Then we are in tune with the imbalances of the struggle, rather than living in ignorance.

Next, the Torah goes into some very basic things about how to live one's life. It talks about a man who has two wives, one he loves and one he hates. He may not allocate a bigger inheritance to the children of the woman he loves. This really represents two aspects of the person, and implies the understanding that both are one and the same. In other words, one cannot just say I like this and I do not like that, and that is the way it is. One must accept everything as it is.

Then there is a section about concern for people's property. It is clear that the light will not honor us if we do not honor other people and their things. It talks about the ox and the donkey: They should not be hitched together under the same yoke, because that is cruelty to them since each has a different pace and rate of working. So, this is about protecting the wellbeing of animals, and being careful not to cause them pain or discomfort. The Torah talks about how linen and wool should not be woven together; I assume that it was because they have different vibration rates and one is from plant, the other from animal. All of these teach us to have moment-to-moment awareness of all the things that are going on around us. It also says that when you build a house and you have a porch, you need to have a barrier on it. Why? So people do not fall off the porch; it is about having concern for others. What is the message? The more we care about others, the more we are creating light in the world.

Ki Thetze also talks about lashon hara (slander). When a husband gossips about his wife, it creates a negativity that does not belong anywhere. It also talks about adultery and rape, and in a deeper level this is really about the original "sin" with Kayin and Hevel, and the importance of correcting this on all levels. Ki Thetze says that, because of the presence of God moving through the camp one should not defecate in the camp. One needs to step outside the camp to defecate. It talks about how you should always have a spade to bury your feces, which is clearly about ecological awareness, and it talks about one's responsibility not to pollute the public commons, or the community environment. These are some of the everyday ins and outs covered in this parashah.

We are all slaves until we begin the path of liberation. So, when the Torah says that one should not return an escaped slave to his or her owner, it is saying something very unique: "Once you start to wake up, don't turn back!" One has to keep that energy going.

The Torah also introduces us to the prohibition against charging interest on loans. This mitzvah has been consistently violated. It is not simply about avoiding usury; it is about not charging interest. It does not refer only to loans, but when you do someone a favor, you should not expect a favor in return; otherwise, it would be more akin to a business deal and would lack the positive energy born of sharing from the heart. So, when we loan money to someone or do someone a favor, we should not expect that there ought to be, or will be, a return on that.

It also talks about the importance of the first year of marriage. That is the foundation of the relationship. If the relationship is difficult in the beginning, it is not considered a good sign. So, this is why an Israelite warrior, in those times, did not have to go to war, or even have to work very much during the first year of marriage, so that he and his wife would have space to create and firm up the foundation of their relationship. After a year, one can better surmise whether the union is positive or negative. So that year is crucial. It is foundation-building time. Again, the parashah is focused on merging the heavens and the earth, the walk between the b'limah and the mah, as a general approach to spiritual life, so it necessarily includes the practicalities involved in healthy relationships—relationships with partner, neighbor, enemy, and with people in general—in terms of helping others become free.

This also includes the law about kidnapping. The prohibition against kidnapping is clear: one should not kidnap. But subtle kidnapping also happens when someone completely controls another person even in a relationship, and this can happen between husband and wife, and/or between parents and children. There is a balance. This is why I teach the family-centered approach, in which everybody is honored. The child-centered approach is a reverse form of kidnapping, where the parents find themselves dominated by the child. This has a high probability to create difficulty and rebellion.

The parashah also addresses the importance of treating debtors with dignity. If we are in a better financial position than another, we need to be humble. In kabbalistic thinking, it is possible that the person who lent the money may have come into the world solely for that purpose. In fact, what that would mean is that the lender would need the debtor, but we do not exactly always see it that way as part of the bigger picture.

In the final section, Ki Thetze refers back to our age-old enemy, Amalek, who, kabbalistically, represents doubt. The power of doubt can undermine the spiritual path. The parashah teaches about the importance of certainty. That is one of the roles of the spiritual teacher: to be in that place of certainty and to inspire the people to overcome their doubt with certainty.

The haftorah for this parashah is from Yesha'yahu, suggesting that no matter what our status is, physically or spiritually, we still have the power to do good acts, and we should take advantage of it. The story never ends.

So, it is interesting how the Torah takes us from the very beginning in Bereisheet, the universality of all and the merging of heaven and earth, right down to the physical plane of domestic life in Devarim, and how our spirituality needs to resonate in an enlightened way with our domestic life. In other words, our domestic life must reflect our spirituality. This is also known as walking our talk. May we be blessed as we read this section, that we become empowered with the consciousness, determination, or willpower to walk our talk and become the living expression of the Great Torah Way of multi-dimensional enlightenment.

Amen

Ki-Tavo

Tʜɪs parashah is an important part of Moshe's final communication to the people, laying out the two possible destinies for Am Yisrael. It is the summation of the teachings Moshe had given to the people, gleaned from what he had learned from his personal life and from Hashem. It is the essence of the teaching of the divine way. The parashah starts very simply with the blessing of bikurim, the first fruits of the harvest. The people were going into the Promised Land, and Moshe was giving a message about the different levels of consciousness they would need to exercise while living on the land. One lesson involved the offering of the first fruits on the altar, which demonstrates basic gratitude to God for allowing Am Yisrael to be in this land. It also served as a ritual reminder to the people of the source of their harvest, which, in turn, helped them maintain a certain level of humility. The offering of the first fruits also was related to the unity of the relationship of the secular to the spiritual in Am Yisrael. The spiritual gave meaning to the secular and the secular gave meaning to the spiritual. That was the beauty of a coherent Am Yisrael. Just making a fruit offering, as if it were a tax, had no meaning, but when offering the first of the fruit harvest as a symbol of relationship to God, the land, and all the people on the land, something different happened. It takes us into the meaning of Eretz Yisrael, where we had the potential to fuse nationality with spirituality, and in that way be aligned in the service of God. The Israelite farmers understood this. They knew that without the Levites and the Beit HaMikdash, all that they would strive to do would not have very much meaning. The fruits and the seasonal rains coming at the appropriate times were understood as not just about the farmer and his produce; they were about the spiritual health of the whole nation.

The bikurim were an occasion for public celebration. The bikurim were connected to the Levi'im, who breathed life into the nation spiritually as much as the farmer did physically. Each had their job, and this joint offering ceremony represented the synthesis of the two. The farmer was affirming his connection to the land of Israel and the spiritual essence of Am Yisrael. The bikurim gift to the Beit HaMikdash symbolized the ability to survive as a nation. In order to enter the land, the people had to fuse the spiritual world with the physical world within their consciousness, and in that way they would be fruitful in the land of Israel. The importance of gratitude, humility, and awe in our spiritual evolution cannot be emphasized enough.

What most people associate with Ki-Tavo are the blessings and the cursings. At a deeper level of understanding, Moshe relayed the consequences of their choices of action. Consequences are not punishments, as many would interpret them. Consequences, whether positive or negative, are the result of the natural laws of Elohim known as midah k'negid midah (measure for measure) and the higher level of YHWH, which is the power of grace, or *yad Hashem* (יד יהוה)—"hand of God" (Shemot 9:3 and Devarim 2:15). The power of the hand of God can create a more or less severe consequence than "measure for measure." Hard to understand in Moshe's prophecy is the degree of the severity. We would like to think of this in a Newtonian way: Action brings an equal and opposite reaction. The description of the positive consequences seems wonderful, but the negative consequences, while they defy the imagination, actually happened in the way the Jewish people ended up suffering during the Holocaust. Moshe's prophecy is too painfully and literally close to what we suffered in the Holocaust not to be noticed. And as prophesied, after paying this price we have been returned to Eretz Yisrael. The concept of grace, like measure-for-measure, which is more of a Newtonian physics concept, can be understood through the world of quantum physics. This includes the Heisenberg uncertainty principle, for instance, which is the physics explanation of the hand of God, or grace. In this case, the consequences of not following the Torah Way were far more severe than what we would call an equal and opposite reaction.

Being "chosen" for God's assignment, as was Am Yisrael, has a magnificent upside, but also the reverse. It was, and is, a profound spiritual opportunity that we could not grasp at that time in history, nor do we well understand today. Today there are more who may be ready. Being around a strong tzaddik is like being near a warm fire on a winter day. The fire is warming, but one can also get burned. Ultimately, Am Yisrael chose, at that time, to follow their lust and their egos rather than the Great Way of the Torah. We have suffered for 2,500 years as a result of not being focused on deveikut. Moshe was clearly saying that when people are on the spiritual path, they will receive the blessings and sustenance: "As long as you listen to God your Lord, all these blessing will come to bear on you" (Devarim 28:2). On the other hand, if they choose to follow their selfish desires and receive for self, alone, rather than receive in order to share, then they will bring chaos. This is a warning: If you are going to be on the spiritual path, take it seriously; do not take it lightly. Make your commitment from a very reasoned judgment; knowing in your heart that this is what you truly want to do, because once you begin, you no longer have the privilege of "ignorance is bliss."

This brings us to some questions. What does it mean to follow the way of God? What does it mean to dwell on God's holy mountain? Does it mean to ritually and mechanically follow the 613 mitzvot, or does it mean something else? These are questions that we have struggled with for thousands of years. Rabbi Simlai, in the third century, was the first to mention the number 613 (Talmud Bav'li, Makot 23b–24a). However, people took it out of context. He actually said something far more profound than there are a bunch of specific practices that you must follow.

In a translation from Rabbi Gershon Winkler, Rabbi Simlai's whole message was as follows:

> 613 precepts were given to Moses at Sinai: 365 prohibitions according to the 365 days of the solar cycle, and 248 imperatives corresponding to the 248 organs of the human body.
>
> Then came David, and narrowed it down to eleven, as it is written: "Oh God, who shall merit living in your tent, who shall dwell on your holy mountain?" [This, incidentally, is the essence of what we are talking about here.]
>
> He gives the answer: "The one who walks the path of simplicity and performs acts of benevolence and his heart resonates with truthfulness; whose speech knows no deceit, and who does not wrong fellow creatures nor shame those who are kin; who

despises those who are sinister, and honors those who appreciate the gifts of the creator; who keeps promises to others and will not renege even at personal hardship; who does not exact interest for money loaned, nor accept bribes at the expense of the innocent" (Psalm 15).

Then came Isaiah and narrowed them down to six, as it is written: "The one who walks with deeds of benevolence and resonates with righteousness; who despises profits gained from oppression; whose hands recoil at the offer of bribes; whose ears are muffled from hearing of destructive schemes; whose eyes are shut from gazing upon evil" (Isaiah 33:15).

Then came Micah and narrowed them down to three, as it is written: "Perform justice, love benevolence, and humble your walking with your creator" (Micah 6:8).

Then came Isaiah again and narrowed them down to two, as it is written: "Be ever so cautious to do justice, and do charity" (Isaiah 56:1).

Then came Amos, who narrowed them down to one, as it is written: "Seek God, and live" (Amos 5:4).

And then came Habakkuk, according to Rabbi Nachmon ben Yitzchak, and narrowed them down to one in another way: "The just [righteous] person shall live by faith in God" (Habukkuk 2:4).

Rabbi Simlai was pointing out how these prophets and king—David, Yesha'yahu, Mikha, Amos, and Habakkuk—were looking at the foundations of the mitzvot, and that the mitzvot is not the goal in itself, but serves as a way of how to live a fully human life. We can say the mitzvot are, in a sense, pathways of becoming a full human being on the planet. The halakhah, or Jewish law, was never the sole definition of the Way of the Torah. It is a means, not the end, to spiritual devotion and aliveness. Actually, the word halakhah itself translates literally not as "law" but as "the walk." Torah is the showing, or the teaching, of this. Torah is a guide for how to be a full human being on the planet, rather than how to be religiously correct. It was never meant to be a vehicle for whipping people into a desired, mindless form, but as a vehicle of spiritual journeying that would keep people in their individual aliveness and collective harmony in a context of responsible behavior. Moshe's message was, "Make God the context for your life; make God your way of life"—not "Here is a set of rules you have to follow." It is really about what King David declared— "I will rejoice in the Lord" (Tehillim 104:34); in other words, "I will make God the context of my life and my frame of reference." That is what brings us true noncausal love, noncausal joy, noncausal peace, noncausal bliss, noncausal oneness, noncausal compassion, and noncausal contentment, all of which are our natural emotions and are the essence of the experience of chey'rut and deveikut. This is what automatically fills us with simcha, "spiritual joy," and tuv levav, "goodness of hearts," which implies spiritual contentment (Devarim 28:47).

Devarim 26:11 says, "You, the Levite, and the proselyte in your midst shall thus rejoice in all the good that God your Lord has granted you and your family." Devarim 26:16–17 adds: "Today God your Lord is commanding you to obey all these rules and laws. You must carefully keep them with all your heart and with all your soul. Today you have declared allegiance to God, making Him your God, and [pledging to] walk in His paths, keep His decrees, commandments and laws, and to obey His voice."

This is an explicit direction of the intention, or kavanah (כונה), with which we are to be lived by the mitzvot. Devarim 27:9 says: "Moses and the Levitical priests spoke to all Israel, saying: Pay attention and listen, Israel. Today you have become a nation to God your Lord." This includes incredible benefits (out of proportion to actions) or severe negative consequences (out of proportion to actions). This is the great offering given to the "chosen people." It implies that the primal cause for a negative outcome would be "You would not serve God your Lord with happiness and a glad heart" (Devarim 28:47). In other words, performing rote ceremony will result in a negative outcome. Your heart must be in it, too, and you have to serve God with joy, not out of duress (Tehillim 100:2).

The Ba'al Shem Tov refused to even go into certain shuls or places of worship because he saw the prayers of the people lying on the floor "like birds with broken wings." The simcha and tuv levav come from a complete heart devotion to Hashem and from "broken hearted prayers" and from being lived by the mitzvot, in which God is the living center of our life's actions. They arise when we are in gratitude and appreciation of the wonderful and mystical ways the Torah has given us for drawing the divine experience of Hashem into our lives. This is further activated by our experience of ourselves as divine beings radiating with the presence of God within, which becomes deliciously heightened through mitzvot and prayer. When we walk around filled with the presence of God, we become lived by God in every moment of our lives and consequently are joyously filled with the noncausal love, contentment, joy, peace, oneness, and compassion of the Divine dancing in the center of our hearts. Living this way fills us with the ecstatic pleasure of God. If people had experienced how sublimely wondrous they would feel they may have been able to live in the Great Torah Way.

The Talmud teaches us that the presence of the God is referred to as the shekhinah within us, but it does not come into people when they are not in that right relationship to the Divine, such as when we are sad, lazy, or mindlessly talking (Talmud Bav'li, Shabbat 30b). She inspirits us only when we are happy and serving God's purpose. Part of that is doing a mitzvah, but part of it is also perhaps connected to a bigger piece. When we are feeling the infinite Divine working through us, our life has meaning. When we are participating in the unfolding of the divine will from keter, then we do feel meaning. We feel alive, and we are able to dance on God's mountain.

The Torah is our guideline. The book of Iyyov (Job) says, "But the stupid man shall become wise, when a wild ass's colt shall be turned into a man!" (Iyyov 11:12). The Torah teaches us that our natural inclinations have a divine purpose, but that our task, guided by the Torah, is to transform our wild drives into the highest octaves of how we can be as human beings. When we start to understand this, we start to get a different grasp of what it means to live on God's mountain, as David said in Tehillim (Psalms). This is what it means to merit living in the divine tent: "A Psalm of David. Lord, who shall abide in thy tent? Who shall dwell in thy holy hill?" (Tehillim 15:1). It is about becoming a mensch. A mensch is an authentic, full human being who is honest with himself, sensitive to others, just, loving and living in right ethical and spiritual relationship to the world.

As we live these practices with the right consciousness and intention, we are no longer "doing" them, but rather we are being lived by the Torah Way of life. When we are being lived by love, being lived by chey'rut, being lived by the holiness in the joy of kedusha, of holiness, then the grace of God, which some also call *Ey'ma Ila'ah* (אימא עלאה—"the ancient one of the many cycles"), may at the right time appear and take us into the state of God-merging. This is the purpose of the Torah, to take us into God-merging, into deveikut. As it says in the Talmud, "Whether you do a lot, or whether you do a little, what matters is that your heart is directed toward the heavens" (Talmud Bav'li, Berachot 5b). So it is not actions that we are talking about; it is the context of our life and the love in our heart for God. That is what establishes us in God's tent. So, another way of looking at the spiritual path as it is outlined in the Torah is not so much about actions but about transforming our character so that we can live on the planet, in God's tent, at the highest level. All these mitzvot serve the purpose of transforming our character (midot), as well as establishing energetic channels to the heavens through which the shefa (divine heavenly influx of the shekhinah) nourishes our soul with the joy and love of God.

What is interesting about parashah Ki-Tavo is that the entire section of the blessings and curses is being spoken in the first person, in the singular. It is not talking about the people in general, but about how we as individuals bear responsibility for the fate and merit of the entire kol Yisrael. As it says, "If only you keep the commandments of God your Lord and walk in His paths, God will establish you as His holy nation, as He promised you" (Devarim 28:9). The summation of the mitzvot is then simply to walk before God and be whole, to be a blessing to God in every action that we do. This establishes us on the holy mountain. If we live that way, we will never be kicked out of the land again. What is important in the latter verse is that it does not say *kol*, or "all" mitzvot. It really just says "Walk in the ways of Hashem," and that is the key to living in God's tent or the holy mountain. It is actually considered a mitzvah to "walk in the ways of Hashem" (Bereisheet 18:19). This is what Maimonides, the great twelfth-century rabbi and physician, emphasized in his famous treatise on Jewish law and practice, *Mishnah Torah*. There, in his discussion about proper behavior and character development, he provided us with a detailed recipe for becoming a mensch (Mishnah Torah, Hilchot

Deʿot, 1:3). He believed that Judaism begins and ends with the challenge of becoming a mensch. It is about changing one's character to become a living embodiment of kedusha. He considered it an obligation, without which we are not fulfilling one of the basic ingredients of the Torah Way. It is menschness, rather than any particular actions performed correctly, that keeps us on the holy mountain.

In the time of the year when this parashah is read, we are approaching the period of Rosh Hashanah. Our focus is not just on our actions of the past, but on developing our basic character traits, so that our actions and our character traits become a living blessing to the Divine, which establishes our living on the holy mountain. It is about living in a way that we hear the voice of Hashem emanating from every human being, and we are motivated to become the full kedoshim (קדושים) that we were meant to be (VayYiKra 19:2).

Another little piece to the secret of the blessings and cursings that fill this parashah is that nothing is unattainable, and everything can be easily lost, if we are not paying attention and striving for that holiness in every moment. This depends also on our sense of appreciation, awe, and wonderment of the Divine. The Hebrew word elul (אלול), which is the name of the month in which this parashah is read, is very interesting because it is also an acronym for an intimate phrase out of King Solomon's *Shir Hashirim: "Anee l'do'dee v'do'dee lee"* (אני לדודי ודודי לי)—"I am my beloved's, and my beloved is mine" (Shir Hashirim 6:3). It reflects the beauty of what we are talking about here, the intimacy of merging with God, of deveikut. In this way, we raise ourselves above the slavery of the ego and our self-centered way of life. It is interesting that the number of verses in Ki-Tavo equals the numerical value, or gematria, of *avadav*—"His [God's] servants." Ki-Tavo helps free us from the slavery of the world so we become the expression of the Divine in our lives. "Receiving in order to share" is another way of understanding the full meaning of all this. In every blessing we get, we want to renew our commitment to our spiritual life. The bottom line of the Torah is "Her ways are ways of pleasantness, and all her paths are peace" (Mishle 3:17). In other words, the core of the Torah and the core of living on the holy mountain, is living in loving-kindness to ourselves and to those around us. This is achieved by refining our character so that we are walking in balance, specifically in the balance of gevurah and chesed, to be in that place of beauty, the place of compassion and of loving-kindness in everything we do. It means being fully conscious so that in every step we take on the planet, as we walk before God, we are a blessing and are merging with the Divine—deveikut in every moment. That way, we will always live on God's holy mountain, because then walking in the way of God becomes our way of life, and not a separate practice that we do in order to "feel religious." May we all be blessed to continue to live on God's holy mountain and in the bliss and awe of God's tent.

Amen

Netzavim

T HE word netzavim means "we are standing gathered." As this parashah opens, all the people were standing before God and before Moshe, ready again to make their commitment anew. Said Moshe:

> "Today you are all standing before God your Lord—your leaders, your tribal chiefs, your elders, your law enforcers, every Israelite man, your children, your women, and the proselytes in your camp—even your woodcutters and water drawers. You are thus being brought into the covenant of God your Lord, and [accepting] the dread oath that He is making with you today. He is establishing you as His nation, so that He will be a God to you, just as He promised you, and as He swore to the ancestors, Abraham, Isaac, Jacob."
>
> (Devarim 29:9–12)

A prime message here, and there are many levels of it, of course, is that no one is any holier than anyone else; everyone stands before God equally. What is interesting is that it mentions also the woodcutters and the water carriers. That was very specific, because in those times, the woodcutters and the water carriers were to be the tribe of Giv'on, who would later enact a treaty with Yehoshua. Their story is related in the book of Yehoshua, Chapter 9. Actually, they were already living in the land of Canaan, but they pretended to be coming from a far distance so they would not be harmed, and Am Yisrael made a treaty with them. Only a few days later did Yehoshua discover that he had been tricked by the Giv'onites, but Am Yisrael chose to create a peaceful solution, and the people of Giv'on agreed to be the woodcutters and water carriers in their role as members of Am Yisrael.

Everyone who chose was included, and that is the point. No one was considered any more holy than anyone else. There is no monopoly on kedusha (קדושה), holiness. No individual or subgroup, according to these principles, could ever claim to have exclusive possession of the spirit. Every individual, tribe, and subgroup was, by this oath, linked to God in the Torah, because all entered the covenant at that time. The Torah is teaching us a very important lesson: that kedusha belongs to everyone, to the most sophisticated and the most simple, to both men and women, Jew and non-Jew (Midrash Tana D'bei Eliyahu Rabbah 10:1). Each person is said to have his own letter in the Torah and his own gift to give. Of course, the purpose of the gathering in this parashah is for the people to see themselves as one full nation, secular and spiritual, a totality, and a wholeness. No particular group was to serve God to the disadvantage of any other group; rather, the entire nation was to serve God together.

This is a powerful model and statement of what needs to happen in Israel today, and in the whole world, because no one person, no one nation, no one country, in any way, has any monopoly on holiness or on relationship with God. The covenant is made with the whole world, and it is a universal message that the Torah is teaching at this moment. We also should understand that the whole world, and not just Am Yisrael, will suffer the consequences of not aligning with the universal teachings emerging from the Torah template.

Moshe then went on to warn the people once more not to worship idols. Idol worship means giving power to something other than God as our source. Idol worship includes anything that distracts you from your spiritual life, from knowing God, from deveikut, the direct merging with God. Money, power, sex, ego, pride—all these pull us away from the source and can become idols. So, an idol is not just some graven image or statue. It is something far more profound: what we attach more importance to, consciously or unconsciously, than serving and merging with God.

This parashah, like the previous one, is usually read in the latter part of the month of Elul, close to Rosh Hashanah. Moshe was reminding the people to look very closely at all the ways that they were living so that they might become completely focused on God-merging. Rav Soloveitchik writes that this parashah is the source of the personal covenant between Hashem and each individual. In Devarim 29:11–13 Moshe made this oath clear:

> "You are thus being brought into the covenant of God your Lord,
> and [accepting] the dread oath that He is making with you today.

He is establishing you as His nation, so that He will be a God to you, just as He promised you, and He swore to your ancestors, Abraham, Isaac, and Jacob. But it is not with you alone that I am making this covenant and this dread oath. I am making it both with those who are standing here with us today before God our Lord, and with those who are not [yet] here with us today."

We read this parashah, then, as a way of entering into a state of awe and hitlahavut (ecstatic frame of mind in the service and worship of God), so that by the time Rosh Hashanah comes around we are prepared and have the potential to enter into the realm of the Holy One.

The theme of this parashah is not about a spiritually light matter. It is a difficult one. It is difficult because we are being asked for a total commitment. In this way, Netzavim lays out the deeper meaning of teshuvah (תשובה), which involves more than simply reviewing and righting wrongs. In Ramban's teaching, the Jewish people are only redeemed through teshuvah (Mishnah Torah, Hilchot Teshuvah 7:5). I have to add that acts of charity (צדקה—tzedakah), love (אהבה—ahava), intense spiritual focus with prayer (תפילה—tefilah), meditation (התבודדות—hitbodedut), repeating the name of God (הגיה—higia), and being lived by the mitzvot (מצות) and halakhah (הלכה) also play a powerful redemptive role. This is about each individual engaging in a covenantal relationship with the creator. That is what becomes the source of one's personal holiness.

Netzavim is very much about redemption and the order of the prophecies leading to redemption. In Devarim 30:1–10, Moshe said to us:

"There shall come a time when you shall experience all the words of blessing and curse that I have presented to you. There, among the nations where God will have banished you, you will reflect on the situation. You will then return to God your Lord, and you will obey Him, doing everything that I am commanding you today. You and your children [will repent] with all your heart and with all your soul. God will then bring back your remnants and have mercy on you. God your Lord will once again gather you from among all the nations where He scattered you. Even if your diaspora is at the ends of the heavens, God your Lord will gather you up from there and He will take you back. God your Lord will then bring you to the land that your ancestors occupied, and you too will occupy it. God will be good to you and make you flourish even more than your ancestors. God will remove the barriers from your hearts and from the hearts of your descendants, so that you will love God your lord with all your heart and soul. Thus will you survive. God will then direct all these curses against your enemies and against the foes who pursued you. You will repent and obey God, keeping all His commandments, as I prescribe them to you today. God will then grant you a good surplus. In all the work of your hands, in the fruit of your womb, the fruit of your livestock, and the fruit of your land. God will once again rejoice in you for good, just as He rejoiced in your fathers. All this will happen when you obey God your Lord, keeping all His commandments and decrees, as they are written in this book of the Torah, and when you return to God your Lord with all your heart and soul."

The real meaning of teshuvah is clearly then to merge with God. It is not only to undo wrongdoings. And here, teshuvah is divided into three phases: First, "return to your heart" (Devarim 30:1); second, "return to God" (Devarim 30:2); third, "then you will be brought to the land of your ancestors" (Devarim 30:5). We see here how returning to the land is an integral phase of a complete teshuvah, and, thus, interdependent on the other two phases, returning to the truth of Self and returning to the truth of God. Clearly, then, Am Yisrael will merit full divine support when it has experienced a full teshuvah of deveikut. May we be so blessed.

In Devarim 30:6, Moshe continued: "God will remove the barriers from your hearts and from the hearts of your descendants, so that you will love God your Lord with all your heart and soul. Thus will you survive." To have a circumcised heart means to let go of all your lusts and cravings. The prophecy here is that if the people will repent after their exile, they will be returned to Eretz Yisrael. There is a more refined stage of teshuvah involved here, which is that of the circumcised heart. This is about the spiritual revolution that will take place in the messianic times. As Ramban pointed out:

> From the time of creation, each person has been given free choice to be a saint or an evil doer … but in the messianic period it will be natural to choose only good (we will not have desires and lusts). This is the circumcision of the heart…. At this time people will become like Adam before the sin.

It means they will no longer hold the evil inclination. On a deeper level, this means that people will be so filled with God, they will no longer be subject to the evil inclination. The battle between good and evil within ourselves will be over, because it will be natural to choose the good. Until that time, the battle between the yetzer tov and the yetzer hara (between good and evil and free will) goes on as part of our evolutionary process. At the end of that process, we will be so filled with God that we will not have those yetzer hara desires anymore. At the end of his life, Moshe was an example of this; he became free of evil desire and the illusory concept of free will on the physical plane. His essence becomes the unique enlightened expression of the Divine, completely linked with keter (will of God).

Another implication of Devarim 30:6 is that parents and their children have different hearts, which is actually true as each generation is shaped by different circumstances and understandings on every level of being. This is one of my reasons for writing this level of Torah interpretation, which is to speak to members of the newer generations, who may consider themselves spiritual, but are not able to relate to the previous generation's understanding and way of life. Malakhi 3:24 implies that Eliyahu, the harbinger of the messiah, will be able to touch and blend with the hearts of each generation in a way that will "restore the heart of the fathers to the children, and the heart of the children to their fathers." Until this process is complete, we use the illusions of free will and the evil inclination to best serve our evolution. In this context, the illusion of free will separates us from God, and yet is also part of our spiritual evolution. But in the process of deveikut/chey'rut, we naturally transcend this illusion. We are so moved by the t'shukat deveikut (תשוקת דביקות—the driving urge to merge with God) that nothing can hold us back from the draw of the Divine. At this point, the illusion of free will, as the unique expression of the Divine (as the Yehuda archetype, as the enlightened One) disappears, and we simply become the will of God expressing itself through our unique body-mind complex, also known as the personality.

During the season when this parashah is read, we prepare ourselves for Rosh Hashanah. Rav Shlomo Carlebach taught that we do so by transforming the vessel and actions of the previous year into a vessel that can contain the light of the upcoming year. Ultimately, this is about being in deveikut. The more we are in deveikut, the more light we contain and the higher we can go. The struggle to transform ourselves is to be taken seriously. Teshuvah applies to everybody, and, in the fullest sense, teshuvah means to return to Hashem. Its ultimate expression is God-merging. On one level of teshuvah, we can go back in time and dissolve those things that have created trouble. We can change the future by rectifying the seed thought forms that have misdirected our actions in the past, so that they will not be around to create the same missing-the-mark actions in the future. This allows us to eliminate misdeeds that cause us to miss the mark to begin with. In so doing, we are better able to forgive ourselves and others. We can create a healthier body and soul. We can achieve longevity through eliminating stress. We can rescind unfavorable edicts. There are many good things that come from teshuvah.

Ramban (thirteenth-century Rabbi Moshe ben Nachmon) taught that in Netzavim, everyone is standing before God, ready to be initiated into the divine covenant. Everyone is treated democratically. Everyone joins in making the covenant happen, and everyone is responsible for honoring it. Devarim 29:17–19 says:

> "Today, there must not be among you any man, woman, family
> or tribe, whose heart strays from God, and who goes and wor-
> ships the gods of those nations. There must not be among you a
> root whose fruit is gall and wormwood. When [such a person]
> hears the words of this dread curse, he may rationalize and say,
> 'I will have peace, even if I do as I see fit. Let me add some mois-
> ture to this dry [practice]!' God will not agree to forgive such
> a person. God's anger and demand for exclusive worship will

be directed like smoke against that person and the entire dread curse written in this book will lie [at his door], so that God will blot out his name from under the heavens."

This is an interesting point because when the individual hears other people imprecating themselves with these oaths, he will, in his imagination (his own world of personal spiritual delusion), believe he can do whatever he can rationalize in his mind, with whatever temporal socially accepted morality, and be okay. That person will not be pardoned, and the divine anger will surely come against him. As it is publically stated, the illusion that one can have inner peace without accepting the oath of the covenant does not work. "The Lord will not spare him," because he did not accept the warning and sincere oath to Hashem (Devarim 29:19). Yesha'yahu 11:1 says, "And there shall come forth a rod out of the stem of Yishay, and a branch shall grow out of his roots." The metaphor here is that the father is the root and the son is the twig that will grow out of the root. The "root that beareth gall" suggests that from a sweet root, no bitter herb will issue after all hearts are perfected with the glorious name. We are talking about a different time. Rosh v'la'anah, gall and wormwood, are poisonous herbs. This is talking about those people in the coming generation who are not ready to take the oath of commitment to make God the center of their lives to, and who prefer to join the service of the Sit'ra Ach'ra, "the other side."

In Yirmeyahu 31:13, we read, "And I will satiate the soul of the priests with fatness, and my people shall be satisfied with my goodness, says the Lord." This implies that when we downplay our physical lusts, the cravings of our soul will grow greater, and the more we feed our physical lusts, the more our hunger increases. The more we channel our desires into healthy pursuits, in other words, the more we become free from the urgency of those desires that serve to derail us on our spiritual walk. No matter how holy or spiritual we think we are, we are not exempt from following the mitzvot and working at teshuvah. People will commonly ask "Why has this trouble come to me?" It has come because they did not commit to the main purpose of life, which is to know Hashem. Consequently, they then became deluded in this life and past lives by the Sit'ra Ach'ra. The difficult times we may experience now are the result of the seeds of past actions coming to fruition. Devarim 29:28 says: "Hidden things may pertain to God our Lord, but that which has been revealed applies to us and our children forever. [We must therefore] keep all the words of Torah." These secret things on the p'shat level are the mysteries of Hashem and the sins that are hidden from those who commit them. For sometimes we are completely unaware that we are creating separation and missing the mark, and our faith tells us that God will cleanse us of those (Tehillim 19:13). The things that are revealed, however, mainly our conscious sins, "belong to us and to our children forever, that we may do all the words of the Torah as an eternal statute."

The message of Netzavim is clear. No matter how spiritually sophisticated we may think we are, the basic message from Yah is clear about what needs to be done in our daily lives if we are to be a blessing to ourselves, to the planet, and to God, and so that we may merge back into the One in deveikut/chey'rut. The Great Torah Way to enlightenment asks us to simultaneously keep our feet on the ground and our head in the heavens. No one is above the p'shat teachings of the Torah as the basic kedusha foundation of the Great Torah Way, although we may have significant variations in our philosophical and practical understanding of it, depending on our level of consciousness. One can apply these teachings in a harsh way or a sweet way for long-term evolution of spiritual awareness and for the creation of kedusha on a mass level. The Way of the Torah is the way of *ham'takah* (המתקה), sweetness and pleasantness. As King Sh'lomo wrote of the Torah, "Her ways are ways of pleasantness, and all her paths are peace" (Mishle 3:17).

The process of deveikut, of covenanting with God, of walking the Torah Way, is not out of reach. It is user-friendly and accessible to us at all times. In Devarim 30:11–14, Moshe said:

> "This mandate that I am prescribing to you today is not too
> mysterious or remote from you. It is not in heaven, so [that you
> should] say, 'Who shall go up to heaven and bring it to us so
> that we can hear it and keep it?' It is not over the sea so [that you
> should] say, 'Who will cross the sea and get it for us, so that we
> will be able to hear it and keep it?' It is something that is very

close to you. It is in your mouth and in your heart, so that you can keep it."

In summation, if you open up our heart to God, "God will circumcise your heart," meaning that when you are ready to purify yourself, God will support you.

Thus says God to us:

> "Open for me a passageway of turning your life around even if it is only as narrow as the eye of a needle, and I shall in turn open for you passageways wide enough for entire caravans of coaches and wagons to pass through with the greatest of ease."
>
> (Midrash Shir HaShirim Rabbah 5:3)

In the messianic times, people will naturally choose good. The nature of humanity will have shifted. The heart will not desire the improper and we will not have any cravings. Yehezqel 36:26–27 says:

> "A new heart also will I give you, and a new spirit will I put within you: and I will take away the stony heart out of your flesh, and I will give you a heart of flesh. And I will put my spirit within you, and cause you to follow my statutes, and you shall keep my judgments and do them."

But we do not have to wait for the messianic times. A new heart means a new understanding; it means having a heart that is open to God. A new spirit means being free from desire and will. In Kohelet 12:1, Solomon, who had access to the fulfillment of every conceivable desire, wrote "I have no pleasure in them." These are the days of the messiah, and they will offer opportunity for either merit or guilt.

Evil desires will have no power over us at this time if we stand firm in our commitment to the covenant. May everyone be blessed with this strength and the teshukah (yearning) in our lives now to do this sacred work.

Amen

VaYelekh

VAYELEKH is the shortest parashah, yet in certain ways it has a tremendous amount of strength in it, and it has great value for us. The parashah has only thirty verses. Moshe was ready to leave his body. He shared again how he was not to enter Eretz Yisrael, and I view this as a trial. All of the great teachers in this tradition are always going through trials. There is no one perfect master, and the process of spiritual evolution never ends, even if one is half angel like Moshe. There is also another message connected with Moshe not entering the Promised Land. It comes down to what Moshe said:

> "God your Lord will be the One who will go across before you. It is He who will destroy these nations before you, so that you will expel them. Joshua will be the one who will lead you across, as God has promised. God will do the same to [these nations] that He did to the Amorite kings, Sichon and Og. [As you know,] He annihilated them and their land. When God gives you power over [these nations], you must do to them everything required by this mandate that I have prescribed to you. Be strong and brave. Do not be afraid or feel insecure before them. God your Lord is the One who is going with you, and He will not fail you or forsake you."
>
> (Devarim 31:3–6)

The eternal teaching here is about having faith that whatever God does is for the best. God is the One who will lead us in the way that is best for our spiritual evolution. God was not going to uproot the nations; God was going to lead the Jewish nation to battle, and then they would be the ones who would do the physical fighting. In this context, Am Yisrael is God's messenger in the world. Again, Am Yisrael was given the task of forming a nation from the diverse parts of the secular and the spiritual, in a way that would infuse the mundane with kedusha, holiness. God would fight for them, and thus the war would be part of the divine will. If they could understand the meaning of this, they were ready to enter Eretz Yisrael and lead a national life of holiness. It meant God was not only present in times of war, but also in times of peace, that all of our activities would be sanctified by God.

We are riders of the merkavah (מרכבה), the vehicle of divine manifestation. The merkavah is the mystery that carries all existence. It is the mystery that steers and guides all of us. The merkavah is the embrace of the four winds and the four breaths that emanate from the single primordial breath of God, which brings all into existence. It is what carries Am Yisrael and all peoples on the journey through life. Literally, merkavah means "that which carries." In a sense, it means to be carried rather than to walk or run. It means to have faith that we will get there—wherever and whenever. Moshe was laying out the mystery of the spiritual path, which is to surrender to the mysterious merkavah energy fully and completely. *Merkavulim* are ones who are completely surrendered. They act and live in complete faith. At its highest octave, this is also what it means to be in deveikut/chey'rut. It means there is no "you" who is doing this work, but you are simply surrendered to the unfolding of the merkavah as it carries you to your assigned destiny. This is what Moshe is subtly telling Yehoshua and the people: "Don't worry, be strong, have faith, have courage, and the merkavah, as an expression of the Divine, will carry you through all of existence."

The other piece to this, of course, is that one has to be an active participant in the merkavic ride. This is not a passive position. It means to be open to being led by the Divine as it unfolds. As is pointed out, God will lead you, but you must do the actual fighting; you must do the work, and you must tune in to what it means to be led. This requires a certain amount of surrender and thoughtfulness. As the parashah unfolds, this appears to be a practical message to Yehoshua, who, at this point, was probably in his mid-sixties. He had led the battle against Amalek. He had gone up on the mountain. He had been the completely faithful disciple of Moshe for at least forty years. He was probably living in merkavah consciousness and was completely surrendered to God. And he had achieved this level of awareness in a very authentic way, being Moshe's number one disciple for forty years. Yehoshua had the humility of netzach, which allowed him to fully "cook" with the awareness of deveikut/chey'rut and be prepared to take on the leadership of the next generation.

There are also some subtleties here, because in Devarim 31:23, God was saying to Yehoshua, "Be strong and brave, since you will bring the Israelites to the land that I promised them, and I will be with you." Yehoshua was also appointed to be commander in charge by Moshe, who also said he would be supported by the seventy elders. Moshe told Yehoshua he must also be with the people, and that they too are part of the leadership. It seems like a contradiction, but it really is not. It speaks to the whole paradox of spiritual leadership, where one must be a leader and at the same time an integral part of the people.

The message to Yehoshua was to have faith and have courage. He would always be in charge, but he must honor the group process in order to keep the people focused on becoming a light unto the nations, and to ultimately usher in the messianic times. The goal was not his leadership or staying in power; it was transforming this group of people beyond becoming an ethical role model into becoming a spiritual role model, where the secular and the spiritual are infused into a single unit. Yehoshua was now the vehicle to achieve that objective. His goal was the transformation of the people; their goal was the transformation of the world. Moshe was not just passing on the position of leadership; he was handing over a dream, a mission, and a goal for Yehoshua to accomplish.

As this parashah falls between Rosh Hashanah and Yom Kippur, it also inspires us to examine our own dreams and goals, and pray that this coming year, as a people and as a planet, we will succeed at finding the balance in our life's walk. Finding and maintaining the balance is a major point of spiritual life in general. The process begins with lekh lekha (לך לך), "go to the self"—leave your family, leave all your concepts, leave your sectarian viewpoint, leave your nation, leave your ego, leave your ethnocentric ways of being ... and wake up to the One. Sh'ma Yisrael, YHWH Eloheinu, YHWH Echad (אלהינו יהוה אחד שמע ישראל יהוה) (Devarim 6:4). It also means walking every moment of your life attuned to this awareness. "When you are sitting in your home and when you are walking along the way" (Devarim 6:7). Spiritual life is not separate from your life; it is integral to the "walking along the way." All is sacred, and all is the expression of the spiritual. Therefore "sitting in your home" is included here because that is the mundane life that we can nevertheless spiritualize by bringing our consciousness to it. It is about participating in the continual merging of the heavens and the earth. In this context, the real message of the sh'ma is that spirituality and our focus on God is absolutely an inherent part of ourselves. Merging with God is the point of life in every moment, not just when doing "spiritual practices" or mitzvot.

As we deepen our journey, we begin to see how all of this is actually inherent in our natural self, our innate understanding. We do not journey to Gan Eden; we *become* Gan Eden. In our walking on the way, the light of Yah is always shining within us. In that sense, we no longer make an effort to "be spiritual," but we are living in the divine presence as our true nature in every moment. Moshe saw the future and was warning the people that the consequences of not following this natural Torah Way are severe, and that we will be removed from the land if we do not follow the path of teshuva and return to God. Unfortunately, we could not sustain the inner Torah Way, and we were eventually removed from the land as prophesied. Over time, Am Yisrael had to suffer immensely (from the Crusades, the Inquisition, and the Holocaust), before returning from the diaspora to the Holy Land. But there was a promise in the prophecy, as stated in parashah Netzavim, that "the day will come when you shall return"—"you will then return to God your Lord" (Devarim 30:2).

May all be blessed in sincerely living the Great Torah Way, so that if a root of gall is growing inside of us, we may root it out. May all who read this be blessed to make the transition to deveikut/chey'rut in every moment, and may the heavens and the earth become one as we walk on the way.

Amen

Ha'azinu

Parashah Ha'azinu opens: "Listen heaven! I will speak! Earth! Hear the words of my mouth!" This is very interesting. Moshe was basically saying "Before I begin to speak, you need to be ready to listen." The word ha'azinu (האזינו) means "listen," but what Moshe was really saying was: "Your heart has to be open to be able to receive what I am going to say. When I see your heart is open, then I will speak."

In Ha'azinu, there are fifty-two verses; these verses correspond to the fifty-two weeks of the yearly cycle, which is in the realm of malchut (מלכות), and it is twice the numerical value of the Tetragrammaton (יהוה), which is 26. Tetragrammaton times two implies that our world is essentially a mirror. In this section, Moshe sings his final song, which also mirrors their past to the people. In order to understand ourselves, we need to see each other in the context of our past. That is the shamanic way. We honor the past and then move beyond it.

In this song, Moshe gave the people two blessings, as he was getting ready to leave his body. The first blessing was the song itself; the second was the blessing he gave to each of the tribes. The song he sang came from his heart. It encapsulated his understanding of the nature of this people he had led for forty years. In a sense, it encapsulated Jewish history past and future. As such it gave the people all they needed to know to be successful in their lives and to survive throughout their turbulent history. This song came from his direct prophecy. It is through song that we create prophecy. In the song, he warned the people before they entered the Promised Land, how Yeshurun (ישורון) (Israel) would become fat and then rebel. "Jeshurun thus became fat and re-belled. You grew fat, thick and gross. [The nation] abandoned the God who made it, and spurned the Mighty One who was its support. They provoked His jealousy with alien practices; made Him angry with vile deeds" (Devarim 32:15–16). Moshe warned the people regarding a tendency toward which they were prone: "You get to be a fat cat, and you become complacent and forget

God." This is why it is often the case that a person whose primary focus is his wealth "has as much a chance of getting into heaven as a camel has of passing through the eye of a needle," because such people tend to think that they have created all their riches, that they are responsible for their wealth. Now, we have to understand that the Israelites in Moshe's time had been carried in a divine atmosphere for forty years. The people's camp was surrounded on all sides by the clouds of divine glory, so they could not possibly forget the presence of God. But in settling down in Eretz Yisrael, that would all go away. Behind their success, they might forget God, so Moshe warned the people through his song.

Song in Hebrew is *shirah* (שירה). Moshe was singing the song to protect the people against the tendency to grow ignorant. The song was designed to enlighten them to the pitfalls and to serve as a warning to all the future generations—in other words, to be a witness to the people. That is why Moshe was directing his warnings to every single person, as his song was primarily composed in the singular vernacular. With the power of song comes the power of prophecy, because song overrides the resistance that people have toward experiencing the Divine. Through shirah, the individual enters the inner chambers of existence and reveals the divine self, and so allows it to become part of prophecy. That was the way Moshe wanted to leave the people: with a song of prophecy that came straight from the heart. Once we appreciate that, we understand why he chose to garb his words in song. His song helps us to hear the song of our own soul, and to listen to what our soul is trying to tell us. If we could hear the song of our soul, we would not have any questions. We would know where we stand, and what we have to do.

Song has other meanings as well, and I am very moved by what is apparently a true story I heard about Chaim Shapiro. When World War II had started, Chaim was living in Poland, happily married with eight children and a large extended family. By 1945, Chaim had gone through four different concentration camps. By the time the war was over, seven of his eight children had been murdered along with seventy other relatives. All that remained were Chaim and one son, Baruch. Chaim and his son came to Israel on one of the blockade-running boats. When they reached Israel in 1948, they were fighting a war for survival, as is usually the case, and all the young men and women went off to battle. Baruch, who was seventeen at the time, went right into the war. He served under Yitzhak Rabin, did well in battle, and was awarded a field commission. Still, the war eventually took its toll and Baruch was killed in battle. Chaim had one request: that his son be buried on Mount Herzl, which is the national military cemetery in Jerusalem, so that even though Baruch never made it to Jerusalem while alive, he would at least get there in a pine box.

Word soon spread that Chaim's last son out of eight children had been killed, and it drew a tremendous amount of support from all kinds of people. When they were going to bury his son, hundreds of people showed up, most of them total strangers. Yigal Yadin, who was then Israel's Army Chief of Staff, attended the funeral as well, and positioned himself alongside Baruch's grieving father—the head of the entire military was standing by Chaim's side. Then, as people became silent, Chaim began to sing. People thought his mind was blown, that he was surely falling apart. Yigal put his arm around him and asked him if he wanted a cup of water. But Chaim said: "No, there's a reason I'm singing. Because, you see, I lost everyone and everything I had in Europe: my wife, my seven children, my parents, brothers, sisters, in-laws, my wife's family—more than seventy relatives in a single year—and, ..." he continued slowly, "I have no idea why they died. For me, in my understanding they died for nothing. I cannot even mourn them. There are no graves, no ashes; they are scattered all over Europe. But with my son Baruch, it is different. He has a grave, he is in Yerushalayim, in a new state of Israel. And at least I know why he died. He died so that after 2,000 years we can come home. He died so that we can put an end to our pain, our wandering, and our suffering. And that is a reason not to cry, but to sing." Again, he began to sing, and this time hundreds of people joined him in singing and eventually in dancing. What were people singing and dancing for back in 1948? They sang because they had a song of a new home and were dreaming of a new day.

The question that arises is, where does one find the strength to sing in the midst of such pain? Chaim exemplified how important song is in the Jewish tradition. On Shabbat, for example, we chant from Tehillim 96: *"Shiru la'Hashem shir chadash!"*—"Sing unto God a new song!" What is this new song about? Why do we have to sing it? Why do we need a new song? Because

Shabbat is when we get a taste of this harmony, and that is why we want to sing as much as we can on Shabbat.

The end of Moshe's life was the completion of his mission to prepare the Jewish people to enter the land of Israel. This song he sang to the people was a new song because they were coming into a new space. This song was a testimony reminding the people that they were prone to the very temptations that would result in evil and distressing consequences. Summoning the heavens and the earth as his witnesses, he addressed all of the people, and repeated the prophetic warning about how they are bound to grow complacent after settling into the land, then lose their interest in God: "You'll get fat, you'll be removed from the land, and in the end, you'll come back to the land." His prophetic admonishment was mostly done in prose, and nobody was allowed to enter the land until they had learned this song.

So, how important is song? Well, let us examine another song attributed to Moshe, the *shirat ha'yam* (שירת הים), the song that Moshe, the Jewish people, and Miriam sang at the Sea of Reeds after it was split and the people were saved. It was a big transition event, and it was, again, about rejoicing in God and welcoming the new. When the people escaped from Egypt after 210 years of oppression, where did they get the energy to sing this song? It was the Divine speaking through each one, giving each person the power to remember how to sing and connect to the unity. In World War II, we did not sing when we were finally rescued from the concentration camps, but in 1948 we began to sing because everything started to come together. A home was created, and our ancient language was restored into a modern spoken language, which apparently is a first in human history.

All the different pieces began to come into focus, and we got a sense of meaning and purpose to the whole picture of the last 2,000 years of our tumultuous and often tragic history. So we sang a new song filled with renewed hope and faith. In Ha'azinu Moshe inspired us to do this. He taught us that even if bad things happen to us, we need to be ready to sing a new song, an expression of our faith that things will get better, be different. He taught the people about the power of song, which is to transform fragmented consciousness into unity. He inoculated them against the mistakes that his prophecy told him they were going to make. That is why it is said that every time we sing, we revisit those nodal times before we entered into the Promised Land following our exodus from Egypt.

The liberated one is always singing to God, always singing and giving thanks for liberation. Because song opens up the heart to newness.

Now, what is the difference between saying something versus singing it? The word for song, shirah (שיר), is related to the word yashar (ישר), which means straight, honest, connected. Song has the power to cut through the resistance of the mind and take us directly to the truth. When we speak, we risk dissonance and separation, whereas song takes us beyond speech and creates peace, brotherhood, and love. So, when a true song is sung, it creates a sense of unity, balance, and symmetry in the world, particularly when it reflects a truth. The mystical nature of a song is that it allows all the different notes and all the different harmonies to blend together. They become part of a complete symphony, which is again like the song of the Jewish people. Each person has a particular note in the symphony of the nation that needs to be expressed in its own unique way. When it comes together it creates great unity among the diversity of the notes, which is a great message that Israel is still trying to understand at the time of this writing. That is the difference between speaking and singing: Speaking involves thoughts and ideas, and that often creates dissonance because everybody has to be heard, and not all are in agreement. Singing, however, creates togetherness, and a wonderful sense of harmony and unity. It is where the energy of unity within each person comes from.

There are two songs, mizmorim (מזמורים), that declare a new song, with the dream of singing to Hashem. The first was to be revealed when the Jewish people understand the message that Moshe gave them. The second song addressed the time after the deepness of the Divine is accepted throughout the entire world, when all the nations of the world finally grasp the oneness of God. Our dream is not just about coming home, but it is to be a vehicle for inspiring the whole world to come home to the truth, to wake up to the eternal truth of "I Am that I Am."

May we all be blessed that we wake up to the eternal truth of lekh lekha, and know the Self that God put us on this planet to know.

Amen

Vezot HaBerakha

THIS parashah is simultaneously the end of Devarim and the end of the To-rah. It is a statement of the ongoing existence of Am Yisrael as the carrier of the Torah lineage as a guide to enlightenment, and the beginning of the Torah as a living and evolving expression of the word of God. There are really two aspects of this lineage: (1) the inheritance, or varun morashah, which is the deep connection that Am Yisrael has with it as the direct descendants of Ya'akov (Devarim 33:4); and (2) the share in that inheritance held by gey'rim, or converts, who have joined their souls to Am Yisrael and to the great lineage of the Torah Way of Enlightenment. This lineage is both an inheritance, morashah, and a betrothal, ma'urasa (Midrash Shemot Rabbah 33:7). The lineage was passed down energetically from Avraham to Yitzhak, from Yitzhak to Ya'akov, from Ya'akov to his twelve sons, who fathered the twelve tribes of Am Yisrael, to Moshe, who received the Torah and direct s'micha (סמיכה—initiation) from YHWH, and who passed its powers and secrets on to Yehoshua. Yehoshua continued to transmit the lineage to Pinchas, from Pinchas to Eli, from Eli to Shemu'el, from Shemu'el to King David, from King David to Ahiyah ha-Shiloni, and from Ahiyah ha-Shiloni to Elijah ha-Tishbi, and from Elijah ha-Tishbi to Rabbi Shimon bar Yochai, and eventually to the Ba'al Shem Tov from both Elijah ha-Tishbi and Ahiyah ha-Shiloni, and on to this present day. On another level, the betrothal aspect of the lineage is our own heart connection to the Torah and also our chiddushei torah (חידושי תורה), which are the unique Torah interpretations that we individually add, such as with this book. The transmission of the Torah energy from generation to generation also comes from the blessing of Moshe to Am Yisrael before he left his body: "Torah zivah lanu Moshe morashah kehillat Ya'akov," meaning "Moses prescribed the Torah to us, an eternal heritage for the congregation of Jacob" (Devarim 33:4). It means that God gave us the Torah via the transmission of Moshe. The Ramban, the thirteenth-century Rabbi Moshe ben Nach-mon (Nachmanides), interpreted this to mean, as I also do, that this not only addresses all of genetic Am Yisrael, but equally all the heartfelt converts who would link their souls to Am Yisrael throughout the ages.

In this context, parashah Vezot HaBerakha is the manifestation of the Torah and represents the Torah prior to the beginning and without ending. As the Talmud points out, Moshe never died (Talmud Bav'li, Sotah 13b), yet he: (1) left his body and was mysteriously buried in an unknown place (Devarim 34:5-8) so that people could not worship his grave; and (2) at the same time, he is here with us in every generation. This suggests that he was, and is, connected to both worlds. In this understanding, Moshe returns to us in every generation to support our spiritual evolution (Midrash Shemot Rabbah 28:6).

In parashah Vezot HaBerakhah, Moshe blessed everyone as a group and all the tribes separately. These blessings were for us not only in this world but also the next world, as Moshe was, and is, in two worlds at once. After he blessed the tribes individually, he blessed all of the people. This was a collective blessing for the whole world.

It is said in the oral tradition that Moshe's neshama was empowered by the energy of the highest of angels, Metatron (מטטרון), who, in turn, was the angelic incarnation of Hanokh (Enoch). In fact, in its original Hebraic spelling, Moshe (משה) is the abbreviation for מטטרון שר הפנים—"Metatron, Prince of the [Divine] Faces" (Sefer HaSh'lah ahl Sefer Vayikra, Perek Torah Ohr, M'Sefer Torat Kohanim, No.14). It is also taught that the soul of Hanokh/Metatron will return to the planet as the force behind the messianic energy (Zohar, Vol. 1, folio 27a). This is the even greater blessing for which the whole world is waiting and which the world needs to bring forth.

Moshe's humble greatness was beyond ordinary human capacity:

> No other prophet like Moses has arisen in Israel, who knew God face to face. [No one else could reproduce] the signs and miracles that God let him display in the land of Egypt, to Pharaoh and all his land, or any of the mighty acts or great sights that Moses displayed before the eyes of all Israel.
>
> (Devarim 34:10–12)

Moshe's unabated devotion to God and to the people was the highest level of service. This was, and is, a model of the highest service, which is why the Zohar refers to Moshe as ra'aya mehaim'na, "the faithful shepherd" (Zohar, Vol. 1, folio 106a). He lived for the people, not for himself. His service to God was so complete that he not only died "at God's word" (Devarim 34:5), "by divine kiss," (which is also the way his brother Aharon and sister Miriam died) (Midrash Shir Hashirim Rabbah 1:16), but he was buried by God himself (Devarim 34:6): "[God] buried him in the depression in the land of Moab, opposite Beth Peor. No man knows the place that he was buried, even to this day."

The "faithful shepherd's" service was higher than the service of the kohan'im, who were analogous to the mystical tzaddikim, carrying the secrets of the universe and giving forth energy to the supernal worlds by being its expression as the humble greatness of the divine presence. The power of the kohan'im doing their priestly service helps to uplift the world (BeMidbar 18:7). Below this is the service of the Levites, who spread the Torah teachings as the carriers of the halakhah. Moshe, in his service to Am Yisrael, and ultimately the world, was the bridge of the continuing connection between Am Yisrael and God. He built the first mishkan, which eventually was a focal point for the divine presence and a way to channel the energy of the Divine into the community. This later manifested as the Beit HaMikdash (the first Holy Temple in Jerusalem).

Moshe activated the tradition of s'micha m'shefa (סמיכה משפע) or hanihah, which was the energetic transmission of the Torah's liberation lineage energy to the seventy elders and was used to transfer the energy of the lineage leadership energetically to Yehoshua, son of Nun, who then became "filled with the spirit of wisdom" (Devarim 34:9). As mentioned earlier, this tradition of energetic transmission of lineage was carried on from Yehoshua to the judges and then to prophets such as Shemu'el and down to modern-day energetic carriers of the lineage. The energetic transmission of this Torah enlightenment lineage is a constant reminder of the living energy of the Torah as the unbroken energy of the Divine. It is the divine Torah energetic transmission for all time and ultimately for all people.

The Torah makes a clear statement here that Vezot HaBerakhah is not the end, but the beginning of a journey of the Great Torah Way of enlightenment that is reactivated in every generation.

May we all be blessed that we are able to receive the spirit of Ruach Ha-Kodesh, of the Divine in our lives to take us individually and globally toward deveikut/chey'rut.

Amen

References

To create consistency, all Torah quotes are from *The Living Torah: The Five Books of Moses and the Haftaro—A New Translation Based on Traditional Jewish Sources,* translated by Aryeh Kaplan and published by Moznaim Publishing Corporation, Brooklyn, NY (1981). However, many different Torah interpretations, in both English and Hebrew, were used to stimulate my inspired understanding.

Scripture quotes from the nevi'im (prophets) and the ketuvim (writings) are from *The Jerusalem Bible,* revised and edited by Harold Fisch and published by Koren Publishers, Jerusalem (2000).

Due to my lack of scholarly Hebrew translation expertise, all quotes from the Midrash, the Talmud, the Zohar, and the Mishnahs cited in the text were translated from the original Aramaic and/or Hebrew source texts by Rabbi Gershon Winkler in order to keep a consistent language style. The folios and volumes indicated for these texts are based on the standard traditional Aramaic and/or Hebraic original editions, not from English translations, as they are the most aligned with the understanding presented in this book.

Aaron, David, *Endless Light: The Ancient of the Kabbalah to Love, Spiritual Growth, and Personal Power.* New York: Simon & Schuster, 1997.

Aaron, Rabbi David, *Seeing God: Ten Life-Changing Lessons of the Kabbalah.* New York: Jeremy P. Tarcher/Punam, 2001.

Ackerman, C. D., trans., *Even Sheleimah: The Vilna Gaon Looks at Life.* Jerusalem: Targum, 1994.

Bar Yochai, Rabbi Shimon, *The Zohar,* edited and compiled by Rabbi Michael Berg. Jerusalem/New York: Yeshivat Kol Yehuda, 1993.

Ben-Amos, Dan, and Jerome R. Mintz, trans. and ed., *In Praise of the Baal Shem Tov: The Earliest Collection of Legends about the Founder of Hasidism.* Lanham, MD: Jason Aronson, 1970.

Berg, Rav Yehuda, ed., *The Kabbalistic Bible: Technology for the Soul.* Los Angeles: The Kabbalah Center International, 2004.

Bialik, Hayim Nahman, and Yehoshua Hana Ravnitzky, eds, *The Book of Legends (Sefer Ha-Aggadah): Legends from the Talmud and Midrash,* translated by William G. Braude. New York: Schocken Books, 1992.

Bitan, Harav Yisrael, *Yalkat Yosef: Hilkhot Shabbat,* Volume 2. Jerusalem: HaKeter Institute, 2007.

Bokser, Ben Zion, trans., *Abraham Isaac Kook: The Lights of Penitence, Lights of Holiness, the Moral Principles, Essays, Letters, and Poems.* Mahwah, NJ: Paulist Press, 1978.

_____, ed. and trans., *The Essential Writings of Abraham Isaac Kook.* Amity, NY: Amity House, 1988.

Buber, Martin, *The Legend of the Baal-Shem.* Princeton, NJ: Princeton University Press, 1955.

Buzbaum, Yitzhak, *The Light and Fire of the Baal Shem Tov.* London: The Continuum International Publishing Group, 2005.

Carlebach, Shlomo, and Susan Yael Mesinai, *Shlomo's Stories.* New York: Jason Aronson, 1994.

Chavel, Rabbi C., trans., *Ramban Nachmanides: Commentary on the Torah.* Brooklyn, NY: Shilo Publishing House, 1975.

Citron, Sterna, *Why the Baal Shem Tov Laughed: Fifty-Two Stories about Our Great Chasidic Rabbis.* New York: Jason Aronson, 1993.

Cohen, Seymour J., *The Holy Letter: A Study in Jewish Sexual Morality.* Lanham, MD: Jason Aronson, 1976.

Collins, John J., and Michael Fishbane, eds., *Death, Ecstasy, and Other Worldly Journeys* (includes the essay "Weeping, Death, and Spiritual Ascent in Sixteenth Century Jewish Mysticism" by Elliot R. Wolfson). Syracuse: SUNY Series in Religious Studies, 1985.

Cordovera, Joseph, *Pardes Rimonim, Orchard of Pomegranates.* Saskatoon, Canada: Providence University, 2007.

Culi, Rabbi Ya'akov, *The Me'am Lo'ez Haggadah.* Brooklyn, NY: Moznaim Pub. Corp., 1978.

Doron, Pinchas, *Rashi's Torah Commentary: Religious, Philosophical, Ethical, and Educational Insights.* New York: Jason Aronson, 2000.

Drob, Sanford L., *Symbols of the Kabbalah: Philosophical and Psychological Perspectives*. New York: Jason Aronson, 2000.

Finkel, Avraham Ya'akov, trans., *Ein Ya'akov: The Ethical and Inspirational Teachings of the Talmud*. Lanham, MD: Jason Aronson, 1999.

Glazerson, Rabbi Matityahu, Joel Gallis, Robert M. Haralick, and Dr. Robert Wolf, *Light Out of Darkness: Surviving the End of Days*. Pischai Olam Publishers, 2003.

Glazerson, Rabbi Matityahu, and Robert Haralick, *The Mayan Culture and Judaism*. Leonard Himelsein Torah Foundation, 2009.

Glick, Rabbi S. H., trans., *Legends of the Talmud*. Chattanooga, TN: H & M Book and Gift Shop.

Hertz, Chief Rabbi Dr. J. H., ed., *The Pentateuch and Haftorahs: Hebrew Text, English Translation with Commentary*. New York: Oxford University Press, 1936.

Heschel, Rabbi Abraham J., *God in Search of Man: A Philosophy of Judaism*. New York: Farrar, Straus and Giroux, 1976.

_____, *The Prophets*. Philadelphia: The Jewish Publication Society of America, 1962.

Ibn 'Arabi, Muhyi-d-din, *The Wisdom of the Prophets (Fusus al-Hikam)*. Northleach, Cheltenham: Beshara Publications, 1975.

Josephus, Flavius, *The Jewish War*. New York: Penguin Classics, revised edition 1984.

Kantor, Mattis, *The Jewish Time Line Encyclopedia: A Year-by-Year History from Creation to the Present*. New York: Jason Aronson, 1992.

Kaplan, Aryeh, *Immortality, Resurrection, and the Age of the Universe: A Kabbalistic View*. Jersey City, NJ: KTAV Publishing House, 1993.

_____, *Jewish Meditation: A Practical Guide*. New York: Schocken Books, 1985.

_____, *The Light Beyond: Adventures in Hassidic Thought*. Brooklyn, NY: Moznaim Pub. Corp., 1981.

_____, *Meditation and the Bible*. New York: Samuel Weiser, 1978.

_____, *Meditation and Kabbalah*. New York: Jason Aronson, 1995.

_____, *Sefer Yetzirah: The Book of Creation*. New York: Samuel Weiser, 1990.

_____, trans., *The Bahir Illumination*. York Beach, ME: Samuel Weiser, 1979.

Kook, Chief Rabbi Abraham Isaac, *Olat RIAH*. Jerusalem: Mossad Harav Kook, 1963.

Kook, HaRav Avraham Yitzhak HaCohen, *War and Peace*. Jerusalem: Torat Eretz Yisrael Publications, 5757.

Kurinsky, Samuel, *The Glassmakers: An Odyssey of the Jews—The First Three Thousand Years*. New York: Hippocrene Books, 1991.

Lamsa, George M., trans., *Holy Bible: From the Ancient Eastern Text*. San Francisco: Harper & Row, 1985.

Leshem, Rabbi Zvi, *Redemptions: Contemporary Chassidic Essays on the Parsha and the Festivals*. Southern Hills Press, 2006.

Luzzatto, Moshe Chayim, *The Path of the Just*. Nanuet, NY: Feldheim Publishers, 1990.

Mandelbaum, Yitta Halberstam, *Holy Brother: Inspiring Stories and Enchanted Tales About Rabbi Shlomo Carlebach*. New York: Jason Aronson, 1997.

Matt, Daniel C., *The Essential Kabbalah: The Heart of Jewish Mysticism*. New York: Harper One, 1996.

_____, trans., *The Zohar: Pritzker Edition*. Palo Alto, CA: Stanford University Press, 2003.

Michaelson, Jay, *Everything Is God: The Radical Path of Nondual Judaism*. Boston & London: Trumpeter Press, 2009.

Morrison, Rabbi Chanan, *Gold from the Land of Israel: A New Light on the Weekly Torah Portion from the Writings of Rabbi Abraham Isaac Hakohen Kook*. Jerusalem: Urim Publications, 2006.

Naor, Bezalel, trans., *When God Becomes History: Historical Essays of Rabbi Abraham Isaac Hakohen Kook*. Spring Valley, NY: Orot, 2003.

Oratz, Rabbi Ephraim, *... And Nothing but the Truth: According to the Rebbe of Kotzk*. New York: The Judaica Press, 1990.

Raz, Simcha, *An Angel Among Men: Rav Avraham Yitzchak Hakohen Kook*. Israel: Kol Mevaser Publications, 2003.

Rosner, Fred, *Maimonides Medical Writings*. Haifa, Israel: The Maimonides Research Institute, 1987.

_____, *Medicine in the Mishneh Torah of Maimonides*. New York: Ktav Publishing House, 1984.

Schochet, Jacob Immanuel, *Tsava'at Harivash: Testament of Rabbi Israel Baal Shem Tov*. Brooklyn, NY: Kehot Publication Society, 1998.

Schroeder, Gerald L., *God According to God: A Physicist Proves We've Been Wrong About God All Along*. New York: Harper One, 2009.

_____, *Genesis and the Big Bang: The Discovery of Harmony Between Modern Science and The Bible*. New York: Bantam Books, 1990.

Schwartz, Richard H., *Judaism and Vegetarianism*. Marblehead, MA: Micah Publications, 1988.

Seeskin, Kenneth, *Maimonides: A Guide for Today's Perplexed*. Springfield, NJ: Behrman House, 1991.

Serkez, Kalman, *The Holy Beggars' Banquet: Traditional Jewish Tales and Teachings of the Late, Great Reb Shlomo Carlebach and Others in the Spirit of the 1960s, the 1970s, and the New Age*. New York: Jason Aronson, 1979.

Steinsaltz, Rabbi Adin, *The Talmud: Steinsaltz Edition*, translated by Rabbi Israel V. Berman. New York: Random House, 1989.

Telushkin, Rabbi Joseph, *Jewish Literacy: The Most Important Things to Know About the Jewish Religion, Its People, and Its History*. New York: William Morrow, 1991.

Touger, Eliyahu, trans., *Mishneh Torah: Hilchot Deot—The Laws of Personality Development* and *Hilchot Talmud Torah—The Laws of Torah Study* (English and Hebrew Edition). Brooklyn, NY: Moznaim Publishing Corp., 1991.

Tzadok, HaRav Ariel Bar, *Protection from Evil: Exposing and Neutralizing Harmful Spiritual Forces in Light of Torah and Kabbalah*. Tarzana, CA: Kosher Torah Pub., 2008.

_____, *Walking in the Fire: Classical Torah/Kabbalistic Meditations, Practices and Prayers*. Tarzana, CA: Kosher Torah Pub., 2007.

Vital, Chaim, *Shaarei Kedusha: Gates of Holiness*. Saskatoon, Canada: Providence University, 2007.

_____, *The Tree of Life: The Palace of Adam Kadmon—Chayyim Vital's Introduction to the Kabbalah of Isaac Luria*. New York: Arizal Publications, 2008.

Weitzman, Gideon, *Sparks of Light: Essays on the Weekly Torah Portions Based on the Philosophy of Rav Kook*. Lanham, MD: Jason Aronson, 1999.

Winkler, Gershon, *The Golem of Prague: A New Adaptation of the Documented Stories of the Golem of Prague*. New York: Judaica, 1980.

_____, *Kabbalah 365: Daily Fruit from the Tree of Life*. Riverside, NJ: Andrews McMeel, 2004.

_____, *Sacred Secrets: The Sanctity of Sex in Jewish Law and Lore.* Lanham, MD: Jason Aronson, 1998.

_____, *The Way of the Boundary Crosser: An Introduction to Jewish Flexidoxy.* New York: Jason Aronson, 1998.

_____, et al., *Magic of the Ordinary: Recovering the Shamanic in Judaism.* Berkeley, CA: North Atlantic Books, 2003.

_____, and Lakme Batya Elior, *The Place Where You are Standing Is Holy: A Jewish Theology on Human Relationships.* New York: Jason Aronson, 1994.

About the Author

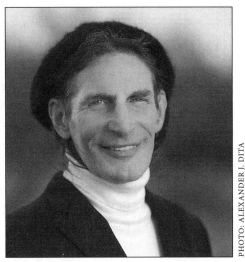

PHOTO: ALEXANDER J. DITA

RABBI Gabriel Cousens, MD, was brought up with a Reform Jewish background under Rabbi Siskin of North Shore Congregation of Israel in Glencoe, Illinois. When Cousens was eleven, the leading Conservative rabbi in the area, Rabbi Lippis, strongly recommended that he become a rabbi rather than a medical doctor. But Cousens was destined to become a physician first. Although his interest in and study of Judaism remained strong, the next major phase of his Jewish life did not begin until he was forty, on the fortieth day of a fast when an unexpected divine voice whispered that it was time to return more fully to his source and serve Am Yisrael.

Cousens then began to study Torah and kabbalistic texts intensely. He studied under several orthodox rabbis and also acted as medical doctor for Rabbi Schlomo Carlebach. In 1996 he officially began rabbinical studies under Rabbi Gershon Winkler, whose grandfather had been the chief orthodox rabbi for Copenhagen, Denmark. (Rabbi Gershon Winkler's rabbinic lineage goes directly back to Rabbi Elimelech, the third generation from the Baal Shem Tov, and down to Rav Eliezer Ben Tzion of Yeshivat Bait Yosef-Navaradok in Israel.) It was also about this time in, 1996, that Cousens became fully observant (frum), which he has been ever since. Under Rabbi Winkler, Cousens received semicha in 2008, after twelve years of rabbinical study and training.

He founded the Tree of Life Foundation in 1993 and over time a mikveh was created and the center began serving kosher food to the public. Rabbi Cousens started to lead Shabbat services in order to meet the needs of his shul, Etz Haim, in Patagonia, Arizona, where he now holds weekly public Shabbats and ceremonies for all the holidays. He also began teaching in Israel twice a year and made aliyah in 2007. In a personal aliyah ceremony he spent seventy-two hours in the Negev desert without food and water, and it was there that he had a vision of Abraham in which he received Abraham's energy of universal love and living in all four directions of one's open tent. This furthered his inspiration to serve all levels of Jewish people.

When in Israel, Rabbi Cousens holds regular public Shabbat services as well as classes on Torah and spiritual fasts. He also holds kabbalat shabbats around the world and lectures to Jewish groups on Judaism, veganism, and the Torah. His particular emphasis is on Shabbat, which he feels is a sacred cornerstone of Jewish life.

At the Tree of Life Rejuvenation Center, where is serves as director, he has developed a world-famous program to heal diabetes naturally (healing up to seventy percent of Type 2's). He lectures about this program at many medical schools and centers around the world and provides spiritual and nutritional teaching in a wide range of countries including the United States, Israel (where he founded a Tree of life Europe/Israel center), Canada, Egypt, Morocco, Lebanon, Nicaragua, Costa Rica, Panama, Mexico, Peru, Ecuador, Brazil, Hong Kong, Australia, New Zealand, Bali, Japan, Argentina, Nigeria, Ghana, and almost every country in Europe. Cousens is the author of numerous books including *There Is a Cure for Diabetes, Creating Peace by Being Peace, Spiritual Nutrition, Conscious Eating, Rainbow Green Live-Food Cuisine,* and *Depression-Free for Life* (which contains his ninety-percent-effective program to heal depression naturally). In addition, he offers a free, two-hour internet TV show called *Alive with Gabriel* in which he lectures and discusses spiritual, family, and relationship matters as well as spiritual nutrition issues.

His other major humanitarian service efforts through the Tree of Life

Foundation are the establishment of programs in various communities and countries that contain a cluster of interrelated services for sustainable, healthy living. These include diabetes prevention and holistic nutrition centers, schools, orphanages, community center complexes, and small organic farming complexes. Cousens is already working successfully on such initiatives with the Hispanic communities in Mexico, farm workers in Arizona, and the African communities in Ghana and the Biafra region of Nigeria, where, through the West African Rural Empowerment Society, a NGO of which he is a co-founder, he has reintroduced Judaism to one of the genetically identified lost tribes. Rabbi Cousens is happily married and an appreciative father of two and grandfather of three.

Information on his work and his programs can be found at:
www.drcousens.com